D1520695

The Search for Negotiated Peace

In this engaged and insightful narrative of the internationally-minded citizens' peace movement of the Great War era, David Patterson helps us appreciate that we can, indeed must, study flawed efforts to achieve peace in past times to help us fashion a more humane and peaceful world for the future.

—Frances H. Early, author of *A World Without War: How U.S. Feminists and Pacifists Resisted World War I*

Patterson's study, weaving diplomatic records with private papers, provides a thorough appreciation of that unpopular but far-seeking commitment where women's initiatives were crucial. It shows what was visionary and "utopian" in 1914 became received wisdom by war's end.

—Sandi E. Cooper, author of *Patriotic Pacifism: Waging War on War in Europe, 1815–1914*

Set against the backdrop of the gruesome trench warfare and massive carnage of the First World War, *The Search for Negotiated Peace* is the absorbing story of high-profile Americans and Europeans, led by women, who launched a vigorous movement to persuade neutral governments to mediate for peace and a better world order. David S. Patterson skillfully develops the interactions of such leaders as Jane Addams, Aletta Jacobs, and Rosika Schwimmer into a dramatic narrative that brings together for the first time the history of women's activism, international diplomacy, and peace. *The Search for Negotiated Peace* is an essential read for anyone interested in the transatlantic dimensions of the Great War and the foundations of citizen activism in the world today.

David S. Patterson is a historian who has served in both academia and government. Besides teaching at several major universities, he was for many years chief editor of the *Foreign Relations of the United States* series at the U.S. Department of State. He is author of *Toward a Warless World: The Travail of the American Peace Movement, 1887–1914.*

The Search for Negotiated Peace

Women's Activism and Citizen Diplomacy in World War I

David S. Patterson

 Routledge
Taylor & Francis Group

NEW YORK AND LONDON

First published 2008
by Routledge
270 Madison Ave, New York, NY 10016

Simultaneously published in the UK
by Routledge
2 Park Square, Milton Park, Abingdon, Oxon OX14 4RN

Routledge is an imprint of the Taylor & Francis Group, an informa business

© 2008 David S. Patterson

Typeset in ErhardtMT by
RefineCatch Limited, Bungay, Suffolk
Printed and bound in the United States of America on acid-free paper by
Walsworth Publishing Company, Marceline, MO

Library of Congress Cataloging in Publication Data
Patterson, David S., 1937-
The search for negotiated peace : women's activism and citizen diplomacy in World War I /
David S. Patterson.
p. cm.
Includes bibliographical references and index.
ISBN-13: 978–0–415–96141–7 (hbk. : alk. paper)
ISBN-10: 0–415–96141–6 (hbk. : alk. paper)
ISBN-13: 978–0–415–96142–4 (pbk. : alk. paper)
ISBN-10: 0–415–96142–4 (pbk. : alk. paper)
[etc.]
1. World War, 1914–1918—Diplomatic history.   2. World War, 1914–1918—Protest movements.
3. World War, 1914–1918—Women.   4. Mediation, International.   I. Title.
D613.P38 2008
940.3′1—dc22
2007040873

ISBN 10: 0–415–96141–6 (hbk)
ISBN 10: 0–415–96142–4 (pbk)

ISBN 13: 978–0–415–96141–7 (hbk)
ISBN 13: 978–0–415–96142–4 (pbk)

For Scott, Alix, Emmett, and Tucker

CONTENTS

ILLUSTRATIONS

ACKNOWLEDGMENTS

Writing a book is a solitary undertaking, but in the course of my project I also found solace and support from many other individuals and institutions. During my research in many manuscript collections in the United States and abroad, a host of librarians and archivists provided indispensable help. I am grateful to the many kindnesses of the staff at the Rothermere American Institute, University of Oxford, where I was a visiting research fellow during the winter term of 2006; and I explored with profit additional European sources at its Vere Harmsworth Library. Roberta Staples also provided personal attention to my research needs at Lady Margaret Hall Library at Oxford. During various trips to the United Kingdom, I also conducted research at the National Archives (Public Record Office), The Women's Library, the British Library, John Rylands Library at the University of Manchester, and the Cumbria County Record Office in Carlisle. On a visit to Holland many years ago, I also perused collections in the Netherlands Ministry of Foreign Affairs and the International Archives of the Women's Movement.

Of the many American libraries visited for this project, I am particularly indebted to the staff at the Swarthmore College Peace Collection, who warmly welcomed me on several research visits beginning many years ago. Much of this material was used for a previous book, but some too has proved very useful for this one. Wendy Chmielewski, the current curator at Swarthmore, and her staff helped to fill in some missing information in the final stages of my research, and Mary Beth Sigado assisted with arrangements for the reproduction of several photographs. The staff at the manuscript division of the Library of Congress obligingly responded to my often picayune requests for manuscript sources from their enormous collections. James H. Hutson, chief of the division, listened patiently to my ruminations about my project and shared his wisdom on scholarly publishing. I am also indebted to the newspaper and prints and photographs sections of the library and to Bruce Martin, who provided an office for my research and writing.

The staff of the manuscripts and archives division of the New York Public Library was very helpful during my research visits, and archivist

Laura Ruttum went out of her way in locating relevant photographs for the book. The Walter P. Reuther Library at Wayne State University sent me photocopies of relevant documents. In assisting my research, I also thank the archivists and archivists at the National Archives and Records Administration, the Bentley Historical Library at the University of Michigan, the Wisconsin Historical Society, the Hoover Institution, Hull House Archives, Princeton University Library, Yale University Library, Ford Motor Company Archives, and the Friends Historical Society at Swarthmore College.

For other photographs, I appreciate the cooperation of Elkie Jordans at the International Archives of the Women's Movement, and the staffs at Brown Brothers, the University of Wisconsin Archives, the Wisconsin Historical Society, the National Archives in England, the London School of Economics, and University Museum, Grönigen. I thank the Trevelyan Trustees and Newcastle University for permission to use a photographic portrait of Charles P. Trevelyan, and Jennifer Balme obligingly sent me one of Emily Hobhouse for the book.

I am grateful to Lawrence S. Wittner and Robert D. Schulzinger for their encouragement and support. John A. Thompson shared with me his extensive knowledge of Woodrow Wilson and his foreign policies. Several individuals read sections of the manuscript at various stages in its preparation. I am particularly indebted to Roger Chickering, Peter van den Dungen, James T. Patterson, and Barbara Tufty, who read all or parts of the manuscript; each saved me from mistakes and also offered substantive suggestions. Any remaining errors of fact or interpretation of course are mine alone.

Jill Liddington answered my query concerning a photograph selected for the book, and Mineke Bosch generously provided me with an English translation of the introduction to her biography (in Dutch) of Aletta Jacobs. Daniel Lautenslager translated or summarized additional parts of this biography for me.

In the course of my writing, I delivered papers on aspects of my topic to seminars or conferences at the University of Bremen, the International Peace Research Association, the Rothermere American Institute, the Society for Historians of American Foreign Relations, the Transatlantic Studies Association, and the Peace History Society. The subsequent comments and questions at these sessions stimulated my rethinking of key interpretive points.

Kimberly Guinta, acquisitions editor for history at Routledge, expressed confidence in my project from the outset and, assisted by Matthew Kopel, cheerfully guided me through the several intricate steps leading to publication. Chris Smith performed the copy editing, which was ably coordinated by Bob Banbury and his colleagues at RefineCatch Limited.

Finally, I thank my family for enduring my mental and physical absences in the course of my research and writing. Without my wife Mary Margaret's forbearance and encouragement, this project would have remained in limbo; the dedication to my son and his family can only begin to express the inspiration they have given me to finish the book so that I can enjoy their presence more.

David S. Patterson
Chevy Chase, Maryland
July 2007

PREFACE

The First World War was an epic event of cataclysmic proportions that burst upon an unsuspecting continental Europe in August 1914 and soon spread to the farthest reaches of the globe. Lasting more than four years, the fierce fighting eventually involved more than 20 nations and resulted in 30 million casualties, including more than 8 million killed.[1] The extended human tragedy had dramatic impacts on many aspects of political, social, and intellectual life worldwide. Among its many far-reaching consequences, it led to the political collapse of Europe and sowed seeds of bitterness that would foster the rise of fascism and produce another world war and the Cold War. But if the First World War produced right-wing, nationalist movements and the expansion of communism, it also gave birth to active citizen-led efforts seeking alternatives to the scourge of war. Initially, it was women who gave the modern peace movement its first truly visible presence.

The unique life experiences that prompted American and European women to make peace and international reform their major concerns are a major focus of this book. Before the outbreak of the First World War, most of these pioneering women had been engaged in various social reform movements or the women's suffrage campaign, including their international dimensions. The perspective of many of these women reformers thus already transcended national boundaries before 1914. Thereafter, these progressive internationalists increasingly made "peace" their major concern.[2]

Comprising a relatively small but very energetic transatlantic network, these women—at least in the neutral nations where peace movements were not censored or curtailed—were well positioned to counter the belligerents' war propaganda and to initiate new organizations and programs seeking peace and international reform. The female activists deserve to be studied for their self-image as women and their involvement in various domestic reform movements, but they were also seriously engaged in world politics. Several male private citizens of course were also involved in peace activity from the beginning, and they collaborated with their female counterparts in the search for a negotiated end to the conflict. This mixed gender element to the mediation movement is also incorporated in the narrative.

The reformers' proposals for changing the international system, parallel-
ing those of other pacific-minded liberals and socialists—the Left generally—in Europe and the United States, made them part of what has been
called the "parties of movement." They supported non-annexationist war
aims and attempted to discredit nation states' secret diplomacy, militarism,
and narrowly nationalistic practices that in their minds had caused the war.
They became engaged in a struggle against the "parties of order" (the
Right), which wanted to preserve their privileges and power domestically
and promoted imperialism and expansionist war aims. In place of traditional diplomatic norms and practices, the reformers wanted to develop a
"new diplomacy."

Accounts of this ideological struggle have centered almost entirely, however, on the climactic phases of the war, 1917–1919, with the dramatic
impact of the Russian Revolution providing an alternative, Communist
challenge to liberals' vision of a new world order.[3] Except for biographies
and studies of individual groups, historians have not explored in any detail
the liberals' international reform movement before 1917, including the
circulation of their ideas in the transatlantic world and their possible
impact on political elites.[4] This book serves to fill at least some of that gap.
It focuses on the activists' interest in the principles of a liberal peace
settlement from the first stages of the conflict, although largely within the
context of their active quest for neutral mediation of the horrific conflagration before it became a prolonged fight to the finish. In other words, the
peace advocates searched for creative proposals that would initiate peace
discussions, indirectly through an intermediary if not directly, between the
two belligerent sides. Such negotiations would include discussions not
only of territorial adjustments and other specific peace terms, but also
lead to agreement on many reform proposals for a new international order
that in their view would significantly reduce postwar tensions and the
prospect of future wars. My account concludes with the U.S. entrance into
the conflict against Germany in April 1917, which ended citizens' hopes
for a comprehensive mediated end to the war.

A sub-theme of the book is a wider view of the foreign policies of the
United States and the European neutral nations in the early years of
the war, and for this purpose I integrate peace history with international
diplomatic history.[5] My account goes beyond traditional U.S. diplomatic
history to look at the attitudes of European governments toward the large
question of possible mediation of the horrendous conflict. The prospect of
peace parlays in a stalemated military struggle was always a diplomatic
option and would have occurred even without outside public entreaties,
but the citizen advocates had some success in confronting governments
with their proposals and requiring justifications of their inaction. For the
European neutral governments, mediation meant assessing the desirability

and practicality of offering their good offices for peace talks; for the belligerents it involved weighing their desired war aims against the possible benefits and costs of pursuing an early, and perhaps inconclusive, peace settlement. The question of "war aims" alone is a vast subject and in this study is treated only in summary fashion to suggest the enormous complexity of international diplomacy during a multistate war.[6]

The advocates of neutral mediation had personal interviews with the heads of government and foreign ministers of all the major European belligerent and neutral nations, and the Netherlands and Sweden were prepared to explore neutral mediation further if the Wilson administration supported it. I detail what the belligerent and neutral government leaders said directly to the citizen activists about their interest in or hopes for "peace," but also explain their real wartime goals and constraints as debated confidentially within their foreign ministries. This comparative perspective shows more clearly the degree of realism of the activists (who, to be fair, were of course not privy to the internal governmental discussions) in their assessments of the actual chances for a negotiated end to the war.

In addition to the transnational mediation movement, there were two other peace movements limited to American citizen activists during their nation's neutrality. The first involved the domestic debate over military preparedness, and the second had to do with citizens' efforts to prevent U.S. belligerency, first against Mexico and then against Germany. The American mediation advocates, some centrally and others peripherally, also participated in these peace actions. Thus I cover in one chapter the preparedness controversy in the first half of 1916 and the activists' proactive responses to U.S. crises with Mexico, which nearly brought the two nations to full-scale war. Throughout the public discussions over preparedness they clearly expressed their strong antimilitary prejudices and the negative implications of a military buildup for their vision of America's future role in world affairs; and they perceived successful mediation of the contentious issues with Mexico as a test case for an eventual negotiated settlement of the much larger European conflict. The final chapter details the antiwar citizens' desperate attempts to persuade President Wilson to stop short of full U.S. belligerency against Germany. I provide concise accounts of the mediation advocates' involvement in these issues to provide a full picture of their ideas and activities, but the common, unifying theme throughout until the final submarine crisis with Germany is the pacifists' search for a negotiated peace.

As hopes for a U.S. peace initiative became central to the mediation movement, another secondary theme is the reactions of Woodrow Wilson. In an ever-expanding military conflict, involving at any one time hundreds of thousands of fighting men on the front lines and the belligerents' nearly total commitment of their material resources to the war effort, the chances for meaningful peace talks were slim at best, but Wilson, the head of the largest Western neutral, made U.S. prospective mediation a major policy aim from the first stages of the war and ultimately proffered mediation in late 1916–early 1917. The mediation advocates had more than 20 private meetings with the American president from the outbreak of the war until his peace initiative, during which they encouraged his commitment to a negotiated peace and argued for international reform. I look at Wilson's intellectual and psychological makeup that contributed to the development of his liberal internationalism.

As the story unfolds, it becomes in fact a genuine hybrid account: women's, but also partly mixed gender history as the main theme, and within that framework it is also part American and part European (or transatlantic), part peace and part diplomatic, and some Wilson and some (though less) European political leaders. Readers accustomed to historical works focusing on one or a few fields may be uncomfortable with this broader perspective, but I believe that my approach is closer to the complex, real world than a strong emphasis on a single element, such as gender, peace or diplomacy, would be. Analytical narrative history requires careful attention to the many direct as well as subtler influences that motivate the behavior of the author's principal subjects.

The ideas and actions of the peace advocates surely contain all the ingredients for a compelling storyline. Even if their campaign for mediation had had no impact on Woodrow Wilson or international diplomacy and had proven historically insignificant, their movement would still constitute an engrossing account worth telling. I argue, however, that the proponents of mediation did have an impact on the American chief executive. It is of course a tricky business to try to measure the effects of various pressures on a head of government. Moreover, if such influences exist, they may not only persuade a political leader and affect his ideas and policies, but may also induce negative reactions. Something of both, I believe, was the case with Woodrow Wilson. My narrative looks at the nature and extent of the pacifists' relationships with the American president and their possible significance.

In one sense, this book is microhistory. Covering a relatively short time period, it provides a close look at how at least one significant peace effort got started and its main organizing modes, strategy, and tactics. It also examines tensions and disagreements within the movement and evaluates its effectiveness. The extraordinarily large number and wide variety of relevant manuscript collections as well as government documents of many nations allow for an intensive investigation of the movement.

The temporal frame of 1914–1917 may at first glance seem constrained. And Wilson's independent mediation initiative—the culmination of our story here—had barely begun when it ran head-on into Germany's announcement of unrestricted submarine warfare. But the First World War also had major longer term effects. It inexorably undermined old modes of thinking and behavior and spawned new ones that are still with us today. My study treats a phase of this transformation to the modern world of our time. Wilson's emerging vision of a reformed world politics in particular, of which his mediation initiative was an integral part, remains today, for better or worse, an important variable in international politics. Peace movements went through a similar reorientation. Internal strains within them have always existed, but they took a new form after 1914. In their strategy, for example, the radicals and more adventuresome in the peace movement added a new, activist dimension that made it more visible and vibrant, but their initiatives and behavior also created difficulties with more moderate participants who placed greater emphasis on organizational structure and longer range educational goals.

At the same time, the spatial frame is broad, as the international dimensions of the movement provide a wider panorama of the story. My narrative, while using the war experience as the defining period in the major peace activists' lives, also details their prewar backgrounds. My purpose is to elucidate the motivating influences that shaped their peace activism. And in a final section providing an overview of their postwar careers, I try to enlarge our understanding of the effects of the war on them, including their perspectives on war and peace questions in the interwar period and their possible impact on peace advocacy in their own and later generations.

This book treats major citizens' peace initiatives during the First World War, but does not cover all mediation activity and peace moves. I concentrate on the ongoing efforts by private individuals to persuade governments to promote diplomatic initiatives that might produce negotiations leading to a comprehensive end to the fighting. More attention is given to citizens' pressures for mediation in America than in the European neutrals because it became increasingly apparent to the peace advocates—including some Europeans—that the U.S. Government offered the best, and perhaps the only, hope for initiating peace parlays. I also do not relate, at least not in any detail, other private schemes (sometimes with the collusion of very self-interested warring governments) to restore peace between only a few combatant countries.

Finally, I use the words "citizen," "pacifist," and "feminist" in an inclusive sense. Thus "citizen" in my account applies to all private individuals (as distinguished from government officials and diplomats) involved in the quest for a negotiated peace. It includes women activists in this search, even though nearly all of them, not having the right to vote, were less than fully-fledged citizens.

I also often employ the word "pacifist" in these pages, interchangeably, with the words "peace advocate," "peace activist," or "peace worker."

"Pacifist" goes far beyond absolute pacifists or conscientious objectors to include all those who actively sought a negotiated end to the war. In the case of the United States, for example, some advocates of peace talks during the period of American neutrality supported U.S. belligerency after the nation entered the war in April 1917. Pacifists were also not a monolithic entity in their views on collective security and a postwar association of nations. Similarly, the word "feminist" herein extends to all those who worked for the advancement of women's rights. "Feminists" could be those females whose reform agenda was limited to women's suffrage, but could also encompass those pursuing more far-reaching social and economic changes in the status of their sex, such as the improvement of women's working conditions and equal rights with men. (Some men in this account could be considered "feminists," although I apply the word only to women.) The unfolding narrative will delineate the specific content of the major participants' "pacifist" and "feminist" perspectives.[7]

Prologue

In early 1914, leaders of the American peace movement looked forward to a stimulating and fruitful summer. Caught up in the burgeoning international peace cause, they were preparing to attend one or more formal convocations of peace gatherings in Europe at which they would exchange ideas and develop plans with their European compatriots. By July 17, only a few weeks before the beginning of the Great War, a half dozen American university students were already immersed in meetings near London with scores of British peace advocates and other European young people. They faced 10 days of discussions on foreign policy issues in an ambitious program sponsored by popular internationalist writer, Norman Angell, and his like-minded British associates.

Angell's book, a bestseller called *The Great Illusion* (1910), had set forth several foreign policy propositions, which argued in essence that, in an increasingly internationalist and interdependent world, war was unprofitable and was (or should be) outmoded. His stimulating theories had soon led to the founding of Norman Angell (or international polity) clubs in British universities and the creation of a quarterly foreign affairs journal. Angell himself gave lectures to businessmen and bankers to try to win over elite opinion to his views. An industrialist created a foundation to finance his efforts, and the result was this gathering of his young disciples to debate and refine his internationalist ideas.

Accompanying the American students was George W Nasmyth. A recent graduate of Cornell University, Nasmyth had been active as a college student in the Association of Cosmopolitan Clubs, which was composed of foreign and American students dedicated to promoting international understanding. In the decade before 1914, the Cosmopolitan Club movement, whose motto was "Above All Nations is Humanity," had expanded to several American universities and beginning in 1909 held biennial conferences with its European counterpart, Corda Fratres.[1]

Another American overseas visitor at the conference was Edwin D

Mead, a peace advocate for 20 years. Mead spoke at the Angell conference before heading off to an interdenominational convention of American and European religious leaders set for the first days of August in Constance, Germany. Sponsored by the Church Peace Union, which Andrew Carnegie had liberally endowed earlier that year, the gathering of many Protestant and Catholic clerics was to be a path-breaking peace initiative in the nascent ecumenical movement. Still another planned peace convocation was the annual meeting of the Interparliamentary Union in Stockholm in early August. Founded in 1889 by lawmakers from several Western democracies, this internationalist group had no official authority, but its participants, including several members of the U.S. Congress, supported arbitration treaties for resolving disputes among nations along with the development of international peacemaking institutions. Many American peace workers were also making travel arrangements to join their European cohorts in Vienna in mid-September for five days of sessions at the annual meeting of the Universal Peace Congress.

———

On the surface at least, Americans active in peace causes had good reasons for their hopeful perspective. Although peace advocates and anti-imperialists had protested without immediate success the U.S. imperialistic foray at the turn of the century and, subsequently, in Panama and the Caribbean, the number of peace societies and members had soared after 1900. In the first decade of the new century, for example, the oldest and largest organization, the American Peace Society, had increased its membership by over 600 percent to nearly 7,000 members.[2] Conferences held each spring at Lake Mohonk, New York, which had begun in the mid-1890s as small gatherings of high-minded international reformers, had grown by 1914 to 200 or more participants, including prominent educators, foreign diplomats, and political leaders, and beginning in 1907 American peace advocates held biennial national peace congresses at which diplomats, international lawyers, congressmen, and business leaders addressed the well-attended sessions.

New peace entities, supported by wealthy benefactors, proliferated. Edwin Ginn, a Boston textbook publisher, created the World Peace Foundation in 1910; with an annual budget of $50,000 (equivalent to about $1 million in 2007), it promoted peace education, arbitration, and world federation. Even more impressive, Andrew Carnegie, once he sold his steelworks in 1901, began over the next decade to spend his millions on a number of peace projects. The former ironmaster's most generous peace philanthropy was the founding in December 1910 of the Carnegie Endowment for International Peace with an endowment of $10 million ($200 million today). Domestically, the endowment began giving annual subventions to the American Peace Society, which used these funds to provide financial support to its affiliated groups. Among the beneficiaries of the endowment's largess was the Association of Cosmopolitan Clubs, which the World Peace Foundation also supported financially. Another Ginn ally in the Boston area was Rose Dabney Forbes, a wealthy patron of the arts and humanitarian causes, who contributed generously to his foundation and the Cosmopolitan Club movement and also sponsored the American School Peace League, which Fannie Fern Andrews, a professional educator, had founded in 1907. Soon Andrews' focus on peace education, supported by the U.S. Commissioner of Education, was making modest inroads in the curriculum of many schools around the nation.[3]

Americans traditionally expressed their peace concerns through local societies. Alexis de Tocqueville, commenting in the 1830s on the relentless democratization in America, had pointed to the role of voluntary associations in the United States in tempering its citizens' individualistic, anti-institutional proclivities. Having no strong family lines, clearly defined class structure, and controlling traditions, Americans early on found associational activity a source of socializing and psychological support.[4] On a small scale, peace societies became the organizational format for the joining together of citizens in pursuit of a peaceful society. But if their purposes were initially almost wholly social and educational, they inevitably began to debate foreign policy issues resulting from the nation's emergence as a major world power. By 1914, some peace groups came to explore more active ways to proselytize their programs and were taking the first, hesitant steps toward becoming political pressure groups.

If the pervasiveness of voluntary associations, including peace societies, was a specially American phenomenon, such groups also existed in some measure in all political democracies. Thus, before the outbreak of the European war there were as many as 50 peace societies in Great Britain. In 1904, British peace leaders had formed a National Peace Council to coordinate the programs of religious, socialist, and radical parts of the peace movement. Cooperation with the Council was halting, however, as individual groups still valued their automony, and the influx of "neopacifist" Angellist elements further complicated the effort. Still, by 1914, membership in this coordinating body had increased greatly to 10 thousand members, and its journal, *The Peacemaker*, had a circulation of 67,000.[5]

Similarly based peace movements existed in Scandinavia, France, and elsewhere on the European continent. There was even a middle-class peace movement in semi-democratic Imperial Germany. The movement there was part of the growing agitation among progressives for political and social democracy; it was engaged in a serious struggle against the still dominant autocratic institutions and traditions. Among the many groups, the German Peace Society was the largest, with an estimated 10,000 members in some ninety-eight branches. Only about one-third of the local groups were really active, however, most existing only on paper. Moreover, those committed to spending much time or money on peace activity probably numbered only two to three hundred, of whom only a few dozen could be considered peace activists. Not surprising, therefore, the political impact of peace advocacy in Germany was marginal. Some leaders in the German peace movement in fact—Ludwig Quidde and Walther Schücking, for example—were academics who were as interested in the theoretical bases of international law and arbitration for international relations as in broadening the public appeal of the peace movement. German pacifists were not radical war resisters and had at best only tenuous contacts with the German working class, although the rapidly expanding labor and socialist movements in Wilhelmine Germany had begun by 1914 to remonstrate against the burdens on workers imposed by the escalating armaments race.

Within their relatively narrow liberal base, however, German peace advocates tried to mobilize public opinion and financial resources behind their vision of war as a senseless and declining anachronism and of nations' financial and economic interdependence and their growing morality and cooperation. Their efforts utterly failed, however, because, as an historian of the German peace movement writes, "their campaign lacked any cultural foundation and the images they sought to popularize clashed frontally with images being promoted officially." In truth, numerous patriotic societies, the major public institutions, and other elite groups—especially the educational system, the army, and even large segments of the clergy—inculcated stark images in Germany of a proud, but beleaguered, people surrounded by hostile enemies who were envious of German accomplishments and conspiring to attack whenever Germany relaxed its defenses. These conservative elements saw international conflict, even war, as natural, inevitable, and necessary to preserve the domestic status quo, and emphasis was placed on domestic unity, suppression of debate on national security issues, and acceptance of political authority.[6]

Until the war came, however, peace advocates throughout Western Europe and America pointed to some promising signs of peace sentiment permeating world politics. The Hague Peace Conferences of 1899 and 1907 were unprecedented government-sponsored international gatherings to discuss arms limitation, the rules of war, and the development of peacemaking machinery. While the conferees failed to reach agreement on armaments, they established the Permanent Court of Arbitration at The Hague to which nations could voluntarily submit their disputes for settlement. The prospect of a third international peace conference at The Hague in 1915 seemed an especially hopeful opening for further progress toward a more authoritative arbitral court and the goal of a world without war.[7]

Peace advocates vigorously promoted these promising new developments.

Transatlantic peace reform had indeed come a long way in just a few decades, transforming the traditional meaning of "peace" as the absence of war to the promotion of positive programs in relations among nation states. Advocates often claimed with some justification that the peace movement had entered a "practical" phase. "The peace idea has passed the period of prophecy and intuitional exhortation which marks the early stages of every great reform, and has entered the field of practical politics," Nasmyth proclaimed.[8] Such prewar discussions on the development of authoritative international institutions would later provide some of the intellectual foundations for the creation of the League of Nations and the World Court after the Great War.

Before 1914, however, "internationalism" was still more an amorphous state of mind than a clear vision or program, and most internationalists emphasized formal legal and diplomatic procedures over bold political programs to reform the international system. Many were lawyers, but even non-lawyers supported the glacial codification of international law and the ultimate development of a world legal system. The central aim of the peace movement was the substitution of peace through law for force in world politics. The emphasis of the peace leaders on arbitration treaties to resolve international disputes, which with a very few exceptions required no compulsion or sanctions against nations refusing or rejecting arbitration or its awards, suggested their limited internationalism. Even the American advocates' modest emphasis on voluntary international arbitration became a victim of their nation's constitutional system. Thus, when every American President since the late 1890s, culminating in Taft, had tried to extend the scope and powers of arbitration in treaties with friendly nations, the Senate always emasculated them with crippling amendments or rejected them altogether.[9]

Peace advocacy in these prewar years suggested a progressive force, and a few internationalists like Edwin Ginn (who died in early 1914) and the New York journalist Hamilton Holt advanced audacious programs calling for a politically oriented world organization, which would have at its disposal an international police force that could be used against aggressive or recalcitrant states. But they were a tiny minority among American and European internationalists before 1914, and much of the leadership of the peace cause, at least in the United States, was not particularly bold or questioning. Old timers drew upon the non-resistant doctrines of the peace churches or the humanitarian antislavery and anti-imperialist traditions, and some newer recruits to international reform—Cosmopolitan Club members and certain social gospel clergymen, for example—expressed the most idealistic expectations of the new reform era. On the whole, however, those joining the movement after about 1900 were cautious reformers and had no well-developed antiwar credo beyond a general belief in the desirability of peace over war. The prewar American peace movement had benefited from the domestic progressive reform impulse. Reform activity seemed to be manifest everywhere, and some peace people perceived the attainment of international peace as a harbinger of man's moral improvement. Peace became a socially respectable outlet for upper middle-class Americans' mildly reformist inclinations. But unlike progressive reformers in the domestic sphere who were trying to break up or regulate big businesses, support the needs and rights of urban workers and immigrants, attack prostitution and the liquor interests, or push for more direct democracy, the patrician reformers joining peace associations in these twilight years of peace posed no challenge to the existing social or political order. Membership in this genteel reform allowed newcomers to rub shoulders on occasion with wealthy benefactors or to share ideas with the conservative minds of its more erudite spokesmen.

As part of its growing conservatism, the American peace movement in the decade before 1914 continued to eschew contacts with ordinary citizens or the working classes and instead stressed closer ties with elite opinion, including influential government leaders. Nicholas Murray Butler, President of Columbia University and Director of the Carnegie Endowment's education division, conceded this elitism: "We must face the fact," he commented in 1913, "that our rather scientific and intellectual program is on too high a plane to be understood and sympathized with by large numbers of persons."[10] Increasingly, concludes a historian of the prewar peace movement, the recent recruits looked to government and advanced policies of government as their peace strategy.[11] This approach at worst made its proponents susceptible to manipulation by national leaders; at best it sacrificed the critical perspective the peace forces as outsiders could have brought to the government's nationalistic or self-serving foreign policies.

Moreover, the Carnegie Endowment's annual subventions to the American Peace Society and its affiliated groups had given the peace movement a newfound affluence, but a countervailing result was a decline in private donations to peace groups and their increasing dependence on the endowment for financial support. Some peace leaders perceived their groups' loss of independence and the endowment's not always subtle efforts to discourage all but the most "practical" peace initiatives. In the event of a major war threatening the nation's neutrality, including the possibility of U.S. military involvement, what would happen to these peace groups if the endowment's conservative trustees opposed their antipreparedness and antiwar programs?

Even before the European war, those peace spokesmen opposed to the large navy proposals of the Roosevelt and Taft administrations began to chafe at the growing conservatism in their movement. They articulated antipreparedness arguments at peace congresses and in their societies and foundations, but almost always after 1907 they found themselves in the minority. In consequence, none of the groups officially opposed the arms race, and the dilution of antipreparedness sentiment gave the movement a distinctly mushy, diffuse orientation.

Exceptions to the elitist, conservative drift of the American peace movement included the more youthful and idealistic reformers. They were sometimes joined by progressive-minded women who were willing to reach out to the churches, trade unions, and immigrant groups. Despite women's numbers in peace societies, male assumptions about females' traditional position in the home denied them positions of leadership and ready access to men of power and influence. During peacetime, however, most American women involved in the peace movement suffered the sexist barriers without much protest, perhaps because they were much more engaged in the advocacy of suffrage, social welfare programs, temperance, and other domestic reforms.[12]

Peace societies in Europe welcomed women members, and Bertha von Suttner, the Austrian pacifist who persuaded Alfred Nobel to create the Nobel Peace Prize, became widely known for her writings denouncing militarism and war. Much more than their American counterparts, in the twilight years of peace European women particularly criticized the skyrocketing arms race, which in their view was deflecting resources from necessary social programs affecting women and children, and crushing ordinary citizens economically with burdensome taxation. Further, they sometimes articulated widespread assumptions at that time that women were different from men, particularly in being less aggressive and more altruistic, nurturing, and committed to the worth of human life. Maternalist thinking permeated Victorian society as an argument for women's special province in fostering peace in domestic life. Olive Schreiner had extended the argument to social policy in her *Women and Labour* (1911). A South African living in England, she had criticized the British army excesses in the Boer War at the turn of the century. Her book particularly crusaded for females' right to satisfying work but also emphasized that women naturally opposed war because they were mothers.[13]

But like their American counterparts, many European women were also actively involved in the feminist movement. Thus, promotion of peace and arbitration inevitably competed with feminists' simultaneous involvement with a wide range of other social and political questions affecting their sex. These issues included not just suffrage, but the legal rights of married women, jobs in the public sector, and working rights. Peace was an integral part of their program for equal citizenship, but except for Suttner and a few others, was not singled out as a special issue requiring more urgent attention. Neither in the United States nor in Europe was there a separate woman's peace organization to try to focus public attention on the dangerous escalation of European tensions.[14]

As long as general peace existed, American peace advocates could debate their differences in a relaxed atmosphere and avoid intense self-scrutiny of their assumptions. The similar social origins of the leading peace advocates helped to disguise the differences among them. The overwhelming majority was male and lived in the major cities of the northeast or Chicago and came from professional, Anglo-Saxon, and Protestant backgrounds. Besides their common upper-class standings, they assumed inevitable moral progress. If they differed somewhat in how much mankind's own exertions could speed up the pace of social improvement, they all believed that progress was inexorable.[15]

To be sure, they realized that man was selfish and could easily be caught up in a spirit of war, and many of them were well acquainted with the dangers to peace from the European imperial rivalries, tightening alliance systems, and spiraling arms race. David Starr Jordan, the first president of Stanford University (1891–1913) and then its chancellor, understood the potentially explosive European situation. Trained as a natural scientist, he had used "science" in support of the peace cause. Though steeped in that generation's interest in heredity and racial theories, he came to reject the widely accepted social Darwinian notions of "natural selection" and "survival of the fittest" as justifications for war and imperialism. Turning social Darwinism on its head, he claimed instead that wars badly disrupted the processes of natural selection because they killed off the healthiest and strongest fighting men who were most fit to propagate the human race while sparing those unfit for military service. The deplorable result, he argued, was reverse selection, racial decay, and an undermining of the nation's republican principles.

Jordan was already well known as an outspoken anti-imperialist and peace advocate. Between 1910 and 1914, he had traveled extensively throughout Europe and Japan under the auspices of the World Peace Foundation and wrote and lectured about the real European tensions, especially in the Balkans. Munitions makers and other self-interested businessmen, he charged, might easily manipulate the potentially explosive nationalistic passions to bring about a general European military conflict. His analyses exposed the lineaments of what a later generation would call the "military-industrial complex."[16]

Most American peace workers, however, were sheltered from the virulent national rivalries permeating Europe and easily projected their optimistic, sometimes naïve views of domestic progress onto the world stage, and they downplayed the most unpleasant features of a pervasive European insecurity, which threatened to touch off a general war on the continent. Even Jordan recoiled from the implications of his depiction of parasitic business, banking, and armament interests leading Europe toward war and instead developed an elaborate argument that general European hostilities were "impossible." Echoing Angell's theories on the deleterious economic consequences of war, he contended that the self-interest among business-men and bankers alone would prompt these elites to resist governments' willingness to countenance military combat. Moreover, he asserted that the growing democratic movements in Europe were steadily empowering ordinary citizens who preferred peace and would restrain their governments from going to war.[17]

All but the most cautious American peace advocates remained optimistic, even in 1913–1914. In 1913, the secretary of the Chicago Peace Society dreamed wistfully of a fund of $100,000 ($2 million in 2007), "not for endowment, for the peace reform will be consummated during the present generation," but to double its spending to $12,000 a year in hurrying along a movement that might well succeed in 10 years.[18] Nasmyth perhaps best articulated this confident attitude. Traveling through Europe at the end of the first Balkan War in the spring of 1913, he wrote that the continent was "in the throes of an international reign of terror," but he then not only suppressed this gloomy prognosis, but also expressed his rapturous vision of a coming "wonderful period in the world's history . . . A new era in human history is dawning – the era of the unity of the world."[19]

———

While some American peace advocates had not yet embarked for Europe when the general war on the continent began, the 35 American peace advocates who had already made it to the continent were to witness first-hand the mounting diplomatic tension, frenzied street crowds, upsurge in popular hysteria, and heart-wrenching farewell scenes as soldiers left their families and loved ones for the front lines.

For Louis Lochner, a young American pacifist, the plunge of Europe into the ensuing Great War was an eye-opening experience. Like Nasmyth, Lochner had been active in the Cosmopolitan Club movement, which he had joined while an undergraduate at the University of Wisconsin. Though of German-American background and fluent in German, Lochner abhorred German militarism and was a true internationalist. Following his graduation in 1909, he had edited the club's monthly magazine and served as its general secretary before accepting the position of secretary of the Chicago Peace Society in early 1914. As he assumed his new post, he was beginning to investigate possible new activist strategies for expanding the appeal of the peace cause.[20]

Though only 27 when he and his wife set off in late July for the Vienna peace congress, Lochner was already deeply involved in the international peace movement and was well acquainted with its leaders. He had believed

p.1 Convention of the Association of Cosmopolitan Clubs, Ann Arbor, Michigan, December 1908. George W. Nasmyth is in the next to last row, third from left, and and the president of the association, Louis P. Lochner (with high forehead), is two rows in front of him. (University Archives, University of Wisconsin-Madison) In subsequent years, some women students also became members of the association.

that the flurry over Austria's ultimatum to Serbia, which it had issued on July 28 in response to a youthful Serbian zealot's assassination of the Austrian archduke a month earlier, "would soon pass over" and dubbed the very thought of a general European war as "too stupendous for earnest consideration." As the European powers began general mobilization the Lochners, who disembarked at Cherbourg on July 30, could get only as far as Paris. After witnessing Parisians singing the "Marseillaise" and wildly waving tricolor flags in street demonstrations that degenerated into unruly mobs rioting in "an orgy of wanton destruction of everything that seemed German," they made it to Le Havre for the ocean passage back to the United States.[21]

Meanwhile, European peace advocates watched the rush toward war with increasing anguish and dismay. At first they also wanted to downplay the crisis. As late as July 31, the president of the Interparliamentary Union, Philip Stanhope (Lord Weardale), still wanted to believe that general European war could be avoided. "The prevailing nervousness is natural," he commented, "but I hope and believe, exaggerated. Neither France nor

Germany desire war. I do not think that the court circles in Russia desire it either."[22]

The *Bureau International de la Paix* (International Peace Bureau) became the focus for the most concerted pacifist effort to avert war. Encouraged by the meetings of the first universal peace congresses, European peace workers had created the bureau in 1891 as a central clearinghouse for peace initiatives. With headquarters in Berne, Switzerland, the bureau had struggled along with miniscule funding, but thanks to vigorous leadership, its winning of the Nobel Peace Prize in 1910, and an annual subvention from the Carnegie Endowment, it was on a fairly solid financial and organizational footing by 1914. As the diplomatic crisis escalated, the Berne bureau president, the Belgian Henri LaFontaine, called an emergency meeting of the bureau in Brussels on July 31. Despite the difficulties of travel, about 50 pacifists made it to the meeting. Most were from Belgium, but bureau representatives also came from Germany, France, England, Italy, and the Netherlands. Edwin Mead delayed his journey to Constance to participate as an American member in the bureau's deliberations on the critical situation. The International Peace Bureau sent appeals urging the heads of government and foreign ministers of Russia, Austria, and Germany to avert war and also cabled President Wilson requesting his mediation.[23]

Despite delays and detours caused by the diplomatic crisis and confusion, about one-half of the 150 clerics, including most of the American delegates, had made it by August 1 to Constance, where the church peace congress was scheduled to open the next day. Although the major nations on the continent were already beginning general mobilization, one of the American delegates reported that most of his country's colleagues "were light-hearted and laughed at the idea of leaving Constance at all; we discounted the war scare."[24] As the nations continued the inexorable plunge toward war, on August 2 the delegates sent a telegram to the heads of the European governments and the United States urging them to work to avert war and save Christian civilization from disaster.

The social gospel clergyman Frederick Lynch, secretary of the Church Peace Union, recounted his reactions to the unfolding events in great detail. He had believed before the war that the hard work and moral fervor of like-minded clerics and social reformers, who were trying to ameliorate the abuses of urban-industrial America, could apply their talents to bring about the abolition of war. Peace on earth, Lynch felt, was the great reform movement of the future. Witnessing Europe's descent into full-scale fighting was, needless to say, a sobering experience for him. He saw it from the French side on his way from Paris to Constance in the last days of July and among Germans on his way out, just as Germany's mobilized armies were amassing to invade Belgium and France. He observed several demonstrations of Parisian workingmen crying out "A Bas la Guerre" and noted the sad resignation of ordinary French civilians as the force of arms descended on them. Like Lochner, he saw other French crowds shouting "Viva la France" and, when he reached Germany, crowds denouncing France. He also observed soldiers on both sides being particularly rough, even aggressive, toward suspected enemy aliens with whom they came in contact. All these experiences left Lynch awestruck and dumbfounded at the seeming ease with which soldiers, often intoxicated, hurled epithets and behaved violently against enemy nationals in their presence and were willing to rush off to war.[25]

The outbreak of the European war forced all peace advocates to consider their future roles in the peace movement. Those from the belligerent countries had little choice but to accept the war as a *fait accompli*. The warring governments, with the partial exception of England, tolerated little freedom of expression. Before the war, the German police had monitored pacifists' activity in some parts of the nation, but on the whole pacifists there were treated indifferently or dismissed as politically irrelevant. The initial popular war enthusiasm—what was called "the spirit of 1914" in the belligerent countries—also made any dissenting German voices seem totally isolated. Germans often referred to *Burgfrieden*—the notion of social peace permeating a besieged medieval castle—to explain the universal popular support for a united war effort.

German pacifists were initially part of this solidly pro-war consensus. At the outset of hostilities, for example, the German Peace Society issued a pamphlet which declared: "Now that the question of war and peace is no longer an issue and our nation is threatened from all sides in a life-and-death struggle, every German must fulfill his duty to the Fatherland regardless of whether or not he believes in peace." And a history of the German peace movement concludes more broadly, "all German pacifists were convinced that their country was fighting in the name of humanity, justice, and international law." They refused to accept guilt for their nation, claiming that Germany had to defend itself from uncontrolled Russian and Slavic invaders. They also believed that the violation of Belgian territory was a necessary preemptive attack because French troops were preparing to invade Germany through Belgium and that the British quest for European hegemony and imperialism had to be resisted.[26]

Unlike its French neighbor, Germany had experienced no full-blown democratic revolution enshrining liberal and egalitarian beliefs; nor did it have, like England, any well-established tradition of a loyal opposition that allowed some toleration of dissenting opinions. Instead of personal freedoms and liberty, Germans more often thought in collective terms. The individual was subordinate to the community and the state, and conscientious objection did not exist. Because of its narrow social base in Germany, bourgeois liberalism posed no major difficulty for the nation's political authorities taking their citizens to war. Their greater concern would be the socialists and their politically powerful Social Democratic party (SPD). Though the SPD approved war credits at the outset of hostilities, it expected that a quid pro quo for its support would be the enactment of constitutional and social reforms. Conservatives used the *Burgfrieden*, however, to uphold the status quo. Whether socialists would continue to endorse a war whose aims might become imperialistic and whose burdens fell largely on unrewarded German workers would remain an ongoing big question mark.[27]

Among the German liberal minority, the German peace advocates, even while approving of the war, did not necessarily participate in the war enthusiasm, and several among them were the first to entertain some misgivings about the conflict. To be sure, the doubts expressed were mostly very muted, their speeches and writings carefully avoiding discussion of Germany's possible responsibility for the conflict or its army's conduct.

For their part, the German governmental authorities at first did not vigorously impose full-scale repressive measures again dissident behavior. The early widespread public support for the war, together with pacifists' expressions of support, allowed them to continue their scornful disregard of the peace movement. The assumption of quick and victorious military campaigns also seemed to obviate the need for seriously restrictive measures on pacifist activity. In addition, the decentralized nature of military authority in Germany partially shielded pacifists from blanket restrictions. Under German (and in the south, Bavarian) law, during wartime deputy general commanders overseeing military districts had emergency powers over all national security matters and public discipline. These powers included the imposition of press censorship, banning of organizations, breaking up meetings, and curtailing foreign travel. An emergency decree in Berlin of July 31, 1914, for instance, required 48-hour advance notice for all public meetings. And of course the military, having no sympathy for pacifists, would be inclined to impose and enforce restrictive measures.

In practice, however, the repression was at first far from complete, even in Berlin. Each deputy commander had to determine case by case whether a proposed pacifist publication or activity was tolerable or not. This inevitably resulted in some regional variations on the curtailment of pacifist actions. Moreover, fearing notoriety, unneeded attention, and perhaps even martyrdom to pacifists, the Prussian War Ministry also issued guidance to the districts to avoid wholesale persecution of the peace movement. Some pacifists could not live with these restrictions, even when unevenly applied, and moved to neutral countries. Alfred Fried, a long-time leader of the German peace movement, settled in Switzerland, for example, but no longer had an organizational network for trying to counter the belligerents' propaganda.

The result of these government actions was that some branches of the German Peace Society continued to hold meetings, albeit regularly monitored by police authorities. The police's meticulous reports showed, among other things, that 35–55 people, about one-half of whom were women, regularly attended the meetings at the Munich branch. The small number at this local group, which under Quidde's leadership was one of the most active, suggests its very limited public support (and perhaps also the subtle effects of the threat of intimidation and harassment), but also women's interest in the peace movement. Government officials also reviewed the prospective periodical editions of German peace groups, which were allowed to continue publication with occasional blank columns for those articles that were suppressed as too controversial.

The government's restrained behavior even allowed the founding in Berlin in the fall of 1914 of *Bund Neues Vaterland* (New Fatherland League). Its members came from a wide range of backgrounds; most were left-leaning pacifists, socialists, and intellectuals, but some businessmen, bankers, experienced diplomats, and aristocrats also joined the new organization. Thinking internationally, they hoped for an early negotiated peace, but what most united them was their opposition to the annexationist war aims promoted by German patriotic veterans, and other ultranationalist groups. Though the membership never numbered more than a few hundred, the *Bund* set forth its moderate views in highly articulate pamphlets, and its public presence became quickly more visible than the Peace Society. By early 1915 German authorities, perceiving these developments as undermining the war effort, would begin the systematic tightening of controls on peace-oriented or "defeatist" groups as well as increased harassment of suspected individual pacifists.[28]

This repression also existed in the other belligerent nations on the continent, and peace advocacy of any kind under these conditions was out of the question. In France, however, almost all the pacifists, sure that Germany was to blame for the war, supported their government's prosecution of the war and opposed any kind of negotiated truce. Baron d'Estournelles, a leading French peace advocate before the war, strongly condemned Germany's actions. "The world can now measure what Prussian militarism cost: peace can only be re-established by war to the finish," he wrote. "Better to die, better to lose everything, than to let ignoble German militarism win." Other French pacifists were just as uncompromising. The noted French novelist Romain Rolland was virtually alone in denouncing the conflict and, like Fried, resided in Switzerland during the hostilities. Proclaiming he stood "au-dessus de la mêlée" (above the fray), he tried to isolate himself intellectually as well as physically from the war passions; but his self-imposed alienation instead resulted in his bitter condemnation both in his native country and in Germany, a country he professed to revere.[29]

Escaping from the advancing German armies in his native Belgium, LaFontaine became a refugee in England. In October he published a strongly worded manifesto, "What the Pacifists Have to Say," which expounded on Germany's responsibility for bringing on the war. He nonetheless urged pacifists to support neutral mediation if it would lead to a genuinely democratic peace, including the abolition of the armaments industries, the transformation of armies into militias, and the creation of tribunals to try violations of human rights. About one-third of the International Peace Bureau commission members from Belgium, France, Netherlands, Italy, Great Britain, and the United States signed his manifesto, and others likely would have supported it if they could have been reached. However, all German members and several others refused to endorse the document.[30]

The International Peace Bureau soon became irrelevant. Conservative and elitist, the Carnegie Endowment backed away from possible public controversy. It cut off all funding for peace groups during the war, and irreconcilable differences among the bureau's commission members quickly surfaced. At its meeting in Berne in early January 1915, the Allied conferees passionately argued for a resolution squarely blaming the Triple Alliance of Germany, Austria-Hungary, and Italy for causing the war, while the German members just as ardently opposed it and wanted to discuss instead the activities the bureau might undertake during wartime and to consider principles for a lasting peace. Some, though not all, neutral members supported the resolution. Counting proxies (French members did not attend the meeting but had expressed their views blaming Germany in writing), the members split evenly, 10:10, on the resolution.

The members also discussed whether the bureau should support neutral mediation of the war. Joseph Alexander, the lone British delegate, was willing at least to consider joint mediation by the United States and European neutrals, brought together by the Swiss Government. Representatives from other Allied and some neutral members, however, argued against neutral mediation without the withdrawal of the Central Powers from Belgian and French lands. The incompatible views resulted in the bureau's public neutrality during the war. "Although that outcome was preferred by French pacifists," a study of the European peace movement concludes, "in the long run, it undermined the remaining prestige and moral presence of the Bureau international de la paix as a force in peace circles." The bureau conferees did agree to call for an end to secret diplomacy and other democratic principles needed for a just and durable peace settlement and issued an appeal to intellectuals of the belligerent nations "to hold aloof from the slough of hate" and to work for the restoration of goodwill among the combatant nations. The situation of the bureau further deteriorated, however, once Italy entered the war on the side of the Allies in May 1915. For all intents and purposes, the expanding Great War shattered the prewar peace movement in Europe, and the Berne bureau held no more meetings during the war.[31]

———

Peace workers from European neutrals and the United States had more freedom of action. Would they stand aside, admitting by their behavior if not their rhetoric that the peace movement had failed and was no longer a relevant factor in international politics? Alternatively, would they suspend public comment on the immediate pressing issues of the war, such as the rights of neutrals or military preparedness, while trying to influence decision-makers in their governments to adopt their reform programs for the postwar world? Or would they choose a third course, which would focus mainly on efforts to revitalize and redirect the peace movement in a sustained search for a negotiated end to the conflict?

Those citizens who became involved in the last effort, the search for a negotiated peace, are the main concern of this narrative, which along the way will also show these liberals' and socialists' support for liberal international-ist principles for a new world order. But while they often cooperated with other moderate promoters of a new postwar order to prevent future con-flicts—the second group—they were prepared to go further in reforming the international system. They were also more actively engaged in trying to prevent the spread of the European war to neutral nations, including the United States. The primary focus will consistently be on the activists' ideas, programs, strategy, and frustrations in trying to persuade neutral governments to support their initiatives for bringing the belligerents to the peace table.

Lochner and, to a lesser degree, Jordan would play active parts in the search for a negotiated end to the fighting, but George Nasmyth, his ideal-ism deflated by the ongoing human slaughter on the battlefields, focused more on peace education among young people as a long-term antidote to the recurrent human problem of warfare. Edwin Mead and Benjamin Trueblood, the venerable secretary of the American Peace Society for two decades, would have participated, but old age and illness curtailed their involvement. Believing human misunderstandings and accidental missteps on both sides had brought on the war, Mead struggled mightily back in the United States to commit the World Peace Foundation, of which he was the chief director, to take a strong antiwar position.

But the trustees in his foundation, wishing to avoid public positions on the many controversial questions facing American neutrality, required the trustees' approval before issuing any official statements. Effectively silenced, Mead confided to a friend about his struggle with the trustees: "I have been sadly overworked, and at the moment am paying the penalty for it." He soon suffered a nervous breakdown and became incapacitated. He remained under doctors' care until the early 1920s when he gradually recovered his mental and physical health. His wife, Lucia Ames Mead, was also a veteran peace worker. She would also promote an activist peace strategy and would zealously support the emerging women's peace movement during American neutrality, but her husband's illness would necessarily curtail her full-time involvement in the cause.[32]

The caution of the World Peace Foundation also afflicted the American Peace Society and Carnegie Endowment for International Peace, which avoided taking official positions on controversial issues such as neutral rights, military preparedness, and the arming of American merchant ships. More important for this account, they shunned the question of neutral mediation as a method to negotiate an end to the war before its horrors continued unabated and perhaps spread to other nations.

A minority of the prewar peace advocates, already chafing under the inaction of the prewar movement, rather quickly realized after August 1914 that the existing groups were either too confused or too conservative to assert any influence during the war. This realization became particularly strong among those women peace reformers who were already dissatisfied with the caution of the peace societies. For example, Anna Garlin Spencer, a Unitarian minister and social reformer, objected to the New York Peace Society's timidity on the armaments question. "We have no reason for existence as a peace society," she had complained in 1908, "if we are silent when there is talk all over the United States of the need of keeping up our navy."[33]

Disaffected women peace advocates like Spencer were to be joined by many other women and some men, too. Indeed, the nature of the peace movement in the United States changed significantly in its membership and goals after 1914. None of these new recruits had shown sustained interest in peace questions before the war, but thereafter channeled their energies into the formation of new pacifist and internationalist organizations that were prepared to advance fresh perspectives on the issues arising from the war, including the nature and shape of the postwar world.

An immediate issue that concerned many of them was the immense scale of the battle lines on two extensive fronts on the continent that involved some 18 million combatants in three months. Most troubling were the reports of rapidly escalating deaths on the bloody battlefields. The French suffered 11,000 casualties (dead, wounded, or missing) in an offensive in mid-August, for example, and the first battle of Ypres, two months later, resulted in 50,000 German and 24,000 British dead. All told, in the first five months of the war, the French had over 500,000 casualties, one-half or more of whom were fatalities; Germany lost 241,000 lives, the British and Belgians 30,000 each. Those numbers were only for the Western front, but the casualties in the East during 1914 were higher. Austria-Hungary's casualties were 1.2 million, for example, and Russia's were perhaps as many as 1.8 million. The belligerents often did not report or verify the human losses, but everyone knew from newspaper reports and other sources that the death toll on both sides was startlingly high and rising daily.[34]

Labeling the other side responsible for the European catastrophe might help to motivate the armies to fight on for a "just" cause. But with no early end to the mounting bloodshed in sight, the finger-pointing only exacerbated the bitterness and made efforts at reconciliation more tenuous. To be sure, some peace advocates even from neutral nations early endorsed the Allied position. Reverend Lynch sympathized with those individuals who would seek a negotiated end of the conflict and stayed in touch with several of its leaders. He was not an active participant in the ensuing mediation movement, however, in part because he early concluded from his reading of documents, including the British "white paper" justifying Britain's decision for military intervention, that the British and French Governments had made valiant efforts to maintain peace while Germany was most responsible for the war, especially for its violation on Belgian neutrality. His patron friend Andrew Carnegie similarly concluded that Germany was the guiltiest nation and that Britain was honor bound to protect Belgium. He surmised, fairly accurately most historians would now agree, that Kaiser William II wanted peace but, blustering and indecisive, had refused Britain's last-minute peace overtures and allowed his advisers to out-maneuver him until he found himself authorizing Germany's involvement in a two-front war.[35]

By contrast, those citizens who would participate in the ensuing search for a negotiated peace found the question of "war guilt" or the Allied charges (and German countercharges) of enemy atrocities in Belgium almost irrelevant. They believed almost from the start that this unparalleled tragedy in human history would require creative and insistent diplomatic initiatives to try to counter the national misunderstandings and hatreds that a long war would engender.

Many European citizens shared the perspective that the issues arising out of the war required new efforts to change the nature of international politics. To these individuals, the lights had indeed gone out in Europe, and Western civilization, as they knew it, seemed at risk. A counter-effort, they early concluded, was needed as a healthy antidote to the destruction of humane values and the escalating poisonous national hatreds that prolonged, murderous trench warfare would foster in Europe. Some of these reformers would soon become involved with like-minded Americans in an urgent and persistent movement of private citizens to persuade neutral governments actively to search for a negotiated end of the conflict before it became a fight to the finish.

1

First Efforts

During the 32-month period of American neutrality in the First World War, advocates of peace devised several plans for bringing the belligerents to the conference table, but all were variations of two central proposals: independent mediation by the United States or a European neutral or joint mediation by two or more neutral nations. The idea of mediation by non-belligerent third parties was nothing new in 1914. Neutral states had offered their good offices to mediate between hostile powers going back to ancient times, and they had frequently made mediation offers to try to resolve international conflicts and end wars in the eighteenth and nineteenth centuries. President Theodore Roosevelt had served as mediator in ending the Russo-Japanese War in 1905, and Article 3 of the conventions of the Hague Peace Conferences of 1899 and 1907 had stated: "Powers, strangers to the dispute, have the right to offer good offices or mediation, even during the course of hostilities. The exercise of this right can never be regarded by one or the other parties in conflict as an unfriendly act."[1] Most immediately, the United States and Mexico had accepted the good offices of Argentina, Brazil, and Chile (ABC) to mediate their contentious dispute following President Woodrow Wilson's impulsive decision, in response to a slight to the nation's honor, to send U.S. marines ashore at Vera Cruz, Mexico, in April 1914. The incursion had cost lives on both sides, but the ABC powers had successfully mediated the issues and defused the situation.

President Wilson had been aware of the intense national rivalries in Europe, and his chief aide, Colonel Edward M. House, had visited its major capitals in the spring and early summer months of 1914 to see whether the Wilson administration could serve as an honest broker in bringing about a reduction in interstate tensions. In reports to Wilson of his talks with leading statesmen, House confessed that he was making little headway, at one point writing presciently, "The situation is extraordinary. It is jingoism run stark mad. Unless someone acting for you can bring about an

understanding, there is some day to be an awful cataclysm." The assassination of the Austrian archduke occurred a month later, but House, Wilson,
and Secretary of State William Jennings Bryan did not focus on the
approaching "awful cataclysm." During the final week of July, House was
shipboard on the Atlantic en route to his Massachusetts retreat, while
Wilson was increasingly preoccupied with the rapidly deteriorating health
of his wife, Ellen. Her illness, which led to her death on August 6, kept him
close to the White House where he could keep abreast of the rapidly
changing European situation, but it also distracted him from close attention
to public affairs. When the guns of the first few days of August commenced
in Europe, Wilson had not proposed any démarche to the European powers
and still refrained from any public comment on the diplomatic situation.[2]
On August 4, he finally wired House, asking whether he should offer his
good offices of mediation. By the time House advised the same evening
"doing nothing for the moment," Wilson had already cabled the belligerent
leaders offering his mediation. His message specifically cited Article 3 of
the Hague conventions as justification for his offer of August 4, 1914 of his
nation's good offices, "either now or at any other time that might be
thought more suitable," to the European belligerents.[3]

The President explained to House the next day: "Events moved so fast
yesterday" that he felt he had to act. He did not elaborate, but a Senate
resolution on August 4 declaring that body's judgment that the President
should offer mediation may have prompted his message. Earlier press and
individual inquiries asking whether he would offer his good offices or suggesting that he do so probably influenced him too. Whether Wilson saw the
cables from the Constance church conference or the International Peace
Bureau appealing for his mediation is unclear; in any event, the American
President never acknowledged their existence.[4]

———

Wilson's very belated mediation offer of course had no impact on the Great
War, which had already begun in Europe, but many peace workers still
wanted to believe that a way might be found to end the bloodshed. Those
individuals who had actively participated in the peace movement before the
outbreak of the European war recalled the legal sanction given mediation
under the Hague conventions as well as previous examples of neutral peace
efforts. Some of the most concerted American citizens' appeals for mediation in the first few months of the European hostilities came from a small
group of social justice advocates who, with a few exceptions, had shown
only a secondary interest in the American peace movement before 1914,
although many of them understood and supported its aims and specific
policies. These reformers believed that a prolonged war would undermine
Christian values, disrupt the social fabric that had previously facilitated

human progress, and endanger all efforts for social reform. Like the prewar peace seekers, they were unprepared emotionally for a major war and were shocked by the outbreak of the European conflagration. They were already somewhat discouraged by the limited success of their domestic reform efforts, and the war added to their demoralization. War is a "demon of destruction and a hideous wrong – murder devastating home and happiness," Lillian Wald, the head of the Henry Street Settlement in New York, lamented. It was "the doom of all that it has taken years of peace to build up."[5] Jane Addams, who had shown more interest in the peace cause before 1914, now questioned her previous struggle for domestic reform. Compared with the wholesale slaughter and human suffering of the belligerent peoples, her own efforts for human betterment seemed insignificant:

> When a million men are suffering in trenches wet and cold and wounded, what are a few children suffering under hard conditions in the factories? Take old age pensions, upon which England, France, and Germany have been working. With widows and fatherless children numbered by the thousands in each of those countries, what are a few old people more or less? It will take years before these things are taken up again. The whole social fabric is tortured and twisted.[6]

But if they remained somewhat discouraged, they were also activists temperamentally unsuited to overlook any major social problem. As Wald's and Addams' remarks attested, they perceived from the onset of the conflict that war had social consequences reaching far beyond the battlefield. They clung to their interests in domestic reform, but the continuing bloodshed increasingly diverted their energies into the area of international reform. They projected their social concerns from the national arena onto the international stage.

In some ways, Jane Addams was fairly typical of the American women who became actively involved in the peace movement during the war. Like Addams, most came of age in the late nineteenth century when young women began to attend college in much greater numbers. Like her, too, most of these college-educated women pursued professional careers and were unmarried or, if married, had supportive husbands and no small children. Compared with men with family responsibilities, these professional women, as one of them, Emily Balch, much later wrote, "were far freer in general to risk their jobs for the sake of unpopular principles and tabooed forms of activity."

A commitment to peace was one of these "unpopular principles." Many of the American women in this generation also thought a challenge was involved. They had, Balch continued, "a quite special spur in the desire to prove incorrect the general belief that they were congenitally incapable. They found a tingling zest in discovering that it is not true, as woman had been brought up to believe, that she was necessarily weaker and more cowardly, incapable of disinterested curiosity, unable to meet life on her own merits."[7] These qualities help to explain why many women were prepared to take an active part in the peace effort.

Two other observations can be added to Balch's account. One was the direct experience of many of them, as reformers and social workers in urban slums and settlement houses, in helping poor people, unassimilated immigrants, and disadvantaged people generally. In resisting the military demands of the state and broadening their humanitarian concerns for domestic social concord, they extended their commitment to social justice issues to include international peace. A second involves religion. Although some of the women attracted to the peace cause were non-believers or Jewish, the great majority grew up in Christian households. Religious influences existed, but in most cases were not so much doctrinal as a stimulus to do good works. A historian of British humanitarian reformers in this era, including 40 of the leading pacifists and internationalists, writes that the Christians among them "were not great, practising humanitarians because of their Christianity, but rather that their Christianity was a religious manifestation of their humaneness."[8] While private religious beliefs are not easily discerned, enough is known about the women peace leaders to apply this rough generalization to most of the European and American women pacifists.

Jane Addams fits this social profile. But she was also an exceptional person, and she would quickly become the acknowledged leader of the mediation cause—or at least of the women involved in it. By 1914 she was the best-known woman in America and was widely respected, even idolized throughout the nation. To many, she was "Saint Jane." She was also highly respected in Europe, especially among women reformers and social workers. It is not easy to explain her appeal. Slight of stature at five feet three inches tall, always dressed modestly in matronly attire, and not a charismatic orator, she did not appear at first glance to be a commanding presence at meetings. Indeed, as many commented at the time, her demeanor conveyed a profound sadness and humility. Behind her reserved and soft-spoken manner, however, lay a resolute determination to help immigrants and the working poor.

One of her greatest assets was her long-term experience in making Hull House, the settlement house she cofounded on Chicago's West Side in 1889, a haven for immigrants. Through her active involvement in Chicago's urban–industrial problems, she developed a network of loyal liberal friends, including intellectuals and some politicians, who came to admire her dedication and her vision of a participatory democratic order. This vision was another asset. In some ways, Addams was more important as an innovative social theorist than as an activist. At best, some historians downplay her ideas, saying she should be remembered for her "administrative talent," "shrewd business sense," and "genius for compromise and conciliation" and her contributions as a social worker. She surely possessed these qualities and accomplishments in abundance. These historians also argue that she was more important as an articulate speaker and publicist than as a careful thinker,[9] and at worst some have distorted her ideas.[10] Her ideas were often original and insightful, however, and always serious. Her career in the peace movement would display the fine tension between her bedrock beliefs and her more practical role in trying to harmonize and reconcile the views and strategies of the growing numbers of activist feminists who joined the peace cause.

Though a nominal Presbyterian, Addams distrusted religious dogma as well as political doctrines (including socialism) as too rigid, and she derived her pacifism, which crystallized over several decades before the war, from her practical experiences. These included her father's idealistic internationalism and her small-town upbringing where a sense of community and self-government prevailed. Her own mediation of familial disputes as a young adult may also have nourished her later interest in the resolution of disputes in the wider world. Other influential experiences were her wide reading of the writings of well-known European communitarian, democratic, and feminist thinkers. These authors reinforced Addams' ideas on reform, her belief that she could break out of the societal stereotype restricting women to the home, and her strong sense of social justice. Most important for her maturing pacifism was Leo Tolstoy. She read his pacifist writings and had a personal meeting with him, although she rejected his non-resistant lifestyle. The American imperial takeover of the Philippines and the forceful suppression of its people at the turn of the century, which she condemned, further nourished her interest in peace.

Addams fully articulated her insights on this subject in her *Newer Ideals of Peace* (1907). As a social evolutionist, she argued that "military ideals" and presumed virtues of war were giving way in an industrial age and would gradually disappear. In Addams' view, just as the serious conflicts between inner-city immigrant groups would erode and lead to a new cosmopolitanism, so would nation-states eventually find ways to interact peacefully. A key word in her lexicon was "fellowship." The neighborliness and fellowship at Hull House represented a successful experiment that could have a wider significance. What she had in mind was a projection of fellowship and community at the city level, which involved respect for diversity, to cooperation among peoples internationally. It can be argued that Americans' individualism and restless mobility, both vertical and horizontal, rather than a sense of fellowship and community, have been the defining traits of the American character, and her thinking on these matters was surely overly sanguine. She was nonetheless correct in emphasizing the key importance of intimate local communities as important, if not indispensable, elements in nourishing social stability and the peaceful resolution of conflicts.

Another element in her developing pacifism was her belief in the importance of "experts." Like many progressive reformers, she supported the reliance on highly knowledgeable citizens, usually in the form of nonpartisan commissions, who, divorced from political pressures and class biases, devised rational and workable solutions to complex domestic problems; she would perceive the same mediatory role for "experts" in the international sphere.

Women's increasing involvement in public life, Addams also believed, would push militarism into further decline and nourish and sustain a new

1.1 Jane Addams, about 1915. (Swarthmore College Peace Collection)

social morality. Women's right to vote was part of this process. Her writings pointed out that the industrial city had undermined women's control over their traditional roles of child-bearing, child-rearing, education, and family health and forced working women into a new, dehumanized environment of factory labor where they suffered industrial diseases and had no control over hours or wages. Women should have the suffrage because of the new conditions and because they were different from—more gentle and nurturing—not similar to men.[11]

As the human slaughter escalated in Europe after August 1914, her views seemed increasingly irrelevant, but somehow her hopes and actions for a resolution of the conflict short of a victory by one side or the other sustained her. Her intellectual acumen, long experience with social problems, and organizational talents would serve her well in the neutral mediation campaign, which would become her and her supporters' most immediately important goal—at least until her own nation entered the war in April 1917.

The movement for mediation of the European war developed slowly. Still unsure of their bearings, those most disturbed by the violence and suffering at first only demonstrated against the war. One of the first to take action was Fanny Garrison Villard. Married to the wealthy railroad magnate Henry Villard and living in Manhattan, Mrs Villard participated in the city's philanthropic activities and the social whirl of parties and receptions. She was, however, mainly a crusading reformer. She had imbibed from her father, the abolitionist William Lloyd Garrison, not only his liberal racial views, but also his non-resistant pacifism and feminism. A committed pacifist, she had joined the newly founded New York Peace Society in 1906, but soon found that male establishment figures dominated it while women's voices were ignored. Convinced that the society's masculine leaders "certainly do not know what peace is," she took more comfort in her suffrage work. Like many feminists of that era, she assumed that women were a real force for peace. "Men can protest at the ballot-box against the fearful waste of war-powers," Villard said in 1911, "but only in a few states can women do so." She and other like-minded New York women had formed a woman's antiwar committee to protest the Wilson administration's military incursion into Mexico in April–May 1914, which provided a foretaste of her activism during the European conflict.[12]

Although nearly 70 years old at the onset of the conflict, Fanny Villard soon joined Lillian Wald and other New York women in forming a Peace Parade Committee. Chaired by Villard, the committee quickly enlisted the support of well-established left-leaning feminist networks of suffragists, social reformers, trade unionists, and socialists, and on August 29 Villard, Wald, and her liberal friends at the Henry Street Settlement in New York led more than 1,200 women, dressed in black or in white clothes with black arm bands, to the beat of muffled drums in an otherwise silent march down Fifth Avenue as a moral protest against the European maelstrom. This antiwar demonstration, however, offered no positive proposal for ending the bloodbath. Indeed, Wald, fearing the parade might embarrass President Wilson, who had just issued an appeal for Americans' impartiality on the European strife "in fact as well as in name . . . in thought as well as in action," had solicited Wilson's approval in advance of the demonstration. Wald promised that the leaders of the parade would prohibit speeches and partisan displays for peace, and the President, thankful for the safeguards, cautiously approved the venture. Wilson's guarded endorsement probably helped to publicize the peace march and contributed to its modest turnout of marchers and onlookers.[13]

Given an ethnically diverse and divided citizenry free to comment on the many emotion-charged issues of neutrality—private arms sales to the Allies, for example—the President's neutrality proclamation was unrealistic. It would have been, however, more idealistic—and probably disastrous to him politically—to support one side openly or encourage citizens to champion their biased views on the war. In any event, historians usually overlook the second part of his appeal, which expressed his hopes for future U.S. mediation. Only a nation seemingly unified, dignified, and dispassionate, he believed, could be "ready to play a part of impartial mediation and speak

1.2 Women protesters against war in parade down Fifth Avenue, New York, August 29, 1914. Fanny Villard, dressed in white dress and black hat, is alone in the first row of the marchers. (Bain Collection, Library of Congress)

the counsels of peace and accommodation, not as a partisan, but as a friend."

Initially, Wilson's private views were not impartial. He went "even further," House noted on August 30, "than I in his condemnation of Germany's part in this war, and almost allows his feeling to include the German people as a whole rather than the leaders alone. He said German philosophy was essentially selfish and lacking in spirituality." But at the same time Wilson also was coming to see the causes of the war as complex and not a simple question of German war guilt. He personally deplored the German army's destructive actions in Belgium, which were highly publicized by the Allies (and is now better understood, not always exaggerated) but refrained from public comment on them or the question of Germany's alleged war crimes. Despite his Southern upbringing, as a young scholar he had written a relatively objective history (though not based on archival research), in an era where sectional prejudices were still intense, about the causes and consequences of the American Civil War. In much the same way, he disciplined himself to repress his pro-Allied sympathies. He soon was remarking that scholarly detachment was required until much more documentary evidence had been assembled, disclosed, and carefully evaluated. "When the time for summing up comes, . . ." he wrote an aggrieved Belgian minister, "we shall be upon very much firmer ground in coming to conclusions" concerning Germany's military behavior in that country.[14] Already he was turning away from looking backward to war causation; soon he would be looking forward to the creation of new internationalist principles that would emerge ascendant out of the ashes of the European maelstrom.

Following the parade, the peace advocates gradually became bolder. Addams made the first effort to meet the issues raised by the war when she suggested to Paul Kellogg, editor of *The Survey* magazine, the quasi-official journal of social workers, that social reformers and others committed to peace jointly draft a statement outlining the harmful consequences of the war and supporting the President's neutrality proclamation. Kellogg shared her desire for action, but thought that so much was at stake in the war that the social workers "ought to express themselves voluntarily and privately in some great affirmative way." As a start, he suggested "a gathering of first men and women of the United States" to frame a manifesto on the war. Hopefully, such a manifesto would:

> make known that the New World has a message for men which the old world would take to heart, a message which would breathe the spirit of democracy; would challenge . . . dynasties, armaments and commercialism; which would enunciate a world policy to take the place of commercial exploitation which goes under the name of

colonialism; which would set forth a social conception for the reconstruction of Europe as broadly as Lincoln in his Gettysburg address set forth the conception of liberty and self-government.

Kellogg added that the failure of any other American group to make such an appeal increased the need for some kind of affirmative action on their part. "Neither from the government," he wrote, "nor from the more conservative peace people nor from any other group that has commanded a national hearing has, so far as I know, come such a message, instinct with the youth and vision of America."[15]

While Kellogg continued to offer encouragement and advice, Addams traveled to Boston to confer with some well-known peace workers. When she discovered that the Boston peace advocates had not yet taken any steps to issue a peace manifesto, she encouraged Kellogg to continue his organizational efforts.[16] She then enlisted Wald, her social worker friend in New York, behind their proposal, and the two and Kellogg invited about 30 prominent social reformers, literary intellectuals, scientists, and educators to attend a series of roundtable discussions at Wald's Henry Street Settlement.[17] In issuing the invitations, they said that the main purpose of the meetings was to clarify their minds on the European situation, but if possible they also hoped to draft an affirmative statement expressing certain guidelines for the peace settlement and European reconstruction after the war.[18]

Thus far they had made no suggestions for mediation of the war. Their hopes for a short war and the President's standing offer of August 4 to help in terminating the war whenever the belligerents desired peace, which his neutrality proclamation had reaffirmed, probably constrained them from any discussion of peace proposals. This avoidance of the question of mediation continued throughout the Henry Street meetings, which convened irregularly throughout the fall.[19] The conferees would finally issue a statement in early March 1915, which detailed the baneful effects of the war on all efforts toward human progress and offered very general principles for the healing of Europe's divisions and for the construction of a more peaceful world order after the war; but it said nothing about mediation.

The meetings had far-reaching importance, however, because they brought together many prominent liberals, social workers, and pacifists, at least 18 of whom in the following months were to become directly involved in the mediation movement. In addition to Addams, Wald, and Kellogg, the most active participants in the cause thereafter consisted of Boston social worker and professor of sociology at Wellesley College, Emily Greene Balch, the liberal Unitarian minister John Haynes Holmes of New York City, and three prewar peace leaders, Hamilton Holt, editor of *The Independent*; William I. Hull, a Quaker and professor of history at Swarthmore College;

and George W. Nasmyth. Their presence at the Henry Street meetings early symbolized a common commitment to action on behalf of peace, which lasted for the duration of the war.[20] For Addams and Balch, however, peace remained their main concern long after the conclusion of hostilities. Starting with the Henry Street meetings, the two women would become lifelong close colleagues in the peace cause.

———

More immediately, the Henry Street meetings served as a nucleus for possible support of peace proposals from other individuals and groups who later expressed themselves on the question. This support initially came entirely from women. The key initiator in Europe was the fiery Hungarian feminist Rosika Schwimmer. Though from an upper-middle class Jewish family, Schwimmer did not have a comfortable childhood. Her father suffered financial misfortunes, and Schwimmer, the oldest of three children, from age 18 had to support herself by working as a bookkeeper and secretary. Lacking a university education, she had a particular gift for learning foreign languages, becoming fluent in German, English, and others. She organized women's labor unions and feminist groups in Hungary, and by 1904 was pursuing a career as writer and lecturer on a number of reform causes, particularly the rights of working women, suffrage, child labor legislation, and birth control. Schwimmer married in 1911, but was divorced two years later. She had no children. Wearing bright-colored, loose-fitting dresses without a brassiere or corset, she was a devotee of the dress reform movement among women, which defied Victorian conventional etiquette. Because of her quick wit and caustic criticisms of the masculine sex, women especially enjoyed her presentations, and she became known in Europe as the *comédienne* of the women's movement. That label barely concealed, however, Schwimmer's strong will and serious purpose. Indeed, she championed her causes as though the survival of humanity depended upon their success. And having also served as a journalist, she knew how to get the attention of the press to publicize her causes.[21]

Even before the Great War, Schwimmer showed some interest in the peace movement. Her uncle had founded the Hungarian Peace Society, and she was acquainted with many prewar peace leaders, such as Bertha von Suttner. In 1913, she attended the annual congress of international peace workers in The Hague at which she criticized the delegates for their endless talking and theorizing about peace questions at the expense of political action.[22]

Only 36 years old in the summer of 1914, Rosika Schwimmer was in London where she was acting as a newly appointed organizing and press secretary for the International Woman Suffrage Alliance (IWSA). Founded in 1902, the alliance had grown by 1914 to become a loose affiliation of some 26 national suffrage groups. With headquarters in London, the organization published *Jus Suffragii* (The Law of Suffrage), a monthly journal (a French edition was published in Geneva), and held biennial meetings in European cities; both became vehicles through which members exchanged information on feminist issues, debated suffrage strategy, and publicized IWSA activities. Schwimmer herself had played a major role in helping the alliance expand into the Hapsburg Empire by hosting the IWSA congress in Budapest in 1913, the first time the group had held its meeting outside Western Europe. Nearly all the IWSA leaders came from relatively privileged backgrounds, and many showed little interest in the labor questions affecting women or in the non-Western world. Schwimmer's radical advocacy of full equality for women and the extension of democracy to all classes was an obvious exception. There were in fact divisions on social and economic issues in the suffrage alliance, which belied their ideological solidarity. Nevertheless, the members did form an international community. Most significantly, a continuity in the IWSA leadership meant that its most active participants were well acquainted with each other and carried on an ongoing, lively correspondence, even when they disagreed, on feminist questions.

The IWSA adherents also discussed other women's issues, including temperance and prostitution. Moreover, in the half-decade or so before the Great War, they increasingly debated questions of war and peace. Part of their mounting interest in peace before 1914 was a visceral reaction to rising European tensions: an escalating Anglo–German naval arms race, colonial crises, the tightening rival alliance systems, and the upsurge in violence in the Balkans. These developments, which portended ceaseless conflict, perhaps even major war, naturally disturbed these liberal women. But in addition to their private correspondence, *Jus Suffragii* and the biennial meetings facilitated the ongoing dialogue on foreign policy issues. In consequence, the international alliance became an educational laboratory for suffragists beginning to explore the transnational dimensions of the relationship between feminist issues on the one hand, and militarism and war on the other.

In addition to Schwimmer, other IWSA leaders who would subsequently become involved to a greater or lesser degree in the mediation movement included Carrie Chapman Catt, its president, and Anna Howard Shaw (United States), Thaura Daugaard (Denmark), Lida Gustava Heymann (Germany), Aletta H. Jacobs, Wilhelmina van Wulfften Palthe and Rosa Manus (Netherlands), Baroness Palmstierna (Sweden), and Chrystal Macmillan, Catherine Marshall, Emily Hobhouse, Mary Sheepshanks, Kathleen Courtney, and Helena Swanwick (Great Britain).[23]

Because of her first-hand knowledge of southeastern Europe, Schwimmer made the intense ethnic rivalries and tensions in the Austro–Hungarian Empire, particularly as they affected her native Hungary, one of her specialties. The London *Sunday Times*, for example, published in May 1914 her personal portrait of the Austrian Archduke Franz Ferdinand, whose political views, she emphasized, were important to understand because he would succeed the aged Joseph as Emperor-King "probably very soon."[24] A month later, on June 28, Ferdinand and his wife fell victim of a Serbian fanatic's bullets in Sarajevo, and their violent deaths unleashed the chain of events that would propel Europe into war. On July 9, only 11 days after Ferdinand's assassination, Schwimmer gained an interview with David Lloyd George, Chancellor of the Exchequer in the Asquith government of Great Britain, at which she warned him that the archduke's murder had inflamed Austrians and that the impending Austro-Serbian diplomatic crisis could easily escalate in a chain of events leading to general European hostilities unless energetic diplomatic efforts were undertaken to avert them. Lloyd George, like other British leaders, dismissed such talk as alarmist, although later he gave her credit for her prescience. In fact, the British Cabinet did not even meet to discuss the crisis until July 24.[25]

In the last, desperate days of July, Schwimmer worked with British suffragists in trying to keep Britain out of the onrushing maelstrom, but the suffrage alliance became an early victim of the surging war passions. On the European continent, the national affiliates supported their governments' decisions for belligerency. Great Britain was somewhat a special case. Living in an island nation and unaware of their government's secret obligations to its continental allies, especially France, many Britons still hoped that their country could avoid military involvement. Large numbers of British suffragists were horrified at the prospect of hostilities. At an emergency meeting on July 29, the British branch of the alliance drafted a desperate manifesto appealing to European governments "to leave untried no method of conciliation or arbitration for arranging international differences which may help to avert deluging half the civilized world in blood." Schwimmer argued at the meeting that the women should personally present the manifesto to Foreign Secretary Sir Edward Grey and the ambassadors of the states mobilizing for war in London if it was to have any possible effect. Millicent Fawcett had long served as president of the National Union of Women's Suffrage Societies, the official British arm of the suffrage alliance (she was also an IWSA vice-president). She opposed hand delivering the appeal when "a penny stamp would suffice," but Schwimmer's position, supported by Macmillan, a Scottish lawyer specializing in women's issues and an activist IWSA secretary, and others, prevailed. Fawcett mostly got her way, however, when she hired a cab and, to the horror of Schwimmer and Macmillan who accompanied her, just delivered the appeal to the footmen at the gates of the Foreign Office and the embassies.

The British section of the alliance, the National Union of Women's Suffrage Societies, and other women's groups also cooperated in scheduling an August 4 antiwar protest rally against British involvement in the conflict. Eager to broaden the peace campaign, Schwimmer even wanted to invite to the meeting anti-suffragist women as well as Emmeline Pankhurst, leader of the Women's Social and Political Union (WSPU), and other militant suffragists, who had performed such radical acts as chaining themselves to the gates of Parliament, disrupting debates in the House of Commons, smashing windows in government buildings, and holding hunger strikes in jail. Mrs Fawcett and other organizers were almost convinced, but finally rejected Schwimmer's inclusive strategy. Schwimmer was more successful in persuading the organizing committee to add Olive Schreiner and Emily Hobhouse to the invitations list. Like Schreiner, Hobhouse had been a vocal critic of the British army's cruel practices during the Boer War. The NUWSS executive committee voted, however, that their group would not officially support any particular policy at the demonstration and that that the views of each union speaker would be solely hers or the affiliated organization she represented.

By the time of the rally, Germany had invaded Belgium, and England was poised to declare war. The frustrated women realized that time had run out on them. The meeting unanimously passed resolutions urging mediation by the nations not yet at war and asking women's groups to "offer their services to their country," which a delegation took to the prime minister's residence. But when Germany ignored the British ultimatum to withdraw its troops from Belgium, England declared war a few hours later. Many of the same antiwar women protesters, including Fawcett, henceforth loyally supported their government's decision for war.[26]

Fawcett's attitudes toward the coming war paralleled those of many British women reformers. At the August 4 meeting, Fawcett had called war "insensate devilry" and claimed that voteless women could not be held responsible for the events leading to the conflict. (She later wrote that her government's declaration of war was "the most miserable day of my life.") But at the end of her speech, she also made clear that women should put aside their "highest and most precious of national and international aspirations" and do their "duty" as citizens in supporting the war effort. The next day she received a letter from Lord Robert Cecil, a conservative supporter of women's suffrage in Parliament, criticizing her for allowing the NUWSS to promote a "peace" meeting and complaining that the society's "unreasonable" action made male supporters of female suffrage question whether women could be entrusted with the franchise.

Cecil's stinging rebuke served as a stark reminder to Fawcett that opposition to the war would gravely jeopardize the suffrage cause, which would require parliamentary support. It is likely, however, that she would have begun to distance herself from the suffragists' peace faction even without Cecil's reprimand. She had already declared her support for her government's decision for war at the August 4 meeting, and as an experienced and politically astute committeewoman she well understood that Parliament might reward suffragists' loyal support, but punish their opposition. Just as important, her feminism extended only to the admission of women to the existing male political system, but beyond that gender and societal relationships needed no further redefinition. Despite her suffrage proclivities, she was in fact a very respectable, upper-middle-class Victorian woman who admired British imperialism—she was appalled, for example, at the invitations to Schreiner and Hobhouse, who were considered "traitors" in British conservative circles—and the nation's political elite. Given her class loyalties, it was not difficult for her to endorse her country's war effort, and a majority of the group's executive committee would support her.

Even so, Fawcett had to tread carefully at first, because large segments of the NUWSS membership, and perhaps nearly one-half of the executive committee, including Mary Sheepshanks, who ran the IWSA office in London and served as editor of *Jus Suffragii*, Selina Cooper, Marshall, Macmillan, Hobhouse, Courtney, Swanwick, and Maude Royden, editor of the national union's weekly magazine, opposed their country's involvement in the war. While it was of course possible for British citizens to accept their country's participation in the war while still wanting an early negotiated end to it, in practice the most active proponents of mediation had all opposed their nation's military involvement. Many of these advocates of a negotiated peace had experience as social workers or had otherwise early identified with the working poor, and they were on the whole younger and more recent participants in the suffrage movement than the more traditional leaders. In the immediate prewar years they had helped to make the NUWSS organization more democratic and to bring the suffrage cause more actively to trade unions and women's cooperatives. As energetic advocates of social change, they brought critical perspectives to both domestic and foreign policy issues. Though supporters of the Liberal party, they were disappointed in its opposition to women's suffrage and its seeming reluctance to support lower- and working-class Britons, and they were increasingly attracted to the rising Labour party. They were also beginning to see connections between the discrimination against their sex and class oppression and, internationally, between their second-class status and the inhabitants of imperial-controlled Ireland and India. Some went a step further to argue that militarism and war fostered masculine, violent values and the continued subjugation of women. Their feminism extended far beyond the franchise, but they perceived their emphasis on respect for women's personality and rights as a humanitarian movement that would lessen tensions in domestic society and among nation states.[27]

Once war commenced, Schwimmer immediately resigned from her paid position as IWSA organizing and press secretary to devote herself to peace work. She could no longer be the *comédienne* when "a whole world shall be killed and thousands of men should never see again the sun and enjoy the smell of flowers, and millions of women and children shall be thrown into the utmost misery." Turning away from other reforms as well as refugee work, she became a single-minded, radical pacifist. Schwimmer was above all else a passionate personality. The causes of her emotional intensity, beyond perhaps her difficult childhood, are not easily explained. It is understandable, however, why her strong feelings, combined with her left-ist political views, could make her a committed peace activist after August 1914, and more than any pacifist she would provide creative initiatives—as well as difficulties—for the emerging citizens' peace movement.

Schwimmer at first found herself in a difficult position, because she was an enemy alien in England after Britain declared war on Austria-Hungary. Xenophobia in the belligerent countries became rampant, and her pacifistic views made her situation even more intolerable. Knowing she had to leave England, she decided against trying to return to her belligerent homeland and instead to launch a campaign to end the war. Her British suffragist friends arranged with their American colleagues for her to find a safe haven in the United States where she would support herself on the lecture circuit. Schwimmer obtained permission from British authorities to remain in London until she could find passage on a ship sailing to America. Meanwhile, she drew up a petition, which she cabled to woman suffrage leaders throughout Europe and the United States. The petition urged President Wilson to lead a movement to end the European war. "We entreat you," the crucial section read, "in the name of our common civilization to combine the neutral nations under your own wise leadership in an insistent demand to all belligerent powers to call an immediate armistice until mediation has been given a fair opportunity to find a just settlement of international differences."[28]

Schwimmer had scant financial resources and had to scrounge for money to pay for boat passage to America. But because of her extensive lecturing and writing before the war, Schwimmer had developed a network of sympathetic and influential reformers in Britain and on the continent. Some encouraged her mediation initiative or, more cautiously, asked her for more details. In any event Schwimmer, who was reluctant to beg for money, found that none would support her financially. Others just disagreed with her. She wrote Andrew Carnegie at his summer castle in Scotland, for example, asking him to meet with her to discuss her proposed visit to America to see Bryan and Wilson. Though she reminded him that he had met her the previous year at the dedication of his munificent gift of the Peace Palace at The Hague and had then expressed great sympathy for her native Hungary and its national hero Louis Kossuth, Carnegie coolly replied that he could not join a mediation committee that would "pass judgment upon the [belligerent] nations." Impatient with such excuses, Schwimmer penned "Idiots!!" on his response. The International Woman Suffrage Alliance gave her three months' severance pay, and a Yorkshire friend loaned her £50 (about £3,300 today) in increments, even though she disapproved of Schwimmer's spending "recklessly" on telegrams for her

1.3 Rosika Schwimmer in the United States, September 1914. (Schwimmer-Lloyd Collection, New York Public Library) Ethel Snowden, who lectured with her in the United States a year later, described Schwimmer's "peculiar style of dress . . . the loose, flowing robe more suggestive of the boudoir than the public platform." Ethel Snowden, *A Political Pilgrim in Europe* (New York: George H. Doran, 1921), p 43.

stop-the-war movement. From such help and the selling of some personal items, she managed to raise enough money to pay for her boat ticket and living expenses in America until she hoped to be able to meet with President Wilson.[29]

In the face of the conflicting loyalties and confusions in the first days of wartime, Schwimmer's petition did not get very far. The officers of the IWSA branch in Holland, for instance, unanimously refused to endorse Schwimmer's petition for neutral mediation. As Aletta Jacobs, its president, wrote her: "We do not believe in the practicability of your plan."[30] Internationally, the suffrage alliance, its national leaders explaining they needed time to divine their members' views on the war, refused to endorse her appeal. Believing mediation too urgent and important to await slow-moving, formal consideration by the national suffrage bodies, Schwimmer simply claimed to have secured the personal endorsements of suffrage leaders from 13 nations, including several neutrals and most of the belligerents. She then sailed for the United States to present the petition personally to President Wilson.

The septuagenarian May Wright Sewall, a longstanding pacifist, greeted Schwimmer upon her arrival in Boston.[31] Sewall had long been an active member of the International Council of Women (ICW), which she had helped to found in 1889. The ICW's avoidance of controversial issues like suffrage had in fact contributed directly to the founding of the International Woman Suffrage Alliance. Despite the ICW's more conservative orientation, Sewall had established a peace and arbitration committee for the American National Council of Women and in turn a similar committee for the international body, which she chaired. With Sewall's support, Schwimmer was soon in New York seeking the backing of Carrie Chapman Catt, the IWSA president.

An experienced ally in the suffrage struggle, Catt had always admired Schwimmer's enthusiastic commitment to women's causes. As she had written Schwimmer in 1913, "When I remember the young girl who could understand no English and who knew so little about the movement for the enfranchisement of women only nine years ago, and then see the wonders of your own development and growth, and the great work you have accomplished in Hungary, I am filled with amazement, gratitude and pride." Her endorsement of Schwimmer's petition would have carried considerable weight in the suffrage alliance. Catt had in fact been in London in late July 1914, and Schwimmer had given her a friendly send-off for the start of her return trip to the United States.

But Catt differed markedly from her Hungarian colleague in temperament. While Schwimmer was intent on diverting all her energies into the cause of peace, Catt was more circumspect. She sympathized with the peace cause, had given occasional speeches on the subject before the war, and had joined in the women's peace march down Fifth Avenue. During the World War, however, Catt's highest priority was always suffrage. The onset of the European conflict initially seemed to simplify her role as a suffrage leader. With the war imposing a suspension of transatlantic suffrage activity, she could direct her energies entirely to the cause in the United States, which was then entering its climactic phase. Rising peace agitation among women, however, soon introduced a new variable that threatened to complicate her politically shrewd direction of the suffrage movement. In particular, she was at the moment deeply involved in organizing suffrage campaigns in New York State and, recognizing the divisiveness of the peace and military preparedness issues in the United States, was in no mood to jeopardize her long-time commitments to that end. She had declined the peace parade chairmanship, for instance, that Fanny Villard assumed. The parade promoters were deluded, she warned, if they believed that "a thousand, five thousand or a million women marching through the streets of New York or speaking upon the abstract subject of peace" would impress European opinion. She epitomized in fact a newer breed of pragmatic women reformers who were noted for subordinating all other reforms to the panacea of suffrage.[32]

Catt was willing to aid Schwimmer's peace mission to the extent of putting her up in her home while she was in New York and arranging lectures for her before American women's organizations. But she stopped short of committing herself, and by implication the international suffrage alliance, to her Hungarian colleague's call for mediation of the war. She even helped Schwimmer initially by using two friendly intermediaries, Senator Charles Thomas (Democrat, Colorado), a sympathetic supporter of woman's suffrage, and pacifistic Secretary of State William Jennings Bryan, to arrange a meeting for Schwimmer and herself with the President on September 18.[33] She reconsidered, however, and two days before the appointment told Schwimmer that she had to return to New York. As she explained to Schwimmer, "My heart ached to go off" and "desert you, but I could do nothing else." What she recognized was that her presence with Schwimmer at the White House might seem to Wilson, as well as to her suffrage compatriots, to tie her suffrage organizations to Schwimmer's petition. (Left unsaid was that Wilson might resent Catt's seeming sponsorship of Schwimmer, a citizen from a belligerent country, when he was trying to appear truly neutral.) Catt's consistent position throughout the mediation campaign would be that her leadership positions in suffrage groups made her first and foremost a spokeswoman for suffragists whose organizations had not officially endorsed neutral mediation. She even tried to convince Schwimmer to cancel the interview with Wilson and to convey her message to him in a letter. When Schwimmer persisted with her plans, Catt encouraged her to call alone on the President, assuring her the interview would be cordial and routine. Schwimmer felt "crushed" by her friend's desertion but kept her appointment with the President.[34]

When Schwimmer arrived at the President's office, the fact that Wilson expressed his surprise and disappointment at Mrs Catt's absence perhaps suggests that he was more interested in developing friendly ties with American suffrage leaders than with earnest peace advocates. That he agreed at all to see Schwimmer, a private citizen from a belligerent nation, when he was trying to project a truly neutral stance, is somewhat remarkable. Schwimmer was likely a beneficiary of the small, informal White House staff monitoring the President's visitors. Today, literally scores of special assistants, deputies, and staff people surround the President and carefully monitor access to the Oval Office, but gaining an audience with the President in Wilson's time usually required only the approval of a close adviser or two. Joseph Tumulty, Wilson's private secretary, or, less often, Colonel House, served as gatekeepers. Their perception of the caller's importance for domestic political purposes or for providing information on issues that interested the chief executive, or perhaps both, usually guided their decisions on whether outsiders would be given entrée to their boss.

In any event, when Schwimmer appeared at the White House without Catt, she was shown in to see the President. Schwimmer presented him her petition for an immediate armistice and outlined an alternative proposal that urged the President to form a committee (she suggested the name International Watching Committee) of official representatives of the European neutrals and the United States. Meeting in some European neutral country, perhaps Norway as most removed from the actual fighting, this committee would formulate peace proposals and then transmit them daily to each of the belligerents until both sides agreed through their confidential replies upon some basis for negotiations. She admitted that the plan would involve unconventional diplomacy, but argued that the totality and intensity of the hostilities required new approaches to peace. When she emerged from the interview, she told reporters: "The President told me he was thinking day and night about the possibility of peace in Europe. He seemed to be deeply interested in the movement and said that he would lose no opportunity of taking practical steps to end the war."[35]

Wilson did not reveal what he said in the interview, but it is safe to say that Schwimmer, who throughout the war consistently magnified the very slim prospects for peace, exaggerated his hopes for successful mediation. Certainly he contemplated no bold peace move from the United States, for he assumed any mediation proposal that did not receive the support of belligerent statesmen would fail. Nearly a month earlier he had discouraged the Niagara section of the New York Peace Society after its officers had telegraphed Wilson that they had an opportunity to raise 1 million dollars to pay the expenses of a commission of inquiry appointed by neutral governments to investigate the causes of the European war and develop a peace plan that the belligerents might accept as a basis for peace talks. Even before he had received a full description of the proposal, Wilson had found the society's plan "very dangerous," probably because it raised the specter of a well-financed, and blundering, private initiative meddling in government business. Wilson's suspicion was correct, as he soon learned that the peace group had already solicited the reactions of the embassies of the belligerents in Washington. Besides the society's indiscretion and the hostility such a commission would arouse from one or both belligerent sides in assessing the responsibility for the war, the President believed that the formula for mediation was impractical.

Even the pacifistic Bryan agreed. The secretary would soon express greater hope for joint efforts with other neutrals leading toward mediation, but in the first month or so of the war he believed that the other neutrals were already deeply influenced by one belligerent side or the other and that the United States alone could best mediate impartially. To Bryan, the belligerents' professed declarations of their opposition to war and their regret that it had occurred "would seem to make it easier when an opening to present the matter again" arose, and he argued that Wilson could decide according to the circumstances at the time of his second peace initiative whether it would be best to mediate jointly with other neutrals or independently.

Wilson had another reason for rejecting Schwimmer's proposal. Ten days before this interview, he had approved preliminary peace feelers, using Secretary Bryan and the former American minister to Turkey, Oscar Straus, as confidential mediators between the British and German ambassadors in Washington, and he did not want to jeopardize the outcome of these discussions by an indiscreet endorsement of any specific proposal for mediation.[36]

Only a few days after the Schwimmer meeting, the President even went out of his way to lecture the press about their writing of foolish stories about his presumed intention to call a peace conference. "[O]ther things that I am earnestly, let me say prayerfully, trying to do for the peace of the world may be blocked by all this talk of things that are impossible and unwise, and in themselves unworkable . . . ," he commented. "We may make it impossible for the United States to do the right thing by constantly saying that she thinks of silly things to do." Quickly falling in line, the newspapers were soon reporting that Wilson would initiate no movement for peace until the belligerents indicated that they would be well disposed toward one.[37]

Secretary Bryan, however, warmed to mediation even as his chief was pulling back from it. In early October, he surveyed three possible mediation scenarios for the President—the United States alone, a U.S. initiative in cooperation with major Latin American nations, and one also including European neutrals—and he reported that certain Latin American nations and several European neutrals were prepared to join in a Wilsonian initiative. Cautious, Wilson replied that it was the belligerents who would decide which nation or nations would mediate, and when:

> I think that when the time comes [he continued] we shall receive an intimation that our intermediation would be acceptable and I think, speaking confidentially, that it is very desirable that a single nation should act in this capacity rather than several. The difficulties and complications would be many and the outcome much more doubtful if there were several mediators.[38]

The President demonstrated the same cool attitude toward joint mediation schemes while his personal emissary, Colonel House, went abroad in the winter months of 1914–1915 to continue with the British, French, and German leaders the inconclusive mediatory efforts of Bryan and Straus. Once he had decided upon House as his personal envoy, Wilson refused to see any peace workers, for he surmised that such presidential hearings would only arouse unrealistic expectations among them and confuse or annoy the belligerent leaders whose confidence he needed before any American offer of mediation could succeed.[39]

———

In this same interim, women advocates of peace expanded their movement even without the administration's support. In October, the British suffragist and pacifist, Emmeline Pethick-Lawrence arrived in the United States. She had left her privileged family in her twenties to found cooperatives and social settlements in London to help poor workingwomen obtain a living wage. Her socialist beliefs served as the mainspring of her feminism, and she espoused women's suffrage as necessary to help women gain some control over their lives. Beginning about 1906, Pethick-Lawrence had become a cause célèbre in Britain because of her association with the militant suffragist activities of Emmeline Pankhurst. In her strident activism, Pethick-Lawrence was imprisoned six times and at one point was forcibly fed in jail during her participation in a hunger strike. Pankhurst, whose forceful personality dominated the Women's Social and Political Union, had deposed Pethick-Lawrence from that group in 1912, but the latter did not renounce militancy.[40]

When the European war erupted, Pethick-Lawrence was 47 years old. Criticizing the prewar peace movement as "passive and negative," she was ready for peace activism. She endorsed Schwimmer's petition for an armistice and decided to organize sentiment for mediation of the war. Most militant suffragists supported Emmeline Pankhurst's vigorous endorsement of Britain's belligerency, while only a few among them opposed it. Besides Pethick-Lawrence, other prominent antiwar militants included Sylvia Pankhurst, one of Emmeline's daughters, Charlotte Despard, whose brother, Sir John French, commanded the British Expeditionary Force, and the Glasgow socialist, Helen Crawfurd. Pethick-Lawrence had been in fact something of a misfit in the WSPU, as her militancy was limited to violence against government property, but stopped short of more extreme measures, such as destruction of private property and arson, which might threaten lives. Pankhurst's autocratic leadership also did not sit well with her belief in democratic government. (Despard had much earlier left the WSPU for that reason.) Accompanied by her wealthy husband Frederick, she came to the United States because she believed that it was the neutral nation having the best opportunity for ending hostilities. Upon her arrival, she joined up with Schwimmer, who had already undertaken a speaking tour to women's groups in New York and Ohio. Much more than the suffrage question, the consistent appeal of the Hungarian's speeches was for peace. The two women, one from each belligerent side, launched a new and more extensive speaking tour of women's organizations in cities from the East coast as far west as Chicago and Milwaukee and as far south as Nashville.[41]

While Schwimmer consistently emphasized the horrors of war in Europe and the early cessation of hostilities either by neutral demands for an armistice or some kind of joint neutral mediation, Pethick-Lawrence focused on the substantive features of an enduring peace. She brought with her to America the four cardinal principles of the Union of Democratic Control (UDC), which prominent left-wing Liberal and Labour intellectuals, publicists, and politicians in Britain had formulated in September 1914. Many of the union's leaders had promoted political and social reform before the war and had also worked for a more accommodating, anti-imperialist foreign policy. They were shocked by the events of July–August 1914 which, they were convinced, had quickly smashed their vision of a peaceful future. Frederick was also a suffragist as well as a member of the UDC executive committee. Blaming the European war on a small elite of diplomats and armament syndicates, the British group called for the democratization of foreign policy. Specifically, it advocated no transfer of territory without the consent by plebiscite of the inhabitants (self-determination), parliamentary control of foreign policy to replace secret alliances and agreements, the nationalization of armament manufacture as a prerequisite for international agreement on disarmament, and the replacement of "balance-of-power" politics with the creation of an "international council" (that is, a democratic league of nations).

The UDC believed that these principles constituted the sine qua non for the peace settlement at the end of the war and for postwar diplomacy. Embodying liberals' faith in man's rational nature, its leaders also believed that Germany's civilian rulers were reasonable. Peace by negotiation with Britain's enemies was thus eminently possible and should not be rejected out of hand, although the union was not an antiwar group and did not emphasize this point during the first year of the war when pro-war feeling in Britain was quite predominant.[42] Drawing on the UDC principles, Mrs Pethick-Lawrence championed international reform in her early speeches and urged governments to appoint women to a permanent international committee that would serve as the mouthpiece for women's views at the final peace settlement.

Despite the different emphases, the two women cooperated effectively during their speaking tour. Each drew upon similar ideas growing out of the feminist movements in which they had participated. They especially emphasized the "maternal instinct." As Pethick-Lawrence wrote:

> The bed-rock of humanity is motherhood. The solidarity of the world's motherhood, potential or otherwise, underlies all cleavages of nationality. Men have conflicting interests and ambitions. Women all the world over, speaking broadly, have one passion and one vocation, and that is the creation and preservation of human life. Deep in the hearts of the women of the peasant and industrial classes of every nation, there lies beneath their readiness to endure their full share of their nations' toll of sacrifice and suffering, a denial of the necessity of war. There is a rooted revolt against the destruction of the blossoming manhood of the race.

Pacifistic feminists may have self-consciously employed this powerful, emotional rhetoric as a rallying cry to attract women to the peace movement, but there is little doubt that they believed it. Some even extended it to women without children. Thus, while Schwimmer stressed that mothers best understood the life-creating process, she also argued that women who had not given birth were like mothers in nurturing the young in child rearing and as teachers. As Schwimmer expressed it, "Even women who are not physically mothers, feel all as the mothers of the human race." Perhaps because neither she nor many other women pacifists had borne children, they felt obliged to expand maternalism to a more inclusive sisterhood. More likely, they were simply elaborating on the common thought of the time that women were naturally more peace loving than men and could articulate these feelings in the peace movement.[43]

During the European war, antiwar feminists particularly championed two arguments: men were responsible for the conflict, and women and children were its chief victims. One of their chief polemicists was feminist

Helena Swanwick, former editor of the NUWSS monthly journal, who forcefully argued that "men make wars, not women," and she later wrote that man was "the Playboy of the whole World." He was playing the "silly, bloody game of massacring the sons of women." That seeming man-hating rhetoric could be misleading, as Swanwick was happily married and, "sick of segregation" of women in activist associations, had prevailed upon the UDC to accept women members. Its male leaders were not feminists and did not welcome the opposite sex with open arms. E.D. Morel, the prime mover in the new organization, wrote Charles P. Trevelyan, also a founder, early on that Norman Angell, another prominent member, was "a little afraid of women," which, Morel added, "within limits, is a proper frame of mind." But Swanwick became a valued member of the UDC executive committee, and on her own also published pamphlets forcefully articulating the maternal theme.[44]

Actually, numerous research studies since about 1900 have confirmed that, in the Western world at least, women are more likely than men to be peace-oriented, but that this trait stems mainly from the different socialization of men and women. Thus, the "maternal instinct" for peace is probably more sociological than biological in origin. Historically, the gender gap has been very evident on issues involving a nation's military action in geographically distant conflicts, but has vanished in cases where the warfare directly and immediately affects the nation's security. Many female pacifists recognized fairly early in the European conflict that most women in the belligerent countries strongly endorsed their nations' war efforts, a few even saying they were glad their sons had gone off to combat.[45]

Some women rejected the "maternal instinct" ideology. On the radical fringe, feminists demanded complete sexual equality. Believing men and women were no different in intelligence, emotional makeup, and physical endurance, they opposed protective legislation for women (except perhaps for maternity leave) in the workforce. Similarly, they thought men and women equally peace loving, and some of them, such as the passionate pacifist, Crystal Eastman of New York City, had difficulty in accepting women acting separately in the peace movement. Almost six feet tall and athletic herself, Eastman believed that if women were expected to be agile, strong, and courageous, they could develop those qualities. She likewise deprecated women's fascination with fashion, which, she argued, served to limit their freedom of movement. Actively involved in the Congressional Union, a militant suffrage group always opposed to the party in power—at this time, the Democrats—she was not averse to direct action techniques challenging political authority.[46]

As these varied stances suggest, in their mounting angst over the unfolding human tragedy in Europe, women pacifists seized on a number of feminist arguments in support of their antiwar positions. They sometimes

intertwined their maternalist rhetoric—and its obverse that men were naturally more violent and warlike—with equal rights. Thus Schwimmer,
Pethick-Lawrence, and others championed equality for women while simultaneously arguing that their sex was more peaceful. Further to confuse
the maternalist rhetoric, on the opposite side of the political spectrum
there were women patriots and antifeminists who also cited the instinct of
motherhood, but came to very different conclusions. Backing national self-
defense, they argued that women's moral responsibility for the "conserva-
tion of life" and the "protection of the home" required their support of
military preparedness.[47]

In an era when women were not enfranchised anywhere worldwide,
except for a few U.S. states and the Scandinavian countries, however, antiwar women could claim with some justice that their sex bore no responsibility for the horrific conflict, which masculine governments had begun
and were prosecuting with a vengeance. It was easy (though not so easily
proven), especially for those women distant from the battlefields, to go a
step further to argue that the empowerment of naturally peace-loving
women would bring about a gentler, saner world. Moreover, because
almost all women were not liberated from the home, Schwimmer and
Pethick-Lawrence's emphasis on the notion of a nurturing feminine sex
was directly relevant to most women's own life experiences.

In any event, the argument in their talks that women should have a
special concern for calling on governments to initiate peace discussions
managed to stir up considerable interest among reform-minded women,
who soon began to organize peace committees in several cities. These
groups attempted to arouse American public opinion to demand their
government's mediation of the war. In early December the two women
formulated bolder plans. Shortly after Pethick-Lawrence helped to found a
peace committee in Washington, DC, its leaders began to contemplate
calling a meeting in their city of all women interested in peace.

Not all friends of peace applauded the efforts of the two foreign women.
Catt was increasingly concerned over Schwimmer's seeming fixation on
mediation and "shocked" at her extravagant expenditures on cables to get
foreign women to support her cause. Instead, she urged her zealous friend
to champion women's suffrage on her tour. She advised her, for instance,
not to talk about peace to a German-American bazaar, but attempt to "turn
the Germans to thinking kindly of woman suffrage." But Catt's appeals
were of course in vain, and she wondered whether Schwimmer "is a little
mad over all this world's madness. Her plans for peace are impractical."[48]

Schwimmer's total dedication to the question of an early peace especially
upset peace workers who were more moderate in temperament and less
confident in the feasibility of negotiations in the near future. At a Chicago
peace meeting, after David Starr Jordan had given a speech in which he

blamed the war on Europe's professional military leaders, Schwimmer replied by roundly denouncing American peace workers for their "petty theories," which never resulted in action. "You talk and talk," she complained, "but you accomplish nothing for we sufferers on the other side." This emotional outburst startled Louis Lochner, the energetic young secretary of the Chicago Peace Society, which had sponsored the meeting. Following the meeting he apologized to Jordan, describing her as "evidently unstrung and nothing short of hysterical." Lochner dismissed Schwimmer's behavior at the time as much more exceptional than typical of her, but the incident foreshadowed difficulties Lochner would encounter a year later when he would attempt to deal with her mercurial temperament on the peace venture organized by Henry Ford.[49]

If Schwimmer's confrontational approach served to distance her from many peace reformers, her magnetic personality also attracted many women who admired her outspoken ways and penchant for peace action. Among the first of many women endorsing Schwimmer's mediation campaign was the well-known British novelist and art historian, Violet Paget, who wrote under the pseudonym, Vernon Lee. Having also lived in Germany, Italy, and France, she appreciated the cultural traditions of each and, assuming a humanistic–internationalist perspective, came to believe that people were very much alike. She had witnessed Europe's diplomatic crises and military escalation before the war, which tended to divide Europeans, and, like other pacifistic women, had sharply criticized them. The Great War confirmed her worst suspicions. In an open letter to Schwimmer, which Oswald Villard, Fanny's pacifist son, obligingly published in his *Evening Post*, Lee applauded Schwimmer's mediation plan as a healthy antidote to the current war enthusiasm. She would continue to speak out against the war and would soon join Swanwick as a female member of the UDC executive committee.[50]

Schwimmer's most intimate and loyal supporter, however, was Lola Maverick Lloyd, who agreed wholeheartedly with Schwimmer's radical politics and pacifism. With four small children, Lloyd was perhaps an unlikely peace activist. But her marriage to a Chicago industrialist, the son of muckraker and socialist Henry Demarest Lloyd, was falling apart and heading for a divorce, and she was also attracted to radical causes. (She was after all a Maverick whose family name, derived from her unconventional, unorthodox Texas grandfather, had become synonymous with independent thinking.) Having some means, Lloyd provided financial backing for some of Schwimmer's peace exploits, and the two would remain lifelong friends.

Addams, who kept her finger on the pulse of the women's movement, watched the developments growing out of the Schwimmer and Pethick-Lawrence lecture tour with a mixture of admiration and consternation. The pair's speeches in Chicago had already inspired her to cooperate with

Lochner in organizing an Emergency Federation of Peace force in her home city, and she was frankly pleased that women elsewhere were showing enthusiasm for peace. Like many other female pacifists of her day, Addams believed that the "maternal instinct" defined women as love-giving and life-giving—in short, they were naturally peaceful. As she had remarked shortly after the outbreak of the war, "I have never advocated, even in my suffrage arguments, that women were better than men; but there are special reasons why women are more sensitive to the sacrifice of human life than men." Distrustful of ideology, she did not promote maternalism but, ever practical, recognized the ideology as a powerful motivating force for women's interest in peace work.

Still, she at first hesitated to endorse a national women's peace movement. In the first place, she recognized that the chances for successful mediation of the World War were remote. Earlier she had endorsed Schwimmer's mediation plan "reluctantly as a member of the National Suffrage Board, simply because I don't like to damp any plan which is so widespread, but it doesn't seem very feasible." Addams believed that calling a national meeting for the creation of a women's peace organization would be "most difficult." As she confided to Schwimmer, "I dread a large and ill-assorted assemblage and doubt if we could do anything with it." Moreover, she feared that her unqualified support of a national women's peace movement might conflict with the work of the Henry Street group, which was quietly drafting its own statement on peace and international reform.

But if Addams was cautious in her appraisal of the situation and frankly "perplexed" about what to do next, she always inclined toward activism and did not wish to see women's enthusiasm for peace dissipated. For quite different reasons, both Schwimmer and Catt actively nourished Addams' interest in the women's burgeoning peace movement. Schwimmer realized that she, a foreigner, could not become its leader and that Catt was too committed to suffrage to assume this role. Addams, a well-known American woman peace advocate, became her choice, and she urged Catt to prevail upon Addams to take on this leadership role. She exaggerated claims of Addams' interest in spearheading the movement, even writing Catt that Addams had agreed to call a women's mass meeting when Addams was still undecided about the issue. At the same time, Schwimmer, telling Addams incorrectly that Catt had already endorsed a national women's peace organization, tried to cajole her to organize a mass meeting in Washington, DC.[51]

Catt's entreaties to Addams, however, were directly related to her suffrage concerns. Having been deluged with letters from suffragists urging her to lead a women's peace movement, she continued to believe that peace concerns could greatly complicate the suffrage campaign. "It is enough to drive a dry to drink," she complained. Most immediately, Catt worried that the militant Congressional Union was already planning a peace meeting to coincide with its annual convention in Washington, DC, in January 1915. Fearing that the militants would co-opt the women's peace movement to popularize their radical suffragist strategy and detract from her own main-stream suffrage efforts, she began bombarding Addams with letters telling her that she (Addams) was uniquely qualified to guide American women's enthusiasm for peace. She also tried to dissuade her from deferring the leadership role to other prominent pacific-minded women, particularly Lucia Ames Mead who had been involved in full-time peace work for a decade and headed the peace and arbitration committees of two women's organizations. Having remained in Europe until November, Mrs Mead had not been actively engaged in the women's groundswell for peace and was not a logical candidate, but Catt proceeded to discredit her anyway. She argued that Mead was suspect as a leader because of her too "conspicu-ous" position in the "overmasculinized" prewar movement and then demeaned her as "an extremely unpopular woman. I confess that while I cannot name a single sensible reason for my feeling, I always want to run when I see her coming." Very willing to have Addams relieve her of peace concerns, Catt encouraged her to use her name to enlist suffragists' support for peace.[52]

Schwimmer's and Catt's efforts likely had some effect; for when the Washington group continued with its plans for a national peace meeting, Addams decided to promote the movement. It was not that she believed women were more uniquely qualified for peacework (the Emergency Peace Federation in Chicago included men as well as women), but she recognized that many more women than men had shown enthusiastic commitment to the cause. When Catt wrote her sharply criticizing the inertia of the exist-ing peace societies, Addams replied, "I quite agree with you as to the masculine management of the existing Peace Societies. I have been identified with them for years, and while I believe that men and women work best together on these public measures, there is no doubt that at this crisis the women are most eager for action." Together with other pacific-minded women, she addressed appeals to prominent women in existing reform groups to convene in Washington on January 10, 1915, to organize a new women's peace organization. Three thousand women answered the call and founded a new group, which they titled the Woman's Peace Party.[53]

The spontaneous groundswell for a female peace movement and its rapid crystallization into an organization was a heady, almost ethereal experience for some women attracted to the new undertaking. Thus, one of them, Belle La Follette, wife of the Wisconsin progressive senator, exulted, "[T]he Women's [sic] Peace Party is *taking* like a prairie fire and I am like an imprisoned spirit set fire!!!," and in response her good friend, the Boston reformer, Elizabeth Glendower Evans, extended the same imagery:

"I have jumped in with my whole soul. Doubts and self-disparagement are all swept away – I am so on fire that I can pass the flame along."[54]

———

Fortunately for the movement, the women channeled their newfound emotional intensity toward the development of a constructive program. At its Washington meeting, the Woman's Peace Party adopted a platform of 11 planks. While some of them, such as limitation of armaments, democratic control over foreign policies, and a "concert of nations" to supersede "balance-of-power" in diplomacy, were similar to the platform of the UDC, the women drew on a wide range of international reformers' critiques of the "old" diplomacy and their search for "new" principles to guide foreign affairs. Even the one "domestic" plank endorsing women's suffrage was framed in the context of the "further humanizing of governments." The foreign policy provisions actually anticipated the liberal internationalist principles later espoused in Woodrow Wilson's Fourteen Points of 1918. Most important for the mediation movement, however, the first plank called for "The immediate calling of a convention of neutral nations in the interest of early peace." This idea of a neutral conference, almost identical to Schwimmer's original appeal to Wilson, thereafter became the *idée fixe* of almost all American peace activists.[55]

As the new peace group publicized the proposal for a neutral conference, Julia Grace Wales, a 24-year-old Canadian instructor of English at the University of Wisconsin, was spelling out more fully its implications and possibilities. Deeply religious, Wales had assumed before 1914 that Europe was developing an enlightened and progressive civilization, and the outbreak of the war had shocked her tender-hearted sensibilities. She found it difficult to comprehend why Europeans would defy their humane heritage and participate in mass murder. Surely, she reasoned, someone would devise a plan that would allow the belligerents to come to their senses and end the bloodshed.[56] When she found that nobody else came forward with proposals for mediation of the war, she began to search for possible ways to end it.

Apparently independent of Schwimmer's or other peace proposals, in December 1914 she completed a draft of a plan that called for the neutral nations to appoint delegates to a conference for continuous mediation.[57] Although similar in many respects to Schwimmer's plan, Wales' did not mention an immediate armistice. Instead, it emphasized that the neutral conference would explore the issues involved in the conflict and serve as a clearinghouse for peace proposals from both sides. It would invite suggestions from the warring nations and also submit its own proposals to them on the difficult questions of territorial boundaries, indemnities, disarmament, and postwar security. However small the short-range accomplishments of the conference, Wales believed that it would stimulate intelligent discussion on the present war situation and offer the belligerents some opportunity, involving neither prior commitment to any definite program nor humiliation because of any one of them, to consider the possibility of peace. The hope was that the neutral conference would succeed in "tempting" the belligerents into peace negotiations before the continuing slaughter on the battlefield resulted in either a military victory for one side or the exhaustion of both.[58]

Wales discussed her plan with several of her university colleagues, some of whom were members of the Wisconsin Peace Society, and early in 1915 the society published her plan (anonymously because she was a Canadian citizen) as a 12-page pamphlet. Originally entitled International Plan for Continuous Mediation Without Armistice and later given the simpler title, the Wisconsin Plan, her pamphlet was distributed to the nation's foremost pacifists, including Addams, Jordan, and Lochner. All of them were impressed with her plan and urged her to distribute it more widely.[59] It was endorsed, for example, by the Woman's Peace Party and a National Emergency Peace Conference attended by 2,000 individuals representing some 200 liberal, socialist, labor, and pacifist organizations in Chicago in late February 1915. Shortly thereafter the governors of six states, the Wisconsin state legislature, and more than a score of congressmen endorsed the Wisconsin Plan. Moreover, Paul Kellogg and Hamilton Holt publicized the joint mediation proposal in their journals, and the latter lectured extensively on the plan in the East and Middle West.[60]

Bolstered by this support, one of Wales' Wisconsin friends, John A. Aylward, former Democratic nominee for governor of Wisconsin, and Addams sent her plan to Woodrow Wilson. Addams had visited the President two months earlier to voice social workers' objections to pending restrictive immigration legislation, and she had warmly thanked him for his veto.[61] If she had anticipated a friendly White House reaction to the Wisconsin Plan, however, she was to be disappointed. Wilson replied that he would look at it but, holding to his previous decision to avoid interviews with mediation proponents, refused their requests to see him personally. He frankly explained his dilemma to her: "I think I do not exaggerate when I say that requests of a similar sort come from different quarters at least every week and I should have to draw some distinctions which would become invidious before I got through with them, unless I granted interviews to all who applied for them in this matter. You will understand the delicacy this situation places me in. I should welcome a memorandum from you with all my heart."[62]

Aylward forwarded a two-page synopsis of the plan to Wilson who, despite his earlier expressed confidential objections on joint mediation, refused in his reply to comment on the proposal beyond again saying he would carefully consider it.[63] He was moving cautiously on mediation and obviously did not want to say anything that might become public knowledge and close off his options. In this case, for instance, his stated objections to joint mediation could have jeopardized support from neutral nations for any uses of his good offices for mediation the belligerents might sometime request or that he might initiate independently. For peace advocates committed to joint mediation, however, the President's noncommittal reply intimated that he was not firmly wedded to any particular mediation strategy and could still be won over to their views. Wilson's response also seemed to suggest that he was not yet convinced the mediation movement had aroused any widespread support at home or abroad. In truth, despite their organizational efforts the peace workers had made only modest progress by the early spring of 1915. It was obvious to them that they would have to stimulate more public interest in their cause before they could command a presidential hearing, much less action on mediation.

2

Women at The Hague

Rebuffed during the first months of the war, the peace advocates nonetheless continued to expand the mediation movement. Once again it was women who seized the initiative. Even as President Wilson was refusing to see a delegation regarding the Wisconsin Plan, several American women were preparing to attend a large international women's congress in the Netherlands. Aletta H. Jacobs, president of the Dutch National Society for Women Suffrage, had unwittingly promoted the congress when, upon hearing that the war compelled the German women to cancel the biennial meeting of the International Woman Suffrage Alliance scheduled to be held in Berlin in June 1915, she convened an emergency meeting of the Dutch alliance's foreign affairs committee to consider an IWSA meeting on neutral territory.

Jacobs contemplated nothing more than the discussion of the alliance's routine business matters and a symbolic demonstration of the solidarity and friendship among women suffragists during wartime. When Chrystal Macmillan, an activist secretary of the alliance in Great Britain, received the invitation, however, she immediately wrote these same auxiliaries suggesting that the suffrage alliance should invite women from a wide range of national and international societies to consider all aspects of the peace question. She proposed that the meeting discuss the subjects of international arbitration, democratic control of foreign policy, principles underlying the revision of territorial boundaries, reduction of armaments, and world organization. She also indicated that if the alliance refused to sanction such a meeting, she would urge women interested in these issues to convene one on their own.[1]

While expressing her personal convictions, Macmillan knew that many alliance members shared her general sentiments. In the previous months, issues of *Jus Suffragii* contained letters from European women expressing their unwavering faith, in the face of raging national passions, in women's solidarity and internationalism and their hopes for an early peace. Especially noticeable were two actions. The first came from two German pacifists, Frida Perlen and Lida Gustava Heymann. Both women, along with Heymann's lifelong companion Anita Augspurg, had long been radical pacifists and even before 1914 had often brought serious discomfort to their feminist friends for trying to commit suffrage organizations to international understanding and against militarism. In 1909, Heymann and Augsburg even resigned for a time from the International Woman Suffrage Alliance, because they believed the organization allowed itself to be "carried along in the wake of the warlike character of male politics, and was governed by the petty fear that a stand for pacifism might damage the prospects for female suffrage." As the war began, Perlen had cabled the Kaiser to stop the war, while Heymann had visited Bavarian war ministry to ask the minister to send a telegram to Czar Nicholas for the same purpose. On both occasions, the women were treated politely, but their entreaties were ignored. Undeterred, they used the pages of *Jus Suffragii* to make passionate pleas for a massive women's protest against the war. Perlen's appeal concluded, for instance, that women should "join the peace movement in thousands and tens of thousands."

The second event was an open Christmas letter to German and Austrian women, which the British pacifist Emily Hobhouse circulated and was published in *Jus Suffragii*. Signed by 101 British women, the letter expressed their firm faith in the common humanity of womanhood and their dedication to the active search for an early and just peace settlement. "Sisters, . .," it read in part, "Do not let us forget that our very anguish unites us, while technically at enmity in obedience to our rulers, we owe allegiance to that higher law which bids us live in peace with all men . . . Do not humanity and commonsense alike prompt us to join hands with the women of neutral countries, and urge our rulers to stay further bloodshed?"[2]

The replies to Macmillan's appeals soon indicated, however, that her views represented a distinct minority of European suffragists, most of whom either feared the radical implications of a women's peace movement or considered it impractical. The thrust of the many negative responses, Jacobs later recalled, was, "Personally I think it's a good idea but my organization just doesn't want to hear about it."[3] Nevertheless, more than 150 German and Austrian women sent a reply to the British Christmas letter warmly endorsing its sentiments for peace; and several women from many European neutral and belligerent nations, distressed at the apparent reluctance of neutral governments to promote mediation of the war, enthusiastically endorsed Macmillan's proposal for a peace meeting.[4]

When Jacobs learned of women's support for Macmillan's initiative, she viewed it as an opportunity to organize a large women's congress. Because the International Woman Suffrage Alliance would not officially sponsor such a gathering, she decided to help interested women call one of their own. She used the Amsterdam planning sessions to issue invitations to the national auxiliaries of the alliance and affiliated groups suggesting the convocation of the meeting in Holland.[5] Jacobs thus became the key figure in implementing Macmillan's proposal. One of the few women physicians in Holland, Jacobs was widely respected in feminist circles for her professional attainments and her advocacy of birth control and attacks on prostitution. She befriended the American feminist and economist Charlotte Perkins Gilman and translated into Dutch Gilman's *Women and Economics* (1899). Gilman's argument in this pioneering work, considered quite radical at the time, was that women needed to go beyond suffrage to attain economic independence and suggested cooperative ventures that would free women from household drudgery. (Jacobs' translation inspired Schwimmer's translation of Gilman's book into Hungarian a few years later.) In 1913, Jacobs performed the same task for Olive Schreiner's *Women and Labour*. Jacobs was also a leading suffragist and had served as prominent member of the International Woman Suffrage Alliance since its founding in 1902 and in 1911–1912 had traveled around the world with its president, Carrie Chapman Catt.[6] Along with Mrs Catt, she was at the time probably the best-known suffragist in the worldwide suffrage movement.

Dr Jacobs' endorsement of a women's conference on peace questions stemmed directly from her experiences during the first stages of the European war. With the outbreak of hostilities she and her Dutch colleagues had immediately devoted most of their time to arduous relief work for thousands of Belgian refugees streaming across the Dutch border. Suffrage work stopped altogether and seemed insignificant compared with the sufferings and miseries arising from the war. Appalled at the cruelties of warfare, especially as they affected defenseless women and children, she took a deep interest in the cause of world peace. She cooperated with men and women in organizing Holland's most active peace group, the Nederlandsche Anti-Oorlog Raad (Dutch Antiwar Council); and because of her intimate contacts in the suffrage movements, she also wrote to alliance friends asking them what women could do "to stop this scandalous bloodshed. Ought not the women of the whole world . . . send a strong and serious protest to the different Emperors, Kings, and other responsible men?" Preoccupied with relief work, she did not find time to devise and circulate a women's antiwar petition, and Schwimmer, who might have coordinated such an effort, was on her way to America to promote her own campaign for ending the war.[7]

Jacobs was already familiar with the international peace movement before 1914. Absorbing her father's antimilitarist views, she grew up opposed, as she later put it, to the military's "blind obedience" and "impersonal devotion," which "completely contradicted my own sense of self-respect" and "offended my dearly held belief in freedom." She was

2.1 Aletta Jacobs, standing, and Carrie Chapman Catt in Capetown, South
Africa, 1911, during their world tour. (University Museum, Grönigen)

also familiar with the best-selling novel, *Die Waffen Nieder* (*Lay Down Your
Arms*) by Bertha von Suttner and, then a dedicated suffragist, carried on
an ongoing friendly debate with Suttner, who believed feminists had to
choose between the peace and suffrage movements, but could not become
involved in both, until shortly before Suttner's death on the eve of the
European war. Moreover, through her husband, a member of the Dutch
Parliament, Jacobs often attended the annual conferences of the Interparliamentary Union, where she was exposed to progressive internationalist
views.[8]

Nevertheless, before the war she did not question imperialism, including
the excesses of her own government's colonial policy, and had shown little
real interest in peace movements. Partly, it was her assumption that the
notion of war among the so-called advanced powers was anachronistic. "At

the time," Dr Jacobs later wrote, "I was so idealistic I even believed that in
Germany, a military state par excellence, the people were simply too highly
developed to allow its participation in a European war."[9] More important,
her total immersion in the Dutch women's suffrage campaign absorbed her
attention. Her single-minded devotion to obtaining the vote for women led
her to ridicule a resolution passed at the 1913 IWSA meeting urging the
member nations to request their governments to institute national inquiries
into the extent and causes of prostitution. Such requests, she protested,
only diverted attention from the suffrage crusade: "There are many
important questions besides commercialised vice, and if we begin to work
for one of these there is no reason not to take up others – for instance, peace
by arbitration, temperance, sweating of women and children by employers,
etc. – and what then, finally, would become of our work for suffrage?"[10]

While the war in Europe greatly aroused her emotional sympathies for
peace, her loyalty to the suffrage cause remained strong. During the height
of her revulsion against war, she urged women to "combine and try at least
to make an end of this war;" but she emphasized that in the long run the
"ballot will give us the greatest power to work for this end. As soon as
possible we must let our cry for enfranchisement be heard again." And if
the prospects for winning the vote in Holland seemed at any moment to
outweigh the chances for an early peace, she might downplay the latter.[11]

In addition, Jacobs was a strong-willed, frequently uncompromising
woman who might refuse to cooperate with fellow peace activists if she did
not share their views on a given issue. Alice Hamilton, one of Addams'
close American friends, would soon describe her, only a little unfairly, as
"very decided, fairly irritable and quite able to see that her own comfort is
attended to."[12] Such qualities did not bode well for close cooperation
among women pacifists during the war years.

But these were long-range problems, which fortunately for the peace
movement did not affect its short-run prospects. Indeed, because of Dr
Jacobs' prominence in the international suffrage movement, her endorsement of a congress of women virtually assured widespread support for the
proposal.[13] Supported by many like-minded Dutch feminists, especially
Rosa Manus and Dr Mia Boissevain, she invited leading women from
neutral and belligerent nations in Europe to convene in Amsterdam on
February 12–13 to consider the convocation of an international women's
meeting. In addition to several Dutch women, handfuls of representatives
from Britain, Belgium and Germany answered her call for this preparatory
meeting. The women worked out the details of planning the congress,
appointed a committee to frame the resolutions for a preliminary program,
and then in the name of the Dutch women issued a "Call to the Women of
all Nations" to attend a peace congress at The Hague.[14]

As drafted by the committee, the preliminary resolutions reflected the emerging consensus among women friends of peace throughout the Western world on the principles of the eventual peace settlement. While formulated without direct American advice, they expressed aims quite similar to those of American and British international reformers. Like those of the Woman's Peace Party and the Union for Democratic Control, the Amsterdam resolutions called for the belligerents to define their peace terms, the referral of future international disputes to arbitration and conciliation, the use of "international pressure" against any nations that resorted to arms without referring its case to arbitration or conciliation, and the democratic control of foreign policy. They also proposed no transfer of territory without the consent of the inhabitants and the promotion of international goodwill and of peace education for children. Finally, the preliminary program included resolutions on women's relation to the war: a protest against their sufferings in wartime, women's responsibility for war prevention, and the political enfranchisement of women.

Unlike the Woman's Peace Party, however, the European women had not yet devised a formula for ending the bloodshed. The best they could offer was a resolution by Perlen and Theodora Wilson Wilson, an English Quaker and successful novelist, calling for an immediate truce until the belligerents publicly defined their peace terms. After much debate the resolutions committee included this proposal for a truce on the preliminary program, but the wide difference of opinion on this question at the Amsterdam meeting mirrored the larger divisions among women interested in the upcoming congress at The Hague.[15] As Macmillan explained, "Over this resolution on the preliminary programme it was that so much controversy was waged. Not a few of those who wished to attend the Congress said they would not think it worth to go if it had not been for this resolution since it was the one which asked for action to be taken towards ending hostilities. On the other hand it was because of this resolution that many women refused to attend the Congress or even to express any sympathy with it."[16]

The prospect of a truce was not completely far-fetched, as during Christmas the opposing armies over wide sections of the Western front had imposed a general cease-fire. The origins of the Christmas truce, as it was called, are somewhat obscure, but apparently began on Christmas eve, with German troops putting up their traditional *Tannenbäume* topped with lights along the front lines and singing carols in their trenches. Hearing the yuletide music from their own bunkers nearby, French, Belgian, and British soldiers responded with their own caroling. Soon a few daring souls from both sides, announcing that they were unarmed, ventured into no-man's-land. No shots were fired, and fraternization between the two sides ensued. The truce quickly spread to cover large portions of more than hundreds of miles of front in Flanders and France. The opposing soldiers exchanged photographs and other souvenirs, food, and tobacco, sang popular folk melodies, cooperated in burying their dead, and even engaged in games of football amidst the shell holes.

The participants were hardly pacifists, but were likely expressing surviving nineteenth century notions of civility, chivalry, and morality. A common Christianity among the enemy combatants also facilitated the peaceful interlude. In any event, the truce was an extraordinary manifestation of the soldiers' uncertainty about the purposes of their fighting, if not their active yearning for peace. The French and Belgian forces could at least claim they were defending their lands from invasion, but the belligerent governments, all claiming to act from self-defense, had not yet publicly clarified their war (or peace) aims.

The Christmas truce, which had percolated up from the rank and file, of course did not last. Senior officers acquiesced in the one-day reprieve from fighting, but none in the affected areas emerged to champion a permanent ceasefire. Commanding officers on both sides also objected to the demonstrations of peace sentiment and could use the threat of courts martial to silence future peace demonstrations. Along with government authorities, they opposed publicity of the truce, but soldiers sent home details of the experience, and several newspapers and magazines (except in France where censorship mostly kept the story out of the press) published first-hand accounts of the episode.

Reports of the Christmas ceasefire briefly heartened those revolted by the mounting carnage on the continent. Lady Kate Courtney of Penwith, a British Quaker, confided in her diary: "The stirring and most touching accounts from many sources of the spontaneous Christmas truce by the common soldiers, English and German, with exchange of souvenirs, of talk, of carol signing, have made one feel happier. Surely it will catch people's imagination and be infectious!" Curiously, however, the women activists rarely referred, then or later, to the Christmas truce publicly or in their private correspondence as a valid demonstration of frontline sentiment in support of their quest for a negotiated peace. The women chose to overlook the Christmas events, perhaps because they sensed that public references to them would spark an unproductive debate with incensed ultranationalistic opinion for seeming to impugn the soldiers' courage or patriotism, and the resulting controversy would deflect their attention from the development of their own organization and program.[17]

———

When Jane Addams received the Dutch invitation urging "you and your whole peace party" to participate in a women's congress at The Hague, she immediately cabled her acceptance. She also forwarded the invitation to the members of cooperating organizations of the Woman's Peace Party, urging them to join her in the undertaking. She then set out for New York to persuade American women to attend the congress.[18] To those she could not see personally, she sent letters encouraging their participation. Anticipating the objections and reservations of skeptical women to their attendance at a European conference during wartime, she frankly admitted that "the undertaking has about it something of a certain aspect of moral adventure and may easily fail – even do harm" to the peace cause. But she went on to emphasize that American women, farthest removed from war-torn Europe, had a special obligation to respond affirmatively to the European invitation. She also offered the possibility of constructive results from the congress. Whatever the short-run failure, the congress might lead to long-range positive gains for the peace movement. Women "willing to fail" in the experiment might help to "break through that curious hypnotic spell" and the inhuman irrelevances of traditional diplomacy that paralyzed the belligerents from considering peace proposals.[19]

Once again demonstrating her organizational talents, Addams succeeded in persuading several reluctant women to journey to the congress. She especially encouraged the participation of experienced peace advocates and prominent professional women who would make up a "coherent" delegation, thereby giving it some "chance of success."[20]

Winning the endorsement, if not the participation, of Carrie Chapman Catt, IWSA president, would have gone a long way toward committing the organization to the upcoming women's peace meeting at The Hague, but Addams had no luck. In mid-November 1914, Mrs Catt had written Jacobs, "We of the neutral nations ought to do something – but what? Can we hold a meeting in a neutral country and there make plans for something practical?" But she was instinctively cautious about more radical women activists. Part of Catt's strongly negative views of militant suffragists involved in the founding of the Woman's Peace Party, she had confided to Addams, was that they were "extremely out of favor" with the IWSA. (The alliance had consistently recognized the British militant WSPU as "fraternal" members only, for instance, ostensibly on the grounds that membership was limited to one group per country.) "My prayer has been that I might walk so straight a path that I could help pull that body [the alliance] together at the end of the war. Especially is it important to keep my skirts clear at this particular moment, for a vote is on its round to determine whether or not we should hold an international peace conference in Holland in April. I should lose my only hope of help in the International situation if I manage to get tangled" in a row with militant groups.

Catt at first seemed favorably disposed toward the Hague congress, but when Dr Jacobs asked her to preside over it, she claimed that her suffrage work prevented her absence from New York. Indeed, Catt continued to back away from pacifist activity almost as quickly as she had seemed hesitatingly to endorse it. Almost simultaneously, she began receiving letters from suffrage alliance members in Europe loudly affirming their support of the war effort in their countries, denouncing the nation's enemies in the conflict, and deploring the talk of peace in *Jus Suffragii*. Under these circumstances, Catt thought any meeting would split the IWSA, which she wanted to avoid at all costs. She thus opposed any meeting bringing women from the warring nations together, complaining that the effort "would be too much like trying to organize a peace society in an insane asylum." When plans for the Hague meeting developed anyway, she took a neutral position, finally informing Jane Addams laconically that "I have no feelings in the matter."[21]

Another prominent suffragist, Anna Howard Shaw, president of the National American Woman Suffrage Association, also declined the Dutch invitation. She pleaded financial exigencies and poor health, but left no doubt that she disapproved of the venture. She and Mrs Catt were then consulting regularly on the women's peace movement as it might affect the suffrage cause (partly perhaps because Catt was going to take over the NAWSA presidency later in 1915), and she agreed with Catt's fear of dividing the international suffrage movement. "I have not the least hope," she wrote Jacobs, "that it would be possible to hold such a meeting even among the neutral nations; a spark would create a blaze in a moment that would make any future meeting of the Alliance impossible . . . I feel that my first duty is here. That the best thing I can do for peace and a thousand other things is to get votes for women."[22]

Some who could not attend were nonetheless supportive. Addams wrote Wald three times, and Addams' good friend Mary Rozet Smith wrote the New York social worker once, to try to get her to join the expedition, but she held firm that her obligations at the Henry Street settlement prevented her participation. She nonetheless strongly endorsed the undertaking and came to the pier in Hoboken, New Jersey, to bid the delegation *bon voyage*. Similarly, Anna Garlin Spencer pleaded previous commitments, and Lucia Ames Mead had to care for her ailing husband; both strongly regretted their non-participation. Neither could Belle La Follette nor Elizabeth Kent, wife of another pacific-minded member of Congress, join the expedition. Other women, however, responded affirmatively to Addams' entreaties.

Emily Greene Balch wanted to join the venture from the start, but she at first claimed that her obligations teaching sociology and economics at Wellesley College prohibited her extended absence from the United States. Addams refused to treat her letter as a demurral and immediately wrote her again, emphasizing that the success of the venture depended largely upon the participation of women who could contribute their expertise to the congress. "We should have delegates conversant with the racial and nationality situation, and I know of no one who could meet these requirements better than you would . . . Don't you think that there is a certain obligation on the women who have had the advantages of study and training, to take this possible chance to help out? I don't want to be too insistent but won't you please consider it again?" Addams' second appeal worked, for Balch managed to hire a substitute for her classes and then successfully persuaded the president of Wellesley to grant her a leave of absence.[23]

Balch later described her decision to go to The Hague as "a turning point in my life." That it was. She had been awkward and hesitant in the Henry Street peace discussions, confessing at one point that she felt "so ignorant" on foreign policy questions.[24] She learned quickly, however, and her European experiences in connection with the Hague congress led her to irrevocable commitment to the peace movement. She spent the rest of her life as a peace worker.

Her deepening involvement in the peace cause, however, was not entirely a matter of chance. Balch was the second oldest of six siblings in a warm and loving family. Growing up in the Boston area right after the Civil War, she was exposed in her youth to the idealistic views of antislavery reformers and the writings of New England transcendentalists. Her maturing interest in literature developed at newly founded Bryn Mawr College where she graduated in three years. Alongside her intellectual pursuits, Balch was also an intensely religious person and was attracted to humanitarian causes. When she decided to attend the Hague congress in 1915, she was already searching for new outlets for her benevolent impulses—and the Hague congress would satisfy these aspirations. In the previous two decades Balch had confided in her diary her dissatisfaction with the routineness of her teaching and "a certain passivity or dullness" in her inner life. She had lost none of her faith in God or in Christian service and for a time considered the ministry as a new career. Her friends discouraged her from this idea, saying she could accomplish her goals outside the church. But her search for personal meaning persisted, as did her strong feelings of guilt for her aloofness from the misfortunes and sufferings of less fortunate peoples. Even her involvement as a volunteer in a Boston settlement house did not entirely fulfill her notions of service. In a sense, her increasing involvement in the peace movement satisfied her personal quest for inner peace.[25]

Moreover, Balch's turn to peace rather than some other humanitarian reform was not fortuitous. Following graduation from Bryn Mawr, she spent two years of graduate study in Paris and Berlin in the 1890s as well as one-and-a-half years of postgraduate research in southeastern Europe in the following decade. Her European sojourns had helped to nurture a cosmopolitan outlook, and her studies on the assimilation of Slavic immigrants in the United States emphasized the virtues of cultural pluralism to newcomers and natives alike and presaged aspects of her later idealistic internationalism.[26] Nor was she ignorant of peace questions before 1914. Her minister for more than 25 years before the Great War was the Unitarian Charles F. Dole, an uncompromising pacifist and anti-imperialist, and he had helped to impress on her the racism and greed motivating America's domination of Filipinos and Latin Americans at the turn of the century. She had early perceived that preoccupation with foreign policy adventures diverted attention from pressing domestic questions, and she had signed a petition to Congress protesting proposed armament increases in the budget in early 1914. The destruction of the whole network of reform efforts in Europe following the outbreak of the Great War, dramatically confirmed what she already believed.[27]

Emily Balch was one of the 47 American women who journeyed to The Hague. The list of American participants further illustrated the transformation of the peace cause since the outbreak of the war. Only two active participants in the prewar movement, Addams and Fannie Fern Andrews, attended the congress. More interested in international education and world organization than in mediation, Mrs Andrews had already agreed to serve as the lone American delegate to the founding meeting at The Hague in early April of the Central Organization for a Durable Peace, an international group started by the Dutch Anti-War Council for the formulation and dissemination of internationalist principles for the peace settlement and postwar world order, and she departed for Holland several weeks ahead of the American delegates bound for the women's congress.[28]

Julia Grace Wales also bolstered the list of active participants in the mediation movement who joined the delegation. Among other members were three professional colleagues of Addams in Chicago, who were also top scholars in the fields of social work and industrial relations: Grace Abbott, a Hull House resident and lecturer on immigration at the University of Chicago; Dr Alice Hamilton, a physician specializing in industrial diseases who was also living at Hull House; and Sophonisba P. Breckenridge, dean of the Chicago School of Civics and Philanthropy (later absorbed into the University of Chicago Graduate School of Social Service Administration). Florence Holbrook, school principal and reformer, and Harriet P. Thomas, social worker and executive secretary of the Woman's Peace Party, were additional reform-minded Chicago friends accompanying Addams.

Other delegates included Madeleine Z. Doty, lawyer and prison reformer, who reported on the women's congress for the New York *Evening Post*; Angela Morgan, author of the popular poem "The Battle Cry of Mothers," Elizabeth Glendower Evans; social workers; suffragists; and teachers. On the whole, the Americans were well-educated, solidly liberal, and strongly pacifistic middle-class women. Even organized labor had a modest representation, however, with a member from the Telephone Operators Union and two from the Woman's Trade Union League participating, and the delegation also included some socialists and advocates of working America, such as Alice Thatcher Post, a leading single-tax advocate, vice-president of the Woman's Peace Party, and wife of Assistant Secretary of Labor Louis F. Post, and Mary Heaton Vorse, who was a labor activist as well as a suffragist and journalist.

Although suffrage organizations sent some representatives like Vorse to the congress, suffrage was not a major issue to the Americans. Balch's brother had tried to discourage his sister from joining the Hague venture, offering several objections, including the linking of suffrage and peace issues. "What are those quite single-mindedly in favor of peace, but who oppose woman suffrage, now to do?" he had queried. Balch was relieved to find that her brother's fear was groundless. A few, like Dr Hamilton, were skeptical of the undertaking, but their loyalty to Addams and their adventuresome temperament carried them along. Despite its pronounced liberal orientation, the group was neither overly rebellious nor radical, Doty modestly labeling it "sane, sound, and safe."[29]

Lola Maverick Lloyd and four other American delegates, along with Rosika Schwimmer, sailed from New York in early April. Shortly before their departure, they sent a telegram to the Chicago headquarters of the Woman's Peace Party urging Louis Lochner to accompany the remaining 42 American delegates, who along with Mrs Pethick-Lawrence and her husband were to depart a week later, April 16, on the Dutch steamship *Noordam*. Always inclined toward activism in the peace movement, Lochner approved the suggestion. His mounting concerns over the European

2.2 Emmeline Pethick-Lawrence, left, standing next to Jane Addams and other American delegates embarking on the *Noordam* to the Women's Congress at The Hague, April 1915. (Bain Collection, Library of Congress)

slaughter had pushed him leftward toward what he called "aggressive paci-fism," and he was meeting resistance from the conservative executive committee of the Chicago Peace Society, which opposed his attempts to commit the group to an activist antiwar position. His friends in the Chicago Peace Society helped him negotiate a leave of absence from his administrative duties; but Lochner, finding a new haven with the women peace seekers and other activists for mediation, would soon resign from the Chicago group.

During the *Noordam*'s trans-Atlantic crossing, Lochner gave lectures to the women on the aims and history of the prewar peace movement. Because of his writing skills as well as his close association with Jane Addams' Chicago peace work, he also served as her private secretary and as ghost-writer of her press dispatches to the *New York Times* throughout the entire venture.[30]

The women's peace efforts of course received prominent press coverage. Beginning with Schwimmer's peace petition, her lecture tour with Pethick-Lawrence, and the founding of the Woman's Peace Party, newspapers increasingly reported the women's activities. As a large-scale venture, the proposed Hague gathering was a newsworthy event, which explains why newspapers and magazines hired American delegates to write first-hand, freelance accounts of the events. Editorial opinion in the United States on the upcoming congress varied considerably. Only a few publications like *The Survey* unqualifiedly endorsed the women's program, while others, believing the participants would fail, nonetheless gave them credit for their organizational efforts and willingness to confront the major issues of peace and war.

Among the women's critics, none was harsher or more quoted in the press than Theodore Roosevelt. His strongly negative views of pacifism were already well known. His public papers as president are filled with references to peace advocates' "shortsightedness," "folly," "sentimental-ity," "selfish indifference," "fanatical extremism," demagoguery," and "hysterical pseudo-philanthropy." His vitriolic rhetoric escalated during the World War. As the women prepared to journey to The Hague, for example, he charged that the women's peace movement was "both base and silly. It is silly because it is absolutely futile." It is base, he went on, because, like the Northern Copperheads opposing the nation's Civil War 50 years earlier, "there is nothing more repulsive than to see people agitating for general righteousness in the abstract when they dare not stand up against wickedness in the concrete."

As an example, Roosevelt cited the women pacifists' failure to protest Germany's "frightful wrongs" in Belgium. Fanny Villard and Gertrude Pinchot, chairman of the New York branch of the Woman's Peace Party, among others, replied in the press, attacking Roosevelt's "sorry" and "dangerous" militarism and scorn for human life, while asserting that women reformers worldwide were involved in "heroic efforts" to protest the brutality of war and seek international reforms that would address its causes and prevent its recurrence. Roosevelt's strident pro-Allied and prowar views and his unrelenting criticism of the Wilson administration's "weak" foreign policy increasingly alienated him from his more dovish progressive supporters. While his colorful remarks continued to provide good copy, he was becoming something of an anachronism politically and unrepresentative of Americans' mixed and often conflicted opinions about the war.[31]

The women on the *Noordam* were aware that their transatlantic adventure was controversial, to say the least. As Balch confided to her journal en route, "We know we are ridiculous," though adding that "even being ridiculous is useful, sometimes . . . [to] say what needs to be said but is not discreet or 'the thing' to say and which important people will not say in consequence." The women wasted no time in deciding "what needs to be said." During the daytime they drafted and discussed resolutions that the American delegation might want to introduce at the congress. Then each evening they gave addresses on the peace question or debated foreign affairs subjects. Madeleine Doty described one such debate between Jane Addams and Emmeline Pethick-Lawrence on the subject of whether war was ever justifiable, Addams taking the negative:

> Totally unalike in appearance and action, by very contrast they vivify each other . . . Gentle, modest, clad in a dark silk dress, with hair pulled back from the pallid face, the light of a spirit shining in her tragic eyes, she [Addams] seems hardly of the earth. With charm and sweetness she pleads for the sacredness of life and the policy of non-resistance. To turn from her to Mrs Lawrence is to turn to a glowing, burning flame. The English woman, in her Oriental dress of red and green, is all passion, all fire. Every gesture is full of emotion and meaning. Spirit and body are one. Joyfully would she face any danger and go sinking to death, if in doing so she might hasten the world's peace.
>
> Both women are animated by the same ideal – the sacredness of life. But one looks at life as a saint, and pleads let there be peace. The other, living and suffering with humanity, facing reality, flings body and soul into the fight for peace, and for liberty, which is dearer than life itself.

During the ensuing discussion, a consensus emerged "that it is no disadvantage if we do not all agree on these theoretical points."[32]

The women devoted most of their time on board to a discussion of the resolutions the American delegation would present to the congress. Alice

Hamilton compared these discussions with "a perpetual meeting of the Woman's City Club, or the Federation of Settlements, or something like that." A self-described "doubting Thomas and a pessimist," she nonetheless conceded that the absorbing talk made her "never . . . so little bored on a trip." And from her rough-and-tumble experiences as a labor organizer, Vorse was initially skeptical of the undertaking. In particular, she had little confidence in mediation of the war. Writing home to her husband, she mocked: "Today a little Miss Wales, small, dark and slender, a thin little flame of emotion surrounding her, read a pamphlet on Armistice Without War. It is so simple and so naïve that it is as though a wee child ran into one of the cabinets of Europe and with a word showed the way out of all difficulties. Such things haven't happened in real life since Jeanne d'Arc." By the end of the Hague adventure, however, Vorse would become more sympathetic to mediation initiatives.[33]

During their voyage the women thrashed out resolutions, which accepted most of the preliminary program, including Wales' mediation plan, and added planks of their own. Grace Abbott recommended, for instance, the abolition of preferential tariffs. In clarifying the plank of the Woman's Peace Party platform urging the "gradual organization of the world to substitute Law for War" and the appointment by the American Government of a commission to promote international peace, Addams proposed a resolution advocating the establishment of an international agency to adjust economic, social, and political controversies among nation-states. She argued that the conciliation of such disputes, as distinct from violations of treaty rights and international law, would help to restrain national passions and reduce the chances for violent confrontations. In addition, the American delegates, recognizing "the idealization of the military and the undervaluation of the civilian aspects of life," proposed a resolution vaguely urging "the necessity of clarifying and moralizing the conceptions of patriotism, heroism, and honor." The American women agreed to all these resolutions.

In such a large group, there were of course some tensions, mainly over social class. During the discussion of resolutions, for example, Breckenridge and the labor advocates proposed a resolution making the investments of "capitalists" in foreign nations wholly at the risk of the investors, but by majority vote the more moderate women prevailed in substituting "citizens" for "capitalists" in the resolution. Moreover, when Balch found Pethick-Lawrence, from a well-heeled British background, patronizing in her talk about poor working girls and slum children, she gently retorted with a story of how a shirtwaist worker had dismissed Wellesley students eager to help during a strike as hapless innocents.[34]

Mostly, however, the American delegates noted the remarkable unity of spirit and purpose permeating their deliberations on shipboard. Wales marveled at the "undercurrent of absolutely united feeling" among the American women, and Alice Thatcher Post agreed that they "had worked without personal feeling or even pride of opinion." Most extravagantly, Angela Morgan exuded, "this whole experience has been simply wonderful – yet perfectly natural, as if it were preordained . . . It seems to have been a charmed voyage." Always cautious in her judgments, Addams nonetheless was pleased by this harmony. Just before leaving American shores, she had called the proposed trip "a fools' errand perhaps;" but toward the end of the voyage she admitted that "I have felt all kinds of ways about the mission itself, but the women on the whole are as nice and friendly as 40 [odd] women, thrown suddenly together, could possibly be – and so far, so good, whatever happens next."[35] In their common dedication and cooperation, the women in short approximated the ideal of a united sisterhood.

Two months before the *Noordam* crossing, Germany had proclaimed a war zone around the British Isles. Ostensibly in retaliation for the British mining of the North Sea, the German announcement threatened to sink all enemy ships in the zone. It exempted neutral shipping; but hoping to scare away neutral shipping from British waters, it warned neutrals that the torpedoing of their vessels could not always be avoided. Mistakes in fact occurred, and during early April 1915 German U-boats prowling the sea-lanes had sunk six neutral steamships, including the Dutch steamer *Katwijk*, without warning. The American women were aware of the dangers, but outwardly at least tried to seem blasé. "It is really amusing to think," Dr Hamilton wrote home, "that we are actually in the danger zone now, in this gray, still, monotonous ocean, with everything as ordinary and reassuring as can be. One cannot have a single thrill." They may have felt more secure because the *Noordam*, hoping to minimize a possible U-boat mistake, emblazoned its name in big electric lights on each side. The *Noordam*'s safe passage may also have been a beneficiary of the *Katwijk* sinking, which provoked a violent reaction in Holland and caused the German authorities in mid-April to send urgent new instructions to its submarine commanders to take extra care in sparing neutral ships, especially those under the Dutch flag. The American women of course knew nothing about shifts in German U-boat policy. Indeed, the captain of the *Noordam*, fearing controversy among the passengers, refused to divulge any news on the war situation he was regularly receiving in wireless reports.[36]

The women had a "thrill" or two toward the end of the trip. First, two German stowaways were discovered, captured, and searched. As British authorities were preparing to remove the prisoners to an awaiting naval vessel, one of them shouted, "Hoch der Kaiser, Deutschland über Alles." Then the next day the British Admiralty, without explanation, held up the *Noordam* from completing its passage through the English Channel. With their ship sitting motionless in the water, the passengers got their first, small glimpse of war alert, if not actual combat, as they came close to all kinds of ships, not only of the British military – torpedo boats, destroyers, and dirigibles looking for German submarines – but also neutral ships with large flags painted on their sides. The American delegates worried that the delay would force them to miss the Congress, but after four days the British, just as inexplicably, released the *Noordam*. The women finally arrived safely in Rotterdam, only hours before the opening session the same evening at The Hague.[37]

———

The Americans joined representatives from all the western and northern European neutrals. Twelve delegates from Norway, six from Denmark, and sixteen from Sweden attended. Of the belligerents on the continent, Germany had twenty-eight, Austria six, and Hungary ten. No women from France, Russia, and Serbia attended, but the absence of women from these countries did not necessarily mean opposition or lack of interest. As in England, Germany, and elsewhere, suffragists in France had increasingly embraced pacifism before the war, and all the major French suffrage groups then included peace sections to coordinate women's work for peace. After 1914, however, the French feminists' commitment to peace largely dissolved in the face of the patriotic groundswell among their compatriots, although a handful of prominent feminists in those countries held to their pacifist convictions. They were among the more leftwing feminists who perceived—and sometimes denounced—the conflict as a triumph of men's militarism and lust for power and the subjugation of women.[38]

Some socialist women had already initiated peace action. Defying their governments as well as their male socialist comrades, about 25 of them from European countries, including several from England and Russia (four of whom were Bolsheviks) and one from France, held their own international conference in Berne, Switzerland, in late March 1915 to protest against the war. Clara Zetkin, the leader of women socialists in Germany, initiated the meeting. The outbreak of the fighting in August 1914 profoundly shocked Zetkin. "I thought I would go mad, or that I would have to commit suicide," she later wrote. The war, and its widespread support among German socialists, made her more radical. Using her position as secretary of a small international socialist organization, she called the Berne meeting, the first international gathering of socialists since the beginning of the war, to bring together antiwar socialist women. The participants drafted a peace manifesto declaring that "the workers have nothing to gain from this war, they have everything to lose, everything, everything that is dear to them," and called on women to demand peace.[39]

The socialist women did not propose mediation of the war, however, and

their emphasis on class interests was far removed from the bourgeois pacifist feminists at The Hague. Indeed, many socialist women perceived the
suffrage movement and feminism as distractions from the class struggle,
while feminists, seeing socialist working men as uncommitted if not hostile
to women's issues, focused on attaining the vote for their sex as the path
toward liberation. The social backgrounds and ideology of the feminists
and socialist women were in fact widely divergent. Jacobs urgently wanted
French participation at the Hague congress, but she rejected the suggestion
of Dutch socialist women to invite Louise Saumoneau, the lone French
delegate at the Berne meeting, or any other French socialist. Saumoneau
was no more accommodating. When she heard of Jacobs' decision, she said
she would not cooperate with the bourgeois pacifist women under any circumstances. From a very poor working family, Saumoneau was a seamstress,
while Jacobs was a proud feminist from a privileged background. Similarly,
Jeanne Halbwachs, who became identified with the feminist peace movement in France, was the daughter of a college professor and a philosophy
student. Though she too was a socialist (she and Saumoneau were both
members of the same section of the socialist party), Saumoneau had refused
Halbwachs' request before the war for help with a feminist project.
Halbwachs remarked at the time that Saumoneau "had something of a disagreeable expression; no coquetry; the simplicity of a woman of the people:
dull, drab, truly a woman of the people. But of course we were students and
had very little contact with the workers in the [party] section."[40]

To be sure, in the first year or so of the war feminist pacifists and some
women socialists expressed similar antiwar opinions. Both believed that
women, having no political rights, bore no responsibility for the war, and
had a special responsibility for advocating peace. As Zetkin expressed it, "If
men kill, women must fight for peace; if men keep silent, our socialist duty
is to raise our voices." These socialists' and feminists' common struggle for
peace was far ahead of men's efforts. But the class and ideological differences between antiwar feminists and socialist women would continue to
inhibit any close cooperation between them.[41]

An additional reason for the absence of French and Russian women at
The Hague was the vigorous opposition of their governments, whose officials had increasingly censored feminists' publications and correspondence,
searched their homes, and generally harassed those women suspected of
disloyal activities. The German authorities first opened Zetkin's mail and
searched her home and then sent her and many of her German supporters
to prison for distributing the Berne manifesto. French officials also arrested
Saumoneau for circulating the manifesto and other pacifist tracts. Such
intimidation was sufficient to discourage all but the most determined
women pacifists from direct contacts with like-minded citizens in enemy
countries.

The belligerents could also make it virtually impossible for suspected disloyal citizens to travel abroad. If any Russian women seriously planned to attend the congress, it is doubtful whether their government would have permitted their participation. The government in Berlin was no more accepting than other belligerents of the women's meeting, but the decentralization of enforcing powers over matters of public order, which extended to the issuing of passports, meant that regional variations could sometimes occur. Thus some German women, including Frida Perlen of Stuttgart who had attended the Amsterdam meeting in February, could not get to the congress when military officials in her city refused to grant her the necessary papers, but in other areas of Germany women had little difficulty in gaining permission to travel to Holland. Immediately following the Hague congress, the German women had a German edition of the resolutions printed in Holland; German authorities in Munich, Hamburg, and Frankfurt, however, prohibited a second printing. The German women finally managed to publish the resolutions in Stuttgart and to distribute them widely throughout Germany.

Nevertheless, by the fall of 1915, censorship of "peace" propaganda, whether advanced by feminist or sexually mixed groups, was becoming pervasive throughout the empire. Evidence of the growing repression, while gradual, was not unsubtle. Perhaps the most visible example was the *Bund Neues Vaterland* (New Fatherland League), which was increasingly harassed on all sides and banned altogether in early 1916. Overall, women pacifists on the European continent were so severely hampered in their communications and travel that they could not publicly support, let alone actively participate in, the movement for a negotiated peace.[42]

Nevertheless, the most important reason for the small representation from these belligerents at both the Berne and Hague conferences was the absence of widespread support for peace among feminists in their homelands. Russian women sent the Hague congress a letter firmly endorsing their nation's war effort. And in declining their participation at The Hague, two of the largest feminist organizations in France sent a manifesto, which stoically declared that "in order that future generations may reap the fruit of this magnificent display of self-sacrifice and death, French women will bear the conflict as long as it will be necessary. At this time united with those who suffer and die, they do not know how to talk of peace." A historian of the French women's suffrage movement concludes that the feminist pacifists in France "remained a small minority surrounded by nationalists . . . The same women who had planned to go to Berlin for the IWSA congress in 1915 fervently hoped that the French army would arrive there instead." That minority included a few suffragists who said that they would have come to Holland if the authorities had not denied them passports, and 57 international-oriented women who managed to get together to sign a quite different manifesto endorsing the congress and regretting French absence from it. Their statement also espoused the maternal ideology of women as peacemakers, affirmed the importance of expressing their humanitarian views and opposition to national hatreds—"We must speak – we must act," the manifesto proclaimed—and endorsed the women's international reform proposals.[43]

Feminist organizations that had accepted pacifist views at the outbreak of the war no longer tolerated them. The leadership of the League of German Women's Associations, a federation of some 56 women's groups, unanimously approved a resolution declaring "propaganda for the [Hague] congress or participation in the congress to be incompatible with the patriotic sentiments and national duties of the German's women's movement." The league's leaders made clear that none of the 28 German women venturing to Holland was an officer of the league or its member organizations and thus "the German women's movement was not represented at The Hague." The claim was somewhat disingenuous, as prowar executives of women's groups could, and did, use their positions of authority to assist the government in intimidating those citizens engaged in seemingly unpatriotic endeavors. The president of the German National Council of Women, for instance, told Alice Salomon, a leading social worker, an Addams' admirer, and also an officer of its worldwide federation, the International Council of Women, that if she and other members attended the Hague meeting, they could no longer serve as council officers. "There we were faced," Salomon recalled, "with the crucial question which public servants have had to answer for themselves in every age: Is it better to keep an office in order to use its influence from within or to resign and accept open opposition? I am certain that those who submitted to the German Council's order, as I did, were wrong."

There is no denying, however, that most German women reformers at this stage in the war remained firmly committed to their nation's military effort. Lida Gustava Heymann belonged to the antiwar German Women's Suffrage League, which before the war had only 2,000 members, or one-sixth the membership of the two largest suffragist groups in Germany, and soon after the start of the conflict she conceded that only the involvement of her group in relief work allowed it to keep even 10 percent of its members.[44]

Meanwhile, the approaching Hague congress further exacerbated the growing split between the more internationally minded British suffragists and their erstwhile nationalist colleagues. In the first months of the war, Millicent Fawcett promoted humanitarian relief work for suffragists in response to the hunger, unemployment, and general social dislocation caused by men going off to the front lines. But such emphasis, while demonstrating suffragists' patriotism and good works, failed to satisfy the large numbers of British internationalists in the National Union of Women's Suffrage Societies, many of whom opposed the war and military solutions, even at the risk of seeming to be disloyal. Simultaneously finding patriotic allies, Mrs Fawcett gradually hardened her position against accepting any internationalist initiatives. Convinced that the peoples of all the belligerents believed they were fighting for "the cause of justice and freedom" and were prepared "to sacrifice and suffer more," she objected to an international women's peace congress, believing it would degenerate into "violent outbursts and fierce denunciations." She even wrote Catt that "I feel so strongly against the proposed convention that I would decline to attend it, and if necessary would resign my [vice president's] office in the IWSA if it were judged incumbent on me in that capacity to take part in the convention."

Some moderate internationalists in the national union sought to broker a compromise between the internationalist and nationalist wings at the group's annual council meeting in London in early February 1915. The internationalists might have represented a majority of the more than 1,000 British women in attendance. The meeting passed resolutions, for example, asking the ISWA president to call a convocation of the international group in a neutral nation, although it did not say whether peace would be a topic of discussion. It also endorsed resolutions supporting in principle educational courses on the causes and consequences of war and war prevention and a new postwar international order to include arbitration and conciliation of international disputes before the resort to war, and urging its members to "take every means open to them for promoting mutual understanding and goodwill between nations and for resisting any tendency towards a spirit of hatred and revenge."

Nevertheless, the council meeting rejected the internationalists' key provision—the NUWSS's active sponsorship of an educational program in support of those principles. Although the union's executive committee had voted to send delegates to the Hague convocation as representatives of the suffrage society, Fawcett argued that the congress was a peace gathering and the executive had no authority in that area. Ultimately, a compromise was reached in the larger council meeting, allowing members to attend, but not as national union representatives. Moreover, Fawcett spoke strongly of women's duty in supporting the war effort to drive the Germans out of Belgium and France. "Until that is done," she declared to the assembled women, "I believe it is akin to treason to talk of peace."

Fawcett's firm stance against the international reformers forced the issue, but her patriotic rhetoric revealed the real gulf in their views on the war. Her strong words rankled even some of her loyal supporters. A liberal male newspaper editor, for instance, wrote Fawcett that she had violated her own guidance, adopted by the council meeting, not to discuss the merits of the war when in her talk she proclaimed the government pro-war position on its causes and purposes. "If you will recall the views regarding the war held by many members of the executive," he wrote, "you will realize, I think, how painful such as interpretation must have been to them."[45]

Having failed to prevail at the meeting and in the face of Fawcett's determined opposition, many of the internationalists found their continued participation in the national union intolerable. Separation from the organization was nonetheless a difficult experience for them. They had loyally supported and assumed positions of leadership in the group and did not lightly sever their relationships with it. They had also respected Fawcett's inclusive, democratic management of the suffrage organization and liked her personally. One of their more thoughtful and articulate spokesmen was Kathleen Courtney, the union's honorary secretary and a friend of Fawcett. As she explained in her resignation letter:

> I feel strongly that the most important thing at the present moment is to work, if possible, on International lines for the right sort of peace settlement after the war. If I could have done this through the National Union, I need hardly say how infinitely I should have preferred it & for the sake of doing so I would gladly have sacrificed a great deal. But the Council made it quite clear that they did not wish the Union to work in this way.[46]

Fortunately for Courtney, she had the support of like-minded internationalist women in the NUWSS, including Swanwick and Maude Royden, a close friend from their years together as students at the University of Oxford. Both Swanwick and Royden also resigned from the executive committee. Indeed, more than a dozen members of the NUWSS executive favoring a more inclusive, internationalist direction began over the next several weeks resigning from the NUWSS executive committee and from the society itself. Rather than continue fighting the Fawcett-led faction, they perceived that most local affiliates identified with Fawcett as the embodiment of the national union and would continue to support her. Because Fawcett would likely not resign, they would be hard-pressed to prevail on issues arising out of the war. They also did not want to be identified with Fawcett's vigorous pro-war views, which seemed to equate dissent with treason. And finally, they thought the organization was becoming undemocratic and was making a mockery of suffragists' commitment to the "consent of the governed" principle. As Emily Leaf wrote Marshall in early April:

> I don't know what is going to happen at the next Executive [meeting] . . . Personally I feel more and more . . . that the older section of the

NU who want to do nothing (other) than ask for the vote – and feel that it is undemocratic to commit NU suffragists to the UDC or the International Congress must be left to go their own way . . . [They] will wish less and less to adapt themselves to new ideas as time goes on – I don't consider that they are carrying out the resolutions of the Council by taking the line they do – but they either do consider it – or else they don't care.[47]

As the internationalists resigned from the NUWSS executive committee, Fawcett succeeded at the March 18th meeting to get the more loyal executive committee, by a nearly two-to-one margin, to decline to send delegates to the Holland convocation. Nevertheless, 180 women, mainly from the internationalist wing of the British suffrage movement, signed up for the trip to The Hague. Like their similarly motivated American compatriots, these women were overwhelmingly well-educated, professional, and middle-aged feminists who had transcended gender and psychological constraints to escape the home and become active in public life before 1914.[48]

Besides its own propaganda machine boosting the war effort, the British Government of course had the means to monitor the views and behavior of its citizens, and it gradually moved to control the communications and movements of nonconforming or dissident citizens. At the very beginning of the war, it cut the cables linking North America and the European continent, so that all direct telegraphic traffic had to go through Britain where it could be suppressed. Moreover, less than a week into the war it pushed through the House of Commons—without debate—the Defence of the Realm Act, which gave the government broad powers, among other things, to suppress dissident publications and restrict travel. In practice, censorship initially did not go much beyond information going to and from enemy countries, and British authorities tolerated the continued publication of *Jus Suffragii* and other communications about the impending women's gathering at The Hague. But they drew the line in permitting any large group of its citizens, male or female, to travel abroad to a peace convocation. The Cabinet thus at first denied travel permits to all 180 women.

One of the rejected applicants was Kate Courtney. Lady Courtney immediately contacted a political friend, the Lord Chancellor, who agreed to talk to Home Secretary Reginald McKenna the same evening about the women's plight. When she called on McKenna the next day, she found him "a bit relaxed;" and he soon relented slightly by selecting 24 for the trip to The Hague.[49] Even this small group could not attend, however, because the British Admiralty then closed the channel to passenger traffic from Britain during the few weeks preceding the congress. In consequence, only three British women, Kathleen Courtney and Macmillan, both of whom had

2.3 Four British suffragists sometime before the Great War. From left: Helena Swanwick, Margaret Ashton, Kathleen Courtney, and Maude Royden. After 1914, all four became part of the internationalist wing of the National Union of Women Suffragist Societies. (Schwimmer-Lloyd Collection, New York Public Library)

already traveled to Holland before the British restrictions to assist their Dutch cohorts with the conference preparations, and Pethick-Lawrence were able to represent their country at the congress.[50]

Reflecting on the preparatory work for the Hague meeting, Aletta Jacobs gave full credit to Courtney, Macmillan, the Germans Anita Augspurg and Heymann, and several of her Dutch compatriots. "It was largely due to these energetic and talented women," she recalled, "that, despite all the difficulties, the delays in the mail, the lost, censored, and confiscated letters, we still managed to organize an international conference in just two months that was to be attended by a great many women from twelve different countries."⁵¹ Altogether, about 1,100 delegates, 1,000 of whom were from Holland, attended the four-day convocation at The Hague.

———

According to the call of the congress, a woman could qualify as a delegate by expressing "general agreement with the resolutions" on the preliminary program. Because several had asked for clarification of this requirement, the resolutions committee had interpreted the phrase to mean support for the pacific settlement of international disputes and the extension of suffrage to women. These two principles indicated the clear link between the woman's suffrage and peace movements. Like Balch, some European delegates to the congress, especially from Holland, worried that the assemblage might become a suffrage as well as a peace meeting, but their fears were unfounded. While feminists occasionally cited the special problems facing women during the war or the enfranchisement of women as a remedy for war and militarism, the broader question of peace predominated. Helene Stöcker, a German delegate, perhaps best represented that viewpoint. Having participated in mixed gender groups for sexual reform and, less actively, for peace before 1914, she was comfortable with collaborative efforts with like-minded males. The war tragedy made her a passionate peace advocate, and she early worked with men in the *Bund Neues Vaterland*. At the Hague congress, she disagreed with participants who claimed that if women had had a political voice, the war would not have occurred, and she opposed giving prominence to suffrage at the Hague congress. "It is not the time to place the rights of women at the forefront . . . for we must not delude ourselves about the results of the right to a political voice: women's suffrage will not protect us from the outbreak of war." In addition, the congress accepted the resolutions committee's suggestion to prohibit the discussion of a few controversial subjects: the belligerents' responsibility for and conduct of the present war as well as rules relating to the conduct of future wars.⁵²

At the first session of the congress, the delegates unanimously elected Addams the presiding officer. The choice was obvious, for she was widely respected and represented the largest neutral. Her selection was also wise, for she possessed the even temperament and fair-mindedness so necessary for resolving controversial questions among such a large and diverse group. On several occasions her tact and sincerity of purpose smoothed over potential hassles among the delegates. The American delegates, thankful for her skillful leadership, labeled her conduct as presiding officer "impressive," "magnificent," "masterly," "perfectly wonderful."⁵³

There were additional reasons for the harmonious spirit pervading the congress. One was the essential moderation of the delegates. Vorse explained that the participants "were for the most part well-to-do women of the middle class. It was an everyday audience, plain people, just folks, the kind you see walking out to church any Sunday morning . . . women full of inhibitions, not of a radical habit of thought, unaccustomed for the most part to self-expression, women who had walked decorously all their days, hedged in by the 'thou shalt nots' of middle-class life." Because no self-styled anarchists or doctrinaire socialists attended the congress, there was little possibility for disruptive demonstrations or inflammatory rhetoric. The European participants were, if anything, more "sound and safe" than the Americans.

There was, however, a small minority of socialists and radicals, particularly among the Dutch delegates, who distributed militant anti-war circulars, and some Austrians, who proposed a resolution calling for women to refuse any personal or financial support to the war system. The latter's proposal never made it through the resolutions committee, and no record of the activities of extreme left-wingers appears in the official conference proceedings. But a few sympathetic observers, especially Vorse, recorded their actions, and Schwimmer would draw upon this radical undercurrent in the closing hours of the congress.

Further, the fear of the war spreading to the neighboring neutrals induced a cautious attitude among the delegates from the European neutrals. This timidity at times bordered on paralysis. Wales wrote home about "how terrified the little neutrals are. They are afraid that in spite of everything the terrible war will come to them too." Besides "fear," Vorse perceived a pervasive sense of "grief," especially among the women representatives from belligerent nations. Everyone from those countries, she discovered, had relatives, friends, or neighbors who had been killed or wounded in the fighting, and in several cases had witnessed the destruction of their towns and real suffering among women, children, and other civilians. These Europeans more often projected a certain stoicism—"a spirit of terrible endurance," Vorse called it—than rebellious behavior. Thus while a strong undercurrent of emotion certainly existed at the congress, the Europeans' fear and grief somewhat muted their voices of protest. The resulting sense of paralysis permitted the Americans, already well prepared from their shipboard discussions, to dominate most of the proceedings.[54]

Throughout the congress various delegates affirmed their solidarity, their passionate human sympathy for the women of the belligerent nations, and their idealistic internationalism. Belgian and German women, for instance, appeared on the same platform and exchanged greetings and expressions of friendship. Many of the specific resolutions embodied these feelings.

The congress passed two types of resolutions: protests against war, and principles necessary for permanent peace; both included advocacy of feminist concerns. Specifically, the delegates protested "the madness and the horror of war," "the odious wrongs of which women are the victims in the time of war, and especially against the horrible violation of women which attends all war." Resolutions also demanded women's enfranchisement and espoused putting into practice nationally and internationally "the principle that women should share all civil and political rights and responsibilities on the same terms as men." As part of their seriousness and moderation, however, the delegates did not flaunt the rhetoric of the maternal instinct or their sex's moral superiority; an exception was a loud hissing from the delegates in response to the claim of a British woman living in Holland that women in belligerent nations supported the war as much as men.

Also adopted without dissent were resolutions calling for open diplomacy, democratic control over foreign policies (which of course included the enfranchisement of women), the education of children "directed towards the ideal of constructive peace," no transfer of territory without the consent of the inhabitants, and self-determination for all peoples and their right to choose their form of government. In addition, they further endorsed an international agreement on government manufacture of munitions and control of their international traffic as important first steps toward eventual disarmament, freedom of the seas and free trade, investments of capitalists of one nation in the resources of another wholly at risk of the investor, and the convocation of a third international peace conference at The Hague immediately after the war.

The congress also passed resolutions urging the formation of a league of nations, which would include a permanent international court of justice to adjudicate "differences of a justiciable character such as arise on the interpretation of treaty rights or of the law of nations," and periodic meetings of an international conference involving the participation of women. The conferees agreed that this body should not discuss the rules of warfare, which had severely limited the scope of the two Hague Peace Conferences, but should promote "practical proposals for further international cooperation" that these two conferences had only begun to foster. They also proposed that this international conference should "formulate and enforce those principles of justice, equity, and good-will," not only for the benefit of the great powers and the small nations, but also on behalf of the recognition of the rights of colonial and "primitive" peoples.

The women's congress further urged all nations to reach an agreement referring future international disputes to arbitration and conciliation. For this purpose it proposed that the peace conference appoint a permanent council of conciliation and investigation for the settlement of international controversies arising from economic, social, or political differences. Finally, the conferees adopted a resolution urging governments to negotiate an agreement in which they would unite in bringing "social, moral and

2.4 Leaders on the dais at the Women's Congress at The Hague, April 1915. From left: Mme Thoumaian (Armenia), Leopoldine Kulka (Austria), Laura Hughes (Australia), Rosika Schwimmer (Hungary), Anita Augspurg (Germany), Jane Addams (United States), Eugénie Hamer (Belgium), Aletta Jacobs (Holland), Chrystal Macmillan (Britain), Rosa Genoni (Italy), Anna Kleman (Sweden), Thora Daugaard (Denmark), and Louise Keilhau (Norway). (Swarthmore College Peace Collection)

economic pressure" against nations resorting to arms instead of arbitration or conciliation. The omission of military sanctions to enforce the peace against recalcitrant states once again underlined the pacifists' revulsion against power politics in general and military power in particular.[55]

Looking ahead, the delegates passed a resolution requesting the convocation of another women's congress at the same place and time as the official peace conference at the end of the war. As part of their preference for citizen diplomacy, they also agreed that "representatives of the people," including women, should be involved in that peace settlement. Until then, they authorized the women members to organize popular support for their peace resolutions in their countries. Further to their moderation, the delegates recognized "the desirability of the cooperation of men and women in the cause of peace" but, as an expression of their active, ongoing commitment to these principles, decided to create their own organization, an International Committee of Women for Permanent Peace with headquarters in Amsterdam. The executive committee consisted of a maximum of five women from each of the participating nations. The congress elected Addams chairman, Jacobs and Schwimmer vice-chairman, and Macmillan secretary of the international committee.[56]

Toward the end of the conference the delegates discussed the difficult subject of bringing the war to an early conclusion. The preliminary program had urged the belligerents to "define the terms on which they would be willing to make peace and for that purpose to call a truce," and some women came to The Hague to support the measure. Many Dutch and Scandinavian delegates, however, objected to an armistice because they feared it might result in a status quo peace. Such a settlement, they believed, would be intolerable because it would tend to subordinate standards of justice to raw military power. Ultimately, they feared that the perpetuation of such injustices would subvert their hopes for permanent peace. The women from Belgium and Poland (which was not then a nation-state) most strongly objected to any resolution that might seem to tolerate German occupation of their soil. Expressing this fear of becoming a subject people, a Belgian cried out, "[J]e suis Belge avant tout." The delegates therefore agreed that any cessation of hostilities would have to be "permanent and therefore based on principles of justice, including those laid down in the resolutions adopted by this Congress."[57]

But the women were willing to discuss mediation proposals that might facilitate the consideration of peace by the belligerents. They therefore agreed to consider the mediation formula contained in Grace Wales' pamphlet, Continuous Mediation without Armistice, which the author had distributed to the delegates in English, French, and German. By prearrangement Schwimmer proposed a resolution requesting the neutral nations to create an official conference that would invite suggestions for settlement from each of the belligerent nations and in any case submit to all of them simultaneously reasonable proposals as a basis of peace. After Wales seconded and Pethick-Lawrence warmly endorsed the resolution, the conference adopted it unanimously.[58]

That was as far as the women seemed willing to go. Had they stopped there, the congress would have adjourned without impinging directly on traditional diplomacy. But Schwimmer had another idea that resulted in a surprising sequel to the Hague gathering. At its final session she introduced a resolution calling for the appointment of envoys who would personally present the women's resolutions to the premiers and foreign ministers in the major European belligerent and neutral capitals as well as to the president of the United States. She proposed that the presentations could test the receptivity of heads of state to a neutral conference without armistice.

Alice Hamilton recalled that when the American delegates first heard about Schwimmer's proposal, they believed it was "hopelessly melodramatic and absurd and we said Miss Addams would never consent to go from court to court presenting resolutions."[59] Schwimmer's initiative first prompted the question whether it could be considered at all. Under the rules of the congress, new resolutions since the printing of the program could be presented if recommended by the resolutions committee. In this case, Schwimmer had presented her proposal to the committee, which did not vote on it. As chair, Addams could have squelched further consideration by ruling the resolution out of order, but she allowed it to be discussed. Although she did not explain her decision, she likely perceived a groundswell of interest in the proposal and did not want arbitrarily to frustrate ambitious schemes that might receive popular support. While the proposal could result in acrimonious debate, denying discussion would also lead to dissension. Either way the harmony and goodwill permeating the congress might be seriously compromised, so it was better to allow for democratic discussion and accept the result.

Schwimmer's resolution touched off a lively debate among those who opposed any presentation of the resolutions of the congress to governments, those who wanted to give them only to the ministers and ambassadors represented at The Hague, and those who were in favor of Schwimmer's more ambitious scheme. Schwimmer had lined up many women from the European neutrals to speak in support of her resolution. A few radicals from belligerent nations may also have favored it, but most women from the warring states believed the plan was unrealistic and feared potential ridicule. Among those opposed to the proposal, Kathleen Courtney argued, for example, that Schwimmer was the only delegate from a belligerent nation who spoke out in its support and that anyone using their heads instead of their hearts would see that the resolution was "not practicable." Mild-mannered Wales thought Schwimmer's proposal was

too radical and supported Macmillan's more modest alternative of presenting the resolutions to the Dutch and foreign diplomats at The Hague.

With the congress deadlocked, Schwimmer delivered an impassioned
appeal for acceptance of her proposal. "Brains – they say – have ruled the
world till to-day," she exuded. "If brains have brought us to what we are in
now, I think it is time to allow also our hearts to speak. When our sons are
killed by millions, let us, mothers, only try to do good by going to kings and
emperors, without any other danger than a refusal! (*Hear, Hear, Hear!*)"
Unlike the high seriousness and restraint characterizing almost all speeches
during the congress, her appeal throbbed with emotion. Its directness and
simplicity successfully won over many wavering delegates, and her resolution passed by a narrow margin. Schwimmer's American friend, Lola
Maverick Lloyd, recorded in her diary, "It was a close shave. Most exciting
crisis of the whole Congress . . . We trembled for its fate. The victory was
all Rosika's but she wanted to go away and let them forget how she had
forced things."[60]

The congress then authorized Addams to appoint envoys to visit the
foreign governments. In deference to the strong sentiment in favor of her
participation, she reluctantly agreed to serve as an envoy. She also appointed
two other envoys from neutral nations, Dr Jacobs and Rosa Genoni, the
lone Italian delegate at the congress, although Italy would soon become a
belligerent on the Allied side, thus ending Genoni's "neutral" status.
These three comprised the delegation to the war capitals of Great Britain,
Germany, Austria-Hungary, Italy, France, and Belgium, and a lone neutral,
Switzerland. In addition, two unofficial delegates, Alice Hamilton and
Wilhelmina van Wullften Palthe, of Holland, accompanied them on their
travels. Addams also selected two neutral envoys, Balch and Cor Ramondt-
Hirschmann of Holland, and one from each belligerent side, Macmillan
and Schwimmer, to journey northward to the neutral capitals of Denmark,
Sweden, and Norway, and to Petrograd, the capital of belligerent Russia.
Wales went along nominally as secretary of the delegation for the Scandinavian part of the journey. Altogether the two delegations were to have
interviews with 25 European leaders.[61]

3

Private Diplomacy in Europe

Although the idea of private citizens calling on the heads of European governments struck the American envoys as very unconventional, they rather easily adjusted to their assignment. They had already ventured to Holland, and the realization that the women at the Hague congress took their missions seriously encouraged them to extend their adventure to the European capitals. As Jane Addams began her travels, she wrote her friend Mary Rozet Smith: "The whole experience has been tremendous. I don't think that I have lost my head – there is just one chance in 10 thousand."[1]

The women emissaries faced imposing difficulties. Logistically, each group experienced cumbersome travel arrangements to get to the various capitals. For example, Addams and her fellow envoys traveled from the Netherlands to Britain, and then back to Amsterdam before setting off for Berlin. They next proceeded to Vienna and Budapest, then back to neutral Switzerland before entering allied Italy and France. Finally, to return to Amsterdam, they first had to cross to England for the necessary passage around the battlefront. Sometimes they had to endure long delays at the borders while their passports and luggage were scrutinized, and to deal with mostly unsympathetic diplomats at embassies and legations in arranging the interviews and getting permissions to enter the next countries.

These inconveniences were minor irritations compared with the daunting task of persuading the government leaders to consider peace negotiations. Among the belligerent nations in the spring of 1915, however, there was little evidence of a desire for peace. For the frontline enlisted men, the Christmas truce might have indicated some reluctance to fight, but the troops were well provisioned and mostly dutiful. Even the unending labyrinth of deep trenches, despite their unsanitary and grisly conditions, saved lives, and the largely unspoken recognition of the stalemated military situation reduced, at least for a time, the frequency of massive suicidal charges and loss of men. These developments may have facilitated soldiers' uneasy acceptance of the grim realities of trench warfare. Compared with the frantic battles in

1914, casualties on the Western front on both sides would be lower per month in 1915 and would not rise sharply again until the massive military campaigns in 1916. The conflict nonetheless became more total and global during the year, and the killing machine continued unabated. Italy entered the war on the side of the Allies, for instance, in May 1915; by the end of the year 62,000 of its troops had been killed. The deaths of German soldiers numbered more than 430,000 that year. And on the eastern fronts alone, Austria-Hungary's casualties in the Carpathians from January to April totaled almost 800,000 men, and in the year-long, abortive Gallipoli campaign beginning February 1915, Allied losses exceeded 250,000 men. Altogether for the year, Russia's casualties in the east were about 1.4 million and the Central Powers' more than one million.

Despite these losses, the civilian populations in the warring nations still seemed supportive of the war. Although no clear measures of public opinion then existed, there was much evidence suggesting the belligerent peoples' firm support of their nations' war efforts. Intellectuals, religious leaders, and a wide array of civic groups in the various warring countries issued manifestoes elaborating on their nations' just cause (or the enemy's unjust one), and their arguments rendered relatively easy the task of warring governments in convincing their civilian populations that they were fighting a righteous "defensive" war against outside invaders. In Britain, for example, support for the war was broad-based, with voluntary enlistments coming from its colonies abroad and from all social classes domestically. In consequence, the government did not need to introduce conscription until early 1916. In a sense, the peoples were self-mobilized, and the political leaders on both sides, aside from the Allies' publicity of German atrocities in Belgium, had only begun to ratchet up propaganda to bolster possible sagging civilian morale behind the war effort.[2]

Given this pro-war consensus in the warring countries, their political leaders would not feel unduly defensive or pressured by the women emissaries' presentations. They could speak respectfully, sometimes even frankly, to the women, and hopefully not see them again. The ladies' timing was also not auspicious. Unluckily, they would arrive in London on May 9, only two days after the sinking of the British luxury liner *Lusitania* by a German U-boat, with the loss of 1,200 lives, the great majority of whom were British citizens. British opinion raged against Germany for this act, and the British Government initiated a series of reprisals against Germans living in Great Britain. In such an inflamed atmosphere, talk about mediation seemed rather pointless.[3] Moreover, they would cross into Italy just after that nation had entered the war on the side of the Allies. Needless to say, they would find the Italian leaders in no mood to talk about peace.

Despite the difficulties, the women emissaries found certain compensations. In particular, they derived a certain satisfaction in trying to initiate personally what the diplomats scrupulously avoided. The whole thrust of their ideas and actions suggested a distrust of conventional diplomacy and a search for both a new style and content to international relations. As Mary Heaton Vorse commented: "The great value of the envoys to the nations is this breaking away from tradition, that instead of being content to make resolutions and go home, the women should go on this journey and that for the first time women, representing an international congress of women[,] should approach the great governments of Europe, voicing to them women's protest against war." Committed to reform the international system, they were easily critical of diplomats who to them represented the old order. Emily Greene Balch, for example, frequently emphasized that the failure of diplomats to confront seriously the unprecedented problems arising out of the war required "fresh" approaches. The envoys' trips to the capitals would confirm their low estimate of the diplomatic corps whom they found on the whole to be closely tied to the aristocratic classes and absorbed in formal protocol and the artificial conventions of high culture. These influences, according to the envoys, accentuated both the diplomats' aloofness from the enormous human tragedy of the war and their ingrained conservatism leading to automatic skepticism of possible peace parlays.

Balch expressed this sentiment following an unsatisfactory interview with Maurice Francis Egan, American minister in Copenhagen: "the diplomatic world seems so far away and so incredulous to all that does not answer to the preconceived notions – everything really different from the past is impossible, inconceivable." Following the same meeting with Egan, Julia Grace Wales commented that "the diplomats have a tendency to see the thing [mediation] *more difficult* than it really is, might fail to see the wood for the trees. I said that to the ordinary mind it seemed foolish that the world should destroy itself without any collective effort at systematic thinking. 'Perhaps,' I said, 'that simple, human way of looking at it is the right way . . .' He is too much of a diplomat to see anything in that light. It is curious how the diplomats all seem to have that thing Lowes Dickinson calls 'The Governmental mind.' " Egan also struck her as "just a little too reverential toward 'continental culture,' overtimid, perhaps, about being 'insular,' a little lacking in the *courage of his Americanism.*"

Wales received a similar impression from her visit with the British minister in Copenhagen. It was, she remarked, "the most uphill interview I have ever had. His whole manner was hostile and his eyes were as hard as glass." Chrystal Macmillan, who also called on the British minister, gave Wales this assessment: "A narrow young aristocrat! And the whole house looks like it."

The women perhaps expected too much from the overburdened diplomatic corps who were confronted with real and pressing problems growing out of the war, but some of their assessments were not far off the mark. Even

British diplomats found, for example, that their minister in Copenhagen had a prickly personality and narrowly nationalistic views. And although Egan was a former professor of English literature, he had served as the U.S. minister in Copenhagen since 1907 and had grown comfortable with traditional diplomatic procedures and etiquette.[4] The women had more serious—and often accurate—complaints about some of Wilson's appointments of chiefs of mission to European nations. They would be particularly hard on James W. Gerard, ambassador to Germany. A dilettante in Tammany politics, Gerard was totally lacking in diplomatic savoir-faire. His blunt and impulsive personality served his nation poorly at the Berlin post during these months of delicate German-American negotiations. Following the sinking of the *Lusitania*, for example, Gerard began openly predicting war between the United States and Germany, while his wife started packing their belongings for a quick departure out of the country. When Lochner relayed this information to Balch, she complained, "Is this not criminal under the circumstances?"[5]

———

Before setting out on their missions, five of the envoys—Jacobs, Addams, Schwimmer, Macmillan, and Rosa Genoni—first interviewed Dutch Prime Minister Cort van der Linden. Addams explained the decision of the congress to appoint women envoys to visit all the European governments and present the resolutions of the congress, including their proposal for a neutral conference of continuous mediation. The prime minister was a well-known opponent of women's suffrage, but on the war issue Jacobs recalled that the interview revealed him as "a committed pacifist," who wanted a cease-fire. His perception was, however, that the belligerents were uninterested in peace talks. In any event, a mediation move, he emphasized, was a matter of delicate timing. If the Netherlands pushed for peace discussions too early and were refused, its influence in offering mediation at a later time would be undermined. As the women were to learn from other neutral governments, his reply served as a standard objection of diplomats who were reluctant to promote peace overtures. Perhaps seeking further justification for his inaction, Cort van der Linden also complained that the women in the belligerent countries might be just as warmongering as their male counterparts. The envoys countered that women in the warring countries could not vote, and thus their opinions were not being heard. "What you read in the newspapers are the opinions of only a handful of female writers," Addams added.[6]

Following this interview the first delegation—Addams, Macmillan, Genoni, Jacobs, and Wulfften Palthe—departed for Great Britain. Although the recent *Lusitania* sinking would squelch any serious talk about mediation, the envoys believed, as Addams put it, that the incident "should be made the occasion of pressure for the co-operation of all neutral nations to end the war." They proceeded with their mission in the hope that their plan might help prepare the way for peace when public passions subsided.[7] The Dutch and American embassies agreed to schedule interviews with British leaders, although the American ambassador to the Court at St James, Walter Hines Page, was a confirmed Anglophile and opposed any mediation overtures.[8]

On May 13, the women met with British Foreign Secretary Sir Edward Grey, who throughout the war demonstrated a very resilient attitude toward neutral opinion. He was mildly encouraging. While insisting beforehand that their talk had to be "entirely private and of a personal nature," he seemed to exhibit interest in the women's congress and their mediation plan. When he asked whether German women attended the congress and about their difficulties in getting there, Jacobs explained some German localities granted passports to the women and that those who came to the congress showed more courage than the British women because they would have a very hard time in Germany afterwards. Grey volunteered that he was "mostly astonished to hear that." He told them that it was impossible for the belligerents to begin negotiations, and he intimated that he personally believed the war would be fought to the finish. He conceded, however, that he could see no harm in neutral nations submitting propositions, one of which might provide a starting point for peace talks. He added that President Wilson could be very useful in initiating discussions on peace terms.[9] On the following day Jane Addams saw Prime Minister Herbert Asquith. Privately, Asquith viewed the women pacifists with bemused contempt, labeling their peace activities the "twittering of sparrows." During the interview, however, he was courteous and noncommittal and, like Grey, admitted that some good might result from the women's mediation scheme.[10]

Their interviews in Berlin were friendly, but unproductive. Gerard, absorbed in the prospect of war between the United States and Germany, had lost all faith in mediation and privately considered the women envoys "cranks." Nevertheless, he dutifully arranged for their interviews with Chancellor Theobald von Bethmann-Hollweg and Foreign Secretary Gottlieb von Jagow, who privately agreed that they should see the emissaries because a refusal would create a bad impression on neutral opinion if they were well received in the other war capitals. Although Gerard recalled that the two German leaders looked forward to the meetings "with unconcealed perturbation," they managed to repress their annoyance and remained cordial during the interviews.[11]

Jagow told the emissaries that he preferred an early peace, but emphasized that the German people would demand a settlement providing for Germany's future security. He added that only the neutral countries, especially the United States, could take the first steps toward peace. Somewhat paradoxically, however, he then attempted to discredit America's potential role as mediator. He especially complained about the shipment of American munitions to the Allies. The U.S. policy was freedom of its merchants to trade with both belligerent sides, but in practice almost all trade went to the Allies who controlled the sea lanes and searched and confiscated cargoes destined for enemy ports. While Jagow did not deny the legality of the American policy, he explained its harmful effects on German opinion. Under these circumstances he doubted whether Germany could consider the United States as an impartial mediator.

Bethmann-Hollweg spoke more freely but offered little more encouragement. He had lost a son during the war and seemed to favor a negotiated peace, but he made no promises to support a neutral conference and strongly defended Germany's high-minded motives in the war. Jane Addams correctly perceived that for all Bethmann-Hollweg's good thoughts, he, like so many other German civilians, found the influence of the military "too strong for him."[12]

> He said he had never heard a German say he wanted to crush England. I said I had never heard an Englishman say he wanted to crush Germany, but that they wanted to crush German militarism. He said that was a distinction but not a difference. The army in Germany is part of the government, and he went on to talk in that half mystical way they do – so difficult for us to understand. It is as if their feeling for the arms was that of a church for its procession. It is a part of it.[13]

Most of the other war leaders were no more satisfactory on mediation. The leaders of the new Italian war ministry, Sonnino and Salandra, were in no mood to consider a negotiated peace. The French and Belgian statesmen were just as discouraging. Viviani claimed he was a pacifist and feminist but France could not then consider peace, and D'Avignon said he was completely dependent on Belgium's allies on the subject. Most hostile was the French Foreign Secretary Theophile Delcassé, who declared that he wanted to destroy Germany "so that she would not come up for 100 years."[14]

Even the Swiss leaders, fearing the rival armies near its borders, were "rather timid" about a neutral conference for continuous mediation. Obviously unwilling to speak freely, Foreign Minister Alfred Hoffmann greeted the women coolly, remained silent throughout their presentation, and then escorted them to the door. Their interview with Swiss President Motta was little more satisfactory. Taking a hardheaded position, he declared that the time for peace talks was premature and that the warring powers would not agree to a peace settlement until one side achieved a clear-cut military victory. He said that it would be "impossible" for the warring governments to reach a peace agreement and then be able to face their countrymen and admit, "we erred." He further emphasized that Switzerland would neither call nor participate in a conference of neutrals until the other neutral states agreed to one.[15]

A few leaders, however, showed more than polite interest in the proposal for a neutral conference for continuous mediation. Because the envoys arrived in Vienna on the same day Italy declared war on the Central Powers, the fear of Italy's military hostilities may have in part prompted the encouraging responses of the Dual Monarchy's Foreign Minister Stephan Burian, the Austrian Prime Minister Karl Stürgkh, and the latter's counterpart in Hungary, Stephan Tisza. Perhaps, too, their concerns about their nations' dependent, vassal status to a predominant German partner and the prospect of nationalistic forces in any prolonged conflict disintegrating their empire may have motivated their seeming receptivity to mediation moves. The statesmen only hinted at specific explanations, but claimed that they had genuine reservations about the war and hoped for an early peace. Following their presentation to Count Stürgkh, for example, Addams remarked that perhaps he thought their mission to the governments was foolish. "Not at all," was the answer. "You are the only sane people who have been in this room for ten months," he said, bringing his fist down on the table until everything rattled.[16]

According to Aletta Jacobs, Burian "even more resolutely" favored neutral mediation. He believed that President Wilson did not grasp the complexities of the European situation, but a conference of European neutrals including an American representative should be formed immediately and continue to advance definite peace proposals until the belligerents found some basis for agreement on peace discussions. Tisza was just as encouraging. He had earlier displayed his abhorrence of war when he had momentarily refused to sanction the aggressive designs of the Austrian Government on Serbia during the crisis of July 1914, and he had not renounced his antiwar sentiments. Addams noted that Tisza "expressed the feeling that the Hungarians were getting nothing out of the situation. Let Germany settle with the Belgians. He would welcome negotiations."[17]

Although the congress did not instruct the envoys to visit the Vatican, they met unofficially with the Vatican Secretary of State Cardinal Gasparri and on the following day with Pope Benedict XV. Elected pontiff in the first days of the war, Benedict had previously served the Vatican as a diplomat in several European capitals. A veteran envoy wrote, for instance, that he was "a diplomat of exceptional brilliancy and experience." Other observers thought he was mediocre and in any case untested in his new position. In any event, because he had refrained from taking sides, he was widely rumored as an acceptable and suitable mediator of the conflict. All four women took part in the interview with Benedict, who praised their mission and spoke of his deep grief over the war, which involved massive

Catholic fratricide. He nonetheless spoke cautiously about the prospects for mediation. Sensitive to accusations from both warring alliances of his alleged partiality to the opposite camp, he emphasized his "difficult position" in initiating peace discussions. He feared such an effort would be misunderstood and might do more harm than good, but he told them to convey to Woodrow Wilson his deep interest in an early peace and promised to support the American President if he took the initiative.[18]

Following these interviews Jane Addams and Aletta Jacobs had previously planned to rendezvous with the second delegation in Amsterdam, and the envoys to northern Europe asked Addams to wait for their return. But after crossing to England for the necessary passage around the battlelines to Holland, Addams decided against returning to the Netherlands and booked passage directly to the United States. Reluctant to refuse the entreaties of the envoys to Scandinavia and Russia, she nonetheless was tired of the hectic traveling and was anxious to return home. Beyond rationalizing that she wanted to report about her travels to the Woman's Peace Party and to make arrangements to see President Wilson, Addams offered no clear explanation for her decision. But her resolve to return to the United States unquestionably suggested her lingering reservations concerning the usefulness of her private diplomacy.[19] Her decision disappointed her colleagues and particularly annoyed Rosika Schwimmer who began calling her "slippery Jane" for her seeming hesitant commitment to peacework.[20]

While awaiting the departure of her ship the following week, Addams wrote British Foreign Secretary Grey, asking whether he would hear her account of their interviews in the other European capitals. Because Grey had retired to his country estate to rest his deteriorating eyes, he replied that he could not see her but intimated that her impressions of the European statesmen were important, and he referred her to his subordinates in the foreign office. Once again he assured her that he had "great respect" for President Wilson and had tried to keep him fully informed "of my own personal views about the war and the future peace." To his assistants, Grey noted that he had already shared his views on peace talks very candidly with Colonel House, the president's most intimate adviser, and thus did not need to meet with her again. But he urged his Foreign Office subordinates to see her in his absence. She could provide interesting information on her interviews with the continental statesmen, and, just as important, it would be "very undesirable" not to talk to her after the other belligerent leaders had received her.[21]

It was Lord Crewe who received Addams at the foreign office, and he first listened attentively to her impressions of the responses of the European belligerent leaders and the Pope to the proposal for a neutral conference for continuous mediation. The ensuing discussion was lively. When Addams asked for the position of the British Government on the proposed conference, Crewe replied that "the question was not so much one of the opinions and hopes of the particular individuals who formed the Government as of the sentiments of the British people generally; and that the views of the people about a possible peace were conditioned not only by the fact that we were at war, but by the atrocious conduct of the war and the outrages against international law by the enemy." Addams rejoined that the Germans were similarly indignant over the British "barbarous" blockade, which was starving the civilian population. Crewe refused to accept the parallel, saying that the German excesses were "admittedly cruel, besides being unsanctioned by precedent," while it was impossible to see a distinction between the sufferings to civilian populations caused by the German siege of a great city, such as Paris, and their own naval blockade. Addams did not dispute Crewe's argument but reiterated that the British blockade greatly embittered German opinion. During their conversation, Addams also reaffirmed her personal opposition to neutrals' export of munitions by the belligerents, but also allowed that Jagow had admitted to her both the legal and moral right of the United States to export munitions, while regretting the lasting rancorous feelings among Germans.

Regarding possible peace talks, Crewe was frankly skeptical, though he conceded that if an absolute victory to either side were long deferred, the desire for peace would gain strength intellectually. Then "more people might begin to ask whether it would not be stupid to continue fighting when the profit of doing so was not evident," but he doubted that "an overwhelming moral objection would be taken to the continuance of the struggle." Meanwhile, he believed that joint neutral mediation would not carry much weight with the belligerents, and he reiterated the British preference for Woodrow Wilson's good offices in any consideration of mediation. The British Government, he told Addams, "would not desire to throw cold water upon any suggestion that President Wilson might make, though it was useless for us to deny that the difficulties in the way of any such step were simply enormous."

Before her departure her British friend, Lady Courtney, also arranged for Addams to have short talks on the peace question with the conservative internationalist Lord Robert Cecil, the undersecretary of state in the foreign office, the recently appointed minister of munitions David Lloyd George, who, Lady Courtney noted, "was full of his munitions, and went for the complete crushing of Germany," and the Archbishop of Canterbury, who showed keen interest in the women's interviews, especially the one with Pope Benedict XV.[22]

———

Meanwhile, Emily Balch, Cor Ramondt-Hirschmann, Chrystal Macmillan, and Rosika Schwimmer had begun their trip to the northern capitals. For the neutral countries, the purpose of their journey was somewhat different than the other envoys' visits to the warring powers. As Balch put it: "Now, what we are asking the Scandinavian government[s] is: 'Would you three with Switzerland and Holland send out an invitation to a neutral conference if you knew that the United States would be glad to respond?' " These envoys met with the King of Norway for nearly two hours and had shorter meetings with political leaders of all three Scandinavian nations.[23] The diplomats made no definite promises and were at best mildly encouraging. The Danish statesmen cautiously received the women and replied to their presentation with a very vague written statement affirming that their government would "gladly render their cooperation when possibilities might offer themselves for endeavors on the part of neutral States aiming at the restoration of Peace."[24] More favorable was their interview with Gunnar Knudsen, the Norwegian Prime Minister, about whom Balch wrote: "He is very much in sympathy, I think. He asked many questions and promised that the cabinet would consider our plan."[25]

Of all their contacts, however, by far the most encouraging was Knut Wallenberg, the Swedish foreign minister. This interview, Emily Balch exuded, "was worth all the others put together." Wallenberg, leading the women to believe that he hoped Stockholm would become the site of the final peace negotiations, expressed considerable interest in a conference of neutrals. While he refused to take the initiative at present, he promised to call a neutral conference if he received definite assurances that it would not be unacceptable to the belligerents. Upon further questioning he indicated that if the women could bring him a note expressing interest in an early peace from an official spokesman from each belligerent side, he would call a neutral conference for continuous mediation.[26]

Greatly encouraged, the women envoys departed for Petrograd. For the Russian part of the journey Baroness Ellen Palmstierna, a Swedish delegate to the women's congress, substituted for Rosika Schwimmer who, nominally representing the other belligerent side, was of course *persona non grata* to the Russians. Although Russian Foreign Minister Sergei Sazonov spoke temperately to the women, he dominated the interview. Even before the envoys could present their mediation proposal, he began a lengthy discourse on Russia's role in the war. He believed that the war would be fought to a finish; he also claimed that while Russia wanted peace, it was willing and able to fight on indefinitely because of the army's good morale and large reserves. He asserted that his government wanted only security of free transit through the Dardanelles and disclaimed any territorial aims beyond the independence of Poland under some kind of Russian influence. When the envoys finally presented their mediation proposal and mentioned in general terms their interviews with the other statesmen, Sazonov seemed mildly interested in the proposal but refused to endorse it. After some

3.1 Women envoys to the northern capitals—Emily Balch, Cor Ramondt-Hirschmann, Rosika Schwimmer, and Chrystal Macmillan—outside the royal palace in Christiania (Oslo), Norway. (International Archives of the Women's Movement)

prodding, however, he reluctantly approved a written statement declaring that the calling of a neutral conference "would not be unacceptable" to Russia, although he personally doubted whether it would lead to any constructive results. When the women returned to Stockholm and confronted Wallenberg with this statement, he refused to act. He told them that Sazonov's statement was too ambiguous and cautious (as indeed it was) to warrant agitation for a neutral conference.[27]

The four envoys did not abandon the effort. Recalling Wallenberg's initial promise, they refused to believe that the second interview ended the matter. Balch gave this overly optimistic assessment of their second meeting: "All this . . . sounds more negative than the first interview perhaps, but I think he was taking the whole thing even more seriously."[28] Before undertaking further action, however, the women returned to Amsterdam to discuss the situation with Dr Jacobs. After exchanging reports of their interviews, the five women concluded that the belligerents believed only the neutrals could take the first steps toward mediation, but the neutrals were afraid of reprisals if they acted without at least the prior tacit consent of the belligerents.

They also reassessed their assumptions on the creation of a neutral conference. At the onset of their travels the women assumed that President

Wilson, as the leader of the one great neutral power, would be the most suitable initiator of the neutral conference, and this feeling had persisted among the envoys to the northern capitals despite the submarine crisis between the United States and Germany which seemed to preclude his acting as impartial arbiter. Immediately following the *Lusitania* disaster, for example, Wales had written, "The little neutrals will follow where America leads," and Chrystal Macmillan agreed when she remarked of Wilson: "I think we are all putting our chief hope in him." Yet the serious crisis in German–American relations seriously diminished the prospect of the United States acting as an impartial mediator. Moreover, Dr Jacobs emphasized to the women envoys that Jagow had questioned America's neutrality and opposed its mediation. The women thus agreed that they should direct their main efforts toward the conversion of European neutrals to their mediation plan.[29]

But the problem remained: how could they convince a neutral government of the desirability and feasibility of calling a neutral conference? Dr Jacobs suggested that the Netherlands offered the best hope for action on their proposal. She was eager to have her own nation convoke a neutral conference and along with Rosika Schwimmer, who had returned to Holland while the envoys were visiting Russia, had already held a second interview with Cort van der Linden on this possibility. The Dutch prime minister expressed interest in their reports of interviews with European statesmen and asked them to inform him of any additional information on their views concerning mediation.

The other women believed, however, that no European neutral would unilaterally take the diplomatic initiative on mediation. They argued that a single neutral's invitation to a neutral conference of continuous mediation would immediately raise embarrassing questions about its real motives and probably jeopardize the last shreds of its neutrality, but the five neutrals acting together would both safeguard the neutrality of each and provide strong evidence of their good faith in an early peace. Before the European neutrals would begin to consider a joint initiative on mediation, they would need to gather assurances in writing, similar to the one they had already received from Sazonov, from the British and German leaders that they would not regard the creation of a neutral conference for continuous mediation as an unfriendly act. They wanted to return to these belligerent capitals and obtain such written assurances. The women deferred to Dr Jacobs' suggestion to call again both on the Dutch prime minister and foreign minister, but they also decided to go again to Berlin and London "unless Holland is so promising that it does not seem worthwhile."[30]

No record exists of these interviews, but the Dutch leaders apparently refused once again to commit their government to a neutral conference. Thus Schwimmer and Ramondt-Hirschmann set out for Berlin, while Macmillan and Balch went to London.

Their missions were only partially successful. Jagow attempted to reassure the women that Germany was fighting only to safeguard its future security and did not desire military victory. He also consented to put the following statement in writing: "Germany would find nothing unfriendly in the calling of a conference of neutrals but questions whether it would have practical consequences." He best summarized all the belligerent leaders' assumptions on the imposing obstacles to mediation when he remarked, "at this moment neither side is so weakened that it has to sue for peace."[31]

In London, Balch and Macmillan saw Crewe on July 14 and Grey, who had returned to the Foreign Office, a day later. On each occasion the envoys explained that as a result of their interviews in the Scandinavian capitals they believed that the European neutrals were afraid to undertake any independent mediatory action that might jeopardize its neutrality or have its good faith questioned by one side or the other, but that a group of five neutrals "acting together would safeguard the neutrality of each and would at the same time give confidence to the belligerents that each of the five were acting in good faith." The women argued that the European neutrals were prepared to cooperate in forming a conference if they could be convinced *"that their action would be useful and that it would not be resented by the belligerents."*

Reiterating what he and Grey had earlier told Jane Addams and Aletta Jacobs, Crewe replied that it was "impossible for the Government to invite the formation of such a body because it would be thought equivalent to an indirect proposal for terms of peace," nor could his government unequivocally "accept" the proposition of joint neutral mediation. He reiterated, however, that Britain would neither hinder the formation of a neutral conference for continuous mediation nor protest its existence after its formation. Most significantly, when the women wrote Crewe asking him whether their interpretation of the interview was correct, he replied on July 22nd confirming their account and reiterating that Britain could not invite the formation of a neutral conference "because it would be thought equivalent to an indirect proposal for terms of peace," but that "the Government would place no obstacle in the way of the formation of such a body."[32]

Foreign Secretary Grey elaborated on the position of the British Government. Accepting the possibility of a neutral conference, he warned that his government would deny all reports, including those that might be factually accurate, of the Allies' willingness to accept peace proposals if any such reports appeared before a neutral conference actually began to introduce peace proposals. Although he apparently did not volunteer the real reasons for this remark, he obviously wanted to prevent suspicions and perhaps disunity among the Allies until they could work out a common posture toward any such neutral conference.[33]

One can discredit any substantive importance to these interviews. Skeptics would point out that the envoys' travels lasted only a month, and the effects of their individual interviews were as transitory as attempts to write with a stick in water. One can plausibly argue in fact that the European statesmen did not take the women seriously and only humored them in order to make a good impression on neutral opinion. Delcassé's outspoken opposition to any negotiated peace, the many reservations of other war leaders, and their vigorous defense of their high-minded motives in the war would seem to indicate that they either resented talk about mediation or had little faith in a neutral conference. It was easy for them to assume that the women were too idealistic and too removed from the bases of power to get very far with their proposal for a neutral conference.

While still believing that their interviews were worthwhile, the women admitted the limitations of their influence on the governments. During their travels they talked with feminists and other private citizens in every belligerent capital and found that the vast majority supported their country's war effort and unquestioningly accepted their leaders' explanations of their high-minded motives in attempting to prosecute the war relentlessly to a victorious conclusion.[34] Even pacifistic liberals readily conceded overwhelming popular support for the war efforts in the belligerent nations. Much as the fanatical patriotism troubled them, the envoys readily admitted its pervasive existence. If they instinctively wanted to minimize pro-war sentiment, European pacifists reminded them of its dominance. Emily Hobhouse told Addams that in the warring nations, "Most of the Peace Societies don't want Peace – they want Victory," and she pointed out that the International Committee of Women for Permanent Peace could not even find five women in neutral Switzerland, let alone France, to represent their nations on the executive committee.[35] Balch concluded years later that the envoys "meant to leave no stone unturned but I doubt if any one of us was even hopeful for success."[36]

Balch's retrospective view may have served as a partial rationalization for the ultimate failure of mediation, for during and immediately following their interviews the envoys were slightly more sanguine. Their recent experiences had encouraged their cautious optimism. Expecting to be turned away at the chancelleries or to gain only brief, perfunctory interviews there, they were pleasantly surprised at the diplomats' cordial reception of them and their willingness to exchange views. As Balch remarked: "I may say that what was planned as a comparatively formal presentation of the resolutions of our Congress developed into something more than this." Speaking for her delegation, Addams agreed: "We do not wish to overestimate a very slight achievement nor to take too seriously the kindness with which the delegation was received, but we do wish to record ourselves as being quite sure that at least a few citizens in these various countries, some of them in high places, were grateful for the effort we made."[37] Of course, the women wanted to believe that their efforts might open the way to peace talks, but there seems little reason to doubt the essential veracity of their reports. If they were temperamentally inclined to exaggerate the importance of the most favorable statements in support of neutral mediation, their accounts of the interviews strove toward accuracy and agreed with one another.[38]

Moreover, with a few exceptions the leaders honestly expressed their general attitudes toward peace talks at the time. The fact that the women were without much actual influence in their own governments and obviously represented no particular nation officially enabled the statesmen to speak rather candidly on the subject of mediation. As Addams noted, "Perhaps the ministers talked freely to us because we were so absolutely unofficial." It was also difficult for the statesmen of the belligerent nations to refuse all prospects for neutral mediation after the women asked whether they would consider feasible propositions for peace or would steadfastly attempt to obtain by bloodshed what they might be able to win through negotiations. Even the French leader, Viviani, conceded that he did not oppose a neutral conference as a possible alternative to a war to the finish, although he spoke hesitantly and without conviction.[39]

Of the belligerents only Sasonov and Tisza deliberately lied to the women. The wily Sazonov attempted to mislead them when he asserted, contrary to Russia's secret agreements with France and Britain in March 1915, that Russia had no expansionist aims in the Dardanelles. In this and other respects, the envoys were at a serious disadvantage in their lack of confidential information on the belligerents' war aims, although the women did not interpret their missions broadly enough to broach this delicate area.

Tisza was hypocritical. A staunch Calvinist, his expression of pacifistic sentiments to the women envoys could be seen as religiously inspired. Such sentiments also seemed in character with his momentary refusal to sanction the aggressive designs of the Austrian Government on Serbia in July 1914. His opposition to war on that occasion derived not from pacifism, however, but from his fears of Hungary's increasing dependence on Germany in an extended war and the possible harmful consequences to the existing Hungarian political and social order and its national interests. Representing the dominant Magyar faction in Hungary, he was a reactionary politically, who spent much of his time as Prime Minister trying to crush liberal and democratic movements in the Empire. In any case, Tisza was indecisive in the final diplomatic crisis and, shortly before Austria-Hungary's declaration of war against Serbia, agreed vigorously to support the decision. Thereafter, he became an unyielding war hawk right down to the final dissolution of the Empire. Although the emissaries had heard from other Hungarians that he was a fire-eater, they were nonetheless taken in by his protestations of opposition to the war on religious grounds. They apparently made no attempt even to probe his alleged Calvinism or its tenuous connection with pacifism.[40]

It is also questionable whether Jagow was really sincere in discounting annexationist aims, but he and Bethmann truthfully indicated their general reservations about either American independent mediation or joint mediation by several neutrals. What they did not tell the envoys was their deeper reasons for opposing any mediation leading to a general peace settlement. For one thing, following the *Lusitania* sinking, German officials believed that any negotiated peace, short of complete repudiation of its military victories, was impossible. As early as September 1914, when Germany seemed poised to defeat France, Bethmann had approved a program of aggressive war aims in the continental west, which included taking territory from Belgium and France and making them economically subservient to Germany, and France's payment of a war indemnity. Historian Fritz Fischer argues that even after the allied forces soon checked the German armies at the Marne, the September program remained "the essential basis of Germany's war aims right up to the end of the war, although modified from time to time to fit changing situations." Germany's admirals and generals mostly agreed with these expansionist aims, although more vigorously demanded outright annexation of conquered territory.

Historians still debate whether Bethmann-Hollweg was ideologically committed to an expansionist program in September 1914 or just pragmatically acquiescing in maximum gains from an anticipated victory. Although he probably favored major territorial annexations, he could not say so publicly; to do so would undermine the very fragile domestic unity behind the German war effort. He was in fact beleaguered on all sides by conflicting crosscurrents. To sustain popular support for the war, he had to try to preserve the *Burgfrieden*. But in the face of mounting pressures from both the left and right, the task of maintaining the domestic truce forged in the summer of 1914 required extraordinary interpersonal skills—and Bethmann, a career civil servant who had advanced through the bureaucracy, was neither gifted intellectually nor particularly decisive. For a time, he maintained Socialists' support by espousing moderate peace aims and sympathy for their domestic reform goals. But he also had to be concerned about the military situation and to deal with the generals and their nationalist allies who favored expansionist goals for their nation. Because Germany had no institutional mechanism for reconciling military strategy and political aims—for example, whether to give priority militarily to the eastern or western fronts or to expand submarine warfare—the Chancellor often became involved, even as the generals and admirals resented civilian involvement in military matters and tried to encroach on his authority. There was also the erratic Kaiser, who would make major decisions on strategy and policy but whose many moods Bethmann had to deal with.

Jagow and Bethmann were also probably correct in telling the women envoys that national public opinion, inflamed to ultranationalistic heights from their military's initial triumphs, would likely topple the whole system of government if there was no recognition of Germany's successes in any final peace settlement. In addition, the two civilian leaders believed that any neutral effort leading to a comprehensive peace settlement would work to the disadvantage of Germany. Fearing unfriendly neutral opinion, which generally assumed Germany's greater responsibility for the war, disliked its militarism, and condemned its submarine warfare, they believed that any neutral mediation looking toward peace, no matter how impartial its motives, would result in a settlement favorable to their enemies.[41]

Instead of a comprehensive peace settlement, Germany's goal was to split the Entente powers, and throughout the war its leaders pursued a diplomatic strategy calculated to lead to a separate peace with one of its members. Because each of the Entente powers was bound under a September 1914 agreement not to make a separate peace or to discuss peace terms without the other allies' prior consent, German diplomats were under few illusions about the difficulties of inducing one or more of its enemies to consider peace. France was unmoved while the enemy occupied its territory, and the British Government was seemingly more united behind the war after Prime Minister Asquith formed a coalition government in mid-May 1915. But German political leaders and diplomats began to explore the possibility of a separate peace with Russia. Seeking to exploit the long-standing mistrust between Britain and Russia, they tried to sever Britain's link with Russia, which, Bethmann hoped, "on its part could win over France."

When the women first visited Berlin, the German Government had already begun to encourage the efforts of Hans Neils Andersen, a Danish shipping executive and a close friend of King Christian of Denmark to arrange for a separate peace with Russia. After much diplomatic maneuvering the Russians finally broke off Andersen's peace feelers in June 1915, but the German leaders continued to hope that they might use him to revive the possibility of a separate Russo–German peace. As Jagow wrote Brockdorff-Rantazau, the German minister in Copenhagen who was coordinating the Danish peace effort with the German Foreign Office, "It is because we do not mainly want a general peace but a separate peace with Russia that Andersen should try in Petrograd to move Russia toward peace."[42]

Germany correctly surmised England's lack of interest in a negotiated peace, but British leaders were unwilling to dismiss outright the possibility of neutral mediation. Acutely aware of the many intangibles in the war situation, they realized that the United States or European neutrals might eventually adopt the neutral conference or some other mediation proposal.

Sir Edward Grey, perhaps the most flexible of the European diplomats, understood that neutral nations, either through their economic policies, mediation initiatives, or outright military involvement, might eventually determine the outcome of the war, and he thus avoided policies that might irreparably alienate neutral sympathies. He especially recognized the importance of the United States, the largest and most powerful neutral, as the major outside supplier of the Allies' military resources, and his policies of pegging the price of confiscated cotton at a profitable level, which appeased its growers in the American South, and devising other British maritime practices favorable to the United States, indicated his willingness to compromise Britain's rightful claims under international law when they would help to appease American opinion.[43]

During the *Lusitania* crisis Grey tried to persuade Colonel House that only U.S. military involvement against Germany would enable Wilson to exercise "all the influence that is possible of the terms of peace." Yet because he correctly gauged the strong neutralist-isolationist sentiment in the United States, as well as Wilson's own strong preference for diplomatic intervention, both of which reduced the probability of American belligerency, he continued to express mild interest in any mediation plan under Wilson's leadership. If American military intervention on the side of the Allies was unlikely at present, he could still try to cultivate Wilson's goodwill in preparation for some later mediation move by the President. Grey never lost an opportunity to speak kind words about him, especially when they might eventually reach his ears, and almost certainly Grey had this ulterior motive in mind when he twice remarked to Jane Addams that he had great faith in Wilson's leadership. Grey conceded to House that several neutrals had pressed him for his opinion on a conference of neutral states to undertake mediation at the opportune moment, and he was even willing to contemplate this possibility if, but only if, the United States joined it.[44]

The envoys realized that the European neutrals were individually too small and weak to undertake any policy that threatened their fragile neutrality, but they still assumed that collectively these neutrals could withstand possible threats from one or both warring sides. Actually, the European neutral states were interested in cooperative action, but their primary motive was self-interest, not idealism. Cooperation for preservation of their trading rights and strict neutrality against belligerents' actual and threatened incursions rather than altruistic service as peacemakers most concerned them.

In December 1914, for example, the three Scandinavian monarchs had held a meeting in Malmö, Sweden, at which they agreed to consult on questions involving their nations' trade and navigation before initiating policies in these areas, and in early 1915 the three governments dispatched joint notes protesting Britain's mining of the North Sea and Germany's initiation of submarine warfare. However, these notes were temperate and did not even hint at reprisals, mainly because the neutrals feared that stronger protests would lead to drastic retaliatory actions by the belligerents.[45]

One can argue that close cooperative action among the European neutrals would have convinced the belligerents that the risks of war with these several neutral states resulting from flagrant violations of their legal rights would greatly outweigh any military, diplomatic, or economic benefits accruing from these violations. More probably, however, even the combined strength of the European neutrals would not have deterred the belligerents from extending their incursions on neutrals if they felt the ultimate success of their war effort demanded such action.[46] The neutral leaders were often at pains in discounting press reports and rumors of favoritism to one side over the other in the war. Dutch diplomats, for instance, went out of their way in denying to their British counterparts that they were unneutral and might even be cooperating confidentially with the Central Powers.[47] In any event, if the neutrals could cooperate with little effect on critical matters involving their national honor and economic well-being, it is no wonder that they failed to cooperate on mediation.

Yet the women correctly perceived that Sweden and Holland among the neutral governments were most interested in an early, just peace. The envoys' visit to Sweden nourished underlying sentiment there for peace talks. The Swedish delegates to the Hague congress organized 343 peace meetings on June 27 to enlist support for the calling of a neutral conference for continuous mediation. A deputation from one of these peace meetings called on Wallenberg and urged him to initiate the proposal. Wallenberg candidly warned them that Sweden's neutrality was precarious and that necessity to defend "our rights and our liberty" could bring Sweden into the war. Even if Swedish belligerency never occurred, he had to think first of his own nation. He understood that "the pacificists think that Sweden's role as pacifier would be both desirable and natural. But," he went on, "it isn't so simple. There is a saying that goes, 'The one who comes unasked, goes away unthanked.' Worse than that, stepping in at an unsuitable time or in an unsuitable manner might do irreparable harm."[48]

———

The Dutch Government more earnestly attempted to prepare the way for an end to the war. In early May 1915 it sent an unofficial emissary to the Vatican, and a month later it introduced a bill in the Dutch House of Commons establishing a temporary embassy at the Vatican. Both measures, Cort van der Linden acknowledged, would open communications with the Vatican and enable the two powers to cooperate when one or both belligerent groups expressed interest in peace talks. The Holy See welcomed the arrival of the Dutch envoy, promised to lend the Pope's moral influence to any Dutch peace initiative, and urged the appointment of a minister. The Netherlands quickly responded by appointing L.W.H. Regout as temporary minister to the Vatican in August 1915. Regout soon reported on his very friendly personal audiences with Gasparri, the Pope's influential secretary, and Benedict XV himself. All three recognized the desirability of close Vatican–Netherlands cooperation in preparation for possible future mediation opportunities.[49]

The Netherlands was a strongly Protestant nation, but Catholic numbers and influence had increased by the early twentieth century. Moreover, because the Catholics, with their own political party, were sufficiently strong in the Dutch parliament to hold the balance of power, the political leadership could not easily ignore them. Even more influential in the decision for the Vatican contacts were Holland's proximity to the actual fighting and its leaders' mounting fears over belligerents' possible restrictions on Dutch sovereignty in the Scheldt River, a vital trade route extending into German-occupied Belgium. Another self-interested motive was the Dutch leaders' desire for the Vatican's support for holding eventual peace talks at The Hague which, having hosted the two Hague Peace Conferences and serving as the home of the Permanent Court of Arbitration, would continue the nation's peacemaking tradition. In sum, considerations of national self-preservation and prestige as much as pacifistic sentiments underlay the Dutch Government's interest in mediation.

Catholic members of the Dutch parliament, with some Protestant support, had in fact initiated the suggestion of restoring relations with the Vatican in February 1915, and Loudon, who at first resisted the idea, changed his mind only when he learned that a definite, "even if only embryonic peace action" was taking place there. Moreover, the mission to the Vatican was temporary (though it ultimately was prolonged until 1925), and exchange of information between the two powers was not binding, but had the limited aim of enabling each party to know in advance the attitude of the other on possible peace talks. Neither did the Papacy nor the Dutch Government harbor illusions about the extremely slim hopes for peace discussions in the foreseeable future.[50]

But the desire of Holland's leaders for a close working relationship with the Vatican made sense for two reasons. First, because the pontiff's authority among Catholics transcended national boundaries, he could be a powerful influence for peace if he exercised his influence forcefully at an opportune moment. (The belligerents too maintained their diplomatic presence at the Vatican—or in the case of Britain sent a special emissary there in early 1915—to deal with issues arising out of the war, including possible papal mediation.) Second, Dutch cooperation in a peace initiative would counterbalance the Central Powers' assumption of the Netherlands' pro-Allied sympathies with the Entente's belief in the Holy See's pro-Austrian connections. But even granting their self-interested motives or fragile hopes, the Dutch leaders' desire for peace was genuine. As the Prime Minister Cort van der Linden argued before the Dutch House of Commons, "when we declare, not in secret, but openly, that because we are neutral, we associate ourselves with all efforts that are made to put an end to the war, I think we interpret the feelings of our nation . . . As the territory not yet swept by the waves of war becomes smaller, it becomes more important that all those who honestly desire peace, should unite themselves more closely," so that they would be ready to help end the war "when all the belligerents long for peace." Loudon had written Grey much the same thing a few weeks earlier: "if at any time I acquired the conviction (which I certainly have not at present) that peace openings were possible, I should be happy to approach the various Ministers of Foreign Affairs by means of a personal letter." He also was receptive to the offers of some members of the Society of Friends in Great Britain to extend peace offers of a conference of neutrals to Berlin "at the appropriate time."[51]

Minimizing the importance of the Dutch Government's requirement of genuine belligerents' interest in peace talks before launching any mediation offer, the Dutch Anti-War Council pursued the matter. While still at The Hague, the envoys conferred with the council's energetic leader B. de Jong van Beek en Donk, who had read with great interest Wales' pamphlet on continuous mediation. The Anti-War Council had proposed a similar, though less explicit, mediation plan at the beginning of the war and the Hague congress' adoption of Miss Wales' proposal renewed his interest in cooperative mediation by the several nations. He had invited Addams and Wales to one of the Anti-War Council's meetings to explain the women's neutral conference scheme. Following the envoys' visits to the European capitals, the peace group issued a statement to the press urging the Dutch Government to take the initiative for a conference of neutrals preparing the way for possible peace talks.

On August 12 Macmillan, who had come to Holland with Lord Crewe's statement endorsing mediation by a conference of neutral powers, and Jacobs called on Cort van der Linden. The Prime Minister thought Crewe's statement was important and wondered about the U.S. position. Jacobs' notes of the interview continued:

He could not take the initiative to form such a comm. of neutrals as long as he did not know if Pres. Wilson himself preferred to take the lead or if Pres. W. was willing to join the combined 5 Europ. neutrals when they invited him and other neutrals for a combined action. If you can bring me as soon as possible unofficial[ly] a statement of Pres. Wilson's attitude, I consider this as an act of great importance. I than

[then] told him that I in this case was willing to leave for U.S. the next day, Friday 13th. He encouraged me to do [so].

The two women immediately met separately with Foreign Minister Loudon. According to Jacobs, he too thought Crewe's written statement was "of *great* value" but wanted a similar statement from France. "If that was given and we knew the attitude of the US, than [then] there could be a beginning," he said. Unwilling to wait for the French statement (which they must have known would not be forthcoming anyway), Jacobs and Macmillan argued that they would ask Benjamin F. Battin, a Quaker and professor of German at Swarthmore College, who was going to France, to obtain such a letter from the French Government. Battin had traveled through Europe in 1914–1915 under the auspices of the Church Peace Union to organize national branches of the World Alliance of Churches for Promoting International Friendship. During his European trip he had come into contact with Quaker pacifists and other church figures sympathetic to a compromise peace. Unofficially sounding out government leaders of European belligerents and neutrals, he already had had two interviews with Sir Edward Grey, who authorized Battin to use the substance of their second conversation in early August in Paris, Berlin, and Berne. While Professor Battin traveled to Paris to see the French leaders, Loudon acquiesced in having Jacobs proceed at once to the United States, and he gave her a letter of introduction to the Dutch minister in Washington.[52]

Rumors of the Netherlands' growing interest in mediation and the Anti-War Council's publicity campaign greatly alarmed Allied ministers at The Hague, who opposed any mediation move at present and feared that Germany had inspired the Anti-War Council's activity. Calling on Loudon, the Entente ministers collectively warned him that any mediation attempts would be considered as an "unfriendly action" by their governments. Loudon hastened to assure the Allied representatives that the Netherlands had no intention of promoting any peace move unless requested by a majority of the belligerent powers. Although this Dutch response was not a blanket rejection of all possible future peace initiatives, it appeased the Allied diplomats. The Netherlands in fact continued to develop cordial ties with the Vatican for possible future cooperation on peace initiatives, but the Dutch leaders' seeming public reluctance to promote mediation talk persuaded the Anti-War Council to abandon its agitation for peace talks for more than a year. The Swedish Government, hearing reports of the Anti-War Council's propaganda efforts in Scandinavia, also denied that it had any connection with the peace proposals of anti-war groups.[53]

4

Peace Workers and the Wilson Administration

With prospects for peace overtures coming to a standstill in Europe, peace advocates turned their attention to the United States. The women's interviews with European leaders were a prelude for face-to-face meetings they hoped to have with Woodrow Wilson concerning prospects for neutral mediation. Having been politely put off by the President before their European adventure, the peace advocates knew that he was not easily influenced. As the women had set off for the Hague congress in mid-April, he had publicly intimated in fact that he did not want to "discountenance it in any way, but it has no official sanction of any kind." Certainly they knew that he had not thus far expressed any real interest in their proposal for a continuous conference of neutrals. He had shown the same reserve in his reactions to the discreet inquiries of other neutral governments about possible peace initiatives, although the peace advocates were unaware of the details. In November 1914, for example, he had rejected the feeler of Switzerland to begin negotiations with the European neutrals on the feasibility of calling a conference of neutral states. The Swiss Government had suggested that the American delegate would preside over this conference in some European city, which would agree on a mediation offer to be presented to the belligerents at an opportune time. A month later he had also squelched the request of the King of Spain for cooperation on a possible mediation overture.[1]

Outwardly, Wilson seemed to approach the issues arising out the European war in its first several months with hesitation. Compared with his aggressive and frequently decisive leadership on domestic questions in Congress from the very outset of his presidency, his dealings with the unfolding European catastrophe seemed by comparison curiously reactive. His inexperience in foreign affairs contributed to his caution. Unlike Theodore Roosevelt, who from an early age assiduously prepared himself for international politics and reveled in diplomacy, or Wilson's predecessor, William Howard Taft, who also had had considerable pre-presidential foreign policy experience, the new president was a student of American government and history and had devoted little attention to world affairs. Before his presidency, Wilson had taken only several brief trips to the British Isles and Bermuda, had never traveled to the European continent, and was fluent in no foreign language. He had never served in a national administration, and his political career consisted solely of a two-year term as governor of New Jersey. When he remarked just before his inauguration as president that "it would be the irony of my fate if my administration had to deal chiefly with foreign affairs"—words that virtually every historian of Wilsonian diplomacy has quoted—he was expressing his genuinely uneasy feelings about the conduct of foreign affairs. His handling of crises with Mexico in the first year or so of his administration, which was excessively moralistic and erratic and led to a U.S. military intervention with the loss of scores of American and Mexican lives, showed his inexperience.[2]

After saying nothing during the final diplomatic crisis in July 1914 and only belatedly offering his good offices for mediation, Wilson did not focus on the European conflict. In October, House found him "singularly lacking in appreciation of the importance of this European crisis" and "difficult to get his attention centered" on it. For the rest of the year, Wilson showed no disposition to question traditional views of neutrality, as defined by precedent and international law, although the introduction of the submarine by early 1915 would seriously challenge previously accepted notions of cruiser warfare. Specifically, it was risky for fragile submarines to come to the surface to stop and search enemy merchant vessels, which was the legally accepted practice in wartime, because the ships could falsely carry "neutral" flags or conceal powerful guns—and the Allies increasingly resorted to these practices during the war. The U-boats thus usually remained submerged and fired their torpedoes at suspected enemy craft. Because American seamen and passengers were sometimes aboard these merchantmen, the threat to amicable U.S.–German relations was ever present. Nor did he comment on the desirability of allowing American citizens to travel on belligerent or neutral passenger liners, although German U-boat attacks on such ships, which sometimes also carried war materiel to the Allies, would obviously seriously complicate the Wilson administration's professed desire to stay out of the war.

While the American president issued a proclamation calling for neutrality in thought as well as deed, he publicly refrained from commenting on the administration's acceptance of loans by private U.S. banks or the shipment of munitions to the belligerents. Because the Allied ships controlled the high seas, almost all of the loans, which the Entente powers used to pay for the U.S. goods, and the munitions went to the Allies. These supposedly neutral policies were distinctly unneutral to the Central Powers. This is not to say, however, that Wilson was deliberately pro-Allied; the effects of alternative policies—an embargo on munitions shipments, for example—would have been decidedly pro-German. Indeed, it is hard to see how he could have devised more truly neutral policies.[3]

Contributing to Wilson's seeming indifference to the issues of the European war was the severe depression he experienced for several months after his wife's death. He suffered grief and loneliness, guilt, and hopelessness, telling House in early November that "he was broken in spirit . . ., and was not fit to be President because he did not think straight any longer, and had no heart in the things he was doing." A week later he remarked that he was "so lonely and sad" that he hoped someone would kill him. "He has told me this before," House commented. "His eyes were moist when he spoke of not wanting to live longer, and of not being fit to do the work he had in hand." Wilson had suffered bouts of depression in his pre-presidential years, but his personal distress following the loss of his beloved Ellen was particularly acute. In trying to overcome his depressed mood throughout much of the fall of 1914, he threw himself into his work, wrote letters to sympathetic women friends, and increased his recreational diversions—motoring trips around Washington, excursions on the presidential yacht, and golf—and somehow managed to conceal his distressed state from public view. Only gradually, however, did he pull himself out of his depression and again think clear-headedly about domestic and foreign issues.[4]

Actually, even during the first months of the European conflict, there were signs of an evolving Wilsonian foreign policy. Whatever twists and turns he might make in reaction to specific events or crises, two thoughts predominated in his thinking. The first was to stay out of the war if humanly possible, and the second was the hope of serving as mediator between the two belligerent sides, if an opportune moment arose, to bring about a negotiated end to the conflict. The first was of course a prerequisite for the second. Colonel House's confidential mission to Europe even before the war was an innovative diplomatic initiative signaling the Wilson administration's sincere interest in trying to reduce the general insecurity; when war came anyway, the president did offer, however tardily, his good offices for mediation.

Some of the reasons for Wilson's determination to avoid involvement in the war for his nation are fairly obvious. To Wilson and the overwhelming majority of Americans, the European maelstrom was the result of age-old rivalries and hatreds; many Europeans had in fact immigrated to the United States to escape them. Even the militaristic Roosevelt and other Americans who wanted a more assertive U.S. foreign policy agreed in the first months that their nation should keep the complications of warfare away from American shores. The sentiment of most Americans was distinctly pro-Allied (or, more accurately, Anglophile), but the presence of many Germans and Irish (altogether, "hyphenated" Americans constituted

30 percent of the population) required presidential caution on foreign policy, if he was to maintain a semblance of domestic unity.[5]

Much more was involved in Wilson's approach to the Great War, however, than just the maintenance of social peace and vague hopes for his possible role as mediator. Deeper impulses in his psyche were in fact at work that would reinforce his antiwar views and motivate him to aspire to become the world's peacemaker. Some historians suggest that he may have developed an aversion for warfare from his vivid memories of bloodshed and death during the Civil War. As a seven-year-old, he saw wounded soldiers in his father's church in Augusta, Georgia, and Union soldiers imprisoned in the churchyard. He witnessed Confederate troops marching through the town en route to resisting General Sherman's invasion, and he remembered standing "for a moment at General Lee's side and looking up into his face." Wilson himself later commented that "A boy never gets over his boyhood, and never can change those subtle influences which have become a part of him." Perhaps these "subtle influences" included his unhappy memories of the American Civil War and his determination to find alternatives to war.[6]

Even more important was the spiritual influence of his father, Joseph Ruggles Wilson. Firmly adhering to the stern Presbyterian tradition, Reverend Wilson imparted to his son a sturdy Christian faith. "*My* life would not be worth living," the younger Wilson later declared, "if it were not the driving power of religion, for *faith*, pure and simple . . . No, never for a moment have I had one doubt about my religious beliefs." His father also nourished a comprehensive covenant theology in his son. Woodrow grew up accepting this divine "theology of politics" for the individual, church, and society, which provided a rational explanation for every aspect of human life. It even involved a covenantal relationship between God and the American nation. "It provided a comprehensive view of the world and the individual's place within it," the biographer of his formative years writes, "and for Wilson, it was most frequently employed to provide structure and wholeness in the midst of personal and social disorder." Throughout his life he showed a special fascination and fondness for covenants, compacts, and constitutions. The direction of his thought was toward finding ways to develop more perfect constitutional governments at all levels. His later fervent promotion of a league of nations would be the capstone of this covenantal ethos.[7]

Being a good Presbyterian, however, did not inevitably make Wilson a peacemaker. Christian attitudes toward peace and war have ranged from the nonresistant peace churches, which profess absolute pacifism, to crusading fervor to impose the Christian message forcibly, if required, on infidels, and Presbyterian theology espoused neither nonresistance nor militant messianic interventionism. It was Wilson's application of the covenant theology that nourished his interest in peacemaking. In a more secularized era the covenant theology was sufficiently vague and ambiguous to allow Wilson to apply it in several different ways as long as it did not conflict with what he felt was "right" or "moral." The flexible doctrine even permitted him to think in terms of "Providence" or "natural law" instead of specific reference to "God."

Wilson's education also exposed him to secular writings, which became more predominant in his thinking about American politics. Chief among them was Edmund Burke, the late eighteenth century British political theorist. Wilson came to revere Burke's hostility to abstract reasoning and his emphasis on practical experience and evolutionary change. Much as he appreciated the British philosopher's utilitarian and expedient bent, he also came to value the central role he gave to moral issues underlying political behavior. But if Wilson early found Burke an invaluable guide in his interest in conservative reform, he would gradually see the possibilities in a more progressive politics to deal with the many problems associated with a rapidly urbanizing and industrializing America.[8]

Wilson's responses to the American peace movement in his pre-presidential years reflected his slowly growing interest in a "practical" reform for the gradual amelioration of world politics. Beginning about 1907, he warmed to the burgeoning movement and its promotion of international arbitration treaties; but while endorsing its activities, he remained mostly on its fringes. A host of domestic issues were more pressing to an ambitious politician at a time when foreign issues to most Americans seemed dull and far away. Typical of his involvement, he joined the American Peace Society in 1908, only to allow his membership to lapse sometime before his presidency. He also gave a few very general and highly intellectual speeches on the theme of "peace," in which he extolled mankind's spiritual strivings for enlightenment, justice, truth, and industrial peace within nations as prerequisites for the pursuit of international goodwill.[9]

Moreover, Wilson had a lifelong fascination with leadership. In aspiring to become "a leader of men," he sought during his rising career to become the commanding statesman who, combining personal integrity and high principle, would inspire others to follow him. In a scary metaphor revealed to his fiancée Ellen, he compared himself to the "selfish" and "lonely" eagle soaring above the ordinary and mundane; "it[']s better to swing in independent flight from [mountain] top to top than to be all your life flocking and nest-building and chattering with innumerable commonplace little birds in the branches of a tree which is, even at its highest twig, very near the ground after all." More frankly, he confided to her that "I have a strong instinct of leadership . . . I have a passion for interpreting great thoughts to the world."[10]

His striving for moral leadership at Princeton often drove him to

overwork and exhaustion, and likely contributed to recurrent physical ail-
ments, including digestive problems, hemorrhoids, headaches, and, most
alarming, many strokes between 1896 and 1913. His strokes—a few apparently serious—strengthened his religious faith but did not dim his ambition.
Was this drive for personal achievement a natural tendency to a committed
Calvinist to "prove" that he was one of the "elect"? It is hard to say, but he
became almost obsessed with the nature of leadership and his desire for
authoritative positions, first in academia as reform-minded president of
Princeton and then in politics. His strong Presbyterian faith could also
make him very rigid. Once he was convinced he was right, he could be
obstinate and unyielding toward his opponents. It was his self-righteous
refusal to compromise on educational issues at Princeton that brought
about his downfall there.[11]

Wilson's seriousness and sense of moral purpose made him seem prig-
gish and holier-than-thou to some observers. That side to Wilson was
sometimes present, but he also was a warm family man and could be a
delightful, engaging companion in small groups. There was in fact a fine
tension between two personality tendencies in him. One side was essentially clear-headed, rational, and measured in weighing different opinions,
and it would find expression in his most highly articulate and carefully
argued speeches and official papers. Another Burkean maxim contributing
to this side was the importance of expressing the best thoughts and ideas of
dominant public opinion. It was useless to appeal to a minority in a democracy or to try to change their minds for some future time. "If you would
be a leader of men, you must lead your own generation, not the next," he
had written in 1890. Moreover, the ideas should be expressed in simple,
direct terms and have moral appeal. The other side of his personality was
more intuitive, idealistic, committed, and susceptible of emotion, including
strongly negative feelings toward those who seemed to disagree with his
proposals. Wilson's somewhat dreamy, intuitive bent was present throughout his presidency, but it would become more dominant during his second
presidential term when he became less accepting of reasoned argument and
more stubborn and egotistical in pursuit of his liberal peace aims and a
postwar league of nations.[12]

Robert Lansing, Bryan's successor as secretary of state, would later write
that Wilson had a "feminist mind," by which he meant the president's
thought processes were nonlogical or intuitive rather than rational. In other
words, according to the gender stereotypes of that era, he thought more like
women than men.[13] During his first term, however, President Wilson was
mostly rational and sensible and was often receptive to outside advice. His
dispassionate analysis of the causes of the European war, for instance, was
an early expression of this side, and even in his depressed mood following
his wife's death his self-prescribed antidote was not isolation, but more

socialization. In any event, during the World War the juxtaposition of Wilson's search for a better constitutional association between nations, his moral principles, and his desire for inspired leadership would gradually propel him to become a major champion of a new peaceful world order.

Despite his lingering hopes for a peace initiative, in the first several months of the European maelstrom Wilson was pessimistic about prospects for mediation. Indeed, as late as the early spring of 1915 he wrote that "there are no terms of peace spoken of (at any rate in Germany) which are not so selfish and impossible that the other side are ready to resist them to their last man and dollar. Reasonableness has not yet been burned into them, and what they are thinking of is, not the peace and prosperity of Europe, but their own aggrandizement."[14] Despite such cautious appraisals, he remained interested in his possible mediation, and this interest would very gradually intensify. As early as mid-September 1914, he gave his Christian friend, John R. Mott, a letter of introduction to U.S. ambassadors and ministers in several European countries for his upcoming trip to the continent to explore possibilities for religious and social services to the belligerent troops. He told Mott of his "strong desire" to preserve U.S. neutrality so that he could mediate at the appropriate time. In that regard, he quoted a remark attributed to Napoleon, "No lasting peace [was] ever secured by force," and Secretary Bryan's comment that "Nothing is final between friends."

Wilson opposed a decisive triumph by the Central Powers, which would elevate the legitimacy of military force in world affairs, but even an Allied victory would not be an ideal solution for him. A military deadlock would show the futility of the resort to arms, however, and over time persuade the warring powers to consider a just and equitable peace settlement. The chief executive continued to believe that by maintaining self-control and impartiality, the United States, "the servant of mankind," might eventually come to the assistance of Europe in restoring peace. Already he was thinking in terms of what he would later call a "peace without victory."[15]

More specifically, Wilson had reacted favorably to the suggestion of the Venezuelan minister in Washington for a conference of neutral nations called together by the United States to formulate propositions on neutral rights that would later be submitted to a conference of all nations, including belligerents. The Venezuelan minister also believed that such a neutral conference might open the way to mediation, and Secretary Bryan endorsed the suggestion mainly for this reason. Colonel House of course did not share Bryan's hopes for joint mediation, but he enthusiastically supported the idea of an inter-American treaty pledging the signatories to "a common and mutual guarantee of territorial integrity and of political independence under republican forms of government" and their cooperation in resisting aggression both from within and outside the hemisphere.

House hoped that the example of pan-American cooperation "would serve as a model for the European Nations when peace is at last brought about," and he easily won the president's firm support for the concept. This vision of a new pan-Americanism began to gestate actively in Wilson's mind, and he immediately drafted two articles (soon expanded to four) of a pan-American treaty. The first, and most important, article called for the mutual guarantee of the hemispheric nations' territorial integrity. Historians rightly focus on this article as a kind of multilateralization of the Monroe Doctrine and, later, as the origins of Wilson's notion of collective security, which would be embedded as Article 10 in the Covenant of the League of Nations, but it also had more immediate relevance to the issue of mediation. The prospect of a pan-American pact could focus attention on U.S. relations with Latin America at the expense of its possible cooperation with European neutrals, and in the following months Wilson would argue more than once that he could not commit the United States to a conference of European neutrals before he had developed a common policy of cooperation with its Latin American neighbors.[16] But he would also recognize that the interests of neutral American republics and the European neutrals in avoiding war and pursuing peace were not exclusive, and that cooperation with Latin America could indeed be enlarged to include the European neutrals.

Even while the women envoys were visiting the European capitals, President Wilson was considering another mediation initiative put forward by Francis van Gheel Gildemeester, the son of a former court chaplain at The Hague and a Dutch citizen. From all accounts, Gildemeester's peace initiative was entirely his own. He apparently had no contacts with Dutch peace groups, such as the Anti-Oorlog Raad, or with his nation's political leaders but claimed he had well-connected citizen contacts in America. The German minister at The Hague had initially recommended Gildemeester to his Foreign Office to help the nation's propaganda effort in the mid-western United States "as an inauspicious neutral." By the time he called on Chancellor Bethmann and other German officials in Berlin, however, the *Lusitania* disaster had occurred, and Gildemeester may have also used his trip to Washington more immediately as a personal emissary to help defuse the crisis in German–American relations. Historians who have closely perused the documentary record of Gildemeester's initiative agree that the purposes of his U.S. trip as well as Ambassador Bernstorff's association with it are somewhat "mysterious," but not on whether Wilson actually received Gildemeester in person. There is some circumstantial evidence, which can be interpreted to indicate a meeting, but nothing definite despite the considerable correspondence surrounding the private emissary's appearance in Washington. Whether Wilson and Gildemeester actually talked directly may not be particularly significant since the substance of the German Foreign Office's proposals to be conveyed by Gildemeester were clearly conveyed to Wilson personally by Bernstorff on June 2 and in a follow-up letter from the Dutchman five days later.[17]

What Gildemeester brought with him was information on Germany's peace terms as well his impressions of German attitudes toward the war. He believed, as he was also to relate to an American acquaintance, that there was "a sharp cleavage between the militarist or war party in Germany and the moderate or peace party" and that the latter (whose position he represented) "is already strong and gaining in strength." As Gildemeester emphasized in a follow-up letter to Wilson, he particularly valued the opinion of Professor Clemens Delbrück, German Interior Minister, who had stressed to him his government's willingness "to come into negotiations if a real neutral, with a neutral point of view, will help us. I can assure you," Delbrück had written, "that we will leave Belgium the moment that peace negotiations are entered into."[18]

More significant, however, were the views Wilson expressed to Bernstorff at their June 2 meeting. He then indicated that he hoped to settle the *Lusitania* incident favorably and then try to find a modus vivendi between Britain and Germany on the observance of traditional international sea law. In that regard, he mentioned calling a conference of neutral nations, starting with the Latin American states that were then meeting at a Pan-American Congress in Washington, and then extending to the European neutrals, to discuss measures for the joint protection of their rights in wartime. Wilson told the German ambassador that if he succeeded in bringing all the neutrals together and committing them to the protection of neutral rights, he would then ask the belligerents to participate. The league of neutrals would cut off all trade, including munitions and foodstuffs, from those warring powers refusing to participate in the peace conference. Thus Wilson was thinking of a conference of neutral nations with very different purposes than continuous mediation, but that might ultimately bring an end to the fighting. The peace terms he envisioned included the status quo antebellum in Europe, adjustments of colonial possessions, and, as Bernstorff described it in his report to the German Foreign Office, "freedom of the seas to such an extent that it would be equal to a neutralization of the seas."[19]

Wilson's plan thus was both another alternative to war and a search for some feasible stratagem that might pressure the belligerents to consider peace. He seemed to recognize that the peace conditions were very favorable to Germany, which because of the British blockade was already cut off from supplies from neutral nations, and it would be difficult, short of a defeated England, to get that nation to accept unfettered trade by neutrals of noncontraband goods. Despite Gildemeester's optimism and Bernstorff's messages to Berlin urging his government to take advantage of this "favorable" opportunity in German–American relations, nothing in fact came of the initiative. For one thing, Bethmann's influence in the German Government was so tenuous that he could not respond positively to Wilson's thoughts; for another, Italy's entrance into the war upset hopes for peace based upon prewar conditions. And finally, Germany soon concluded that Britain would never accept even partial freedom of the seas.[20]

The American women returning to the United States had no inkling of Gildemeester, who disappeared from view as quickly as he had emerged,[21] but even in their unawareness they were far from cocksure about the feasibility of their mediation proposal. Not only had the European interviews proved inconclusive, but the *Lusitania* crisis in German–American relations ended all hopes for early American participation in a neutral conference for continuous mediation. Nevertheless, the women decided to press on with their proposal in the hope that the crisis would soon pass without irreparable damage to America's neutrality.

Jane Addams, their most influential spokesperson, realized that many obstacles lay in the way of any kind of mediation, but she remained cautiously optimistic. In her homecoming address to a packed audience of 3,000 well wishers at Carnegie Hall on July 9, 1915, she emphasized that the European war resulted in so many emotional and contradictory opinions that she wished to avoid making any generalizations that were "not founded upon absolutely first-hand impressions and careful experience." To attempt authoritative statements on the conflict, she warned, would only add to the overwhelming confusion and passions. She tried, however, to draw upon her personal experiences to formulate tentative conclusions.

One promising sign, Addams said, was the revolt of a growing proportion of the civilian population against militarism within all the belligerents. These indicators of peace sentiment were not obvious, and the "civilian party" was censored and overshadowed by the predominant "military party." The longer the war continued, she feared, the more the military would gain control, expand censorship, and break down "all the safeguards of civil life and for the rights of civil rights and of civil government, and that consequently it will be harder for civil life and the rights of civil life to resuscitate themselves and regain their place over the rights and power of the military." The importance of starting peace talks now, she asserted, was to prevent the military party from entrenching itself, and she focused particularly on the favorable indicators for a negotiated peace that she found among the "civilian party" in the course of her European travels. She related several examples of soldiers' conscientious scruples against shooting enemies.

Another component of this "civilian party" was the women of the belligerent nations. Addams conceded that the commitment of women to their nation's war effort seemed to contradict the feminist notion that the instinctual love of mothers for their sons would prompt their opposition to military combat. She nonetheless continued to pay lip service to the feminists' pacifist ideology when she remarked, "That curious revolt comes out again and again, even in the women who are most patriotic and who . . ., when they are taken off their guard, give a certain protest, a certain plaint against the whole situation which very few men I think are able to formulate." While Addams' report of women's stillborn revolt against war was undoubtedly accurate, she had also encountered many women in belligerent countries who strongly endorsed the war and were glad their sons had gone off to combat. Like other feminists, Addams would continue to complain that defenseless women were victims of rape and other cruelties at the hands of occupying enemy soldiers, but she did not stress the notion of women's exclusive role as peacemakers. It was not difficult for her to downplay the "maternal instinct," however, as she had always worked well with male reformers domestically. Indeed, she continued to argue "that men and women should work together on all questions of public interest. It has a better effect on both, and it is moreover the ideal condition that men and women shall do things together."[22]

In her talk, Addams went on to report the recent revolt against war among the younger people in Europe. Less inclined than their elders to accept the abstract slogans of their war leaders, many of them judged the war on pragmatic grounds and found it wanting. It was in short "an old man's war; that the young men who were dying, the young men who were doing the fighting, were not the men who wanted to war, and were not the men who believed in the war. . . . This is a terrible indictment, and I admit that I cannot substantiate it, I can only give it to you as an impression." Because of her belief in direct experience, which Addams as a woman and noncombatant of course had not faced herself, she provided some examples from her conversations with belligerent soldiers, who were prepared to die, but were very reluctant to kill other young men. She concluded her address with a report on bayonet charges. Soldiers had told her what was already widely believed—that the soldiers on both sides were given stimulants of alcohol or other "dope" (absinthe to the French, rum to the British, and a regular formula to the Germans) to dull their sense of horror before the inevitable face-to-face killing.

Addams' speech drew a strongly critical reply from Richard Harding Davis, a writer on military affairs who had recently returned from Europe, and several others. Overlooking her remarks that the soldiers did not fear dying but in killing their adversaries (though she later admitted she should have more clearly made that distinction), these critics accused Addams of besmirching the courage and gallantry of the soldiers in warfare. A New York lawyer and founder of a settlement house, and with a son in the French army, wrote, for example, that "Miss Addams evidently knows nothing of the joy of combat; whatever faults the soldiers have, they are not cowards." The soldiers on both sides did "not need any 'dope' to stimulate their courage, or to drown their fears. Someone had told Miss Addams this gruesome tale and she believed it." They may not have needed stimulants, but they were readily available, as alcohol of some type was a part of the food rations of soldiers on both sides. Clearly, some denunciations of her came from antifeminists who objected not only to her antiwar views, but because these came from a woman who dared to comment on military matters, which they perceived as an exclusive male preserve. In his earlier criticism of the women's peace movement, Theodore Roosevelt had not singled out his former domestic reform ally, but he now began attacking her "as one of the shrieking sisterhood," "poor bleeding Jane," and "Bull Mouse."

Addams probably hoped that her remarks would discredit the shibboleth that military combat was a glorious and exhilarating experience. What she learned instead was that Americans still firmly adhered to the long-cherished, popular myth of the heroism and nobility of the soldier on the battlefield. Some of her friends came to her defense, and in the following few weeks she tried more specifically to document the sources for her remarks. Addams also sought to redirect attention to the main message of her talk: the need for neutral nations, especially the United States, to promote mediation, which the beleaguered and righteous belligerent governments could not initiate themselves. But her explanations served only to unleash more criticism. She found the entire experience discomforting to say the least, and the attacks brought her, as she later wrote, "very near to self-pity, perhaps the lowest pit into which human nature can sink." The negative reaction to Addams tarnished her image as "Saint Jane" and presaged even more scathing attacks on her for her later opposition to U.S. military involvement in the conflict.[23]

Addams' address was the prelude to her intention of gaining a meeting with President Wilson. Already her pacifist friends were attempting to weaken his opposition to personal interviews. Louis Lochner wrote Wilson a long letter in which he quoted a note he had recently received from Adolf Montgelas, head of the American section in the German Foreign Office, replying to Lochner's earlier inquiry about the neutral conference proposal. Montgelas had written that while he had discussed the plan with his superior, Undersecretary Arthur Zimmermann, and appreciated the idealistic motives behind it, he could not see its feasibility. Among the objections, he wrote Lochner candidly, "I would in the first instance place the somewhat clumsy apparatus of the conference, the difficulty of uniting all the neutral powers upon one program, and – last, not least – the even greater difficulty in persuading all the belligerent powers to accept the program. To me it seems . . . that direct negotiations, opened at the right moment through a skilled mediator, give promise of quicker results." In forwarding this information to President Wilson, Lochner acknowledged that Montgelas' objections had some validity, but added: "that, after all, is not the real question. Whether you as the head of the largest neutral nation call a halt to the war, or whether it be done by joint action of a number of neutrals, is immaterial." Since Lochner had just received a long letter from Emily Balch describing her interviews with statesmen in the capitals of northern Europe, he also enclosed a copy of her account in his letter to the President.

Wilson replied that he had noted "with the deepest interest the implications of the interesting messages you enclosed," but he gave no hint that he would budge from his previous position of watchful waiting.[24] The mediation advocates became more persistent in their requests for a presidential hearing. When Addams arrived in New York, she found that her cohorts in the peace movement had already attempted to arrange an appointment with the President at which she could present the Hague resolutions and her impressions of her European interviews. For example, Charles R. Crane, a Christian friend of Wilson, wrote:

> Mr President, wouldn't you like to ask Jane to come to see you soon after she returns? The women are very proud of her and I feel that she has gotten by the very dangerous work they crowded her into with a good deal of grace and dignity. Of course she is the best we have and has really been received everywhere as a spiritual messenger. Later on she and Mott [who had just been appointed general secretary of the YMCA] may help you in a great service to the world. Added to her great spiritual power is wonderful wisdom and discretion. Every woman in the land and most men would be cheered by knowing that you and she were in conference.

From his summer retreat in Cornish, New Hampshire, Wilson wrote Crane and Lillian Wald that it was "impossible" to see Addams there, but he would surely try to see her upon his return to Washington.[25] Because the length of Wilson's stay at Cornish was indefinite, his replies did not give the peace advocates the assurance they wanted. Consequently, some of them attempted to see Colonel House, who might in turn persuade the President to make a definite appointment to see her. House first learned of these plans on July 17 when he received a letter from Norman Hapgood, the liberal editor of *Harper's Weekly*, who was on friendly terms with House and Wilson, asking if he would see Addams. House agreed; but even before meeting with her and learning more about the plan for a neutral conference, he had personally rejected it. More than that, before the interview he wrote his chief that "She has accumulated a wonderful lot of misinformation in Europe. She saw von Jagow, Grey and many others and for one reason or another, they were not quite candid with her so she has a totally wrong impression."[26]

House's views were important because of his key role in the Wilson administration. His relationship with the President was undeniably very special. From their first meeting in 1911, the two had forged a personal bond that was arguably the closest between a president and an adviser in American history. They read poetry to each other and engaged in searching discussions of religion, death, and love. Wilson actively asked his friend for advice on intimate personal matters as well as weighty policy subjects. When House was in Washington, they would dine and go to the theater together, and House would stay at the White House. When he was away at his residences in New York or New England or in Europe, the two men kept up a lively correspondence, Wilson's letters usually beginning "Dearest Friend." Wilson commented truthfully to a politician in 1916, "Mr. House is my second personality. He is my independent self. His thoughts and mine are one."[27]

Because House played such an important role in Wilsonian foreign policy, it is worthwhile analyzing his ideas on the European war. Certain dominant assumptions underlay his thinking. He began with the belief that the United States was a major world power and could thus afford to stand firm in defending the nation's neutral rights under existing international law. He wanted the Wilson administration to uphold these rights and equated their defense with defense of the nation's honor. He opposed as demeaning any substantial concessions on America's rights to Germany, such as imposition of an embargo on munitions, a ban on loans to warring nations, and official warnings to or prohibitions of American citizens traveling on belligerent passenger liners. When Germany initiated submarine warfare against enemy merchantmen (with obvious dangers to neutral commerce as well) in February 1915, ostensibly as retaliation against Britain's legal blockade, House refused to contemplate a change in America's neutrality policies, although the submarine was not covered under existing rules of cruiser warfare.[28]

His defense of neutral rights dovetailed nicely with his Anglophile predilections, which he shared with the majority of Americans, and by the winter months of 1914–1915 almost all of the United States' major neutrality policies directly or indirectly aided the Allies. The sinking of the *Lusitania*, far from shaking House's faith in the wisdom of his pro-Allied proclivities, only served to reinforce them. He began to identify the "success" of the United States with that of the Allies. "If we lost their good will," he wrote Wilson, "we will not be able to figure at all in peace negociations [sic], and we will be sacrificing too much in order to maintain all our commercial rights."[29]

House's mention of possible peace talks indicated the third element in his approach to war. Despite his favorable disposition toward the Allies, he did not want a smashing Allied military victory. He understood the advantages of maintenance of a European balance of power to American interests and the explosive potential of a Carthaginian peace on Germany. House thus continued to hope for a negotiated settlement of the outstanding issues. His desire for the United States to serve as an honest broker between the two power blocs dated back to his visit to Europe in the winter and spring months of 1913–1914. He had then tried to get Germany to agree to limitations on naval building in return for Entente concessions on commercial and colonial matters.[30]

His attempts at accommodation between the two alliance systems continued after the outbreak of the European conflagration. The *Lusitania* crisis convinced him that any formal mediation initiative would fail dismally while the critical German–American negotiations dragged on; but if he began to muse increasingly about the prospect of "a long war" and possible American belligerency against Germany, he continued to encourage talk of a mediated peace. He pursued this objective even though he wished to satisfy the Allies' basic demands before trying to harmonize them with those of the Central Powers. Mediation based on Allied preconditions would have been unacceptable to the German leaders and in retrospect appears incompatible with peace negotiations, but House steadfastly believed that the combined military pressure of the Allies and diplomatic pressure from the United States could eventually force Germany to retreat from submarine warfare and annexationist demands and adopt a more flexible, conciliatory posture from which peace discussions might begin.[31]

Realization of his mentor's emotional and intellectual responses to the World War also probably motivated Colonel House's interest in mediation. Wilson continued to struggle to maintain a detached view of the war and to uphold strict neutrality, and even after the *Lusitania* disaster showed little desire for military intervention in the conflict. His impromptu reference in a speech about being "too proud to fight" expressed his sense of personal restraint, although he tried to downplay its impact on policy. While he continued to prefer procrastination to assumption of the burdens of foreign policy, events increasingly forced him to devote larger amounts of time to the nation's external relations. He sensed, however, that compared with domestic matters the consequences of his foreign policies might be far-reaching and relatively unmanageable. Because House believed that the European war vitally affected the present place and future role of the United States in world affairs, he faced the arduous task of trying to overcome his chief's seeming indifference to its courses. Shrewdly perceiving Wilson's need for approval and encouragement and his instinctive preference for those policies he could reconcile as "right" in his own mind, the colonel tried to focus Wilson's attention on the World War by appealing to his egotistical and idealistic proclivities.[32]

House especially stressed that Wilson's moral leadership could make him the world's peacemaker. As early as his 1913–1914 trip to Europe, House wrote back that the president's successful mediation between the two alliance systems could make him "the world figure of your time . . . the prophet of a new day," and he sprinkled his letters to Wilson with similar messages during the first years of American neutrality. In the first stages of the war, he told him, "The world expects you to play the big part in this tragedy, and so indeed you will, for God has given you the power to see things as they are." Thereafter he continued to reiterate his mentor's future role as savior of the belligerents from their own destruction. A few months later, for example, he remarked to Wilson, "When I think of the things you have done, of the things you have in mind to do, my heart stirs with pride and satisfaction. You are the bravest, wisest leader, the gentlest and most gallant gentleman and the truest friend in all the world."

At least part of his mission in Europe, House perceived, was to undermine the prospect of other third parties' mediation and thus clear the way for Wilson's. Pope Benedict XV was interested in serving as mediator, but House, considering him guided by the Central Powers, frankly reported to Wilson that "I am trying to make sure that the Allies will never accept him." Likewise, he worked to "eliminate" the King of Spain from any such initiative and instead was trying to get him to assume the more modest role of seconding any future Wilsonian peace move. Simultaneously, he sought to assure Wilson that when the opportune time for peace talks came, because of Allied disunity "you will be able to largely dominate the peace convention."[33]

Because House had few illusions concerning the warring nations' self-interested objectives in the conflict, his appeals to Wilson as the world's peacemaker were somewhat misleading. One can argue that House magnified the slight hopes for successful mediation, even in the distant future, because his continued role as a go-between on foreign policy questions depended directly on his ability to convince the President of hopeful prospects for peace talks. Although his motives in stressing the possibility of a negotiated peace may have been more subconscious than conscious, either way his appeals to Wilson as possible peacemaker served to justify his own importance as Wilson's special emissary to the belligerent capitals of Europe. But it is doubtful whether House was deliberately hypocritical. Once he convinced himself of the importance of the war for American interests, he sincerely believed that he was justified in using the prospect of mediation to arouse Wilson's interest in the complexities of the war situation generally.

Given his views on mediation, House was understandably critical of the neutral conference scheme. In the first place, he believed that the crisis in German–American relations during the summer months of 1915 made the timing unsuitable. Moreover, a neutral conference did not square with his full appreciation of power realities—in particular his understanding of the material weakness of the small European neutrals and his corresponding faith in the independent leadership of the United States. He was willing to consider a conference of neutrals sponsored by the United States to discuss cooperative measures for the protection of neutral rights in the war, but he was too much the realist to contemplate the more lofty purpose of peace-making for such a body. Additionally, the neutralism implied in the conference plan conflicted with his pro-Allied orientation. Although these reasons sufficed for House's opposition, he might also have perceived that Wilson's serious consideration of its possible merits might jeopardize his own role as *persona grata* among the belligerent statesmen. To tell the President, even before he had heard Addams' views directly, that the European statesmen had not talked openly with her was, intentionally or not, self-serving. Valuing highly his own importance to the Wilson administration, he certainly did not want the President to deprive him of his role as confidant on the European situation.

House acted swiftly to squelch the neutral conference idea. In his letter to the President preemptively discrediting Addams' views on mediation, he also summarized his consistent approach to mediation during the summer months of 1915. While sincerely desiring American mediation, he argued that it was still a long way off. He also reemphasized that Germany was the real obstacle to peace talks and that until the military situation changed or Germany voluntarily agreed to some kind of status quo antebellum, the United States should develop any proposals for mediation only in cooperation with the Allies.[34]

Two days before House's meeting with Addams, he received Oswald Garrison Villard, editor of the New York *Evening Post*. Son of Fanny, Villard shared his mother's absolute pacifism. He became the first of a long line of pacifistic individuals who were to confront House in the last six months of 1915. House's impressions of Villard, while unsympathetic, correctly depicted the latter's incurable pacifism and annoyance with the President's deliberate avoidance of mediation proponents outside his administration:

> We talked for an hour. There was nothing he knew or said that was worth repeating. He has a vague and visionary idea as to how peace should be initiated. He has much misinformation, and has it so fiemly [sic] fixed that it was not worth while trying to dislodge it. He was disturbed because the President would not see Miss Addams, and would not answer his telegrams in regard to her. I told him when the

President returned to Washington, perhaps his misgivings would vanish and that the President would see Miss Addams there. I tried to make him understand that if the President was to have rest at Cornish, he must not be compelled to see people and answer letters or telegrams or do any of the ordinary things, each one of which seemed so important to someone.[35]

Villard's pacifism accounted for his impatience, but even Alice Hamilton who was only vicariously interested in the mediation movement did not easily tolerate Wilson's seclusion. "It really seems too absurd that he should do himself up in cottonwool for fear of any influence except his own," she complained.[36]

Because Wilson had denied Addams' request for an interview earlier in the year, seemed to be doing it again, and would later be reluctant to receive women pacifists, he may have seemed to have had little respect for women's views on public questions and that perhaps gender bias was involved. It is true that Wilson had never advocated women's rights and had doubts earlier about feminism. As a young academic, he had found teaching women students at Bryn Mawr "about as appropriate and profitable as would be lecturing to stonemasons on the evolution of fashion in dress." He even wondered if higher education for women was desirable and thought co-education was "even under the most favorable circumstances . . . most demoralizing." He believed women were as intelligent as men, but their mental qualities were different. Men were naturally patriarchal, forthright, and courageous, while women were gentle, modest, and sympathetic. Though "strongly" opposed to women's suffrage, as a reformer in New Jersey politics he began to waver, telling one suffragist that "I am honestly trying to work my way toward a just conclusion" on the issue.[37] Well into his first presidential term, however, Wilson remained skeptical of the benefits of suffrage for women. Politically, he came to believe it would have little effect but perceived, albeit only dimly, that the enfranchisement of women only masked women's quest for equality in other areas. In particular, suffrage would "disastrously" impact on home life. "Someone has to make the home and who is going to do it if the women don't," he mused.[38]

Wilson's unpleasant experiences with women activists earlier—Rosika Schwimmer's interview and, much more discomfiting, a White House meeting in mid-1914 with a huge throng of suffragists, who had aggressively questioned his position on the vote for women, some even hissing when he left the room at the end of the meeting—could have hardened his antifeminist prejudices.[39] President Wilson consistently treated men and women advocates of mediation much the same, however, and the women pacifists never felt discriminated against because of their sex. He neither patronized nor spoke disparagingly to them.

In any event, the question of Addams' access to the President soon evaporated. When she called on House, the latter wrote condescendingly in his diary that "She had nothing of value to tell that I did not already know." The interview went smoothly, however, both because of Addams' "great poise and good sense" and because she received word during the interview from the White House that Wilson would see her later that week.[40]

Wilson did not say why he agreed to see Addams, but he probably realized that he could not in good conscience refuse to see the women envoys after their courteous reception in the European capitals. This explanation probably accounts for Wilson's decision to receive Addams in July and Emily Balch a month later. Other motives surely prompted his willingness to lift his ban on such interviews, however, for he met six more times with other mediation proponents in the following three months. Because he would display no great enthusiasm for these meetings and on occasion would even make half-hearted attempts to avoid them, it is tempting to say that he had not relaxed his opposition to a conference of neutral nations, but had submitted to the interviews because he was too indecisive during the last half of 1915 to continue to refuse their entreaties.

Nevertheless, we know enough about the President's approach to public issues during these months to advance more plausible reasons for his acquiescence in these interviews. One explanation is that the emergence of the submarine issue, which starkly dramatized the danger of war with Germany, more directly intensified Wilson's interest in the subject. A common thread throughout the neutrality period was Wilson's revulsion against war as well as his strong conviction that the vast majority of Americans wanted, if at all possible, to stay out of the European imbroglio. The submarine crisis with Germany caused Wilson to hope, almost in desperation, that some kind of American peace initiative might bring an end to the war before its horrors engulfed his own nation.[41] His contact with Gildemeester revealed not only his real interest in neutral mediation, but also his thinking on how mediation and diplomatic pressure might move the belligerents toward peace. While Colonel House was attempting to devise a mediation formula, perhaps the mediation advocates could provide some useful information on the European situation and some suggestions as a starting point.

Other influences contributed to Wilson's reopening of direct contacts with advocates of an early peace. Their persistence convinced him that the mediation proponents were in earnest and would persevere until he clarified his position on mediation. As he wrote Lansing before his interview with Balch: "I know these good people are not going to let the matter rest until they bring it to a head in one way or another. I must, I suppose, be prepared to say either Yay or Nay."[42] Moreover, he realized that continued denials of their appeals for interviews might alienate these activists whose sincerity he respected and whose support he would need whenever he decided to offer mediation. Even if he never proposed mediation, he would want them to understand first-hand both his personal sympathy for their laudable aims and the many practical difficulties accounting for his inaction.

Related to his personal feelings were domestic political considerations. Social reformers, many of whom participated in or sympathized with the mediation movement, were politically important in a reform era. Despite House's polite disdain for the women's views on peace, he recognized the political folly of deliberately alienating Addams and her "large and influential" following, and he was glad his mentor agreed to see her.[43] Widely accepted as the first lady of the land and the shining symbol of social justice advocates, she could influence the votes (even if only mostly male votes) of many liberals. Wilson's courteous treatment of her throughout the period of American neutrality indicated that he understood her political importance.

More generally, Wilson may have recognized that he would have to demonstrate clearly his strong commitment to peace if he hoped to gain their support for future domestic legislation and perhaps for his reelection bid the following year. Political expediency may not have been an overriding motive in the last half of 1915, for Wilson had not yet precisely chartered his future strategy in the domestic arena, but it could not hurt him politically to try to appease potentially critical voices and keep his options open. Since he already knew that his forthcoming announcement for military and naval expansion would threaten to alienate pacifists and antimilitarists from his administration,[44] he probably reasoned that his decision to meet with them in the last months of 1915 might help to restore their confidence in his leadership. If nothing else, it might enable him to strike a delicate balance between the preparedness and antipreparedness factions outside his administration. Whatever importance Wilson attached to these political realities did not require any hypocritical reassessment of his relationship with mediation advocates, for he admired many of them personally and fully sympathized with their hopes for restoring peace in Europe. It was another instance where "politics" and "morality" happily coincided in Woodrow Wilson's career.[45]

In preparation for Addams' interview with the President, 23 friends of the peace movement met at the Henry Street Settlement to formulate a specific mediation proposal, which she and Lillian Wald, who was to accompany Addams as spokeswoman for the Henry Street group, could present forcefully to Wilson. The conferees considered many alternative courses of action. As Paul Kellogg described the meeting:

Discussion hung on whether we should move for an international conference which would be official and instituted by the President; or on one nonofficial, growing out of private initiative; and whether it should be limited to sea law and the immediate issues [e.g., the submarine] now to the fore; or on broad humanitarian grounds; and whether it should be limited to [the] America[s], or neutrals of all nations; and finally, whether it should be a large or a small one.

These were indeed knotty questions, and the mediation advocates, very unsure of their priorities, debated them at length without agreeing definitely on any one program. References to sea law and the submarine crisis with Germany indicated how easily questions of national self-interest impinged on the idealistic goal of a negotiated peace.[46] Their confusion mirrored their lack of harmony on all issues of neutrality. Beyond a desire to find a reasonable balance between the legitimate rights of neutrals and the pressing economic and military needs of the belligerents, most peace workers did not have any firm ideological convictions on neutral rights in wartime. With absence of forethought they shared President Wilson's desire for a true neutrality for the United States, and the administration's decisions to extend credits to the belligerents did not seem at first inconsistent with this goal.

They had discovered, however, that because the Allies controlled the seas, almost all American credits (later extended to loans as well) went to the Allies who could use them to buy American goods, including munitions, for their war effort. Most peace workers were torn between their desire to sympathize with Germany's moral indignation over the munitions traffic and their belief that the result of an embargo would be more unneutral because it would abruptly change policy in the middle of a war and deny the Allies from exploiting their one military advantage, control of the seas, to counteract Germany's military domination of the European continent. A few Germanophiles in Congress, numerous German-American organizations, and some insurgent progressives, Socialists, and radicals, most of whom came from the Middle West and Plains states, urged Congress to enact an embargo on the sale of munitions, but vocal opponents of such legislation were even more numerous.[47]

Peace advocates were similarly divided. Kellogg's magazine, *The Survey*, editorialized against the shipment of munitions on humanitarian grounds, and Addams and a few other peace people likewise deplored the practice. They did not abandon their position following Germany's initiation of submarine warfare and the *Lusitania* incident.[48] But because they received little support on the issue outside the German-American community, they never campaigned vigorously for it. Everyone knew that the humanitarian arguments of German-Americans were secondary to the practical advantages of an embargo for Germany's war effort, and the peace people carefully avoided any association with German-American groups on the issue.[49] Other peace advocates just as consistently cited arguments opposing any embargo.[50] They were sincere in believing their views were more truly neutral than proponents of an embargo, but because existing international law simultaneously benefited American prosperity and the Allies' legal argument, the position of these peace people reflected their underlying, if sometimes unconscious, sympathy for the economic well-being of the United States and the moral claims of the Allies over the Central Powers. The thrust of their argument, as carried out by the Wilson administration, would help to prevent an easy military triumph of the Central Powers and in a prolonged war might lead to American involvement to assure the triumph of the Allies in the face of repeated German violations of international law.

Even William Jennings Bryan did not provide a clear perspective on the U.S. neutral position. His ideas on neutrality in the First World War were later cited as an authority for the congressional neutrality legislation in the mid-1930s, which would prohibit loans and shipment of munitions to belligerents and the travel of U.S. citizens on belligerent passenger liners, but he was not so explicit on these points in 1914–1915. He acquiesced easily in the lifting of the ban on private credits and opposed an embargo on munitions, arguing that it would be unneutral for the United States to change such policies during wartime. Although he wanted the United States voluntarily to relinquish the legal right of U.S. citizens traveling on belligerent passenger liners or of neutral ships carrying munitions, he thought it would take an act of Congress to institute this policy.[51]

The inconclusive discussions at Henry Street on the many questions affecting neutral America were a poor prelude for the interview of Addams and Wald with President Wilson. The two women arrived at the White House without any specific instructions from the Henry Street conferees and unsure of their own thoughts. When Addams gave Wilson the Hague resolutions, he seemed interested, but gave her no special encouragement on mediation. As the conversation developed, Addams even admitted that she had no mediation plan of her own beyond the rather general principle of a neutral conference, and she agreed with him when he objected to any concerted American mediation move. As the spokesperson of the Henry Street group, Wald had little to offer to the discussion and remained silent throughout most of the interview. In a follow-up letter to Kellogg, Addams summarized her quiet frustration, which had contributed to her ineffective presentation: "I am sorry I was so dull when I got back [from Europe]. I was so filled with many contradictory impressions that I didn't seem to be quite clear beyond one or two points, and I was also held in the grip of the conviction that it was so easy to still further confuse the situation."[52]

Nevertheless, the peace workers continued their mediation campaign in the hope that when the military situation and other circumstances changed, Wilson might be persuaded to act. The Henry Street conferees soon devised an alternative plan that Addams had first tentatively considered.

They formulated her thoughts into a draft proposal to be presented to the Wilson administration.[53]

The new plan was really a variation of the proposal for a continuous conference of neutrals. It began by reaffirming their belief in the desire of the "civil leaders" in the warring nations for mediation overtures that might eventually lead to a just peace and the advantageous geographical position and moral responsibility of the United States for assuming leadership of this task. Specifically, it called for the creation of a committee of three or more Americans "of recognized international spirit and qualified by experience in great human and economic activities of inherently international character," who would seek the cooperation of like-minded men from other nations, both neutral and belligerent. Together these individuals would "examine the situation with patience and fair-mindedness, and in the light of this study begin making propositions to the belligerents in the spirit of constructive internationalism. If first efforts fail, they should consult and deliberate, revise their original propositions or offer new ones, coming back again and again, if necessary, until a basis may be reached upon which actual negotiations looking toward peace could begin." They believed that the commission would not commit the President to any specific policy. But before appointing the American commissioners, they wanted the private sanction of President Wilson. Only some kind of semiofficial endorsement would allow them to "go to the belligerents with all possible weight and dignity" and "clearly express the earnest desire of the whole American people to be of service."[54]

This formulation did not resolve the questions of scope and alternative courses of action for the neutral conference. It said nothing, for example, about the number of nations represented in the commission. Addams preferred to limit it to the United States and the European neutrals, but this conflicted with the Wilson administration's recent emphasis on pan-American cooperation and the need to exemplify harmony in the Western hemisphere before attempting concerted action with the Europeans. Rather than risk disunity among their own members or premature rejection by Wilson, they simply avoided the question.

Nor did the formulation confront squarely the problems inherent in a quasi-official endorsement by the President. Presumably, neutral governments would view a neutral conference as either official or unofficial, while a halfway endorsement would appear an anomaly. The conferees nevertheless attempted to apply their experience with independent commissions in internal affairs to the field of foreign affairs. They reasoned that just as fact-finding, investigative agencies—on railroads and immigration restriction, for example—created for domestic problems during the Progressive era, both interacted with and assisted the executive branch without committing the President to specific courses of action, so would an international commission with quasi-official support allow for the opening of lines of communication among the belligerents and perhaps lead to peace parlays without binding in advance the United States or the other governments to any settlement.[55]

On August 6, Oswald Villard handed the written proposal to Secretary Lansing, but failed to arouse his interest. Lansing believed that the belligerents were not yet interested in peace parlays and, like House, thought they had misled Jane Addams. When Villard asked him to pick his own committee, perhaps appointing to it House and Crane (Lansing had just appointed his son as his private secretary), Lansing remained deeply skeptical. He promised only that he would present the proposal to Wilson, but considering Lansing's and House's objections to their proposal Villard had little hope that it would interest the President.[56]

Lansing forwarded the written statement to the White House, saying he had declined to express any opinion about it, and Wilson immediately realized that the pacifists, now better organized, would continue to demand presidential hearings for their proposals. Only a few days earlier he had agreed to see Balch, but he probably hoped that this prospective interview would end their agitation. Unsure how to handle these appeals, Wilson returned the proposal to Lansing and asked him for his opinion.[57]

Before Lansing replied, Balch made the final arrangements for her appointment with the President. In anticipation of this interview, she called on Colonel House. She told him that Aletta Jacobs would soon arrive in the United States and hoped to see Wilson. She also gave him a detailed report of her own European experiences. Although he appeased her with assurances that the chief executive "had his hand on the pulse of the situation and, at the first favorable moment, would intercede on behalf of peace," she failed to alter his negative assessment of possible peace talks.[58]

Following this meeting Balch was about to leave for Washington when she received a telegram from Addams urging her to cancel her appointment with the President. She argued that such interviews would be futile and perhaps harmful to the peace movement since Wilson was not interested in an official conference of neutrals and had not yet responded to their appeal for a quasi-official one. Addams' discouraging interview with Wilson motivated her opposition to Balch's appointment, for Louis Lochner had related her pessimistic appraisal of Wilson only a few days after her meeting with him. "Miss Addams is afraid the President will not act until he personally has made up his mind that it is time to act," he wrote. "She fears that no amount of pressure makes any impression on him."[59]

Respecting her colleague's judgment, Balch considered canceling the interview. But before making a final decision on the matter, she phoned Colonel House for his opinion. He assured her that Wilson was "wedded neither to the idea of acting alone or of acting jointly" and would welcome her views and information about Dr Jacobs' imminent arrival.[60] Since he privately scoffed at their specific proposals, it is curious that he gave Balch this gentle encouragement. Apparently House, who was unaware of the President's growing vacillation on mediation, believed that Wilson agreed with his own discouraging assessment of mediation and could easily convince her of the present American difficulties prohibiting any U.S. peace initiative. Realizing "her good sense and temperate views," he correctly surmised that she would be deferential and not embarrass the President. Moreover, he was politically astute and realized that the President would need strong support in his own country whenever he offered mediation. House was already cultivating his contacts with British pacifistic liberals for the time Wilson would mediate,[61] and their American counterparts might also prove helpful.

Buoyed by House's words, Balch set off for Washington. Wilson received her cordially and the two talked for an hour. He assured her that he would offer his services for peace whenever he saw a favorable opportunity. He also expressed interest in the plan for a quasi-official conference of neutrals and suggested that pacifists, who tended to overlook or minimize military realities, should not serve on such a body. When she gave him a five-page summary containing extracts of the two delegations' interviews with the European statesmen, her own report of her interviews, and other memoranda describing alternative methods for choosing delegates to a neutral conference, its scope of action, and a list of 45 British pacifists and liberal supporters of the proposal,[62] Wilson thanked her but made no definite promises.

In fact, he tried to avoid commitments of any kind. When she told him that Dr Jacobs would soon arrive in the United States, he said he could not see a foreigner. Wilson had consistently maintained this position ever since his interview with Rosika Schwimmer, but Balch pointed out that Dr Jacobs' status was different. "What, not a neutral?" she queried. "Colonel House had seemed to think there would be no difficulty." But Wilson complained that newspapers would misrepresent such an interview and that she could explain her mission to Balch or Addams who could then relay the information to him. Still seeking some definite assurances, Balch asked whether an interview could be arranged officially with herself or Addams while still allowing Dr Jacobs to come along nominally. Wilson finally promised that he would consider her request further and give her a definite answer later.[63]

The interview was inconclusive, but revealed Wilson's dilemma. On the one hand, he wanted to avoid further interviews with mediation advocates and thus tried to discourage a later meeting with Jacobs. Such meetings, he believed, might embarrass him and encourage rumors in the press misrepresenting his position. On the other hand, still without a mediation policy, he did not want to cut off all contact with peace workers, most of whose sentiments he respected and whose support he desired. Consequently, he temporized. He assured her of his eagerness to mediate at the first favorable opportunity and also seemed interested in the proposal for an unofficial conference. At the same time, in refusing to commit himself to any specific mediation scheme, he maintained his freedom of action.

During these interviews, the President had not really engaged in extensive discussion about the merits or liabilities of the various mediation proposals, but he was at least as forthcoming in his one-on-one conversations with Gildemeester, Addams, and Balch, all private citizens, as he then was with his closest government advisers. But Wilson had another outlet for his thinking, which was often the most revealing of his real thoughts. This conduit was Edith Bolling Galt, a wealthy widow, with whom Wilson had fallen passionately in love in the spring of 1915, and by late June the two had become secretly engaged. Wilson's emotional makeup included strong narcissistic needs, which favored women best fulfilled. In his courtship of Ellen a generation earlier, he had written her passionate letters espousing his love and pining for reciprocated devotion. And during his final years at Princeton he had developed an intimate relationship with a married woman with whom he carried on a warm and extensive correspondence. Now the fair object of his affection was Edith Galt, and in daily, often very lengthy letters to her, he gushed with expressions of ardor for his betrothed, but he also often digressed with intimate comments on affairs of state. In one such aside, for instance, he reflected on his meeting with Balch, which revealed his clear understanding of the dynamics of the neutral conference proposal as well his skepticism about it.

> I had a visit today, by the way, from Miss Emily Balch, who, like Miss Addams, has been visiting European prime ministers and foreign secretaries in the interest of peace, wants me to assemble a conference of neutral nations (which I am expected and invited to "dominate") which shall sit (and I with it, I wonder? I did not inquire about that) continuously till the war ends and all the while, patiently and without sensitiveness to rebuffs, and by persistent suggestion, heckle the belligerent nations about terms and conditions of peace, until they are fairly worried (I suppose) into saying what they are willing to do. I can't see it. And yet I am quite aware that they consider me either very dull, very deep, or very callous. Alack and alas![64]

On the same day Lansing's opinion on the Henry Street proposal, which Wilson had requested of his secretary of state nearly two weeks previously, arrived at the President's desk.[65] Predictably, the secretary disagreed with all the pacifists' premises for a peace initiative. He felt that the civilian leaders of the belligerents opposed mediation at present; and even if they favored it, the military parties on both sides dominated the situation and wanted to continue the war. He conceded that the Germans might welcome a peace move by neutrals because they dominated the military situation and were in a position at any peace conference "to demand compensation in territory and treasure." But, Lansing argued, "Every reason which would induce the Teutons to make peace would make the Allies unwilling." Until the Allies had forced their opponents back to their borders, he assumed that any peace move would "not only be rejected but resented" by the Allies. Therefore, he concluded that "it would be folly to approach the belligerents on the subject at the present time." More important, in reject-ing Wilson's peace move the Allies would thereafter discredit Wilson as a friendly or disinterested mediator and thus seriously hinder his ability to mediate at a later time.[66]

In this opinion Lansing openly summarized his disdain for peace pro-posals. More than this, he did not entirely conceal his real sentiments toward the belligerents, which were profoundly pro-Allied. In Lansing's case, how-ever, his personal views coincided neatly with his long-standing traditional beliefs on international relations. To him, sovereign nations were entirely free agents and thus not obligated to follow moral principles or legal conven-tions in world affairs; in an anarchic international system only public opin-ion and military force could change nations' behavior.[67] Despite his personal bias, Lansing's letter displayed considerable common sense (the pacifists would have said, too much common sense) and immediately appealed to the President's practical side. As Wilson replied, "I need only say that I entirely agree with the conclusions you have yourself arrived at." Much as he pro-fessed sympathy for the purposes of the mediation workers, he thought Lansing was correct in urging him to hold back and maintain his freedom of action until the psychological moment for peace arrived.[68]

On the afternoon following his interview with Balch, Wilson learned that a German U-boat had torpedoed the British steamship *Arabic* with the loss of American lives. The *Arabic* incident on top of mounting evidence in the administration of widespread German espionage in America again raised the prospect of a rupture in U.S.–German relations as an intermedi-ate step that, fearing the worst, might lead to U.S. military involvement, which neither he nor the American people desired. Just as he had earlier shown some interest in a neutral conference, but not for mediation, in his exchanges with Gildemeester and Bernstorff shortly after the *Lusitania* sinking, so did the reemerging submarine issue in late August.[69] As he wrote Mrs Galt:

After breaking off diplomatic relations, if we wished to go further, probably the next step would be to call a conference of neutrals, not to do what Miss Addams and Miss Balch suggested (though it could do what it pleased when once it was constituted), but to consider the present treatment of neutrals by *both* sides in the war and concert some action, to be taken either severally or jointly, calculated to make neutral rights more secure. The one thing that is clear, or, rather, the two things that are clear are that the people of this country rely upon me to keep them out of war and that the worst worst [sic] thing that could possibly happen *to the world* would be for the United States to be drawn actively into this contest – to become one of the belligerents and lose all chance of moderating the results of the war by her counsel as an outsider.[70]

Nearly two weeks later, while the Wilson administration was still trying to moderate the new German–American crisis, Emily Balch and Aletta Jacobs asked to see the President. From the women envoys' interviews as well as her own contacts with the Dutch political leadership, Dr Jacobs believed that the neutrals wanted the Netherlands to take the initiative in calling the neutral conference. Before taking any action, however, the Dutch prime minister had sent her to the United States confidentially to obtain Wilson's views on mediation. Just prior to her departure, she and Chrystal Macmillan drew up a list of seven questions that asked in effect whether President Wilson preferred mediation initiatives by the United States, by European neutrals jointly, or by a single European neutral. If the first alternative, would he want the cooperation of European neutrals? If one of the latter two, what would be the position of the United States, or more specifically, what was his preference among the European neutrals and his preconditions, if any, before sending American representatives to join in the peace effort?[71]

But Wilson, bolstered by Lansing's opinion and in any event fully engrossed in the German situation, was in no mood to discuss peace proposals. He politely refused to see the ladies, saying the meeting would arouse too much speculative publicity. He referred them instead to Lansing and House, who could convey Dr Jacobs' message to him confidentially. Unwilling to alienate the two women entirely, he anticipated their interview with Lansing by sending him careful instructions:

> I would be obliged [Wilson wrote] if you would say to Dr Jacobs and Miss Balch, that I highly appreciate the whole spirit and purpose with which they have acted, and need not say that my interest in bringing about peace, when that is possible, and in any way that may prove feasible, is profound. But I do not feel that at this time it would be wise for the United States to take the initiative in calling such a conference, and that the question whether we should respond to such a call, if made upon the initiative of some other nation is one which I

do not feel I can wisely answer beforehand. It would necessarily depend on the occasion and on the whole European situation as it stood at the time of the call. I am sorry to give them a reply to their suggestions which will, I fear, appear to them so unsatisfactory, but, all things considered, I might be misleading them were I to give any other.[72]

It is possible that Lansing did not receive this letter before seeing the two women, for he never mentioned it in his report of the interview to the President; more probably, he chose to emphasize Wilson's reservations on a neutral conference and ignore his request for a sympathetic hearing of their presentation. Whatever the facts, Lansing, contrary to the chief executive's intentions, made no effort to appease them with kind words. Indeed, probably believing Wilson's recent directive to him showed the President's stiffening against mediation in general and his outright rejection of the neutral conference idea, he was even more hostile to the women than he had been to Villard nearly four weeks earlier. Emily Balch reported that Lansing considered a neutral conference impractical. He was in fact "scandalized at the idea of proposing terms. This was meddling in other people's affairs. The United States would never do anything like that." He emphasized that nations acted from self-interest in foreign affairs and would never accept mediation for humanitarian reasons. When Balch cited Roosevelt's mediation of the Russo–Japanese war and America's "disinterested" motives in returning the Boxer indemnity as recent examples of morality in foreign relations, Lansing bitterly condemned the harmful consequences of the former (presumably referring to the anti-American reaction in Japan to the Treaty of Portsmouth which ended the Russo–Japanese conflict) and complained that no European nation had followed the American example in the Boxer episode and returned any money.

He was no more agreeable with Dr Jacobs. When she began asking him questions about his government's attitude toward a neutral conference, Lansing at first refused to comment. He remarked only that he could not accept her credentials as an unofficial representative of the Netherlands although she had a third person statement (unsigned) from the Dutch minister in Washington. If the Dutch Government really wanted to know the views of the Wilson administration, he insisted that its minister could personally approach him "unofficially and confidentially," which was the traditionally accepted diplomatic procedure in such cases. Upon further questioning, however, Lansing relented and, in Emily Balch's words, "finally gave straight, definitive answers to various of the questions we had come to ask." He said that the United States would not object to or try to prevent the calling of a neutral conference. He added, however, that the United States definitely would not take the lead, and he remained noncommittal in the event the European neutrals invited the United States to join a neutral conference.[73]

When Secretary Lansing reported this interview to the President, he made little attempt to conceal his entire disagreement with the women. In fact, he deliberately emphasized his negative views on mediation in hopes of disabusing the President of his sympathy for a negotiated solution. He stressed the impractical features of the proposal for a continuous conference of neutrals, especially the women's failure to consider the "perversity and selfishness of human nature" in the situation, but refrained from elaborate remarks on their discussion. "I shall not bore you with an account of the conversation which took place," he wrote his chief somewhat testily. Since Balch and Jacobs expected some kind of answer from the President, Lansing reiterated his earlier warnings against any hasty movement toward peace. "I hope that you can make some sort of reply which will discourage them from renewed efforts to secure action by this government."[74]

Balch's and Lansing's reports confirmed that the two had widely differing assumptions on and approaches to foreign relations. However, they only hinted at Emily Balch's shock and entire anger at Lansing's attitude. Normally charitable toward those who disagreed with her, she found Lansing's attitude contemptible, and she poured out her indignation to Oswald Villard:

> The talk with Secretary Lansing was a disheartening experience. I hate to think of his representing our country. What he said to us was on an unspeakably lower moral level than what was said by any of the European statesmen with whom we talked. Of course words are not everything, but to openly take an absolutely amoral and cynical attitude and defend it seems to me to unfit him for any large or constructive action in international affairs, however shrewd and capable he may be as an international lawyer.[75]

The two women's interview with Colonel House was little more successful. House agreed with Lansing's opposition to any peace move at present, but he wanted to leave the door open for a Wilsonian mediation offer in the future. Thus, he attempted to dampen the ladies' zeal but, unlike Lansing, was much more careful in his choice of words. "I tried to show them," he noted in his diary, "how utterly impractical their plan was, while evidencing the deepest sympathy with their general purpose."[76]

In the midst of these unprofitable discussions, the reappearance of Schwimmer and Macmillan would bring some dissension to the women's ranks. Coming to America as a confidential, private emissary of the Dutch Government, Aletta Jacobs perceived her mission as part of a quiet diplomatic strategy to learn directly Wilson's views on neutral mediation. The last thing she wanted was public attention given to activists' agitation for mediation. At best, such publicity might torpedo her hopes for an inter-view with the President; at worst, exposure of her mission might embarrass the Dutch Government and confirm Wilson's dubious opinion of publicity. The result at a minimum would be that the President would shy away from further contacts with the citizen mediation advocates. When she left for the United States, Jacobs had sent a letter to Schwimmer and Macmillan ask-ing them to delay their visit until she had completed her own; once in America, she and Addams followed with cables making the same request. Members of the International Women's Committee for Permanent Peace (IWCPP) in Amsterdam likewise pleaded for restraint from Macmillan and Schwimmer. An articulate academician, Macmillan was the more sensible of the two. She had in fact opposed Schwimmer's proposal at the Hague congress to send envoys to the belligerent and neutral capitals. But once the congress endorsed the initiative, she came to believe in the effectiveness of direct action and consistently supported her Hungarian cohort's more radical tactics. Rejecting her feminist colleagues' pleas for moderation, Schwimmer argued that the full delegation of women envoys should call on Wilson, just as they had with the European leaders, and she produced a letter from Maurice Francis Egan, the American minister in Copenhagen, making the same case. She and Macmillan then proceeded to persuade the IWCPP executive committee, of which Schwimmer was acting chairman in the absence of Addams and Jacobs, not only to authorize, but to pay expenses for their journey to the United States. (Schwimmer broke a 2:2 tie vote in favor of their trip, thus in effect voting twice.)[77]

Upon their arrival in New York, Jacobs once again begged them to maintain a low profile until they could study the situation in the United States or before they saw Addams, and the latter, who was recovering from an illness compounded by pleurisy at her summer retreat in Maine, sent them a telegram saying that Wilson had been quite definite in telling her that his reception of a belligerent was "quite impossible" and would make her "embarrassed if it were suggested." But these entreaties were to no avail. Reporters interviewed the two women, and at least three newspaper photographers took their pictures.[78] As Schwimmer's and Macmillan's publicity-seeking continued, which included mentioning Jacobs' name in their interviews, Jacobs went into a blue funk. In total exasperation, she wrote Schwimmer and Macmillan:

> I am sorry to say that I feel very angry this morning after I read the papers. I told you that I took the greatest care not to be mentioned in the papers in connection with the work I hoped to do here, and I asked you not to give any publicity to your plans before you have seen Miss Addams. Have you than [then] the right to use our names for publicity without informing us? You know that you cannot see the President,

now you will make it impossible for me too. Miss Macmillan knows that I never would have gone to the U.S. if I could have presumed that you were coming. What does this all mean? I have now spent my money, time etc. for nothing else than a dangerous trip.[79]

As it turned out, Jacobs overreacted to the harmful consequences of publicity, for only hours after writing this letter she learned that Wilson would receive her at the White House. But Jacobs' outburst was the culmination of her frustration over Schwimmer's determination to pursue her own strategy, even if it jeopardized the efforts of her erstwhile allies. In her view, Schwimmer's headstrong behavior had irreparably subverted their long friendship, and soon she permanently cut off all contacts with her.

Why Wilson agreed to see Jacobs is not easily explained. If he had seen articles in metropolitan newspapers implicating Jacobs with Macmillan's and Schwimmer's publicity campaign, he would have had sufficient grounds for denying her an interview. Wilson usually read the daily papers only very briefly and selectively, however, and may have been unaware of this public effort. More likely, he changed his mind because he felt obliged to see the neutral envoy who had come all the way from Europe and had received no satisfaction. Perhaps, too, he realized after reading Lansing's report of his interview with Jacobs and Balch that the secretary had been too outspoken in his opposition to a neutral conference and thus had given a badly misleading impression of his own attitude. A personal interview might correct any misconceptions she might have and retain her confidence and, more importantly, that of her government in his leadership.

Whatever the reasons, when Dr Jacobs arrived at the White House, she found Wilson "very kind and manlike as well as gentlemanlike." She asked him the several questions the women envoys had drawn up before her departure from Amsterdam, but as usual he made no promises of any kind during the interview. He merely pointed out that recent difficulties with the belligerents precluded any peace move at present. Although he did not elaborate, he was thinking about the *Arabic* and other German blunders, and these crises did not subside until early October. Besides, noting that the changing circumstances in Europe could alter his approach to the question of mediation, he feared that "even a quick unofficial statement in one way or another could bind him in a certain degree." Following the interview, Dr Jacobs correctly summarized this attitude: "He want[s] to remain free to act in the best way as he sees the thing himself."[80]

None of these three interviews with Wilson in the summer satisfied the women, but Wilson's dignified and respectful demeanor had temporarily mollified them. If they did not agree with him, they at least deferred to his difficult position. It remained to be seen whether his deliberate procrastination would continue to satisfy them in the future.

5

More Momentum and New Directions

The women's three personal contacts with President Wilson in the summer months of 1915 appear in retrospect rather sterile. All three repeated their desire for Wilson's mediation, and on each occasion the President insisted that the time was inopportune. He was sure on this point, much as his polite demeanor in these interviews and his vacillation on other foreign policy issues might have suggested an indecisive and pliable chief executive. Wilson confirmed his skeptical attitude toward peace talks in an interview with Benjamin F. Battin, who met with him only five days after he had seen Dr Jacobs. Persuaded by Macmillan and Jacobs at their August meeting, Dutch Foreign Minister Loudon had sent the Swarthmore College professor to Paris to try to obtain France's views on neutral mediation. Battin hoped to see the French political leaders and then convey this information to the German and Swiss Governments. He was unsuccessful, however, in seeing any high-level officials, because of "a combination of illness, cabinet crises, and absence from Paris," as Battin put it, and without first-hand information from that government he decided it was inadvisable to proceed to Berlin and Berne.

Upon his return to the United States, Battin nonetheless sought to obtain the President's views on the subject. During their meeting Wilson authorized him to give the foreign ministers of the Netherlands, Germany, Britain and Switzerland a statement asserting explicitly that "International conditions are at present of such a nature as to preclude the United States Government from enunciating any position on the question of a conference of neutral powers." Before Dr Jacobs returned to Holland, Battin gave her this statement, which was included in his account of his many interviews with European political leaders, to present to Loudon and Cort van der Linden. He did not forward it to the British, German, and Swiss foreign offices, but suggested that the Dutch leadership should make further unofficial inquiries about peace prospects in the belligerent capitals. Jacobs presented Battin's document to the Dutch leaders along with her own discouraging assessment of the prospects for Wilsonian leadership on mediation.[1]

Collectively, these unsatisfying encounters with Wilson might have convinced the peace activists that their entreaties would not deflect him from his watchful waiting. Actually, some of the more cautious or "realistic" peace advocates, especially in the Henry Street group, would gradually accept Wilson at his word and begin to divert most of their energies into domestic reform issues and resistance to military preparedness. In particular, the issue of an enlarged navy and army would become a heated controversy in domestic politics following Wilson's endorsement of a greatly expanded military establishment in early November, and the peace people would see it as a national crisis that required their urgent attention.

Those most committed to the quest for an early and just peace also would participate in the antipreparedness campaign, but did not slacken their mediation efforts. Indeed, their activity gave the movement greater momentum. There were several reasons for this vitality. First, and most important, peace workers remained confident that human intelligence and goodwill would ultimately triumph over brute force and hate, and that this triumph would result in a negotiated peace. Because they sensed some vacillation in Wilson's responses, they continued to believe that concerted pressure might yet win him to their cause. Wilson himself did not really attempt to discourage this interpretation; on the contrary, he conveyed the impression that he was interested in their campaign and would continue to welcome their suggestions. Following his interview with Dr Jacobs, for example, he wrote to Jane Addams, "You may be sure it gave me great pleasure to meet so interesting a woman."[2]

In the second place, Dr Jacobs' mission reporting Holland's alleged desire to call a conference of neutrals (Sweden also remained mildly interested) brought a ray of hope to the pacifists' campaign. Battin and Jacobs believed that of all the neutrals the Netherlands was best positioned to offer mediation and, when it acted, could count on the support of the other European neutrals. Meanwhile, they urged mediation advocates to educate U.S. public opinion on the neutral conference proposal so that Americans could effectively pressure the Wilson administration to endorse a European peace initiative. Assurances of Holland's real interest in mediation helped to reunite almost all peace activists behind the proposal for a governmentally sponsored neutral conference, and Addams' plan for an American commission working with like-minded private citizens of both neutrals and belligerents, which the Henry Street group had tentatively endorsed in its petition of August 4, temporarily receded into the background. Rosika Schwimmer and Chrystal Macmillan seemed to confirm this consensus when they went to Maine to see Addams, who was recovering from pleurisy, and convinced her to support an official conference of neutral nations.

The two women argued that since the women's congress at The Hague had already endorsed the plan for a conference of neutral nations, the American delegates at that gathering, and certainly its president, should continue to stand behind it. To entertain other proposals, they pointed out, would cause dissension among their foreign cohorts who were still promoting a joint neutral conference among the European neutrals.

Despite Addams' commitment to the joint neutral conference, the Henry Street group did not endorse it. At its September 27 meeting, those most impatient for action, such as George Foster Peabody, a nonresistant pacifist and businessman–philanthropist, and the Unitarian minister John Haynes Holmes, proposed to send abroad a group of private citizens, who would meet as an unofficial conference with like-minded citizens from the European neutrals. (Unlike the earlier proposal for a conference of private citizens, they did not consider inclusion of belligerent representatives.) Supporters of this plan hoped that the citizens would dramatize the public interest in mediation and prompt the neutrals to create an official conference. But Battin, Schwimmer, and others sought to commit the conferees to the plan of a government-sponsored conference of neutral mediation. A few, like the veteran diplomat Oscar Straus, objecting to any further agitation, argued that when any belligerent wanted mediation, it would let its wishes be known "in the right quarter," and until then bruiting over the question was fruitless. Paul Kellogg believed "the meeting was not satisfactory. In a way," he concluded accurately, the conflicting voices made it seem "as if we were back where we were at the beginning."[3]

Actually, the official and unofficial proposals were not so far apart. Emily Balch and other proponents of the official one argued, for example, that the delegates appointed by the governments would not be subject to instructions. Once appointed, they would not have to clear proposals with their nation's political leaders, nor would their proposals commit their governments. They would be entirely free to make public proposals for peace terms. Their thinking reflected their faith in the power of public opinion in influencing diplomats on the structure and content of a new postwar international order. And if they could not get an official conference, they were prepared to support a semiofficial one, "blessed," if possible, by President Wilson or, failing that, one composed of private citizens named by peace groups and other voluntary associations.[4]

Moreover, proponents of both the unofficial and official plans remained committed to moving forward. They agreed that because the belligerents would not initiate peace talks, which would seem to acknowledge defeat, then novel methods to bring about mediation were still required. As Hamilton Holt noted at the meeting, the neutral conference approach was new. "There is nothing about it in international law books. It is without precedent . . .; we should try the new." He believed, further, that the two proposals were not mutually exclusive and were both worth trying, and Kellogg rationalized that both plans had elements in common and might help one another. The two strategies would in fact both be promoted in the following months, but the failure of governments jointly to establish the neutral conference would stimulate more attention to the unofficial one—how and where it could be established and how it would operate.[5]

Third, the continuing military stalemate, growing war weariness, and the approach of the winter months with the repetition of the previous year's unavoidable human suffering and probable futile fighting nourished the pacifists' hopes for peace. They pointed out that the war was causing massive economic dislocation and intensifying internal social conflicts. The continuing slaughter and imposed sacrifices, which were already awakening the masses politically, might well lead to catastrophic social upheavals. When Balch had earlier asked the leader of the Dutch social democrats, for example, whether the war would cause revolutions, he replied, "If the war closes soon there will not be revolts, but if it goes on long there will not be absolute revolutions, but anarchy . . . I find here in the highest quarters that there will be revolutions everywhere," including even in European neutral countries. Agreeing with this prognosis, she nonetheless hoped that belligerent leaders, for reasons of self-preservation if not altruism, would come to their senses and realize their governments "can well afford to make peace before too late."

Somewhat paradoxically, they also believed that they could not wait patiently for presidential action, for they surmised that the European bloodbath was rapidly intensifying national and ethnic hatreds. While still believing in the reality of human rationality, they acknowledged that prolonged warfare tended to suffocate moderate opinion. The longer the European war continued unabated, the more the prospects for a negotiated peace would diminish while the influence of the fight-to-the-finish proposals of the military parties would increase. Already, the peace workers perceived a marked tendency toward purely military solutions and the further suppression of all peace sentiment in the belligerent nations. They believed that if they could not induce Wilsonian mediation while sane and reasonable voices still exerted some influence on belligerent governments, then mediation at a later date would surely fail.[6]

Finally, underlying this mixture of hopes and fears lay their deep-seated sense of moral responsibility, almost approaching a massive guilt complex, for all the human suffering unleashed during the war. However impractical their program, they felt a burning compulsion to press for neutral mediation as long as the slimmest chances for success existed. Addams referred to the "undeniable duty" of pacifists to continue their search for peace, and Balch summarized this inner dynamism that drove them on even during moments of discouragement: "If, in the wisdom that comes from the event, we see that the United States was dilatory when it might have helped to open a way to end bloodshed and make a fair and lasting settlement, we shall have cause for deep self-reproach." Or as Balch and Addams later wrote, "Nothing could be worse than the fear that one had given up too soon and had left one effort unexpended which might have saved the world."[7]

———

In the summer and fall of 1915 several actions of peace leaders indicated the movement's new sense of urgency. At a Panama–Pacific Exposition in San Francisco in early July, May Wright Sewall presided over a conference of women peace advocates, which the officers of the exposition had authorized her to organize even before the outbreak of the European war. Since meeting Schwimmer upon the latter's arrival in Boston in September 1914, Sewall had mentioned the neutral conference proposal in scores of public talks, many of which she gave on the Pacific coast. Although several American women declined to participate in the San Francisco gathering after the submarine controversy threatened to involve the United States in the war, and others, especially those women who had only recently returned from The Hague, found the West coast too distant, more than one hundred American and a few foreign women participated in the conference.

Moreover, David Starr Jordan, the Stanford chancellor, had arranged speaking engagements for Lochner in the Bay area as part of the conference events, and Lochner in turn managed to scrounge funds from peace groups to underwrite the travel expenses of Schwimmer and Macmillan to give speeches to the women's conference. In addition, William Jennings Bryan, now a private citizen and free to promote his pacifistic beliefs, warmly endorsed the women's movement for peace at their banquet and concluding session. The assembled women endorsed "the Woman's Peace Party as their specific channel of influence" and adopted 11 resolutions, patterned very closely after those previously approved by that peace group and the International Congress of Women at The Hague. Most important for the mediation movement, their last resolution urged "that the governments of the neutral nations create a Conference of the Neutral Nations for the purpose of mediating between the warring Powers until Peace can be secured."[8]

In mid-October the fifth biennial American Peace Congress, composed of many of the nation's leading peace workers, also met in San Francisco. It endorsed the proposal for a neutral conference and commissioned its president, David Starr Jordan, to take the resolution to the White House.[9] A few days later the five chief officers of the International Committee of Women for Permanent Peace issued a manifesto that reviewed in general terms their interviews with the European leaders and reaffirmed the most optimistic prospects for a neutral conference. Aimed directly at President Wilson the crucial section read:

> we believe that of the five European neutral nations visited three are ready to join in such a conference, and that two are deliberating the calling of such a conference. Of the intention of the United States we have as yet no evidence. . . . The excruciating burden of responsibility for the hopeless continuance of this war no longer rests on the will of the belligerent nations alone. It rests also on the will of those neutral Governments and people who have been spared its shock but cannot, if they would, absolve themselves from their full share of responsibility for the continuance of the war.[10]

In addition, Oswald Garrison Villard publicized all these actions in the New York *Evening Post* and became more outspoken in his demands for presidential action.[11]

On November 3, 1915, nine days before Jordan's scheduled appointment at the White House, Mrs Sewall called on the President. A generation or more older than the core leaders of the mediation movement, Sewall was not well connected with them, and they scarcely took notice of her interview with the chief executive. Wilson received her graciously, accepted the resolution of the women's peace conference at the Panama–Pacific Exposition, was properly sympathetic, but promised her nothing.[12] Wilson seemed in fact largely immune to the pressures of American public opinion on the war. To the extent that he was receptive to others' views on the conflict, he appeared to prefer the counsel of "front line" observers of the European scene, especially Colonel House, but also the reports of Mott, Battin, and the women envoys who likewise had traveled extensively in Europe. He again revealed this preference, for instance, only an hour before his meeting with Mrs Sewall, when he had received Herbert Hoover, then a very successful mining engineer who had been residing in London at the start of the Great War and had become chairman of the Commission for Relief in Belgium. Hoover visited Wilson to report on the financial pressures facing his commission's relief efforts, but, detained by Wilson, answered his many questions about the war and the prospects for U.S. mediation. Though Hoover strongly shared the President's desire to stay out of the war, he advised the chief executive that "the emotional situation" among the belligerent peoples made a peace effort "hopeless" at the time.[13]

Unaware of Wilson's other private sources of information on the European situation, mediation proponents continued to rely on their own members' direct contacts with the President. Most immediately, they placed faith in Jordan's upcoming presentation of their case. Like Wilson, Jordan had had a long career as a scholar and university administrator. He also was a long-time personal acquaintance of the President and had already sent him several letters, urging him to implement non-interventionist and idealistic foreign policies. If anybody could impress upon the President the many advantages of joint neutral mediation, the peace advocates reasoned, then surely Jordan could.

But Jordan was not an ideal choice for forceful presentation of the proposal. In the first place, Wilson's promotion of domestic reform and his highly moralistic foreign policies before the World War had made him an uncritical admirer of the President, and Wilson's restraint in weathering the several crises with Germany over the submarine during the first year of neutrality had strengthened Jordan's favorable estimate of him.[14] The Stanford chancellor was thus not predisposed to rebut any objections Wilson might raise during the interview. Jordan was also realistic enough to understand the many imposing obstacles to successful mediation. However much he supported neutral mediation in principle, he already had reservations concerning its practicality.

During the previous summer he had already displayed the tension between his strong love for peace and his more sober assessment of international realities. Lochner, believing Wilson respected the views of the intellectual community, had then persuaded Jordan to draw up a petition urging mediation for circulation to his many contacts on college and university faculties throughout the nation. This petition had argued that the war was a stalemate, that in any case a military victory for one side "would not contribute to the solution of the problems of Europe, being sure to leave an increasing legacy of hate with the seeds of future wars" and that therefore Wilson should offer mediation at the earliest opportunity.[15] Jordan, however, never had high hopes for its success; and after several hundred academics from more than 50 colleges and universities had signed the petition, he had failed to forward it to the President. He had written him instead that he had not sent it to him because he was sure Wilson best understood the prospects for mediation and did not need to be guided by private appeals.[16]

Jordan again revealed his second thoughts about mediation when, two weeks before his scheduled interview with Wilson, he visited Colonel House in New York to learn more about the administration's attitude toward a neutral conference. Jordan arrived in an acquiescent mood, and House quickly convinced him that the President, "probably the best-informed man in the world" on the prospects for mediation, was eager to serve as peacemaker and would make a peace initiative at the first favorable moment. More than satisfied with this explanation, Jordan told House that he would not argue the case for a neutral conference with the President, but would merely give him the resolution of the peace congress.[17]

When Jordan informed Lochner of this interview, the latter expressed dismay at his older friend's weak-kneed behavior and tried to restore Jordan's enthusiasm for a neutral conference. He explained Jordan's declining confidence in the proposal to Grace Wales, and both wrote him forceful letters reaffirming their faith in neutral mediation and urging him to recommit himself to the proposal. Lochner's letters to Jordan emphasized the "personal element" with Wilson. He wrote that Wilson would surely value Jordan's international experience, intellectual qualities, and advice. The President, he argued, "has not traveled the globe as you have, and I feel certain that Mr Wilson must respect that superior knowledge of yours. . . . Your word, I know, will go further with him than that even of Col House" whose influence on the President Lochner minimized. His view of House is both interesting for his partial insight into the relationship between the President and Colonel House, and amusing for his absurd understatement of House's importance in the administration. "I have tried to impress upon Dr Jordan," he wrote Wales, "that Colonel House, because of his relation as a sort of flunky to Mr Wilson (I understand that he even attends to the purchase of wedding rings and all that sort of thing), is perhaps not to be taken seriously by the President when grave matters of state are pending."[18]

Lochner also hoped that evidence of public support for a neutral conference might convince Jordan of its merits. He had already begun to organize a nationwide demonstration for peace on November 8, four days before Jordan's interview with the President, and he now became more vigorous in the effort. From his office in the Chicago Peace Society, he sent out a circular letter to the heads of several thousand churches, schools, civic groups, and labor and farm organizations, asking them to call meetings four days before Jordan's interview at which they would pass resolutions urging President Wilson to summon a conference of neutrals.[19]

About 200 individuals and organizations, responding favorably to Lochner's appeal, passed resolutions endorsing neutral mediation and sent them to the White House. But the impact of this effort was more superficial than real. The call for the demonstrations went out on such short notice that many individuals and groups never had an opportunity to arrange for the meetings. And those that were held usually passed these resolutions as routine business and were too thinly scattered throughout the nation to convince Wilson that the demands for peace were irresistible. The press scarcely mentioned the meetings and gave little indication that a national demonstration for peace had occurred.[20]

Moreover, even much of the enthusiastic public response to these particular meetings was more temporary than lasting. The idea of a negotiated peace might be initially attractive, but the European conflict remained an intellectual abstraction to the overwhelming majority of Americans. Some of those attempting to arouse support for peace rallies complained of the "extraordinary apathy" of a "morally sterilized" public. With most Americans it was business as usual, and the uninterrupted human slaughter on the European continent merely confirmed their assumptions about the corruptions of the Old World. Following his escape to England in the first stages of the war, the Belgian peace advocate Henri LaFontaine visited the United States to lecture on the issues of the European war. While speaking on the West coast, he found the people "willing to support a movement tending to secure a lasting peace, but I did not find anybody anxious to help . . . General ideas and world politics do not impress strongly the western Americans." A University of Colorado professor attempted to organize a committee of faculty and townspeople for consideration of Lochner's petition, but encountered even greater indifference, if not hostility.

> I was astonished at the difficulty of getting any cooperation [he reported]. There are some who do not take any active interest in the war at all, some who regard it with cynicism or pessimism, some who see in it the working out of mechanical laws which cannot be interfered with, some who are preoccupied with other matters, some who fear to stir up the animals. The *issues* of the war, i.e. the merits of the two sides, were not discussed. The essential difficulty was not one arising out of these issues, but out of the inertia or inhibitions of individuals.[21]

Given this public lethargy, the mediation movement understandably failed to sustain the active interest of more than a few high-minded citizens. As Julia Grace Wales dimly perceived, "the strength of our cause has been in its very weakness, in the very fact that it has been led by a few idealistic citizens of the world."[22]

Many Americans, especially in the northeast, did not want to remain wholly isolated from European developments. Neutral mediation seemed a remote issue to most Americans, however, while other questions of foreign policy—Germany's submarine warfare, the munitions traffic, and military preparedness—aroused strong emotions and dominated the public imagination. As early as December 1914, for instance, many of the New York members of the Henry Street group, reacting against the mounting propaganda activities of so-called national defense leagues, had joined with other like-minded Americans in organizing the American League to Limit Armaments (soon renamed the American Union Against Militarism), which thereafter absorbed ever larger amounts of their time. While they still cooperated with the other proponents of mediation, divisions in their meetings over strategy weakened its influence, and by late 1915 they were no longer the central actors in the mediation movement.[23] By that time it had become clear that President Wilson would soon ask Congress for large increases in the army and navy, and the Henry Street conferees along with many other worried pacifistic Americans, believing an enlargement of the military establishment was unnecessary, a dangerous step toward "militarism" and perhaps war, quickly concluded that preparedness was the most important issue of the moment and required their strenuous opposition.

The antipreparedness forces protested publicly and in private appeals to the President, but Wilson went ahead and announced the essential features of his upcoming message to Congress on the subject in a speech on November 4, only four days before Lochner's public meetings. With public attention focused on the administration's preparedness program, Lochner's ill-timed campaign became a victim of this new issue.[24] Even the radical pacifist Oswald Garrison Villard, who considered himself an expert on military matters, wrote and spoke almost exclusively on the preparedness question in the final months of 1915, and the Woman's Peace Party began to emphasize antipreparedness as a central, unifying issue in rough proportion to the failure of the mediation campaign.[25]

But if Lochner's promotional efforts did not convert many Americans to the possibilities and desirability of a negotiated peace, they at least temporarily won back Jordan to the pacifist ranks. He was so deeply impressed with Lochner's zeal that he agreed to make a vigorous presentation of the case for joint neutral mediation to the President. As if to sustain his new enthusiasm, he even asked Lochner to accompany him to the White House.[26] Lochner accepted, and Wilson received the two on November 12.

Jordan formally presented the San Francisco resolution and then advanced arguments for a neutral conference of continuous mediation. He reviewed his own long-standing contacts with peace advocates in Europe, Lochner's contacts with moderate, antiannexationist voices in Germany during his European trip the previous spring, and the information gathered in Europe by Jane Addams and her co-workers. In response to a question, Wilson said he had read the accounts of the envoys' interviews with the heads of European governments, which Emily Balch had earlier left with him. Lochner and Jordan also mentioned the Central Organization for a Durable Peace, which planned an international conference in Berne, Switzerland, in December to formulate specific proposals as guidelines for the eventual peace settlement, and Wilson carefully studied the names of the individuals identified with the movement. Jordan then attempted to convince the President that the European neutrals were "ready and anxious to call the conference" and might act even if the United States refused to cooperate. In that event, it would be unfortunate if the United States refused to join. Wilson replied, "I have been revolving this proposal in my mind dozens of times," but he had finally decided not to endorse a neutral conference because he believed many of the European governments did not accurately reflect their peoples' sentiments; one side (the Allies) would probably object to such a conference as a partisan measure, and the United States might be outvoted by the other neutrals and more harm than good done.

Jordan and Lochner attempted to refute these objections. They argued that because of its wide influence the United States would naturally dominate in the selection of the commissioners to such a conference and that it would begin on a higher plane than temporary military advantage. Lochner remarked that the President was best remembered for his unconventional leadership, such as reading his annual messages in person to Congress, and his cooperation with Argentina, Brazil, and Chile in resolving difficulties with Mexico following U.S. military intervention in Vera Cruz in 1914, and that the peoples in Belgium and Holland were waiting constantly for his leadership on mediation. The young peace activist added that he had talked with reasonable German officials like Hans Delbrück and Bernhard Dernburg and leaders of liberal groups within the belligerent nations, such as *Bund Neues Vaterland* in Germany, and found all of them opposed to extreme territorial annexations as war aims. (Lochner, it will be recalled, had earlier sent Wilson his report of these contacts, which the President had gratefully acknowledged.) What these moderate voices desperately needed, however, was some actual peace machinery to which they could direct their governments. A neutral conference, Lochner argued, would release the hopeful idealism in the belligerent nations and direct it into constructive channels.

Wilson listened patiently, but ultimately remained unconvinced. He remarked that these individuals and groups might support a conference only if it accorded with their own wishes. Jordan and Lochner rebutted that a year of war had sobered all of them, and as moderate individuals would accept any reasonable plan leading to peace. Wilson then suggested that the press in the belligerent countries would misrepresent the purpose of such a conference, but Jordan argued that the press would at least have to report the existence of such a conference. "And probably its recommendations," admitted Wilson. Lochner pointed out that news of peace sentiment in the warring nations kept leaking out in spite of the rigorous censorship, and he believed the editors in the belligerent nations would publish the deliberations of a neutral conference "even at the risk of their lives."

Jordan and Lochner pressed their case in this lively but friendly fashion for about half an hour. Finally, the President terminated the interview, saying "I assure you gentlemen that you have done me real good." Overestimating Wilson's friendly reception to their presentation, Lochner then asked if he could say that the President would act. But Wilson remained noncommittal: "No, that is for me to say when the right moment, in my judgment, arrives." He even refused to comment on his probable response in the event some other neutral initiated a conference and invited the participation of the United States.[27]

Despite the President's final remarks Lochner was optimistic. He was convinced that Wilson was playing a "lone hand" in his approach to mediation and was afraid that immediate mediation by the United States would alienate Great Britain. But Lochner also surmised that Wilson, having no proposal of his own, was decidedly interested in the pacifists' presentation. As Jordan remarked to Lochner following the interview, "I have known the President for 25 years and never have I seen him so human, so deferential, and so ready to listen. Usually he was difficult to talk to, and rather haughty." From these favorable impressions Lochner concluded that Wilson could still be won over to the proposal for a neutral conference, but more public pressures along the lines of the November 8 demonstrations were necessary.[28]

However, Lochner surely exaggerated Wilson's receptivity to a neutral conference. Certainly from any but the most utopian perspective, Wilson had raised important, almost unanswerable objections to any such body. Moreover, because he was temperamentally predisposed to independent executive leadership, he had little faith in cooperative action on mediation with neutral nations. He had earlier confided this attitude privately on several occasions and implied as much again when he told Lochner and Jordan that the European neutral governments were out of sympathy with their peoples. Given this belief, for Wilson to endorse a neutral conference under such conditions would have contradicted his sturdy faith in "democracy." He perhaps best indicated his real disinterest in the neutral conference approach when he did not even bother to open a small packet containing information on this approach that Lochner sent him the day after the interview.[29]

Yet for all his passionate commitment to pacifism, Lochner was still close to the truth in his assessment of Wilson. Having excellent reportorial skills that he would put to good use in his postwar journalist career, he correctly concluded that Wilson never discussed mediation in cabinet sessions and confided only in a few trusted advisers. And there is no reason to question Lochner's appraisal of Wilson's sincere interest in the presentation, although he misjudged the President's motives. Wilson was in fact focusing more intently on the mediation question. Only a day earlier he had tentatively endorsed Colonel House's proposal for an American peace initiative that Wilson would advance with the prior knowledge and support of the Allies.[30] Lochner discerned Wilson's fears about a neutral conference offending Great Britain, but was only partly right in believing that Wilson still was undecided on a mediation formula. It is probable that Wilson was so friendly during the interview because he sought a full discussion with concerned individuals outside his administration on the problems involved in any mediation move. He also wanted to maintain the sympathetic support of peace workers in case his own cautious plans for mediation culminated in a specific peace note.

House's proposal, which resulted in the House–Grey Memorandum three months later, provided the first clear evidence that Wilson really intended to implement a specific mediation policy. Wilson had found that the longer the United States attempted to resolve each submarine crisis separately and safely, the greater the likelihood that the United States would drift into the war. Some kind of American mediation, however, might bring an end to hostilities before American participation became necessary. With German–American relations still very strained, he accepted House's proposal to link American mediation of the war to Sir Edward Grey's desire for full American participation in promoting a postwar settlement based on disarmament and collective security. Wilson's tentative commitment to this course thereafter meant that he would downgrade semantic and ultimately futile arguments about neutral rights and take the first hesitant steps toward American mediation, which would be tied to some still vaguely defined changes in the international system.[31]

———

Immediately following the interview, Louis Lochner wrote down his recommendations for future tactics.[32] Above all, he pinned his hopes on Henry Ford, the millionaire automobile manufacturer, who a few months earlier had begun articulating pronounced pacifist views and his vehement opposition to military preparedness. Speaking of militarism and the European war in a *New York Times* interview, Ford argued that "the word 'murderer' should be embroidered in red letters across the breast of every soldier. . . . I am opposed to war in every sense of the word." He soon began talking about active support of antiwar and antipreparedness efforts.

> I will do anything in my power [Ford emphasized] to prevent murderous, wasteful war in America and the whole world; to fight this spirit which is now felt in the free and peaceful air of the United States, the spirit of militarism, mother to the cry of "preparedness" – preparedness, the root of all war. I have prospered much, but I am ready to give much to end this constant, wasteful "preparation."[33]

A few weeks later Ford announced that he had set aside one million dollars for an educational campaign for peace and against preparedness, a figure he increased to ten million dollars. Beyond a brief reference to a large cash prize for the best history of the war that "shall not make the demigods of soldiers and shall show war in all its horrors," he was vague about a peace strategy, but he recognized the wide-ranging ramifications of his commitment to peace when he remarked, "I confess I do not know how it is best to undertake this work in an organized manner. I realize it is a vast undertaking." Ford also promised to develop his program after consulting with William Jennings Bryan and his luminary friends, the inventor Thomas Edison and John Wanamaker, the department store entrepreneur.[34]

Lochner and his pacifist allies of course already had a peace plan, and he hoped that if he could persuade Ford to furnish the mediation movement with unlimited funds, its leaders could organize "an overwhelming series of demonstrations in favor of neutral mediation" in the United States and the European neutrals and begin the formation of an unofficial conference of neutrals. "Then," Lochner surmised, "I am sure I could secure another interview with the President and show him how all plans are laid for action, and that it is up to him either to get into the game or be forever left out."[35]

This desire to enlist Ford's financial support behind the peace movement of course occurred to all peace workers as well as many other pacifistic and isolationistic Americans who were not involved in the mediation effort, and several sent him their peace plans and attempted to schedule interviews with him. Florence Holbrook, a school teacher and member of the Chicago Peace Society, who had become another of Schwimmer's loyal followers, wrote Ford asking him to underwrite the expenses of foreign peace workers in America—for instance, Schwimmer, LaFontaine, Jacobs, Macmillan, and Ethel Snowden, a leading British feminist and wife of Philip Snowden, well-known Labour leader in Parliament, who was currently lecturing in America. "I wish Ford would finance you all to sweep the country with your splendid unanswerable arguments for peace," Holbrook wrote Schwimmer in September, but conceded, "No one seems to know Mr Ford's plans."[36]

Ultimately, it would be the pacifist crusader, Rebecca Shelley, who would win pacifists' access to Ford. Twenty-eight years old in 1915, Shelley had been the youngest of the American delegates to the women's congress at The Hague. The basis of her maturing pacifism was religious. One of eight children of a minister of the Evangelical and Reformed Church in eastern Pennsylvania, she was reared on the Bible and was well acquainted with the pacifist passages in the New Testament, including the beatitude "Blessed are the Peacemakers," her mother's favorite, and Jesus' admonition, "Put up again thy sword into his place; for all that take the sword shall perish with the sword." In the midst of her pacifist activities, Shelley explained to her father that she felt divinely inspired to do God's will and that after the outbreak of the European war convinced herself that He had selected her as a missionary for peace. "I believe that God has laid his hand upon me and is leading me to help bring about peace," she wrote him. This divine calling provided the religious inspiration for her peace action, which was unique to her family. None of her brothers or sisters expressed interest in the peace movement, and her parents, while emotionally supportive and appreciative of her Christian commitment, did not encourage her single-minded devotion to peace work.[37]

Nevertheless, without any premeditation, several experiences in her early life had prepared her for total involvement in the peace cause after 1914. Part of Shelley's commitment to the mediation movement might have been intensely personal. A Phi Beta Kappa graduate in German from the University of Michigan in 1910, she taught German for the next four years in high schools in Wisconsin, Washington, and Illinois. During a summer in Europe in 1911 she had fallen in love with a young German, Franz Willmann, and the couple became engaged in 1913. They planned to marry in Germany the following fall, but the war abruptly interrupted their plans. She came to abhor war in part because it separated her from her fiancé, and she later admitted that the chance of seeing her beloved helped to attract her to the Hague congress.[38]

She also conceded retrospectively, however, that other influences figured very prominently in her decision to go to The Hague. She had shown little haste in wishing to exchange wedding vows. She had even rejected Franz Willmann's first marriage proposal, then renewed correspondence with him, and finally consented to betrothal. Profound admiration for Franz's long and unfailingly interesting letters as well as dissatisfaction with her teaching career temporarily reunited them.[39] But while Franz obviously respected Rebecca's intellect as well as her advanced views on women's rights, he could not entirely discard the influence of the German males' traditional view of the wife's role as that of *Kinder, Küche, Kirche*. Given these fluctuations and tensions, her lengthy periods of separation from Franz, far from making her heart grow fonder, only increased the strain in their relationship. The outbreak of the European war exposed their real differences, for he loyally fought in the war for the Fatherland while she increasingly moved toward radical pacifism. She managed to see him briefly in Munich following the Hague congress, and they agreed to break off their engagement indefinitely.[40]

There was another influence drawing Shelley toward peace work. During her senior year at Michigan, she learned that university administrators had forbidden Jane Addams to speak on the campus because her subject, woman's suffrage, was considered too controversial. An admirer of Jane Addams' social settlement work, about which she had read in a sociology seminar, Rebecca Shelley was appalled at this indignity to her heroine. "On that day," she later recalled, "I became a militant suffragist." Thereafter Addams became her "visible symbol" in the struggle for woman's rights. When she learned that Addams was leading a delegation of women to The Hague, Shelley resigned her teaching position and sailed with them on the *Noordam*. In analyzing her motives for this impulsive action, she later remarked: "Had there been no other attraction, adventuring for peace and freedom with Jane Addams might have drawn me to that momentous Hague congress."[41] But it is conceivable that she would have gone to The Hague even without Addams' participation, for she was already developing her pacifist position independently and was beginning to perceive her "calling" for peace.

In a larger sense, the major formative experiences of her early years—her religious zeal, her decision to leave a sheltered home environment for the challenges of university life, her intellectual curiosity, her cautious approach to marriage, her growing identification with feminism and peace—suggested the development of a remarkably free spirit. She even became partially disillusioned with Jane Addams after her half-hearted endorsement of sending envoys to the governments, and she found a new inspiration in the activist Rosika Schwimmer, becoming her "humble messenger" in the peace movement.[42]

The new relationship between Shelley and Schwimmer soon brought concrete results. Following Ford's pacifistic pronouncements, Shelley directed her zeal toward winning his moral and financial support for the neutral conference proposal. She began to knock on his door. Surrounded by numerous secretaries and aides, Ford was inaccessible to outsiders, and Shelley was no exception. One of his secretaries told her that she could see Ford if she could get a statement endorsing a neutral conference from the German ambassador, Johann von Bernstorff. She immediately left for New York and managed to gain an interview with Bernstorff. Although he regretted that he could not give her a written endorsement, Shelley was not in the least discouraged. Assuming that diplomats had to be guarded in their official statements, she persuaded herself that the interview was a "wonderful triumph."[43]

When Shelley returned to Detroit, Ford was on vacation in California. Nevertheless, she began to prepare for his return. With the pacifist poetess, Angela Morgan, who had also participated in the women's congress at The Hague, she held street meetings to dramatize the peace issue. She also organized a public peace meeting and invited her new idol, Rosika Schwimmer, to give the main address.[44]

Once in Detroit, Schwimmer attempted to arrange an appointment to see Ford upon his return from the West coast, but his secretaries rebuffed her. Very discouraged, she was ready to abandon the effort when Shelley finally found the entrée they needed. The resourceful young feminist looked up an acquaintance, Ralph Yonker, a young cub reporter on the Detroit *Journal*, which of all the Detroit papers had given the women's street and mass meetings the fullest and fairest coverage. She poured out her heart to him about Rosika Schwimmer's inability to see Ford. Yonker then persuaded another reporter, Theodore Delavigne, who was on friendly terms with Ford and knew his private telephone number, to urge Ford to see Schwimmer. Shortly after Ford's return to Detroit, the journalist prevailed upon him to grant an interview to the Hungarian pacifist.[45]

Rosika Schwimmer arrived at Ford's factory on November 17. Escorted into Ford's office, she found him meeting with the Reverend Dean Marquis, an Episcopal minister who served as Ford's personal spiritual adviser and confidant, and Frederic Howe, a well-known social reformer. At lunch, Yonker and three of Ford's advisers joined them. With so many others present, most of whom disapproved of Ford's interest in peace, Schwimmer found it impossible to get the millionaire's attention. She was also surprised to hear Ford's views on the origins of the European war. "I know who caused the war. The German-Jewish bankers," she recalled him saying at one point. "I have the evidence here," he said, patting his pocket. "Facts." We do not know why Ford made such a statement in Schwimmer's presence; whether he then knew that she was Jewish, or what constituted his "facts," but his remark was a bad omen for the future support, financially and otherwise, she would seek from him for the peace movement.

Schwimmer spent the entire day with Ford, during which she managed to press her case for neutral mediation. She marshaled every conceivable argument in support of a continuous conference of neutral nations. She apparently stressed in particular Jane Addams' identification with the movement for an early peace, the most sanguine conclusions of the women envoys' visits with the European political leaders, the pacifists' friendly interviews with President Wilson, and their hopes for winning him to their cause. While Ford still wavered, Schwimmer summoned Lochner to Detroit, and to Ford he obligingly confirmed Schwimmer's evidence and the private and public support for joint mediation by neutral nations.[46]

Schwimmer's and Lochner's arguments won over Ford who became an enthusiastic partisan of the scheme. With Ford's moral and financial support assured, mediation proponents acted swiftly to intensify pressures on the Wilson administration. Within the span of a few short weeks their efforts would push the mediation movement to the peak of frenzied activity. But the climax of peace action would prove ephemeral and be followed by an equally speedy anticlimax.

6

Climax and Anticlimax

Henry Ford's endorsement of the mediation movement brought new life and vitality to the peace forces, whose leaders began to discuss how they could best harness his personal and financial commitment to the cause. Hoping to put Ford's support to good use, the mediation proponents above all wanted to redouble their pressures on the Wilson administration. They first prevailed upon their patron to seek an interview with President Wilson at which he could push for the administration's endorsement of a neutral conference. Even if he could not convince the president, they told him, he could still inaugurate and underwrite an unofficial conference composed of private citizens from the United States and European neutrals.[1]

As part of this effort, Rosika Schwimmer left for New York City where she conferred with Jane Addams and Lillian Wald. The three of them gained an interview with Colonel House on November 21. Without mentioning Ford's commitment to the movement, they once again appealed for House's endorsement of a conference of neutrals. The President's confidant, who had recently won Wilson's approval of his own mediation formula, privately viewed the pacifists' persistent appeals with a mixture of weariness and amusement:

> It was the same old story of trying to get the President to appoint a peace commission jointly with other neutral nations, to sit at The Hague and to continue making peace proposals until accepted. I explained that the President could not do this officially. They then wanted to know whether he would object to an unofficial commission doing it, and I thought he would not. As usual, I got them into a controversy between themselves, which delights me since it takes the pressure off myself. . . .[2]

House did not explain the cause of dissension between the three women or what he meant by "as usual," since his women visitors had not previously argued among themselves in his presence. Despite his self-congratulation over his performance, House did not openly criticize their scheme. Instead, he continued to feign interest and asked them to state their case more fully in writing. Addams sent him a statement, which emphasized the key role of public opinion in mediation. A neutral conference (whether official or unofficial) was important, she wrote, as the vehicle for citizens' input into the peace process and the necessity of a public forum in a neutral city to circumvent the censorship imposed by the military parties in the belligerent countries. As an example, she pointed out that many people in England were prepared to talk peace once German forces had been driven out of Belgium, while a large German antiannexationist league was declaring that Germany must not keep Belgium. Although their positions were not far apart, each group, unable to communicate, might assume the other was unwilling to negotiate. Without a neutral venue, her argument continued, "the people will know nothing of the terms of peace until they are practically ratified; and the only way popular opposition could then express itself would partake of the character of revolution."[3] However, House did not forward her statement to Washington.

Meanwhile, he received two other visitors, Lochner and Ford, who had followed Schwimmer to New York. House still posed outwardly as the reluctant friend of a neutral conference and wanted the pacifists to convince him of its soundness. Lochner at any rate reported that House listened to them courteously and attentively, acknowledged that the plan for a conference of neutrals had merit, and even remarked, "I agree with you that something of that sort ought to be done." Lochner then challenged the Colonel to win a public endorsement from the Wilson administration. House, taken by surprise, floundered and finally replied, "You see, I am not the Government." House's answer failed to satisfy Ford who concluded the interview with a terse rejoinder, "But you are pretty close to it."[4] This encounter strengthened House's impatience at the stream of pacifists flocking to his door. He found Ford's views on mediation "crude and unimportant." While conceding Ford's genius in mechanical matters, he concluded that the automobile magnate was so lacking in good judgment that he might "become a prey to all sorts of faddists who desire his money."[5]

Undismayed by House's equivocal attitude, Ford and Lochner journeyed to Washington to arrange an interview with the President. Ford had already telegraphed the White House requesting a meeting on November 26, just before one Wilson had already scheduled for a delegation of women promoting the neutral conference scheme. It was Wilson's personal secretary, Joseph Tumulty, who arranged for Ford to meet with the President.

Tumulty's role, then and later, would have a subtle, but nonetheless important, impact on the President's relationship with the mediation advocates. An Irish-Catholic, Tumulty had served in the New Jersey legislature and had joined Wilson's campaign for governor of the state. His reward following Wilson's triumph was his appointment as the governor's private secretary. Devoted to Wilson, he actively supported his mentor's presidential ambitions, and Wilson kept him as his secretary when he moved to the White House. Bright, gregarious, witty, generous, and politically savvy, he more than made up for Wilson's more cerebral demeanor and deficiencies in political instincts and public relations. He served not only as the gatekeeper severely restricting the flood of congressmen, office seekers, and other callers who wanted to see the President, but he also commented on drafts of Wilson's correspondence and speeches. Moreover, having an office adjacent to the President's, "Tumulty alone enjoyed free access to his chief." Perhaps most important, Tumulty was confident of his own skills in assisting the President, and he was not intimidated by his chief's superior education and intellect. He saw his job as fearlessly giving the President his best opinion on issues, even when it might conflict with his mentor's.[6] He would intercede more than once on behalf of mediation advocates' requests for presidential interviews when he saw them as politically desirable.

When Wilson first heard about Ford's request for a meeting, his instinctive reaction was decidedly negative. "Mr Ford has proved himself so unwise recently that I think this interview ought to be avoided if possible," he noted to Tumulty. But his personal secretary, perceiving the automobile manufacturer as a high-profile personality, replied that "We could not afford to turn Ford down." Tumulty prevailed and, once persuaded, Wilson sent word for Ford and Lochner to meet with him at the White House.[7]

The interview began with pleasant conversation. Always informal, Ford sank down into an easy chair with his left leg dangling over the arm and told a joke, and Wilson, also fully relaxed, responded with a limerick or two.[8] Ford then told the President that he had decided to back the plan for a neutral conference of continuous mediation. He urged the chief executive to appoint a commission from the United States and offered his unlimited financial support for its expenses. Wilson patiently reiterated the same objections to such a conference that he had earlier given other peace workers. He especially objected to any premature endorsement of their plan, which might restrict his freedom of action in case he later found a better formula.

I am by no means saying [Wilson explained] that the plan for continuous mediation is not the best one that has yet been offered. But as the head of a neutral nation I must also preserve neutrality of judgment when dealing with various proposals regarding the war. Suppose I commit myself to your plan. Who knows? Tomorrow a better plan may be offered which I shall be prevented from adopting because I have already committed myself to yours.[9]

Wilson's response was too sophisticated for the plain and straightforward Henry Ford. Because the President would not act, Ford replied deliberately, "Tomorrow at ten, in New York, representatives of every big newspaper will come to my apartment for a story. I have today chartered a steamship. I offer it to you to send delegates to Europe. If you feel you can't act, I will. I will then tell the newspaper men that I shall take a shipful of American delegates to Europe." Lochner, who already knew of Ford's decision, was nonetheless almost as surprised as Wilson by Ford's blunt announcement. Lochner could not recall whether the President made any comment, but Wilson obviously did not approve of Ford's sensational plan, even if he felt he could not stop it. Whatever his immediate reaction, the automotive manufacturer emerged from the interview with a negative impression of the President. "He's a small man," was his only comment following the meeting.[10]

Ford had decided to charter an ocean liner the previous day after Schwimmer had mentioned it at a planning session in New York with Lochner as well as Addams, Kirchwey, and Kellogg of the Henry Street group. Schwimmer's notion of a peace ship for transporting his private peace commissioners to Europe was probably a revival of her earlier hope in finding a millionaire to finance a ship to transport a large women's peace expedition to the Hague congress earlier that year.[11] Lochner endorsed the proposal half-jokingly, but the Henry Street representatives were opposed. They envisioned instead the appointment of a few well-qualified Americans who would agree to go abroad only after the selection of European delegates and a conference site. Ford seized upon the suggestion of an ocean liner, however, and ordered Gaston Plantiff, his company's East coast manager, and his lawyers to make arrangements for the charter of his peace ship.[12]

On the day following the presidential interview Ford announced to the press that since the Wilson administration refused to back a neutral conference, he had decided to organize one of his own. To dramatize his venture, he had reserved all the first- and second-class rooms on the Scandinavian-American liner *Oscar II*. He hoped his peace ship would awaken the soldiers' deep yearnings for peace, result in their refusal to continue fighting, and, in Ford's famous words, "get the boys out of their trenches and back to their homes by Christmas Day."[13]

Schwimmer's promotion of a peace ship as the precursor to an unofficial conference of neutrals was a curious reversal of her earlier insistence that the women leaders should steadfastly support only a governmentally sponsored conference. Her turnabout probably resulted from her frustration over getting any neutral government to initiate the proposal. By early November, she was thoroughly discouraged and ready to abandon her crusade. Indeed, she had already booked passage for her return to Hungary at the end of the month.[14] Only something big and dramatic could change her mind, and the peace ship certainly seemed to give the mediation campaign new vigor and to highlight her importance in the effort. Her suggestion of the ship may have also been a tactic to maintain Ford's support for the mediation cause in a large, concrete way. From her first promotion of an immediate armistice in the first days of the war through her proposal at the Hague congress to send women envoys to the European capitals, Schwimmer always championed bold initiatives.

Schwimmer, Lochner, and of course Ford, immediately began working long and hard to recruit individuals for the upcoming voyage. In the midst of their frenetic activities, Schwimmer also journeyed to Washington for a presidential hearing. It was Schwimmer's persistence and an accommodating Tumulty that brought her and Wilson together for the second time. Dissatisfied with Jane Addams' statements following her July interview with Wilson that he would not receive women from belligerent countries, Mme Schwimmer had nonetheless connived to find a way to gain a presidential interview. At one point she rationalized that she and Chrystal Macmillan could be received, not as belligerents, but as envoys of the women's international congress. But since Wilson had already received information about the women's peace movement from Addams, Balch, and Jacobs, Macmillan refused to sign her joint draft letter to Wilson requesting an interview.[15]

It was Schwimmer's friend, Rebecca Shelley, who found a more indirect route for the ladies' entrée to the White House. Even before Schwimmer had won over Ford's support of the mediation movement, Dean Marquis, who was initially impressed with the neutral conference plan, had taken Shelley to the offices of the *Detroit News* and explained the proposal to E.G. Pipp, the city editor, who, according to Shelley, replied that the conference idea "was the biggest thing he had ever heard." When Shelley said that Wilson would not see citizens from belligerent nations, Pipp wired the *News*' correspondent in Washington to ascertain the administration's position. When Tumulty was confronted, he claimed that the President had never declined to see the women and that if Schwimmer wanted to see the President, she had only to ask. Perhaps Tumulty was sensitive to the women's assumption that the President had refused access and wanted to straighten out a "misunderstanding." In any event, he promised an interview with the President without consulting him, and Wilson, though nonplussed when he heard about it, decided to receive Schwimmer.[16]

Initially, Schwimmer had envisioned her White House appearance as her final attempt to get the President's support for the conference of neutrals before she returned home to Hungary. Ford's action, however, had given her an additional opportunity to push for Wilson's endorsement of a neutral conference. Because Chrystal Macmillan, who would have given balance as a representative of the opposing belligerent side, had just left to return home to England, Schwimmer prevailed on Ethel Snowden to accompany her to the White House. Mrs Snowden revised her lecture schedule so that she could join Schwimmer for the presidential interview. Though support-ive of neutral mediation and of "mother-love" as a force for peace, Snowden was also a realist. She believed, for instance, that British women were as supportive of the war as men and that even British peace advocates did not want peace "until the wrongs in Belgium have been righted."[17]

Schwimmer carefully laid her plans for the interview. While she was in Detroit, she had persuaded Ford's wife, Clara, to contribute eight thousand dollars to the Woman's Peace Party, and the women leaders agreed that they should spend the entire sum on telegrams, which they sent out to eight thousand women, all of whom were officers of multifarious women's organizations. The telegrams asked the women to bolster the appeal of Mme Schwimmer and Mrs Snowden by telegraphing the President urging him to convene a conference of neutral nations.[18] Many women officers responded affirmatively by sending thousands of telegrams to the White House. Although Wilson probably never saw any of these messages, the women's activities bolstered the confidence of Ford's supporters. As if these efforts did not suffice, Schwimmer organized a mass meeting at the Belasco Theatre before their interview at which she, Mrs Snowden, and Ford gave the main addresses.[19]

Following the meeting the two women drove to the White House through a crowd of their well-wishers. The President received them graciously and talked with them for more than an hour. The women did not mention the peace ship because they assumed he disapproved of the venture and because they specifically wanted his official endorsement of a neutral conference.[20] According to Ethel Snowden, Wilson clearly expressed his hatred of the war, his desire to avert American participation, and his earnest wish to restore peace in Europe. "You need not plead with me," he reportedly told them. "I am anxious, most anxious to do all that I can for peace. I shall earnestly endeavor to unite official and unofficial opinion to that end."[21] Yet he raised practical objections to any precipitate creation of a neutral com-mission. Should China and Latin American nations be invited to such a conference, he asked? On what basis should the nations be represented? Would the belligerents approve of the conference? He said he kept looking for tangible signs of peace sentiment but found few, and Ethel Snowden, who came prepared to like and believe in him, silently agreed. However, Schwimmer vehemently dissented and began to berate the President for his inaction. At one point, when she hinted at America's munitions profit-eering, Wilson barely restrained his anger. "Surely," Mrs Snowden recalled him replying, "there are profiteers in other countries."[22]

In this meeting Wilson not only reiterated his objections to a neutral conference; he also raised many procedural obstacles to any such body. These latter arguments Wilson advanced more as reservations than outright objections, for he obviously wanted to justify his inaction. He probably hoped that the sheer quantity of objections—however minor or illogical—might dampen the ladies' enthusiasm for a conference of neutrals without alienating them from his administration. If that was his intention, he only partially succeeded. Only a forceful denunciation of the scheme would have discouraged the women; and since Wilson was unwilling to squelch high-minded proposals for ending the war, his objections had little lasting effect. Indeed, Schwimmer (Snowden was much less certain) left the interview convinced that he deeply shared their laudable objectives and might later be won over to their proposal.[23]

Wilson's failure to endorse the expedition did not discourage Henry Ford. His sensational publicity for his peace ship suggested that he considered the unofficial conference of respected private citizens from the European neutrals and the United States relatively unimportant. Ford did nothing in succeeding days to dispel this impression. He even convinced himself that the troops on both sides were so tired of war that the mere arrival of the peace ship in Europe during the Christmas season would provoke a widespread revolt against war. "I have all faith," he claimed extravagantly, "that on Christmas Day the world will see a general strike – that on that day of days war-worn men will climb from the trenches, throw down their arms and start home. And then militarism will be dead – dead for evermore."[24] Such remarks obscured the pacifists' original purpose of forming an unofficial conference as a clearing house for peace feelers.

———

Ford's frequently erratic and contradictory direction of his peace expedition would baffle his contemporaries, and his biographers have since advanced several explanations, not always convincingly, of his behavior. At least some aspects of his personality, however, are understandable.[25] For one thing, Ford's mind was not logical and rational, but a bundle of impulses and hunches. As early as his first meetings with Ford, Lochner sensed the millionaire's undisciplined mind, which "jumps," he wrote David Starr Jordan, "from one idea to another, so that we have quite a job to hold him to the thing in hand."[26] Reverend Marquis, one of Ford's close aides, later remarked of him: "He does not reason to conclusions. He jumps at them."[27] Without first asking the advice of his subordinates, Ford would endorse causes, including the peace movement, about which he had little knowledge, because he intuitively believed they were good and right. (Later he would champion unpleasant causes, such as anti-Semitism, also in an unthinking manner.) The many far-reaching implications of such endorsements did not concern him. It was the idea, not its implementation, which was important to him.

Unfortunately for Ford, even his ideas were not well developed. Although some of his forbears had tried to avoid military service, were killed or wounded in combat, or, in one case, deserted the army, Ford's background provides no clearly defined antimilitarist or pacifistic influences on him. Specifically, he had no philosophical or religious basis for his pacifism beyond a strong emotional hatred of war, as did more systematic peace seekers, and thus had little to sustain it in practice. This meant that if his peace ship failed to hasten an end to the war, he might become even more erratic and unpredictable.[28]

In addition, Ford believed in action for the sake of action. Ford's acquaintances noted his physical hyperactivity: his seemingly inexhaustible nervous energy, never sitting still for very long and constantly on the move. Similarly, what was normal for him intellectually was mental agitation, never focusing on an issue for very long, but constantly moving from one to another. "He has little patience with processes that take time and that cannot be measured by the ordinary standards of measurement," Lochner later wrote. For that reason, the automobile executive distrusted the incremental effects of education ("history is bunk" became one his best remembered quotes) and thought it was unnecessary, even a waste of time. He probably had no more than six years of schooling and, becoming a successful self-made man, thought that others could do the same. Abysmally ignorant of European history and power politics, he would be seen by many commentators as a childlike innocent abroad.[29]

A peace ship involved bold and unconventional action. To give it some chance of success or at least to minimize the public ridicule, Ford could have worked out in advance the details of the venture—deciding who would be invited (including giving sympathetic invitees sufficient time to make arrangements to join the peace ship), who would serve as the U.S. citizen representatives on the unofficial neutral conference, how many commissioners there would be, how delegates from other countries would be selected, in which neutral city the conference would be located, what public relations strategies they might pursue to get the sympathetic attention of neutral and belligerent governments, and countless other issues. The main promoters of the mission perceived the peace ark as only the first stage in the creation and workings of the unofficial neutral conference for continuous mediation in Europe, but Ford, delighting in surprise and unconventional action, announced his peace initiative before lining up support for his plans and then allowed only 11 days until the departure of *Oscar II* for Christiania (Oslo), Norway. At the New York press conference announcing his peace ship, Ford had appeared flanked by Lochner and Oswald Garrison Villard. An experienced journalist, Villard had told Ford that he should give out a prepared statement because the press was not known to treat pacifists and their initiatives fairly. But Ford had refused and simply spouted his "from the trenches" statement. Because he deferred to Lochner and Villard on the details, he left the impression that he was an uninformed visionary.[30]

Once Ford had decided on the peace ship, he seemed to assume that his famous friends—Thomas Edison, horticulturist Luther Burbank, naturalist John Burroughs, and John Wanamaker—would join the expedition, and their involvement might have given the venture some semblance of prestige and respectability. But Ford made no effort to get their allegiance in advance, and despite Ford's subsequent entreaties they all respectfully declined his invitation. Edison's refusal particularly hurt Ford; and when his inventor friend visited the *Oscar II* just before sailing, he again tried unsuccessfully to persuade him to stay on board and make the voyage with him.[31]

Throughout the venture, Ford took little interest in organizational matters. For him, the details and processes of peace machinery were boring in comparison with active demonstrations for peace. His compulsion to act in fact superseded any hopes for success. He also failed to delegate clear responsibilities to others. He appointed Schwimmer "expert adviser" and Lochner "general secretary," but he also allowed Liebold, Plantiff, and Marquis, all of whom also accompanied Ford and his party to Europe, to play important administrative roles. Ideally, the undefined roles of Ford's senior advisers on the peace venture required his conscientious oversight to resolve disagreements and coordinate activities, but Ford was relatively uninterested in administrative discipline. In his business, to be sure, he wanted a profitable and growing company, but he met shortcomings by replacing managers rather than reorganizing the bureaucracy. The haphazard organizational management of his peace undertaking in fact duplicated the unstructured business leadership of the Ford Motor Company. Because Ford's business associates involved with the peace venture were hostile to the undertaking, Schwimmer and Lochner would face a difficult uphill battle to maintain Ford's commitment to the conference scheme. Even Clara Ford was opposed. When she failed to persuade her husband to give up the peace ship, she refused to accompany him, fearing a torpedo might sink the *Oscar II* and leave son Edsel an orphan.[32]

Related to his interest in action was his preference for the tangible and love of publicity. In his automotive business, he eschewed theoretical notions of organizational management in favor of obsessive hands-on tinkering with auto parts. His introduction of the continuously automatic assembly line to mass-produce a mechanically reliable Model T car for the common man was correctly perceived at the time as a very progressive and efficient innovation, but it derived not from textbook notions of "scientific management." Similarly, he had an innate sense of what made "good copy" for the media. The peace ship was both something tangible and sensational

6.1 Masterminds of the Ford Peace Expedition: Rosika Schwimmer, Henry Ford, and Louis Lochner, December 3, 1915, the day before the sailing of the *Oscar II*. (Swarthmore College Peace Collection)

news for the metropolitan papers, while the neutral conference was only a cerebral "scientific commission."[33]

Discernment of Ford's dominant personality traits makes him more understandable, but does not really explain how he became quixotic and unpredictable. Perhaps, as at least one historian strongly suggests, psychic factors were involved in his sudden fixation on a peace expedition to Europe. One possible explanation is that a guilt-ridden Ford, who had rejected his father, tried to atone for his ungrateful behavior by pursuing good works like his peace ship. Ford's strange behavioral patterns certainly lend themselves to a psychological explanation of his personality, but the interpretation is not clearly developed and the evidence for repudiating his father is fragmentary. Indeed, the dominant portrait of Ford in the prewar years was not one of a repressed and angry son, but of an effusive and forward-looking entrepreneur.[34]

A more plausible explanation comes from modern psychiatry. Psychiatrists have developed the term "hypomanic" to describe restless, hyperactive individuals, and have postulated that hypomania is probably related genetically to bipolar disorder, a psychiatric condition more popularly known as manic depression, though in a much milder form. Unlike the gloomy and even reckless or destructive behavior of manic-depressives, however, hypomanic people tend to be exuberant, confident, optimistic, and creative. Known for his restless, emotionally charged energy and his supreme optimism, Henry Ford certainly fits this personality profile. And although he did not originate the idea of the peace ship, he seized on it so that the entire venture became the epitome of the confident risk-taker. Because hypomania is on one edge of a psychiatric continuum with bipolar disorder, however, it is not far removed from its more negative, despairing relative. While some hypomaniacs may never experience the downside, others suffer psychological setbacks, perhaps because they are more inclined to initiate new projects than to finish them. Ford's peace ship for ending the war surely set impossible goals which, when not met, would have debilitating results. Fortunately in Ford's case, he already had a successful business to which he could return and loyal subordinates who would help to soften the depressive effects of his failed peace venture. He nonetheless would continue to be susceptible thereafter, as a hypomanic person, to infectious enthusiasms, such as anti–Semitism, that would have disastrous consequences.

Because of its relative newness in psychiatry, hypomania requires more scientific studies to test more conclusively its relationship with depression. There is little doubt, however, that many well-known historical individuals, including Ford, have experienced sustained periods of high mental activity and exuberant behavior.[35] In any case, in addition to his psychological makeup, there is another link between his mental outlook and aspects of his political culture. Ford grew up on farms in Michigan and like many rural inhabitants of the Middle West and Plains states absorbed the ethos of the populist movement, which blamed their sections' economic problems on special interests—in particular, Eastern capitalists and the moneyed power of Wall Street. Unlike many economically downtrodden and indebted populists who were reacting angrily to their plight, Ford was more representative, even before his business successes, of a middle-class reform perspective that was more typical of Middle Western progressivism. Despite differences between populism and progressivism, a mood of rebellion and hostility to "special interests" pervaded both reform movements, and progressivism co-opted many aspects of populism. Ford's professed "pacifism" was to a major extent an outgrowth of hostility to these interests, especially the armament makers, which he deplored because they were "wasteful" and "war breeding." Military preparedness, he argued, "is really a plan to keep the munition factories busy after this war ends. In reality war is a device of big financiers, the biggest cowards in the world. Those fellows run if you drop a hat, but they don't care how much the other fellows – the little ones – fight, or how many are killed."[36]

Like many populist-progressives of the time, he made sharp distinctions between these conspiratorial "interests" and the "people," who, he strongly believed, did not want preparedness or war.[37] By the "people" Ford was thinking mainly of those like himself and his workers who were products of the rural and small-town American heartland.[38] The "interests", by contrast, were far away; unseen and unfamiliar, the worst could be believed of them. He envisioned his inexpensive cars and tractors as helping to alleviate the drudgery of farmers' lives. Ford's thinking embodied nostalgic views of an agrarian Eden. The irony was that the automobile, which he believed would help rural and small-town America, did more than any other technological change of his era to stimulate the process of suburbanization and urban sprawl. Similarly, just as some populists made nativist and anti-Semitic remarks (though many populists were immigrants and were often victims of these prejudices, and anti-Semitic feelings were not limited to populists), so could Ford equate the Eastern "interests" with a conspiracy of Jewish capitalists. During the Great War, Ford occasionally mouthed anti-Jewish rhetoric that was fairly common among his friends and associates, including even the local businessmen and bankers who had supported his early enterprises. Thus his outburst to Schwimmer at their first meeting about the "German-Jewish bankers" causing the war was an inchoate prejudice, which would gradually harden into obsessive anti-Semitism after the war.[39]

—

Ford's hastily devised and extravagant plans for his expedition threw the peace forces into confusion. Some of the more cautious among them like David Starr Jordan and Hamilton Holt, believing that only quiet diplomacy by the neutral governments could bring the belligerents to the conference table, refused to join the expedition. Lochner bombarded Jordan with flattering telegrams of the crucial importance of having him, an "original champion" of the neutral conference plan, on board, but the Stanford chancellor was unwilling to risk his reputation with an amateurish entourage. He well expressed many peace workers' surprise and bewilderment at Ford's spectacular announcement. Much as he admired Ford's idealism and courage, he sensed the futility of the projected venture. "I fear," he wrote half-seriously to his wife, "that even a relay of Ford automobiles will not 'get the boys out of the trenches for Christmas.' "[40] Others, including William Jennings Bryan and Lillian Wald, expressed greater faith in the expedition, but claimed that previous commitments, especially their involvement in fighting military preparedness advocates in Congress, prevented their participation.[41]

Even many of the most dedicated peace people, including the rest of the Henry Street group, while marveling at Ford's vision and bold plans and welcoming the potential propaganda value of the peace ship for the mediation movement, recognized that the peace expedition was too hastily and poorly organized to achieve any real success.[42] Jane Addams, for example, perceived that the sensational publicity surrounding the undertaking would discredit the unofficial conference, but her efforts to influence Ford toward a quieter, more careful organization of a conference of private citizens failed. As a leading symbol of the proposal for a continuous conference of neutrals, she felt obligated to join the expedition, but fate intervened. A sick woman for much of the previous summer and fall, she succumbed to a tubercular infection of the kidneys and on the date of the ship's sailing was bedridden in a Chicago hospital. Many wrongly suspected, however, that she was not really so seriously ill and only used her poor health as an excuse to back out of the enterprise.[43]

In the end, besides Lochner and Schwimmer, Julia Grace Wales, May Wright Sewall, and Shelley were the only peace people prominently associated with the mediation campaign who joined Ford's undertaking. Schwimmer noted that the absence of experienced women peace workers like Addams and Balch put the expedition "into a very disagreeable position." Trying to overlook these inauspicious beginnings, Ford and his associates nonetheless pressed forward. Schwimmer, of course, made certain that her women supporters would be included among Ford's guests. Among her disciples joining the voyage were Lola Maverick Lloyd, Lloyd's brother Lewis Maverick, Shelley, Florence Holbrook, Katherine Leckie, a New Yorker who had coordinated Schwimmer's lecture schedules, Alice Park, a suffragist from San Francisco who had been attracted to Schwimmer's peace campaign, and two Finnish women reformers, who then happened to be in the United States. Because the custody of Mrs Lloyd's children was at issue in her pending divorce suit, she even brought along, thanks to Ford's largess, her three oldest, ages seven to eleven, and their governess.[44]

From a suite of rooms at the Hotel Biltmore in New York, Ford, Schwimmer, and Lochner also sought to recruit others. They sent out a flood of telegrams to well-known public figures in America asking them to join "leading" Europeans in establishing an international conference for peace negotiations. Most of the invitees were identified with social reform movements or had political ties to the Wilson administration. Ford refused to include any members of Congress, who, he argued, should remain in Washington to fight preparedness, but otherwise the recruitment of the politically powerful was the order of the day. The governors of all the states and territories were invited, for example, though only one governor and a lieutenant governor accepted. Over the next few days they also traveled to Washington, DC, Baltimore, and Philadelphia, to appeal personally to others. In the end, however, nearly all the well-connected and prominent invitees turned Ford down. The result was that the delegates were mostly a motley collection of peace advocates, moralistic uplifters, and pacifistic clergymen. None of the delegates had any significant international experience. To fill out the passenger list, the organizers recruited international-minded college students to observe and learn about private diplomacy in action.

Regardless of its personnel, the Ford peace expedition would have had to endure considerable ridicule from the press, but the absence of the most respected peace leaders and the presence of mostly inexperienced and eccentric individuals, however sincere and well-meaning, made such criticism sharper and more widespread. Press commentary on the undertaking was sure to be widely disseminated because the contingent of journalists was in fact overrepresented on the *Oscar II*. Realizing the adventure would provide an ongoing human-interest story, almost every major newspaper in New York, Boston, Philadelphia, Chicago, and San Francisco as well as the three main wire services and several national magazines appointed correspondents for the trip, and there were many others on board from other cities and towns across the nation. Altogether there were at least 44 journalists (including five photographers and newsreel cameramen) on the ship accompanying some 55 delegates (including 11 on the Lochner-Schwimmer staff), 25 students, and 31 members of Ford's business and clerical staff. Ford barred foreign journalists and could have limited the number of American journalists; instead, however, he opened the ship to most accredited journalists who applied. Because Schwimmer, Shelley, and Leckie were careful to invite journalists who had sympathetically covered their earlier peace activities, he may have believed that the coverage, which had heretofore been sympathetic to Ford's business exploits, would be mostly favorable. Most journalists in fact liked Ford personally; it was the expedition (and only by implication Ford himself who was bankrolling it) that they attacked.

There were some reputable reporters on the ship—for example, Elmer Davis of the *New York Times* and the celebrated muckraker S.S. McClure, who admired Ford and was also a delegate. Others like William C. Bullitt of the Philadelphia *Public Ledger*, a well-educated socialite who would later serve as a controversial U.S. envoy, tried to provide full and some semblance of balanced coverage, but their negative judgments about the expedition nonetheless were prominently featured. Journalism was just beginning to develop into a profession and did not have high reporting standards, and journalists were not as a rule well educated. Many of them on the expedition were in fact simply inexperienced or biased against the undertaking, or both. Moreover, regardless of their personal views, many were under pressure from their publishers, who objected to the venture, to provide sensational copy, highlighting the bizarre aspects and internal bickering. The unfavorable segments of the press reported, almost gleefully at times, the more sensational sidelights of the expedition, but gave short shrift to its avowed aim of neutral mediation.[45] Lella Secor, a young journalist herself who strongly believed in the purposes of the expedition, wrote home that she found the reporters "so scurrilous and vicious that I have entirely severed all connection with them."[46]

Unfavorable publicity, however, was not the only problem faced by the peace pilgrims. Indeed, internal dissension developed on the peace ship itself.[47] One of the better publicized disagreements involved the party's reaction to Wilson's message to Congress on December 6 in which he urged great increases in military preparedness for the coming year. According to exaggerated and ill-informed press accounts, a major "war" developed on board between those supporting Ford and those agreeing with the President. The delegates finally elected a committee to draft resolutions to be sent to Congress as embodying the views of the peace ship; but instead of submitting it to the delegates for discussion, the committee announced that the document would be left with the delegates and other guests for their voluntary signatures. Though a well-meaning effort to avoid further controversy, it created an uproar from those who charged that the antipreparedness forces were using "steamroller" tactics to get their own proposals adopted intact. Ford shortly circulated a letter to the delegates reaffirming the relevance of antipreparedness to his peace mission: "What could be more absurd and inconsistent," he wrote, "than for us to ask Europe to stop adding to her own military burdens, while supporting either actively or passively a proposed increase of them in our own country." His argument did not persuade a dozen or more in the party who believed that increases in U.S. military and naval preparedness were necessary until international disarmament agreements could be negotiated. But because his letter also affirmed that those remaining in disagreement would "still be his welcome guests to the end of the trip," he at least quieted rumors that the opponents would be asked to leave the expedition upon landing in Norway.[48]

Ford's intervention resolved this controversy, but thereafter he provided little guidance during the Atlantic crossing. Occasional displays of his leadership, including some indication of his future plans for the mission, would likely have shown those on board his ongoing commitment to the enterprise. Throughout most of the voyage, however, Ford remained in his cabin, even eating his meals there, and held no meetings with Lochner, Schwimmer, or other delegates to discuss future strategy. In a strange reversal from his earlier publicity seeking, he even shunned the press. The journalists found him generally incommunicado and only occasionally engaged him in inconclusive conversations during his few brief forays on deck. Because of Ford's isolation, they became more prone to rely on rumors and the disagreements among his undisciplined guests for their "news" reports.

As the squabbles on board materialized, Ford failed to intervene. Instead, perhaps because of the internal bickering he began to realize that it would take much more than publicity to inspire peace talks, and he became partly disillusioned with the venture. During the last stages of the voyage, Ford caught a bad cold. Dean Marquis, who early became hostile to the expedition and had accompanied his boss at Mrs Ford's request to protect him from zealous pacifists, cleverly manipulated this turn of events to his own advantage. As soon as the peace party disembarked in Christiania, Marquis hurried to the hotel and engaged a two-room suite for Ford. He put the indisposed Ford in the inner room, which with its bleak, northern exposure was hardly conducive to raising Ford's sagging spirits. Marquis himself stayed in the outer room and kept Ford virtually isolated from the pacifists, including Schwimmer and Lochner. Exploiting Ford's forced dependence on him and his wife's misgivings about his European venture, Marquis within a few days prevailed upon him to use his illness as an excuse for leaving the expedition and returning to the United States. As Ford shortly informed Lochner, "Guess I'd better go home to mother [his wife]. I told her I'd be back soon. You've got this thing started and can get along without me."

Marquis' task was facilitated by Ford's increasing disenchantment with the factionalism among his party and its lukewarm reception in Norway. Even then the pacifist leaders remonstrated with Ford, reminding him of the upcoming meetings in Norway and his other obligations, and Ford said he would reconsider. Ford chose to leave, however, and Marquis engineered his actual departure from the hotel at 4:00 a.m. the following morning, December 23, only four days after arriving in Norway. He hoped that his nocturnal exit would avoid further controversy, but word of his planned exodus leaked to some members of the delegation who, assembling in the hotel lobby at the departure hour, urged him in vain to change his mind.[49]

Once back in the United States, Ford told reporters that the experience of the peace expedition had shaken his pacifism. "A marked change has come over my whole viewpoint since I went away," he confessed. "Before going to Europe I held the views that the bankers, militarists, and munition[s] manufacturers were responsible [for the war]. I come back with the firm belief that the people most to blame are the ones who are getting slaughtered. They have neglected to select the proper heads for their Governments – the men who would prevent such chaotic conditions." Although the automobile magnate emphatically denied that he had "deserted" his peace party and urged the remaining members to continue his venture in Europe, his lukewarm moral and financial support thereafter would do little to bolster the sagging spirits of the peace pilgrims who were attempting to establish an influential congress of neutrals.[50]

One can believe, of course, that the peace ship venture was totally impractical from the outset and doomed to failure, but a well-developed and smoothly operating neutral conference could have at least provided a visible forum for the expression of belligerent nations' peace feelers whenever they might intimate their interest in a negotiated settlement. And if nothing else, through its publicity and demonstrations it could help to keep alive the hopes for a negotiated and just peace as an alternative to purely military solutions. From the outset, however, the leaders of the Ford peace venture spent an inordinate amount of time in a series of conflicts and hassles over the details of the conference.

———

Much of the writing trying to explain the failings of the peace ship and its sequel, the unofficial neutral conference, focuses on the conflict of personalities. In these accounts, Rosika Schwimmer is usually portrayed as the principal villain. Ample evidence exists to support that perspective. Even those writers who have not blamed Schwimmer alone for the shortcomings have still emphasized the factionalism and bizarre behavior of the members. The diaries and reminiscences of participants contain a catalogue of personal squabbles over the military preparedness issue, Schwimmer's habits and deceptions, and the Schwimmer–Marquis struggle for Ford's attention. The efforts in creating the unofficial conference in Scandinavia and The Hague are also full of juicy intrigues among the Ford party. Moreover, the unsympathetic journalists accompanying the group focused on the personality conflicts; and without access to Ford or Schwimmer for authoritative information, they could more easily play up and exaggerate the disagreements among individual members.[51] Even Lochner's letters at the time reveal his preoccupation with personality conflicts and factionalism, and his later book about the expedition emphasized Ford's unpredictable, "quixotic" personality as the fundamental weakness of the undertaking.

The exclusive focus on personality conflicts, however, tends to highlight the superficial and the sensational at the expense of other fundamental reasons for the ineffectiveness of the Ford peace expedition. In the first place, some conflict is inevitable in such a large group of people, and it can even be beneficial if held within reasonable bounds and channeled into constructive debate over alternative courses of action. It is more instructive to inquire into the reasons for excessive conflict rather than for its existence. As Lochner, admittedly a strong defender of the expedition, later put it, "Show me any community in which there is not healthy disagreement over details," even though he readily conceded later that "the closing days of our voyage were not a symphonic poem!"[52]

Leaders of associations frequently cite personality conflicts as the cause of organizational problems, although closer inspection reveals that the real causes are just as likely to be faulty organizational design, poor communication, and ineffective leadership, all of which derive as much directly from ignorance, self-deception, and stupidity and are bound to increase interpersonal tension, confusion, extreme frustration, and ultimately some kind of blowup. From the beginning, in fact, the Ford peace venture can be viewed as a classic case of organizational ineffectiveness. The lines of authority should have been clear. Henry Ford was providing all the money, and he alone could direct how much should be spent and for what purposes. Even if he might delegate authority on occasion, as indeed he had to do after he left the expedition, his control of the purse strings gave him an absolute veto. His name and ultimately his reputation were too closely identified with the venture to abdicate leadership to an unpredictable group.

Had Ford, following his return to America, remained in regular contact with his neutral conference of private citizens or clearly designated the responsibilities of its principal leaders, he might have helped the conference to become a viable forum for popularizing mediation as an alternative to the escalating European bloodbath. But having few ideas on mediation and little interest in the details of managing his nascent organization, the automotive entrepreneur gave little direction to his chosen representative, Gaston Plantiff, a Ford manager, for providing on-the-scene financial administration of the venture in his absence. Caught in the crossfire of competing views on the organization and direction of the neutral conference, Plantiff had a thankless task in dealing with many details and controversies over the financial aspects of the conference. Moreover, he was a businessman with little commitment to the conference. He was also weak-willed and often consenting to self-seeking requests. For example, the Rev Charles Aked, formerly the pastor of John D. Rockefeller's Baptist church, from the outset of the expedition tried to assume a leadership position. Impressing the pliable Plantiff with his ideas and abilities, Aked persuaded him to pay his salary as an American delegate, including expenses for him and his wife, even before he had been elected.[53] But for all his weaknesses, Plantiff at least understood that he was Ford's agent and most of all wanted to please him. Besides Plantiff in Europe, there was Ford's private secretary, E.G. Liebold, who served as the go-between in Detroit. Liebold was hostile to the conference of neutrals and was well prepared to issue instructions, supposedly in Ford's name, which placed obstacles in its way. Liebold and Plantiff quickly agreed on a scheme, which they assumed would simplify the communications between them. Liebold, claiming to represent Ford in all matters, signed all messages coming from Detroit, and Plantiff, acknowledging Liebold as the conduit to their employer, wrote him, "Pay no attention to any information coming from anyone connected with this party beside myself."[54] Thus Plantiff, with Liebold's connivance, early tried to extend his reach beyond purely financial matters.

In putting another layer between Schwimmer and Ford, Liebold and Plantiff were circumscribing her authority. Schwimmer believed, however, that Ford had given her his personal mandate to lead the neutral conference subject only to his personal intercession with other instructions. She even claimed that he had privately confirmed her leadership as "expert adviser" at the time of his abrupt return to America. Because Ford upon his arrival in New York had publicly expressed his continued confidence in her, perhaps her claim was accurate. In any event, she was, not surprisingly, reluctant to share power with Ford's intermediaries. For a time, she used flattery and exploitation of her "expert" role in successfully bamboozling the weak-willed Plantiff to provide the funds for her publicity initiatives, gifts to political leaders and peace advocates in the neutrals in gratitude for their sponsorship of receptions and other favors, honoraria for delegates elected from the neutral countries, and many other expenses. Moreover, she successfully challenged the authority of another Ford executive, Frederick Holt, who arrived to serve as co-financial manager with Lochner and tried to impose new administrative procedures that threatened to curtail the scope of the undertaking. Even Lochner, distrusting orders from Ford's agents in the absence of written instructions coming directly from Ford himself, acquiesced in Schwimmer's forceful espousal of her and the conference's authority. She also wrote long reports directly to Ford detailing the plans and progress in forming the neutral conference but received no reply.[55]

Unlike her patron's shapeless perspective on neutral mediation, Schwimmer at least had good knowledge of Europe and a general strategy for the expedition. At an early meeting on the *Oscar II*, she had told the American delegates that from her experiences as an envoy of the Hague congress to the European neutrals, she anticipated that the entire Ford party would visit the three Scandinavian capitals for several days each, at which they would attend banquets and meetings, before proceeding to The Hague where she predicted a warm reception. Vaguely intimating that the plans of the local organizations would affect the next phase of peace-work, she had refused for the moment to give further details. Nevertheless, Schwimmer's talk had raised the spirits of the young, committed, and unquestioning. Even Julia Grace Wales, who had earlier seen her at close range on a number of occasions, was impressed by her performance. "In her black hair and eyes, her powerful voice, the solid bulk of her figure, the great strength of her head and neck, the emotional vigor of her speech," she wrote her family after the meeting, "she suggested the natural force of the super-woman."[56]

As Schwimmer had outlined, the Ford peace party took a 16-day excursion en masse from Christiania to Stockholm, Copenhagen, and, through German territory, to The Hague, Netherlands. Peace groups and other well-wishers generally gave the Americans as well as some Scandinavians who had joined their pilgrimage a warm welcome, but during their travels the factionalism intensified, mainly because of Schwimmer. From the outset she in fact consistently overplayed her hand. Her behavior and actions increasingly annoyed members of the expedition, who became convinced that she was a negative factor in the undertaking. Specifically, they criticized her insistence on overseeing the establishment of the neutral conference when she came from a belligerent nation. Despite her obviously passionate pacifism and sincere attempts at true neutrality, her Hungarian nationality predisposed many people to perceive her as partial toward the Central Powers. Much as most members understood her disinterested motives, they recognized that Allied outsiders who might be tempted to use the neutral conference would shy away from it as long as she was one of its leaders. Schwimmer, however, saw no problem and ignored hints that she step aside to improve the neutral conference's chances of success.

Many also came to object to her secretive behavior. She always carried with her a black bag, inside which, she claimed, existed solid evidence of governments' support for a conference among European neutrals, but she refused to divulge its contents. There was in fact nothing more in the bag than the confidential statements of European statesmen in support of neutral mediation, which the women envoys had received during their visits to the European capitals. Although she was not at liberty to divulge the names of the persons who had made the various statements, she could have revealed their contents, as indeed the women's manifesto had already done a few months earlier. Her black bag came to symbolize false hopes and empty promises. Similarly, just as she had earlier annoyed her women cohorts with her lavish expenditures on cables and her own living comforts, she spent Ford's money with abandon while concealing any valid justification for their relevance to the expedition. Following her departure from the Ford venture, Lochner found the financial books in total disarray. Her accounting, he remarked, reminded him "of the Parvenue . . . Opera Parties, Banquets, and vouchers for several thousands of Kroner;" and where the vouchers called for justification of expenses, Schwimmer had simply marked "confidential."[57]

Finally, colleagues came to resent her arbitrary behavior. She snubbed those who she thought were unsympathetic to her leadership, and generally appeared in the guise of an autocrat. As delegates early on began asking her more questions about the "secret documents" in her possession and other details about their peace mission, she avoided future meetings and, no less than Ford, remained in her cabin during most of the ocean voyage. In isolating herself from other viewpoints, she wasted several days when skillful leadership might have educated the other delegates on the purposes and proposed workings of the neutral conference for continuous mediation and developed a coherent organizational strategy for promoting its acceptance on European shores. "To reach her presence was more difficult than to embrace the Dalai Lama," Bullitt reported.[58]

6.2 Delegates and some staff people at the first formal session of the Neutral Conference for Continuous Mediation, February 1916. Except for Emily Balch, who had not yet joined the conference, there would be no women delegates six months later. (Wisconsin Historical Society)

Some members of the expedition believed that her devious, aloof behavior stemmed from her upbringing in Central Europe, which lacked a strong liberal tradition. Her Hungarian background undoubtedly affected her personality, but she had spent much time in Western European nations and had admired their open, democratic processes. More important, her behavior was psychologically compulsive. Schwimmer was a highly intelligent and resourceful woman, but because her remarkable successes had come almost entirely from her own initiative and inventiveness, she had become increasingly infatuated with her talents. After persuading Ford to join the mediation movement, for example, she told Lochner, "I feel as though I were in Fairy-land. All I have to do is wave my wand for what I think is necessary for our Peace Mission, and lo! it appears." Her egotism led her to believe that her leadership was indispensable and that Ford would withdraw his financial support from the neutral conference if she resigned. Others disagreed with that assessment but failed to move her.[59]

At the same time, Schwimmer developed a conspiratorial view of those not entirely converted to her plans. Since there were several journalists as well as a few members of the expedition eager to discredit the entire undertaking, her concerns were legitimate, but Schwimmer's fears were obsessive, even paranoid, and extended even to those supporting the venture. Irving Casear, a student member of the expedition (and later a very successful song writer), wrote in his diary that "Mme Schwimmer wants to annihilate Newspaper men." The Rev Charles Aked, who became one of her severest critics among the American participants, commented that "she is wholly lacking in magnanimity. She will never assume a higher, or nobler attitude. Prick her with a pin, and she will go in search of a sword to retalliate [sic] with."[60] Indeed, anyone who was not totally loyal to her was suspect, and Caesar connected her Hungarian background to her conspiratorial countenance. "[B]eing a Central European," he later reflected, "she could not divorce herself from the idea of imaginary espionage, which resulted in her putting into operation a system of intrigue to counteract what she felt was a conspiracy – first to dethrone her, and second to defeat the purpose of the expedition. So there was set up an autocracy of which Ford knew nothing."[61] Caesar did not doubt that she made enemies who wanted to get rid of her, but believed that the other delegates wanted the expedition to succeed. He soon found himself very depressed and "absolutely exhausted by the stifling atmosphere of plot and counterplot, intrigue, and secrecy that has permeated the air for the past few weeks." He tried to like Schwimmer, but finally labeled her, "at her best . . . a benevolent despot" and a "deluded" woman when she continued to meddle in the affairs of the conference even after she had resigned from it.[62]

Those who believed she lusted for power were only half right. She assumed her own motives were entirely selfless in trying to promote a successful expedition, but unfortunately for the venture she personalized any opposition as direct attacks on her authority. Even Louis Lochner and Grace Wales, among others, who had supported Schwimmer's positions and tried to work with her, became alienated. Lochner found that "Schwimmer's mind had slowly become poisoned." Frankly admitting her disillusionment with democracy, she now claimed that only secret methods in the neutral conference would succeed.[63] Winning over Plantiff, her opponents bypassed Schwimmer and soon had effectively neutralized her power. The ensuing problems stemmed from the uncertainty over Ford's true wishes and the real lines of authority in the conference.

Following Ford's return to the United States, the conferees had to decide upon a permanent site for the neutral conference for continuous mediation. The debate over location was between Stockholm and The Hague. The latter's proponents cited the advantage of tradition, with the Hague Conferences and the interest of the Dutch Government in mediation, but Stockholm was selected because of the active lobbying of the pacifistic Stockholm mayor, the Scandinavians' inclination to try new and more activist approaches to the mediation question, and the easier travel and communications among the delegates from the northern neutrals. By late

1916, the delegates had begun to set up conference headquarters in the luxurious Grand Hotel.

Despite this accomplishment, the organizational defects began to show up in the pressing issues facing the American pilgrims. A major one involved the selection of the permanent representatives to the neutral conference. It had been agreed that each of the six neutrals would select five commissioners and five alternates. The European neutrals could perform the election according to their own procedures, but the American entourage had to select delegates before the non-delegates disbanded and returned home. With her allies on the committee of administration, Schwimmer tried to maneuver the selection of a "slate" of American delegates, subject to Ford's approval, but others on the committee were more independent and demanded a more open democratic election procedure. Plantiff, tired of the wrangling, finally declared that because Ford would want an open election, that is what they would have.

Actually, the American conferees easily agreed on three delegates—Ford, Bryan, and Addams—but none of them was likely to join the conference for some time, if ever. Ford said he hoped to rejoin the conference, perhaps in connection with a tour promoting his company's tractor, but his wife's continued opposition to the peace venture and her fears for his safety in submarine-infested waters worked against his return. Moreover, he claimed that for the immediate future he had to remain at home to fight military preparedness, which had become a predominant domestic issue. Bryan, a vigorous opponent of major military increases, also was fully engaged in the preparedness debate, but intimated that he would become a delegate if Ford or Addams did. When neither joined the conference, he felt no special obligation. In any event, the Ford people let the Great Commoner know that he should not to go to Stockholm unless Ford so requested. Aked, already in the pay of Ford, had pushed himself forward as the fourth delegate. Thus the dispute over the election of the final American delegate and the alternates assumed immediate importance. Lochner decried the brazen politicking, later calling the "forced" election of Aked and the alternates "the most disgusting chapter in the history of our peace crusade."[64]

In the end, Schwimmer would not relinquish her position until Ford removed her. She had used the threat of her resignation several times to cow delegates who were unwilling to depose her against her patron's explicit wishes. Until the question of her leadership was resolved, the delegates were hamstrung among those on one side, who opposed and wanted to proceed without her, and her few loyal supporters on the other; and in the middle were those who were unwilling to alienate her until Ford's real wishes were clarified. As her alienation became complete, however, she cabled Ford that she did not want to embarrass him and, if he so decided, would take his request for her withdrawal "impersonally." "But," she added, "I cannot act so irresponsibly as to leave before I have been discharged by you, who have put me in charge." Finally, perceiving that the delegates saw her as the main obstacle to an efficient conference, she actually resigned as "expert adviser" at the end of February over an unimportant administrative issue before Ford had sent word asking her to step aside. But he had already obliquely intimated—appointing a new business manager, for example, who would effectively curtail her control over finances—that he was unhappy with her management of the undertaking, and he quickly accepted her resignation. Even after she stepped down, Schwimmer tried to exert her influence. Sulking in her Stockholm hotel room, she railed to her loyal friends against Lochner and others and conspired with her supporters, mostly without success, to affect the course of the conference.[65]

—

Following Schwimmer's resignation, which the conference accepted unanimously, Lochner took over as general secretary. He was a logical choice, both because of his intimate involvement in the Ford endeavor from the outset and the confidence of almost all those involved had in him. They respected him for his commitment to the cause and for his good humor, competence, and fairness. A Danish delegate complimented him as "Lochner of the white heart."[66]

Despite the problems, plans for the conference of neutrals made some headway as an organizational entity. Even under Schwimmer's stormy tenure, its members managed to agree on a constitution defining the structure and basic procedures of the conference. The document called for a conference chairman, an executive committee, a publicity committee, and a committee of experts, which was divided into sections to refine the principles of international reform and territorial issues for the eventual peace negotiations. Another committee was to advise on the preferred options for submitting their peace proposals to the belligerents. By the end of February 1916, the assembled delegates began regular sessions in the Grand Hotel. Most of the European representatives were from the intellectual elite of their countries and held advanced degrees. They included jurists, university professors from the humanities and social sciences, several members of national legislatures, and businessmen. Notably, one-third of the delegates were women, one-half of whom had attended the Hague congress the previous year, and all were leaders of women's reform organizations in the areas of suffrage, social work, and the labor movement.[67]

As the conferees moved forward, they found themselves debating the preferred strategy for mediation. Was the neutral conference for continuous mediation going to stay out of the mediation business and expend their efforts in trying to persuade the neutral governments to assume that function? That strategy would provide a moral presence for the neutral conference but limit its authority at best to the role of expert advisers. Or should the conference offer its good offices, which would mean trying to develop direct contacts with the governmental leaders of both belligerent sides? And would the contacts be undertaken quietly and discreetly in the hope of gradually finding some common ground on the two sides for an eventual *rapprochement*? Or would they risk alienating the belligerents by also engaging in publicity to stir up latent popular feelings against the war, which might erode war morale and put pressure on the belligerent authorities to consider peace talks? The conference never entirely resolved these issues, with Schwimmer and other delegates, mainly from Sweden and Denmark, championing the activist course, while Dutch members, led by de Jong van Beek en Donk, the Norwegians, Aked, and some others favored a quieter role as expert commentators and facilitators. Caught up in the whirlwind of developing a functioning conference and the creation of new initiatives, Lochner had no time to contemplate alternative organizational arrangements. He later commented, however, that in their haste and zeal he and his cohorts had erred:

> The mistake we made in those days of the conference was that we did not realize that the various methods proposed were not necessarily incompatible with each other; that, in fact, there was a large field for publicity, for popular agitation, for professorial investigation, and for semi-diplomatic mediation. All these lines of work might have been pushed with greater vigour from the beginning had we, instead of insisting upon plenary sessions day after day, broken up into commissions or committees, each pursuing one of the lines above suggested and autonomous within its own sphere.

He also acknowledged that a strong permanent chairman would have provided much needed stability and direction to the conference.[68]

Despite the unresolved issues, under Lochner's tutelage the newly assembled neutral conference began to make itself heard. For all their differences the conferees agreed that they could promote aspects of the various mediation strategies. First, in March it addressed a public appeal to neutral governments to propose joint mediation, and a delegation from the conference presented the appeal personally to the Scandinavian foreign ministers who were then meeting in Copenhagen. Already warned by the French minister (and perhaps other belligerents' envoys) there not to discuss mediation, the Scandinavian diplomats finally accepted the document but said they could not discuss it in their meetings. Undeterred, the neutral conference subsequently presented the appeal to the same diplomats in their ministries and to the president and parliament in Norway, the head of which endorsed the appeal and lamented the failure of the United States to lead the mediation effort. "In general," Lochner later wrote, "it may be said that all the Governmental representatives visited stated that their Governments were ready to do anything within their power to mediate whenever the occasion presented itself. They made it perfectly plain, however, that it was incumbent upon the United States to create the occasion."[69]

At the same time, most of the neutral conference representatives did not envision mediation leading to a brokered peace based on traditional diplomatic practices. As activist international reformers, they wanted instead to press the belligerents publicly to state their war aims. Many of them did not believe the neutral conference would partake in the peace talks, but wanted it to publicize the peace terms of the Allies and the Central Powers. It could also try to cut through military censorship and relay the proposals of peace-oriented citizen groups to the other side—the Germans could read the proposals of the Union of Democratic Control, for example, or the British the programs of German antiannexationist groups. They hoped that their efforts would force the warring nations to abandon secret diplomacy and accept much greater transparency in international dealings. Lochner concurred, writing Ford at one point that the neutral conference itself was "too ponderous, slow-moving, professorial," and he believed that moneys now squandered on honoraria "should be used for *publicity, publicity, publicity*, and for keeping *a few skilled persons in constant and living touch with the warring governments.*"

The delegates also agreed that a new, forward-looking, and comprehensive settlement was required, if a just and durable peace was to be achieved. In April, the neutral representatives issued a detailed manifesto outlining their criteria for such a peace: postwar disarmament, democratic control of foreign policy, freedom of the seas, and economic guarantees such as free trade and the open door. The manifesto also advanced requirements for territorial adjustments, including the restoration of Belgium and occupied French territory, reconsideration of the question of Alsace-Lorraine, the independence of Serbia and Montenegro, creation of an independent Poland, and adjustments of borders in eastern and southeastern Europe as much as possible according to the determination of the inhabitants. Most important, it called for creation of a new world organization to which nations would agree to submit all international disputes.[70]

Cooperation with peace societies in the European neutrals improved markedly. Despite his preference for quiet diplomacy, de Jong, for example, became actively engaged in the work of the conference. Ada Morse Clark, Lochner's secretary, commented in July that the Dutch peace advocate "has plunged into the work heart and soul. He and Lochner are like brothers, and Miss Balch is also one of the sisters. Everyone leans on her, and she is on nearly every committee." Balch, after arranging for a long-term leave of absence from Wellesley, had arrived in Stockholm in mid-April. Although she was only standing in as a delegate during Addams' absence, she was coming into her own as an accomplished peace worker. Mrs Clark called her "a splendid member of the Conference and full of ideas for constructive work." Though not disposed to commend her colleagues, even Schwimmer, who had traveled with Balch as private envoys to the northern capitals in mid-1915, valued her talents. And after Schwimmer withdrew into the background, she still sought her friendship and support. For her part, Balch tried to be accommodating but offered this assessment of the Hungarian activist: "Such power, such emotional fervor, such capacity, and all shipwrecked and made to work at least as much for harm as for good, by other qualities perhaps not in her power to control. It is a great tragedy."[71]

Despite these achievements, the organizational health of the Neutral Conference for Continuous Mediation remained shaky. Gaston Plantiff had considerable respect for Lochner's abilities and commitment, but as Ford's agent wanted him to reduce expenses considerably. Liebold even more strongly wanted to rein in costs. Given Schwimmer's extravagance, Lochner could readily agree to considerable trimming of outlays and tighter financial management. But like Schwimmer, though on a more modest scale, he recognized that honoraria and bills for hotels, restaurants, and travel had to be paid, and the conference also needed considerable funds for publicity. Even after Lochner gained some administrative control, he had to deal with Plantiff and Liebold as additional layers of company representatives between him and Ford. Always, it seemed, he was spending an inordinate amount of time trying to wheedle money from the tight-fisted Ford agents. The Ford headquarters later calculated that the expense of the peace ship and the pre-neutral conference organizational efforts was $400,000 ($8 million in 2007), or less than a month's interest out of the automobile magnate's personal wealth at the time of about $150 million ($3 billion). But the neutral conference was costing an additional $30,000 or more a month, and as businessmen, Ford's lieutenants sought to limit costs of a faction-ridden operation that appeared to have little chance of success.[72]

As Schwimmer before him, Lochner felt frustrated at the human barriers between the conference and its benefactor. While constantly prodding Plantiff to get better directions from Ford, he also often wrote to his patron to urge him to return to the conference, even if only for a short time, and to inform him directly of its work and problems. He did not know whether Ford's aides forwarded all Lochner's messages to their boss, whether Ford, who often ignored his mail, read them, or whether his replies, if he made them, were intercepted and confiscated by the government censors. Actually, Dr Jordan, who had a long private meeting with Ford in April 1916, found the Detroit automotive magnate very well informed of developments at his conference. Ford had frequently said that money was no object in his undertaking, and he felt obliged to continue to finance it, albeit on a more modest scale. Having started the undertaking, he would now allow the American and European activists to try to make something of it. At the same time, however, because he never remained focused on his enthusiasms, especially one that had lost its publicity value and seemed to produce recurrent internal crises, he remained in the background, preferring to delegate administrative oversight to his chosen managers.

In April, Ford ordered the reduction in the number of delegates from each country from five to two. Already disturbed by Ford's departure, the European members were dismayed by this decision. They had relied on Ford's leadership of the expedition as sufficient reason for their decision to weather personal criticism for committing themselves to the undertaking. Several had resigned their regular positions in order to join the neutral conference, only soon to find themselves without income. This action of course further aroused the Europeans' suspicions of his devotion to his mediation plans. Lochner professed surprise at the reduction, but it had earlier been discussed as part of the required belt-tightening for the conference. While Schwimmer was still in control, for example, she had successfully resisted Frederick Holt's attempt to impose the same decrease of delegates.[73]

The delegates had barely recovered from the reduction when Plantiff, returning in June from a trip to Detroit, informed them that he had instructions to move the entire conference from Stockholm to The Hague. No reasons were given for this drastic change, which Lochner and the delegates surmised might have been another ploy of Liebold or Mrs Ford to try to destroy the conference. This time, however, the delegates were prepared to resist the order. From its earlier factionalism, the conference had gradually settled down and was moving forward with ambitious plans, which even Frederick Holt, Ford's business agent, had endorsed. When a committee of the conference forcefully detailed these plans to Plantiff, he had to concede that the conference was making headway. "Visibly worried," as Lochner later remembered, Plantiff put off a final decision while he went off to Russia to explore business opportunities for the Ford Motor Company.

By the time he returned in late July, Lochner had developed a compromise, which consisted of dividing the conference into three "peace centers" —one in Stockholm for the three Scandinavian countries, another in Berne, Switzerland, and the third (with the headquarters) in The Hague. Each city would have one or two delegates and some secretarial help, and Lochner as general secretary would move to The Hague headquarters. Expenses, he further proposed, would be kept to a more modest $10,000 a month for the three centers, which was at least a specific amount for the indefinite future. The young American believed that the delegates who now knew and understood each other could still perform effective work in accordance with already generally approved plans. Plantiff, for his part, accepted the compromise because he could tell Ford, who knew none of the European delegates, that the headquarters had been moved to The Hague and that a smaller budget had resulted. Both were supposedly his employer's main interests.[74]

Despite Lochner's ingenuity in keeping the conference alive, he still felt in the dark about Ford's commitment, noting that he had received only one cable from him in more than three months since his benefactor's return to Detroit. As he labored on without Ford's direct blessing, the doubts persisted. He found, for example, that Liebold was writing instructions to Holt to look into certain problems but ignoring him. Finally, he complained, "Plantiff, you have said Ford has great confidence in me, but what evidence is there for it? Where do I stand?"[75] Lochner would receive some answers directly from Ford himself two months later, but they came not because of his complaining, but as a result of his own creative initiatives that would involve him directly in mediation activity between the two belligerent sides.

7

Two Discomfiting Episodes

Ford's private diplomacy seriously discredited the honest efforts of all proponents of neutral mediation, but the movement did not collapse entirely. While the Ford pilgrims were attempting to recruit prominent citizens from the European neutrals to serve as delegates for a private neutral conference, American devotees of the cause continued to promote the proposal at home. Advocates of neutral mediation would have two interviews with President Wilson in January. Before they could launch a new mediation campaign, however, they would confront two new issues that diverted their attention. The first was the question of military preparedness, which would result in a fierce public debate throughout the first half of 1916. No sooner was the issue being resolved in Congress than peace advocates confronted a crisis over military incidents on the nation's southern border that threatened war with Mexico. To the peace proponents, the outcome of the preparedness debate would have serious implications for the future foreign policy of the republic, while the Mexican crisis would provide a practical test of their faith in the efficacy of mediation as an alternative to war.

Throughout 1915 and 1916, the Woman's Peace Party provided much of American citizens' energy for the reformation of U.S. foreign policy. Following its rapid formation, the new group had become the most vibrant entity in the American peace movement. Using mass mailings and meetings throughout the nation, the WPP publicized its sponsorship of the neutral conference for continuous mediation and other principles of international reform as well as its opposition to military preparedness. Still, its vitality derived mainly from its loyal core of dedicated peace advocates, most of whom lived in the Northeast and Middle West. Although the group claimed 165 group memberships, of which 33 were local branches, it had only about 500 dues-paying members, and its program secured the endorsements of only a very few women's clubs. More conservative women believed on patriotic grounds that they should not oppose the President's preparedness program, and many liberals were already committed to the suffrage cause. In consequence, despite many meetings and lecture tours few new state branches were formed. The WPP was more effective educationally in disseminating its program among American women than politically in winning activist support for antipreparedness. Internationally, the International Committee of Women for Permanent Peace, which the women activists had endorsed at The Hague, had already created sections in 15 countries, including the Woman's Peace Party in the United States.[1]

Jane Addams' illness would continue to constrict her movements throughout the first half of 1916, much of which she spent convalescing in California, but she managed to journey to Washington, DC, in mid-January to preside over the group's annual meeting. During her stay in the capital city, she also called on the President at the White House. Wilson's repeated objections to a neutral conference and the recent Ford debacle had convinced her that the immediate prospects for a conference of neutral nations were slight. Thus she merely reviewed the mediation question with the President and reminded him of the possible advantages in calling a neutral conference in the future.[2] But if the interview was inconclusive on mediation, it revealed another side of President Wilson that was significant for his later peace program. During their talk Wilson drew out the list of resolutions of the women's congress at The Hague, which she had presented to him six months earlier. Addams recalled that they had been much handled and read. "You see I have studied these resolutions," he remarked. "I consider them by far the best formulation which up to the moment has been put out by anybody."[3]

Wilson's comment was correct in the sense that the resolutions of the women's congress at The Hague were likely the most comprehensive statement of the general principles for a "new diplomacy" to make a favorable impression on him. But as already noted, by early 1915, ideas for international reform were well known in liberal and radical circles throughout the Western world. In January 1915, Newton Baker, former Democratic mayor of Cleveland and Wilson's friend, had called the President's attention to a magazine article by G. Lowes Dickinson. Prominently involved with the Union of Democratic Control and a founder of the Bryce Group, a group of British Liberals who were exploring alternatives to traditional diplomacy and the creation of a postwar league of nations, Dickinson expounded in the article on the bankruptcy of European statecraft and the need for a "new diplomacy." The President told Baker that he would look up the piece immediately. Whether he in fact read the article is not clear—he never subsequently referred to it—but he began to formulate principles for postwar international relationships about that time, which was a few months before the women's Hague meeting.

In addition, Wilson did not accept all the women's general proposals for international reform. His thoughts on the postwar international order were in fact moving in the direction of accepting the implementation of military sanctions by an association of nations against aggressor states. These notions went beyond what the women pacifists could readily accept. Skeptical of concentrations of power to impose peace, they wanted to limit international cooperation to the imposition of economic sanctions and boycotts on recalcitrant states. It is likely therefore that Wilson's complimentary remarks to Addams about the women's resolutions, while sincere, were also intended to flatter her and win her confidence. Although her foray into the controversial area of peace activism had somewhat tarnished her saintly image, she was still the best known American woman with ties to many like-minded reformers, and Wilson wanted her on his side. No longer simply reactive to her entreaties, he would more actively seek her approval. When he learned that Addams suffered another relapse in the spring of 1916, for instance, he sent her a box of red roses.[4]

Two weeks after his interview with Addams, the President received three leaders of the American Socialist party, who urged Wilson to call a neutral conference for mediation of the war. The Socialists' promotion of a neutral conference was not coincidental. To be sure, they had not actively participated in the mediation campaign, but they were familiar with the neutral conference of the bourgeois pacifists and had early sympathized with it. Several prominent members of the American Socialist party had attended the Emergency Peace Federation Conference in Chicago in late February 1915 at which the peace workers had boosted Grace Wales' proposal for a neutral conference.[5] In May 1915, the National Committee of the Socialist Party had voted that "the President of the United States convoke a congress of neutral nations, which shall offer mediation and remain in permanent session until the termination of the war." In addition, it had adopted a manifesto embodying many of the women pacifists' proposals for international reform as the best hope for constructing a more stable, postwar order.[6] Despite socialist leaders' lauding of the American revolutionary tradition and their bias toward collectivism, most of them shared liberal reformers' democratic values and cooperated easily with them in advancing a progressive internationalist perspective.

When Congress convened in December of that year, the lone Socialist congressman, Meyer London of New York, introduced a joint resolution in the House calling on the President to convene a congress of neutral nations to offer mediation of the war, and at one of the January hearings Addams had testified in its behalf.[7] Later that month three leaders of the Socialist party—London, Morris Hillquit, and James H. Maurer, president of the Pennsylvania Federation of Labor—appeared at the White House specifically to urge Wilson's endorsement of the London resolution.

Scheduled as a courtesy call by the executive committee of the Socialist party, Wilson was unaware of the real purpose of their visit,[8] and he appeared at first too preoccupied and weary to give them more than a perfunctory greeting. But when the Socialists began to talk about a neutral conference, Hillquit recalled that Wilson "became interested and animated and our interview developed into a serious and confidential conversation." They argued that the belligerents, especially the socialists and laborers, had tired of the war and were now receptive to peace talks. They also outlined their peace program and emphasized that their provisions for gradual disarmament and an international court of justice would supplant the present anarchy and provide for a just and lasting peace. Linking mediation to a durable peace settlement, they insisted, would considerably weaken the objections of those who argued that any immediate peace move would favor the Central Powers, which still held the military advantage on the continent.

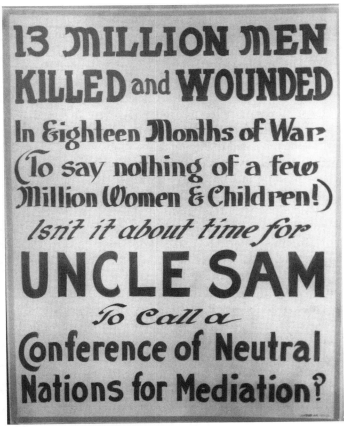

7.1 Call for Mediation, by the New York branch of the Woman's Peace Party, early 1916. (Swarthmore College Peace Collection)

The President was again impeccably polite, expressed his deep interest in restoring peace, and said he differed with them only on the method of approach.[9] He reiterated what he had previously told the peace workers: the other neutrals were too dependent on one belligerent side or the other to mediate dispassionately. He hinted, however, that he might make a direct offer of mediation. His comment failed to satisfy James Maurer, who bluntly remarked, "Your promises sound good, Mr President, but the trouble with you is that you are surrounded by capitalist and militarist interests who want the war to continue; and I fear you will succumb to their influence." This socialist rhetoric mildly amused the President who, placing his hand on Maurer's shoulder, replied candidly: "If the truth be known, I am more often accused of being influenced by radical and pacifist elements than by the capitalist or militarist interests."[10]

Wilson's self-assessment of outside influences on him was much closer to the truth than Maurer's, and his relationship with pacifist and radical opinion would become more intense and complicated during the year. His interview with the socialists on this occasion failed to inspire presidential action for a neutral conference, but he was already exploring the possibility of implementing another mediation formula. He had begun to study the reports of Colonel House, whom he had recently sent to Europe, on the attitudes of the Allied leaders toward American cooperation in ending the war. But House's mission failed to bring about Wilson's mediation. House overestimated the Allied leaders' receptivity to an American peace initiative; and while he managed to negotiate the House–Grey Memorandum in February 1916, which promised American moral, economic, and perhaps even military pressure on the Central Powers when the Allies were ready for peace, Grey never took the agreement very seriously. Much as he seemed to sympathize with the notion of a negotiated peace, his influence in British ruling circles was rapidly declining, and in any event he was a prisoner of Britain's pledge to make peace only jointly with the other Allies. Still wanting to defeat Germany, the Allied leaders would not accept American mediation unless their alliance was in danger of military defeat or political disintegration—and they then perceived no such danger.

Furthermore, despite his high-sounding utterances for a just peace, President Wilson never promised to support any of the Allied war aims, and without ironclad assurances they believed that any outside mediation would involve too many risks for their side. It was all the more risky during the early months of 1916 when the armies of the Central Powers still dominated the European continent. Their forces were entrenched in nearly all of Belgium as well as much of northeastern France extending to the Swiss border; in the East they controlled much of present-day Poland. Enemy troops then occupied no German territory—a military reality that would continue until the end of the war. Finally, the Allies believed that

Germany's submarine warfare might eventually bring the United States into the war on the side of the Allies and tip the balance in their favor. As long as that possibility existed, the Allied leaders were determined to maintain their war effort.[11]

———

In the meantime, public agitation for military preparedness further deflected the attention of the American mediation proponents. The outbreak of the European conflagration had resulted in growing claims of the nation's insecurity and public demands for enhanced military preparedness, but many Americans believed the preparedness agitation had profoundly disturbing implications for America's political culture. The officers of the Woman's Peace Party responded by petitioning Wilson against the dangers of preparedness. Opposing "a preposterous 'preparedness' against hypothetical dangers," they focused on its harmful effects internationally. It would force poorer nations to imitate us, resulting in "rivalry, suspicion and taxation in every country." They also linked the preparedness issue to mediation. "Most important of all," they warned, "it is obvious that increased war preparations in the United States would tend to disqualify our National Executive from rendering the epochal service which this world crisis offers for the establishment of permanent peace."[12]

The President's unveiling of the administration's defense program in early November 1915 galvanized the antipreparedness opposition. To a much later era, in which U.S. military power is projected worldwide, the fierce controversy over military preparedness during the first years of the Great War has an aura of political unreality to it. Considering the nation's large coastline, geographical size, and responsibilities in protecting the Philippines, Hawaii, and Puerto Rico, the U.S. military establishment during the first year or so of American neutrality was not particularly large. The navy was already the second or third largest in the world, but its standing army was miniscule.[13]

The debate over preparedness brought directly into the political arena what had actually been distinctive crosscurrents in the foreign policy of the United States since its emergence as a major world power at the turn of the century. The nation was in fact between two worlds. The first revealed its continuing reluctance to jettison deeply ingrained isolationist and antimilitarist attitudes, and the other world was much more outward-looking but exemplified its own internal tensions between the pursuit of imperial glory and a desire to be the harbinger of a new, peaceful international order. The nation had gotten over its imperialistic moment during and immediately after the Spanish–American War, with the annexation of new territories as far away as the Philippines, and the Wilson administration was successfully sponsoring legislation that would prepare the Filipinos for eventual independence. The more positive aspect of this outward-looking was the nation's long-standing irenic mission that included advocacy of arbitration, conciliation, and mediation for the peaceful resolution of international disputes.

In the early years of the European war, American opponents of preparedness comprised an uneasy mixture of the isolationist world and the pacifistic side of its internationalist one. The United States had a widely revered antimilitary tradition and had experienced a century of "free security" without overt European interference. Suddenly to countenance an enlarged military establishment, even in the face of new dangers to the nation's security growing out of the European conflagration, was an unsettling development and, for many Americans, not to be blithely accepted. These opponents of preparedness found the President's call for a greatly enlarged and accelerated five-year building and recruitment program for the Navy very unsettling, but even more troubling was his plan for a drastic reorganization and expansion of the army, complete with the creation of a national reserve force of some 400,000 men over three years. While Wilson only talked of the "enlistment" and brief training sessions each year of these "citizen soldiers," opponents saw it as a prelude to "compulsory" military service, that is, a draft, since the army could not come close to recruiting sufficient volunteers.

By the end of 1915 a group of New York antimilitarists met at the Henry Street settlement to organize the Anti-Preparedness Committee. Many of the same activists who had participated in the Henry Street meetings on mediation were in the forefront of the new voluntary association, which soon was renamed the American Union Against Militarism (AUAM). Although Kellogg, Villard, Wald, Crystal Eastman, George Foster Peabody, and others prominently identified with the pacifists' mediation campaign were active members, the orientation of the new organization was as much antimilitarist as pacifist. The New York millionaire lawyer Amos Pinchot—younger brother of Gifford, the reform-minded conservationist—was not an absolute pacifist, but he joined the new group because he was convinced that the interests of organized wealth and privilege he was then fighting were behind the preparedness agitation. "[T]he shouters of exorbitant armament are using preparedness as an argument with which to entrench more firmly the doctrine of the sacredness of monopoly and extortion," Pinchot wrote the President. Another loyal supporter, Rabbi Stephen S. Wise, an idealistic liberal reformer, declared, "I am not a peace at any price man."[14]

The AUAM deliberately avoided the ideologically laden word "peace" in its title and tried to project a message that would find a responsive chord in mainstream America. It rejected the old Jeffersonian "bugaboo" against a standing army and would accept "sane" preparedness, but its members objected to a large-scale army or major military increases. They also strenuously opposed military education in the public schools and compulsory military training. The "union" in the title referred to the purposeful joining together of many interest groups and common citizens nationwide in that fight, and the AUAM invited a wide range of associations—granges, labor unions, church groups, social clubs, for example—to cooperate with their new organization. It had some success in organizing branches in several cities and in states extending to California and Washington on the West coast. Despite its outreach efforts, the AUAM never had more than several thousand members, and only a fraction of them contributed financially to the group. Not surprisingly, the AUAM was usually in debt, but made up for its financial weakness with an articulate and energetic leadership.[15]

The antimilitarists' main arguments were all appeals to their conception of the nation's "traditions." In their view, military programs in the schools were new and radical departures from the past. Since the outbreak of the European war, the antipreparedness movement had attracted some conservatives who feared that the preparedness agitation, if successful, would undermine the American antimilitarist tradition.[16] But the main drive and force behind the AUAM were pacifistic liberals and moderate socialists. They shared the conservatives' fears of the deleterious impact of an extensive military program on their vision of the good society, but were more willing to become actively engaged in the AUAM's grassroots challenge to the preparedness forces. They perceived that their efforts to reform American capitalism also encompassed the taming of the private armament interests, which profited from military preparedness and war. More than the conservative preparedness foes, they emphasized that the main promoters of compulsory military training were businessmen who advocated conscription as a vehicle for social control.

Preparedness advocates indeed argued that military training would impose discipline and obedience on young men who in their view otherwise tended to be slouchy, ill-formed, and independent-minded, and they hit a nerve among moderate opinion that could well be shaken from its materialism and complacency over the European war. As a newspaper editor wrote Pinchot, the preparedness campaign would be worthwhile "if it only served for a time to lift this nation out of the sordid pot-bellied, fat-joweled state into which it is getting as a result of its orgy of money-making." Moreover, in an undisciplined, multi-ethnic, and flabby society, preparedness might promote social unity, renewed virility, and a sense of adventure and national purpose. In a sense, it would be the moral equivalent of war. Even some advanced progressive reformers, including Walter Lippmann and Herbert Croly of the liberal *New Republic*, expressed such views.[17]

The opponents of preparedness claimed, however, that its advocates really wanted unthinking individuals to behave as machines, automatically obeying authority. In its baldest terms, they asserted that "preparedness is militarism," and the issue at hand was "democracy versus militarism."[18] Some critics went further in trying to show intimate, self-interested links between the munitions firms, on the one hand, and the Navy League, National Security League, and patriotic societies, on the other. They saw a parallel between preparedness agitation in America and the European experience with German militarism and ruinous arms races that had culminated in the current bloodbath on the continent. Crystal Eastman charged, for instance, "The whole 'preparedness' campaign is built upon a lie, which is that a two-power navy and great army would assure liberty, prosperity and peace. Millions are dying in Europe to prove that is a lie." These critics claimed that under the guise of defending the nation's security, the preparedness forces tried to whip up fears of foreign invasion and jingo patriotism to further their own imperialistic aims and profits.[19]

Despite its nonpacifist emphasis, the AUAM cooperated closely with the Woman's Peace Party on the preparedness issue, especially its activist New York branch. Some women, like Alice Lewisohn, Gertrude Pinchot (Amos' wife), and Crystal Eastman were active in both groups. Despite her aversion to single-sex peace groups, Eastman quickly rationalized that a woman's peace organization filled a practical need and became president of the WPP's New York branch. Above all, she valued the WPP's international perspective and extolled the warring women meeting at The Hague. That they could discuss "the war problems sanely and in friendship while all their male relatives were out shooting each other," she wrote, "is to my mind a great and significant event in history," and she called for women to support and strengthen the women's peace movement. At the same time Eastman also actively supported the AUAM's national perspective by serving as its executive secretary.

At its annual meeting in early January, the WPP leadership decided to make 1916 the year of Congress, and it developed a congressional program that included opposition to increases in military preparedness and to compulsory military service. The AUAM likewise focused on the Congress, and despite its New York base located its headquarters in Washington, DC, and hired Charles T. Hallinan, who had earlier served as a publicist for the NAWSA, as its lobbyist on Capitol Hill. AUAM–WPP cooperation included their common use of a pâpier-maché model of a dinosaur named "Jingo." The model displayed the caption, "all armor plate – no brains. This animal believed in full military 'Preparedness' – He is now extinct!" The WPP had created the dinosaur for an exhibit, and the AUAM borrowed it for display at its public meetings.[20]

In the first months of 1916, antipreparedness advocates testified at several congressional hearings. The thrust of their testimony was that the nation's

7.2 Crystal Eastman and Amos Pinchot, about 1916. (Bain Collection, Library of Congress)

security was still protected by two enormous oceans, and the continuing European conflagration had exhausted the major European powers militarily and financially. They argued that the current agitation for a greatly enlarged military and naval establishment was emotion-based hysteria, since even if one side, already seriously weakened by the military conflict on the continent, should emerge victorious, the logistical obstacles would preclude any invasion of the United States. And preparedness, far from preventing war, became synonymous with it. As Addams remarked, "If we get ready for war, it will surely come."

Aware that their opposition made them seem negative, if not obstructionist, the preparedness foes also lost no opportunity to describe more positive, alternative programs to an enlarged military establishment. They emphasized the importance of reason and sanity to revive respect for old peacemaking mechanisms, such as The Hague Court, and the promotion of enlightened principles of a "new diplomacy," which would be embedded in the peace settlement. For example, Addams predictably focused on the constructive role of independent commissions in resolving complicated policy issues. Arguing historically from domestic policy, she noted that the Labor Department put out many valuable reports, but an industrial commission established by the Congress had profitably investigated labor conditions "in quite a different way and from a different viewpoint." So, too, she believed that the War and Navy Departments could not investigate themselves impartially, but a congressionally mandated commission could study the entire question of military preparedness. Such a commission, she was confident, would establish the "facts," which would expose the supposed dangers to the nation's security as very remote, and defuse the "panic" on the issue. She also suggested that Congress should create commissions to study the question of aliens and recently increased tensions in Asia, as they impacted on foreign nations. Finally, she reviewed for the lawmakers the neutral conference proposal, another "scientific" innovation, which would receive recommendations from the warring nations, open communications between them, and hopefully facilitate public discussion of the proposed peace terms as a valuable organ in the transition between the war and the peace settlement.[21]

As Congress began intense debate on preparedness, Wilson, temporarily distracted by his marriage to Mrs Galt and subsequent honeymoon, had not paid careful attention to the growing opposition to his program. Prodded by his advisers and leading Democrats, however, he came to realize that a hard fight for preparedness lay ahead, and he soon embarked on an eight-day speaking tour stretching from New York through the Middle West to drum up public support for his program. Wilson was reacting less against the antipreparedness forces on the left than the partisan attacks by Republicans to his right who were hoping to make his seeming indifferent leadership on preparedness a political issue in the coming presidential election. Avoiding details in his speeches, the President appealed in general terms for public support for his "necessary," "practical," and "reasonable" preparedness program. Only at his last stop in St Louis did he mention his antipreparedness opponents, referring to them rather contemptuously as "hopelessly and contentedly provincial," and he challenged them to "hire large halls" to argue for their position. He had little doubt that exposure of their views would demonstrate their "folly."[22] Taking the President's remarks as a challenge, the AUAM assembled a group of speakers, including Rabbi Wise, Amos Pinchot, and the Congregationalist minister A.A. Berle, on a speaking pilgrimage that followed most of Wilson's earlier route. They hired "large halls" and spoke to overflow audiences in 11 cities.[23]

Despite the antimilitarists' strong and sometimes angry rhetoric, the antipreparedness advocates were far from inflexibly opposed to Wilson. They mostly approved of his policies and had no desire to break with him on preparedness. Shortly before the announcement of the administration's preparedness program, for example, Peabody effused that Wilson was "all in all the wisest and greatest leader this country has ever had." A lifelong Democrat and former treasurer of the national party, Peabody perhaps was predisposed to like the President, but his personal admiration of him was also heart-felt and genuine. Like Peabody, David Starr Jordan also opposed preparedness but, believing the President was "the most precious asset of the cause of peace," refrained from public criticisms of him.[24] Indeed, despite the preparedness foes' disappointment with the President, they engaged during the national security debate in a kind of elaborate dance in which the "partners" circled and parried each other, but never came close to leaving the dance floor.

To be sure, in his determination to get a robust preparedness program, Wilson occasionally got carried away. His sneering at the opposition in St Louis was one example; another was his exhortation in the same address for the United States to have "incomparably the greatest navy in the world."[25] Moreover, toward the end of the debate, he led a preparedness parade down Pennsylvania Avenue, which to his detractors made him appear as a superpatriot who was far removed from his posturing as a humanitarian and internationalist. Watching the parade with a jaundiced eye, Ellen Slayden, the wife of a pacifistic Texan congressman and a WPP member herself, depicted the President, dressed in "white trousers, a short blue sack coat, and straw hat . . . in the forefront switching a little [American] flag like a drum major's baton" and walking "with a swagger, not a vestige of the Presbyterian elder left about him."[26]

On the whole, however, Wilson maintained a moderate posture. When he realized that the army continental plan had very little support in Congress, he told key Democratic congressional leaders that he was not committed to any single plan but would consider alternatives, including legislation to enlarge the National Guard. And when his secretary of war, Lindley Garrison, intractably committed to the continental army plan, made it an issue of principle, Wilson allowed him to resign. He also came out early against compulsory military service. Throughout the debate he also remained mostly respectful of the antipreparedness opposition. Early on, for instance, in response to Rabbi Wise's complaints about administration's preparedness program, Wilson replied that their disagreement "does not affect in the least my estimate of you or my personal feeling."[27] For their part, many preparedness foes tempered their criticisms of the President. On the antipreparedness tour, Wise attacked "militarism," not Wilson, and disapproved of those colleagues who criticized him.[28] The antimilitarists also believed that the appointment of Newton Baker as the new secretary of

7.3 President Wilson leading preparedness parade, Washington, DC, June 14, 1916. (Brown Brothers)

war, signified that the President was moving in their direction on the issue. Believing war was an anachronism, Baker had been a strong critic of the army and had early joined an antipreparedness group. When Wilson appointed Baker, he was unaware of his pacifistic leanings, but his new secretary, a proven administrator, would be a good team player and would not disappoint him.[29] The antimilitarists only gradually came to realize that despite Baker's professed "antimilitarism," he faithfully supported the President and his defense buildup.

The antipreparedness tour confirmed that despite the AUAM's eastern base, its arguments against military preparedness resonated more clearly further west. Indeed, among its most vigorous champions were many southern and western members of Congress. And William Jennings Bryan, still a leading spokesman for rural and small-town America, claimed that the administration's preparedness policy was a "revolutionary" departure from "the traditions of the country," and many of the Great Commoner's loyal followers as well as other inland or rural progressives echoed his sentiments.[30] They differed mainly in emphasis from their eastern allies. The latter considered themselves true internationalists, while the opposition among some southern and many western congressmen focused mainly on military preparedness as a movement that would betray the nation's traditional isolationism. Both agreed, however, that the nation faced more danger from business and reactionary supporters of preparedness inside the country than from outside powers.

Isolationist sentiment in Congress was already showing its strength in a threatened revolt against the administration on the issue of American citizens traveling on armed passenger vessels. Following Germany's announcement in early February that its submarines would soon begin to attack armed enemy merchantmen, congressmen introduced resolutions requiring the administration to warn Americans traveling on such ships. Many members of Congress, and probably a majority in the House, believing it was unnecessary to go to war to vindicate Americans' rights to travel on armed merchantmen, wanted to acquiesce in the German announcement. This attitude was particularly pervasive among congressmen from the Middle West. Correctly seeing the resolutions as pro-German, Wilson at first objected to them because they angered the Allies and would quickly derail the pro-Allied House–Grey mediation understanding. A larger reason was that the resolutions were a threat to Wilson's authority in the foreign policy arena, which he perceived as a presidential prerogative. He acted quickly, but it took all of his energy and leadership skills in late February and early March to beat down the resolutions and to reassert his control over American diplomacy.[31]

The AUAM speakers were pleasantly surprised and encouraged by the enthusiastic public reception they received during their journey through the Middle West, and they asked Wilson to hear their report of their tour. The President's immediate reaction was negative, telling Tumulty that it was "literally impossible for me to have these people come and make speeches to me." Tumulty replied, however, that he did not see how his chief could turn down Lillian Wald, who as AUAM president was to lead the delegation, and, once persuaded, Wilson agreed to see them. A pattern was emerging in which Wilson initially refused meetings with activists, but eventually ended up seeing them. Much of his resistance derived from the certainty of his position. Once he had made up his mind on issues, there was in his view little reason for further discussion. Throughout his career, he was in fact much more comfortable articulating his well-developed views on current issues to large audiences than debating small groups who had different views. House generally agreed with the President's personal physician, Dr Cary T. Grayson, who remarked about that time that Wilson "is intolerant of advice" and "ceases to have any liking for" people who urged him "to do something contrary to his own conviction." House also observed that Wilson "does not like to meet people and isolates himself as much as anyone I have ever known."[32] Wilson's confidants exaggerated somewhat, for at least in the case of the mediation advocates Wilson had met with many of them over the previous 18 months and had listened to them patiently. He also allowed his advisers, particularly Tumulty, to persuade him on occasion to see prospective visitors. Nevertheless, Wilson was not naturally outgoing and did not readily socialize with members of Congress or his cabinet. He also had agreed to see most of the peace advocates reluctantly—Addams was an outstanding exception—and only after his objections had been overcome.

In preparing for the interview, the AUAM delegation had at first agreed to submit to Wilson a broad petition including discussion of democratic control of foreign policy and "the necessity for calling a conference of neutral nations," but Hallinan set them straight. If they covered other issues besides preparedness, he argued, they would "be bathed in the typical Wilsonian speech, all generalities and righteousness," and the press would dismiss them as a women's pacifist organization "begging the President to stop the war." Preparedness, he continued, was the political issue of the moment, especially because their own recent tour as well as Bryan and Ford, prominent public figures, were stirring up opposition to the administration's program in the Middle West. Hallinan's argument was on the mark. Returning home from his European peace adventure, Ford had continued his outspoken opposition to military preparedness, even expounding his views in full-page advertisements in metropolitan newspapers. More importantly, he had recently won the GOP presidential primary in Michigan without even announcing his candidacy, and he attributed his electoral success there (as well as a close second to another peace and isolationist candidate in the Nebraska primary) as a victory for peace and antipreparedness. If the prospects of Bryan challenging the President's candidacy or Ford as Wilson's Republican opponent in the November election were very remote, the wellspring of organized public opposition to preparedness might move him to make concessions to Democratic antipreparedness elements to maintain a semblance of party harmony.[33]

Stiffened by their lobbyist, several AUAM members went to the White House. Headed by Lillian Wald, the delegation also included Pinchot, Wise, Berle, John A. McSparren, master of the Pennsylvania State Grange, and Max Eastman, Crystal's brother and socialist editor of the *avant-garde* magazine, *The Masses*.[34] The delegates gave the President a prepared statement summarizing their arguments against preparedness and then spoke at length about their trip and their concerns. They particularly emphasized the opposition to preparedness among organized labor and farm organizations like the National Grange, and they discussed their real fears over recent legislation in New York State, requiring six weeks of military training for all young men by the National Guard. Wilson, emphasizing in his replies the distinction between reasonable preparedness and militarism, had little difficulty in dealing with the delegation. When Wise remarked, for example, that an army of 250,000 was an increase of

150 percent, Wilson conceded that the number might be too large, but when you started from a "wholly inadequate number," then the percentage addition was not "extravagant." Historical traditions, he argued, could not be a guide in the current time of "madness" and "excitement, more profound than the world has ever known before. All the world is seeing red. No standard we have ever had obtains any longer." The "facts" and "circumstances" required an enlarged military establishment, and he was confident that the administration would "act on those facts with restraint, with reasonableness." He also distinguished between military training and universal service. The latter would impose military discipline and could threaten democratic values, but the former, involving only six weeks of training, would not really warp recruits' thinking.

Wilson also made interesting remarks on the place of force in international affairs. The antimilitarists placed much faith in the power and influence of moral suasion in world politics, but Wilson conceded only that the moral force of the people permitted a somewhat smaller military establishment than the nation's enormous territory might otherwise require. He then went on to give a glimpse of his own vision of the role of force in the postwar world. If the nations in the postwar world created an international organization for the preservation of peace, as he hoped, then it would require the physical means to make it "bite." Moral force would provide the opinion that would authorize the ultimate application of military force to preserve the peace, and he concluded, "Now, in the last analysis the peace of society is obtained by force."[35]

The President's interview with the AUAM members worked to his advantage. Just agreeing to see them indicated that he was not shying away from argument, and he showed interest in their presentation, especially about the New York legislation and the Grange's opposition, without compromising his views on preparedness. Seeming to speak for the delegation following the interview, Lillian Wald conceded that "we know at heart he is an anti-militarist." Max Eastman wrote in *The Masses* that the AUAM participants "agreed that we had been handled beautifully. The President had taken us into his intellectual bosom ... The whole interview in his hands became a friendly harmonious discussion of how 'we' could meet the difficulties of national defense without the risks of militarism." More than that, Wilson indicated that he was searching for international arrangements that would check the current worldwide militaristic fervor. To Eastman, Wilson, "sensing the tragedy of the world today and apprehending a road out into the future," stood in stark contrast to Roosevelt's preparedness message of rapid nationalism, the same jingoist spirit that had brought on the war.[36]

Of the AUAM delegates, only Rabbi Wise seemed unmoved by the President's arguments. Picking up on Wilson's "seeing red" comments, he remarked: "Because the world sees red must we, too, see red? . . . Are we to enter the armament gamble, in which every nation loses and hell alone is victorious?" He even commented privately that Wilson had "undergone a grave moral deterioration." Substance was more important than form to these antimilitarists, but Wilson's friendly demeanor and reasoned argument surely softened their opposition.[37]

In the end, the antipreparedness forces could take a little satisfaction in the military programs Congress authorized. The final army legislation provided for only a modest increase in the regular army and a much larger expansion of a federalized National Guard as a reserve force. Compulsory service, military training in the schools, and a draft were avoided, the AUAM gratefully reported, but its leaders criticized the generous "subsidy" to the Guard as encouraging an entrenched Washington lobby that would bilk Congress for more funding in the future. Congressman Slayden told his wife that a vote on the army bill "showed a curious influence of the Ford Peace Movement. Strange," she commented, "if a thing so shallow and fantastic should have done good after all. Perhaps the legislature heard by this means that there was such a thing as a peace movement."[38] Ford's highly publicized views on peace and preparedness, more than any movement, may have had some effect in helping to solidify isolationist sentiment that was already well rooted in Congress.

The naval program was initially not as contentious, but the Senate added tonnage to the administration's proposal and wanted to begin the building program over three years instead of five. Wilson came to favor the larger, more accelerated Senate bill and exerted steady pressure on the congressional conference committee to report on an agreed version, which the Congress finally passed in late July. Wilson did not indicate the specific reasons for his acceptance of a larger naval program. Protecting his right flank from Republican criticisms in the upcoming presidential elections may have been involved, although Wilson never directly mentioned domestic politics as a factor. His recent speech to the League to Enforce Peace had articulated his general support for America's involvement in a postwar association of nations, and a robust navy would demonstrate this commitment. He was also becoming fearful of Japan's expansionist pretensions and the possibilities of reactionaries gaining control in Britain. In any event, Claude Kitchin (D-N.C.), the House Majority Leader and a strong critic of preparedness, was bitterly disappointed with the new legislation. "Approval of this building program," he charged, "means that the United States today becomes the most militaristic naval nation on earth" and "condemns our provisions for National arbitration and world peace as hypocrisy and mockery."[39]

Kitchin's criticism went further than that of even the most dedicated AUAM members, who admitted failure overall, but still saw a few positive features for which they legitimately claimed some credit. The final naval legislation provided, for example, for the construction of a government armor plate factory, which would dilute the private armament companies' profits and influence on the government. It also contained a rider, introduced by Representative Walter Hensley, a "small navy" Democrat from Missouri, authorizing U.S. participation, with funding, in a postwar international conference to consider disarmament and new machinery for the peaceful settlement of disputes. Thus if the war ended during the multi-year construction program, an arms reduction accord might make its completion unnecessary. Hallinan called the Hensley clause "a pacifist victory;" while Crystal Eastman argued that if acted upon after the war, it would make the naval legislation "so much waste paper." Curiously, when Charles Levermore, a graduate school colleague of Wilson's and a professional peace worker, had earlier suggested such legislation, Wilson had objected, calling it a "mistake" because the belligerents were "most resentful" of U.S. suggestions relating to the postwar world, but Congress proceeded to include it anyway.[40]

The antipreparedness forces soon found additional comfort for their efforts a few months later. To pay for the military increases, reform-minded congressmen, predominately from the South and West, argued that if the more affluent classes, mainly in the Northeast, wanted military preparedness, ostensibly for patriotic reasons, but also because it would provide additional security for their wealth, then they should be willing to pay for it. Acting on this thinking, Congress passed a revenue measure that sharply increased inheritance and normal income tax rates for the wealthy, including a surtax on much higher incomes, and raised the tax on munitions manufacturers to a maximum of 12½ percent. Wilson did not intervene in this very contentious wrangling in Congress and signed the bill into law in early September.[41]

———

Even as the preparedness issue was playing out in Congress, the United States faced a more immediate crisis over Mexico. President Wilson had learned from his early experiences in Mexican–American relations, especially the Vera Cruz encounter, to be more patient and forbearing toward his southern neighbor. Venustiano Carranza, the First Chief of the constitutionalist forces, emerged as the dominant political force in Mexico. After the Wilson administration recognized the Carranza government in October 1915, the situation had seemed to stabilize somewhat, but the rise of Pancho Villa, a renegade army officer challenging the Carranza regime, again threatened the prospect of U.S. military intervention. In January 1916, his bandits had stopped a train in northern Mexico and ruthlessly gunned down 18 Americans on board. Two months later, he and his followers invaded the border town of Columbus, New Mexico, looted and wreaked destruction and killed 19 Americans, many of whom were innocent civilian residents. Excited opinion in the United States demanded revenge for the massacres, and Congress drafted resolutions authorizing the president to send armed forces into Mexico.

Following the Columbus attack, Wilson sent a punitive expedition under General John Pershing into northern Mexico to protect American lives and property. Fortunately for Wilson in that case, Carranza, with steady pressure from Washington, ordered his army to pursue the murderers and soon had successfully captured or killed many of them. With the Carranza commander threatening to resist the punitive expedition's pursuit of Villa into Mexican territory, however, the prospect of war escalated. Wilson meanwhile resisted pressures from his cabinet, Congress, and his close advisers, all of whom argued that war was the only honorable and politically acceptable course. In an impassioned talk with his secretary, he explained the reasons for his restraint:

> Tumulty, you are Irish, and, therefore, full of fight. I know how deeply you feel about this Columbus affair. Of course, it is tragical and deeply regrettable from every standpoint, but in the last analysis I, and not the Cabinet or you, must bear the responsibility for every action that is to be taken. I have to sleep with my conscience in these matters and I shall be held responsible for every drop of blood that may be spent in the enterprise of intervention . . . I came from the South and I know what war is, for I have seen its wreckage and terrible ruin. It is easy for me as President to declare war. I do not have to fight, and neither do the gentlemen on the Hill who now clamour for it. It is some poor farmer's boy, or son of some poor widow away off in some modest community, or perhaps the scion of a great family, who will have to do the fighting and the dying. I will not resort to war against Mexico until I have exhausted every means to keep out of this mess. I know they will call me a coward and a quitter, but that will not disturb me. Time, the great solvent, will, I am sure, vindicate this policy of humanity and forbearance.[42]

More practical considerations likely reinforced his caution. He well knew that Villa and his compatriots, hoping to benefit politically at home from U.S. military intervention, were deliberately trying to provoke the Wilson administration. For Wilson to overreact would only be doing the desperadoes' bidding. In the back of his mind, too, was his realization that a full-scale war against Mexico would render his nation vulnerable in any diplomatic showdown with Germany, which was his major preoccupation, and hapless militarily against that nation if U.S. forces were fighting in

Mexico. He already had some intimations (though none ever conclusively verified) that German agents were secretly trying to encourage Villa, if not the Carranza government, to foment a U.S.–Mexican war. The Mexican situation was a vexing foreign policy distraction, but Wilson did not want it to escalate to the point where it would consume his administration. He thus needed to act to forestall more extreme congressional action, but simultaneously try to avoid full-scale military involvement by seeking some possible accommodation with the First Chief.

Again, Carranza saved Wilson from testing his patience by temporarily allowing Pershing's men to enter Mexico. Nevertheless, the continuance of the U.S. troops in Mexico in futile pursuit of Villa increased the tension with the Carranza regime, which was criticized on all sides at home for permitting American soldiers' incursion on their soil. Diplomatic exchanges between the two governments only further exposed their real differences and ratcheted up the crisis.[43] A showdown was expected, and it soon came in the wake of a cavalry patrol, which Pershing sent out on a scouting mission to investigate reports of Mexican troop movements. As the U.S. forces tried to pass through the town of Carrizal on June 21, they confronted forces of the de facto government and firing began. Many American and Mexican soldiers were killed and wounded; 17 American soldiers were taken prisoner.

While still trying to ascertain the specific actions leading to the Carrizal incident, Wilson was led to believe from sketchy and somewhat conflicting first reports that either the Mexicans deliberately wanted war or that the Americans had been the aggressors. At a minimum, however, he believed he had to uphold the right to defend American citizens on Mexican soil and to demand the return of the American prisoners with an apology. On June 26, five days after the Carrizal encounter, an American captain's report reached Wilson. Although the report clearly confirmed that the U.S. commanding officer (who had been killed in the fighting) had exceeded Pershing's clear instructions to avoid confrontation with Mexican forces, if at all possible, and had attacked the Mexican troops after being refused permission to pass through Carrizal, Wilson was convinced that Carranza would reject his demands and, even if he yielded, be unable to restrain his soldiers in northern Mexico. On the same day, he drafted a lengthy war message asking for authority to use the nation's military forces to restore order in Mexican states along the U.S. border and, if required, go further into Mexican territory until a constitutional government had been established that could restore order. Still, before going before the Congress, he waited until he received a report from General Pershing as well as a reply from the Carranza government on the scene.

Meanwhile, those hoping to avoid war were raising their voices. Pacifists and antimilitarists would have objected to war in any event, but some of them were intimately acquainted with Mexico and thought they had a good understanding of the difficulties facing the Mexican people during its current revolution. Peabody had invested heavily in Mexican railroads and mining concerns for a generation, Dr Jordan had taken extended visits in that country, and Amos Pinchot had once lived there for several years. Peabody in particular had reason to advocate U.S. military intervention to protect his business interests and foster law and order, but his pacifism led him to oppose U.S. military action. They were all acutely aware of Mexico's difficult social and economic problems and would have special personal reasons for wanting to avert major bloodshed with their southern neighbor.[44]

Almost immediately after hearing of the Carrizal incident, the AUAM and other peace groups wired Wilson that continued U.S. troops in Mexico were a national humiliation to Mexicans and to withdraw them and seek mediation. More positively, the AUAM appointed an unofficial committee of "representative" private citizens, three from each country, to meet in El Paso and investigate the incident. They named Bryan, Jordan, and Frank P. Walsh, former head of the U.S. Commission on Industrial Relations, for the U.S. side. Speaking for the committee, Amos Pinchot remarked that such a body "can get at the facts, present them with fairness to both sides, and give the President and the people of both countries a chance to avoid a wicked and senseless war."[45]

The antimilitarist group also sent telegrams to the embassies of the ABC powers (Argentina, Brazil, and Chile), asking them to offer mediation. The Latin American governments needed no prodding and, recalling the mediation by the ABC powers that had earlier helped to resolve the Vera Cruz crisis, were already sounding out the Wilson administration on accepting their good offices for mediation of the dispute. Wilson was well aware of the AUAM-sponsored joint commission and probably also of its pleas for Latin American mediation. Lansing argued, however, that because the de facto government was "wholly responsible for the lives lost and for the capture and imprisonment of American soldiers," the U.S. demand for justice was "not the proper subject for mediation." Wilson seemed to side with his secretary of state, even though his refusal of mediation—it was also problematical that the Carranza government would have accepted it—effectively sabotaged the administration's policy of pan-American cooperation and might bring on war.[46]

Because of the U.S. Government's hostility to mediation, the AUAM's unofficial body got off to a poor start. The Mexican appointees and Dr Jordan, who had been lecturing in Oklahoma City, immediately went to El Paso, but Bryan, not wanting to embarrass Wilson without official approval, refused the invitation when his government sources indicated the administration's opposition. And Walsh accepted at first, but then declined, when he learned of the War Department's objections. Ultimately,

Moorfield Storey, the septuagenarian Boston anti-imperialist, and Paul Kellogg joined Jordan as the Americans on the unofficial commission, and the indefatigable Crystal Eastman served as secretary. After moving to the Willard Hotel in Washington, the commissioners first sent identical telegrams in Spanish to Wilson and Carranza on July 4, urging a cooling-off period, both militarily and diplomatically, until the official joint commission could deliberate soberly on the controversial questions.[47]

Meanwhile, the crisis was also galvanizing many other concerned citizens who began sending messages urging restraint to the White House. On June 27, the AUAM published a half-page advertisement in major newspapers, which reprinted the captain's report to show that "the Carrizal episode does not constitute a just cause of war" and argued that the Mexicans could not be blamed for resisting further U.S. advances on their soil. It further urged citizens to contact their congressmen to resist war. The advertisements provoked much public comment and also likely stimulated more appeals for peace to the White House.[48] The AUAM also cooperated with the local WPP branch, labor, and other antipreparedness groups at public meetings, which passed resolutions urging U.S. restraint and acceptance of third-party mediation. The WPP executive committee endorsed a peace resolution in Chicago, and additional public meetings in Boston, New York, Philadelphia, Seattle, and elsewhere passed similar petitions. Many of these groups were AUAM and WPP branches, but socialist, labor, and religious groups, especially Quakers and other Protestant denominations, also expressed opposition to a military solution. Telegrams and letters embodying antiwar sentiments and earnest suggestions for arbitration or mediation poured into the White House.[49] Besides the Hearst press and a few jingoes, there was little public enthusiasm for war, while antiwar sentiment gained full expression. Altogether, Arthur Link calculates, the telegrams to the President "ran ten to one against any form of war with Mexico."[50]

Some deputations also went to Washington hoping to present their petitions to Wilson personally,[51] although apparently only one group—consisting of Irving Fisher, the reform-minded Yale professor of political economy, Harry Overstreet of City College, and Gertrude Pinchot—got to see him. Wilson seemed to believe war might still occur, however, telling his visitors at their June 28 meeting that in the present crisis "acts must follow words." While expressing sympathy for the difficulties of the Mexican people and their desire for self-government, he continued to insist "that the lives and liberty of our own people shall be safe from the depredations of Mexican bandits."[52] In response to the WPP antiwar resolution, he wrote Jane Addams in a similar vein on the same day: "My heart is for peace, and I wish that we were dealing with those who would not make it impossible for us."[53] In the evening of June 28 or the next morning, however,

Wilson learned that Carranza had agreed to return the prisoners, which somewhat defused the crisis. More messages poured in to the White House calling on the President to continue his forbearance and to push for a peaceful settlement. As one journalist reported, "Hundreds of telegrams were delivered to the White House this morning urging the President to take all possible steps for peace with Mexico. Many of the telegrams suggested that the United States ought to be willing to arbitrate the questions in dispute. White House officials seemed to regard the great bulk of telegrams as a pretty marked indication of the feeling of the country."[54]

The return of the prisoners removed Wilson's most immediate serious problem, but he still had to decide whether to continue to press his larger demand for assurances from Carranza of no further attacks on U.S. forces in Mexico under any conditions. Nevertheless, even without such assurances Wilson immediately began to move rapidly away from military action against Mexico and to strike out boldly for a peaceful solution.[55] Wilson read many if not all the appeals for peace coming to the White House, and he personally acknowledged many of them. His replies strongly suggest that the rising antiwar chorus had clearly moved him.[56] He wanted a peaceful solution from the outset, but had sent Pershing into Mexico to defend American honor and to protect himself from partisan attacks on his seemingly ineffectual foreign policy. Perceiving the absence of strong outcries for war with Mexico and the widespread public antiwar sentiment, he moved quickly toward a resolution of the crisis once Carranza had returned the prisoners. Wilson's pursuit of peace was undoubtedly aided by the similar restraint of Mexico's First Chief, who also did not want war, but felt he had to resist further incursions of Pershing's forces on Mexican territory. Shortly, the two leaders agreed to establish a joint commission, which would allow for passions to cool while trying to resolve the contentious issues.[57]

The appointment of the U.S.–Mexican commission was of course exactly what the antimilitarists and pacifists had proposed in the first place. It too was composed of private citizens but, appointed by the two governments, had official sanction. The mixed commission met first in New London, Connecticut, and later in Atlantic City, after the AUAM-appointed unofficial peace commission had already begun its sessions in Washington. The unofficial body made clear that it did not want to meddle in the governmental negotiations, but was prepared to share its information and insights with the official commission, if desired. It solicited testimony from scholars and others well acquainted with aspects of U.S.–Mexican relations—for example, on the origins of U.S. concessions in Mexico— and issued statements designed to educate Americans on the sources of the Mexican revolution and the possibilities for constructive engagement between nongovernmental organizations in the two countries. Jordan's later assessment of the role of the private commission was modest: "Whether or not the unofficial efforts contributed to the final result I do not know."[58]

Actually, the unofficial body had no discernible impact on the Wilson administration, but one of its main contacts, the well-known muckraking journalist Lincoln Steffens, attended many of its meetings and made himself generally useful to the unofficial commissioners. And ultimately he gained access to President Wilson. A socialist, Steffens was an ardent supporter of the Mexican revolution. He had been living in Mexico since late 1915 and had abhorred the thought of war between the two countries. He knew Carranza personally and enthusiastically supported him. "In fact," one historian asserts, "to all intents and purposes he became a Carranzista public relations officer."[59] Traveling with Carranza during the Mexican leader's extensive politicking trips across his country, Steffens had gained his confidence. Having some insight on Carranza's reactions to the U.S.–Mexican crisis, the American journalist was convinced that the First Chief did not want war with his northern neighbor. At the time of the Carrizal incident, Steffens had been in New York and had spoken at an antiwar meeting there. When hostilities seemed imminent in late June, he had hurried to Washington. He conveyed Carranza's antiwar perspective to Secretary of War Baker and other cabinet officials but was told him that the President had already decided on war. The President, he learned, would not see him.[60]

Convinced that war was inevitable, Steffens for a time, perhaps a few days, gave up and finally went to the American lawyer representing Carranza in Washington to console one another over the violent fate that would soon befall Mexico. During Steffens' visit, the lawyer showed him several deciphered private wires from the Mexican leader indicating his "innocence of warlike intentions" as well as his "despair and sorrow" over the prospect of a major military encounter with the United States. This written evidence revived Steffens' activism, and he went directly to the White House. Denied access to Wilson, he proceeded to dictate a message to the President's stenographer, saying in effect that a war based on misinformation was unforgivable and before plunging into hostilities the President should receive his valuable information about Carranza with whom he was well acquainted. Steffens' persistence succeeded, for Wilson agreed to see him the next morning, July 6. Although the height of the crisis had passed, the situation was still tense, with Wilson and Carranza still unsure about the other's intentions. The members of the official joint commission had not yet been appointed, and agreement on the withdrawal of Pershing's troops and other contentious issues was far from certain.

Steffens told Wilson that the information the President was receiving about Carranza's desire for war was incorrect, and that he knew from his sustained personal contacts with the Mexican leader that he wanted to avert war. He also cited the gist of Carranza's telegrams to his Washington lawyer, even quoting from memory those that were most pertinent, but Wilson declined the journalist's offer to retrieve the messages from the law office for his personal perusal. Steffens also mentioned the meetings of the antiwar activists' unofficial commission in the city. According to Steffens' recollection, Wilson replied, "Keep them away . . . Don't let them come near me. I won't see them. Those pacifists make me feel warlike." The cause of Wilson's outburst was likely his mounting frustration over the pacifists' recent attacks on his preparedness program and perhaps also his awareness that they were more idealistic than he on foreign policy issues generally. But he did not hold Steffens' involvement with the unofficial commission against him. Indeed, he continued to press him for more information about Carranza. Steffens' briefing managed to persuade Wilson of the Mexican leader's peaceful intentions, and Wilson thanked him profusely for the "very valuable information, information which prevents a war . . . Yes," he smiled, "there will be no war with Mexico."

Because Wilson had already decided to move away from a bellicose response to the Carrizal affair, his effusive compliments to Steffens were overly generous. Nevertheless, Wilson acknowledged that Steffens' firsthand account of Carranza's attitude and his presentation of "some facts I lacked" strengthened his determination to pursue a peaceful resolution.[61] The negotiations were tortuous and painstakingly slow, however, and Villa's episodic attacks on towns and cities in northern Mexico continued to terrorize the local populations. In the end, the official commission resorted to ambiguous language to finesse the most sensitive issues, and even then Carranza refused to sign the accord because Pershing's punitive expedition was still in Mexico. Villa's weakened forces were unable to sustain the initiative from their raids, however, and as he gradually became less of a threat to the United States, Pershing's forces slowly withdrew from Mexican territory. By early 1917 the crisis in U.S.–Mexican relations had subsided.[62]

8

Reappraisals and Political Realities

The military preparedness controversy and Mexican imbroglio were foreign policy concerns that temporarily diverted the peace movement from its focus on neutral mediation of the Great War. To the American pacifists, preparedness would lead the nation closer to military involvement in the European conflict and the abandonment of the nation's traditional aloofness from European power politics and civilian control of the military, while recklessly embarking on war with Mexico would needlessly undermine the nation's credibility as a peacemaker. Believing that the outcome of the two issues would have momentous repercussions for the future of the Republic, they did not hesitate to express their views and organize like-minded citizens in support of their positions.

Nevertheless, even as the pacifists confronted these crises, the question of mediation of the European war never receded very far into the background. As early as the spring of 1916, some peace seekers launched a new mediation campaign that would soon gain a wider and more influential following of private citizens than any of their previous organizational efforts. And within the Wilson administration, despite dealing with preparedness, Mexico, and myriad other issues, and, not least, the upcoming national election in the fall, confidential discussions of the President's possible mediation intensified.

The major reason for the rising interest in neutral mediation was the continuing gruesome military stalemate on the European continent. After a disastrous campaign at Gallipoli in 1915, British forces had evacuated from the Dardenelles, but the Allies quickly checked the furious offensive launched by the Germans at Verdun in February 1916. Intense fighting in that sector would rage off and on for many months. Meanwhile, the Allies prepared for their own offensive at the Somme in July. The British assault on the first day alone of that campaign would result in the death of 20,000 of their soldiers. That massacre was exceptional only as a daily total, and the casualties on both sides at Verdun and Somme rapidly mounted during the summer months. As the conflict hurtled on with no prospect in sight of a military breakthrough by one side or an armistice, speculation mounted that the growing military exhaustion among the belligerents was making them increasingly receptive to possible peace negotiations.

The peace forces would respond to this prospect with a new pressure campaign, but unbeknownst to them others closer to the administration were also urging Wilson to offer mediation. House confided to his diary in early May that he was counseling the president "not to allow the war to continue beyond the Autumn. He can so word a demand for a conference that the people of each nation will compel their governments to consent." He and his mentor discussed mediation strategy in some detail, House advising that if the war was still a stalemate by late summer, the President should act. Moreover, the liberal journalist Ray Stannard Baker, who was on friendly terms with Wilson, commended to him the notion of a neutral conference for mediation, but Wilson objected that association with small nations would divide responsibility, which the United States should mainly bear. Wilson also volunteered, however, that he was then thinking "more than anything else" about the timing of a peace move.[1] Further, Tumulty wrote his boss later in May that the warring nations, nearing exhaustion, could not persevere "through another year without suffering of an untold character." Calculating that it would likely take several months to get the belligerents to the peace table, he argued that the most propitious time for a presidential mediation offer should come very soon as the military campaigns began to slog down for the winter. If the President delayed a peace initiative until the fall, however, the pressures for peace would recede, as militaristic influences would increasingly revive in the winter months for coming spring offensives.[2]

It is safe to say that Wilson was doing "a great deal of serious thinking" about mediation prospects, as he told Tumulty,[3] but during the summer and fall he pursued no initiatives. He never really explained why he then made no new mediation overtures, but the main reason was his understanding that the warring parties were still not interested in his good offices. Although the House–Grey proposal had not gone anywhere, it was still on the table. Moreover, the timing for mediation moves was not auspicious, as the upcoming presidential election stood in the way. Even if the belligerents had been mildly receptive to mediation, they would not have seriously considered a Wilsonian initiative when his own future political leadership was pending. They well knew, as did Wilson, that his mediation, even if somehow accepted, would involve long, arduous, and often acrimonious negotiations between the two sides over countless territorial, political, and other questions. He would become absorbed in the details of diplomatic exchanges, perhaps to the detriment of his campaign, and in any event surely nothing substantial would be decided before election day. And if he lost in November, he would be a lame duck for the next four months without creditable authority to speak for the nation. House and Tumulty, both savvy strategists in electioneering politics, would never have suggested a mediation initiative to their chief if they did not believe his assumed role of peacemaker more likely to help than hurt his re-election chances, but they wisely did not press their case in the face of Wilson's resistance.

The practical considerations of election year politics did not deter Rebecca Shelley, who once again became a main instigator in trying to gear up public support for mediation. She had become one of the most enthusiastic participants on the Ford peace ship and returned to the United States in January 1916, determined to advance the peace cause. She found an ally in the young journalist Lella Faye Secor. They had been good friends in their Everett, Washington, days, and it was Shelley who had persuaded Secor to join the peace ship. Of the two, Shelley would be prime mover and more audacious, but Secor, though holding down a job with a New York magazine, was a willing partner.

Initially, their plans for peace action got nowhere. They advanced two schemes, both of which were designed to re-engage Henry Ford in the peace movement. The two women were prepared to move forward without the auto magnate, but obviously his endorsement of their plans as well as his money would help immeasurably to jump-start their organizational efforts. They first planned for a meeting at Carnegie Hall, which would be a welcome home tribute to their heroine, Schwimmer, and publicize the accomplishments and goals of the Ford peace expedition. But the peace ship debacle was viewed with disfavor, even ridicule, and Ford did not bother to respond to their letters asking for his endorsement of their initiative.

Their sequel was more grandiose. Latching onto the current preparedness debate, they tried to interest the industrialist in an international disarmament league, which would pressure Congress to adopt a disarmament resolution and persuade the political parties to include disarmament planks in their platforms. If they failed in these pursuits, Shelley wanted the league to nominate an independent peace candidate for the 1916 presidential election. Because Ford had been unresponsive, they managed to buttonhole several ambassadors and political figures in Washington, including Bryan and Senator La Follette, to try to persuade them to enlist the industrialist's attention and to emphasize the league's support for the neutral conference and antipreparedness. But the politicians, especially Bryan, were skeptical of the neutral conference and Schwimmer's disinterested motives, and the former secretary of state refused to send messages to European leaders asking for their endorsement of the Stockholm conference or to contact Ford. Without this support, the project never got off the ground. The two feminists' strategy, combining both domestic and international elements, was in fact too ambitious.

Shelley then hit on another scheme that offered more promise. As part of the Neutral Conference for Continuous Mediation's emphasis on propaganda and publicity, in April 1916 Lochner had urged the creation of citizen committees in the neutral countries to provide support for the Stockholm conference of private individuals. Probably because their Hungarian feminist heroine was no longer associated with the private neutral conference, Shelley and Secor ignored Lochner's appeal and instead reverted to the pre-peace ship pacifist program of a government-sponsored neutral conference. For this effort, Shelley proposed the creation of an American citizens' committee of "our best brains, wills, politicians, [and] statesmen." Such a committee, she optimistically believed, would have a good chance of success in an election year because it was "simply a matter of making Wilson and his cohorts see that it is to their advantage to call a conference."[4]

The two young women received more backing for this effort. One explanation was that despite their earlier failures they had convinced peace-oriented people of their faith and perseverance. Thus Harriet Thomas, WPP executive secretary, doubted Shelley's judgment but was impressed with her sense of "real mission," which extended back to her successful street rally in Detroit in November 1915 that had presaged Ford's commitment to the peace cause. Believing that it was "the enthusiast who starts things going and not the calm deliberate person who weighs considerations too carefully," she advised peace people to cooperate with her. Lillian Holt, head of the Woman's Peace Party in Michigan and husband of Frederick Holt, a Ford financial manager for the neutral conference in Stockholm, responded positively to Thomas' advice. She gained an interview with Ford who told her that he favored the formation of a new committee lobbying for an official neutral conference. Ford apparently never publicly endorsed the new effort or contributed money to it, but word of his support gave Shelley a psychological boost to move the effort forward.[5]

Though she and Secor were willing to take on the organizing work, they realized that the winning over of established peace people would immeasurably help their effort. They also recognized, and accepted, that the involvement of well-known pacifists in the new movement would inevitably result in their making the policy decisions. Shelley looked up Jane Addams, hoping that she would allow her committee to send out its literature under the letterhead of the National Peace Federation, the coalition of Chicago peace forces. Addams, characteristically cautious, refused, although she gave the young activist the federation's mailing list. She promised her no WPP endorsement, but said she would personally support any new mediation group she could organize. Following their talk, Shelley complained to Lola Lloyd that while she had shown as an experienced school teacher that she could do "man's work single handed, the peace people, or many of them, persist in treating me like a child, to be commended for good intentions, but whose judgment is not to be seriously trusted."

Shelley's appraisal of Addams' opinion of her was basically correct. The Chicago pacifist was always committed to action, but was also wary of half-baked and ill-conceived proposals that might further divide the peace workers. Nervous about, as well as admiring of, Shelley's zeal, she felt she could only give her modest encouragement. But when Shelley set out for New York City to interest others in her plans, Addams followed through by asking Lillian Wald to cooperate with the young enthusiast seeking her support. "She is more devoted than wise," she explained, "but devoted she certainly is, and sometimes her wild plans come out extremely well."[6]

Another reason for the more positive reception to the two women's new plans was that despite their youth they were not exactly neophytes in the peace movement, and even in their first failures had made valuable contacts. In their earlier effort, for example, they had persuaded George Kirchwey, newly installed president of the American Peace Society, Frederick Lynch, secretary of the Church Peace Union, and Hamilton Holt, a director of the League to Enforce Peace, a U.S. internationalist group promoting a postwar league of nations, to sign the appeal for the Carnegie Hall meeting. Lynch in addition had contributed his organization's funds for Shelley's travel to Washington to try to line up support for her disarmament league. When Shelley and Secor arrived in New York, they successfully appealed once again to these three men to support their new plan, and soon they had also enlisted Wald, Oswald Villard, and Rabbi Wise. Together they formed a new group, the American Neutral Conference Committee (ANCC).[7] All of these prominent New York peace workers had refused to join the Ford expedition, but were still interested in ending the European holocaust.

In organizing the new group, the two women searched for an experienced and prestigious peace advocate who, as chairman, would raise its public profile and attract media attention. After several had refused them, Hamilton Holt agreed to serve as chairman. In addition to editing *The Independent* magazine, Holt was primarily interested in expanding the public influence of the more conservative League to Enforce Peace, and he accepted the ANCC chairmanship, only on condition that he did not have to raise funds. But his identification with the committee also indicated his continued involvement with progressive peace forces. Like many peace workers, he believed that mediation and postwar security could form a comprehensive peace strategy. As he innocently wrote Wilson, to whom he forwarded some mediation proposals of the Dutch Anti-War League: "I am wondering if you have considered the possibility of whether it would be practicable to offer mediation now on the basis of a League to Enforce Peace. Perhaps if the future peace of the world can be guaranteed, the immediate problems will become relatively insignificant and can be easily arranged."[8]

8.1 Rebecca Shelley, 1916. (Bain Collection, Library of Congress)

The ANCC was to be a political lobbying group designed to influence President Wilson by adding a neutral conference commitment in both major party platforms. At its first meetings, the committee members proposed to form a press bureau, hire a professional lobbyist, and gain endorsements from civic, labor, women's, church, and other "progressive" groups. Nothing substantial was accomplished in these areas, however, partly because the group never received robust financial support, but also because nobody stepped forward to complement Shelley's and Secor's efforts. The two women did not mind, but they obviously could not do everything. Much of their time was spent in fund-raising just to pay for administrative overheads and Shelley's living expenses and trying to expand the ANCC membership. At the same time, however, the committee early decided to remain totally separate from the American Union Against Militarism (AUAM), although many members had been actively involved in the recent

8.2 Lella Faye Secor, about 1917. (Swarthmore College Peace Collection) Her daughter-in-law later wrote that Secor had "bright blue eyes and flaming hair," and a British friend remembered her as "a freckled American redhead." Quotations in Florence, ed., *Lella Secor*, pp 126, 260.

antipreparedness movement. The decision disturbed some antimilitarists, but the new group consciously sought to appeal to a wide constituency, including military preparedness advocates.[9]

For funding, Shelley and Secor turned first to reliable benefactors. They had befriended Fanny Villard, and she and her son Oswald provided some financial support, as did the Reverend Lynch, whom Shelley gratefully referred to as their "Santa Claus." With such monetary assistance and their own efforts, they continued to expand the movement. They managed to win over some business and professional people who were willing to back the President whenever he attempted either joint or independent mediation, and the ANCC soon became a solidly respectable citizens' group. The two women adopted an organizing strategy of enrolling a few well-known people in the purposes of the committee and then using their names to recruit others. They were nonetheless pleasantly surprised at the seeming ease with which they won the endorsement of prominent citizens. "It never ceased to amaze us that people of such wealth and distinction should lend their names to two inexperienced and unknown girls," Secor later recalled. While the committee specifically endorsed a conference of neutrals, it also emphasized that it would "support our government in any effort it may make toward a just and lasting peace."[10]

The organizational effort developed rapidly, and in June the ANCC had adopted a plank on a neutral mediation conference for inclusion in the Democratic party platform. Although Shelley included the draft plank in a letter to Wilson along with supporting arguments for mediation in the European neutrals and she and Secor lobbied in person for it at the Democratic convention, the President and party leaders paid no attention to the effort.

Public interest in the ANCC continued to grow, however, and soon had attracted the support of several clergymen, university presidents, professors, and businessmen. Two of the new nonpacifist recruits in New York were the clothing manufacturer, Charles L. Bernheimer, and the millionaire Jewish banker, Jacob H. Schiff. Both were naturalized German-Americans, who found the continuing European bloodshed very unsettling. Schiff, for example, was torn between his sympathies for his native country and his opposition to German militarism, and he viewed the committee as a possible vehicle for ending the war and his personal discomfort. Being well connected with New York social reformers, especially Lillian Wald whose Henry Street settlement he had long supported, made it easier for him to identify with the new group, which he backed financially. Another addition to the committee was Professor Irving Fisher, who wrote an article for Holt's magazine outlining the most hopeful prospects for peace talks.[11]

———

In the midst of this new organizational effort, Emily Balch arrived in the United States. The Wellesley professor would soon become deeply involved in ANCC activities, but she first had more pressing reasons for her return to American shores. The ostensible reason for her trip was to counter the criticisms of the neutral conference by the Reverend Aked, who was returning to present his views directly to Henry Ford. When the clergyman complained publicly during his journey about the neutral conference delegates as "incompetent cranks," "mediocrities," and generally "a stupid lot," Balch immediately provided low key and thoughtful rebuttals. Aked was one of the first to sign the April manifesto sent to the belligerent nations, she pointed out, and he was alone among the delegates in thinking that "an unofficial body of citizens can get into the regular old diplomatic game of secret diplomacy;" all the others believed, however, "that the forces making for peace are the forces of public opinion." Moreover, she asserted that the Europeans did not regard the neutral conference delegates as dreamers. Many Scandinavians involved in the peace movement were not idealists, but were hard-headed trade unionists and elected officials who feared war and supported peace negotiations as a feasible alternative to continued bloodshed. "Throughout Sweden," she remarked, "the neutral conference is given credit for being a powerful factor in keeping that country out of war when at times the war question was at the boiling point," and the Scandinavians appreciated the delegates' "radical, constructive" peace work. Ford received Aked in Detroit, but refused to support his ideas or renew his generous contract.[12]

Besides countering Aked, another purpose of Balch's trip was to explain to Ford the differences between the "old" flawed neutral conference and the creative work of the "new" one and to get his personal commitment for additional financing. Ford was not much more agreeable with Balch. He was still disappointed by memories of the wrangling and factionalism among the American participants and of Schwimmer's failings. Moreover, his wife Clara, if not her husband also, believed that the women's peace movement, which had initially promoted the expedition, had misled them, while Jane Addams' illness was contrived. They were thus skeptical of women peace activists. Plantiff also sought to undermine Balch's visit. In a letter to Ford, which arrived shortly before her interview, he conceded that she "is a hard worker and seems to be well thought of," but counseled his boss to "keep her there, because we don't want any more women connected with this movement." Ford asked her, more as a request than an order, to remain in the United States.[13]

Balch also reported to President Wilson on the neutral conference. Addams arranged the meeting, to which Wilson readily agreed, and Balch appeared at the White House on August 9. She provided an update of the reorganized conference and its efforts in mobilizing European opinion in favor of a mediated and just settlement. When she also complained that U.S. diplomats were deliberately trying to obstruct the American delegates' travel and contacts in Europe, the President properly referred her to the State Department. She finally saw Frank Polk, the department's counselor, and followed with a letter to him complaining that the U.S. diplomats in Europe had placed the delegates to the neutral conference on "a so-called 'blacklist' of citizens to whom no countenance was to be shown." Throwing "obstacles" in their path, she asserted, was "in marked contrast" to the European neutral and belligerent governments, which had "gone out of their way to show us courtesy and help us." Polk replied a month later that his department's investigation not only found no merit in her charges, but claimed that the department's position was to provide "all the assistance that it consistently could to individuals and groups interested in a peace movement."[14]

Meanwhile, Rosika Schwimmer sent Ford numerous letters explaining the reasons for her resignation from the neutral conference which, she inaccurately charged, was devoted to "theoretical" peace work, and the program of her newly formed International Committee for Immediate Mediation. She returned to the United States and set out for Detroit to talk to him directly, but Ford refused to see her. She also wrote Mrs Ford asking her whether she had received a necklace she sent her just before the peace ship had sailed. Clara sent a blistering response, complaining that she "did not wish to have anything that reminded me of the terrible nightmare of last December," and charging Schwimmer with endangering her husband's health and squandering his money.

Although the ICWPP had not endorsed the Ford undertaking, Jane Addams, its president, wanted his neutral conference to succeed. On Schwimmer's arrival from Europe, Addams, always the harmonizer, invited her to visit her at her summer home in Maine. Their meeting only temporarily mollified Schwimmer, who shortly displayed once again her propensity for self-destruction. In a stream of letters to Addams, she proceeded to attack many still associated with the neutral conference, including some who had initially admired her. She believed, for example, that Julia Grace Wales was "on the road to insanity," while Balch, having been "fooled" by the timid leaders of the conference, had managed "to spoil the wonderful opportunities." Addams shortly rejected Schwimmer's appeal to wire Ford to change his mind and see her. Schwimmer never got to see Ford, and her new campaign for "immediate mediation" never got off the ground.[15]

When Balch told Addams about her interview with Ford and his reluctance to finance her return to the Neutral Conference for Continuous Mediation, the latter commiserated, "Poor Mr Ford is simply out of his depth and does not know what or whom to believe. I suppose that if you are not expected to go back, I will be disgusted with the situation." A more charitable view of Ford's behavior in the summer of 1916, however, was that he, a besieged victim of contradictory advice, nonetheless continued his financial support of his neutral conference of private citizens, even as he seemed to believe, as he had told Lillian Holt, that he supported an official conference. Lochner, for one, gave him the benefit of the doubt. After reading the press clippings of the Detroit visits of Aked, Balch, and Schwimmer, he commented to a friend that he was amazed that Ford did not end his involvement with the conference.

The European delegates had also asked Balch to inform American peace groups about the neutral conference and to commit them to active support of its work. One thought was to organize peace demonstrations in America, similar to ones already held in the European neutrals. Here Balch turned to the energetic Shelley. Not one to shy away from public agitation, Shelley tried to drum up support for peace rallies among ANCC members, but managed only to enlist Frederick Lynch and his Church Peace Union in promoting "peace services" in some religious congregations the following Sunday.

It became increasingly evident in fact that the ANCC's more moderate, male leadership clearly preferred quiet lobbying to direct action tactics. Holt even went out of his way to assure financial supporters, like Schiff, that the two women could not undertake any initiative without first consulting him. Moreover, even Oswald Villard, a committed pacifist, wanted to keep Shelley and Secor under control. He admired their activism and creativity, but told Balch that he would withdraw his financial support unless she joined the two feminists in the ANCC office. Balch's presence, he believed, would provide a steadying influence.[16]

These measures increasingly irritated Secor and Shelley. Ideally, they would have felt more comfortable as part of a peace movement composed of younger like-minded activists, and they hoped to attract some to the organization. As Secor had written in June, "We are more and more convinced as we see the inertia and conservatism of older people, that this movement . . . is essentially the movement of the young people." Peace education in the schools and colleges was one vehicle for interesting American youth in peace concerns, but that route was too long term for their activist temperaments. Moreover, compared with the swelling interest of older, well-established citizens, they apparently found little interest in the peace movement among their peers. Feeling somewhat isolated generationally and discouraged by the restrictions circumscribing their spontaneity, Secor recognized that part of their problem was that "from the beginning we have been handicapped with youth and sex. I used to think that there was nothing so desirable in the world as to be young and to be a woman. But there have been moments when I have felt that both of these were a curse." Their complaints were also ideological. When the two feminists devised a committee of one hundred citizens supporting mediation, Holt objected that more representation of "the more conservative type citizen" was needed, and he proceeded to strike from their list "many good peace women on the grounds of keeping [the] committee 'non-pacifist'. . . ." They could tolerate Balch in part because she was a woman but also because of her pacifist activism, but they never warmed to the more conservative Holt or his restrictions. As Secor unfairly fumed in a letter to her sisters, he was "one of those old peace workers whom Rebecca and I call 'peace hacks' because of their stupidity and conservatism and fear."

Despite these tensions, Balch agreed to throw herself into the ANCC organizational effort. Using her academic and liberal contacts, she soon helped to enlist new supporters, including John Dewey, Walter Lippmann (though only confidentially), Congressman James L. Slayden, the socialist journalist John Reed, the social gospel clergyman Washington Gladden, and Mary E. Woolley, president of Mount Holyoke College. By August, Holt had managed to complete the list comprising the committee of one hundred prominent Americans, which included the governors of three states. Simultaneously, Balch publicized the work of the unofficial conference in Europe in newspapers and magazines, which highlighted the conferees' solid scholarly, parliamentary, and left-liberal credentials and, even more, the conference's propaganda and educational activities. The latter, she wrote, were "the fire under the boiler," which would "focus and energize opinion" and provide "the Conference a power which governments are the first to realize." At the same time, she characteristically did not claim too much for the conference, recognizing, for instance, the "enormous" difficulties the conference faced in making contacts with governments. She likewise conceded that the effects of public opinion and pressures were "imponderables" and that the neutral conference might influence the future peace settlement "only on the little drops of water principle." Addams, for one, was very grateful for Balch's many efforts. "I think you [are] a perfect trump in the various things you are doing," she wrote her.[17]

Fortified by the growing support, the ANCC leaders asked the President for an interview. Wilson readily agreed to see them, even instructing Tumulty to give the delegation as much time as it needed. The upcoming presidential election undoubtedly helped to account for his willingness to receive them, as it had been for seeing Balch three weeks earlier. But his former reluctance had given way to keen interest in such meetings. He had met off and on with mediation advocates for two years and well knew how to put them off while still maintaining their interest and support. He thus felt confident in dealing with a delegation of 20 members, representing several professional groups and geographical sections, which arrived at the White House on August 30. Encouraged by recent reports that the European neutrals, as well as the Latin-American nations, were now very interested in a neutral conference, the three spokesmen for the delegation, Fisher, Woolley, and Jordan, renewed the plea for American leadership in calling a neutral conference for continuous mediation.[18]

In his response, Wilson readily conceded that two or three neutral governments had approached him about such a conference and admitted that one (presumably the Netherlands) "would be very pleased to take the initiative." But he could not see how his cooperative action with other neutrals would hasten the end of the war. He argued that the participation of the United States in a conference of neutrals without the inclusion of the Latin-American nations would undermine the "hopeful future" of his Pan-American policy; yet if the United States invited all of them, the

European neutral governments, fearful of being outvoted, might reject the invitation.[19] In addition, Wilson believed that the other neutrals, even those of South America, were too much influenced economically and politically by one belligerent side or the other to participate disinterestedly in a neutral conference. He admitted that as far as the United States was concerned, the war was just a fight to see which side was stronger; but the passions and dangers of the war so directly affected the other neutrals that they could not serve disinterestedly in a conference of neutrals. He distinguished between what he considered to be the partisan interests of the other neutrals and the disinterested motives of the United States, and he indicated that he believed only the United States possessed the "independence of judgment and of interest" to act as an impartial mediator. A conference of about 20 neutrals, he argued, would result in a series of squabbles in which the United States, working for the "interest of mankind," would be outvoted by the other 19 neutrals, which favored settlements that would safeguard their narrowly national interests.

Wilson's assumption of the purity of American motives was characteristic of much of his thinking about his nation's high-minded mission in world affairs, but he did not carry his ethnocentrism to the opposite extreme and assume the European belligerents were selfish and corrupt. On the contrary, he attempted to understand their vastly different perspective. He claimed to "honor" the European leaders he had had "a chance to know and test, but their point of view is utterly different from ours, and their object is utterly different from ours." As an example, he cited the belligerents' unfriendly reactions to his speech before the League to Enforce Peace in May 1916 in which he gave a general endorsement of the creation of a new authoritative international organization after the war. In one part of that address, he had stated that the United States was not interested in the specific territorial and political settlements between the belligerents, but would have much to say at a peace conference about the ways the present war affected neutral nations and the world at large. Yet it was precisely his implied disinterest in specific war aims that the belligerents resented. Wilson continued:

> The German feels if you don't sympathize with him you really don't know what modern culture is, and the attitude of the French is that you don't really know what human liberty is if you don't sympathize with them. I don't really blame them. If I were in their place, I would feel exactly the same way, because they are engaged in a terrible struggle, vital to everything that they hold dear and valuable.

Despite the "circle of difficulties and perplexities" in harmonizing conflicting viewpoints in any mediation, Wilson was guardedly optimistic about peace talks. He saw peace sentiment steadily growing every day and believed the "voice that is calling for peace will presently be heard." He was confident that in the near future the belligerent governments would be unable to suppress this peace sentiment any longer and that at "a psychological movement" he might attempt to bring them together. He believed that once peace parlays began, then the belligerents would be unable to continue the war much longer.[20]

The President spoke extemporaneously on these matters for about 20 minutes. It was an impressive performance, and he was privately pleased with his showing.[21] He spoke with confidence and conveyed the impression that he was fully in control of the delicate diplomatic situation. He confirmed this perspective in his handling of Professor Battin, whom the ANCC had summoned to Washington for the presidential interview. Before the ANCC appearance, Battin asked Wilson if he was willing to meet separately with him to hear his confidential report on his recent meetings on mediation prospects with the Dutch prime minister and foreign minister as well as German Foreign Secretary von Jagow and British leaders Viscount Grey, A.J. Balfour, and Bonar Law, but Wilson, who had earlier been receptive to such confidential briefings, did not even bother to respond.[22]

Certainly Wilson's objections to a neutral conference were persuasive, even convincing—if one assumed that its primary purpose was to negotiate the final peace settlement. But few peace workers had ever entertained such a bold function for a neutral conference. Indeed, most of them had frequently stated that a conference of neutrals should serve only in the modest role of a clearinghouse for receiving peace feelers.

Another member of the ANCC delegation was the liberal publisher Benjamin Huebsch, who had been a Schwimmer supporter on the Ford expedition. Besides Shelley, Secor, and Balch, he was the only member associated with the Ford venture at the interview, which suggested the ANCC's preference for prominence and respectability over activism. Huebsch later gave his impressions of the prevailing attitude of his colleagues at the interview on the purpose of the neutral conference. The conference of neutrals, he said, "was to be a bar of justice without the right of jury to decide who's right and who's wrong. We didn't expect that nations, two nations coming before us, say the Allies and Germany, were going to have to stop [fighting] or go on or compromise according to the majority vote of nations. That was far beyond anybody's thought."[23]

It is not entirely clear why Wilson linked a neutral conference to the final peace conference, but he probably thought that the nations in any neutral conference, if successful in initiating peace talks between the belligerents, would also participate in the actual negotiations. He seemed to assume that the two were inseparable when he said, "My hope is that we can get them to talk to each other, and the minute that happens, the war is over. They will never go back to it. They will never revive the forces that will sustain them in it." Moreover, having abandoned thoughts of simple mediation in favor of using his influence to persuade the two belligerent sides, once assembled for negotiations, to develop firm agreements guaranteeing postwar security for all nations, he thought that he would encounter considerable difficulties in realizing this general goal if several other neutral nations also participated in the peace process. Because he had expressed these opinions in earlier interviews—first with Schwimmer and Snowden and recently with the journalist Baker—he was merely reiterating the same perspective.

Granting the sincerity of Wilson's beliefs, one can also discern another possible motive. He may have deliberately misinterpreted their proposal in order more easily to raise objections to it. In speaking of a conference of 20 neutrals, he surely extended the number of participating nations far beyond the number the mediation proponents anticipated in any congress of neutrals, and one wonders why the delegation mentioned the participation of South American nations. The Mexican crisis had seriously damaged the administration's policy of Pan-American cooperation, but Wilson talked as though Latin America could not be ignored in any U.S. mediation offer. It is plausible to assume in fact that he would have mentioned their prospective role, even if the presenters had avoided it. In any event, seizing upon the Latin American aspect, he easily labeled its weaknesses and then cleverly extended them to discredit a neutral conference of any kind.

Wilson's failure to give the delegates a chance to answer his objections to the neutral conference helps to confirm his deliberate distortion of their proposal. Had it been but a misunderstanding, then the delegates could have corrected his misinterpretation. But Wilson did not give them the opportunity for as soon as he finished his remarks, he gently dismissed the delegation.

Like most in the delegation, Lella Secor was overawed by Wilson. As she wrote her sisters, she thought the presenters were very nervous, while the President's "personality, coupled with his assurance, placed him on an enviable elevation . . . During the moments when he was speaking, I thought him a truly wonderful man." Secor, who was only 29, may have been more readily impressionable because of her relative youth. But she also correctly noted "I was not the only one who was impressed for the moment by what he had said." She quickly realized, however, that Wilson had cleverly manipulated the situation to his own advantage. Finding that the other delegates, "whose clear thinking habits I profoundly respect, were fooled in the same way," she concluded that his arguments "could be shot full of holes."[24] As Huebsch remembered it, the delegates were "flabberghasted" [sic] at Wilson's tactics, which had prevented any meaningful dialogue on the matter.[25]

The meeting was in truth more a presentation and rebuttal than a full-fledged interview. Wilson obviously did not want an extensive discussion on the mediation question. Indeed, fearing someone in the room might unwittingly reveal his private thoughts to the press on a very sensitive issue, he had prefaced his remarks with the condition that they be considered "confidential." Public pronouncements of his thinking on peace talks might hinder his freedom of action, especially if he should later change his approach to this complicated subject. With German–American relations greatly improved following Germany's conditional *Sussex* pledge of May 1916 not to attack passenger liners and merchantmen without warning and with growing British incursions on American rights on the high seas, such as imposing a blacklist on American firms that continued to try to trade with the Central Powers, Wilson was already considering the abandonment of the House–Grey Memorandum. If he had not yet rejected it or seriously considered another formula for mediation of the war, he still wanted to keep open all possible options.

Still, if Wilson's interview had not entirely satisfied many participants, he had at least given the fullest account of his personal views on mediation. Above all, he conveyed the distinct impression that he would offer his own mediation at the first favorable opportunity. The main question thereafter for the mediation proponents involved their tactics in bringing about presidential action. Should they continue to advocate a conference of neutrals, even in the face of Wilson's repeated objections, or should they abandon the plan and attempt to induce the President's independent mediation? While still paying lip service to the neutral conference, they increasingly emphasized the latter course.

Following the August 30 interview, the delegates appointed Holt, Fisher, and Lynch to draft a letter to the President asking for another interview at which they could answer his objections to and correct his misconceptions of the neutral conference. But the three concluded that such a letter would probably accomplish nothing. More generally, the committee agreed on the following appraisal of Wilson's intentions: "While he did not say so, our feeling was that President Wilson believes that single efforts by our government will be more effective than mediation by a conference of neutral nations."[26] David Starr Jordan's personal judgment of their meeting was blunt: "The President holds off from Neutral Conferences. I think he means to mediate himself, when a psychological moment arrives. It is pretty clear that he won't want any awkward squad firing in his place."[27] Jordan was in fact embarrassed by the interview. Asked by the ANCC to attend "at any sacrifice," he had participated only because he assumed that "new features" on the European scene raised prospects for mediation, and he subsequently apologized to Tumulty for imposing on the President who better understood that the election campaign in America and "new entanglements in

Europe make present action [on mediation] impossible."[28] The timing of the interview, it turned out, was indeed unfortunate, as Roumania's entrance into the war on the side of the Allies two days earlier momentarily raised their hopes for turning the tide militarily.

Once they reluctantly admitted that Wilson could not be converted to their scheme and would not act anytime soon, they adopted more flexible tactics. While not entirely abandoning the plan for a neutral conference, they decided that henceforth they should "emphasize the mediation idea, rather than any one method of mediation." The committee even began to circulate a petition urging the American Government "to mediate between the opposing belligerents by whatever method seemed most effective." They hoped that the petition would convince the President that he had the public support necessary for any future peace move.[29]

These actions suggest that the ANCC had become less interested in pressure tactics than in serving as a latent cheerleader group for a presidential peace initiative. Moreover, because the Central Powers still held the upper hand militarily on the continent, German-Americans like Schiff kept a low public profile to minimize suspicions that the committee's emphasis on an early mediated peace was serving Germany's interests.[30]

———

The upcoming presidential campaign at first encouraged their cautious optimism. Aware of the implications of any peace move on domestic politics, they hoped that the approaching election might provide an additional incentive for Wilsonian mediation. As early as the spring of 1916, for example, Jane Addams had advanced a political calculus that Tumulty and House shared, but did not articulate in writing:

> if the country is at war before the November election Wilson will be re-elected on the general principle of not wishing to swap horses in the middle of the stream. But, of course, the same thing would be attained if we were in the midst of negotiations; while it could not be put so bluntly as that, and while it would be most unfortunate to have that presented as the motive, yet if it could be presented to someone near the throne, it might become a determining factor.[31]

Similarly, in one of several letters he sent to Henry Ford to try to re-engage the auto manufacturer's interest in his European neutral conference, Lochner mused more elaborately on how Wilson's mediation could assure his re-election. He proposed that Wilson offer his good offices on the basis of certain terms, such as complete German withdrawal from occupied Belgium and France, the independence of Serbia, and discussion at the peace table of territorial and other questions. Because of the enormous economic leverage the United States had over the belligerents, he argued that if either side rejected Wilson's offer, the President could use his influence over the other neutrals to impose an economic embargo on the recalcitrant nations. If this initiative succeeded, Wilson "would be the one who had ended the war, and he would win easy election!!!!"[32] But such suggestions involved only wishful thinking, and they were not conveyed, either directly or indirectly, to President Wilson.

As the election approached, most peace advocates were realistic enough to perceive that Wilson would not make any mediation overtures while his future political status was in doubt. Indeed, in their more sober moments, even Addams and Lochner recognized that Wilson was not predisposed to act. As Addams wrote, "I doubt if any political pressure will hurry the Prest [sic] in his second offer of mediation."[33] Far from being politically beneficial, these peace workers realized that the Republicans would immediately attack any such offer as thinly disguised electioneering. Such criticism would be especially damaging to Wilson's political fortunes if either belligerent side spurned his peace appeal. Given Germany's continued territorial advantage on the continent, the Allies, especially French leaders who privately ridiculed Wilson's pretensions as a new prince of peace, would surely have rejected any offer of his good offices. The peace advocates correctly surmised that the European battlefronts still ruled out all prospects for successful mediation. Until the military situation clarified following Roumania's involvement, hopefully in checking the Central Powers and restoring some kind of military balance on the continent, the peace workers realized that the Allied leaders would probably continue to reject all peace initiatives.[34]

The presidential election illustrated the pacifists' dilemma. In a sense, they had little choice but to support Wilson's re-election. To be sure, because the incumbent had vacillated for two years without offering mediation and had frequently expressed his opposition to a conference of neutrals, the pacifists might have considered deserting him for another candidate. The Socialists involved in the mediation and antipreparedness movements would loyally support their party's nominee, Allan Benson. But having less charisma than its candidate four years earlier, Eugene V. Debs, who had won more than 900,000 votes, or 6 percent of the electorate, Benson was not a realistic choice for nonsocialists. The only meaningful alternative was Charles Evans Hughes, who had resigned from the Supreme Court to accept the Republican party nomination. It was widely assumed that he was the only attractive Republican politician who could keep progressives in the party, and initially, some peace advocates believed they might be able to support Hughes who had earlier compiled a record of moderate reform as governor of New York.

In 1909, for example, Governor Hughes, who had been impressed with

Crystal Eastman's thorough study of industrial accidents, had appointed her as the only woman of a state workmen's compensation committee. In that position, Eastman, then a young lawyer, had drafted the state's first workmen's compensation law. Lillian Wald, who had also worked with Hughes on social welfare issues during his gubernatorial term, recalled that he had given the "same grave attention and wisdom" to the ordinary citizens as he gave to the "business and material interests." Like Addams, she had supported Roosevelt's Progressive party in 1912. She had thought Wilson's campaign speeches rather ethereal, and in her first personal contacts at the outset of his administration she had found him reserved, even distant. During the 1916 campaign, Wald broke off her summer vacation to join an AUAM delegation, consisting of Crystal Eastman, Amos Pinchot, Charles Hallinan, Paul Kellogg, Oswald Villard, and Alice Lewisohn, in a personal meeting with Hughes. Following the meeting, Villard reported favorably about Hughes' "fearlessness, courage, and independence" and his opposition to the nation's involvement in the European war; and despite Hughes' inexperience in foreign affairs, he believed that he was educable to their antimilitarist views.[35]

The antipreparedness forces continued to bother Wilson through the summer concerning an obscure clause in the Army Reorganization Act, which provided for the drafting of members of the National Guard into the army if the voluntary enlistments in the reserves fell below prescribed strength. Introduced by Congressman Carl Hayden (D-Ariz.), it had apparently slipped into the final bill without comment. Labeling it the "Hayden joker," the antimilitarists asked Wilson to repeal this clause, which gave the army the power to invoke a draft. In a letter to Amos Pinchot, Wilson conceded that the clause was "susceptible of misinterpretation," but believed it did not mean conscription, but only "a draft in the more limited sense of the term." Wilson in effect made a distinction between conscription in peacetime and wartime; it would not occur in peacetime, but in war would inevitably result in new conscription legislation. Wilson went to the chairman of the House military affairs committee who confirmed the President's position that a "draft was inevitable in war." Wilson asked his antimilitarist correspondents to keep the matter quiet, but, still unhappy with his position, they proceeded to publicize the "Hayden joker." What disturbed the antimilitarists was that the draft, whether in peace or war, contravened America's traditional voluntary system. The one exception in the nation's history was the draft in the Civil War, which, as Hallinan put it, "proved to be a costly fizzle." The Hayden clause also included no provision exempting conscientious objectors.[36]

Since the President seemed to agree that the "joker" was a mistake, the antimilitarists had persistently asked him to get the Congress to delete the provision, but Wilson, perhaps seeing that any question relating to a "draft," even a seemingly simple one, could provoke emotional debate just before the presidential election, put off the issue. The AUAM found support from some members of Congress, who accused the military committee chairmen in both houses and Hayden for "lack of candor" in including the clause in the army law, but Congress did not formally raise the issue of repeal before the election. In press releases and newsletters, the AUAM publicized the "obnoxious" clause, and socialist publications likewise criticized it; both urged readers to write their congressmen and the President advocating its repeal. The publicity had some effect, as in subsequent months the White House received many messages asking about the clause and indicating their opposition to it.[37]

Lillian Wald also stressed the unpopularity of the clause to the President and intimated that nearly all the AUAM members were sympathetic to him and could influence a significant number of votes in the President's re-election campaign. But Wilson only reaffirmed his opposition to conscription and noted his "entire sympathy with her position that the power to authorise conscription should remain with the Congress and not be delegated, except upon special occasion, to the Executive," and he hoped Congress would change the clause "upon the first suitable occasion." Wald nonetheless judged Wilson's response "entirely satisfactory," and the AUAM dropped the matter for the duration of the presidential campaign. Humoring the antimilitarists with expressions of general concern and vague promises, Wilson had adroitly managed to defer the issue until after the election.[38]

In the end, however, none of the prominent peace and antipreparedness people endorsed Hughes. Uncomfortable in national partisan politics, Hughes did not project a particularly attractive image, and as the campaign progressed, the progressive internationalists found his statements on foreign affairs more erratic, vague, and narrowly nationalistic than Wilson's. Rabbi Wise commented that a campaign speech by Hughes was "appallingly naive, or evasive. It might have been spoken [in] 1906 or 1896 or 1886!"[39] More significantly, they distrusted Theodore Roosevelt's prominent role in Republican party matters. Having gradually given up his Progressive party and returned to the Republican fold by 1916, the former president had abandoned reform and become more closely allied to conservative business interests in the party. The Republican leadership had denied him any chance for the nomination, but his influence in party circles was nonetheless considerable. Pacific-minded Americans particularly found his ultranationalistic and militaristic views on foreign policy matters distinctly offensive. Compared with Wilson's even-handed leadership on foreign policy matters, they believed that if Hughes was elected, Roosevelt's outspoken pro-Allied position would shortly bring the nation into the war against the Central Powers.[40]

Their preference for Wilson, however, involved much more than a choice between the lesser of two evils, for with the exception of Villard, who had become disillusioned with Wilson and voted for the Prohibition candidate, and Holt who privately favored him but for some unknown reason did not vote, the available evidence suggests that every one of them supported Wilson's re-election bid. Indeed, many of them endorsed him with enthusiasm, Pinchot and Wise even serving as "Wilson volunteers" in boosting his candidacy. Their solidarity behind Wilson was remarkable, for some of them had voted for Roosevelt or Taft only four years earlier.[41]

Wilson's domestic reform record helped to move them into his camp. They approved of all his New Freedom programs, but these involved mostly tariff reform and the regulation of big business and banking. They applauded even more warmly his most recent initiatives, which included social justice measures directly impacting on ordinary, working Americans. These included his courageous appointment of the Jewish progressive, Louis D. Brandeis, to the Supreme Court and his vigorous leadership in the enactment of the eight-hour law for railroad employees and the abolition of child labor in business establishments involved in interstate commerce. It is also true, however, that Wilson's cautious handling of foreign problems contributed to their support. Much as they grumbled about Wilson's preparedness program and his reluctance to offer mediation, they recognized him as a man of peace who had patiently weathered a series of diplomatic crises with Germany and Mexico without any military showdown. Lillian Wald had gradually warmed to him, but she and Addams delayed endorsing him publicly, perhaps hoping that Wilson would provide a private statement of his views on conscription. When no such statement came, they came out for him anyway in mid-October. They also joined in a petition signed by Kellogg and 92 other social workers that concluded: "In foreign affairs he has stood for a diplomacy of reason and negotiation, with good will toward all people, rather than one of bluster and the parade of force."[42]

Wilson understood that he was not entirely a free actor in keeping the United States out of the war; major new violations of the nation's rights and interests by the belligerents could require U.S. retaliation, including a declaration of war. He thus privately rejected the popular Democratic party slogan, "he kept us out of war," as shortsighted and naïve. Much more than preserving the peace, his campaign addresses emphasized his vigorous defense of American "rights" as a neutral in wartime. "America is always ready to fight for things that are American," he asserted. The avoidance of war also imparted an isolationist view of negative peace, which was far removed from Wilson's vision of peacemaking. Following his speech to the League of Enforce Peace, Wilson included U.S. membership in a postwar league of nations in the Democratic party platform. Still, his speeches also included repeated references to his proven record of maintaining peace and emphasized that he was the best candidate for staying out of future war. The skillful blending of "Americanism" and "peace" proved to be persuasive with many voters. The peace seekers of course generally shared the Wilsonian internationalist perspective, but the Democrats' avoidance of war theme also summarized the sentiment of the pacifists, who recognized the President's valuable services to the peace of his own nation, if not yet to the world.[43]

Wilson's campaign of peace and progressivism was so attractive that it even won over the erratic Henry Ford, who a year earlier had called Wilson "a small man." After his disastrous venture in private diplomacy, Ford showed a greater appreciation of the many diplomatic and military obstacles standing in the way of peace. Though a life-long Republican who had been successfully entered into presidential primaries without even announcing his candidacy, he found Wilson more progressive, more pacifistic, and generally a more able national leader than Hughes. He gained two interviews with Wilson at the latter's retreat in Shadow Lawn, New Jersey, at which he promised to support the president's re-election.[44]

In addition to his domestic and foreign policies and his proven ability as a national leader, the peace workers admired Wilson as a human being. They had at first half-expected to find the President too intellectual, haughty, and cold for sympathetic consideration of their peace proposals, but after their numerous personal interviews with him they reappraised their earlier judgment. If he still was noncommittal on mediation, by election day they found him engaging, sincere, and compassionate. As Ford exuded these sentiments:

> In upholding the dignity of his office he may have appeared to some to be cold and aloof. But nothing is further from the truth. He's the warmest hearted man in the interest of those who work that I ever dreamed of. I cannot tell you how sincerely he feels for them and desires to improve their conditions . . .
>
> The keeping of Americans alive – out of war – and alive properly, with comfortable working hours and decent wages, is Woodrow Wilson's passion.

Wilson, a professor in politics, of course had had no experience as a laborer, and his identification with working America was vicarious at best. Ford was nonetheless so inspired by Wilson's seeming passion for the common citizenry that he extended pay equality to women workers in his factories.[45]

Overall, Wilson managed to convince the pacifistic liberals that his heart was in the right place. Again, when compared with Hughes' icy personality, Wilson was a clear winner, but their identification with him was genuinely spontaneous and did not require any relatively unfavorable estimate of his political opponent. To sensitive individuals concerned with the preservation of human values, Wilson's humanity was an important, albeit intangible, factor in their decision to support his re-election.

In terms of its short-term political consequences, Wilson had skillfully managed the mediation question. He had pursued a fairly consistent policy of watchful waiting, which he believed European military and diplomatic realities required, without alienating either the peace workers who had consistently urged presidential mediation or the pacifist-isolationist Americans who wanted the United States to remain aloof as much as possible from Europe's problems. Although he was helped along by Hughes' inept campaign, his adroit handling of the European situation undoubtedly won over to his side many more voters than he lost and contributed significantly to the new progressive coalition that gave him the very narrow victory in the election.[46]

———

The support Wilson received from women may have contributed to his electoral triumph. In one sense, Wilson was at a disadvantage in wooing women voters because Hughes had come out strongly for a federal suffrage amendment, while Wilson had merely endorsed his party platform, indicating that votes for women were a state, not a national, matter. Wilson was also educable on women's issues—to a degree. Two of his two daughters were ardent suffragists, and he had long believed that the effective leader could change and grow in response to new issues and movements. Moving leftward as a champion of political reform, he became more receptive to the suffrage movement, saying in late 1915 that he would vote for a women's suffrage amendment in New Jersey. At the same time, despite this endorsement he felt constrained by conservative elements, especially in the Southern states, which had embedded the state-based suffrage plank in the Democratic party platform. To many suffragists, Wilson as the Democrats' standard bearer could have worked harder to secure his party's endorsement of a federal amendment and was hiding behind the platform as a weak excuse for his failed leadership on the question. In response, Wilson told suffragists that if he changed his position, he would seem to be a political opportunist angling for votes. Suffragist leaders did not hold his position against him, some even admiring his "respect for our intelligence." The Woman's Peace Party and National American Woman Suffrage Society officially endorsed no candidate in the presidential election, but their leaders clearly favored the chief executive's re-election. This preference extended even to Crystal Eastman. To the dismay of her radical feminist friends in the Congressional Union, which opposed the incumbent president, she supported and campaigned for him.[47]

During the campaign Wilson gave talks to three large women's groups, the first of which was his warm endorsement of votes for women at the NAWSA annual convention. Downplaying any quarrel over method, he exuded to Mrs Catt's group, "I have come here to fight with you" for suffrage. It was a high point in his long and continuing odyssey on women's issues. Immediately following his talk, he went to a women's charity event. Seated in the audience, he was asked to stand up so the women could have a closer look. Wilson obliged and proceeded to recite a limerick (the same one he had probably told Henry Ford in his office a year earlier), which was a spoof on his lack of "beauty." Wilson's performance, which delighted his audience, was fairly typical of the personal touch he often projected during the campaign.[48]

Many issues were involved in the election. The American economy was buoyant, and the incumbent usually benefits politically from prosperity. Farmers in the South and West were profiting from expanded trade to the Allied nations, which badly needed American goods; they also recognized the Wilson administration for recent legislation expanding rural credit. But people voted for Wilson not simply because of their full pocketbooks or general contentment. Indeed, postmortem commentary on the election agreed that Wilson's reform record and his peaceful diplomacy were mainly responsible for his victory. Of course, those identified with the peace movement represented only a small, albeit elite, minority of social reformers in America, but their views mirrored the general sentiments of the entire moderate left wing of progressives, who solidly supported the President's re-election. Wilson's reform program particularly succeeded in drawing very large numbers of votes away from supporters of Theodore Roosevelt's third party four years earlier. He also won over large numbers of socialists. He skillfully exploited the domestic reform impulse, which may have peaked, but still had remained vibrant throughout his first term. When the votes were counted, Wilson had received a narrow majority in the electoral college. He also won the popular vote, receiving the highest percentage of votes (though just short of a majority) for any Democratic presidential nominee since 1876.

The President's re-election clearly benefited from his record of avoiding war. One detailed study of voting in the Midwestern states concludes that the "peace issue was the most important of the campaign" in that section.[49] It was likely even more important in the Far West. This was true even in the border states of Arizona and New Mexico, where solid voting for Wilson indicated their endorsement of his avoidance of full-scale war against their southern neighbor.

The vote totals also pointed to the importance of the "peace" issue among women. In 1916, women could vote for president in 12 states, all except for Illinois in the Plains and farther west, accounting for 91 electoral votes. Wilson won 10 of those states. In a pre-polling era, there was no detailed analysis of the feminine vote, but the *New York Times*, which conducted an extensive survey of the election returns, reported two broad generalizations. First, although women voted much like the men in their families in Illinois (which Hughes won), in the American West they voted for Wilson in higher numbers than men and particularly accounted for the difference in his very close win in California. If he had lost that state, he would have lost the election. Second, many women voted for Wilson, among other important reasons, because they were attracted to him as the "peace" candidate who had avoided war with Mexico and Germany. In other words, the women's vote seemingly validated their pacifist sisters' rhetoric that women were more peace-oriented than men.[50]

9

Peace Feelers in Europe

While the presidential election campaign became something of an obsession among Americans during the fall of 1916, it was also capturing the
attention of Europeans. It was widely assumed in Europe that Wilson's
re-election would improve the chances of a U.S. offer of mediation of the
conflict, but the continued large-scale bloodletting on the stalemated battlefields fueled speculation about possible peace talks even without him.
The military struggle in the Verdun sector continued throughout almost all
of 1916 until German forces withdrew toward the end of the year. Meanwhile, the Allied offensive at the Somme, beginning in July, would also fail
to achieve a military advantage after nearly five months of fighting. The
casualties on both sides during the extended fierce struggle of these two
campaigns would number more than 800,000 men on each side.[1] As the
drawn-out trench warfare continued unabated, many more citizens in belligerent countries began to yearn openly for peace initiatives that might
somehow lead to a partial or complete end of the fighting. Talk was rife, for
example, about the possibility of Russia concluding a separate peace with
Germany.

The prolonged fighting intensified economic and political divisions
within all belligerent countries, but particularly in Russia and the Central
Powers. Growing discontent in Russia with the failure of the military effort,
food shortages, and social inequality would soon escalate into full-scale
revolutionary activity by early 1917. On the opposite side, government
authorities in the Austro-Hungarian Empire struggled against declining
food supplies, war weariness, and centrifugal pressures of dissident nationalist elements. In Germany, despite the government's severe constraints on
their activities, pacifists tried to nourish public interest in a negotiated
peace. They were particularly encouraged by the women pacifists' activities
and the members of the Central Organization for a Durable Peace, both of
which in their separate endeavors were developing new international networks to promote common internationalist principles that might eventually

guide political leaders toward a just peace settlement. Many nonpacifists among the German middle class shared this disenchantment with the continuing war and opposed expansionist war aims, and even after the suppression of the *Bund Neues Vaterland*, moderate views found some expression politically among liberal parties in the Reichstag.

A much greater danger to the German war effort was labor unrest, which steadily increased during 1916. At a workers' rally in Berlin in 1916 on May Day, a traditional day of labor protest, placards appeared demanding "Bread, Freedom, and Peace!" During the demonstration, Karl Liebknecht, a socialist agitator, shouted, "Down with the war! Down with the government." He was arrested and convicted of treason and sentenced to four years in jail. Workers sympathetic to Liebknecht and his plight went out on strike in many German cities. Industrial strikes became not only more numerous, but involved more workers and lasted longer; the increasing workdays lost to the factories could seriously impair the war effort. The economic and political grievances became in fact more intrinsically intertwined in the latter half of the war. The labor movement was increasingly divided between centrists and radicals, and it was not clear by the end of 1916 how it would all play out.[2]

In Britain, the movement for a negotiated peace witnessed both a coming together and a scattering. Though very disappointed by their government's actions that had prevented them from attending the Hague congress, the British women continued their involvement in the peace cause. Following the Hague gathering, they, along with like-minded women in other European countries, founded national sections of what came to be called the Women's International League. Like the Woman's Peace Party in the United States, the British WIL never approached a mass movement, but it was the largest and most active among the European national federations. Taking the Hague resolutions as its basis, its mission statement combined international goodwill and the women's movement. Beyond the solid nucleus of would-be travelers to the Hague gathering, the WIL attracted many other British women who for various reasons did not sign up for the congress, but were attracted by the new group's blending of constructive peace and feminism and were prepared to support it organizationally and financially. In its first year, the British section altogether expanded to some 2,000–3,000 members and 34 branches.

The WIL's elected officers were already well known for their leadership in the suffrage movement and other reforms: Helena Swanwick, chairman, Kathleen Courtney, Maude Royden, and Margaret Ashton, vice chairman, Catherine Marshall, secretary, and Emmeline Pethick-Lawrence, treasurer. Others who were intimately involved in its activities included Lady Courtney, Helen Ward, Ethel Snowden, and honorary secretary Irene Cooper Willis, who was also active in the Union of Democratic Control, anticonscription campaigns, and labor organizations. The unofficial motto of the new society was, appropriately, "Live Dangerously." Although their contacts with pacifistic women abroad were severely restricted, they published an "international notes" section in their monthly newsletter to document the continuing interest in a negotiated peace even in enemy countries.[3]

The main focus of the Women's International League, at least initially, was the promotion of negotiations that might lead to a just and lasting peace. To that end they held meetings and gave speeches. Their reasoning was that their campaign, combined with the mounting battlefield casualties and economic exhaustion, would stimulate a growing will among "ordinary" citizens for negotiations that the British Government could not ignore.[4]

From the outset, however, the WIL's promotion of a negotiated peace settlement encountered severe difficulties. Watched by the home office and police for possible illegal activities, its speakers at public meetings had to try, not always successfully, to walk a fine line—to avoid the appearance of being antiwar while continuing to promote international understanding and emphasize the need for peace talks. Moreover, sensational segments of the British press, especially in London, waged a bitter campaign against the organization and often ignored its well-attended meetings. Public opinion did not seem to be in the least sympathetic. Self-appointed patriots created an Anti-German League, which organized and incited mobs to invade and violently break up WIL assemblies. "How can we educate people as to the spirit and purpose of our League?" Emmeline Pethick-Lawrence complained in mid-1916. "It is almost impossible to obtain halls or to hold public meetings." Despite the difficulties, the WIL organized hundreds of them throughout Britain at which the members publicized the group's message.

The Women's International League was more successful with its educational programs. Concerned about the deleterious effects of the continuing hostilities on the minds of young people, its members held meetings attempting to educate on the dangers of militarism in the schools. It also sponsored small weekly gatherings to raise women's understanding of foreign policy issues, such as the meaning of freedom of the seas, or the role of finance in international relations. One well-attended WIL conference, for instance, focused on the problem of national bias in the teaching of history and religion.

Although the British Women's International League remained a stable organization, it inevitably had to react to new challenges. One was the Easter Rebellion in Dublin, Ireland, in late April 1916, which suddenly and dramatically escalated the question of Irish political independence. The British Government's ruthless suppression of the uprising and the

execution of many of the rebel leaders inflamed even moderate Irish opinion. Some WIL members turned at least some of their attention to a search
for peaceful initiatives that might help to de-escalate tensions. There were
also strains between the liberal and socialist activists and its more radical
women. Sylvia Pankhurst, for instance, found the WIL too "cautious and
moderate," and she objected to its failure to put "peace" in its title and to
accept foreign women as members. She also had her own women's organization, Workers' Suffrage Federation, which was mostly focused on fighting
the government's repressive measures in general and military conscription
in particular rather than mediation. And while remaining in peace activism,
Pankhurst saw its frustrations and gave as much attention to her fight
against poverty in London's East End. Even when the war finally ended,
she reasoned, helping the unfortunate to improve their wretched lives
would remain a long-term struggle.

Moreover, other issues besides mediation arising out of the European
war were pulling some of its leaders in different directions. These women
did not abandon the peace movement; but frustrated with the WIL's isolation from its female cohorts abroad and perceiving their crusading work
for peace and internationalism as unfruitful, they turned to other pursuits,
which might better fulfill their desire to serve society in meaningful ways.
Because of their solid experience and intellectual talents, they did not have
far to look.[5]

The first to go, albeit only temporarily, was Kathleen Courtney. At the
end of 1915, she signed up for a Quaker relief committee, which sent her to
the eastern Mediterranean and eventually to Corsica to oversee a camp of
displaced Serbians. Much later, she rationalized that her language skills
and administrative experience would be useful in aiding these unfortunate
victims of Britain's ally, but her Mediterranean venture was also an escape
from the painful split with Millicent Fawcett and the national union. When
she returned to England six months later, she became re-engaged in the
mediation movement as well as feminist campaigns for suffrage and pay
equity for women.[6]

During Courtney's absence, Royden and Swanwick had a falling-out,
though the specific issues leading to their disagreement are not entirely
clear. They seemed of one mind on feminism. In separate essays reflecting
on the effects of the drawn-out war on the woman's movement in Britain,
both came to similar conclusions. They welcomed the new economic
opportunities for women, who were flocking to fill jobs previously held by
men now serving in the trenches. Britons, they wrote, were finally discovering that women had intelligence, public spiritedness, and physical stamina
equal to men. In agriculture, they had proven adept at picking up the slack
on farms by producing desperately needed foodstuffs, and other women
were providing indispensable labor for the munitions factories. The result

was that even many formerly skeptical men gratefully acknowledged women's contribution to the war effort. The Asquith government conceded in the fall of 1916 that because of their effective service in wartime the vote should be extended to the millions of still disfranchised men and many women. While the details of the extension of the franchise still had to be worked out (and would not go nearly as far as most suffragists wanted), the announcement signaled the beginning of the end of opposition to women's enfranchisement. At the same time, however, Royden and Swanwick still argued that war was a reactionary force and questioned, presciently it turned out, whether changing societal attitudes and economic opportunities for women would endure in postwar Britain.[7]

A major part of the difficulty between the two women was that both were strong personalities who were temperamentally unsuited to one another. To Royden, Swanwick was "critical, or analytical or destructive, according to taste!" For her part, Swanwick advanced an unflattering portrait of Royden:

> She is an extraordinarily unfair and intolerant person. Nothing she has ever done or proposed has been criticised and turned down but she has some vague scunner at me and apparently can't live in the same room as me. I'm sorry, for the sake of the WIL. I wish she would not so grotesquely misrepresent my opinions. I suppose officially "religious" people are quite hopelessly antagonistic to rationalist minds like mine.[8]

Swanwick's rationalist perspective was in fact well removed from Royden's spiritual bent, which was already carrying her in new directions. Well before the war, Royden had served as a Protestant cleric in London and had begun what would become a long, frustrating battle for ordination of women in the Anglican Church. She also was an early supporter of the Fellowship of Reconciliation (FOR) and the No-Conscription Fellowship (NCF), which Quakers, other religious pacifists, and libertarians had founded in the winter of 1914–1915 in support of anticonscription and conscientious objectors. She found a ready ally in Catherine Marshall, a good friend, who attended her first NCF meeting as a WIL representative in November 1915, and soon threw herself into its activities. Drawing on organizational and publicist's skills from her suffrage days, she became an irrepressible, dynamic force in the new group. A historian of the NCF concludes that "Marshall contributed more to the fellowship's success and survival than any other individual." Along the way, Marshall worked closely with the liberal pacifist philosopher Bertrand Russell, fell in love with Clifford Allen, the first NCF chairman, and, suffering from overwork and internecine criticism, suffered a nervous breakdown in September 1917.[9]

At the same time, the organizational activity supporting peace by negotiation expanded. The UDC spearheaded this effort. In the first phase of the war, the UDC had focused on its causes—blaming Anglo-French secret diplomacy, for example, which had foisted a major war on an uninformed and unsuspecting public—and on the development of new liberal internationalist principles required in any peace settlement. The conduct of the war was not its immediate concern. As the war evolved with no end in sight, however, the UDC leaders became increasingly restive and began to confront the British Government more directly. Some of the opposition developed in reaction to the political maneuverings of the Asquith government, which seemed to them more interested in self-preservation than enlightened policies. In the twilight years of peace before 1914, the Liberal party, wracked by internal conflicts over home rule for Ireland, responses to the militant suffragists, and labor strife, was already in decline, and the war more severely tested its vitality. Lacking solid support for the war effort, Asquith had formed a coalition government in the spring of 1915. This meant bringing Tories into the government, some of whom expressed ultranationalist views on the conflict, and the ousting of some Liberals who were prepared to support peace moves.[10]

Further disenchanting UDC members and sympathizers, in the last half of 1915 the government began preparing the public mood for the introduction of military conscription. This prospect offended many Britons, especially Liberals, as an unprecedented repudiation of individual liberty. These people clung to traditional notions of voluntarism, even though the near totality of the military struggle was moving belligerent governments to further mobilization of their citizens and restrictions on their freedoms.

E.D. Morel was a human dynamo who more than any other founding member provided the UDC with much of its energy and programmatic direction. He understood that conscription would become a hotly contested issue in British politics, but argued that the UDC's straight-out opposition would seem obstructionist and unpatriotic. Outright resistance to the government "would clearly bring the UDC within measurable distance of prosecution for sedition and rebellion," he wrote Charles Trevelyan, and he believed that UDC members agreed with him that "it was useless to oppose measures which would be persisted in despite opposition."[11] A politically shrewder course, he counseled, was to express dissent on the government's war and peace aims. Morel and other UDC leaders were suspicious of the British Government's avowed high-minded purposes of defending the rights of small countries like Belgium and striking down German militarism and correctly perceived that its war leaders were also developing annexationist aims, such as the takeover of Germany's colonies and coveting new possessions for the empire in the eastern Mediterranean and Constantinople.

Conscription thus became not so much an issue in itself, but a vehicle for challenging the government: "what is the object and aim of the war?" UDC members constantly asked. Morel also emphasized that the war could take new turns at any moment, including possible peace overtures, and the UDC had to be ready to exploit any openings for a compromise settlement. The executive committee bought his argument. The result, a UDC history concludes, was that as early as a year into the war "the Union of Democratic Control made peace by negotiation the central theme of its wartime dissent."

The many British peace people who were unhappy with the UDC's failure to take up the cause of conscientious objectors and civil liberties turned to the NCF and FOR to champion these causes. Russell, for one, exemplified the pacifist who was active in the UDC for a time, but by early 1916 had transferred his main loyalty to the NCF, whose efforts he found more immediately relevant. The union, he complained, was "too mild and troubled with irrelevancies. It will be all right after the war, but not now. I wish good people were not so mild."[12]

UDC talk of mediation was undertaken cautiously at first, as the public mood did not yet seem receptive and many UDC branches were reluctant to defend an unpopular position, but by the last months of 1915 a growing war weariness and the introduction of conscription prepared the ground for bolder initiatives. In November 1915, the UDC began publishing as leaflets speeches in Parliament calling for a negotiated peace, and in the same month persuaded a coalition of British peace groups to adopt a mild resolution stating: "That no proposals, made through neutrals or by any belligerent, for negotiation based on the evacuation of invaded territory, should be rejected by the Government without the knowledge of Parliament." In 1916, the mounting human costs of the war, especially after the heavy British casualties during the cruelly disappointing Somme offensive, further nourished the yearnings for peace.[13]

The UDC initiative with peace societies was part of a purposeful strategy of winning over affiliated sympathetic citizen groups. Occasionally these efforts met some resistance. The international polity clubs, which Norman Angell had inspired before 1914, feared being swallowed up by the union and resisted UDC affiliation. Angell, a UDC founder himself, urged the merger, but many of the clubs remained separate and competed for private funds, even though their internationalist aims were virtually the same. On the whole, however, the UDC strategy was overwhelmingly successful. The Society of Friends in particular enthusiastically endorsed the UDC program and also provided sustained financial backing.

The union's most successful inroads, however, lay with organized labor. From the onset of the Great War, the Independent Labour party (ILP), which provided much of the intellectual force and policy direction to the

Labour party, opposed British involvement. The ILP had been in decline before the war, but its antiwar message attracted the attention of dissident workers and intellectuals alike. Much like the radical Liberal dissenters, several ILP leading voices, especially Keir Hardie, Philip Snowden, and Ramsay MacDonald, believed the Liberal government had used the secret obligations of the French alliance to lead the nation into an unwanted war, the burdens of which would be borne disproportionately by the working classes. They resigned from the parliamentary Labour party supporting the war and joined forces with the UDC. The UDC and ILP never formally merged, but their cooperation involved appearances of their spokespersons together at public meetings and circulation of the other's literature. Some links were particularly close. MacDonald was a UDC founder, for instance, and after Hardie's death in 1915 became the indisputable leader of the Independent Labour party.

Their programs complemented one another. Agreeing with the union's foreign policy prescriptions, the ILP adopted them as their own; its leaders also perceived that the support of the union's middle-class intellectuals would provide more breadth and depth to the labor cause. For its part, the union valued the ILP's mass base in the burgeoning labor movement. While the union's main appeal was to intellectuals and middle-class radicals, especially in the London area, the ILP's main strongholds lay among workers in the midland industrial cities, Scotland, and South Wales.

The growing collaboration of the two groups made both a more visible presence in British public life. Largely because of its message of peace by negotiation, the UDC affiliated memberships rose, for example, from 5,000 in November 1914 to 300,000 a year later, and continued to grow throughout 1916. The Independent Labour party also flourished in the same interim. Some UDC founders—Morel, Trevelyan, and Arthur Ponsonby, for example—welcomed ILP cooperation on foreign policy, but did not formally join it, partly because they could not enthusiastically endorse the ILP's socialist orientation, but mainly because they thought the UDC would be more successful in remaining free from identification with any political party. The ILP nonetheless became a haven for Liberals who were disenchanted with the war, and their views on domestic policy were fairly close to those the ILP championed. Some, like Swanwick, initially declined membership, but by early 1916 had joined the ILP which, she said, "is taking so frank & courageous a stand against militarism." Eventually, the ILP program would become more attractive to the Labour party as a whole, which was gradually emerging as a national, and not just a class-conscious, political party. In the meantime, the Liberal party, many of whose members were increasingly caught between their reluctant support for the war and their half-hearted opposition to war measures in violation of their beliefs, would continue its precipitant decline.[14]

The belief of the union's leaders in human reason sustained their hopes for peace negotiations, even when the escalation of the war seemed to bring all belligerent parties closer to social and economic ruin. Thus in August 1916, as the Verdun and Somme campaigns raged across the channel, Morel could still write, "we should be inclined almost to despair of the future were it not that we still preserve our faith in the ultimate triumph of reason over the national and international dementia now prevailing, and that we believe there is a vast mass of opinion in this country represented neither by the politicians nor by the Press, and considerably saner than either."[15] This liberal faith, already strained, would be more severely tested in the last months of that year.

Throughout 1916, however, Morel, and his UDC cohorts remained optimistic, partly because of the organization's rapid expansion but also because of a new, more promising lobbying campaign. In May 1916, the union had taken an active part in the formation of a Peace Negotiations Committee, a coalition of nearly a score of peace, women's, socialist, and labor groups. The committee immediately began circulating a memorial, which emphasized the extended war of attrition as a "moral iniquity, involving cruelty and suffering no words can describe" and "the imperative duty" of the British Government "to seek the earliest opportunity of promoting negotiations with the object of securing a just and lasting peace." Charles Roden Buxton, one of the more radical UDC founders, was a leading activist in the broad-based outreach effort and also served as the committee's treasurer. And Swanwick, serving as chair of the committee, provided ready liaison with the Women's International League as well as labor organizations that joined the enterprise.

The Peace Negotiations Committee almost immediately had to deal with a more radical feminist group, the Women's Peace Crusade, which Helen Crawfurd and other antiwar women had organized in Glasgow, Scotland. The crusade was an offshoot of Crawfurd's earlier feminist and socialist activism. A militant suffragist before August 1914, she had been imprisoned four times for her actions and had survived three hunger strikes. She opposed the war from the outset and participated in a large antiwar demonstration on the Glasgow Green less than a week after Britain's decision to enter the conflict. Shocked by Emmeline and Christabel Pankhurst's support of the Asquith government and the war, she resigned from the WSPU and joined the Independent Labour party. Glasgow, which soon became a prolific producer of war supplies, attracted workers from outside the city, and the resulting acute labor shortage raised rents. If the Glasgow area emerged as a symbol of militaristic Britain, it also had a militant labor movement and had long been known for radical activity. Drawing on the latter, Crawfurd, Agnes Dollan, only 26 years old, and other ILP women proceeded to organize a local Women's Housing Authority, which urged tenants to withhold the rent increases and demanded rent control. Largely because of their organizing efforts, about 25,000 tenants had gone on strike by October 1915, and an appeal the next month attracted 15,000 demonstrators. The government immediately capitulated with a proposal to peg rents.

Crawfurd also opposed conscription but, chafing at the WIL's comparatively mild liberal program and its links with the UDC, wanted a grassroots socialist-oriented peace organization, and she called a "great women's peace conference" in June 1916. The resulting Women's Peace Crusade quickly expanded with open-air meetings in Edinburgh and the Scottish lowlands. The campaign provided a mass working-class base for socialists' opposition to the war, but also appealed more broadly to nonsocialists who were agonizing over the increasingly deleterious effects of the ongoing warfare on their families.

Because of its wide support, the Women's Peace Crusade impressed the leaders of the Women's International League and the Peace Negotiations Committee. Swanwick spoke to the crusade's organizational gathering, and other WIL or UDC feminist members, including Margaret Ashton and Theodora Wilson Wilson, subsequently participated in its meetings. They also tried to link, with some success, the crusade with the recently founded Peace Negotiations Committee. In November 1916, for example, the WIL persuaded Crawfurd to serve as its Scottish organizer. She expanded the membership of the three WIL branches in Scotland and opened a fourth in Aberdeen. Most important for the mediation movement, she helped to circulate the Peace Negotiations Committee's memorial, which by October 1916 had been signed by upwards of 100,000 Britons, with endorsements by several labor groups representing hundreds of thousands more.

Partly because of Crawfurd's connection to WIL and the memorial, less was heard of the Women's Peace Crusade during the winter months, but it would become re-energized with the onset of the Russian revolution in the spring of 1917. Although much of the support for the revolution derived from the hope that it would result in peace talks and an end of the World War, some socialists in the crusade, including Crawfurd, would become communists.[16]

———

In addition to group-based pressures, a few individual private citizens launched pacifist initiatives on their own or in conjunction with established peace entities. The first of these ventures was in some ways the most bizarre of all peace actions during the war. It involved the British pacifist, Emily Hobhouse, in several loosely connected solitary peace missions she initiated during 1915–1916. An indomitable spirit and, less directly, the wartime women's peace movement prompted her adventures. Born in 1860, Hobhouse was the daughter of an Anglican vicar in East Cornwall. Like many of her later pacifistic feminists in England, she had worked with the poor and infirm and in the 1890s even did a stint as an Anglican missionary for Cornish miners working in the Mesabi iron ore region of Minnesota. She fell in love with an American businessman there, but her engagement to him was eventually broken off after he went bankrupt in the depression in that mid-decade. Back in England at the turn of the century, she became an outspoken critic of British military excesses in the Boer War. Traveling to South Africa, she visited the concentration camps for civilians established by the British army and was shocked by the diseased, destitute, and ragged inhabitants, especially the women and children incarcerated in them. She organized humanitarian aid for the victims and also wrote scathing exposés of the deplorable conditions in the camps, which made her a well-known and controversial public figure.

In the following decade, she became greatly concerned about the rising war clouds over Europe, but as a semi-invalid because of a heart condition she generally kept a low profile until the outbreak of the Great War. She objected to British involvement from the start, believing it would ruin the nation, and she quipped that it would be better to put Sir Edward Grey and the German Kaiser on separate battleships and let the fight between them decide the fate of the war. She drew strength from those ministers in the Asquith government who, opposing British involvement, early resigned in protest, as well as international-oriented suffragists and Quaker friends.[17] Sympathizing with Rosika Schwimmer's petition for an armistice in the first stages of the conflict, she then concluded that mediation was premature; but the escalating fighting soon stirred her into action. Her leading role in the drafting of the open Christmas letter to the women of Germany and Austria in late 1914 early exemplified her activism.[18]

Hobhouse also found emotional support from relatives. Leonard, her younger brother, was a sociologist who was becoming a strong proponent of a postwar league of nations, and a distant relative was Lady Courtney. Moreover, a cousin, Stephen Hobhouse, converted to the Society of Friends and following the introduction of conscription in 1916 became a conscientious objector and took an absolutist position against serving even with a Quaker medical unit, since he considered it an appendage of the army. For his uncompromising views, he was incarcerated for several months and eventually wrote two books about the British prison system. Stephen's mother also was converted to Christian pacifism and published a brisk-selling book, probably ghost-written by Bertrand Russell, setting forth the case for conscientious objection.

Emily Hobhouse apparently never became a Quaker by convincement but came to follow its persuasion in accepting everyone as part of common

9.1 Emily Hobhouse, about 1905. (The Hobhouse Trust) In a biography of Hobhouse, her niece notes that of the many portraits of Emily, this was the one she "liked the best." Balme, *To Love One's Enemies*, p 257.

humanity, even in wartime when people were driven apart. As she later explained:

> Holding as I do, that a war is not only wrong in itself, but a crude mistake, I stand wholly outside its passions and feel, while it lasts, a spectator of a scene I deplore, but with which I am in no sense a part. . . . My small means are devoted entirely to help non-combatants who suffer in consequence of war, and in every movement making for Peace. . . . I believe that the only thing is to strike at the root of the evil and demolish war itself as the great and impossible Barbarity. Hence all the Governments concerned in making this war are to blame in my eyes, none better than the others, though possibly some worse.[19]

She also was a pronounced feminist, finding men duplicitous and motivated by fear, greed, and envy. They had brought on the war, she believed, and women should lead the way to peace. In the spring of 1915, Hobhouse was serving with a Quaker relief detachment in France and did not attend the women's Hague congress, probably because it was, among other reasons, logistically impossible for her to get to Holland.

Soon, she was in Rome, where she had regularly visited each year to regain her physical well-being, and she received the women envoys from the congress during their visit to see the Italian governmental leaders. She also had met with the Austrian ambassador to the Vatican to gain approval for her visit to the eastern front in Galicia to see for herself the human suffering and help with relief efforts. When Italy shortly entered the war, that initiative died aborning. During her Italian sojourn she also tried to organize a women's peace movement in the country. Press attention for her pacifist activities prompted the British ambassador to complain to the foreign office that she was a "great nuisance" there.[20]

Hobhouse was already developing bolder plans for carrying a message of peace to enemy countries. "I wanted as far as any one individual may to begin laying the foundations of international life," she confided to her journal, "*even while war was in progress* – to say 'Here I come, alone, of my free will into your country to bear you, even while our Governments are at war, a message of peace and good will.' "[21]

What followed was a kind of year-long cat-and-mouse game in which British government authorities tried to curtail her travel, but because of different perspectives and inefficiency in the government bureaucracy could never quite catch up with her. The various government departments had been in truth largely autonomous fiefdoms before the conflict and still were not well coordinated in the first stages of the war. The persistence of "peace minds" in the various foreign affairs agencies, as a journalist critic called them, and their internecine conflict with those who wanted a more intense and vigorous war effort further hindered interagency cooperation.[22] The first phase of Hobhouse's new venture began in mid-July 1915 when, back in England, she requested permission to visit Dutch friends in Holland for a few months and also to travel again to Italy. The military authorities denied her Italian request, but travel to neutral countries was the domain of the home office, which issued her a visa for the Netherlands before it had digested a foreign office paper arguing that she should be refused any requests for traveling abroad.

Hobhouse's Dutch "friends" were in fact Dr Jacobs and her colleagues in the headquarters of the newly created international women's peace organization (ICWPP) in Amsterdam, which the women's congress at The Hague had authorized, and the purpose of her trip was to provide them with temporary office support. But Hobhouse was too inclined to activism to sit still for very long. This was the time when Jacobs was developing plans with the Dutch political leadership for quiet personal diplomacy with President Wilson on mediation prospects, but was shadowed by Schwimmer and Macmillan who believed in maximum press publicity on the subject. Hobhouse had tried to restrain Schwimmer, but as a temporary secretary her opinion, she noted to Jacobs, "was of course valueless." Despite her brief time at the ICWPP offices, she found the work, as she wrote her brother, "of exceeding interest and value and one day I think the world will own the fact. It grows rapidly despite attendant difficulties." Catching up on the women's peace movement, she wrote the foreword to the published proceedings of the women's congress at The Hague, and from her office correspondence learned directly the names and addresses of the most active women on the continent.

Some women pacifists had objected to her temporary appointment and work at the Amsterdam office, however, and Hobhouse returned to England in October 1915, feeling unappreciated. She was unsuccessful there in pressing her strong views on feminism and peace strategy at two meetings of the WIL executive committee. Lady Courtney successfully moved a resolution thanking her for her Amsterdam work. But when she wrote in her diary, "Her personality always excites extremes of feeling," she was referring not to Hobhouse's nationalistic opponents, but to WIL women who nonetheless had difficulty in working with her.[23] Neither Hobhouse nor the WIL publicly explained her plans, but she may have wanted organizational support for her initiative in mobilizing women's peace sentiment on the continent. For her part, Hobhouse perceived most WIL leaders as "formalists" inspired by "timidity and expediency." The rebuffs by her Amsterdam and British colleagues nonetheless shocked and hurt Hobhouse. The reception from several WIL members, she complained to Addams, "was like a blow in the face," and she wondered how "women *could* have behaved quite like it to one who like themselves was engaged in devoted work for a neutral & sacred cause." She also told her that she desired "to possess *nothing* & so to be set free for the service of humanity."[24] Fully committed to peace activism, she was preparing to make a major personal sacrifice for the cause.

After failing to win over the WIL, Hobhouse decided to travel again on her own to Italy. In this instance, her political connections as well as continuing bureaucratic confusion facilitated her travel plans. The military, strongly supported by the foreign office, rejected her application to return to Italy, but Sir John Simon, the home secretary, was critical of the military and in fact would resign his post when conscription was introduced a few months later. Perhaps his antimilitary and pro-mediation biases as well as his awareness of Hobhouse's well-placed connections in the Liberal Party made him less willing to kowtow to the other responsible departments.[25] In any event, he decided without elaboration of his reasoning that, in the absence of good evidence of her peace activities during her last Italian visit, she should not be prohibited from leaving England. The Italian authorities, he intimated, could decide if she should be allowed to enter their country. He was actually aware of the foreign office's earlier complaints about her peace propaganda in Italy, but neither office had forwarded them to the military departments. In the absence of this information, the military authorities, following the home office's recommendation, reversed themselves and in early November approved her application for a passport with a visa to Italy.

When Hobhouse arrived in Berne, the British consulate asked the foreign office if she should be allowed to continue to Rome. While awaiting a reply from London, she sent a telegram to Ponsonby, a member of Parliament, asking him to see Foreign Secretary Grey about her detention. "No reason assigned," she wrote. "In weak health must get on, wind up affairs in Rome, cannot afford to keep flat there longer nor stay here."[26] In delivering the telegram to the foreign office, Ponsonby vouched for her poor health and modest resources, and argued that, having the proper documents, she should be allowed to go on to Italy. It is true that she was not a wealthy woman, but she had resources to pay for a maidservant to accompany her to Italy. Other supporters, including Lord Courtney, wrote letters to the foreign office affirming that her frail disposition could not long survive the cold Swiss winter. The foreign office finally compromised by giving Hobhouse the visa, but required her to sign a statement promising not to undertake any peace propaganda in Italy and not stay there any longer than necessary to settle her private affairs. Hobhouse accepted these conditions under protest and, after being admitted to Italy, complied with them. If she had at all considered reneging on her promise, she feared she was being closely watched by governmental officials and would be quickly arrested for any peace action. "I should not at all mind an English prison," she remarked half-seriously to Jacobs, "but draw the line at an Italian [one]!" Meanwhile, Simon, having supported her travel request, belatedly wrote to the foreign office after she was already in Italy that if it objected to her behavior abroad, it could cancel her passport.

Her health somewhat rejuvenated by her months in sunny Italy, Hobhouse decided in the spring of 1916 to embark on a mission to Belgium and Germany. Inspecting the camp of civilian detainees in Ruhleben, Germany, seemed her foremost objective; but if the British activist gained entry to Germany, she also wanted to visit German-occupied Belgium. At the Swiss capital, she explained her proposed travel plans to the startled German minister whom she had already met on her way into Italy the previous year. During the month waiting for a decision from Berlin, she visited the Swiss section of the ICWPP to discuss women's peace propaganda. When news

9.2 Leonard and Catherine (Kate) Courtney, September 1916. (British Library, London School of Economics)

of these contacts with pacifists appeared in the Swiss press, the alarmed British authorities decided to impound her passport and give her a new one only for direct passage back to England. They did not know where she was staying, however, and the Swiss police were not allowed to give such information to governments that might be looking for political refugees. When they finally located her a month later and summoned her to come to their legation, they were too late, for just then the German authorities gave Hobhouse permission to enter Germany. She replied to the legation that she was just leaving Berne, but would call upon her return.

Leaving behind her maid, she learned only upon her departure with a German military officer escort of the severely restrictive conditions of her upcoming trip. She had expected to submit to martial law, but later intimated that if she had known of the additional restrictions, which required her always to be in the company of her German escort and not to speak to Belgians, she likely would not have gone there. Hobhouse protested these regulations, explaining to her escort, "Your refusal to let me speak is your greatest condemnation and in one way I learn more from the prohibition than all the people could tell me."[27] But she complained in vain.

Although Hobhouse's trip is sometimes called a "peace" mission, it involved more than an exploration of possible negotiations between the belligerents. It had elements of déjà vu, as her purposes were somewhat similar to those she had pursued 15 years earlier. Just as she had then reported on British military occupation of the Orange Free State in South Africa and the terrible conditions in the camps, so was she determined to investigate the German military's treatment of the Belgian citizenry and the welfare of enemy civilians in a German detention camp.

An added incentive for her Belgian journey may have been the publication nearly a year earlier of the British Government-sponsored Bryce report on the German occupation of Belgium. Headed by James Bryce, England's venerable and highly respected scholar-diplomat, the report documented, sometimes in chilling detail, German war crimes and wanton destruction in Belgium, and it contributed to the British mindset of the evil "Huns" ruthlessly trying to subjugate Europe. When she had first met with the German minister in Berne, he had given her the German report of its version of the alleged Belgian atrocities, which she had then forwarded to Bryce. Having found British rule in South Africa cruel and oppressive, Hobhouse was prepared to believe that Germany's occupation of Belgium also involved excesses. But because British imperialism in her view had shown scant regard for small nations, she was suspicious of the government's claims that it was waging the war primarily in defense of the rights and independence of small nations like Belgium, and the extent of the Bryce report's serious allegations about Germany's human rights abuses in Belgium "troubled" her. She was thus motivated to see the conditions herself. And perhaps also, as she later wrote Lord Cecil, under secretary for foreign affairs, she hoped that her own investigations "would have a softening influence and be a link to draw our two countries [England and Germany] together."[28]

Once in Germany, she was first taken straight to Brussels. Over the next 10 days, she and her escort toured the capital as well as many other Belgian cities and towns. She regretted that she did not speak German, but fortunately had excellent interpreters throughout her journey. Among the many sites visited, Hobhouse took a particular interest in Louvain (Leuven), a large university town, parts of which German forces had burned and destroyed in the last days of August 1914. Allied propaganda cited the destruction of the town, including the university library with its many ancient manuscripts, as a prime example of the German armies' excessively punitive behavior. German military personnel in Louvain recounted for her a very different version of the pretext for the German "defensive" actions. In this view the German army, which had days earlier occupied Louvain, was responding to an unprovoked uprising by Belgian *francs-tireurs* (un-uniformed citizen militia), and the ensuing fighting resulted in a fire that soon spread to engulf the cathedral and much of the library. Finding on her tour only about one-eighth of the city destroyed, she came to believe that the Allies' claims of the physical destruction of much of the city greatly exaggerated. Despite restrictions on her movements, she also observed widespread food shortages for the inhabitants, which without the heroic efforts of the Hoover relief program would have been even worse, and the serious outbreaks of tuberculosis and other diseases. The hungry people standing for hours, day after day, in depressing food lines, she later wrote a newspaper, "faced a bit of war in everyday garb, stripped of glory – war in its ultimate effect upon a civil population, misery and broken lives."[29]

From Belgium, she went to Berlin and had an interview lasting nearly an hour with Foreign Minister Jagow, whom she had befriended before the war when he was the ambassador to Italy and she had begun spending winters in Rome. To Hobhouse, Jagow emphasized Germany's desire for peace, not from weakness, he noted, but from the realization that the fighting was a stalemate, and Britain's responsibility for taking its enemies' peace feelers seriously and making honest ones of its own. In that respect, Jagow's "hint" to Hobhouse made her an unofficial peace emissary who, the foreign minister presumably hoped, would report her conversation to the British Foreign Office. Hobhouse also visited with some German social workers and pacifists, particularly Alice Salomon and Elisabeth Rotten, a Swiss-born pacifist and educational reformer living in Berlin. Rotten had studied in England, but living in Berlin during the war had been a member of the German delegation to the women's congress at The Hague the previous year. She had then assisted the envoys from the Hague congress during their visit to the German capital, and she provided similar hospitality for Hobhouse. As secretary of a committee for the relief of foreigners in Berlin, Rotten was one of few individuals allowed to visit the British civilian detainees at Ruhleben outside Berlin, and she used her contacts to arrange for Hobhouse's access to the camp.

Hobhouse found very crowded conditions and woefully poor nourishment in the camp, but otherwise not inhumane treatment, and her main complaint was the deleterious psychological effects of prolonged captivity on the detainees. De facto reciprocity guided the operation of the camps, with each side providing roughly the same level of conditions as the other, and the right of inspection of the facilities on short notice by neutral American authorities helped to minimize the abuses.

After her 17-day trip, Hobhouse returned to Berne. With her passport stamped showing her visit to Brussels, the British authorities at the legation immediately confronted her with sharp questions about her visit to enemy territory. When reminded that she had been given a visa to Italy in return for her promise not to engage in peace propaganda, she replied that her assurances applied to Italy, but not Switzerland. The British consul reported back to London that though her "quibble" might be "legally valid, it is a piece of sharp practice showing clearly the kind of woman with whom we have to deal."[30] She also freely admitted that she had talked to Jagow in Berlin and had visited the Ruhleben camp. Hobhouse's passport was revoked and a new one issued for her direct passage back only to England and to be surrendered on arrival.

At the consulate, however, Hobhouse made a serious error, which would further undermine her purposes. Perhaps inadvertently mixed in with the papers that she handed over to the consular officers was an envelope containing her letter to Aletta Jacobs. By the time she retrieved the letter, the consulate had made a copy, which was given to British intelligence. In the letter, dated June 24, Hobhouse summarized her visit to Belgium and Germany and particularly mentioned her interview with Jagow, "whom I knew in old days. From this, much I hope may develop. I am to keep open a line of communication with him. Will you help – saying nothing[?]" She asked Jacobs that if she received any communications from Hobhouse in Britain addressed to "Dear Friend" and with contents "either allusive or with not much meaning for you," she should put the message in an envelope and take it to the German minister at The Hague to forward to Jagow. Similarly, if she received a reply to be forwarded to Hobhouse, she asked Jacobs to rewrite and sign it in her own name. Further to expose her intentions, her letter to Jacobs referred briefly to her activities with women pacifists in Switzerland and their news of the work of the Neutral Conference for Continuous Mediation in Stockholm. She noted that she was continuing to establish links with Swiss pacifists, "but posts are so uncertain across France that I think a duplicate line necessary."[31]

Given Jacobs' prominence in the women's peace movement, Hobhouse's entreaty to her to serve as an intermediary messenger was understandable. It was an unfortunate choice, however, as the Dutch physician had decided after serving as one of the women envoys to the war capitals in mid-1915 that she would thereafter be a "good" peace advocate, loyally serving as an unofficial emissary of her government to President Wilson, but refraining from more activist peace activities that might compromise her continuing leadership role in the Dutch women's suffrage movement. Backing away from peace activism, she failed to provide the European press with the report of the women envoys to the European governments and only belatedly allowed it to be published in the British WIL's newsletter. As

Macmillan lamented to Addams in January 1916, "Dr Jacobs seemed to have lost all courage." Given her new priorities, Jacobs, whatever she may have thought of Hobhouse as a person, was unwilling to support her radical proposal. Most women pacifists grudgingly acquiesced in the reality of Jacobs' preoccupation with women's enfranchisement, although her pacifist friends occasionally tried to remind her that the peace cause was still important, too. Thus Balch wrote her in late 1916: "I hear that you are making a splendid suffrage fight [women's suffrage in Holland finally triumphed in 1918], and I am so glad. But do not let the suffrage drive the other so-pressing demand upon women, the effort for world sanity and good will, out of the field."[32]

Although the British had allowed Hobhouse's and her maid's transit directly from Berne back to England, the consul had predicted that the French Government would refuse her passage through their country. That did not occur, although at the French border she and her maid were "stripped to the skin . . . an affair I am getting used to and always make light of," she wrote in her journal; and at Le Havre a British official met her to escort her back to England. "And so again I knew I was under the protection at any rate for the time being of our Foreign Office. But what was to come?" she added.[33]

The stage was indeed being set for the kind of reception she would receive in England. Eager to meet with British government leaders, upon her arrival at Southampton, Hobhouse sent Foreign Secretary Grey a telegram asking him to hear her report of her trip. The immediate reaction of his subordinates, however, was that while she might send in a written account of the information she wanted to convey, the Foreign Office should not see her. When the consul's report from Berne arrived a few days later, the negative reaction was more decisive. She was summoned instead to Scotland Yard. The interviewer's report revealed that Hobhouse gave a mostly accurate account of her wide-ranging activities in Belgium and Germany, including her long meeting with Jagow and the probability "that the Germans regard her as an unofficial peace emissary, from whose visit some results may be expected. I did not press her on the subject of the conversation," he noted, "because she evidently preferred to communicate this to Sir Edward himself, or to someone delegated by him." Because of her letter to Dr Jacobs, with its proposal that she serve as intermediary with Jagow, he recommended that she be treated "with great reserve," but that she should be received nonetheless by the foreign office.

The police shortly informed him, however, that Hobhouse had also written a message to Jagow, which she sent him from Berne, either directly or perhaps indirectly by adding it to her letter to Jacobs once she had retrieved the letter from the consulate and posted it. The police then asked the home office to intern her, as someone communicating with enemy persons, and advised the foreign office against seeing her.

Undeterred by Scotland Yard's suspicions and unaware of the mounting stonewalling in the government, Hobhouse continued to press Sir Edward Grey to receive her. On July 1, she wrote him that she had no message from Jagow and was in no way an emissary of the German Government. In the sense that she had no official title and carried no papers, she was technically correct; and, perhaps hoping her modest pose would soften his resistance, she sought to downplay her mission.

> It is simply this [she continued] – owing to the chance of old friendship I had a long and intimate talk with von Jagow – easy and unofficial in character – of the kind that gives one vivid and deep glimpses. Afterwards it came to me as a certainty that it was my duty – if you permit – to convey to you the gist of that talk – for the day might come when it might be of great use to you.
>
> One cannot convey such things by letter, therefore I have ventured to beg for the honour of an interview.

When Grey did not reply, she wrote Lord Cecil. Again she received no response; but after learning from a sympathetic official in the foreign office that Cecil was interested in her views on the German prison camps, she wrote him again. Commenting on the letter, one of Cecil's aides advised that she was "a mischievous pacifist and I suspect you should not see her. Ask her to write." To which Cecil added, "Please." Hobhouse eventually sent him an explanation of her trip to Germany, but Cecil did not answer her. Ponsonby finally told her at the end of August that the government leaders "won't listen. They don't want to hear of any approaches. They are determined to ignore any indirect overtures because they are under the impression that in time they will be able to force Germany into submission."[34]

As she was being rebuffed by the government, she was also meeting with members of Parliament, leading officials in the UDC, and members of a government commission involved with the care of British prisoners in Germany. And in early August, in an interview with the Archbishop of Canterbury, she confided the substance of her meeting with Jagow and urged him to help advance the German's peace feeler. The archbishop, while sympathetic, felt she had sealed his lips by divulging information Jagow had given her in strict confidence. In reply Hobhouse could only implore: "If the tide of militarism was rising as it seemed[,] at least the Xtian Church should say[,] 'This cannot be tolerated, thus far and no further.' "[35]

Frustrated in her many personal entreaties, Hobhouse then proceeded to voice her views publicly. Her letters to newspapers in October 1916 reporting on her escapade to Belgium and Ruhleben resulted in a short-lived media frenzy, and in response she was often attacked verbally on several fronts in Parliament and in the press. In writing about Louvain, she did not comment on the causes of the destruction, but claimed that the Germans had destroyed only approximately one-eighth of the town. The Belgian Government had earlier charged, however, that "The town of Louvain . . ., which was the metropolis of the Low Countries since the fifteenth century, is today nothing but a heap of ashes." Moreover, in response to her account, the London *Times*, citing accounts of Belgian émigrés, proceeded to side with the Bryce report, which had blamed the Germans for "deliberately" burning a great part of the city. Hobhouse replied that her respondents had not refuted her claim that only about one-eighth of the city was destroyed and one-eighth of the population homeless.

From her Boer War experiences, Hobhouse knew that strident rhetoric complaining about government actions was insufficient to win public sympathy, so she intertwined her factual accounts with remarks explaining her humanitarian motives. She also tried to give a human face to the situation. Thus in the case of Louvain, she went on, even the dislocation of one-eighth of the people was "bad," and she re-emphasized the need of Britons to contribute to the Hoover relief committee to help alleviate the suffering of the civilian population. She said less publicly about conditions at Ruhleben, but some, including inmates from neutral countries who had been released earlier, nonetheless attacked her as an apologist for the German position.[36]

More seriously, some opponents believed that she should be indicted for treason or some other criminal behavior. The Berne consul had told her that her trip to enemy territory might be "an indictable offense," and others charged that she had obtained her visa to visit Italy under false pretenses since her real purpose was to travel to neutral Switzerland, and from there to enter German territory.[37]

There is in fact circumstantial evidence indicating that Hobhouse was thinking of visiting Germany well before she arrived in Berne from Italy, and a friendly biographer who knew her well later wrote that she had "long determined" to visit Germany. And her proposed actions discussed at two WIL meetings in the fall of 1915 could have included sponsorship of sending herself or other women peace emissaries to Germany. Lord Courtney all but admitted that she had early planned such a journey while trying to put the best face on a delicate situation. His impression, he stated in the House of Lords, was that "the intention of going to Germany did not exist in her mind at all when she started for Italy. If it did exist it lay there very dormant all the winter and through the early spring months."[38]

Hobhouse's reaction to her accusers in the fall of 1916 was not at all apologetic. She instead went on the offensive, although still also explaining her unselfish purposes. She wrote several letters to government officials and newspapers setting forth her humanitarian motives and claiming that she had no idea of entering Germany or Belgium until her return journey to Switzerland earlier that spring. In one of these letters to London newspapers, she continued: "I went to Germany quite simply and openly, contravening no law; I went under my own name with a 'humanitarian pass,' in the interests of truth, peace, and humanity; and I am proud and thankful to have done so." She also published a detailed account of her interview with Jagow, whom she identified only as "a high official" in the German Foreign Office. Given his desire for peace and his expressions of German willingness "to be moderate and reasonable in the proposals on their side," she concluded, "does it not seem as if negotiations might easily be opened? If the moral courage of the governments equalled the immortal military courage of their soldiers, private conversations between ministers might begin, and a basis for honorable peace be found by nobler, saner methods than those that shock the world today."[39]

Hobhouse was never interned or arrested, probably because the government decided it did not have airtight evidence and were reluctant to make a *cause célèbre* out of an avowed pacifist professing humanitarian motives. She was far from an isolated, irrelevant voice, as she touched a sensitive nerve among increasing numbers of Britons who were growing restless about the prolonged stalemate on the continent. Besides her friends in both houses of Parliament, she also had allies in the press, especially the antiwar Labour newspaper, *The Herald*, which praised her account about Belgium as a direct refutation of the Bryce report, and the UDC reprinted the record of her Belgian experience.

Moving cautiously, the attorney general advised that it was a punishable offense in England to publish false statements relating to the war, but conceded that the government could not verify her statements about enemy territory. (The British Government seemed to have no knowledge of her earlier thoughts of visiting Galicia.) He also explained that if she had conceived of the idea of going to Germany when applying for the visa, but had not so informed the home office, her trip might be deemed punishable behavior; but contact with the enemy from a neutral country and then entering the enemy territory, "unless it amounts to adherence or is otherwise aggravated by the circumstances," was not a criminal offense under current law. He could find no good evidence, however, indicating when she had determined to travel to Germany. Perhaps, too, the intelligence service hoped it might gather more information if she was allowed to continue her correspondence. In any event, without a passport for the duration of the war, she could cause no further trouble abroad.[40]

One effect of Hobhouse's mission was that on November 7, 1916, the government issued an amendment to the Defence of the Realm Act, which prohibited Britons from traveling to enemy territory without official permission.[41] And an indirect result of her report on Ruhleben was the stimulation of domestic debate, fueled by critical Liberal members of Parliament, on whether the visits of private citizens to such camps might be as useful in learning about actual conditions, as the military and civilian personnel, preparing the official ones, might be more susceptible to self-interested bureaucratic or political influences. She had also urged the exchange of prisoners above military age and the internment of the remainder in a neutral country. Because of logistical and other difficulties, nothing came of this suggestion, but it prompted considerable discussion of the entire internment process between Lord Cecil and his foreign office colleagues with responsibilities on the subject.

In the area of possible peace negotiations, not surprisingly, her efforts had no discernible impact. It required a remarkable optimism for Hobhouse to believe that the private diplomacy of one citizen might persuade belligerent governments in a desperate multicountry war to change course. While in the Netherlands in the summer months of 1915, she had seemed to disapprove of Rosika Schwimmer's preference for a grassroots direct action strategy over quiet personal diplomacy, her own foray into enemy lands went well beyond what Schwimmer or any other activist, including her women friends serving as envoys to the capitals of Europe and the United States a year earlier, had undertaken. She nonetheless felt impelled, because of her peace ideas, to make the effort in the hope that it might open the channels for peace parlays. She was prepared to bear the personal opprobrium for her efforts, but they further impaired her already failing health and left her more discouraged.

—

Hobhouse was agitating for peace when countervailing pressures for further military escalation were simultaneously continuing to build. The mounting frustration among soldiers and citizens alike nourished support for more drastic war measures, such as German all-out submarine warfare on one side or an extended and tightened Allied embargo on the other, even though such measures would be high risk gambles that might provoke neutrals' retaliatory measures, bring about the complete alienation of neutral public opinion, and perhaps even intensify social tensions internally. Because of his less than forceful support for German expansionist war aims, Jagow would be forced out as foreign minister in late November.

Two months earlier, on September 29, Secretary of War Lloyd George, without first consulting his cabinet colleagues, asserted in an interview for an American newspaper that Britain would not countenance any neutral mediation. Designed to head off Wilson's possible peace initiative, he intimated that Britain was prepared to carry on the military contest until the Allies delivered a "knockout blow" to Prussian military despotism. "Time is the least vital factor," he went on. "Only the result counts – not the time consumed in achieving it. It took England twenty years to defeat Napoleon . . . It will not take twenty years to win this war, but whatever time is required, it will be done."

In the interview, Lloyd George claimed he did not seek vengeance, but believed that a compromise peace would leave major issues unresolved and result only in recriminations and instability and a likely resurgence of military hostilities. Nevertheless, his stark language left no doubt that he favored a fight to the finish, and his interview jolted British advocates of a negotiated settlement. Emmeline Pethick-Lawrence objected to his equating the "hell of slaughter and death" on the battlefields of Europe to a boxing match in which the winner achieved "a knockout," and once again she invoked the universal "maternal instinct," along with evidence of non-annexationist public sentiment both at home and among the nation's enemies, as a rationale for more moderate, peace-seeking diplomacy. The UDC furiously offered rebuttals to Lloyd George's arguments.[42] Even Foreign Secretary Grey, while approving of Lloyd George for his vigorous prosecution of the war effort, rebuked him for his impolitic remarks, which might severely limit Britain's diplomatic options. "It has always been my view," Grey wrote him, "that until the Allies were sure of victory the door should be kept open for Wilson's mediation. It is now closed for ever as far as we are concerned." His interview, Grey believed, would only drive Wilson closer to Bethmann Hollweg's position on mediation. Moreover, the Germans could now tell Wilson that because of British hostility to possible peace talks, they had no recourse but to intensify submarine warfare to which Wilson and his supporters might be more inclined to acquiesce.[43]

Grey's reaction was mild compared with that of Lord Lansdowne, a respected former foreign secretary, who beyond urging diplomatic flexibility, also wanted the government seriously to pursue prospects for a peace of accommodation. Many factors seemed to be coming together to point in that direction. Assembling data and opinions from a range of relevant government departments, in mid-November 1916 Lansdowne prepared an internal memorandum for the war cabinet members, which came to very pessimistic conclusions. The food supply was dangerously low, he wrote, and intensified German submarine warfare threatened further to deplete desperately needed imports. The board of trade in fact anticipated a complete breakdown in shipping within six months. In addition, Britain's manpower was also running short, the exchequer had exhausted creative methods to finance the war effort, difficulties with neutrals over the Allied blockade would likely increase, Russia was an unstable ally, its government teetering on the verge of social revolution, and Italy was "always troublesome and exacting." Given these realities, he argued that Lloyd George's "prospect of a 'knockout' blow was, to say the least, remote." With

1,100,000 British casualties already, more appalling losses to its Allies, and no prospect of reduced casualties in the future, he concluded that "neither in their interests nor in ours can it be desirable that the war should be prolonged, unless it can be shown that we can bring it to an effectual conclusion within a reasonable space of time."[44]

British military leaders did not dispute Lansdowne's main facts, but argued that it was better to fight on than to make peace. What was needed was more men, munitions, and other materiel, which, if devoted exclusively to the Western front, would result in an Allied breakthrough in 1917. Other cabinet members, while recognizing that the situation was very grave, nonetheless agreed that an imminent peace would be premature; at best it would result in German predominance on the continent and a major future menace to Britain's insular position. Only a peace providing for the independence and security of all Europe could provide a stable, enduring postwar settlement. When Prime Minister Asquith decided without any cabinet demurrals that the time was not propitious for peace talks, the result was that at least for the foreseeable future the British Government had rejected the prospect of a peace without military victory.

Lloyd George's "knockout" position had come under intense cabinet scrutiny; and while his views were not exactly endorsed, he had at least survived the Lansdowne memorandum. He had in fact cabinet allies, and his leadership skills, combined with the pessimism and indecision of the peace faction in the government, would shortly contribute to his political ascendancy. He had come a long way on his road to power. But for the German invasion of Belgium, he likely would have resigned from the cabinet at the outset of the war. Thereafter, however, he had committed himself to British military involvement and had gradually emerged as the most forceful cabinet official for the relentless continuation of the Allied war effort. While many of his Liberal colleagues could not enthusiastically endorse the war effort and were troubled by threats caused by the extended war to their values of voluntarism and personal freedom, Lloyd George was a charismatic speaker who brought energy, commitment, and a sense of unwavering optimism to the coalition.[45] Before the war, British pacifists had admired his strong liberal credentials, which included advocacy of women's suffrage. They had become increasingly disillusioned with him, however, perceiving him as a political opportunist at worst and misguided at best in his hard-nosed views toward Britain's enemies.

Despite the British cabinet's decision against peace talks for the immediate future, indecision continued, and Lloyd George finally resigned as war secretary in early December 1916. The Asquith coalition, tired and fragile, collapsed, and a new bipartisan government headed by Lloyd George soon took up the reins of government. Given his position as Prime Minister, the prospects for Britain's friendly reception to neutral mediation overtures remained very limited.

—

Meanwhile, another important citizen peace venture would result in more positive prospects for initiating peace talks. As part of his work with the Neutral Conference for Continuous Mediation, Lochner often journeyed to the European neutrals where he discussed the possibilities for mediation with other peace workers and government officials. During one of his trips to Sweden, he came in contact with the British minister in Stockholm, Sir Esme Howard. Unlike other British diplomats, who believed Lochner's German-American background made him a German apologist or stooge, Howard saw him as "an earnest supporter of the cause of Peace," and he had "no criticisms" of him during his tenure in Stockholm. Howard recommended to Lochner that for the work of his neutral conference he should get in contact with his close Hungarian friend, the disaffected journalist Ferdinand L. Leipnik, who was then living in Holland. Lochner was soon in contact with Leipnik, and their cooperative efforts would add a new dimension to citizens' search for a negotiated peace.[46]

During his prewar career as foreign editor of *Pester Lloyd*, a prominent Hungarian-German newspaper in Budapest, Leipnik had met Howard, who had served as British consul-general in Budapest from 1909 to 1911. Howard valued Leipnik for his contacts with important officials in Budapest, Vienna, and Berlin, and the two were deeply suspicious of Germany's heavy-handed policies toward the Dual Monarchy. They also shared common interests in literature, the visual and performing arts, and religion— both were committed Catholics, for example—and developed an enduring friendship.

Leipnik in particular found that German "materialistic thinking," which "does so much harm in the world," was strongly at odds with his Christian idealism. When he severely criticized the virulent nationalism fashionable in that day and refused to support his paper's pro-German policy, he lost his job in 1911. With Howard's endorsement, Leipnik then became a journalist in England. He joined a newly founded international affairs journal; when that enterprise failed, he wrote articles for the London *Times*, sometimes as its Paris correspondent. His fair and low-keyed reporting of European diplomatic developments had won him the respect of several foreign offices, although his pro-British proclivities and his friendly contacts with Howard, Sir William Tyrrell (Sir Edward Grey's private secretary), and others in the British Foreign Office were to prove most important during the World War.[47]

Despite Leipnik's efforts to be an objective reporter, his anti-German biases hardened in the twilight year of European peace, and he privately worried that the "foolishness" of Germanophiles in the British press, which he knew best, might appease opinion in Germany in return "for a German smile." The problem, he wrote Howard, was that "the Germans prefer not to smile but to show their teeth in order to get a higher price." German "impudence" made his hopes for an Anglo–German rapprochement, which might reduce European tensions, "an almost super human task," and he increasingly feared that a European war was inevitable.[48]

At the outbreak of the conflict, Leipnik was still living in England. Professionally, he lamented that because of the war "no German or Hungarian paper would print my articles because they would be pro-British and no English paper would print them because they come from an enemy alien." His latter status made him subject to restrictions and police supervision. Because of his Anglophile views, he was not harassed by the government, but he realized that his situation would become increasingly intolerable if he tried to remain in Britain. His position was even more complicated, however, because he had declared to Hungarian authorities three years earlier that he was emigrating from his homeland, and that fact had been duly inserted in his passport. "So between two chairs I am placed on the floor," he commented to Howard.[49]

Realizing he had to move to a neutral country, the British Government gave him permission to leave England, and he lived during the conflict in Holland. From there he submitted freelance articles to his prewar contacts at the London *Times*, which despite Leipnik's fears of his ostracism by the British press published several of his pieces about the impact of the war on the Austro-Hungarian empire.[50] Moreover, beginning in 1916 Leipnik also sent press summaries of Austrian, Hungarian, and Croatian newspapers to the British Foreign Office, which then asked him to search for prewar diplomatic correspondence on Eastern European countries. When the Hungarian submitted such documentation, Tyrrell noted that his colleagues found some of this information "of considerable importance."[51]

Howard may have recommended Leipnik to Lochner to give his friend some remunerative work. The British minister also knew from the Hungarian's recent letters, however, that he was distressed by the war but, still basically pro-Allied, would not embarrass the British Government if given a peacemaking opportunity. Lochner at any rate picked up on Howard's suggestion and soon realized that Leipnik, with his interesting background, might be a good choice for relaying the Central Powers' peace feelers to the British Foreign Office. Ford delegates had traveled to Berlin and had discussions with officials at the foreign ministry, but the British Government had consistently denied entry to England to all members of the Ford peace party. In his frustration, Lochner had written Lord Courtney in late June 1916, asking him to intercede and try to persuade the foreign office to allow conference members to visit England. The delegates visiting

Germany "had brought back much worth-while information," he commented, but they also wanted to "obtain first-hand an objective picture of the English state of mind." Courtney forwarded Lochner's letter to Lord Cecil, but the foreign office, feeling that "any relations with these people . . . are at the present moment likely to do more harm than good," flatly rejected the request.[52]

Lochner may have perceived Leipnik as a new way to develop a dialogue with the British diplomats. He began daily conversations with the Hungarian exile and tried to interest him in the mediation campaign. Certainly the hostilities revolted Leipnik. As he had written Minister Howard at the end of 1914, the conflict signified nationalism run amok and the vindication of military force:

> To see how Europe was thrown back into utter barbarism from one day to the other proves clearly that all our culture and civilization is a mere coat of paint . . . We all of us behave like brutes and it seems to me very futile to inquire into the rights and wrongs of the slaughter. What a wonderful example we are giving to all those we are pleased to call savage tribes and who are so distinctly our betters . . . Brutal force can lead to no other justice and nowhere do I see a sign of anything else . . . When will the time come that people will refuse being driven like cattle to kill each other[?] Not until the importance of belonging to God will prevail over the importance of belonging to a king. So long as children are being taught patriotism instead of religion the value of human life will not increase.[53]

Leipnik's pessimism made him less hopeful than his younger pacifist contact that Europe could be saved, or was worth saving. He also was more realistic about the slight prospects for an early peace. He believed that the propaganda activities of the neutral conference were "utterly ridiculous," because they amounted to meddling in the affairs of belligerent nations and, besides, played into the hands of the Germans who held the military advantage. But his Catholic faith "saved" him from the slough of despair. "I have undergone a great transformation," he wrote during the conflict, "and I humbly thank God for it." From this more optimistic perspective he hoped for peace talks that might lead to a termination of the human slaughter, and he speculated that revulsion against the killing might prompt a moral rejuvenation of postwar Europe. In any event, he felt an obligation to play his part, however small, in fostering new principles for a reformed Western world. As he wrote Howard early in the war, "what we want is to prepare the public mind for the final settlement to make another [military] adventure impossible." He believed that only the Allies, particularly Britain, offered some hope for a new harmonious, "satisfied Europe." And anticipating

Woodrow Wilson's idealistic internationalism, he rejected the balance of power principle, which to his mind created "antagonism," in favor of a "harmony of power" for postwar Europe.[54]

For his part, Lochner admitted to Leipnik drawbacks in his plans. He nonetheless managed to convince him of his disinterested motives and of Henry Ford's willingness to spend unlimited sums of money if Leipnik could draw up a more constructive scheme that might have a good chance of justifying the automaker's emotional and financial commitment to his European peacework. Leipnik then suggested that Ford should abandon efforts to spread peace sentiment throughout Europe and instead should attempt to prepare European opinion for the "basic principles" of the peace congress when it finally convened. He especially urged the conference to distribute pamphlets, publish a foreign affairs journal, and later an international daily newspaper, all of which would counteract the exaggerated national ambitions of the belligerents and foster a new international reconstruction. He told Lochner that if Ford would consider these changes, he would actively participate in his movement.[55]

Lochner was of two minds concerning these suggestions. On the one hand, he did not want to abandon propaganda activities entirely; to do so would only alienate his pacifist conferees, who believed that public demonstrations and other grassroots tactics could best nourish peace sentiment. He had had enough difficulty in guiding the conference toward an activist agenda. What would his European colleagues think if he seemed to be abandoning that approach? He was in no mood to create further dissension in the conference and perhaps wreck it altogether. On the other hand, he sympathized with Leipnik's view that changes in the conference were necessary if it was ever going to produce constructive results. Further, he liked the Hungarian personally and realized his potential usefulness to the conference.

Lochner thus attempted to meet his journalist contact halfway. He promised to ask Ford to allow him to return to the United States to discuss the entire undertaking, decide upon changes in its organization and purposes, and to consider the possibility of adding Leipnik to its work. In return, Leipnik agreed to join the conference if Ford approved and serve as a transmitter of peace proposals to Great Britain. Lochner hoped that he could persuade Ford to add Leipnik as the Allied counterpart to his own contacts with Germany. Just as Lochner hoped to win grudging respect from Wilhelmstrasse, so did he hope that Leipnik would gain at least equal respect from Whitehall. If both were successful, they might permanently open the lines of communications between the two belligerent sides.[56]

When Ford agreed to see him, Lochner immediately departed for the United States. Meeting Lochner in Detroit on October 21, 1916, the automobile manufacturer reaffirmed his support of the neutral conference.

True, he admitted, the neutral conference had made mistakes, but he excused them as inevitable in an inexperienced body. Ford then proceeded to elaborate his own ideas for the future work of the conference. Sensational publicity had had its place during the peace ship and the Stockholm days of the neutral conference, but now a new strategy was necessary. The conference should abandon all propaganda activities except insofar as they might provoke constructive peace discussions among the belligerents and in its place should substitute quiet mediatory work. Within a year, Ford had in effect come full circle from championing public demonstrations for peace to quiet diplomatic activity. Lochner was nonetheless very pleased with Ford's proposals, for he and especially Leipnik were already thinking along these lines. As part of this subdued approach to mediation, Ford approved the addition of Leipnik to the conference and urged Leipnik's and Lochner's mediative teamwork respectively in London and Berlin. He also promised to return to Europe if the two made progress with either of the belligerents and found some "definite and tangible" action he could take to hasten peace talks.[57]

To promote this activity, Ford wrote letters of introduction to all the belligerent emperors, premiers, or foreign ministers as well as another letter of introduction to whomever else Lochner desired to contact in his mediatory work. He also gave Lochner a letter to his colleagues in the neutral conference, which strongly reaffirmed his entire faith in his venture.[58] Finally, he said he would spend $10,000 (equivalent to $200,000 in 2007) a month on the conference, including the two's private mediatory efforts. This reduction of expenditures by another third would further constrict the range of activities of the neutral conference, especially with the addition of Leipnik to the payroll. Lochner, however, was too pleased with Ford's commitment to his mediation scheme to complain to his patron about the additional financial belt-tightening. He recognized that if Ford insisted on the 10,000-dollar figure, then he would have to tell the neutral conference personnel that the conference had accomplished its purpose and that thereafter Ford would continue his efforts with only a skeleton organization. The reduction allowed Lochner more easily to justify an abandonment of the democratic voting procedures in the conference in favor of a centralized administration with the different departments reporting directly to Lochner, who in turn kept Ford informed. He nonetheless did not give in easily and upon his return to Europe tried to persuade Gaston Plantiff to find a way to get his boss to restore the monthly stipend to $15,000. Only with such funding, Lochner argued, could the conference continue its propaganda activities as well as launch its academically oriented international journal.[59]

Why the auto magnate agreed to see Lochner and then proposed almost the same changes in the neutral conference, which Lochner and Leipnik had already agreed upon, is not entirely clear. It may be that Ford, always unpredictable, had no considered view of the mission of the conference and simply acted on one of his hunches. It is more likely, however, that Plantiff, who wired Ford before Lochner's arrival, summarized Lochner's suggestions for changes in the conference so that Ford could contemplate them. Certainly he had at least forewarned the automobile magnate about the proposal to add Leipnik to the neutral conference.[60] Ford probably decided that the proposed changes would allow him to continue his nominal support of the venture while further reining in his financial commitments. The downsizing would make it less painful for all concerned if he later decided to withdraw all financial support for his neutral conference. In the short term, Lochner's proposal for quiet mediation, conforming to his own more sober reassessment of his peace efforts, was worth supporting.

It is also possible that the Detroit industrialist had briefly discussed the question of mediation with Wilson during their two Shadow Lawn meetings in October. It is clear that the main reason for both interviews was the upcoming election and Ford's efforts to publicize his endorsement of the President. And given the President's low opinion of the "unwise" automobile maker, he may have deliberately refrained from any comments on mediation during their meetings. But because the first meeting lasted three hours, it is hard to see how they could have avoided discussion of some aspects of the Great War. Moreover, the second interview occurred only three days after Ford's Detroit rendezvous with Lochner; the Lochner–Leipnik stratagem was thus fresh in his mind. Ford undertook his second trip east for two purposes: to support Wilson's election and to promote Lochner's plan for initiating discussions with the belligerents.[61] He accompanied Lochner to New York a few days in advance of the latter's sailing. Before going on to Shadow Lawn to see the President again, he conferred with Democratic Party leaders there on the paid advertisement endorsing Wilson's re-election that he planned to publish in several metropolitan dailies. He and Lochner also used that occasion to prevail upon Vance McCormick, chairman of the Democratic National Committee, to persuade Secretary Lansing to give Lochner a letter requesting American embassies abroad to extend him courteous treatment. The state department granted Lochner a new passport, which removed restrictions upon his entry into Germany. As if this did not suffice, Ambassador von Bernstorff gave Lochner a letter addressed to the German authorities asserting the neutral nature of Lochner's mission and requesting that the German Government's order against his free transit in Germany be revoked.[62]

Lochner decided to return to The Hague by way of the Scandinavian countries so that he could visit the delegates of the neutral conference there and then make a side trip to Berlin. He hoped that he could draw out the German officials on their peace terms. Lochner's return to Europe in early

November came at an auspicious time, for the possibility of a negotiated peace was being discussed everywhere. News of Wilson's electoral triumph shortly after Lochner's arrival in Europe bolstered speculation about a negotiated peace. Since Wilson could now try mediation without any immediate embarrassment to his political fortunes, it was widely assumed that he would shortly make a peace move. And with the winter months approaching, all kinds of rumors of peace activity began to circulate.

A few peace leaders emphasized additional indicators of mediation prospects. They uncritically assumed that despite Germany's decisive military conquest of Roumania, the more moderate civilian party still prevailed in German ruling circles and would accept peace terms requiring the withdrawal of the troops of the Central Powers from most of their occupied territories provided their adversaries could guarantee a secure and just peace. In the United States, David Starr Jordan gave one optimistic appraisal of the German situation:

> There is an influential party in favor of such a [reasonable] peace in England, France, Russia and Germany. In Germany that party is particularly powerful. The German war party, the party which until the beginning of the war controlled the great general staff of the Germany army, has now been ousted. The men close to Emperor Wilhelm in these days are in favor of peace with honor, and were against the world war of the old general staff.[63]

In Europe, Lochner believed that the German civilian leaders had strengthened their position:

> All of us who have been in Germany are struck with the tremendous change which has taken place in the country. With Dr Zimmermann as Minister of Foreign Affairs, and with the Chancellor's position stronger than ever, we really feel that German militarism is in check. Even the smash through Roumania does not appear to have shaken the determination of the German government to refrain from the annexation program.[64]

There was some truth in these statements. The military extremists had not yet gained control of German foreign policy. Moreover, although the victories of the Central Powers in Roumania had diminished the Allies' receptivity to peace talks, it had strengthened Germany's moderate leaders in their willingness to consider and even offer peace proposals. As early as mid-August, German civilian officials hinted that they hoped for an American peace move, and they became more interested in American mediation following Wilson's re-election.

Their uncertainty as to Wilson's plans finally led Chancellor Bethmann Hollweg to develop two possible roads to peace, which he later described as *zwei Eisen im Feuer* (two irons in the fire). He would formulate a peace offer of the Central Powers while still encouraging Wilson to develop his own. In developing the German initiative, Bethmann publicly intimated that the Central Powers were prepared to join a league of nations after the war. Not only Lochner, but some Allied spokesmen interpreted the chancellor's statement as another sign of Germany's moderation. Finally, Lochner's favorable reaction to Zimmermann's appointment was understandable, for the new foreign secretary seemed outwardly eager for American peace overtures. In fact, upon Lochner's arrival in Berlin, Zimmermann's first words to him were, "Well, when will President Wilson act?" Typical of his *chutzpah*, Lochner then gave the foreign secretary a document offering the services of Ford's neutral conference for mediation and requesting a personal audience with the German emperor at which he could deliver it. Zimmermann turned aside that request, telling Lochner that these peace entreaties "would necessarily be met with a sympathetic attitude on the part of the whole world, but that, at the moment, he entertained considerable doubt as to these efforts bringing about any practical result." He refused to discuss Germany's peace terms in greater detail until he had a chance to verify Lochner's credibility. He volunteered, however, that disarmament would be desirable and in any event economically necessary for a prostrate Europe after the war, and he indicated that if he found Lochner trustworthy, he would ask the German minister at The Hague, Friedrich Rosen, to communicate further with him. Always looking for the bright side, Lochner assumed that Zimmermann sincerely favored a démarche leading to a compromise peace.[65]

But Jordan's and Lochner's analyses obscured unpleasant realities that should have made them less sanguine. They misjudged Zimmermann, who only posed as a greater friend of the United States than his less decisive predecessor, Jagow. In actuality, Zimmermann had earlier privately mocked Wilson's pretensions as a mediator and was a German nationalist who could, if the circumstances warranted, support many of the annexationist aims of the military party. He was in fact more in sympathy with the military extremists than Jagow had been.[66] The two's faulty appraisal of the new foreign secretary was, however, no worse than other Americans who followed German developments. Ambassador Gerard as well as American newspapermen, for instance, hailed Zimmermann's appointment, claiming that he had always been frank and honest in his dealings with them. These Americans may have been somewhat predisposed to like Zimmermann's supposed "democratic" leanings because unlike the aristocratic lineage of nearly all Germans in the diplomatic service, he was from middle-class origins and had worked his way up through the less prestigious consular service bureaucracy.[67]

Moreover, had Lochner and Jordan studied the German political situation more carefully, they would have noticed that as early as mid-October 1916 Germany had stepped up the submarine campaign against merchant shipping (excluding passenger liners) according to the rules of cruiser warfare. The annexationists, led by the Holtzendorff–Hindenburg–Ludendorff faction, were directly responsible for this policy. Hoping temporarily to appease these annexationists, the Kaiser agreed to a partial resumption of U-boat activity, but was still unwilling to approve further escalation while the military struggle seemed to be going in Germany's favor.[68]

This decision failed to satisfy the annexationists. The military leaders continued to mobilize all their talents in favor of unrestricted warfare, which, they believed, would lead to the defeat of the Allies before their own alliance succumbed to attrition and war fatigue. In particular, Admiral von Holtzendorff, the naval chief of staff, argued that unrelenting German attacks with a new fleet of larger and more powerful submarines could reduce tonnage getting to Britain by 39 percent within five months and force a starving Britain to sue for peace. U.S. entry into the war would be irrelevant, as the war would be over before American troops could reach Europe. Ludendorff and Hindenburg used this reasoning in their mounting attacks on Bethmann Hollweg's opposition and to win over Kaiser Wilhelm.

Frustrated by the continuing dreary stalemate, not only conservative and nationalist elements in Germany, but also the center and progressive parties and even elements of the SPD in the Reichstag, increasingly favored unleashing the submarines on Allied and neutral shipping. The implication of their rhetoric and party resolutions was that Bethmann should be guided by the military high command on the submarine question and that his further resistance to their recommendations would cost him their political support. More broadly, public opinion looked to the submarine as the path to victory. By the fall of 1916, a historian of the German war experience writes, "the submarine underwent a metamorphosis in the popular imagination. It became a panacea, the wonder weapon whose all-out employment promised to resolve the war and bring the British to their knees." When the pressures for all-out submarine warfare continued to mount, Wilhelm, Bethmann Hollweg, and Zimmermann found it increasingly difficult to maintain their more moderate, flexible position. Before making a final decision on the submarine, however, the civilian leaders decided to make a public appeal for peace. The reasons for the German peace move were complex, but basically grew out of the government leaders' uncertainly concerning Wilson's intentions, their desire to exploit the psychological implications of Germany's favorable military situation, most recently the occupation of Bucharest on December 6, and their attempt to delay a decision on the submarine question.

On the last point, Bethmann reached a tenuous understanding with the military authorities. In return for the military's acceptance of a delay on a final decision on the renewal of unrestricted submarine warfare, he promised that if the Entente powers rejected the peace offer of the Central Powers, then he would agree to further discussions of expanded submarine warfare against armed merchantmen without warning. The Chancellor apparently hoped that regardless of its immediate consequences the German peace initiative would receive a friendly reception in the United States and perhaps constrain the Wilson administration from breaking diplomatic relations and going to war after intensification of submarine activity. The German peace offer also had political and moral purposes domestically. If the Allies rejected it, as seemed likely, they would appear to be in the wrong, thereby bolstering the sagging morale of the war-weary German army and citizenry to continue the fight against their recalcitrant foes. With these considerations in mind, on December 12 Germany announced without elaboration that the Central Powers were ready to enter into a peace conference with their adversaries.[69]

Meanwhile, Lochner had managed to involve Leipnik more directly in his peace activity. During Lochner's American visit, his Hungarian contact had continued to develop more modest "substitute" plans for the neutral conference in the area of postwar reconstruction. Believing the belligerent governments were consumed with winning the war and would shun private mediation, he envisioned the neutral conference calling together experts from neutral and warring nations in "the burning task of reconstructing International Law" for the practical settlement of future international disputes. He believed that Ford, if called upon by governments, would "gladly support an *enquete* to this effect." The private neutral conference, he hoped, might thus become "the nucleus of a Comity of Nations which is the precondition of a reconstructed Europe." He also wanted Ford, whose company was noted for the production of affordable tractors for American farmers, to provide material and moral support to the postwar agricultural reconstruction of Europe. He prepared a draft of these plans to present to the British Foreign Office, emphasizing, for example, that the legal basis for postwar reconstruction was "an essentially Anglo–American ideal" already publicly espoused by Wilson and British government officials.[70]

Upon Lochner's return to The Hague, however, Leipnik found that his American associate had seemingly revived the focus on quiet mediation. Lochner told his Hungarian contact about his meetings with Ford and Zimmermann, and Leipnik, encouraged by these developments, formally joined the neutral conference. The Hungarian exile understood that his first task as a private intermediary was to arrange for talks with his friends in the British Foreign Office. This was no easy task, for in British eyes Leipnik was an enemy alien and had to receive special permission to travel to Britain. Realizing his difficulty, Leipnik deliberately exaggerated the importance of his proposed mission. Through the British minister at The Hague, he cabled Sir William Tyrrell, his friend in the British Foreign Office and Grey's confidant, asking if he could convey some "urgent and most important information about Wilson's future policy" to British officials on his way to the United States where Ford had arranged Leipnik's personal interview with the President.[71] Ford had not yet set up any such interview, but Leipnik obviously believed that only a concocted story of his imminent appointment with Wilson would impress the foreign office with the importance of his mission. Despite Leipnik's deception his story was not altogether a ruse, for he had already told Lochner that he wanted to see Wilson if his discussions with British officials in London promised some hope for peace discussions, and both he and Lochner must have assumed that if he continued to the United States, Ford could arrange for his interview with the American President.

The British authorities took Leipnik at his word and agreed to see him on his way to the United States. In the inner sanctums of the foreign office, it was Tyrrell who persuaded his more reluctant colleagues to receive Leipnik. After reviewing the Hungarian's pro-British background for his subordinates and superiors, Tyrrell vouched for his integrity: "I have always found Mr Leipnik reliable and devoted to this country." In fact, he urged that if the foreign office agreed to see him, they should brief him on the British attitude on peace talks. Leipnik would be told that he was going to the United States on his own, but "the value of his seeing President Wilson consists in the latter's preference for the views of amateurs, as it were, as compared with experts."[72]

In mentioning Wilson's reliance on "amateurs," Tyrrell was likely thinking of Colonel House. But his comment also underscored his understanding of the realities of Anglo–American relations. As Sir Edward Grey's personal envoy to the United States in 1913–early 1914, he had frequently conferred with Wilson on the Anglo–American approaches to the unfolding Mexican revolution and matters of common interest to the two nations. Tyrrell was not an amateur, but from his American visit he likely gained an appreciation of the President's reliance on the reports of citizen eye witnesses and his own personal emissaries as opposed to official diplomatic contacts. Colonel House's three missions to Europe as Wilson's personal envoy surely confirmed this impression. In addition, he realized that the American ambassador at St James's, Walter Hines Page, had completely lost Wilson's confidence and could no longer be relied upon to convey

British attitudes to him. Page had only recently returned from the United States where Wilson had put off seeing him for several weeks and then had shown no sympathy for Page's pro-Allied views.[73] If Page was no longer useful, then perhaps Leipnik could relay the British position to the U.S. chief executive.

Tyrrell's arguments won over his ffice colleagues, Eric Drummond, Lord Hardinge, and, most important, Sir Edward Grey. The difficulty, as Lord Hardinge pointed out, was that the British officials were very wary of any peace proposals and thus were unsure what they should tell Leipnik. Grey simply said that they could inform him that Britain would continue to support its continental Allies, which would demand the withdrawal of enemy troops from their territories as well as reparations or security against further aggression.[74]

9.3 Ferdinand L. Leipnik, visa photograph, 1916. (National Archives, United Kingdom)

After also receiving clearances from authorities in the home office and intelligence services, which also had to approve his British visit, the foreign office informed Leipnik in early December that it would see him upon his arrival in London,[75] but a new development delayed his cross-channel trip. This was the invitation to Lochner by the German minister in The Hague, Friedrich Rosen, to meet with him. Realizing the imminent possibility of peace talks, Rosen had returned to Berlin in November and convinced Zimmermann that their government should prepare the press of neutral nations for their peace overtures. Propaganda vaunting Germany's sincere desire for a negotiated peace would create neutral opinion sympathetic to the Central Powers' objectives, in case peace talks actually developed.[76] Because of Bethmann Hollweg's and Zimmermann's obsession with anti-cipating a Wilsonian peace move, it is probable that the German peace offer of December 12 came before this propaganda activity had begun, but the German peace offensive affected Lochner's relationship with Rosen and Leipnik. The evidence is far from conclusive, but it is probable that once Rosen had received Zimmermann's endorsement of his peace propaganda in the neutral nations, he realized that Ford's neutral conference might serve as a convenient vehicle for circulating to the European neutrals German propaganda concerning its receptivity to a negotiated peace. About a week before Germany issued its peace note of December 12, Rosen asked Lochner for a conference, and the two met for more than an hour. The discussion was friendly and led to several more meetings between the two in the following weeks.[77]

When Lochner began his talks with Rosen, he asked Leipnik to delay his departure for Britain until he could obtain more definite information on Germany's attitude toward peace talks. If Germany seemed agreeable to a negotiated peace, then Leipnik could relay this information to his friends in the British Foreign Office. Lochner even urged Rosen to meet with Leipnik, and the German minister agreed to hold an "unofficial" meeting with the Hungarian on Christmas eve. A week before the scheduled session, how-ever, Woodrow Wilson sent his own peace note to the belligerents. This Wilsonian peace move, and his deliberate follow-on efforts for U.S. medi-ation of the war, would of course affect the Leipnik–Rosen informal meet-ing, but would also have marked impact on all succeeding considerations about a negotiated settlement.

10

Woodrow Wilson's Independent Mediation

"The longing for an early cessation of hostilities in Europe is today an honest one, participated in by almost all the [American] press," Count Bernstorff noted in a long report to his government in early December. The German ambassador believed that this sentiment for peace discussions penetrated even Anglophile newspapers like the New York *Tribune*, which had recently editorialized: "For the millions of Americans the present war is a tragedy, a crime, a piece of willful and collective madness, and the greatest service America can render is (to allude to the catch phrase coined in connection with the fruitless peace mission of Henry Ford) to 'get the boys out of the trenches.' " Regarding the extensive press speculation on possible peace negotiations, Bernstorff commented: "Reports of the sessions of many and various peace societies are set out in the greatest detail, and everything bearing upon the question of peace which is to be found in news transmitted from overseas is printed in the most conspicuous places and made the subject of adequate comment in leading articles."[1]

Bernstorff believed that Wilson, owing his re-election mainly to Americans' aversion to the European war, "will have the wish to live in peace with us," and he urged his government to refrain from any escalation of U-boat warfare until Wilson's mediation, which he was confident would come very soon, was given every chance of success.[2] He thus might have been tempted to slant his reporting with disproportionate treatment of the most positive signs of Americans' keen interest in a mediated settlement of the war. But the ambassador's survey of U.S. public opinion fairly summarized the prevailing mood in the country. He did not identify the peace societies, but the Woman's Peace Party had just held its annual meeting in the nation's capital at which some speakers urged U.S. mediation. Moreover, not just ardent peace advocates, but even more conservative voices spoke out in favor of peace talks. Thus the *New York Times* published an extensive series of articles written by Nicholas Murray Butler, under the pseudonym "Cosmos," expounding on the most hopeful prospects for a negotiated settlement, and George Kirchwey, President of the American Peace Society, also publicly endorsed U.S. mediation. In his report, Bernstorff may have been thinking mainly of the American Neutral Conference Committee, which was already receiving consistent press coverage. The ANCC peace activities would intensify in late 1916–early 1917.[3]

When Bernstorff sent off his opinion analysis, Wilson had already decided to make his own mediation move. Any explanation of the American president's subsequent peace initiatives must begin with his two overriding foreign policy aims: keeping out of the war if possible and trying to serve as mediator to end it. In his own analysis of the changing realities of America's relationship vis-à-vis the European belligerents, the two seemed to be more inexorably linked in these months. He perceived that his relations with the two warring sides had developed to the point where for the first time since the first months of the war he might be able to pose successfully as a truly impartial arbiter. Following the German Government's *Sussex* pledge in May 1916, promising to suspend submarine attacks on merchant shipping, German–American relations had improved. Simultaneously, various British actions, especially its increasing violations of America's neutral rights—blacklisting of U.S. companies trading with the enemy, increasing censorship of the mails, for example—had resulted in a marked deterioration of Anglo–American relations. These changing international developments prompted Wilson to consider other mediation alternatives.

As part of this same analysis, Wilson saw less pleasant realities in the international situation. He surmised that the war was entering its final, climactic stage and that if peace did not come soon, then the belligerents would decide on a fight to the finish. Such a decision would surely involve an escalation of both sides' incursions on American rights on the high seas. Minor incidents—the sinking of several Allied merchant ships in early November 1916, with the loss of some American lives—indicated the fragile nature of improved relations with Germany and might portend an escalation of its submarine warfare. Already acutely aware of the recent sea incidents, Wilson believed that a continuation of the war would inevitably result in Germany's decision for an all-out submarine campaign—a decision that would almost surely bring the United States into the war on the side of the Allies. Wanting to avoid another head-on confrontation with Germany over the submarine issue, which would only destroy hopes for a mediated solution, he seemed prepared to compromise his administration's previous insistence on "neutral rights." In early November, for example, he astonished House by arguing that the sinking of merchant ships with the loss of U.S. lives was somehow less serious than lives lost on passenger vessels and that the American people would oppose war no matter how many citizens were lost at sea.[4]

On the other side, there was still the strong possibility, even if the German Government refrained from unrestricted submarine warfare, that the United States would find Britain's violations of America's neutral rights strained to the breaking point. In these circumstances, an American declaration of war against Britain was improbable, but it was at least conceivable. Wilson told House on one occasion that he would not shrink from war with the Allies if they desired it, and House believed he was deadly serious. In either case, Wilson felt that the alternatives would be intolerable for his nation.[5]

Still wanting to avoid American military involvement, he viewed his own mediation as a last, desperate attempt to end the war before its horrors engulfed his own nation. As House recorded their conversation:

> His argument is that unless we do this [mediation intervention] now, we must inevitably drift into war with Germany upon the submarine issue. He believes Germany has already violated her [*Sussex*] promise of May 4th, and that in order to maintain our position, we must break off diplomatic relations. Before doing this he would like to make a move for peace, hoping there is sufficient peace sentiment in the allied countries to make them consent.[6]

Thus Wilson perceived very practical, self-interested reasons for trying to end the war through his mediation. But what form would it take? He could have continued to prod the Allies to accept the House–Grey memorandum as the basis for his mediation, but Wilson had gradually become disillusioned with the British foreign secretary, who had failed to implement the agreement. Although there were good reasons why the Allies would be skeptical of a Wilsonian elusive promise "probably" to enter the war on the side of the Allies in case the Central Powers rejected U.S. peace overtures, the American president increasingly saw the Entente governments' disinterest in his mediation as symptomatic of a general selfishness among the belligerents. As early as June 1916, he had written House, "The letters and glimpses of opinion (official opinion) from the other side of the water are not encouraging, to say the least, and indicate a constantly narrowing, instead of a broad and comprehending, view of the situation."[7]

Wilson pursued this new approach right after his re-election. He then told House that he wanted "to write a note to the belligerents demanding that the war cease," and he clearly hoped to announce his formal peace offer before Germany might issue its own request for formal peace parlays.[8]

Events conspired, however, to delay his initiative. First, in the early fall Germany had begun the forced deportations of many thousands of idle but able-bodied Belgian citizens, to labor service in the homeland, and the issue quickly complicated German–American relations. In response, the

American embassy in Berlin, which represented Belgian interests, made informal complaints on humanitarian grounds at the German Foreign Office but without effect. Reports of the deportations appeared in the U.S. press in mid-November, which inflamed public opinion at a time, Wilson believed, when Americans had become more even-handed than ever before in their approach to the issues of the war. Annoyed that the deportations might delay, even derail, his peace initiative, he tried to downplay the matter, reasoning that it was ridiculous to protest against the German actions when the United States had not objected to its invasion of Belgium. Lansing and House disagreed, however, the latter arguing that the practice "was one of the most brutal and indefensible acts Germany has yet committed. The tearing away of fathers, brothers and young girls from their families to be taken into foreign territory to become practically slaves, is something I thought we might well make a protest about." Having just heard from Wilson of his determination to forge a new departure on mediation, he also used the German deportations as an argument for delaying any Wilsonian peace move.[9]

While Wilson and his confidants debated the correct course, the career diplomat Joseph C. Grew, who was serving as the chargé at the embassy during Gerard's home leave in the fall of 1916, also raised the issue of the Belgian deportations with Bethmann Hollweg, who following Grew's presentation suddenly turned the subject to peace talks. The chancellor, the diplomat reported, spoke in a way "impressive beyond description, . . . sitting at his desk, speaking slowly, deliberately and sadly of the horrors of war. He seemed to me like a man broken in spirit, his face deeply furrowed, his manner sad beyond words . . . I could not fail to feel, although not directly expressed, his clearly intimated disappointment that the United States had not taken steps leading toward peace." Wilson acceded to a formal protest to mollify public opinion but, using Grew's account of his interview with Bethmann, coupled it with a frank request for Germany's cooperation in resolving the issue amicably so that the way would be cleared for possible peace talks. Germany finally rejected the U.S. protest on December 11, but German officials privately promised U.S. diplomats (and began to follow through with) an amelioration of the practice.[10]

Then, in the midst of the deportation question, Wilson caught a very bad cold and, mostly incapacitated for 12 days, severely curtailed his schedule. To his few visitors Wilson appeared tired and unwell, and he did not complete a draft of his peace proposal until November 25. During the same interim he composed a prefatory essay to his draft note. This essay was never issued, but it starkly revealed Wilson's disenchantment with the purposes of the war and his mounting obsession with "peace." Previous wars, he wrote, had involved decisive battles, decorated national heroes, and citizens' "sharing in the glory of the state." But the current "horrible nightmare" was without brilliant victories, heroes, and glory, and "trench warfare and poisonous gases are elements which detract alike from the excitement and the tolerance of modern conflict. . . . Where is any longer the glory commensurate with the sacrifice of millions of men required in modern warfare to carry and defend Verdun?" he wondered. His debunking of the heroic soldier in the current war was not that different from what Jane Addams had espoused in her homecoming speech at Carnegie Hall 17 months earlier.

Wilson further intimated that the triumph of either side was undesirable, as the victorious powers would impose a harsh peace settlement, which would only rankle in the defeated countries until they were strong enough to seek revenge in another military bloodbath. He was convinced, however, that the current slugfest was a complete military stalemate. While continuation of the war might ultimately bring success to one side or the other in a year or two, it would be achieved only with "the attrition of human suffering, in which the victor suffers hardly less than the vanquished." The most striking reality of the war, he emphasized, was this untold human suffering, and the psychological basis for an enduring peace would be the belligerents' recognition of "the uselessness of the sacrifices made." He concluded with a brave vision of an enlightened mediated settlement:

> the aim of far-sighted statesmen should be to make of this mightiest of conflicts an object lesson for the future by bringing it to a close with the objects of each group of belligerents still unaccomplished and all the magnificent sacrifices on both sides gone for naught. Only then would war be eliminated as a means of attaining national ambition. The world would be free to build its new peace structure on the solidest of foundation it has ever possessed.[11]

Wilson had indicated his hopes for a stalemated outcome in a newspaper interview only four months into the war;[12] now after more than two years of inconclusive slogging on the European battlefields he was privately elaborating the same preference more fully. Very soon he would boldly express these thoughts publicly.

———

In his mediation initiatives, Wilson would draw sustenance and encouragement from prominent British Liberals who favored a negotiated peace. Following the President's address to the League to Enforce Peace in late May 1916, in which he committed the United States to a postwar peace league, a number of these Liberals sent him letters and memoranda urging the use of his good offices for mediation of the conflict, and a few of them even journeyed to the United States to try to get his attention. Wilson wanted to do common cause with them, but was somewhat constrained by his decision early in the war to avoid seeing nonofficial representatives of belligerent countries. He briefly considered making an exception in the case of the British Liberals, but decided that he had to apply the exclusion policy consistently. He would not even reply directly to their letters to him. These Britons nonetheless managed to promote their peacemaking ideas indirectly through Colonel House and other Wilson confidants, and House kept some of them informed of Wilson's sympathy for their views.

The earliest among them were Norman Angell and Noel Buxton, both of whom were visitors to American shores. Angell taught and lectured in the United States in 1915 and 1916; he also wrote articles for the *New Republic*, which the President regularly read. The British publicist was more interested in coaxing the American president away from the issues of neutrality and committing him to a league of nations than in mediation.[13] Angell and Buxton were both UDC leaders, and the latter was also a member of Parliament and an earnest active advocate of Wilson's mediation. Buxton met with House as well as Secretary of the Interior Lane during the summer of 1916. The two sent Wilson their accounts of these discussions, and the colonel also forwarded other letters and press clippings from British sources. After receiving such information, Wilson commented on "the stupidity of English opinion," and, clearly intimating his identification with the peace-seeking Liberals, lauded "the brave struggle a few men and a few journals are making to set it right and throw a little intelligence into the discussion of the things that lie at the very foundation of the peace and right administration of the world." Upon Buxton's return to England, he continued to send letters proposing mediation to House, who again informed Wilson of their contents.[14]

John Howard Whitehouse, another antiwar Liberal member of the British Parliament, also journeyed to the United States in the early fall to present his views to the Wilson administration. Shortly after the President's re-election, Whitehouse conferred with House, who reported to his chief: "Whitehouse is a pacifist, is perfectly reliable and is anxious for a move to be made for peace. He gave me as clear insight into the situation, I think, as it would be possible to get even if I were in England." Wilson replied that House's recent messages, including the account of his meeting with Whitehouse, corroborated his own view that "this is very near the time, if not the time itself, for our move for peace."[15]

Another conduit for British opinion supporting negotiations was John Palmer Gavit, publisher of the New York *Evening Post*. Gavit was not a pacifist but, a strong supporter of Wilson, forwarded him his reform agenda for the administration's second term. He had also attended the Henry Street discussions on mediation strategies in the first stages of the war and was well connected to pacifistic liberals on the American Neutral

Conference Committee. During the President's November illness, Gavit was one of his few callers. When he came to the White House, he brought with him a brief typewritten essay by Charles P. Trevelyan, entitled "What the President Can Do." A founder of the UDC, Trevelyan had arranged to have his paper hand-carried to the United States and given to the American Neutral Conference Committee, with which the Union of Democratic Control was already in contact. The ANCC in turn entrusted Gavit with a copy to take to Wilson.[16]

Trevelyan was only 28 in 1899 when he first won election as a Liberal to the House of Commons. Disturbed by reports of British military atrocities in the Boer War, he began to look at foreign policy adventures with a critical eye. By 1906 he was cooperating with dissenting radicals in his party who were increasingly opposed to the anti-German orientation of British foreign policy. He became particularly disillusioned with Foreign Secretary Grey, who in his view had increased the nation's commitments in the entente with France without publicly explaining these obligations. When, despite his advocacy of continued neutrality, England in August 1914 declared war against Germany, Trevelyan, believing he was a victim of his party leaders' duplicity, resigned his position as education under-secretary in the government. He wrote at the time: "when you have reached the depth of dishonesty of Asquith and Grey over the French alliance, you are capable of any immorality." His antiwar stance estranged him from his family, especially his father and his youngest brother George, a historian who had been a close personal adviser. He continued his service in Parliament, however. Believing it was his duty as a citizen not to hamper the British military, he voted for military appropriations. But he also used his elected position and his prominence in the UDC to become an early political voice in Britain for a negotiated end to the fighting.[17]

Trevelyan's paper stressed that all peoples wanted security, and Wilson's address to the League to Enforce Peace in May had provided for a world organization, which offered the only real hope of a secure future. Appealing personally to Wilson, the Englishman wrote that "My countrymen do not yet see – but they will if you are persistent – that your approval of the League of Peace amounts to American cooperation in the objects for which they profess to be fighting – a secure civilization. Sooner or later your espousal of that plan will affect the course of the war. It will shorten it. They do not yet see that your plan ought to be the first of the terms of peace." At their White House meeting, the President thanked Gavit for the message and used the occasion to ask him confidentially to compile and send him more information about sentiment for peace talks in the belligerent nations.

Gavit almost immediately forwarded him a record of a talk he had just had with the former Washington bureau chief of the Associated Press, who had spent much time in Europe since the onset of the war. This journalist mentioned several signs of war weariness in France among the fighting men in the trenches and their families and relatives at home in France, but that censorship and vigilant police surveillance suppressed that information. To this information, Gavit added his own support for a Wilsonian peace initiative: "Of course this must be the state of affairs in all of the armies – the determination to fight to the bitter end is so largely confined to those who aren't doing the fighting! How quickly an end of war would come if the men on the fighting line should suddenly awaken to the absurdity of the whole business, and with a loud laugh rush into each other's arms." Wanting to believe that nonofficial opinion wanted peace, Wilson replied that the reporter's information was "probably very near to being an assessment of the actual facts."

Ten days later, Gavit sent him a detailed account of opinion in England written by a clergyman with connections to the British peace movement. The pastor's comments began with an admission that "the great majority are behind the Government in its determination to continue the war because very few people believe that at the present time real and lasting peace on reasonably satisfactory terms can be made." He also emphasized, however, that the British "people in general would gladly respond to any authoritative suggestion that an equitable peace could be attained without further fighting." Among his many examples of peace sentiment, he cited the memorial circulated by the Women's International League and other British peace groups asking the government to begin peace talks, which had grown to 150,000 signatures. He believed, furthermore, that there were many others, including himself, who did not sign the petition because "the time was not ripe, that no peace worth having was in sight." But he believed that if Germany could provide positive indications that it was willing to treat its enemies reasonably as equals, then the moderate forces in Britain "would at once begin to make their influence upon the Government." Again, Wilson was thankful for the information and reiterated to Gavit, "I want every tip of this kind that I can get."[18]

Recovering from his illness, Wilson read a draft of his mediation proposal to House and shortly re-emphasized his determination to issue it. "The [international] situation is developing very fast," he wrote, "and if we are to do the proposed thing effectively we must do it very soon." But more delay ensued. On December 4 came the resignation of the Asquith cabinet, which precluded any peace initiative until a new government was formed, and he had to prepare and deliver his annual message to Congress. There was also fallout from the conspiring of Wilson's wife and House, who had persuaded Wilson to ask Tumulty to resign and accept another appointment. Although Tumulty successfully pleaded to retain his job, the confrontation with his private secretary was emotionally draining on the President.[19]

Wilson further delayed his mediation proposal while he considered the comments on his draft by House and Lansing. The secretary of state still opposed Wilson's mediation and believed the government should instead be protesting Germany's sinking of merchant ships. Disagreeing with Lansing's tough diplomatic stance, extending back to his willingness to countenance war with Mexico, Wilson had come to regard his secretary as a mere bureaucrat but, as the only other intimate foreign policy adviser besides House, he still had some influence. Wilson continued to ask for the secretary's opinions and even more trusted the judgment of House. Despite the two's strong objections, Wilson proceeded to draft his peace note and to prepare for its dispatch to all the belligerent capitals.

The President's mounting determination to offer his good offices for mediation coincided with the heightened agitation of pacifists for peace. Following Wilson's August 30 interview with a delegation of the American Neutral Conference Committee, the group continued to expand its activities and received more consistent press coverage. Recognizing the necessity for a secure and just peace, it distributed a petition declaring that peace parlays should include the relinquishment of conquered territory, self-determination of national groups, and a world organization to settle future disputes. The petition also urged the United States alone or in conjunction with other neutral powers to "invite the belligerents to state the basis upon which they would be willing to begin peace negotiations." Endorsing the ANCC petition, Addams sent a circular letter to women's groups asking members to sign the appeal.

The ANCC also formed a branch in California to stir up support for mediation on the West coast. Entirely willing to give Wilson time to develop his peace program, the committee attempted to organize public opinion behind mediation so that when he made his peace move, he would find widespread support. Caught up in this expanding activity, Lella Secor quit her magazine position to direct the ANCC's publicity. She summarized the group's tactics in a press statement in early December, only two weeks before Wilson's peace offer: "We are working to arouse, crystallize, and organize sentiment and place it at the disposal of the President of the United States, so that he may take even an unprecedented step, if he chooses, and know that he has the undivided backing of the country."[20]

Of greater importance were the ANCC's contacts with like-minded organizations in England. Woodrow Wilson might be appreciative of Americans' encouragement of his mediation, but he hardly needed their support for what he had already decided to initiate. What he wanted and sought was intimations of public attitudes on the war in the belligerent countries, particularly those intimating a desire for peace negotiations. The ANCC recognized the importance of foreign opinion, but was hampered by slow and uncertain communications. Nevertheless, in a small way the group served as a conduit for several British expressions in support of mediation. As early as September, the American group was reporting on the British citizens' petition calling for peace negotiations, and their own petition was patterned after the British model.[21] In addition to cooperation with Trevelyan, the ANCC also worked with Whitehouse, who long before meeting with House had conferred with ANCC members. Whitehouse's reports of peace sentiment in his homeland encouraged the committee's leaders to redouble their efforts at mobilizing public sentiment behind their mediation campaign. When an anonymous Californian, for example, gave the ANCC 1,000 dollars to circulate in Great Britain reprints of a magazine article urging a negotiated peace, Whitehouse readily agreed to make the necessary arrangements for their distribution.[22]

The ANCC through Gavit had brought Trevelyan's message to Wilson in mid-November, but later the same month the British Liberal also sent him a personal letter in which he repeated his earlier arguments more forcefully. He recognized dangers in such dramatic appeals, but thought they would have a good chance for success.

The difference between you and the other rulers of the world today [Trevelyan wrote] is that you have imagination and faith in what men can do if they can once get out of this welter of hate. As you have trusted the instinct of your own people and won a most remarkable victory because you believed in their capacity to respond to high standards, my earnest prayer to you is to have the same faith in the multitudes of common men and women in our poor countries. Do not be discouraged by the cold refusal of Governments to welcome your offers of help. Do not judge of opinion by the base press of our capitals. Here, in the least ruined country, there is universal war-weariness except among the politicians and the press, and a yearning for a great solution, which will make your opportunity before much time has passed.

Trevelyan then went on to urge the President to eschew confidential diplomatic soundings in favor of public appeals to arouse latent popular voices for peace.

But, as you have faith in democracy, have faith also in its necessary processes. However much you try to influence Prime Ministers and Chancellors, it is far more important that your great, sane policy should be heard and understood by the peoples. They wait for some voice of authority repeating loudly and constantly enough to create conviction that a reasonable settlement is possible which will give them all security, and that their enemies are disposed to agree to it.[23]

As Trevelyan's letter worked its way to Wilson, the ANCC privately aired his earlier message at a large luncheon in New York on November 25, and gave it to the press for release as an "open letter" to the American people nine days later. ANCC leaders asked colleagues to use their influence in securing prominent coverage of the letter in their local newspapers.[24]

Trevelyan had sent his personal letter through William H. Buckler, a U.S. citizen serving as a special agent to the American embassy in London. Buckler was a personal friend of Trevelyan and other members of the British liberal left and since mid-1916 had been serving as a middleman between them and Colonel House, thereby allowing them to avoid British censorship whenever they wrote U.S. officials. In forwarding Trevelyan's letter to House, Buckler commented, "Whether one thinks his policy wise or foolish[,] one cannot but respect his sincerity," and he added that overall the "peace by negotiation" views of British radicals were "distinctly improving." Buckler had sent the letter to House only after Trevelyan agreed to allow House to decide whether to share it with his boss.[25]

Colonel House's position was, to say the least, delicate. He had previously forwarded to his chief the British Liberals' reports of growing peace sentiment in their homeland and their promises of support for Wilson's mediation. But these suggestions were more likely part of House's continuing use of flattery to nourish the President's hopes to serve as the world's peacemaker. When it came to a specific Wilsonian peace initiative, however, he backed away. He wrote the President on November 30 that he considered the time inopportune and estimated the chances of his successful mediation at less than 10 percent.[26]

Besides, for any mediation initiative, House strongly preferred confidential diplomacy between governments, which was quite different from Trevelyan's radical advice of making public appeals for peace over the heads of governmental leaders. House was likely unaware that Wilson had seen Trevelyan's earlier message and, given discretion about forwarding his personal letter, may have had reservations about sharing it with his chief. But House was less inclined to withhold information from Wilson than to give him his own comments on important foreign policy matters. In any event, there was no reason to withhold Trevelyan's letter when the Liberal's first message appeared in the newspapers the day before he received it. In any event, realizing that Wilson was determined to press on with his peace move, House had already sent his chief an account of his earlier meeting that previous day with Whitehouse, who had also expressed considerable optimism for Wilson's successful mediation.[27]

On December 7, House saw Whitehouse again, and the British Liberal, after receiving news of the completion of the reorganized British cabinet, prepared a memorandum arguing that Lloyd George's premiership would unite the moderate forces in Parliament against the new leader and make the new situation even more favorable for Wilson's mediation. Whitehouse's reasoning was dubious, as Lloyd George's leadership of a new coalition government more likely signified the ascendancy of hawkish views in the government. House sent the memorandum to Wilson, but made one last effort to steer him back toward a pro-Allied approach. Recalling a private conversation he had had with Lloyd George nearly a year earlier, in which the latter had talked enthusiastically of Wilson's mediation, he suggested that the new Prime Minister might agree to revive the House–Grey Memorandum. He even enclosed the draft of a letter to Lloyd George that could initiate discussions on that basis. It is hard to see how Lloyd George's "knockout" blow interview could be reconciled with his earlier interest in negotiations (House later conceded that he doubted whether the British leader was "still of the same mind" on mediation), but the President's aide was prepared to advance any viable argument to try to deflect his mentor from a more strictly neutral—and public—mediation initiative.[28]

When Wilson read Whitehouse's and Trevelyan's optimistic forecasts, he had already completed a draft of his mediation proposal. But he had not firmly decided upon the exact form of his appeal or the timing of its release. The two British Liberals' views arrived at just the right moment, however, to strengthen his determination to offer mediation as soon as possible. Wilson indicated their influence at the same time he decisively rejected the House–Grey formula:

> That was a most impressive letter [he wrote House] from
> Mr Trevelyan – and a most interesting memorandum from
> Mr Whitehouse. The time is near at hand for *something*!
>
> But that something is not mediation such as we were proposing
> when you were last on the other side of the water, and therefore I do
> not think it would be wise to send the letter you were kind enough to
> submit to me to Lloyd George. We cannot go back to those old plans.
> We must shape new ones.[29]

Wilson immediately began to rework the earlier draft of his mediation proposal. Another House tactic was admonitions to Wilson to move forward deliberately so as to consider many approaches and to minimize possible mistakes. Though the President was then undeterred by House's and Lansing's opposition to mediation, their arguments made him more cautious in his writing of the peace note. On December 9, he even submitted a second draft to Lansing.[30]

Then came the German note of December 12, asking for a peace conference. Though upstaged and initially somewhat depressed by the German initiative, Wilson moved quickly to get his note issued before the Allies

10.1 Charles P. Trevelyan, pre-1914 campaign portrait. (Special Collections, University of Newcastle upon Tyne)

submitted their replies, probably negatively, to the German one and closed the door to his own peace move. He reworked his draft and, after a further reading by Lansing, had it sent to all the belligerent governments on December 18. An indication of his haste was that he did not wait for another review by House, who was in New York. Unlike Wilson's earlier draft, which had proposed a conference of representatives of the belligerent governments and the most directly affected neutrals, the final text de-emphasized the plight of neutral nations and did not specifically call for a peace conference. It did not even suggest formal American mediation. Nor did it contain the veiled warning in the previous draft that the belligerent replies would affect America's future foreign policy. Indeed, when House saw the marked-up original draft, he commented, "I have seldom seen anything he has written with so many changes."[31]

But even more forcefully than the first draft, his note asserted that "the objects which the belligerents on both sides have in mind in this war are virtually the same," and it proceeded to enumerate some commonly expressed public aspirations of the two opponents: to secure the rights and privileges of weak peoples and small nations, the desire for a secure peace, and willingness to join a postwar league of nations. In conclusion, the note asked the belligerents to state their war aims publicly so that the entire world could see how near the warring sides were in their desire to end the conflict. Such statements, Wilson implied, might prepare the way for a peace conference at which he would be willing to serve as mediator.[32]

It is tempting to argue that the American advocates of peace and British antiwar Liberals strongly influenced Wilson's decision for independent mediation. Obviously, he did not operate in a vacuum and understood that he needed intimations of clear signs of interest in a negotiated peace in the belligerent nations if his initiative would have a chance of success. Citizen advocates of mediation—mostly Americans, but also some Europeans—had regularly expounded on the deep reservoir of peace sentiment in the warring nations in their numerous interviews and communications with the President. Much as he preferred to procrastinate on the subject, there is no reason to doubt his sincerity when he told them that he had thought through their neutral conference proposal "dozens of times" and wrote Tumulty that he had been doing "a great deal of serious thinking" about mediation prospects.

Wilson was not an overburdened chief executive. He worked conscientiously, sometimes well into the evening hours. But he was well disciplined in arranging his schedule, so that he had time for golf almost every morning and to attend to his correspondence and the writing of state papers, and he usually did not go to his White House office until the afternoon. He had time in short to think about the desirability, timing, and form of his possible mediation initiative. Then in the last months of 1916, the Americans, particularly Gavit and the ANCC leadership, probably helped to sustain his attention to the subject, and their British counterparts surely strengthened his conviction that his mediation might bring an end to the hostilities.

It is entirely possible, however, that Wilson would have adopted the same policy, even in the absence of agitation from peace advocates and peace organizations. Following his re-election, he became remarkably unreceptive to outside advice on mediation. Beyond welcoming Gavit's "every tip" on belligerent opinion and expressing his enthusiasm for Trevelyan's and Whitehouse's reports, Wilson never acknowledged any influence outside his administration in these trying days of late 1916. Nor is there evidence that Wilson was aware of the two Englishmen's cooperation with American peace workers.

Wilson's initiative troubled his closest aides. House particularly depre-cated Wilson's assertion in his note of the similar war aims of the two sides. That one comment, the President's counselor complained in his diary, "will give further impetus to the belief that he does not yet understand what the Allies are fighting for. That one sentence will enrage them." He had persuaded his chief to delete "a much more pronounced offense of the same character" in the earlier draft, but the President, obsessed with the thought, had "put it back in a modified form." House thought it would make him more unpopular among the Allies and perhaps rule him out as a potential peacemaker. "I find the President has nearly destroyed all the work I have done in Europe," he ruefully concluded.[33]

Lansing was also dismayed at the President's bold action. Like House, the secretary of state continued to have strong doubts that Wilson's neutral mediation could then succeed, and both he and House also worried that failure would largely negate the President's chances for future mediation moves. The two also feared that the Allies would reject the overture, while the Germans might respond more agreeably, as if it was a follow-on endorsement of their earlier note. The result might tip the United States dangerously close to the position of the Central Powers. The last thing House and Lansing countenanced in these critical days was their nation declaring war against the Allies. As Lansing observed in his dairy, "Our present position is becoming impossible. We are very near the edge of the precipice. When we do go into the war, and we might as well make up our minds that we are going in, we *must* go in on the side of the Allies, for we are a democracy."[34] He had even written Wilson on December 8 that Germany's unsatisfactory responses to U.S. notes over recent attacks on Allied merchantmen justified the severance of relations with that nation, but the President simply ignored his advice.[35]

Lansing had praised his chief's draft of December 9 and substantively advised only for the deletion of the President's commitment of U.S. forces to a postwar league of nations. But he also wrote the President that he was deeply troubled that Wilson's note might work against the Allies. The secretary did not baldly say that he favored their cause, but directly raised what he had written in his diary—that Germany might accept the Presi-dent's initiative while the Allies rejected it. With such a result, he warned Wilson, "can we avoid the logic of our declarations? And if we act in accordance with that logic, would it not be a calamity for the nation and for all mankind? I have told you how strongly I feel that democracy is the only sure guarantee of peace, so you will understand how these questions are worrying me."[36]

House and Lansing privately gave the President their objections to the note, but the day after it was sent out the secretary also voiced them publicly in an unsubtle way. In a statement to the press, Lansing commented that the U.S. note was not a peace initiative and not designed to support the recent German peace note; on the contrary, he asserted, the United States was "drawing nearer to the verge of war," and the purpose of the U.S. note was to elicit statements of belligerent war aims so that the administration could decide on its future course vis-a-vis the warring sides. The secretary hoped that the pro-Allied tilt to his statement might more likely elicit a sympathetic Allied response; in any event, it might reduce the chances of a diplomatic crisis with them.

When Wilson saw Lansing's statement, however, he was livid and thought seriously about demanding his resignation. He did not fire him—it was a Wilson failing not to dismiss disloyal subordinates—but ordered the secretary of state to issue another statement saying he regretted that his earlier one had given "a wrong impression" and that the United States was only interested in the terms of peace and was not intimating any change in the nation's neutrality policies. Lansing complied to the extent of issuing the correction, but he also told the French and British ambassadors, without informing the President, that his first "verge of war" statement reflected the U.S. Government's real fear of Germany's imminent submarine warfare forcing the country into the war. He even offered them advice on what war aims the Allied governments might enunciate in their reply to Wilson's offer. Because of these efforts, Lansing surmised—correctly it turned out—that the Allies valued his first statement and discounted his correction.[37]

Allied opinion hotly resented Wilson's identification of their high-minded, moral war aims with Germany's militaristic and territorial ones, but it would be the German Government that rejected his initiative. Although there were fundamental differences within the German civilian and military ruling circles on the question of submarine warfare and war aims, they generally agreed that the United States was too closely tied to the Allies, both emotionally and commercially, so that Wilson could never, despite his lofty pretensions, serve as an impartial mediator. Some assumed in fact that the Allies must have colluded in Wilson's recent initiative. Above all, they all did not want Wilson at the conference table. "I won't go to any conference!" the German emperor scrawled on Wilson's note. "Certainly not under his chairmanship!" While the Kaiser might have then opposed any mediator, his comments had a special animus when directed against the head of state of the world's largest democracy. The earlier German initiative was designed to try to pressure the Allies to a peace conference, at which they would talk directly without their enemies. Some European neutral site might be feasible, but without U.S. participation. As Zimmermann revealingly confided to Bernstorff: "The interposition of the President, even in the form of a clearinghouse, would be detrimental to our interests and is therefore to be avoided. The basis for a future conclusion of peace we must settle by direct intercourse with our opponents if we do not wish to run the risk of failing to obtain the results desired because of pressure from the neutral Powers."[38]

Bethmann and other civilian leaders also worried about Wilson's call for publication of the belligerents' war aims which, if acted upon, would only expose the deep gulf between the annexationists and antiannexationists and probably seriously undermine public morale. Moving quickly to try to squelch Wilson's likely follow-on peace initiatives, the German Government formally rejected Wilson's offer only a week after receiving it. The response thanked Wilson for his "noble initiative," but made clear that Germany would negotiate only with their enemies. The Germans allowed for his possible involvement in a conference devoted to international security issues, but only after the peace terms were settled.[39]

Germany's rejection represented the demise of its peace offensive, which from the start had been poorly conceived and clumsily implemented. In the first place, the foreign office seemed remarkably insensitive to the Allies' deteriorating relations with the United States and thus failed to try to exploit the differences. Moreover, if Germany was seriously interested in peace talks, it could have launched a diplomatic offensive, calling attention to its moderation and sincere search for accommodation with its enemies. But instead, by late 1916, the influence of the military authorities had greatly increased; and implacably opposed to diplomatic negotiations, they ruined chances for a more flexible, coordinated foreign policy. Their resulting influence easily tolerated the upsurge of sinkings of Allied merchant ships and, more ominously, promoted the Belgian deportations, which had the effect of inflaming American public sentiment against Germany. Finally, the German negative reply removed the sense of urgency among the Allied leaders, who no longer had to fear possible pressure from both the U.S. and German Governments. On December 29, the Allies rejected the German note as empty and insincere and proclaimed they would consider no peace without restitution, reparations, and security guarantees. They then moved more deliberately to prepare their responses to Wilson's note.[40]

Germany's negative response to the U.S. mediation offer did not faze the President, who on the contrary believed that peace was not far off. To advance his mediation initiative, he was already thinking of giving a public address in which he would appeal directly to public sentiment for peace in the belligerent nations. The idea was not a sudden inspiration. As early as May 1916 in fact, House had written in his diary that Wilson "can so word a demand for a conference that the people of each nation will compel their governments to consent." Wilson hinted at the same approach some weeks later when he wrote his friend that when he decided to mediate, the warring powers "will have no choice but to heed [my initiative], because the opinion of the non-official world and the desire of all peoples will be behind it." Perceiving the growing influence of the Conservatives in British ruling circles and their reluctance to accept any American peace move, his aide had seemed to agree with this thinking. In encouraging a Wilsonian peace initiative, for instance, he had written his mentor: "It may be necessary to arouse the latent feeling of the people in both England and France in such a way that they will compell [sic] their governments to act."[41]

One wonders how serious the President's aide was in advocating this strategy. It is just as likely that it was another instance of House trying to sustain the President's interest in mediation by promoting a policy option he might be reluctant to endorse in practice. Confidential government-to-government diplomacy had always been his forte, and he had opposed the President's note asking the belligerents to state their war aims publicly. Why should he now become a convert to a more daring public diplomacy?

One possible reason for his conversion to this approach may have been his realization that his friend was determined to pursue his peace initiative and would not be deterred, even in the face of the belligerents' unhelpful replies. But House more than grudgingly accepted this new direction. Having gotten over his serious misgivings with Wilson's earlier peace note, he became an enthusiastic supporter of his friend's new diplomatic venture. He convinced himself that the President, having sent his first peace note, should follow through with bolder proposals. At least initially, however, House thought the appeal would be made after Wilson had received replies to his December note, hopefully from both sides, of at least their minimum war aims and would be directed mainly at the governments. On December 27, for instance, Bernstorff had told House that Germany could not publicly state its war aims, as Wilson's note had requested, but he thought his government might be able to provide them confidentially.[42]

While waiting for possible German confidences, House and Wilson met to talk over the outline of possible peace and security terms that the President might express in a public speech. They agreed that the key issue from the American side, as Wilson had earlier indicated publicly and privately, was the establishment of new and authoritative international machinery for preserving peace after the conclusion of the present maelstrom. The issues of territorial settlements and indemnities would be subordinate to the overriding security imperative. Wilson also believed, however, that his address might provide at least an outline of his thinking on the principles underlying territorial adjustments, as it would frame the basis of a peace settlement upon which the United States would agree to join a new world security organization.[43]

Accordingly, between January 4 and 11 Wilson wrote out a "peace without victory" address in which he stated his general principles for ending the war and for postwar security. After House commented on his draft, the President ordered the state department to cable his address to the American chiefs of missions in the capitals of the belligerent nations for publication in the local newspapers at the same time as its actual delivery to the U.S. Senate. Convinced that a groundswell of peace sentiment was already evident within the warring nations and only needed nourishment, he deliberately aimed his peace appeal over the heads of the war leaders to the peoples. As House noted in his diary: "The President is not so much concerned about reaching the governments as he is about reaching the people."[44]

The Allied governments' reply to his December 18 note arrived after he had completed the speech, but before he had given it. Wilson found the Allied extreme terms profoundly disturbing. They could not possibly be realized and were mostly bluff, he surmised. Because the Allied note threatened to cut off all possibility of further peace discussions, he was determined to press forward quickly. "I feel," he wrote, "that time is of the essence."[45]

House, meanwhile, continued his discussions with Bernstorff. The German ambassador was at first mostly in the dark about his government's position on peace discussions. While aware that Berlin was determined to exclude the United States from any peace conference, he sincerely believed that Wilson could be helpful in bringing the belligerents to the bargaining table. House for his part believed his discussions with Bernstorff were moving forward in a positive direction. One difficulty was that since Britain had severed the telegraphic cables in the English Channel at the outset of the war, communications between the German Government and its embassy in Washington had to be transmitted circuitously via the German embassy in Stockholm and the Swedish wire to Washington via Buenos Aires, and vice versa. They had to be resent from each place. To speed up the interchange, House directed the State Department to allow the German Government's coded communications between Washington and Berlin to be transmitted over the department's lines via the American embassy in London. Bernstorff and the German Foreign Office frequently used this more direct route during these negotiations.[46]

As he warmed to the President's peace initiative, the colonel assumed a more optimistic view of Germany's leadership. No less than the American pacifists and the American press in Germany, he had little difficulty in persuading himself that Foreign Secretary Zimmermann, whom he liked personally as a result of several earlier discussions with him, and his moderate civilian cohorts still held the upper hand in Berlin. As he told his mentor as late as January 18, "the [German] Government is completely in the hands of the liberals." Presumably, the German civilian leadership would react favorably to a public appeal for peace negotiations as leverage against the recalcitrant military party.[47]

In the five weeks between Wilson's December note and his "peace without victory" address, pacifists continued their agitation for a negotiated settlement. The American Neutral Conference Committee and the Union of Democratic Control in particular expanded their collaborative efforts. The latter group extravagantly praised Wilson's note, and pamphlets calling for peace parlays written by two of its members, Ponsonby and Charles Roden Buxton, who was more radical than his brother Noel, were hand-carried from England to the ANCC office in New York. Given to the press, generous extracts of both were soon reprinted in the *New York Times.*[48] Bertrand Russell also wrote an "open letter" to the President, which likewise was brought to the ANCC. The British philosopher was a fairly well-known name in the United States. He was married to an American and had taught at Harvard before the war, and his unconventional political philosophy had stirred academic debate. He had achieved notoriety for his writings in support of conscientious objectors, which had resulted in the British Government's cancellation of his passport and his dismissal from his college at Cambridge. The ANCC held an impromptu press event at which copies of Russell's letter were given to reporters. Within hours his letter became a front-page story in many metropolitan newspapers.[49] It also sent Balch, Kellogg, and Peabody to Washington to deliver the letter to the President. Whether he actually received them or read Russell's message is unclear.[50]

Common themes in these messages—the many moderates in the German and other belligerent governments, the rising voices for peace among their peoples, appeals for a Wilsonian populist mediation strategy for ending the war, and an array of necessary international reforms for the postwar war world—were familiar, but its authors also more forcefully pressed two arguments. First, the belligerents needed to state their territorial and other war aims publicly. Then people could assess whether their highly moralistic rhetoric was matched by moderation and reasonableness. And Buxton, for one, already suspected, rightly, that secret agreements committed the Allied countries to fight on for imperialistic ends. "*What are these agreements?*" Buxton asked. "Ought we to go on fighting without knowing what we are fighting for?"[51] Second, they emphasized the continuing slaughter of "millions" on the battlefields and the imperative need for peace before European civilization collapsed in civil discord, chaos, and revolution.

George Foster Peabody, an ANCC committee member, had forwarded Ponsonby's pamphlet to Wilson, who replied that he would "look it over with a great deal of interest." Whether Wilson actually read it is not known, but in any case the pamphlet arrived after he had already completed the text of his upcoming speech.[52] There is also no evidence that he followed newspaper coverage of other peace-seeking liberals, but he had no shortage of material, as House was continuing to ply him with reports from Whitehouse, Noel Buxton, Ramsay MacDonald, and other members of what go-between Buckler labeled the "negotiation group" in Parliament.

Buckler believed that these members numbered only about 40 in the House of Commons, but "by their character" had some influence.[53] One printed source that did directly affect the drafting of Wilson's speech was the liberal *New Republic*. He then praised its editors, Herbert Croly and Walter Lippmann, saying "I am in entire agreement with their articles on peace;" and afterwards he graciously wrote Croly: "I was interested and encouraged when preparing my recent address to the Senate to find an editorial in the New Republic which was not only written along the same lines but which served to clarify and strengthen my thought not a little. In that, as in some many other matters, I am your debtor."[54]

———

Five days before he gave his speech, Wilson displayed his mounting determination for a more aggressive peace offensive during an interview with Louis Lochner and Ferdinand Leipnik. This meeting represented the culmination of the two men's activities on the other side of the Atlantic. These efforts began when Leipnik held his "unofficial" meeting with the German minister at The Hague, Friedrich Rosen, on Christmas day. With both the German and American peace initiatives now public, the meeting took on added importance. The two discussed in generalities the basis for a peace settlement, but their language was guarded. Leipnik could say little since he had not yet conferred with the British officials, and Rosen was not much more specific. It is unlikely in fact that Rosen was given any negotiating authority or specific guidance. Lochner surmised from Rosen's remarks, however, that except for Alsace-Lorraine, which Germany refused to relinquish or even discuss at the peace conference, the German Government was willing to negotiate on the basis of the status quo antebellum. First, however, Germany needed definite assurances from the Allies that they would abandon their assumption of a superior moral position and bargain with the Germans on terms of absolute equality.[55]

Leipnik immediately left for London to report this interview to the British Foreign Office. He saw Eric Drummond on January 4 and must have related his recent conversation with Rosen, for Drummond noted to his colleagues that Leipnik "gave some rather valuable information." Drummond also believed the private envoy was honest and sound in his personal views on peace and should be encouraged to communicate any additional information on the peace question to British authorities.[56] He conveyed these impressions personally to Leipnik who prevailed upon Lochner to join him, and together the two departed for the United States where they hoped to inform Woodrow Wilson of their recent interviews. Ford met them in New York and then arranged for an interview for them with the President on January 17.[57]

When the two were escorted into the President's office, they found

Wilson talking to another visitor, and they discovered that Tumulty had reneged on his promise of a private interview, but had included them among several five-minute callers whom Wilson routinely received as part of his official duties. The President greeted the two men formally, but quickly showed interest when Lochner explained his interviews with Zimmermann and Rosen and the latter's sensitivity to the assumption of the Allies' superior moral position. Lochner told how Wilson's peace note had alleviated this problem somewhat because in dealing with "both sides on terms of absolute equality, [it] has acted as a soothing balm to wounded German souls." Wilson seemed pleased with this information and listened intently while Leipnik described his meeting with Drummond and his inquiry into British peace terms.

Leipnik noted that Britain was primarily interested in a league of nations, but because of distrust of Germany, needed American support for the new organization. Without American membership in such a collective security scheme, it would be worthless, but British leaders feared that American opinion was not behind Wilson on this issue. Here Wilson interrupted sharply: "But don't they know that my party has endorsed it? This is very significant. In the very convention which nominated me and which drafted the party's platform, the League of Nations policy was endorsed." Wilson admitted that he could not "prove" that the American people would support it, but he did not doubt that Congress would endorse the league. "This is only a supposition," he added, "but I have every reason to believe that I am right."[58]

Wilson then asked what could be done to convince the British that the Germans were not completely untrustworthy, and Leipnik brought up the matter of a Bryan conciliation treaty. When Bryan had become secretary of state in 1913, he had implemented a peacemaking plan, which had earlier become an integral part of his maturing pacifism. During his tenure at the state department, he proceeded to negotiate a few dozen bilateral treaties with foreign states in which the United States and other contracting parties pledged in any dispute to delay hostilities for a year while the two sides arranged for an investigation of the contentious issues. The treaties had no enforcement mechanisms. Bryan believed, however, that the investigation would allow passions to cool and war would be avoided. One of these "cooling off" treaties was with Great Britain, but Germany had refused the offer.

Wilson of course was very familiar with the conciliation treaties, and his former secretary of state had renewed his proposal in mid-1916 and more assertively immediately after the election as a possibly important démarche in bringing the belligerents together. In recognition of his delivering the West for the President's re-election, Bryan informed House, he should be the President's special emissary for peace talks in Europe, in which he would easily succeed. "They are all Christians and not pagans," he told him, "and I could talk to them in a Christian-like way and I am sure they would heed." Supremely confident in his simplistic pacifist program, he also asked Ambassador Gerard, who was then on home leave, to prepare the way for audiences with the German Foreign Office and the emperor. When Wilson heard of Bryan's proposed missionary diplomacy, he, House, and Gerard in their separate ways persuaded the Great Commoner at least temporarily to defer his bold plans.[59]

It was neither Bryan nor American officials, however, but European sources that revived the idea of a Bryan conciliation treaty. In the summer of 1916, for instance, Ambassador Gerard reported a rumor that the German Government might suggest a Bryan accord to deal with American–German issues over the submarine. Moreover, individuals at the Interparliamentary Union, the internationalist group of national legislators, reminded German officials of the Bryan treaties and urged them to try to negotiate one with the United States. "The Interparliamentary Union people feel strongly," Lochner had written six weeks earlier, "that if Germany is willing to sign such a Treaty, the Entente will then see that in the future no such thing as the invasion of Belgium is likely to happen. This, they contend, will make for a speedier peace."[60]

Leipnik and Lochner had picked up on this suggestion, and Leipnik now pointed out to the American president that if Germany would agree to negotiate a Bryan treaty with the United States, it would be a test of German sincerity to Great Britain. Germany's refusal to sign such an agreement with the United States had been used in Britain to indicate that Germany opposed any pacifistic idea. But, Leipnik added, the Central Powers' willingness to sign such a treaty now could be used by the Allied statesmen to point out to their peoples that a new spirit of conciliation had permeated Germany. When Wilson interjected that the Bryan treaties provided for only a one-year delay in hostilities and that the peace league was "the only true guarantee of peace," Leipnik answered logically, "But you must first lay the foundations for your building. The negotiation of Bryan treaties will make a beginning. On this beginning you can erect your structure."

Wilson wished to remain skeptical, but was obviously impressed by Leipnik's argument. Sensing Wilson's interest, Lochner pointed out that many of his other European friends had also intimated that the key to peace talks was some German act indicating its willingness to function more along internationalist lines. He specifically mentioned the secretary of the Interparliamentary Union, Christian L. Lange, a Norwegian, who despite his sympathies for the Allied cause had urged the Ford neutral conference to persuade the American and German Governments to negotiate a Bryan treaty as a sign of Germany's "international-mindedness." Wilson frankly conceded the merit of this argument. "This is very significant indeed," he replied.

The meeting originally intended to take five minutes lasted more than 20 before Tumulty re-entered and reminded Wilson of his other appointments. In fact, he had come in once previously, but had failed to divert the President who was absorbed in his discussion. Wilson regretted that he had to end the interview, but in parting assured them of his gratitude: "You have indeed rendered me a great service."[61]

The interview pleased the chief executive, not because the two envoys had given him any new ideas, but because they strengthened his belief that he was on the right track with his own peace efforts. He felt that his upcoming speech, scheduled to be made to the U.S. Senate on January 22, would alleviate the Allied fears on the question of collective security, and he had already begun to contemplate the possible consequences of a Bryan treaty with Germany after House had written him only two days before his meeting with Leipnik and Lochner, relaying an important conversation he had had with Ambassador Bernstorff on the subject. Bernstorff had told House that his government was prepared to refer international disputes to arbitration, join a postwar league of nations, promote disarmament, and, as an indication of Germany's good faith on these matters, immediately to sign a Bryan treaty with the United States. He outlined Germany's "moderate" peace terms, which would not include the annexation of any Belgian territory. He was not authorized to mention other terms, he said, but added that he was confident that while Germany would insist on certain boundaries in southeastern Europe to allow for its uninterrupted access to Constantinople, Wilson could count on German acceptance of an independent Poland and Lithuania. He also told House, "if Lloyd George had stated that there should be *mutual* restoration, reparation and indemnity, his Government would have agreed to enter negotiations on those terms."

After explaining this conversation to his friend, House concluded: "To my mind, this is the most important communication we have had since the war began and gives a real basis for negotiations and for peace." He added the next day: "It seems to me that with the German communication of yesterday you stand in a position to bring about peace much more quickly than I thought possible."[62]

Wilson had written House asking him for more specific information from the German ambassador on these matters, but before House could reply Wilson held his interview with Leipnik and Lochner.[63] When Leipnik said that Britain would welcome a Bryan treaty between the United States and Germany as a favorable sign of Germany's conversion to international cooperation, Wilson, like his chief adviser, assumed that the differences between the two belligerent sides had narrowed appreciably and that the chances for successful mediation had distinctly improved.

Immediately following this interview, Wilson wrote another letter to House in which his puzzlement over the vague terms of the German peace feeler tempered an otherwise ebullient optimism over the recent favorable chain of events. He asked House whether Bernstorff had indicated what his government was willing to promise during the year of investigation provided for in a Bryan treaty. If such a treaty could be signed, he was worried that in case of a controversy between the two nations over Germany's use of the submarine, whether the Germans would discontinue such attacks while the international commission inquired into the merits of the case. "That with me is the vital question," Wilson remarked. "I do not want to walk into a trap and give them immunity for the next year."[64] Wilson then related to House his interview with Lochner and Leipnik and the latter's reporting of his conversation with his "friends" in the British Foreign Office.

> His account of his arguments with these friends about my last note at least proved that he really knew the merits of the case and how to present the argument from our point of view. He said that the men in the British Foreign Office felt that if Germany would now offer to enter with us into a "Bryan treaty" they would begin to take notice and believe that she was in fact at last beginning to change her attitude towards international disputes, putting her aggressive principles behind her! What do you think of that?
>
> I agree with you that it is most difficult to see now what our next move should be with regard to the German proposals – how we should handle the changed case which Bernstorff has put in our hands. I hope that you are thinking about it more constantly and to better purpose than I have yet been able to do.
>
> For one thing, it is hard to see how to guide Congress successfully.[65]

This letter displayed Wilson's blend of rising enthusiasm and restrained judgment. Much as he hoped for the best, agreed with Leipnik, and instinctively wanted to negotiate a Bryan agreement with Germany, he was still attempting to think through all the implications of these recent developments. He clearly understood the dangers of precipitous action and thus solicited House's opinion concerning a Bryan treaty with Germany. He also revealed his awareness of congressional opinion. Prominent Republican senators had already questioned his December peace note, especially its call for U.S. membership in a postwar security league, and he likely foresaw more partisan and nationalist attacks on his forthcoming speech elaborating on America's future internationalist commitments. Wilson was directly grappling with the far-reaching implications and potential dangers of any further peace move.[66]

Zimmermann had not discouraged Lochner's obsession with a Bryan treaty and had allowed Minister Rosen to discuss with him the relevance of such an accord as a vehicle for facilitating peace talks. He also instructed Bernstorff to float the proposal to Wilson of the two countries immediately beginning negotiations on a conciliation treaty. These instructions were not sent until January 7, however, and mixed in with them were ominous hints of imminent unrestricted submarine warfare and a request for any advice on how such action might be undertaken without causing a break in relations with the United States. In any case, there were a number of other diplomatic gestures the Germans could have made to indicate serious interest in peace negotiations, but they did not pursue them.

Germany's intimations of interest in Wilson's mediation were in fact insincere. Significantly, Zimmermann's note of January 7, which authorized the ambassador's highly secret talks with House, mentioned only Belgium but said nothing about Germany's territorial goals elsewhere. Bernstorff had in fact exceeded his authority in giving his own thoughts on Germany's territorial and financial settlements, and his comments in this area misled House and Wilson into believing that peace prospects were distinctly brightening. House related to the President that he was "willing to accept Bernstorff's views as official German ones," but wisely had asked the ambassador to put these views in writing. It is possible that the German envoy was not deliberately dissembling, but still desperate for a German–American accommodation that might stave off his government's decision on submarine warfare, had indiscreetly expressed his own thoughts on territorial matters as those he hoped his government also held. But Zimmermann's note had also instructed him, tactically, to drag out his talks on peace terms, and it is more probable that the ambassador decided that an intimation of Germany's specific aims would encourage House and Wilson to continue their peace discussions, which would simultaneously satisfy his Berlin superiors' directive for delay.

The German civilian leaders in Berlin, however, had different purposes. They wanted Bernstorff to convey Germany's continuing interest in Wilson's peace bid so that following the Allies' anticipated rejection of it, then Wilson would become more sympathetic with the German position and might even acquiesce in its renewal of all-out submarine warfare as an understandable response to the Allied intransigent position. Wilson's re-election on a peace platform and his determination to end the war convinced them that he would find it more difficult than previously to lead his nation into the war against Germany. There is some evidence that they even hoped he might constrain his opposition only to a verbal protest.[67]

In any event, Germany failed to follow through on its peace initiatives. Indeed, even before hearing the Allied reply to the American peace note, at a private conference on January 9, Emperor Wilhelm, whose approval as

supreme warlord was required on major actions affecting the military conflict, reluctantly agreed that Germany should begin unrestricted submarine
warfare in the European war zone. Though the emperor was not subject to
public opinion, the rising popular demands, as expressed by center and
liberal parties in the Reichstag, for the full unleashing of the undersea
weapon may have had some effect in causing him to approve the new policy,
as he was reluctant to dismiss patriotic arguments. But more fundamentally, the Kaiser's authority was in decline. Although he had maintained considerable influence on foreign policy matters until the end of
1916, especially in his appointment of key military leaders and an array of
other advisors and his retention of Bethmann Hollweg as chancellor, despite
the militarists' campaign to get rid of him, his erratic and frequently
incoherent or contradictory thinking on war aims and other vital issues of
the war undermined his supreme position. Having no alternative strategy
for military success and, unwilling to embrace the possibility of a compromise peace, he became susceptible to the arguments of more extreme
military measures. The relentless pressure by the military authorities—in
particular, Admiral Holtzendorff and Generals Hindenburg and Ludendorff
—gradually wore him down. Hindenburg argued that the Western Allies
would launch even larger offensives than the Somme campaign and that
Germany could not hold out forever. "Things can not be worse than they
are now," he argued at the conference. "The war must be brought to an end
by the use of all means as soon as possible." Among other arguments, the
admiralty chief had plied Wilhelm with detailed statistics "proving" that
the German submarine fleet, now with many more larger and longer-range
boats, would starve England to submission within a few months, whether
or not the United States entered the war. Even Bethmann, realizing the
military leadership had finally outmaneuvered him, went along with the
decision to avoid a major rupture in the government.[68]

Often shilly-shallying on important policy matters, the Kaiser seemed
almost relieved once he had made the decision, and he rationalized his
approval in terms of a decisive fight-to-the-finish between irreconcilable
Weltanschauunge. "The war is between two world views," he pronounced
to a German writer. "One must win and one must go down."[69] The major
escalation of hostilities was to be announced publicly on January 31, with
the all-out submarine activity to commence the following day.

———

Bernstorff first received word from his government of this momentous
decision on January 19. Not given details surrounding the new policy
direction, the ambassador may have assumed that it was the Allied Governments' reply to the German and American peace notes that provided
the catalyst for Germany's new fateful policy. That response had rejected

Wilson's implication that the two sides were fighting for the same things. And while claiming no desire to dismember Germany and wanting to achieve a peace based upon principles of liberty and justice, the reply was unyielding in its call for the evacuation of all enemy-occupied territories, the Central Powers' payment of indemnities and reparations, and a reorganized Europe involving expulsion of the Turks from the Balkans and recognition of the national aspirations of Italians, Roumanians, Czecho-Slovaks, and Slavs. Though constrained from revealing the contents of the U-boat decision, Bernstorff wanted to prepare House for the worst. He thus tried to put the best face on a difficult situation: "I am afraid," he wrote House, "the situation in Berlin is getting out of our hands." There, "they seem to believe, that the answer of our enemies to the President has finished the whole peace movement for a long time to come, and I am, therefore, afraid that my Government may be forced to act accordingly in a very short time." House conveyed the warning to his mentor, but urged him to press on with his mediation offensive.[70]

Fully determined to pursue his quest for a negotiated peace, Wilson delivered his address before the Senate on January 22. He had decided on his presentation to that body so that his remarks might appear to be primarily a statement on administration policy to an American audience rather than a frontal directive to the European belligerents. And when his remarks included proposals for freedom of the seas, limitations on armaments, and "government by the consent of the governed" for the peace settlement, he was on safe ground in claiming he was emphasizing "American principles, American policies," as they were widely accepted traditional tenets in the nation. It was a prime example of his genius with words in skillfully blending national values with a new internationalism as he moved American opinion in the direction of more active engagement with European politics.

But his address was mainly aimed at public opinion in the warring nations. Although his affirmation that a lasting peace required governments "by the consent of the governed" could be viewed as a criticism of the Central Powers, he was clearly more interested in "peace" than "democracy." In reviewing the belligerents' replies to his December note, he concluded that each side had indicated it did not want to destroy the other. This implied, he noted, that the coming peace would have to be a "peace without victory," and he went on to emphasize the resentment and impermanence of a vindictive peace. "Only a peace between equals can last," he asserted. Noting that both warring sides were prepared to join an international organization after the war, he emphasized the requirement of substituting a concert of power for entangling alliances and a balance of power. The United States, he said, would make an important effort in the creation of "an organized common peace." Wilson went on to claim that he spoke not just for Americans but for liberals, friends of humanity, and "the silent mass of mankind everywhere who have as yet had no place or opportunity to speak their real hearts out concerning the death and ruin they see to have come already upon the persons and the homes they hold most dear."[71]

Wilson was under few illusions that his new course for the American nation would stir up controversy. Predictably, nationalist voices, particularly among Republicans, reacted negatively to his speech, and he continued to worry sometimes about the Senate, whose approval he would need for any peace settlement involving the United States. But he was already preparing for a possible fight. As he wrote a friend, "discouragement is weakness and I do not succumb for long. I firmly believe that I have said the right thing, and I have an invincible confidence in the prevalence of the right if it is fearlessly set forth."[72]

His Senate address generally received enthusiastic public approval, however, and further encouraged the peace workers. "Isn't the President's action *great*?" Balch exuded, and Addams offered similar praise: "Isn't it fine and isn't the cause moving along?"[73] Among their many congratulatory messages sent to the President, perhaps the most rhapsodic came from the American Union Against Militarism: "Never, we believe, in the history of this world has any message of a single individual found its way to so many minds and hearts, and in every case the reader has been compelled whether in complete agreement or not to think and to ponder upon a great and statesman-like proposal to rid the globe of its worst curse – war and militarism . . . To our minds, it is destined to an immortality as glorious as that of the Gettysburg Address."[74]

As AUAM chairman, Lillian Wald had signed this letter, and Wilson responded by asking her whether she might persuade Andrew Carnegie to have his endowed peace organization distribute copies of his address to its many affiliated peace societies. The peace philanthropist had written the President effusively praising his speech, and Wilson saw an opportunity to publicize it. Wald readily agreed, but reported back her "deep regret" that Carnegie was in poor health and unable to communicate with the endowment.[75]

Lochner went one step further. He sent Wilson a note praising his speech and intimating that Henry Ford wanted Lochner to discuss his European work with the President in greater detail so that they could shape their work along the lines of the President's peace moves.

Actually, Lochner's request for another presidential interview was an act of desperation, for he had recently discovered that Ford had lost all interest in his conference of neutrals. The auto magnate had met briefly with Lochner in Detroit on January 19, then put him off, and finally allowed another short meeting four days later. Ford's "hurried talking" in both interviews bothered Lochner, but more disturbing to him was Ford's startling announcement in their first conversation that he now thought peace was a chimera. "I don't think this war ought to stop," he told him. "Those people over there haven't suffered enough yet. So long as they don't themselves refuse to go on with the war, we in America should do nothing to help them."[76] Ford may have been reacting to the belligerents' discouraging responses to Wilson's peace note, but more probably it was simply another stage in Ford's deliberative ratcheting down of his peace action. Lochner perceived him, however, as "a changed man," who was acting more irrationally and illogically than usual. Following the President's address to the Senate, Ford declared that he was now prepared to spend enormous sums to mobilize citizens' support in the United States behind the President's independent peace move, but that his private neutral conference in Europe would have to close. His aides had already convinced him to cut off all financial support to his conference of neutrals; and as a sign of his negative attitude to peacework in Europe, he said Leipnik was "out of date" and stopped paying his expenses.[77]

Lochner understood, however, that Wilson's appeal directly to the peoples in the warring nations made peacework in Europe more imperative than ever. Ready to act, Ford's neutral conference now had its best opportunity to spread peace propaganda to the people in the European neutrals and, so far as possible, to the belligerents to rally behind the President. But the young pacifist's arguments failed to move the auto magnate. "I remonstrated – in vain," he wrote Leipnik. In Ford's absence, Lochner argued his case with Ernest Liebold, the industrialist's slippery aide, emphasizing the critical importance of supporting peacework in Europe behind Wilson's mediation initiative and Ford's moral obligation to continue to support his European co-workers. Seemingly persuaded, Liebold assured the young activist that Ford would continue to finance the neutral conference if Wilson approved. The main purpose of his presidential interview, Lochner believed, would be to secure the chief executive's endorsement of work of the European conference, which might persuade Ford to change his mind and extend his financial support of the European peace effort.[78]

Wilson agreed to see Lochner on February 1, as it turned out only a day after the German announcement of unrestricted submarine warfare. Overnight Germany had dashed high hopes for mediation, and Lochner, realizing that the President would be preoccupied with the new crisis in German–American relations, telephoned the White House and offered to cancel the interview. But Wilson decided to keep his appointments and as scheduled saw Lochner late that afternoon. It was the young pacifist's fourth face-to-face meeting with the President during the war.[79] Earlier the same day, House who had hurried down from New York found Wilson "sad and depressed, and I did not succeed at any time during the day in lifting him into a better frame of mind."[80]

The President's shock was particularly acute because he had convinced himself that the recent improvement in U.S. relations with the belligerents ruled out the possibilities of American belligerency. He had told House less than a month earlier: "There will be no war. This country does not intend to become involved in this war. We are the only one of the great White nations that is free from war to-day, and it would be a crime against civilization for us to go in."[81]

The positive reactions to his Senate address, which extended even beyond private citizens and groups to Allied political elites, had further whet his appetite for peace. Socialists in the French Chamber of Deputies had unanimously voted a resolution urging all belligerent leaders to support the President's initiative, and a senior French Foreign Office official told the American ambassador that if Germany provided its peace terms confidentially to Wilson, which could be accepted with honor, then the awful cataclysm could be ended. In addition, the Russian Foreign Office stated that its government was unreservedly willing to cooperate in his efforts for peace discussions. These calls for peace negotiations were important breaks in the heretofore solid façade of Allied opinion behind the war effort. He believed that if Germany would be more forthcoming, then he was confident the Allies could be coerced to the peace table. As he wrote House on January 24, "[I]f Germany really wants peace, she can get it and get it soon, *if she will but confide in me and let me have a chance . . .* I genuinely want to help and have now put myself in a position to help without favour to either side."[82]

The President was already considering his next steps for peace in this direction when the German submarine announcement arrived on January 31. It is small wonder then, as summarized by House, that Wilson "felt as if the world had suddenly reversed itself: that after going from east to west, it had begun to go from west to east and that he could not get his balance."[83]

When Lochner arrived at the White House, he also found the President looking "haggard and worried." According to Lochner's poignant account of their meeting, the two commiserated over the apparent enthronement of the war party in Germany, which had brought on the submarine warfare. Wilson commented that the militarists' ascendancy in Germany might change the whole world. Because Lochner's ostensible excuse for the interview was his hope for Wilson's endorsement of the peacework of the neutral conference in Europe, he proceeded to summarize the conference's propaganda activities, including the publicity given his peace notes, as well as the more "scientific" work in creating a viable and effective postwar international organization. With the most serious crisis in German–American relations clearly evident, Lochner's discussion of past and future mediation efforts was very academic. Wilson nonetheless listened patiently and seemed genuinely interested in Lochner's presentation, particularly his account of the neutral conference's petitions and influence with citizens' groups in winning the support of the neutral governments behind his peace initiative. Lochner also asked if there was anything the neutral conference could do in the crisis. Wilson replied, "[N]o, I don't see anything. I am merely trying all day to think, and not to form any hasty judgment."[84]

More pertinent was Wilson's comment about the international obligations the United States was prepared to assume in the postwar world. He reiterated that the general propositions he put forward for U.S. membership in a postwar league in his "peace without victory" address were consistent with the nation's values. "This I know for certain," he told Lochner, "that each and every one of them is an American principle." He added that a criticism of his internationalist message was that the realization of his program might require a change in the course of history. "The President was insistent that he did not attempt in any way to undo past history, and that this point should be clearly understood," Lochner recorded. History might not need to be undone, but Wilson was stretching reality in believing that his principles for reforming the international system did not require the major powers to think about world politics in new ways or that the abandonment of America's traditional isolationism would somehow not be a major departure for the nation.

Wilson severed diplomatic relations with Germany two days later, on February 3. No longer was there talk of mediation, but only of possible war with Germany. Ford immediately announced that he would support the President if he decided on war with Germany and in that event would convert his Detroit factory into a munitions plant. He also ended all financial and moral support of his neutral conference as of March 1 and without any personal contact with Lochner had his aides ask him to submit his resignation. Balch empathized with her cohort's plight at the hands of the automaker's rude treatment. "Isn't Mr Ford's fall from grace more complete and sudden than you expected?" she confided to Addams. "The hideous disgrace to America in Europe[,] only ones who were there can fully realize."[85]

———

Wilson's attempt at independent mediation thus failed. If he had begun his diplomatic offensive several weeks earlier or if Germany had given him more time, he might have made more progress. One pressure tactic at his disposal was economic, as Wilson perceived the enormous financial leverage the United States held over the Allies. Shortly before his December peace note, he had encouraged the Federal Reserve Board to warn member banks against further investments in belligerent treasury bills, and the board's statement alarmed the Allied statesmen. It became immediately apparent that if Americans would not buy their bonds, then the British and French gold and dollar assets would quickly shrink to the vanishing point. The Allies would no longer be able to buy munitions and other needed supplies from the United States. Wilson seemed willing to tighten the economic screws gradually to try to make the Entente more acquiescent about peace talks.

But the application of such leverage would also have been fraught with difficulties. Of several possible scenarios, none offered much hope for quick success. Bankrupt governments cannot fight on forever, but even in desperate straights the Allies, believing in the justice of their cause, could have continued the military struggle for a long time if the domestic manufacturers continued to produce and the troops were willing to fight. It is also conceivable that the Allies might have blindly struggled on in the face of Wilson's restrictive economic policies until they were too weakened to resist the German military machine or until Wilson, fearful of a victory by the Central Powers, abandoned the measures. Alternatively, the mounting outrage of the Allies at Wilson's economic pressure, instead of forcing them most reluctantly to peace discussions, could have led them as easily to an irreparable break, and perhaps war, with the United States.

Germany, however, saved its adversaries from their difficult predicament. Its political leadership did not probe the Allies' real financial weaknesses and, focusing instead narrowly on military operational matters, introduced all-out submarine warfare, which dramatically altered the situation. A historian of the war experience writes, "Finance, seen by many [in Germany] before 1914 as the component which would end war sooner, had dropped out of German strategic calculations by 1917." Financial considerations had become the servant rather than the master of German war policy, and the result of the submarine campaign was that the application of U.S. economic predominance was never implemented.[86]

In any case, Wilson's mediation never could have had a chance for success until *both* sides abandoned their thoughts of military victory. The cards were well stacked against Wilson. Despite persistent rivalries and jealousies for example, Anglo-French military cooperation had stabilized and their economic and financial cooperation had in fact intensified by 1917. Except for Russia, which was soon to plunge into revolutionary turmoil, and Austro-Hungarian leaders who feared that continued warfare would dismember the empire, the hard-line interests predominated in all belligerent governments in early 1917.[87]

Just as important, the troops still seemed to tolerate trench warfare despite its horrific and dehumanizing features. Soldiers' grousing was widespread, and their strikes, protests, and desertions occurred intermittently on both sides. But the commands of the Allies and Central Powers had made adjustments to ameliorate the worst conditions. Rotation of units on the front lines and more frequent home leave made assignment in the trenches slightly more bearable for most soldiers. Military discipline also tightened to the point where insubordination could easily result in death sentences by courts martial. This mixture of carrots and sticks had thus far staved off massive soldiers' revolts against the war, and the belligerents' military and political leaders did not perceive irresistible popular pressures for talking peace with their enemies. Mutinies in the trenches would soon occur with a vengeance in Russia, and shortly also among many French divisions (though more in rebellion against the miserable conditions and their officers' treatment of them than in opposition to the war itself) and some German units, but only after Wilson's mediation effort had failed.[88] Wilson can be faulted for failing to see these realities and for offering his good offices for mediation when its chances of success were minimal.

His decision is understandable, however, in the context of the desperate predicament he perceived by the end of 1916. He then believed—accurately as it turned out—that continuation of the war would soon bring the United States into it. Thus a direct mediation initiative was a possibly practical alternative to that very unpleasant prospect. It was, for better or worse, something of a crapshoot, his hope against hope that he might somehow succeed. Only as he became deeply engaged in the diplomatic maneuverings surrounding Germany's and his diplomatic moves did he begin to see peace negotiations as an end in themselves.

Moreover, Wilson's failure was not all his fault. He was poorly informed and was largely acting in the shadows of reality. For views of the public mood abroad in the last half of 1916, he had to rely on the sometimes biased reporting from Ambassadors Page and Gerard—both of whom Wilson distrusted—and newspapers, which reported all kinds of things. There was then no U.S. intelligence agency that might have reported systematically on opinion, whether for peace or expanded war, in the belligerent countries. He also had no national security team to proffer sophisticated analyses and policy options. Additionally, there were no public opinion polls or wartime elections in Europe to serve as barometers of domestic opinion. In the absence of popular elections, for instance, was Lloyd George's ascendancy a result of popular pressure or a coterie of war hawks in the government and press? Wilson knew nothing about Lansdowne's confidential paper proposing peace talks and, despite the grim prognosis for victory in the interdepartmental review, its rather decisive rejection by the cabinet in November 1916. Perhaps more important, he believed the moderates still held the upper hand in the German Government, which might respond sympathetically to his initiative. Gerard, House, and many American private citizens who watched the German political situation all believed that the liberals were still in charge there.

Wilson clearly wanted to be well informed, and he sought out opinions from House who was well acquainted with European leaders, from British antiwar Liberals (often, but not always, through House), and from private American citizens, especially pacifists and advanced progressives. Six months earlier, when he had discussed with Lincoln Steffens his reasons for avoiding war with Mexico, at the end of their conversation Wilson also provided a self-analysis of his decision-making process. The socialist journalist recalled the President saying:

> "An executive," he said, "is a man of action. An intellectual – such as you or I," he smiled – "an intellectual is inexecutive. In an executive job we are dangerous, unless we are aware of our limitations and take measures to stop our everlasting disposition to think, to listen, to – not act. I made up my mind long ago, when I got into my first executive job, to open my mind for a while, hear everybody who came to me with advice, information – what you will – then, some day, the day when my mind felt like deciding, to shut it up and act. My decision might be right; it might be wrong. No matter. I would take a chance and do – something."[89]

Finally, nothing was really lost by Wilson's mediation attempt. There were no long-term costs besides briefly irritating pro-war European leaders and opinion on the two sides. In any case, his attempt to mediate between the extreme war aims of both sets of belligerents was vintage Wilson, and he would continue to resist the Allies' more vindictive and imperialistic goals, even after the United States would enter the conflict on their side.

This is not to say that Wilson's judgment was always correct. He was a liberal and wanted to believe that his reasonable and enlightened perspective could move the warring leaders to accept his mediation. In consequence, he viewed prospects for peace much too optimistically. Already reflexively discounting more conservative opinions at home, he had also gradually hardened his attitude against the belligerent leaders in Europe who, he believed, seemed close-minded and out of touch with the peaceful aspirations of their peoples. In late 1916, House tried to restrain his mentor from his quest for a mediated settlement. He had extensive contacts with more "realistic" opinion leaders among the Allies and shared their views that any Wilsonian peace offer would have to favor the Entente side, which would be reluctant to negotiate while the enemy controlled parts of their lands on the continent. Wilson then moved decisively away from the House–Grey mediation formula and became much less interested in any information that argued against peace negotiations. But such advice, even if provided by House or others, would not have moved Wilson. It might have tempered his growing optimism for successful mediation, but not his determined new course.

House was in fact somewhat a victim of his own liberalism. As he soon reflected:

> I stood back of every liberal movement, both in Texas and in the
> Nation, which seemed rational and headed in the right direction . . .
> Perhaps the most valuable work I have done in this direction has
> been in influencing the President. I began with him before he became
> President and I have never relaxed my efforts. At every turn, I have
> stirred his ambition to become the great liberal leader of the world.[90]

His persistent encouragement of Wilson's mediation and his unwillingness to jeopardize his friendship and his privileged position as the President's most trusted adviser compromised his influence. Like the pacifistic liberals in the United States, House increasingly relied on the British antiwar Liberals. In essence, they all fed opinions to the President that he already wanted to believe. Their sanguine outlook helped Wilson to take the plunge for mediation; and once he made up his mind, he could be very stubborn and willing to embark boldly on an independent route, even if the quest might be visionary and somewhat lonely.

11

Aftermath

Of all of Germany's leaders, Chancellor Bethmann Hollweg offered perhaps the most accurate appraisal of the conflicting crosscurrents pulling American opinion—including that of its president—in different directions, immediately following the German decision to escalate submarine warfare. As he informed the Budget Committee of the Reichstag of Germany's new submarine campaign on January 31:

> America is still aloof. We have done and will continue to do all in our power to keep America out. I do not know whether we will succeed. America is and will be uncertain. I will not speak more optimistically than I think. And I believe that America will enter the war. Wilson has committed himself in his notes. On the other hand, the peace message makes his entrance more difficult. According to his own statements, he wants peace without victory.[1]

Wilson had moved the United States, particularly in his recent Senate address, to a more active interest in the peace settlement at the end of the war, but his commitment to "peace" in his public utterances also seemed to work against any sudden move toward American belligerency. He was in fact torn between his indignation at Germany's new submarine warfare, which indicated, as he told House, that Germany was "a madman that should be curbed," and his strong conviction of staying out of the war. Shortly after receiving the German announcement, he informed Lansing and House that he believed that the world domination of "white civilization" derived largely from the ability of the United States to stay intact and that his country would have to lead in the postwar reconstruction of a devastated Europe.

Because of the President's distraught state, Lochner did not try during his February 1 interview to argue against a break in relations or U.S. belligerency, but J. Howard Whitehouse, the British pacifist, wrote a memorandum for the President strongly arguing that U.S. involvement in the war "would mean the continuance of the war perhaps for years on a scale of unthinkable horror," and he pleaded for Wilson to remain aloof and continue his peace efforts. House later told Whitehouse that Wilson had expressed his "pleasure" in getting the memorandum and "his agreement with its proposals. They were wholly on the lines of his own thoughts. House went on to tell me that the President had no intention of being rushed. He was a firm as a rock."[2]

The President took his time, mainly because he genuinely wanted to avoid full-scale war, but he also understood that public opinion was badly divided along ideological, ethnic, class, and sectional lines, and that opposition to U.S. military involvement was widespread. Guided by his own advice, penned as a young academic, that the political leader should not get too far ahead of the public mood, he had been successful in the political arena, and he would apply the same maxim, instinctively if not consciously, to the current foreign crisis.[3] He would wait to see what German submarines might perpetrate on the Atlantic and the impact on domestic opinion. Lansing continued to argue that the war was between opposing ideological forces, autocracy and democracy, and the United States should decide to enter the conflict decisively on the latter's side. Wilson was not so sure, telling his cabinet on February 2 that the best outcome might be a military stalemate, which would prevent an oppressive peace. In addition, he also consulted the same day with many members of the Senate. These meetings convinced him that he had no recourse but to break diplomatic relations with Germany. He would wait for hostile acts on the high seas, however, before taking further countermeasures.

Though now more aware that the hawks were in control in both alliances, he also believed that the belligerents were in desperate straits and likely could not continue the war much longer. He still held out hope that the German Government would moderate its submarine order and see that he truly wanted to serve as an impartial arbiter leading to an armistice and peace. There is evidence that if the Germans had limited the new campaign to Allied merchantmen, but spared all passenger ships and treated neutral ships according to the rules of cruiser warfare, he was inclined to accept that erosion of the U.S. rights, as confirmed in the *Sussex* pledge. In his message to Congress severing diplomatic relations, he explained that if Germany somehow did not sink American ships or cause the loss of American lives, he was prepared to stop short of full U.S. belligerency. He even seemed prepared to exempt Americans who might be working on belligerent ships, even though submarine attacks resulting in the loss of U.S. citizens' lives on them would become a serious issue in German-American relations.[4]

But Germany's leaders had played their "last card" and were not prepared to pull back. Obviously, they would have preferred continued American neutrality, or at least its armed neutrality, to a declaration of war and the prospect of facing massive numbers of U.S. ground troops on the western front, but only Bethmann Hollweg had questioned the view that even a complete U.S. military response would have any appreciable impact on the continental war. Bethmann's proposal in December to escalate submarine warfare to include Allied merchantmen but exclude passenger and neutral vessels had failed to convince the military elite that was determined on all-out submarine warfare. That campaign would prove in the end to be an unmitigated disaster for Germany.

———

Whitehouse's plea was only the first among many subsequent ones to the President from those who opposed American belligerency. Americans involved in the mediation campaign wasted no time in working frenetically against possible U.S. belligerency. Unlike antiwar Europeans who found war thrust upon them in July 1914 before they could comprehend the multi-state hostilities that were unfolding around them, Americans had had plenty of time, including weathering previous crises with Germany, to decide what their position on the prospect of war might be and the steps they might take. Moreover, only eight months earlier American pacifists had campaigned vigorously against war with Mexico, and they were determined to resist what could surely become a much larger military adventure against Germany.

There were naturally some defections along the way. Rabbi Wise early told a meeting of the American Union Against Militarism that he would support a war against "Prussian militarism." His colleagues of course firmly objected to his position, and Kellogg remarked that the meeting "morally and spiritually was the most gripping experience I have ever been through. As Miss Balch has just said over the phone, it was the struggle for a man's soul." Shaken by the experience, Wise said he would reconsider his decision but would ultimately come out for U.S. belligerency. Others, like William Jennings Bryan and Jordan, intimated that they would resist American military involvement, but would follow Wilson if the nation ultimately entered the fray.[5]

Of particular interest to the women's peace advocates was the position of their nonpacifist suffragist colleagues. Would the National American Woman Suffrage Association refrain from a public position on the crisis, as pacifists hoped, or would it support U.S. military intervention? Carrie Catt left no doubts. Only two days after the German announcement, she had dinner at the White House with President and Mrs Wilson. What they said to each other is not known. It is unlikely that Catt and Wilson made any bargain, but the two understood one another and would stick together. In any event, the next day Catt began preparing letters calling the executive committee to a special meeting, and she and the head of the suffrage campaign in New York State then offered the services of their suffrage groups to the government in the event of war.[6]

The actions of Catt, a nonpacifist, were in keeping with her pragmatic approach to suffrage politics, but they nonetheless stirred up immediate controversy. A Catt biographer indeed writes: "The announcement that the NAWSA would stand by the government in case of war was the most widely criticized act of Catt's life."[7] Many suffragists attacked her decision. Charles Hallinan, a former NAWSA lobbyist, Benjamin Huebsch, Crystal Eastman, and several other pacifistic suffragists denounced these "high-handed" and "undemocratic" actions as an "inexcusable" betrayal of the organization, which in their view was pledged to avoid other issues besides suffrage. As Eastman put it, "When we joined the suffrage associations we joined to work only for the ballot." In repudiating these suffragist leaders, Margaret Lane, executive secretary of WPP's New York section, commented: "I will not make a bandage until war is declared. What I might do then I don't know, but for the present I shall endeavor to keep the shreds of peace together as well as I can." In the exchange of several vitriolic letters with Anna Garlin Spencer, who would head the national peace group in the 1920s, Catt tried to justify her actions, but her main defense—that she was not blindly following the government but was only offering suffragists' services to the administration—failed to persuade the women pacifists.[8]

Somewhat lost in the personal acrimony was Catt's public comment that the experience of the European suffragists had influenced her decision. The confusion among women in the European belligerent countries at the onset of the Great War and the "mistakes" and "blunders" of their governments in utilizing the suffragists, she remarked, at least partly motivated Catt to try to preempt the debate and make a definite proposal to the government that the suffrage organizations could carry out.[9]

Ultimately, WPP's national board sent a message to Catt imploring her to take no action on committing NAWSA to government service "since many women suffragists hope such a calamity may be averted, and feel that this is a time when patriotism may be effectively shown by refraining from any action tending to increase the war spirit." But Catt knew what she was doing. When she had agreed to head NAWSA a year earlier, she had hand-picked many members for the executive committee who would loyally support her and her "winning plan" for the suffrage movement. Thus a meeting of the NAWSA national executive committee on February 23–24 endorsed Catt's position by a vote of 63:13. When the New York branch of the Woman's Peace Party removed Catt's name as honorary officer, Catt wrote Addams that she considered herself deposed from the peace movement and resigned from the national group.[10]

In the nine weeks before Congress voted on a war resolution, a few ideas and strategies permeated the pacifist discussions. One predominant concept was America's peaceful mission. Thus on the first day of the crisis, AUAM members drafted a statement making the case against American belligerency, which it released to the press and placed as advertisements in several metropolitan newspapers. Directed at President Wilson, it expressed confidence in his wisdom and leadership and exhorted: "We believe that the United States, having had the courage to stand apart throughout the duration of the war as the great representative of the interests of civilization at large, should refuse to allow herself to be dragooned into the war at the very end by acts of desperation committed by any of the belligerents." At the urging mainly of Charles Hallinan, the union's lobbyist in Washington, the advertisements did not indicate the AUAM's sponsorship, but were signed by many of its members as well as other nonpacifist citizens mainly in the New York area to suggest antiwar sentiment extending beyond pacifists and antimilitarists.[11] Similarly, the Woman's Peace Party argued that war with Germany "would not only bring the inevitable horrors of international conflict, but by fomenting bitterness and rancor among ourselves would cause us to sacrifice our unique place as the one country wherein many people live together in harmony offering refuge and opportunity to all."[12]

The American Neutral Conference Committee underwent a rapid transformation. From its inception it had made clear that it was not an antiwar organization but a lobbying group for mediation of the maelstrom, but Shelley, Secor, the Villards, and other prominent members were pacifists determined to resist American belligerency. Before the German submarine announcement, it had planned a mass meeting at Madison Square Garden in New York on February 2, with William Jennings Bryan as the featured speaker, to generate more enthusiasm for Wilson's peace moves. With mediation prospects now seemingly dashed, Bryan turned the well-attended meeting into a peace demonstration. "The United States should fight to the last man if invaded," he boomed to the audience, "but all other matters should be arbitrated." He also called for a nationwide referendum on going to war, which would take away the war-making powers from Congress. The gathering also adopted a resolution proposed by George Foster Peabody, which praised Wilson's past peace initiatives and suggested that his next move should be to call a conference of neutral nations to seek a peaceful resolution of the current crisis.[13]

Those firmly opposed to U.S. belligerency found refuge in a new association, the Emergency Peace Federation (EPF). Within a week of the German submarine announcement, the peace forces had coalesced to form this coordinating entity, which would serve as a clearinghouse for peace organizations as well as socialist, trade union, and other sympathetic associations and keep each group informed of the others' activities. Balch and Kirch-wey, the moderately liberal president of the American Peace Society, initi-ated the effort. The American Union as well as the American Peace Society and the Woman's Peace Party had representation on the new group, which other liberals and socialists also joined. The new federation elected Kirchwey as its chairman, and the ANCC, now going defunct, donated its resources and offices, still run by the hardworking Shelley and Secor, to the new bustling group.[14]

The antiwar activists agreed on a proactive strategy, and in the first days of the crisis they suggested all the main tactics that they would champion in the two months before Congress would vote on a declaration of war. The referendum idea was an outgrowth of progressive reformers' agitation on the state level to permit the referral of policy issues directly to a vote of its citizens. The prospect of a war referendum at the national level in the current crisis, however, was very remote. Besides its dubious constitutional-ity, it would require congressional action and, if approved, would take additional time to hold a special vote. The current crisis would likely be resolved, one way or another, long before the measure might be adopted. Despite its impractical features, the referendum idea received strong sup-port from advanced progressives, socialists, and hardcore isolationists, and Senator La Follette and several congressmen introduced resolutions calling for a popular vote for the decision on war. Bryan, who had advocated a war referendum as early as 1915, became the most prominent public figure championing congressional approval of a war referendum during the final war crisis. He believed that Wilson and the Congress wanted "to carry out the wishes of the people," but could not discern what citizens wanted because of the "misrepresentations" in the metropolitan press, including their denunciation of all pacifistic proposals.[15]

While awaiting congressional action on a referendum, some advocates argued for an advisory referendum to show Congress more immediately the strong grassroots opposition to American belligerency. To that end the AUAM initiated a postcard referendum, which the EPF supported. Using lists of registered voters in five geographically "representative" congres-sional districts (Pennsylvania, Colorado, Ohio, Missouri, and Texas), the American Union sent out 100,000 postcards to citizens in the districts urging them to send back an attached return card to their congressmen with their votes on two issues: war with Germany and a nationwide refer-endum. Among others, Amos Pinchot who had formed his own group, Committee for Democratic Control, took out advertisements in news-papers publicizing the results from the districts, which ranged from 3:1 to 11:1 both for a referendum and against war. The advocates of an advisory referendum never explained how such a nationwide advisory vote could be conducted quickly and impartially, however, and the peace groups lacked the financial resources to expand their sample to the entire electorate. Although the referendum idea was unrealistic, it had certain tactical advantages for the opponents of war. It made good "propaganda," Balch noted, and would allow "a way out for members of Congress too cowardly to vote against war" directly.[16]

Meanwhile, the Emergency Peace Federation coalition was gearing up for the next phase of antiwar activity. A second EPF tactic was peace demonstrations. On very short notice it organized an antiwar rally on Capitol Hill during which several hundred participants visited the offices of congressmen and senators to seek their support. A large number also called at the White House, and Tumulty, saying the President was unavailable, nonetheless received them courteously in the President's office. Resolutions adopted at the demonstrations were read, and Fanny Villard and others made remarks, all of which White House stenographers took down for the President.[17] The Emergency Peace Federation also set up branch offices in Boston, Louisville, Washington, and elsewhere and, as a clearinghouse, sent out telegrams each evening informing scores of affiliated associations of the EPF's activities.[18]

Federation representatives also attended a conference of peace societies in New York on February 22–23, the purpose of which was to try to forge common positions on foreign policy questions. The American Peace Society had called the meeting long before the German submarine announcement, but the crisis had caused representatives of more conservative and internationalist groups to stay away from the gathering. In consequence, the more radical peace people assumed full control, but the debate on the war referendum revealed the first real split on strategy among the pacifists. Though a nonresistant, Peabody was also a Wilson loyalist and, opposing the referendum, argued that the President should be "trusted absolutely" in his desire to keep the nation out of the war.[19] At the New York meeting, Kirchway led the fight against the referendum. As he commented to the gathering, "I have a belief in democracy, but this thing [the referendum] is needless, impracticable, and dangerous," but he was shouted down when he tried to defer a vote on the issue.[20]

More typical of the pacifists' proposals for avoiding war was the call for an official conference of neutrals to consider measures for safeguarding their rights before declaring full belligerency against Germany. As Addams expressed it, she hoped that Wilson would meet the present international situation in cooperation with other neutral nations in Europe and South America, whose interests were similarly involved. Such a league could stand for "international rights and would at least form a method of approach less likely to involve any one nation in war."[21]

The main antiwar argument was that the United States was a peace-loving nation and in concert with other neutrals in resisting Germany's submarine campaign should adopt retaliatory measures short of war. They early seized on a proposal written by Carleton J.H. Hayes, professor of European history at Columbia University, for a league of armed neutrals to defend their nations' rights on the high seas. Hayes' paper reviewed the two previous great maritime wars in history—the revolutionary and Napoleonic eras—both of which had resulted in armed leagues of neutral states when the belligerents' violations of their rights on the seas became intolerable. And in the latter, the John Adams administration had unilaterally authorized a quasi-war with France to defend American rights. Naval battles ensued, but there were no formal declarations of war, and a Franco–American treaty soon resolved the issues and brought peace. The neutrality leagues had also directly contributed to a revision of the laws of war and respect for neutral rights at subsequent international conferences. Applying the lessons of history, Hayes argued that in the current crisis the advantage of a league of neutrals was that it could avoid full belligerency and allow the United States to retain its moral power in trying to resolve disputes without following the path of reckless destruction of the European warring nations. It also could be initiated without prior approval of the other neutrals. When Catherine the Great had invited neutrals to join the first league, for instance, Russia had gone alone for six months before other neutrals joined.

After discussing Hayes' argument, the AUAM executive committee authorized Wald, its chairman, to send the plan to President Wilson and arranged to have the full paper published in *The Survey*. Wald wrote him that the President, "a great historian," already knew the facts presented by Hayes, "but your friends have thought deeply upon this matter and hope that they have something that may be of suggestive value to you." Wald also asked the President to receive a delegation to discuss it. Wilson thought an interview was inappropriate in the current circumstances, but he replied that he was "very much obliged indeed" to Wald for sending him Hayes' suggestions, which would "receive the most careful consideration."[22]

Wilson also forwarded the plan to Secretary Lansing, who shortly returned it without comment. House, who had also been given a copy of Hayes' article to forward to his chief, likewise volunteered no opinion on it. Both were in fact in favor of the nation entering the war from the onset of the crisis, though House, aware of Wilson's aversion to precipitate action, remained more respectful of the President's caution. The President's two advisers may have wanted to avoid serious discussion of an arguably realistic alternative to full-scale belligerency with their chief and hoped that Germany's submarine attacks on U.S. shipping would force Wilson's hand.[23]

Wilson managed to suspend judgment throughout most of February and seemed equally determined to discourage pro-war or antiwar opinion.

When a New Jersey clergyman asked him, for instance, for a "word of greeting" that might be read to a new men's defense group, he commented to an aide: "The Church seems to me a very queer unit to build a defense league of any kind on (I think our ministers are going crazy)." At the same time, however, when Rose Dabney Forbes, the head of the Massachusetts branch of the Woman's Peace Party and a generous contributor to the AUAM and other peace associations, inquired about cooperation with the Emergency Peace Federation's (EPF) antiwar campaign, Wilson replied that such peace activities can "in the present circumstances, if continued, do nothing but harm by creating the impression that there are divided counsels amongst us." He reaffirmed his desire to stay out of the war and counseled that "the best way to support my efforts just now is to show that the whole country, at any rate the thoughtful element of it, is back of me."[24] Such self-serving advice persuaded Forbes to abandon the antiwar movement and the Massachusetts branch soon turned to relief work instead. Many other women who loved "peace" in the abstract, but could not bring themselves to oppose their government, also defected from WPP branches in the following weeks. But Wilson's desire for unity could not stop the antiwar surge.[25]

The President was able to avoid further action for the first two weeks of the crisis, mainly because the German announcement had given a period of grace, up to 12 days for ships already at sea and crossing the Atlantic. Though sinking a few U.S. ships after proper warning in that interim, Germany had not yet committed an overt act resulting in the loss of American lives.[26] But part of the reason was that many U.S. ships had remained in port to avoid possible destruction. Recognizing the difficulty for American foreign commerce, Wilson had privately decided by mid-February to ask Congress for authority to arm merchantmen, but waited until February 26 to announce it before the Congress. The option of arming U.S. ships was widely discussed in American opinion circles at the time, but Professor Hayes' cogently reasoned paper—for example, President Adams' authorization of a quasi-war with France on the seas—provided him with some convincing arguments.

Pacifists readily acquiesced in the decision for armed neutrality as necessary under the circumstances and as a live alternative to full-fledged war. Wald said, for instance, that the new policy was a "substitute for war that will not lead to war." Reverend Frederick Lynch of the Church Peace Union also believed it was a "hopeful step, the step of a man who wishes to keep the peace, and a step to keep us out of war," and Jordan commented that Wilson's action was "a tight squeeze, but I think we shall be spared the humiliation, degradation and distress of getting mixed up in this war."[27]

But if the President adopted U.S. armed neutrality, he never seriously considered the strategy of a league of armed neutrals to defend their nations' rights without resorting to full-scale hostilities. He simply ignored the main thrust of Hayes' proposal. Eighteen months earlier Wilson had written Edith Galt, then his fiancée, that in the event of a break with Germany one option would be to call a conference of neutrals to formulate a common policy for the defense of neutral rights. But that was a hypothetical proposition, and Wilson never developed it further. His comment to her at the time that such a conference "could do what it pleased when once it was constituted" hinted at the possibility of an unpredictable outcome. To the extent that he had any control over international events, the last thing he wanted was to have other neutral governments, whose interests he had often remarked were different from America's, circumscribe his freedom of action.[28]

Unbeknownst to the antiwar elements, however, Wilson had already squelched the prospect of a joint neutral response to the submarine war. After halting and uncertain negotiations, the three northern neutrals—Sweden, Norway, and Denmark—had agreed in September 1916 to issue confidential invitations to a conference of neutrals "to consider common interests especially with regard to commerce, neutrality rules and the application of these rules." While excluding mediation, the initiative proposed to cover a wide range of neutral rights, such as the blacklist and submarine warfare. According to the proposal, the other European neutrals (Spain, Switzerland, and the Netherlands), along with the United States, would also be asked to participate in the conference. When Wilson received the proposal in late November, he informed Lansing that he was instinctively "adverse to any participation by our government in the conference proposed," but sought the secretary's opinion. Lansing who had already expressed his hostility to joint mediation with the European neutrals was no more sympathetic to a defensive neutral league. After discussing the initiative with the President, the secretary of state sent the neutrals a polite rejection, which elucidated the same arguments that Wilson had earlier advanced in opposing joint neutral mediation: the American nation's unique geographical position and different interests and its closer ties with the American Republics, which had not been invited to the conference.[29]

Besides endorsement of the referendum, another outcome of the New York meeting of peace groups was the EPF's recommendation for a delegation to call on the President and elaborate on their arguments for staying out of the conflict. Wilson agreed in fact to see two delegations, from the Emergency Peace Federation and the AUAM. Whether by accident or design, the two meetings were scheduled back-to-back on the afternoon of February 28.

The timing could not have been worse. The President had learned confidentially from British intelligence only three days earlier of the so-called Zimmermann telegram, the German foreign secretary's proposal to Mexico and Japan to declare war on the United States. In particular, Zimmermann offered Mexico support for recovering lands lost to the United States resulting from the Mexican War. Upon investigation, the president realized that Zimmermann had used U.S. transmission facilities, which his administration had made available to the ambassador during much of January, to wire the proposal to Bernstorff, with instructions to forward it to the German mission in Mexico City. Wilson was shocked and angered at Germany's perfidy. He took the telegram personally as an affront to his goodwill. Moreover, as a liberal, he wanted to believe that nations, like individuals, would behave rationally and morally, but the Zimmermann telegram made him lose all faith in the German Government. The State Department had verified the authenticity of the telegram and Wilson had approved release of its text for publication in the newspapers on March 1. Instead of claiming that the telegram was a forgery, which might have required the U.S. Government for verification purposes to reveal its intelligence sources, Zimmermann then foolishly admitted his authorship while weakly explaining that his proposal was only a feeler, not a formal proposal, in case of war with the United States.[30]

Of the two delegations descending on the White House, less is known about the President's meeting with the AUAM delegates, Max Eastman, Pinchot, Wald, and Kellogg. Wilson had pledged both delegations to full confidence of what he said during their discussion, and no record of the AUAM discussions apparently exists beyond a long paper by Eastman, which was presumably summarized orally for Wilson. Eastman argued that the United States had no right to assume or declare that it spoke for other neutrals unless it made honest efforts to confer and act with them, and a neutral league would also "greatly strengthen the moral force of whatever position we might take toward the belligerent infringement of maritime rights."[31]

At Wilson's meeting with the earlier EPF delegation, its representatives, William I. Hull, a prominent Quaker peace advocate and history professor at Swarthmore, Joseph Cannon, socialist labor organizer and politician, Lynch, Balch, and Addams, also advanced the collaboration of neutral governments and other arguments for avoiding war, but Wilson was unmoved and stern and severe in his reply. Hull remarked a decade later that the President "enumerated with great emphasis our various grievances against the Hohenzollern government . . . and stressed repeatedly his conviction that it was impossible to deal further in peaceful method with that government." Hull also recalled "with great vividness his tone and manner – a mixture of great indignation and determination – when he said: 'Dr Hull, if you knew what I know at this present moment, and what you will see reported in tomorrow morning's newspapers, you would not ask me to attempt further peaceful dealings with the Germans.' "[32]

Addams later provided additional details. She also noted the President's stern demeanor and his acceptance of the inevitability of war. "He still spoke to us, however, as to fellow pacifists," she remembered after the war. "He used one phrase . . . to the effect that, as head of a nation participating in the war, the President of the United States would have a seat at the Peace Table, but that if he remained the representative of a neutral country he could at best only 'call through a crack in the door.' " Wilson's remark can be interpreted to suggest that his decision for war was in large part an ego trip in fulfillment of his ambition to become the world's peacemaker. The will to personal leadership was surely a part of his personality. A more charitable view, however, is that his action was a big step, after many smaller ones, to commit the United States to an internationalist future. His willingness to send Colonel House to Europe before and during the war, his defense of neutral rights against pacifists' and isolationists' efforts to abandon at least some of them to preserve peace, his advocacy of military preparedness, his pledges beginning in mid-1916 of U.S. participation in a postwar security organization, and his mediation offer—all evidenced an outward-looking leader. Essentially, his projection of American power had shown his willingness to risk war in order to prevent it.[33]

Still, the Zimmermann telegram by itself did not lead him to cast his vote for war, although the document confirmed his view that the German Government could not be dealt with. In his second inaugural address less than a week later, he reaffirmed his commitment to armed neutrality, although he conceded, "We may even be drawn on, by circumstances, not by our own purpose or desire, to a more active assertion of our rights as we see them and a more immediate association with the great struggle itself." Still concerned about public unity, he exhorted Americans to follow him.

Events soon moved him over the edge, however. When a few handfuls of Senators, led by La Follette, tried to filibuster the bill empowering the President to arm U.S. ships, Wilson denounced the "little group of willful men" and authorized the armament of American ships on his own authority as commander-in-chief. News of revolution in Russia with the abdication of Czar Nicholas II and the prospect of a new democratic government removed the autocratic link in the Allied alliance against the Central Powers. But most important was the loss of American lives from the submarine sinkings. News of a German submarine's destruction of a British liner with the loss of American lives arrived in the United States on February 26, and the loss of several more Allied and American and other neutral ships followed in March.

As popular feelings for war surged, the antiwar activists found that time was running out on them. The EPF continued to lobby furiously. Lochner, trying to use his Wilson connection one more time, requested a presidential interview with an EPF contingent on March 31, but was turned down.[34]

The peace federation also sent special trains from New York filled with antiwar demonstrators. Once in Washington, the assembled antiwar throng of more than 1,000 tried to persuade representatives and senators to vote against the proposed war declaration.

The effort was to no avail. The demands for upholding the nation's honor became more widespread, and after his cabinet agreed unanimously for U.S. belligerency, Wilson went before Congress on April 2 to ask it to vote for war against Germany. It would be a war to make the world "safe for democracy," Wilson proclaimed and, after specifying the objects the United States would pursue, he concluded, "God helping her, she can do no other." That final comment was almost an exact paraphrase of Martin Luther's defense of charges of heresy before the Holy Roman Emperor and princes at the Diet of Worms nearly 400 years earlier. Because of Wilson's solid religious training, the Luther connection was almost certainly not an accident, but became his way of identifying himself with a righteous justification for his messianic interventionism. If he had to sin by going to war, he would in effect "sin boldly" as a good Christian, as Luther had also said. It would be a war of redemption—the quest for a league of nations and the hope of a new, lasting peace—and there would be no turning back.[35]

Within a few days of Wilson's message, Congress responded by declaring war against Germany. Though large numbers of lawmakers had serious reservations about going to war, party loyalty, the desire for national unity, and a pervasive sense of the futility of opposition brought many of them to support the President. In consequence, only six senators and 50 representatives voted against the war declaration. One of those in the opposition was Jeanette Rankin (R – Montana), the recently elected first woman member of Congress. A pacifist as well as suffragist, she made her brief maiden speech during the roll call vote. "I want to stand by my country, but I cannot vote for war," she declared. "I vote no."[36]

Wilson's lofty expression of the ideals for which the nation would fight received widespread praise, but one severe critic was Theodore Roosevelt. Believing Germany's attacks on American rights and interests were only more outrageous in the spring of 1917 than earlier in the war, he could easily accept the President's call for American belligerency.

> But what is impossible, what really represents nauseous hypocrisy, is to say that we have gone to war to make the world safe for democracy, in April, when sixty days previously we had been announcing that we wished a "Peace without victory," and had no concern with the "causes and objects" of the war. I do not regard any speech as a great speech when it is obviously hypocritical and in bad faith.[37]

Even if Roosevelt's political and personal animus toward Wilson is discounted, the former president had a point. Wilson had seemingly moved swiftly from an interest in "peace" to a war leader committed to the destruction of German militarism and the construction of a new democratic world order. He brushed aside various peace feelers and, contrary to House's advice, rejected Pope Benedict XV's mediation appeal in August 1917, which called for the evacuation of occupied lands, no indemnities, disarmament, and territorial boundaries based as much as possible on the principle of self-determination. Wilson saw the papal offer, however sincere, as serving the interests of Germany and its allies, and he would not seriously consider peace negotiations until the German militarists had been driven from power.

In a different way, however, Wilson remained a mediator. His principal biographer writes that even during U.S. military involvement in the war the President "sounded more like an arbitrator than a belligerent."[38] Wilson's peacemaking role included resistance to the imperialistic war aims not just of the Central Powers, but of the Allies as well. And increasingly, especially after the successful Bolshevik revolution in Russia in November 1917, he fashioned a liberal peace program that he would champion as an attractive alternative to peace programs advanced by the extreme left and right.

In pursuit of his peace program, his relations with peace advocates took a drastic turn for the worse. During American belligerency, Wilson at first offered pleasant reassurances that he could tolerate the position of pacifists and antimilitarists. But a few months into the war he changed course and minced no words in excoriating them in bitter, stinging remarks. In a Flag Day speech in June, he lumped the entire peace movement with German traitors and schemers, and he branded pacifists and antimilitarists as "the agents or dupes of the Imperial German Government. . . In a Peoples' War, a war for freedom and justice and self-government amongst all the nations of the world," there was "but one choice," he proclaimed. "Woe be to the man or group of men that seeks to stand in our way in this day of high resolution when every principle we hold dearest is to be vindicated and made secure for the salvation of the nations." Later in 1917, he further expounded: "What I am opposed to is not the feeling of the pacifists, but their stupidity. My heart is with them, but my mind has a contempt for them. I want peace, but I know how to get it and they do not." And the next month he added: "I hear men debate peace who understand neither its nature nor the way in which we can obtain it with uplifted eyes and unbroken spirits. But I know that none of these speaks for nations. They do not touch the heart of anything. They may be left to strut their uneasy hour and be forgotten."[39]

His attacks on pacifists probably redounded to Wilson's short-term political benefit in the hysterically patriotic national mood, but left deep wounds among his American victims. A darker side to the nation's history,

which Wilson did little to discourage and even fueled on occasion, surfaced. Congress passed laws suppressing civil liberties and dissent, which
the chief executive signed and his administration ruthlessly enforced.
American involvement in the conflict split liberals and socialists into pro-
war and antiwar factions, and the government prosecuted and sent to jail
thousands of dissenters, including the Socialist party's longtime leader
Eugene Debs. The intimidation and persecution thoroughly alienated the
American left. As Oswald Villard wrote about Wilson at the end of the war:
"At the very moment of his extremist trial our liberal forces are[,] by his
own act, scattered, silenced, disorganized, some in prison. If he loses
his great fight for humanity, it will be because he was deliberately silent
when freedom of speech and the right of conscience were struck down in
America."[40]

On all sides Wilson would find difficulties, some of which would have
occurred in any event. In an era before bipartisan foreign policy, Republicans would criticize his international reform proposals, and isolationists
would attack his willingness to abandon America's traditional avoidance of
international commitments. On the other side, the editors of the *New
Republic* and many other liberal intellectuals would also object to the
Treaty of Versailles as much too vindictive. His deteriorating health culminating in a massive stroke in September 1919, at the height of the treaty
fight in the United States, would also somewhat limit his political
effectiveness.

But his problems would also be of his own making. He would not reach
out to Republicans in any sustained way; he could try to persuade them to
accept his views, but real compromise was not an option. Similarly, those
questioning his emerging liberal international principles were dismissed as
unenlightened reactionaries; that their cautionary perspectives on international reform, including a league of nations, in an anarchic and confusing
world might have some value besides political partisanship eluded him
completely. He likewise came to perceive leaders of the League to Enforce
Peace, who shared many of his views on collective security, as "butters-in"
and "woolgatherers," partly because they were led mainly by conservative
Republicans like former President Taft, but he also objected to their
strongly pro-Allied biases and their acceptance of the primacy of great
power dominance in world affairs.

His own internationalist program, which included the dissolution of
colonial empires, the protection of small states, and what today would be
called human rights, was much more far-reaching. Except for the concept
of forceful sanctions, it was, ironically, closer to the pacifists' vision of an
organic international community, but the war had irreparably dissolved
their earlier affinity of outlook. Colonel House noted that the chief executive had "strong prejudices" against internationalists who did not share his

predilections on the question of a League of Nations, and Lansing commented privately that Wilson was "a wonderful hater."[41] The President would soon break with House, his closest adviser, ostensibly over the latter's negotiated compromises with the Allies at the Paris peace conference, although the compromises did not really undermine Wilson's peace program. More important contributors to the President's disenchantment with his most intimate friend were Edith Wilson, who was jealous of House's rising influence, and Wilson's rigidity, which criticism of the treaty negotiations at home and abroad and his worsening health aggravated. Wilson and House would never speak to one another again. The President would also fire Lansing when he learned that his secretary was secretly convoking cabinet meetings during his physical incapacity.

As he was unsuccessful in his mediation attempt and in keeping the United States out of the Great War, he would also meet defeat in his attempt to commit the United States to membership in the League of Nations. It is a tribute to Wilson's remarkable abilities as a forceful and articulate leader, however, as well as to his personal courage that he nonetheless left an indelible legacy of the active pursuit of peace in a war-torn and revolutionary world.

———

Once Congress declared war, the participants in the mediation movement went in different directions. Those involved only briefly or peripherally moved easily to other pursuits. Ferdinand Leipnik, for instance, turned his attention to the visual arts, which he and his diplomat friend, Esme Howard, had frequently discussed before the war. By the 1920s he was back in London working for a graphic arts magazine, and he also wrote a history of French etchings since the sixteenth century.[42] His more committed pacifist cohort, Louis Lochner, meanwhile joined American left-wing, antiwar groups during the war. Afterwards, he continued to believe in the important role ordinary citizens could play in moving their political leaders away from armaments competition and toward international cooperation, and he championed foreign student exchanges to increase international understanding. By the early 1920s, however, he was no longer directly involved in the peace movement. He turned instead to journalism, winning in 1939 a Pulitzer Prize for international reporting of Hitler's Germany.

Other peace activists like David Starr Jordan saw the vote of Congress for war as the will of the people. He acquiesced in the decision and supported U.S. membership in the League of Nations. After vigorously championing the war, Ford became a vicious anti-Semite in the 1920s. Still others opposed military conscription and worked to defend the civil liberties of draft resisters. During American belligerency, the AUAM went through several transformations; one faction eventually founded the American Civil

Liberties Union in 1919. Some former AUAM members, mostly younger, and many newcomers, both male and female, would become actively involved in this new organization. Amos Pinchot, one of AUAM's leaders, remained a staunch anti-interventionist and would serve on the executive committee of the America First Committee, a high-profile isolationist group, which lobbied in 1940–1941 against U.S. military involvement in the Second World War.

Distressed at the growing leftward tilt to the AUAM, Paul Kellogg and Lillian Wald, among others, would soon resign from the organization. Wald's activism always stopped short of direct confrontation of political authority. She had received President Wilson's approval before going forward with the women's peace parade in late August 1914 and despite subsequent differences with him over military preparedness, believed he was a "pacifist." Given her perspective, it is not surprising that she would later chide the radical pacifists as "freelances" without "weighty responsibilities."[43] She certainly had other constituencies to consider, especially the viability of the Henry Street Settlement, and so did several other pacifistic Americans, such as Kellogg who had extensive social work connections, not least of which was his editorship of *The Survey* magazine.

But several of the more radical pacifists also had major responsibilities, including Addams and her Hull House, and Balch, who because of her antiwar activism was fired from her Wellesley professorship and had to search for other employment in a social environment unfriendly to pacifists. Addams actually supported the government to the extent of assisting with food relief, but her earlier leadership of women's peace activism already branded her in the public mind as an uncompromising radical. One reason for the real differences between the New York social worker and those continuing antiwar activity was that Wald's perspective was limited essentially to domestic social and political questions, while the more radical members, with their extensive international connections and experiences, thought more in transnational terms.

Rebecca Shelley and Lella Secor also moved on to other pursuits temporarily, but did not abandon their peace activism. In the last-ditch efforts to avert war and their subsequent transition to the fledgling civil liberties group, the two, now dubbed the "peace twins" because of their year-long close collaboration, had sometimes put in 16-hour days. Both became overworked, succumbing to what might be called "burnout" today. They suffered breakdowns during the war, although the exact nature of their illnesses is not known.

Diagnosing herself as "exhausted in spirit as well as in body" and feeling "that I could not go on from day to day," Secor took advantage of a physician friend's offer to take a leave of absence from peacework to rest at his Michigan sanitarium. Her illness seemed to be short-lived, perhaps in part because she received devoted emotional support from a new male friend. The man was an American living in England who, upon returning to the United States for graduate study in December 1916, had been given the Buxton and Ponsonby pamphlets to deliver to the ANCC. At the ANCC offices, he had presented them to Secor, and the two struck up a friendship. When she went off to Michigan, he continued his support; the two were married in October 1917. After giving birth to two boys, Secor moved to England with her husband and family, but remained active in British peace and disarmament groups, while her founding of a family planning association gave voice to her feminism.[44]

Shelley meanwhile fell ill in 1918 and had a longer recuperation in the same sanitarium. In addition to her exhaustion from her peace endeavors, she also suffered a personal crisis when she became engaged only to learn that her fiancé had a liaison with an "older woman." Staying in Battle Creek after her recovery, she purchased a trade journal for the poultry industry in 1920, which she edited through most of the decade. Shelley became engaged a third time, on this occasion, to a German engineer whom she married in 1922 just before the expiration of a law, which denied citizenship to Americans marrying Germans. Because she could have delayed her marriage a few days, there is a strong possibility that she deliberately chose to lose her U.S. citizenship and assume the role of dispossessed martyr. She then refused to take the naturalization oath, which included a promise to bear arms, if necessary, for her country. Only after much publicity and legal battles was her U.S. citizenship restored in 1944. In the 1950s, the religious roots of her pacifism found expression in a U.S. branch of the Fellowship of Reconciliation, and in 1964 she ran as a write-in candidate for vice president of a peace party opposed to U.S. meddling in the Vietnam War. Starting in 1968, she continued through the remaining years of the war to dress in mourning as a protest against that war.[45]

At the Hague congress in 1915, the women delegates had agreed to meet at the site of the peace conference to lobby for their international reform program. Because the Allied blockade prohibited women from the enemy powers to travel to Paris, the women pacifists would hastily convene in Zurich, Switzerland, in 1919. Mostly cut off from one another during the war years, those who gathered at Zurich celebrated a kind of homecoming for the women pacifists, including many from the European belligerents whose governments had prevented their attendance at the Hague congress. The assembled 200 women from 17 countries included about 25 delegates each from Britain, Germany, and the United States. They would protest the harsh provisions of the Treaty of Versailles and the Allied blockade on the Central Powers. Imposed to coerce Germany into acceptance of the punitive peace settlement, the blockade also greatly aggravated the enormous human suffering, especially to women and children in the defeated countries. The worldwide connections among the female activists at Zurich also resulted in the formal creation of the Women's International League for Peace and Freedom (WILPF), which is still the best known global women's peace organization today. In the 1920s and early 1930s, the group campaigned for disarmament at the League of Nations, although some on the European side, perceiving more complicated political and security issues, also tried to support that new world organization in its peacemaking efforts.

By 1920, women had attained the suffrage in the United States and limited or full female voting rights in Europe, except for France, Italy, Spain, and several smaller countries. The focus on suffrage had simplified the challenge for those women reformers, and even those who became involved in peace activity during the war had never turned their backs on the vote for women and other feminist issues. Following her activist peace efforts during the war, Chrystal Macmillan continued to serve as secretary of the International Woman Suffrage Association until 1920. She also remained an active WILPF participant and resumed her career as a lawyer involved in feminist issues.

Whether or not women reformers had joined the peace movement during the hostilities, they now, as women citizens, had to make choices. Much of the writing about the women's movement in the 1920s in both the United States and Europe has centered on the many new directions it took. Historians of this phenomenon still debate whether despite the resulting diaspora feminists continued to cooperate and thrive, or felt isolated and weakened in their struggle for greater equality.[46]

For absolute pacifists, the choice was not difficult. Fanny Villard was a feminist, but even more was an uncompromising nonresistant. Concerned immediately after the war about American women pacifists' agitation for women's rights at the expense of peace, she, now in her late seventies, joined with much younger female radicals in founding the Women's Peace Union, a small group dedicated to uncompromising nonresistance, but she also maintained her WILPF membership. Similarly, Lady Courtney of the Society of Friends in Britain lived out her faith. When she died in 1929, her sister Beatrice Webb, who considered her "an incurable sentimentalist," nonetheless noted in her diary: "Kate was the most beneficent of my sisters. She was in a sense faultless – she had no malice, no envy, little egotism."[47]

For others, however, the choices were not so automatic. Maude Royden, for example, was involved in several reform endeavors related to her interests in feminism and religion. Concerned about the dissipation of her energies into several causes, she decided to focus intensively on one after the war. Initially inclined to emphasize feminism, including women's peace activism, she had been discouraged by Swanwick's "inability to meet me half way" in the Women's International League. She had also encouraged her close friend, Kathleen Courtney, to rededicate herself to the international peace movement and was disappointed in the latter's decision to turn down the position of WIL secretary. Turning her attention more to religion, Royden served as a pastor in a nondenominational church in London. Preaching a Christian socialist message to her parishioners, she continued her agitation for ordination of women in the Anglican Church. She also maintained connections with the British peace movement after the war, however, and because of her abhorrence of international violence became a pronounced religious pacifist. Like many antiwar activists in the 1930s, Royden struggled intellectually and emotionally with the reality of the aggression of totalitarian regimes. With the advent of a second World War, she finally admitted in 1940 that her full-blown pacifism was a mistake.

> I NOW BELIEVE THAT NAZI-ISM IS WORSE THAN WAR. IT
> IS HIDEOUSLY CRUEL, MORE BLIND, MORE EVIL – AND
> MORE IMPORTANT. I am still a pacifist in that I believe . . . that
> spiritual power is the right weapon . . . The tragedy of pacifism is that
> it has left the great mass of the unconverted under the impression that
> the use of spiritual power is simply 'doing nothing'.[48]

Royden's earlier appeals to Courtney may have had some effect, as the latter became WILPF's representative at the League of Nations in Geneva after the First World War. Though Courtney had been a strong proponent of an internationalist direction for the National Union of Women's Suffrage Societies, she was not a radical activist. As one of the few British women at the 1915 Hague congress, she had opposed Schwimmer's call for women envoys to present the resolutions to the European political leaders.[49] In the late 1920s, Courtney left her position in Geneva when she found that many of the WILPF women were uncompromising pacifists agitating for disarmament as a panacea for peace; she herself believed that wars might be necessary in some cases.

Courtney continued to support WILPF, however, and corresponded with Addams into the 1930s in trying to resolve ideological differences within the organization. Increasingly, however, she devoted more time to the League of Nations Union, a British advocacy group, giving lectures and radio talks in Europe and America in trying to educate public opinion on the League as a viable collective security system.[50] Consistent with her mainstream feminism, Courtney's internationalist efforts were primarily directed at encouraging women to become more educated and involved in foreign affairs. She also continued her work for equitable treatment for British working women and families.

Other British suffragists who had promoted mediation and peace during

the Great War continued to be actively engaged in the peace cause afterwards. Helena Swanwick stayed with the Union of Democratic Control
(UDC), editing its journal for a time in the mid-1920s, and publishing a
credible history of the organization. In the same decade she also served
twice as a delegate of Labour governments to the League of Nations.
Swanwick then published her autobiography in 1935, which recounted her
roles in the British women's and peace movements. Her husband had died
in 1931, however, and, in failing health herself, she became more despond-
ent with the rising war clouds in Europe that portended another world war
in less than a generation. Strongly opposed to the use of force in international affairs, she rejected the prospect of military sanctions against the
aggression of totalitarian states and ended her career as a political isolationist. She died only a few months after the Second World War began in
Europe.[51]

The union itself became the foreign policy arm of the fledgling Labour
party, which had continued after the war to attract radicals and liberals
from the disintegrating Liberal party. When Labour became the majority
party in 1924, the new government contained 15 UDC members, including
nine in the cabinet. Facing the responsibilities of power, the UDC tempered its dissent. It worked for European conciliation and promised to
inform Parliament of any binding treaties in foreign affairs. The union
continued well into the 1960s, but was much less influential after Morel's
death in 1924.[52]

What is undeniable, however, is that the peace movement continued to
provide a ready outlet for those women who, finding the war experience
profoundly unsettling, decided to become engaged in efforts seeking inter-
governmental cooperation. The motives for this commitment varied, but
for most it consisted of a mixture of idealism and grim awareness of the
imposing difficulties in creating a saner international environment in a
turbulent world where virulent nationalist and ethnic passions were widespread. Some, too, reacted more immediately against the superpatriotism
and suppression of civil liberties they found in their own countries, and
they vigorously sought to protect free speech and provide legal and moral
support to conscientious objectors. Moreover, maternalism—the belief
that women are more peace-oriented than men—continued to have an
attractive appeal to many public-spirited women long after the Great War,
and it permeated the rhetoric of several separate national women's peace
organizations created in the 1920s and later.[53]

Some suffragist leaders, who were well acquainted with women peace
activists, but had shunned close collaboration with them during the war,
now turned their attention to questions of war and peace. In the United
States, Carrie Chapman Catt, like her British counterpart Fawcett, became
an active internationalist. She gave up the presidency of the International

Woman Suffrage Alliance in 1923 (soon to be renamed the International Alliance of Women), which continued to support suffragists still struggling for the vote in their countries, but also focused more broadly on feminist issues, such as married women's property rights, widows' pensions, education, the suppression of the traffic of women, and equal pay. With the backing of many American women's organizations, Catt then founded the National Committee on the Cause and Cure of War, which promoted U.S. membership in the World Court and proposed internationalist initiatives for disarmament and security that would strengthen the League of Nations. Not a pacifist organization, it deliberately sought to educate middle-class American women in the complexities of international politics.

Considering her preoccupation with the American suffrage campaign and her hands-off approach to the peace movement during the First World War, her new interest could be seen as incongruous, but her long-time and deep friendships with foreign women had also given her an internationalist perspective, which she put to work in the interwar years. Because of her commitment to international peace, in 1928 she could call herself a "humanist" who had "not ceased to be a feminist."[54] During the height of the Battle of Britain with the survival of that country still in doubt, she, now 81, could lament to Kathleen Courtney at America's isolationist mood that withheld full support for British resistance to Hitler's tyranny. "Let me say to you, dear friend, that the better part of our people are absolutely united in their sympathy with Great Britain at this time and our hearts are aching with despair over the situation Germany has created . . . Nor do I lose my faith in the peace that is to come."[55] Long after Aletta Jacobs and other IWSA stalwart friends had died, Catt also continued intimate correspondence with its younger members like Jacobs' loyal Dutch colleague, Rosa Manus. Part Jewish, Manus became a victim of the Holocaust during the Second World War and died in a Nazi gas chamber. Catt herself was in the forefront of Americans who early spoke out against fascism and criticized Germany's militarism and its persecution of the Jews.[56]

After Schwimmer's return to her native land, a short-lived liberal government in Hungary appointed her as ambassador to Switzerland in November 1918. As the first woman chief of mission in modern times, she received considerable press attention. Her assignment to a conservative nation where women, who would remain disfranchised until 1971, held a secondary position in society, however, was not a good match for her talents. More immediately, diplomats representing many other governments in Berne objected to a female ambassador, particularly one with advanced feminist views, and refused to deal with her. Finding the doors of the diplomatic world closed to her and fearing that she was jeopardizing her liberal government at home, she resigned her ambassadorship after only two months. Following a right-wing takeover in Hungary shortly thereafter, she narrowly escaped from her native land and made her way to the United States, but in a famous Supreme Court decision was denied U.S. citizenship for refusing in the oath of allegiance to take up arms, if required, in defense of the nation.[57]

Schwimmer's career was like an explosive rocket launched at the onset of the European war, which hit its apogee with the Ford peace ship and abruptly descended with a brief flare-up in the postwar era. Despite her pronounced feminist views, she no longer participated in international women's groups. Supported financially by Lola Maverick Lloyd, she mostly lived the rest of her life in relative obscurity in her New York City apartment. She better controlled her impetuous temperament that had estranged her from many erstwhile friends in the peace movement, although flashes of her emotional personality still surfaced on occasion. She continued to correspond mostly formally with Catt, but bitterly complained that, despite her American friend's "forceful personality" and "organizing genius and personal charm," she had allowed nonpacifist women to make the tepid annual Cause and Cure of War conferences "a most deplorable waste of our time." What was needed, Schwimmer implored, as she had during the World War, were less words and more deeds. True to her activism, in the late 1930s with almost no outside support, she put forward another plan for a conference of neutral states to negotiate agreements between the conflicting fascist and democratic states.[58]

Addams and Balch also suffered for opposing U.S. belligerency. Addams' pacifism was misunderstood, and she was branded a traitor, communist, and anarchist. Balch's dismissal from Wellesley sped up her transition to full-time peace activism.[59] An event at the Zurich conference highlighted this deepening commitment. When Jeanne Mélin of France arrived on the last day of the meeting from her devastated region in the Ardennes, Lida Gustava Heymann, who had already apologized to the gathering for the wartime excesses of the German Government, took her hand and announced, "A German woman gives her hand to a French woman, and says in the name of the German delegation, that we hope we women can build a bridge from Germany to France and from France to Germany, and that in the future we may be able to make good the wrong-doing of men." After Mélin gave an equally moving reply, Balch rose and exclaimed, "I dedicate my life to the cause of Peace!" and all the other women then echoed in their different languages, "We dedicate our lives to Peace!"[60] Balch practiced what she preached, and she became WILPF's international secretary-treasurer in Geneva from the 1920s to 1940s.

The public opprobrium against pacifists continued well into the 1920s. But many of the men and women involved in the mediation movement nonetheless continued their involvement in the peace cause, and Addams and Balch would win Nobel Peace Prizes for 1932 and 1946, respectively.

Serving as WILPF president and then as honorary president in the 1920s, Addams also donated generously to the organization, including her prize money. Before her death in 1935, she wrote her own epitaph, which despite her myriad reform activities and the peace prize she distilled into two bedrock commitments. Her tombstone in a cemetery in her hometown of Cedarville, Illinois, reads simply: "Jane Addams of Hull House and the Women's International League for Peace and Freedom."[61]

Conclusion

The First World War gave birth to the modern peace movement. Citizen movements for peace have historically arisen and expanded in reaction to the enormous human and physical destruction in large-scale hostilities; and not surprisingly the immense scope and mounting military casualties and prolonged suffering among civilian populations in the Great War prompted many people to question the efficacy of the war as a solution to the deep-seated national and ethnic tensions in Europe and to search for alternatives to the continued fighting. Some of the activists participating in the quest for neutral mediation of the conflict, particularly on the European side, had been involved in the prewar peace movement in criticizing imperialism and arms races, but they were increasingly joined by Americans, several of whom had expressed similar concerns before the Great War and, like their European colleagues, had also promoted more authoritative arbitration treaties and new international peacemaking institutions. The expanding intensity of the conflict moved the European and American advocates, however, into a sustained search for a negotiated end to the fighting and, identifying underlying causes of war, to develop prescriptive remedies for the postwar world. Large numbers of citizens with little or no experience in peacework joined this effort after 1914. In organizing themselves to promote their proposals, citizen activists made the peace cause a much more vibrant and visible presence than it ever had been.

Women, drawing on their prewar transatlantic connections, first gave direction to the new movement, which focused on mediation of the expanding military conflict and the liberal principles for an enduring postwar peace. It was American women like Lillian Wald and Fanny Villard who organized the New York peace parade down Fifth Avenue in late August 1914. The Hungarian feminist, Rosika Schwimmer, a press secretary for the International Woman Suffrage Alliance in London, almost single-handedly started the mediation movement in Great Britain and, with Emmeline Pethick-Lawrence, brought their ideas to the United States. The two of them, helped by Julia Grace Wales' pamphlet on neutral mediation and by many American women, spread the message to women's groups. The result of their agitation was the founding of the Woman's Peace Party, headed by Jane Addams, which initially provided an organizational framework for the American women going to the women's congress at The Hague in April 1915.

In Europe, women socialists opposed to the war held their own small international congress to discuss antiwar strategies even before the much larger Hague gathering, but class and ideological differences between the socialists and pacifists worked against close cooperation between them. The increasing suppression of dissent in the belligerent lands further hindered collaborative efforts for peace. Dr Aletta Jacobs and her Dutch suffragist colleagues along with many British and some German women, all of whom were well acquainted with one another from their connections with the International Woman Suffrage Alliance, organized the congress at The Hague and gave momentum to the movement for mediation and international reform. And it was the women envoys from this congress who took their program directly to every European prime minister and foreign minister, Pope Benedict, and President Wilson.

Once back in the United States, Schwimmer and Rebecca Shelley first engaged Henry Ford's attention and commitment to the peace cause. Women's activism inspired the auto manufacturer's peace ship adventure, although the results were mostly unfortunate for the movement. Subsequently, Shelley and Lella Secor were most responsible for launching and administering the day-to-day operations of the American Neutral Conference Committee.

If all these women, supported by many others of their sex, had not been actively involved, it is very likely that the peace and mediation movements would have developed much more slowly and hesitatingly.

Some men of course were also engaged in the movement for a negotiated peace from the outset. Prominent on the American side were the nonresistants Oswald Garrison Villard and George Foster Peabody, as well as Louis Lochner, a committed peace activist, and David Starr Jordan, a long-time peace advocate. They readily cooperated with women activists in the Henry Street meetings to discuss mediation and international reform proposals. Mixed gender collaboration expanded in 1915 and 1916. The American Union Against Militarism included both prominent male and female activists, and some of its feminist leaders like Crystal Eastman were actively engaged in both the antimilitarist group and the New York branch of the Woman's Peace Party. In their organizational work for the American Neutral Conference Committee, Shelley and Secor successfully enlisted many wealthy and well-known men to give the group greater visibility and possible influence. When Germany declared all-out submarine warfare in early 1917, the large numbers of Americans already committed to peace activism quickly transformed the mediation and antimilitarist campaigns into a pacifist coalition opposing U.S. entrance into the raging maelstrom.

On the of America's declaration of war, Ellen Slayden, whose husband had served in Congress for 20 years, marveled at the EPF's lobbying activities on Capitol Hill. "Numbers of young men, women and girls were busy registering names of sympathizers, and handing out white armbands and badges printed large 'Keep Out of War.' Public opinion has certainly advanced since the Spanish War. A young man wearing such a thing would have been mobbed." She was partly right. An antiwar movement had scarcely existed in 1898, and the few who had dared to speak out against America's "splendid little war" had been ridiculed or even hanged in effigy.[1] Even before 1914, the American peace movement had taken on new life, but had been dominated by more conservative political elites. The World War tragedy indeed brought a resurgence in peace activism. But Slayden's belief that public opinion had "advanced" since 1898 was premature. The previous evening a mob numbering perhaps a thousand people had broken up an antiwar meeting in Baltimore and surged forward toward the stage where David Starr Jordan was the featured speaker. The Stanford Chancellor managed to escape the mob's clutches, which pursued him unsuccessfully through the night yelling, "We'll hang Dave Jordan to a sour apple tree."[2] Repression of antiwar activists continued with a vengeance during American involvement in the war, and the movement, which had never developed a massive base, would soon be in shambles.

The new groups founded after 1914 were in fact relatively small in numbers of members, underfinanced, and structurally weak, and some would not survive the war intact. Several pacifist groups would endure, however, or would be transformed into new associations, and a new generation of younger activists would come to the fore to create still others. A small, but distinct, peace culture was emerging during the years of the World War that would involve new ways of thinking about war and militarism, and the American peace movement would rebound to become an important force in the politics and diplomacy of the 1920s and 1930s. The desire for alternative approaches to great power conflict, together with growing popular disillusionment with the World War experience, would nourish this surprising resurgence, which would be further stimulated by fears of the prospect of another World War.[3]

In Europe, many women complemented men as delegates to Ford's Neutral Conference for Continuous Mediation, and following Schwimmer's departure from the undertaking Lochner and Emily Balch cooperated effectively as the primary American representatives. The male-dominated Union of Democratic Control was easily the most prominent citizens' group in Great Britain advocating a negotiated settlement, but some well-known women—Helena Swanwick, Lady Courtney, and Vernon Lee, for example—were active members, and the union sometimes printed their broadsides or those of other women pacifists like Emily Hobhouse.

Peace activists often differed markedly in temperament, strategy, and tactics, with the more radical pacifists sometimes annoying or bewildering their more cautious colleagues. Nevertheless, without the radicals the pacifist impulse would have had few fresh initiatives and little momentum, while the less adventuresome among them provided an organizational structure and interpersonal skills that helped give stable direction to the cause. The pacifists' networks included ad hoc transnational dimensions—for example, in the informal cooperation between the UDC and the ANCC—and, more enduringly, in the creation of the Women's International League for Peace and Freedom. Moreover, the radical and more moderate strategies in some ways complemented one another. Organized peacemaking since the Great War has developed more imaginative and flamboyant tactics to get public and political leaders' attention, but the basic approaches, as they exist today, started with their pioneering efforts.

In essence, the male and female pacifists offered an alternative view of world politics that emphasized international goodwill and various general principles looking toward a reformed world order. That vision was very idealistic, and in more open moments some admitted to "romantic" views of international politics or discerned naiveté among their more inexperienced colleagues. Despite occasionally admitting that their activities for a negotiated peace were a "fools' errand perhaps" or even "ridiculous,"[4] they nonetheless consistently overestimated the prospects for peace negotiations. Later some of them would acknowledge their excessive optimism, which bordered on self-delusion. Bertrand Russell, for example, later wrote "At intervals, the German Government made peace offers which were, as the Allies said, illusory, but which all pacifists (myself included) took more seriously than they deserved."[5] Still, awareness that growing numbers of people both within and outside their organizations had strong misgivings about the war helped to sustain their commitment to negotiations. They stayed on course but in the end were undone by events.

The liberal peace people developed a broad program of international reform and were prepared to campaign for their principles on a wide range of issues at the peace settlement and beyond. They were committed for the long haul. The activists mostly did not waste time in semantic debates with their erstwhile supporters or detractors, but developed their peace programs and used various tactics to advance them: demonstrations, printed propaganda in the form of leaflets, pamphlets, and articles, and personal contact with political elites. Above all, many of them, already experienced social or feminist reformers before the European conflict, knew where the seats of power lay, and they lobbied in their nations' legislatures and appealed directly to the foreign ministers and heads of government in Europe and the United States.

The reality of a postwar League of Nations would challenge their reservations on the use of military force in world politics, and many involved in the interwar peace movement would have considerable difficulty in trying to reconcile their "pacifism" and "internationalism." Peacekeeping institutions, they believed, were necessary and important, but more enduringly significant were the values and sense of "community" that underlay international cooperation. They differed in this respect from more conservative "polity" internationalists who valued power and, working through the political establishment, were prepared to authorize the League to employ collective military force against obvious lawbreaking states.[6] Until the end of the Great War, however, there was no specific government proposal for a new international body, and the pacifists could actively promote the desirability of international organization as an integral part of their reform program without being deflected by debates over specific features of the proposed entity.[7]

The pacifists also focused on immediate questions, and the ideas and motivations propelling citizens toward peace activism after August 1914 and the impact of the newfound recruits in pushing the peace movement in new directions comprise the main part of the story here. They early settled on a concrete program, a conference of neutral nations for continuous mediation, for possible mediation of the European conflagration. Indeed, much of the pacifists' commitment to peace in the first years of the war involved their search for a mediated solution of the conflict before it became a fight to the finish, although in the United States many of them also became active participants in the struggle against military preparedness. Their plan for joint neutral mediation underestimated the self-interest of nation states and the difficulty in persuading them to act together in any sustained manner. Their persistent focus on the neutral conference is understandable, however, as it expressed their rejection of great power dominance of world politics and their hopes for a rational and sane world in which nations, big along with small, would try to cooperate. When Germany's extensive submarine campaign ruined mediation prospects, the American pacifists simply transformed the conference idea to a league of neutrals cooperating in the mutual defense of their nations' rights short of full-scale belligerency.

———

The issue of mediation is also central to an understanding of the Wilson administration. During American neutrality, the citizen activists had some influence on President Wilson, with whom they regularly corresponded and met face-to-face on more than 20 occasions. Their importance derived in part from their prominence as domestic reformers, whose support he wanted for his re-election campaign in 1916 and for his own maturing vision of a new postwar world order. But he also shared their revulsion over the continuing human slaughter on European battlefields and, like them, searched for ways to end the escalating warfare.

The advocates of peace also had relatively easy access to Wilson because of the informal, highly personalized nature of the presidency in that era. The White House consisted of a small staff, which despite the onset of the World War remained free of bureaucratic constraints. Access to Wilson usually required only the approval of his close confidant, Colonel House, or Joseph Tumulty, his private secretary. The colonel disagreed with the pacifists' neutral conference plan, which might also complicate his own mediatory role, and he did not share with the President Jane Addams' memorandum explaining its purposes.[8] But he and Tumulty, as gate-keepers, almost always forwarded the communications of American peace workers to the President or granted them interviews with him because of their high visibility domestically and their presumed nourishment of their chief's known interest in mediation of the European conflagration. Some-thing of an intellectual loner, Wilson often preferred to think things through on his own and often found himself much in tune with the idealistic foreign policy aspirations, though usually not the specific programs, of reform-minded private citizens, including peace workers.

The activists' impact on the President never rivaled that of Colonel House, who had his greatest influence on his mentor during this period. But Wilson remained open to other approaches to mediation besides his close aide's pro-Allied emphasis, and following his re-election assumed a more neutral posture in launching his own mediation initiative. He incorporated in his mediation initiatives the ideas promoted by American international reformers and Britons in the UDC, many of whom were mem-bers of a small, but articulate, group in Parliament favoring peace negoti-ations. Early in the war, American and British peace and internationalist groups had also formulated and well publicized certain salient premises for a "new diplomacy." By 1917, these ideas were well known among liberal internationalists. Wilson would later include several of them among his general principles (as opposed to more specific and territorial ones) in his "fourteen points" address in January 1918.

Perhaps most important, Wilson derived comfort from these liberal left reformers that his own mediation initiatives had their firm support. Clearly, he sympathized more with them than with noncareer diplomats like Ambassadors Page and Gerard whose views he distrusted and mostly rejected out of hand. One can view Wilsonian diplomacy during the neu-trality period not just from the top down, which would include the input from House and his secretaries of state and, to a lesser degree, his other cabinet officers and Tumulty, but also from the bottom up, or as the ongoing interaction between the President and various citizens and groups.

Biographers of Wilson may overstate the originality of his ideas or his political perspicacity, and studies of House may magnify his role at the expense of other influences on the President. Similarly, the focus on Europeans and Americans committed to a negotiated end of the World War may go too far in detailing their possible impact on Wilson's approaches to mediation. Wilson was in fact arguably as close, or closer, to the *New Republic* editors and other nonpacifist liberals who supported U.S. military preparedness as necessary and eventually belligerency as a critical opportunity to embed American liberal ideals in the final peace settlement. But like the more pacifistic liberals, they too would become severe critics of the punitive features of the Versailles treaty.[9] Sometimes the pacifists' impact on official policy is clearly evident; sometimes it can only be inferred or articulated as one of a number of possible influences. The human mind works in mysterious ways, and humility is called for where solid documentation on the origins of Wilson's ideas and policies is lacking. But, at a minimum, the pacifistic liberals' many interactions with him provide a wider—and more complete—perspective of the many contacts of an active chief executive and their possible impact, negatively as well as positively, on him.

Of Woodrow Wilson's dual personality, the thoughtful, reasonable, and flexible side clearly predominated during his first presidential term. He was unfailingly civil in his contacts with the liberal pacifists in these years. When pressed hard on issues, such as his prolonged inaction on mediation, he could summon forth compelling reasons for his seeming caution. His will to leadership was always present, but in his first administration it was mainly expressed, domestically, in giving eloquent expression to widely shared progressive values; he was a consensus builder in the advancement of the American reform tradition. His foreign policies emphasized America's "rights" vis-à-vis the belligerents and the gradual exploration of the suitable application of the nation's values to a reformed postwar world order.

Even in the period of American neutrality, however, there were also hints of his more intuitive, less rational side. As he positioned himself immediately after his re-election to offer his good offices for mediation of the European bloodbath, he moved increasingly toward committing the United States to a leadership role in working toward his vision of a new postwar security system based on new norms of international conduct. Wilson's depiction more than 30 years earlier of himself as the "lonely" and "selfish" eagle soaring above the rest of the bird species was not a total fantasy.[10] Like the eagle, Wilson in pursuit of his lofty goals during his second term could be harsher and more vindictive toward those resisting his policies. His strong religious background would more often blur the line between what he considered right and his own self-righteous behavior.

Once convinced that he was closest to the truth, he could be unyielding toward those with contrary opinions. In his first term, the pacifistic liberals had been Wilson's natural allies in keeping out of the war and promoting mediation, and the President had listened to and even courted them politically. But his relationship with them had not been comfortable, as he had consistently thought in terms of his own independent mediation instead of their program of joint mediation with several neutral powers; and, more fundamentally, he disagreed with them over the questions of preparedness and the role of military force in world politics. Following Germany's all-out submarine warfare, the pacifists became victims of his determined new course, which included U.S. belligerency and membership in an authoritative League of Nations, but their disaffection from him was an early sign of a much wider domestic opposition he would face as war President and peacemaker.

APPENDIX

PROFILES OF PACIFISTIC-INTERNATIONALIST BRITISH WOMEN

Two quite different lists of British women who supported the Hague meeting initiative have been preserved. One contains the names of the 180 women who actually applied for exit permits to travel to the congress. The other list, published a month or so after the congress, consists of the names of 156 British women who formed the national committee in support of the Hague gathering and its resolutions. The names of some women are on both lists. The overlap is not great, however, and Sybil Oldfield finds a total of 275 different women on the two lists, 200 of whom she has identified. One possible explanation for the dissimilarities of the lists is that some women on the committee members' list may have been joiners, but not activists; they were prepared to support the Hague initiative organizationally and financially, but not as frontline participants. Some, too, may have held demanding jobs that prevented them from taking time off to go to The Hague. Moreover, on the committee list many of the oldest women or those with care-giving responsibilities for children or invalid relatives perhaps decided that they could not attend the Hague congress and thus are not on the list of the 180 actually applying for travel permits. (Another list is the 101 British women signing the open Christmas letter to the women of Germany and Austria in December 1914 (see p 52 above). Only 34 (or one-third) of the names from this list also appear on the list of 156 British committee members supporting the Hague congress.

Because the biographical information about the vast majority of the 200 women is fragmentary, generalizations about them are somewhat hazardous. But looking at their socio-economic origins, Oldfield discerns some common features among them. Fifty percent, she finds, came from the educated, professional middle class, and another 40 percent were from the upper-middle class, gentry, or aristocracy. (She unfortunately does not define what constitutes class lines.) Despite these figures, Oldfield warns against the assumption that lower-class women therefore did not support the women's international congress. She believes that those from poor backgrounds are not well represented on the lists because those women did not have the disposable income to travel to The Hague. Indeed, the few among them who did sign up to venture across the channel may have received financial support for the trip from large women's cooperatives or labor unions with which they were affiliated. It is also possible that many of the 75 unidentified women on the lists came from very modest circumstances. (Also, see Chapter 9 for growing antiwar actions among lower class British women.) Apart from their class backgrounds and short references to the Quakers among them, Oldfield does not delve extensively into other common similarities or differences among the 200 women, and of course many feminists who avoided or opposed the peace movement also likely conformed to this sociopolitical profile. Oldfield, *Women Against the Iron Fist*, pp 90–91.

In a separate, more recent biographical dictionary, Oldfield includes 40 of the British committee women supporting the Hague congress in a sample of more than 150 leading British female "humanitarians" (a term she defines) active during the first half of the twentieth century—doctors, nurses, rescue and relief workers, missionaries, medical researchers—who sometimes risked their lives working in famine, diseased, war, or disaster areas. Of these 40, the vast majority were single women or childless, and the children of the few mothers among them were mostly grown up by the time of the Great War. With some exceptions, their ages ranged from the mid-thirties to early fifties, prime years of middle age. Their comparative freedom from family constraints more easily allowed them to risk government and public opprobrium in identifying with the international peace movement during wartime; at the same time, because they were mature, mostly well-educated or professional women already experienced in organized reform endeavors, this new commitment was likely to be serious and thoughtful. Oldfield also suggests in both studies that religion may have influenced these 40 women's commitment to internationalism and other humanitarian causes. Almost all of the 40 appear to have grown up in Christian homes. (Only one was Jewish, for example.) Some were brought up or became Quakers by convincement. Several of the older women were Quakers and had in fact been involved in the British peace movement before 1914. Oldfield cautions, however, that in most cases it is difficult to know the extent of religious influences on them, and she concludes that overall their humanness was more important than their Christian faith. See Oldfield, *Women Humanitarians*, pp xi–xv, 287–292, *passim*.

Whatever the motivating influences on these British pacifistic internationalists, which could have varied considerably for each woman, what ultimately set them apart from other, more nationalist and nonpacifistic women professionals from similar backgrounds was the former's much greater willingness to advocate "unpopular principles," as Balch had put it for the Americans (see text above, pp 21–22).

NOTES

PREFACE

1 Historians do not entirely agree on casualty figures in the First World War. They also differ, sometimes markedly, on the numbers killed and wounded at various battles. The figures given here and elsewhere are not definitive—we will never know more precise totals—but are presented to exemplify the scope of the human tragedy about which there is no disagreement.

2 Thomas J. Knock, *To End All Wars: Woodrow Wilson and the Quest for a New World Order* (New York: Oxford University Press, 1992), chs 2–4, *passim*, uses the phrase "progressive internationalists" to describe the socialist and liberal international reformers engaged in the search for a new world order. He contrasts them with pro-Allied "conservative internationalists," who promoted a postwar league of nations, arbitration, and sanctions against aggressors, but had little or no interest in mediation, disarmament, self-determination, free trade, or democratic control of foreign policy.

3 Arno J. Mayer, *Political Origins of the New Diplomacy, 1917–1918* (New Haven: Yale University Press, 1959) applies the phrase "parties of movement" for those international reformers and groups, although mainly in Europe and after U.S. entrance into the war. His sequel is *Politics and Diplomacy of Peacemaking: Containment and Counterrevolution at Versailles,* *1918–1919* (New York: Knopf, 1967). These books, and others published in the same vein during the 1960s–1980s, were of course fully compatible with the ideological rubric of the Cold War at the time; but the Left–Right dichotomy is a valid organizing principle for the 1914–1917 period, even without the Bolsheviks, who did not yet have any territorial base from which to promote their extreme leftist principles internationally.

4 Specialized studies include Laurence W. Martin, *Peace without Victory: Woodrow Wilson and the British Liberals* (New Haven: Yale University Press, 1958), a pioneering account of the relationship between British liberal internationalists and Woodrow Wilson. Another example on the British side is Marvin Swartz, *The Union of Democratic Control in British Politics during the First World War* (Oxford: Clarendon Press, 1971).

5 Regarding possible contributions of peace history to diplomatic history, see Lawrence S. Wittner, "Peace Movements and Foreign Policy: The Challenge to Diplomatic Historians," *Diplomatic History*, 11 (Fall 1987), pp 355–370.

6 The controversy over Germany's goals took off with Fritz Fischer, *Germany's Aims in the First World War* (New York: W. W. Norton, 1967 edition); an example on the Allied side is David Stevenson, *French War*

Aims Against Germany, 1914–1919 (Oxford: Clarendon Press, 1982).

7 Distinctions between different anti-war viewpoints are developed in Martin Ceadel's publications on pacifism—e.g., *Pacifism in Britain, 1914–1945: The Defining of a Faith* (Oxford: Clarendon Press, 1980). Lelia J. Rupp and Verta Taylor, "Forging Feminist Identity in an International Movement: A Collective Identity Approach to Twentieth-Century Feminism," *Signs*, 24 (Winter 1999), pp 363–86, suggest a typology for categorizing—and understanding—feminists involved in transnational organizations and movements over the past century.

PROLOGUE

1 Keith Robbins, *The Abolition of War: The "Peace Movement" in Britain, 1914–1919* (Cardiff: University of Wales Press, 1976), pp 15–18; George W. Nasmyth, "International Polity Summer School," *Advocate of Peace*, 76 (October 1914), pp 215–216; Louis P. Lochner, *Always the Unexpected: A Book of Reminiscences* (New York: Macmillan, 1956), pp 43–44.

2 Between 1907 and 1914 the number of statewide and local peace societies in the United States had increased from eight to 31, including 16 new ones in 1913–1914. The best known of the new groups founded in the decade before 1914 was the New York Peace Society, which had nearly 1,500 members, including many of the most prominent businessmen, educators, and philanthropists in the city. The total included about 800 nonpaying associate members, who had signed a declaration of their agreement with the general purposes of the society. New York Peace Society, *Year Book, 1913* [1914], pp 20, 27, 32–42.

3 Regarding the founding and early work of these endowed entities, see Robert I. Rotberg, *A Leadership for Peace: How Edwin Ginn Tried to Change the World* (Stanford, Calif.: Stanford University Press, 2007), pp 90, 96–101, 110–111, 141, 175, *passim*; Michael A. Lutzker, "The Formation of the Carnegie Endowment for International Peace: A Study of the Establishment-Centered Peace Movement, 1910–1914," in *Building the Organizational Society: Essays on Associational Activities in Modern America*, ed. Jerry Israel (New York: Free Press, 1972), pp 143–162; and Joseph Frazier Wall, *Andrew Carnegie* (New York: Oxford University Press, 1970), pp 880–881, 885–901.

4 Alexis de Tocqueville, *Democracy in America* (1835), 2 vols (1835, New York: Alfred A. Knopf, 1945 edition), especially vol 2.

5 Robbins, *Abolition of War*, pp 12–18; and Paul Laity, *The British Peace Movement, 1870–1914* (Oxford: Clarendon Press, 2001), chs 6–8.

6 Sandi E. Cooper, *Patriotic Pacifism: Waging War on War in Europe* (New York: Oxford University Press, 1991); Roger Chickering, *Imperial Germany and a World Without War: The Peace Movement and German Society, 1892–1914* (Princeton, N.J.: Princeton University Press, 1975), chs 2, 7, *passim*; and Chickering's concise account, "War, Peace, and Social Mobilization in Imperial Germany: Patriotic Societies, the Peace Movement, and Socialist Labor," in *Peace Movements and Political Cultures*, eds Charles Chatfield and Peter van den Dungen (Knoxville: University of Tennessee Press, 1988), pp 3–22 (quotation on p 11).

7 Two studies on the U.S. perspective are by Calvin D. Davis, *The United States and the First Hague Peace Conference* (Ithaca, N.Y.: Cornell University Press, 1961) and *The United States and the Second Hague*

Peace Conference: American Diplomacy and International Organization, 1899–1914 (Durham, N.C.: Duke University Press, 1975).

8 Nasmyth, "International Polity Summer School," p 215.

9 David S. Patterson, *Toward a Warless World: The Travail of the American Peace Movement, 1887–1914* (Bloomington: Indiana University Press, 1976), pp 36–45, 126–128, 169–180.

10 Quoted in James Parker Martin, The American Peace Movement and the Progressive Era, 1910–1917 (PhD dissertation, Rice University, 1975), p 37.

11 Michael A. Lutzker, "The Pacifist as Militarist: A Critique of the American Peace Movement, 1898–1914" *Societas*, 5 (Spring 1975), pp 87–104.

12 Patterson, *Toward a Warless World*, pp 181–187, 192–195, 198–199; John M. Craig, *Lucia Ames Mead (1856–1936) and the American Peace Movement* (Lewiston, Me.: Edwin Mellen Press, 1990), pp 73–111.

13 Women play small roles at best in Verdiana Grossi, *Le Pacifisme Européen, 1889–1914* (Brussels: Bruylant, 1994). For the "tremendous impact" of Schreiner's ideas on peace, mainly during the Great War, but also somewhat earlier, see Jill Liddington, *The Road to Greenham Common: Feminism and Anti-Militarism in Britain since 1820* (Syracuse: Syracuse University Press, 1991 edition), pp 68–70, *passim*; also Susan R. Grayzel, *Women's Identities at War: Gender, Motherhood, and Politics in Britain and France during the First World War* (Chapel Hill: University of North Carolina Press, 1999), pp 158–162.

14 Sandi E. Cooper, "Peace as a Human Right: The Invasion of Women into the World of High International Politics," *Journal of Women's History*, 14 (Summer 2002), pp 13–18.

15 Patterson, *Toward a Warless World*, pp 197–204.

16 Jordan's best expressed his genetic views in his books, *The Blood of the Nation: A Study of the Decay of Races Through Survival of the Unfit* (Boston: American Unitarian Association, 1902) and *The Human Harvest: A Study of the Decay of Races Through the Survival of the Unfit* (Boston: American Unitarian Association, 1907). For his perspective on the European rivalries, see particularly his *Unseen Empire: A Study of the Plight of Nations That Do No Pay Their Debts* (Boston: American Unitarian Association, 1912) and *War and Waste: A Series of Discussions of War and War Accessories* (Garden City, N.Y.: Doubleday, Page & Co., 1913). For Jordan's ideas in the context of Darwinian thought, see Paul Crook, *Darwinism, War and History: The Debate over the Biology of War from the "Origin of Species" to the First World War* (Cambridge: Cambridge University Press, 1994), pp 119–124, *passim*.

17 Jordan, "The Impossible War," *The Independent*, 74 (February 27, 1913), pp 467–468.

18 Charles E. Beals, in *Report of the Chicago Peace Society, 1913* (Chicago: Chicago Peace Society, 1913), p 36.

19 Quoted in Patterson, *Toward a Warless World*, p 228.

20 See, for example, Lochner, "A Plea for the Small Town," *Advocate of Peace*, 76 (March 1914), pp 62–64.

21 Lochner, "Personal Observations at the Opening of the War," ibid. 76 (October 1914), pp 211–213. Lochner, *Always the Unexpected*, pp 33–51, is his retrospective account.

22 Quoted in Cooper, *Patriotic Pacifism*, p 186.

23 Theodore Ruyssen, "The Final Efforts of the European Pacifists to Prevent the War," *Advocate of Peace*, 76 (November 1914), pp 236–238; Cooper, *Patriotic Pacifism*, pp 80–81, 186–187; Patterson, *Toward a Warless World*, pp 230–231.

24 James L. Tryon, "Church Peace

Congress at Constance," *Advocate of Peace*, 76 (October 1914), p 207.

25 Lynch, *Through Europe on the Eve of War: A Record of Personal Experiences; Including an Account of the First World Conference of The Churches for International Peace* (New York: The Church Peace Union, 1914), pp 6, 28, 48–49, 94–95, *passim*. Additional reactions of American travelers on the continent at the time are detailed in Michael A. Lutzker, "Present at the Outbreak: American Witnesses to World War One," *Peace and Change*, 7 (Winter 1981), pp 59–70.

26 David Welch, *Germany, Propaganda and Total War, 1914–1918: The Sins of Omission* (New Brunswick, N.J.: Rutgers University Press, 2000), pp 138–144 (German Peace Society quoted on p 138); James D. Shand, "Doves Among the Eagles: German Pacifists and Their Government During World War I," *Journal of Contemporary History*, 10 (January 1975), pp 95–96; Chickering, *Imperial Germany and a World Without War*, pp 322–324 (quotation on p 323).

27 Hew Strachan, *The First World War; Volume I: To Arms* (Oxford: Oxford University Press, 2001), pp 111–124, and 1128ff.

28 Shand, "Doves Among the Eagles," pp 96–97; Welch, *Germany, Propaganda and Total War*, pp 138–142, 144. Fried's treatment of his exile is in his unpublished diary, Mein Kriegs-Tagebuch (Hoover Institution).

29 Cooper, *Patriotic Pacifism*, pp 188–192 (quotation on p 192). Historians' accounts of Rolland's pacifism mostly focus on the interwar period (1919–1939) when he was more actively engaged in peace activity, but an overview of the different phases of his pacifist journey, including the Great

War period, is Norman Ingram, "Romain Rolland, Interwar Pacifism and the Problem of Peace," in *Peace Movements and Political Cultures*, pp 143–164.

30 Except for an introductory comment on the military situation and devastation of the war, LaFontaine's statement is reproduced in full in "A Manifesto by Members of the International Peace Bureau," *Advocate of Peace*, 76 (December 1914), pp 250–253.

31 Cooper, *Patriotic Pacifism*, pp 193–198 (first quotation on p 196). For the text of the appeal to intellectuals and other details, see "Extraordinary Session of the Berne Bureau," *Advocate of Peace*, 77 (March 1915), pp 52–53.

32 Mead to William I. Hull, November 4, 1914, and Mead to Hull, March 19, 1915, William I. Hull Papers (Friends Historical Library, Swarthmore College), Box 3; Craig, *Lucia Ames Mead*, pp 125–127.

33 Quoted in Patterson, *Toward a Warless World*, p 186.

34 John Keegan, *The First World War* (London: Hutchinson, 1998), pp 6–7, 103–104, 107, 143, 146, 167–168, 183–184, 187, *passim*; David Stevenson, *Cataclysm: The First World War as Political Tragedy* (New York: Basic Books, 2004), pp 75–76. These two sources, which derive their 1914 figures for casualties (including deaths) from a wide range of earlier secondary works, agree roughly on the totals, except for Germany where Stevenson cites 800,000 casualties; 116,000 of these were fatalities, 85,000 of which were on the Western front.

35 Lynch, *Through Europe on the Eve of War*, pp 61–112.

1 FIRST EFFORTS

1 Carnegie Endowment for International Peace, Division of International Law, *The Hague Conventions and Declarations of 1899 and 1907*,

Accompanied by Tables of Signature, Ratifications, and Adhesions of the Various Powers, and Texts of Reservations, ed. James Brown Scott (New York: Oxford University Press, 1915), p 43.

2 House to Wilson, May 29, 1914, *The Papers of Woodrow Wilson*, eds. Arthur S. Link, *et al.* (Princeton, N.J.: Princeton University Press, 1979), vol 30, pp 109. Hereafter *PWW* followed by the volume number. Wilson's press conferences, July 30, 1914 and August 3, 1914, ibid., pp 317, 331–332.

3 Wilson to House (telegram), August 4 1914, White House press release [August 4, 1914], and House to Wilson (telegram), August 4, 1914, ibid., pp 342, 343, 349. Bryan to the American Ambassadors in Austria–Hungary, Russia, and Germany, August 4, 1914, and in England and France, August 5, 1914, *Papers Relating to the Foreign Relations of the United States, 1914, Supplement, The World War* (Washington, DC: Government Printing Office, 1928), p 42. Hereafter *FR*, followed by the year and, if part of a supplementary series, by *Supplement*.

4 Wilson to House, August 5, 1914, *PWW*, 30, p 345. When Secretary of the Interior Lane suggested on August 2 that Wilson offer mediation, the President replied the following day that he had already done so, "as far as I thought it prudent or possible," but he really made no diplomatic or public overture until August 4. Franklin Knight Lane to Wilson [August 2, 1914], ibid., p 331, and Wilson to Lane, August 3, 1914, ibid., pp 336–337. The petitions sent to Wilson by the Constance conference or the International Peace Bureau (see p 11 above) have not been found in Wilson's published papers, the Woodrow Wilson Papers (Manuscript Division, Library of Congress), or the files of the Department of State.

5 Quotations in Beatrice Siegel, *Lillian Wald of Henry Street* (New York: Macmillan, 1983), p 117, and New York *Evening Post*, December 5, 1914, p 7.

6 Ibid., September 30, 1914, p 3.

7 Quoted in Jane Addams, *The Second Twenty Years at Hull-House, September 1909 to September 1929* (New York: Macmillan, 1930), p 197. Balch was writing, at Addams' request, about women's changing sexual mores by the 1920s, but the extract quoted here provides insights into the first generation of professional women in many countries, including many who became active in the peace movement.

8 Sybil Oldfield, *Women Humanitarians: A Biographical Dictionary of British Women Active between 1900 and 1950* (London: Continuum, 2001), pp xi–xv (quotation on p xiv).

9 For a demotion of Addams' original intellect, see especially Allen F. Davis, *American Heroine: The Life and Legend of Jane Addams* (New York: Oxford University Press, 1973), pp xi, 102–106, *passim*; also, Daniel Levine, *Jane Addams and the Liberal Tradition* (Madison: University of Wisconsin Press, 1971).

10 Jill Ker Conway claims, for example, that Addams was a "ruthless individualist" who promoted "a philosophy of extreme individualism," though everything about her career rejected individualism in favor of advancing social democracy. Jill Conway, "Jane Addams: An American Heroine," *Daedalus*, 93 (Spring 1964), pp 761–780. Quotations on "individualism," pp 767 and 770. Jean Bethke Elshtain, *Jane Addams and the Dream of American Democracy: A Life* (New York: Basic Books, 2002), pp 25–26, 260–261, critiques this article by Conway. Conway charges in another article that Addams' involvement in reform causes, including peace, derived from her "desire for martyrdom." In

emphasizing Addams' alleged "private fantasies", Conway uses the words "martyr" or "martyrdom" five times in 11 lines of text. Her interpretation seems to hinge on an August 1904 letter, where Addams briefly (and as an interlineated aside) mentioned that she "might" become one of the first martyrs for the cause of "economic slavery" in cities, and from other uncited "letters and from notes made while she was working on the first version of *Newer Ideals of Peace*." Jill Conway, "The Woman's Peace Party and the First World War," in *War and Society in North America: Papers Presented at the Canadian Association for American Studies Meeting, Montreal, Fall, 1970*, eds. J.L. Granatstein and R.D. Cuff (Toronto: Thomas Nelson, 1971), especially p 55. For Conway's further criticism and her more recent evaluation (or re-evaluation) of Addams, see note 1 in chapter 3 below.

11 For insights into Jane Addams' ideas, I am particularly indebted to John C. Farrell, *Beloved Lady: A History of Jane Addams' Ideas on Reform and Peace* (Baltimore: The Johns Hopkins Press, 1967), a pioneering work; and Sondra R. Herman, *Eleven Against War: Studies in American Internationalist Thought, 1898–1921* (Stanford, Calif.: Hoover Institution Press, 1969), ch 5, a penetrating analysis. Elshtain, *Jane Addams and the Dream of American Democracy*, provides a sprightly critique of Addams' social thought, but from a present-day "realist" (or abstract essentialist) perspective that slights historical experience. For Addams' life before about 1900, Victoria Bissell Brown, *The Education of Jane Addams* (Philadelphia: University of Pennsylvania Press, 2003), suggests, among other things, her intermediary role in family relationships; and Louise W. Knight, *Citizen: Jane Addams and the Struggle for Democracy* (Chicago:

University of Chicago Press, 2005), emphasizes intellectual influences on her. The relationship between her views on domestic and international issues is explored in Kathryn Kish Sklar, " 'Some of Us Who Deal with the Social Fabric': Jane Addams Blends Peace and Social Justice, 1907–1919," *Journal of the Gilded Age and Progressive Era*, 2 (January 2003), pp 80–96. Among Addams' many published writings, particularly relevant are *Democracy and Social Ethics* (1902), *Newer Ideals of Peace* (1907), *Peace and Bread in Time of War* (1922); and her two volumes of memoirs. The formative intellectual influences on Addams are being developed in a projected six-volume edition of her papers; the recently published first volume is *The Selected Papers of Jane Addams: Preparing to Lead, 1860–81*, eds. Mary Lynn McCree Bryan, Barbara Bair, and Maree de Angury (Urbana: University of Illinois Press, 2003).

12 Harriet Hyman Alonso, *Growing Up Abolitionist: The Story of the Garrison Children* (Amherst: University of Massachusetts Press, 2002), pp 317–319.

13 Ibid., pp 319–320; Wald, *Windows on Henry Street* (Boston: Little, Brown, 1934), pp 285–286; Mrs Henry Villard, Wald, and Lillian Deaver to Joseph P. Tumulty (telegram), August 19, 1914, and Wilson to Mrs Henry Villard, August 21, 1914, Wilson Papers, Reel 254; "Peace Demonstrations and Fighting War's Effects," *The Survey*, 32 (September 5, 1914), p 555. Wald's remarks at the women's peace march are reproduced in *Lillian D. Wald: Progressive Activist*, ed. Clare Coss (New York: Feminist Press at The City University of New York, 1989), p 85.

14 John M. Mulder, *Woodrow Wilson: The Years of Preparation* (Princeton, N.J.: Princeton University Press, 1978), pp 140–142; Wilson's neutral-

ity proclamation, August 18, 1914, *PWW*, 30, pp 393–394; House Diary, August 30, 1914, ibid., pp 462–463; Wilson's remarks to the Belgian Commissioners, September 16, 1914, ibid., 31 (1979), p 34; and Wilson to Louis de Sadeleer, October 7, 1914, ibid., p 131.

15 Kellogg to Addams, September 11, 1914, Jane Addams Papers (Swarthmore College Peace Collection), Box 5, refers to Addams' plan "of getting joint action by social workers and the peace people." All citations to this collection of Addams Papers are in Series I.

16 Addams to Kellogg [September 1914], Lillian D. Wald Papers (New York Public Library).

17 Some of those invited to the first meeting were Felix Adler, Leo Arnstein, Emily Greene Balch, Ernest P. Bicknell, Louis D. Brandeis, Charles R. Crane, Edward T. Devine, Thomas A. Edison, Charles W. Eliot, John Palmer Gavit, Mary Willcox Glenn, Frank J. Goodnow, John Haynes Holmes, Hamilton Holt, Frederic C. Howe, William Dean Howells, William I. Hull, Florence Kelley, Paul U. Kellogg, William Kent, Julia Lathrop, Samuel McCune Lindsay, Owen R. Lovejoy, Julian Mack, George H. Mead, George W. Nasmyth, Graham Taylor, Charles Van Hise, Oswald Garrison Villard, Mornay Williams, and Stephen S. Wise. All but Arnstein, Howe, Hull, Mead, and Villard, who attended the meetings or corresponded with the group, were listed as those invited in Wald to Balch, September 22, 1914, Emily Greene Balch Papers (Swarthmore College Peace Collection), Box 6.

18 Ibid.; Kellogg to Nasmyth, September 24, 1914, Addams Papers, Box 5.

19 Kellogg, Minutes of Meeting at Nurses Settlement, September 29, 1914, and Kellogg to Balch, October 10, 1914, Balch Papers, Box 6; Kellogg to Addams, October 4, 1914,

Minutes of Meeting, October 23, 1914, and Kellogg to Addams, October 24, 1914, Wald Papers (NYPL).

20 Eighteen social workers and pacifists signed the manifesto, which was printed as an eight-page supplement, "Towards the Peace That Shall Last," *The Survey*, 33 (March 6, 1915). The others who signed—Edward T. Devine, John Palmer Gavit, Frederic C. Howe, Florence Kelley, William Kent, Samuel McCune Lindsay, Julian W. Mack, Graham Taylor, Mornay Williams, and Stephen S. Wise—played lesser roles in the mediation movement.

21 Anne Wiltsher, *Most Dangerous Women: Feminist Peace Campaigners of the Great War* (London: Pandora Press, 1985), pp 8–13; Mineke Bosch, with Annemarie Kloosterman, ed., *Politics and Friendship: Letters from the International Woman Suffrage Alliance, 1902–1942* (Columbus: Ohio State University Press, 1990), p 12. Biographical sketches of Schwimmer's life include Rose Rauther, "Rosika Schwimmer: Stationen auf dem Lebensweg einer Pazifistin," *Feministische Studien*, 3 (May 1984), pp 63–75; Edith Wynner, in *Biographical Dictionary of Modern Peace Leaders*, ed. Harold Josephson (Westport, Conn.: Greenwood Press, 1985), pp 862–865; and Susan Zimmermann and Borbala Major, in *A Biographical Dictionary of Women's Movements and Feminisms: Central, Eastern, and South Eastern Europe, 19th and 20th Centuries*, eds. Francisca de Haan, Krassimira Daskalova, and Anna Loutfi (Budapest: Central European University Press, 2006), pp 484–490.

22 *Bulletin Officiel du XXme Congrès Universel de la Paix, Tenu à La Haye, du 18 Août au 23 Août 1913* (Berne: International Peace Bureau [1914]), pp 66–68.

23 Typical of Schwimmer's chutzpah, at one point during the Budapest

congress she brought before the sumptuously dressed delegates a group of Hungarian peasant women wearing farm clothes to remind the privileged IWSA feminists that the fight for women's rights also involved ordinary, lower class women. It is doubtful whether Schwimmer's unorthodox ploy had any immediate effect. The peasant women appear in a group photograph of the women participants at the Budapest congress, Schwimmer-Lloyd Papers (New York Public Library), Box J18. I thank Mineke Bosch and Susan Zimmermann for this information. Catt to Schwimmer, July 25, 1914, ibid., Box A38, is Schwimmer's letter of IWSA appointment. Also, see Schwimmer's interview in *Christian Science Monitor*, August 11, 1914, p 3; Bosch, *Politics and Friendship*, pp 53ff.; Mineke Bosch, "Gossipy Letters in the Context of International Feminism," *Current Issues in Women's History*, eds. Arina Angerman, *et al.* (London: Routledge, 1989), pp 131–152; H.W. Swanwick, *I Have Been Young* (London: Victor Gollanz, 1935), pp 235–236, and Liddington, *Road to Greenham Common*, ch 4. All of the women mentioned in the text here, for example, attended the Budapest congress in 1913. Even Jane Addams, who was then more interested in social issues than suffrage, Fanny Villard, and Crystal Eastman were there. Leila J. Rupp, *Worlds of Women: The Making of an International Women's Movement* (Princeton, N.J.: Princeton University Press, 1997), especially ch 8, covers the founding and early histories of the International Woman Suffrage Alliance and the International Council of Women.

24 Schwimmer, "Austrian Heir," London *Sunday Times*, May 24, 1914, clipping in Schwimmer-Lloyd Papers, Box A36.

25 David Lloyd George, *War Memoirs, 1914–1915* (Boston: Little, Brown, 1933), pp 50–51. Lloyd George could not remember the name of his woman visitor, but correspondence at the time and later in the Schwimmer-Lloyd Papers (e.g., Lola M. Lloyd to Schwimmer, December 19, 1926, Box A37) confirm that it was Schwimmer.

26 Sybil Oldfield, *Spinsters of This Parish: The Life and Times of F. M. Mayor and Mary Sheepshanks* (London: Virago Press, 1984), pp 176–180; Resolution of NU Executive Committee, August 3, 1914, Schwimmer-Lloyd Papers, Box A39; Program of the Great Women's Meeting, August 4, 1914, ibid.; and Wiltsher, *Most Dangerous Women*, pp 13–18, 22–23. In Britain, the militant supporters of Pankhurst's group were called "suffragettes" (initially a pejorative term, though the militants turned it to their advantage as a rallying cry) to distinguish them from the more moderate, law-abiding "suffragists." I have used the latter word throughout; the text will indicate the relative militancy or nonmilitancy of the individual suffrage advocates.

27 Ibid. Several accounts quote Cecil's letter and suggest its various possible influences on Fawcett (e.g., Oldfield, *Spinsters of This Parish*, p 179). Among the British women pacifists, there were of course exceptions to the younger ages, e.g., Hobhouse, 54 in 1914 and perhaps Cooper and Swanwick, both 50. In 1912, Swanwick had resigned as editor of the NUWSS journal, *Common Cause*, mainly because the executive board objected to her inclusion of other feminist questions besides suffrage in the magazine. On the newer, younger NUWSS leaders, see Jo Vellacott, "Feminist Consciousness and the First World War," in *Women and War: Theoretical, Historical and Practical*

Perspectives, ed. Ruth Roach Pierson (London: Croom Helm, 1987), pp 116–121.

28 Schwimmer's letter of resignation, quoted in Macmillan to Schwimmer, October 25, 1922, Schwimmer-Lloyd Papers, Box A39. Her manifesto is quoted in her article, "The Women of the World Demand Peace," *Woman Voter*, V (October 1914), p 9.

29 Aletta Jacobs to Schwimmer, August 18, 1914, and Hobhouse to Schwimmer, August 20, 1914, Schwimmer-Lloyd Papers, Box A41; Schwimmer to Carnegie, August 17, 1914, ibid., Box A40; J.A. Poynton (Carnegie's secretary) to Schwimmer, August 20, 1914, ibid., Box A41; Margaret H. Illingworth to Schwimmer, August 17, 1914, Schwimmer to Illingworth, August 18, 23, 1914, and Illingworth to Schwimmer, August 20, 1914, ibid. Whitsher, *Most Dangerous Women*, p 32, says that Schwimmer ultimately refused Illingworth's loans because of her restrictions on their use. That may be so for the full £50, but the correspondence between the two women suggests that Schwimmer accepted at least the first installments with restrictions and was already spending them.

30 Jacobs to Schwimmer and Macmillan, September 13, 1914, *Politics and Friendship*, p 160.

31 Schwimmer to Sewall, August 17, 1914, May Wright Sewall Papers (Indianapolis Public Library); Schwimmer to Aletta Jacobs, August 21, 1914, and Schwimmer to Catt, August 22, 1914, Rosika Schwimmer Papers (Hoover Institution), Box 1; Sewall to Lochner, January 10, 1916, Louis P. Lochner Papers (Wisconsin Historical Society).

32 Catt to Schwimmer, June 24, 1913, Schwimmer-Lloyd Papers, Box A33. C. Roland Marchand, *The American Peace Movement and Social Reform, 1898–1918* (Princeton, N.J.: Prince-

ton University Press, 1972), pp 189–190. Lillian Wald had also declined the Peace Parade chair. Alonso, *Growing Up Abolitionist*, p 319.

33 Catt to Thomas, September 9, 1914, Wilson Papers, Reel 320; *Washington Star*, September 18, 1914, p 14.

34 Ibid. Schwimmer explained her plan in an interview in the New York *Evening Post*, September 8, 1914, p 6. Also, Catt to Schwimmer, September 14, 1914, Wilson Papers; Reel 62; Catt to Schwimmer, September 17, 1914, and Schwimmer notes, September 16, 1914, Schwimmer-Lloyd Papers, Box A44.

35 *New York Times*, September 19, 1914, p 2. A similar assessment is Rosika Schwimmer, "The Women of the World Demand Peace," p 10. Schwimmer's handwritten account of her September 18 interview with Wilson, written immediately after their meeting, is in the Schwimmer-Lloyd Papers, Box A44.

36 Niagara Section of the New York Peace Society to Wilson (telegram), August 20, 1914, Wilson to Niagara Section of the New York Peace Society (telegram), August 21, 1914, and Bryan to Wilson, August 28, 1914, and September 5, 1914, *Papers Relating to the Foreign Relations of the United States: The Lansing Papers, 1914–1920* (2 vols, Washington: Government Printing Office, 1939), 1, pp 6–8; Wilson to Bryan, August 21, 1914, James H. Rand, Jr., to Wilson, August 22, 1914, Wilson to Tumulty [September 5, 1914], and Tumulty to Rand, September 5, 1914, Wilson Papers, Reel 320. Arthur S. Link, *Wilson: The Struggle for Neutrality, 1914–1915* (Princeton, N.J.: Princeton University Press, 1960), pp 196–200, 202–203. Hereafter, Link, *Wilson*, 3.

37 Press Conference, September 21, 1914, *PWW*, 31, p 63. Wilson did not identify any individuals or the newspaper involved, but it is not unlikely that Schwimmer's remarks of her

interview, which were picked up by the press, fostered speculation of his peacemaking intent. Samples of press opinion on the Wilson administration's attitude toward mediation include *Washington Star*, September 18, 1914, p 1; *Washington Post*, September 21, 1914, p 2; *New York Times*, September 22, 1914, p 3; and New York *Evening Post*, October 7, 1914, p 1.

38 Bryan to Wilson, October 7, 1914, Wilson Papers, Reel 63, and Wilson to Bryan, October 8, 1914, ibid., Reel 139.

39 Several letters in the Wilson Papers, Reels 319–321, from peace advocates in this period present mediation proposals and ask Wilson to act on them. Wilson's replies show that he thought the situation very delicate and did not want to encourage anyone to boost U.S. mediation overtures.

40 Emmeline Pethick-Lawrence, "The Hero and the Heroine of the Suffraget [sic] Militants," *Current Literature* (London), 53 (August 1912), pp 162–164; London *Times*, February 6, 1913, p 6; Emmeline Pethick-Lawrence, *My Part in a Changing World* (London: Victor Gollanz, 1938), chs 9–20.

41 Quoted phrase in Sandi E. Cooper, "European Women's Struggle to Prevent WWI," *Women and War*, p 52. Regarding British suffragists' positions on the war, see Wiltsher, *Most Dangerous Women*, pp 5–6; Liddington, *Road to Greenham Common*, pp 112–114; and Vellacott, "Feminist Consciousness and the First World War," pp 121, 127–128. Shortly after the outbreak of the war, Schwimmer had called on Pethick-Lawrence in England to help her get to the United States. Pethick-Lawrence came to the United States soon thereafter to speak at a suffrage meeting in New York but, perhaps encouraged by Schwimmer's peace campaign, also hoped during her U.S. visit to enlist

suffragists' support for a neutral mediation movement. The two women did not meet in America until both happened to arrive on their separate lecture tours in Chicago and stayed at Hull House. Pethick-Lawrence to Schwimmer, August 14, 1914, Schwimmer-Lloyd Papers, Box A40; Pethick-Lawrence, *My Part in a Changing World*, pp 308, 310; Schwimmer to M. Carey Thomas, October 28, 1914, and Schwimmer to Julia Lathrop, October 28, 1914, Schwimmer Papers, Box 1.

42 Swartz, *Union of Democratic Control*, pp 11–45, 66–74, *passim*. In mid-1916, the UDC adopted a fifth plank advocating the end of economic warfare after the conflict and the promotion of free trade and expansion of the open door. Ibid., p 78.

43 New York *Evening Post*, October 31, 1914, p 2; *Chicago American*, November 25, 1914, p 1; *Chicago Tribune*, December 6, 1914, p 1; and *New York Times*, December 8, 1914, p 3. Several newspaper clippings and copies of letters in the Schwimmer Papers, Box 1, document Schwimmer's extensive speaking engagements in the fall of 1914. Pethick-Lawrence is quoted in her article, "Motherhood and War," *Harper's Weekly*, 59 (December 5, 1914), p 542. Also, see her "Union of Women for Constructive Peace," *The Survey*, 33 (December 5, 1914), p 230. Schwimmer is quoted in Rupp, *Worlds of Women*, p 85.

44 Sharon Ouditt, *Fighting Forces, Writing Women: Identity and Ideology in the First World War* (London: Routledge, 1994), ch 4, treats selective women publicists and novelists who were "maternal pacifists." Quotations in Swanwick, *Women and War* (London: Union of Democratic Control [1916]), p 6; Swanwick, *I Have Been Young*, pp 264–265; and Morel to Trevelyan, September 17, 1914, in Blanche Wiesen Cook, introduction to

Swanwick, *Builders of Peace: Being Ten Years' History of the Union of Democratic Control* (New York: Garland, 1973 edition), p 6. Also see Swartz, *Union of Democratic Control*, p 58. Another European woman linking the maternal instinct and pacifism, especially after 1914, was the Swedish social theorist, Ellen Key. For a discussion of her problematical and sometimes contradictory ideas, see Ruth Roach Pierson, "Ellen Key: Maternalism and Pacifism," in *Delivering Motherhood: Maternal Ideologies and Practices in the 19th and 20th Centuries*, eds. Katherine Arnup, Andrée Lévesque, and Ruth Roach Pierson (London: Routledge, 1990), pp 270–283.

The historical literature on sex differences has greatly expanded over the past generation. The biological differences did not mean male superiority but that men's and women's traits complemented one another. By the early twentieth century, scientific studies were increasingly asserting that their psychological differences were more sociological than biological in origin. Whatever the reasons, the maternalist rhetoric merged the biological and social roles of women's domesticity, and the "maternal instinct" for peace served as a rationale for converting, justifying, and hopefully uniting women's active participation in the peace movement. A concise summary of the scientific theories and their relationship to women's involvement in peace work is Linda K. Schott, *Reconstructing Women's Thoughts: The Women's International League for Peace and Freedom before World War II* (Stanford, Calif.: Stanford University Press, 1997), pp 47–54, including the endnotes thereto.

45 Women over time have committed only a fraction of violent crimes and have been more opposed than men to capital punishment, but these figures do not translate easily to national security questions. Opinion polls in the United States over the past few generations show that historically 10 to 20 percent more men than women have fairly consistently supported an assertive U.S. foreign policy, such as armament increases and military intervention abroad. However, there appears to be little gender differences when an adversary has physically attacked the nation's soil with huge human casualties, as following September 11, 2001, in the United States, or in the Middle East, where the physical security of all nations seems directly threatened. (There is also the nagging difficulty in trying to measure women's attitudes accurately in cultures that are less accepting, if not hostile, to their opinions on public issues.) Examples of support among women in belligerent lands for their nations' war efforts appear in subsequent chapters herein.

46 Blanche Wiesen Cook's introduction to *Crystal Eastman on Women and Revolution* (New York: Oxford University Press, 1978), pp 1–38; Craig, *Lucia Ames Mead*, pp 117–118. Eastman had married Wallace Benedict in 1911, but they were divorced by 1916, and she soon married Walter Fuller. While married to Benedict, she used his surname; but to avoid confusion this account uses only her maiden name throughout.

47 Liddington, *Road to Greenham Common*, pp 87–94; Barbara J. Steinson, *American Women's Activism in World War I* (New York: Garland Publishing, 1986), pp 178–181; and Steinson's article, "'The Mother Half of Humanity': American Women in the Peace and Preparedness Movements in World War I," in *Women, War, and Revolution*, eds. Carol R. Berkin and Clara M. Lovett (New York: Holmes & Meier, 1980), pp 259–284.

48 Catt to Schwimmer, September 24, 1914 and October 28, 1914, Carrie

Chapman Catt Papers (Manuscript Division, Library of Congress), Box 8; Catt to Jacobs, November 13, 1914, *Politics and Friendship*, p 149.

49 Lochner to Jordan, December 22, 1914, David Starr Jordan Peace Correspondence (Hoover Institution), Box 2. Hereafter Jordan Peace Correspondence.

50 New York *Evening Post*, October 3, 1914, III, p 2. Also see Peter Gunn, *Vernon Lee: Violet Paget, 1856–1935* (London: Oxford University Press, 1964), ch 14; and Sybil Oldfield, "England's Cassandras in World War One," in *This Working-Day World: Women's Lives and Culture(s) in Britain, 1914–1945*, ed. Sybil Oldfield (London: Taylor & Francis, 1994), pp 93–95.

51 Lochner's summary of the Chicago activities is in Chicago Peace Society, *Report 1915*, p 21. *Boston Herald*, September 18, 1914, p 13; Addams to Schwimmer, December 11, 1914, Schwimmer-Lloyd Papers, Box A50; Addams to Wald, December 8, 21, 27, 1914, Wald Papers (NYPL); Schwimmer to Catt, November 29, 1914, Schwimmer-Lloyd Papers, Box A49; Schwimmer to Addams (telegram), December 8, 1914, and Schwimmer to Catt, December 16, 1914, ibid., Box A50.

52 Catt to Schwimmer [December 1914], ibid., Box A49; Catt to Addams, December 14, 30, 1914, and January 4, 1916, Catt Papers, Box 4. Also, see Jacqueline Van Voris, *Carrie Chapman Catt: A Public Life* (New York: Feminist Press at The City University of New York, 1987), pp 124–126.

53 Addams to Catt, December 21, 1914, Woman's Peace Party Correspondence, 1915–1919 (Swarthmore College Peace Collection), Jane Addams File. Hereafter WPP Correspondence. Addams soon wrote Schwimmer that it was the latter's lobbying efforts in Washington, including another

interview she had with Secretary Bryan, which convinced her to call the organizational meeting. Addams to Schwimmer, January 6, 1915, Schwimmer-Lloyd Papers, Box A52. Once committed to the meeting in Washington, Addams coordinated the call and program with Mrs Mead, Anna Garlin Spencer, and other women identified with the peace movement. For example, Addams to Lucia Ames Mead, December 23, 28, 1914, WPP Correspondence, Lucia Mead File; Addams to Fannie Fern Andrews, December 28, 1914, Addams Papers, Box 5; and Addams to Mrs J. Malcolm Forbes, January 2, 1915, Jane Addams Memorial Collection (Hull House Archives). Hereafter JAMC. The rapidly developing interest in a separate woman's peace group is reported in "National Efforts Crystallizing for Peace," *The Survey*, 33 (January 9, 1915), pp 393–394. Also, Lucia Ames Mead, "Annual Report of the National Secretary," *Year Book of the Woman's Peace Party: The Section for the United States of the International Committee of Women for Permanent Peace, 1916* (Chicago: n.p., 1916), pp 41–43.

54 Belle La Follette to Elizabeth Glendower Evans, January 15, 1915 (emphasis La Follette's), and Evans to La Follette, January 24, 1915, La Follette Family Collection (Manuscript Division, Library of Congress), Series D, Box 14.

55 New York *Evening Post*, January 11, 1915, p 2; "Women for Peace: The Organization of the First Woman's Peace Party," *The Independent*, 81 (January 25, 1915), p 120. Hamilton Holt received information for this article from Fanny Garrison Villard, who attended the Washington sessions. Mrs Villard to Holt, January 16, 1915, Hamilton Holt Papers (Mills Memorial Library, Rollins College), Box 1. Women's organizational activities leading to the founding of

the Woman's Peace Party are an involved and complex story. Steinson, *American Women's Activism*, ch 1, and Craig, *Lucia Ames Mead*, pp 117–126, provide details of the organizational dynamics, and Schott, *Reconstructing Women's Thoughts*, ch 2, develops the ideological content.

56 Wales to Graham Taylor, September 4, 1914, Julia Grace Wales Papers (Wisconsin Historical Society), Box 1. Ralph W. Owen, Recollections and Description of Julia Grace Wales, typescript manuscript, Ralph W. Owen Papers (Wisconsin Historical Society), is a perceptive character sketch of Wales.

57 Several early drafts of her plan, dated August to December 1914, are preserved in the Wales Papers, Box 1. An unpublished letter from Wales to Editor, *The Cardinal* (University of Wisconsin's campus newspaper), October 1915?, ibid., gave Schwimmer credit for the neutral conference scheme, but Wales added that she did not know of Schwimmer's plan when she developed her own.

58 The drafts of her plan stressed these points, ibid.; Louis P. Lochner, *America's Don Quixote: Henry Ford's Attempt to Save Europe* (London: Kegan Paul, Trench, Trubner, 1924), p 6.

59 Jordan to John K. Bonnell, February 16, 17, 20, 1915, Lochner to Louise Phelps Kellogg, February 25, 1915, Wales to Louise Phelps Kellogg, [February 28, 1915], and Wales, The Record of the Wisconsin Peace Plan – Mediation Without Armistice, unpublished manuscript, pp 1–5, Wales Papers, Box 1.

60 "For a Peace Conference of Neutral Nations," *The Survey*, 33 (March 6, 1916), pp 597–598; "A Conference on the Neutral Nations," *The Independent*, 81 (March 29, 1915), pp 443–444. Holt to Wales, March 6, 1915, and Wales to Louise Phelps Kellogg [probably April 1915], Wales Papers, Box 1; *Kansas City Star*, March 6, 1915, p 2.

61 Note from White House staff, January 5, 1915, *PWW*, 32 (1980), p 20; Addams to Wilson, January 29, 1915, and Wilson to Addams, February 1, 1915, ibid., pp 162, 168.

62 Wilson to Addams, March 8, 1915, Addams Papers, Box 5. Wilson sent much the same reply to Aylward. Wilson to Aylward, March 8, 19, 1915, John A. Aylward Papers (Wisconsin Historical Society), Box 2.

63 Aylward to Wilson, March 16, 1915, Wilson Papers, Reel 69, and Wilson to Aylward, March 19, 1915, ibid., Reel 141.

2 WOMEN AT THE HAGUE

1 Chrystal Macmillan, "The History of the Congress," in International Congress of Women, The Hague – 28th April–May 1st 1915, *Bericht – Rapport – Report* (Amsterdam: Women's Committee for Permanent Peace [1915]), pp xxxvii–xxxviii. Hereafter International Congress of Women, *Report*. Aletta Jacobs, *Memories: My Life as an International Leader in Health, Suffrage, and Peace*, ed. Harriet Feinberg (New York: Feminist Press at The City University of New York, 1996), p 82. In a critical evaluation of Jacobs' *Memories*, which was first published in Dutch (*Herinneringen*) in 1924, Jacobs' biographer points out its significant omissions, distortions, and exaggerations. See Mineke Bosch, *Een Onwrikbaar Geloof in Rechtvaardigheid [An Unshakeable Belief in Justice]: Dr. Aletta H. Jacobs, 1854–1929* (Amsterdam: Balans, 2005), pp 13–33. Professor Bosch graciously provided me with an English translation of her introductory essay. While I have cited Jacobs' *Memories* here and

below, I have tried to verify her account with details from Bosch's biography and other sources.

2 "Dutch Committee for International Affairs of Woman Suffrage," *Jus Suffragii*, 9 (December 1, 1914), p 200; Frida Perlen, "In a Grave Hour," ibid., p 201; Lida Gustava Heymann, "What Women Say About the War," ibid., p 207; Anita Augspurg, Heymann, and others, "To the International Woman Suffrage Alliance," ibid.; [101 British women] " 'On Earth Peace, Goodwill towards Men,' " ibid. (January 1, 1915), pp 228–229; Heymann, "Women of Europe, When Will Your Call Ring Out?" ibid. (February 1, 1915), p 232. On Perlen and Heymann, see especially Richard J. Evans, *The Feminist Movement in Germany, 1894–1933* (London: Sage Publications, 1976), pp 215–223. Amy Hackett provides details on the lives of Augspurg and Heymann in *Biographical Dictionary of Modern Peace Leaders*, pp 42–43, 405–407. The first quotation is in Welch, *Germany, Propaganda and Total War*, p 138. Also, see H.M. Swanwick, "The Basis of Enduring Peace," *Jus Suffragii*, 9 (January 1, 1915), pp 217–218; and C.A. de Jong van Beek en Donk-Kluyver, "The Basis of Enduring Peace – II," ibid. (February 1, 1915), p 234. Mary Sheepshanks, the British editor of *Jus Suffragii* in London, was in a particularly difficult position because her editorial offices were in a belligerent country, and the British Liberal Government's censorship greatly reduced the flow of news from abroad, especially from the Central Powers. She nonetheless strove to continue to make the journal, as much as possible, "entirely international and untainted by national or partisan bias." A true internationalist herself, she was heartsick over the war and bent over backwards to be fair to opinion coming from both belligerent sides. Sybil

Oldfield, "Mary Sheepshanks Edits an Internationalist Suffrage Monthly in Wartime: *Jus Suffragii* 1914–19," *Women's History Review*, 12 (March 2003), pp 119–131.

3 Jacobs, *Memories*, p 83.

4 Ibid.; 66 German and 87 Austrian women, "Open Letter in Reply to the Open Christmas Letter from Englishwomen to German and Austrian Women," *Jus Suffragii*, 9 (March 1, 1915), p 249. The opening sentence of the formal notice for a women's congress stated: "From many countries appeals have come asking us to call together an International Women's Congress to discuss what the women of the world can do and ought to do in the dreadful times in which we are now living." "International Congress of Women, The Hague, Holland, April 1915: Call to the Women of All Nations," ibid., (March 1, 1915), p 245.

5 Macmillan, "History . . .," in International Congress of Women, *Report*, p xxxviii.

6 Jacobs, *Memories*, pp 58, 100–108, 126. Summaries of the Catt–Jacobs tour are ibid., pp 151–163, and Van Voris, *Carrie Chapman Catt*, pp 85–115. Catt's diary of the trip is in the Catt Papers, Boxes 1–2. Catt was IWSA president from 1904 to 1923.

7 Aletta Jacobs, "Netherlands," *Jus Suffragii*, 9 (November 1, 1914), pp 187–188; "Neutral Countries and Peace," ibid. (October 1, 1914), p 171; Nederlandsche Anti-Oorlog Raad, *Telegrams to President Wilson* (n.p. [1916]), p 1; Jacobs, *Memories*, pp 82–83; Aletta Jacobs, "To Miss McMillan [sic], Miss Sheepshanks, Rosika Schwimmer, and Other Suffrage Friends" [dated August 16, 1914], *Jus Suffragii*, 9 (September 1, 1914), p 161; Jacobs to Schwimmer, August 18, 1914, and Schwimmer to Jacobs, August 21, 1914, Schwimmer-Lloyd Papers, Box A41.

8 Jacobs, *Memories*, pp 74–77.

9 Ibid., p 79.

10 Aletta Jacobs, "Resolution on the White Slave Traffic," *Jus Suffragii*, 8 (September 1, 1913), p 8.

11 Jacobs, "Netherlands," p 188.

12 Hamilton to Louise de Koven Bowen, May 16, 1915, in *Alice Hamilton: A Life in Letters*, ed. Barbara Sicherman (Cambridge, Mass: Harvard University Press, 1984), p 192. The editor of Jacobs' correspondence has written: "Jacobs had her own peculiarities and personal pride, which made her several enemies." Bosch, *Politics and Friendship*, p 296.

13 An American delegate later wrote: "When she accepted the chairmanship of the Dutch committee of arrangements, the recognition of the Congress as a serious undertaking was assured." Elizabeth Glendower Evans, "The International Congress of Women at The Hague," *La Follette's Magazine*, 7 (June 1915), p 6.

14 Macmillan, "History . . .," in International Congress of Women, *Report*, pp xxxviii–xxxix; "International Congress of Women," *Jus Suffragii*, 9 (March 1, 1915), p 245; Rupp, *Worlds of Women*, p 27. Dr Jacobs recounted the origins of the Hague meeting and its results in an interview with Crystal Eastman, "Now I Dare to Do It," *The Survey*, 34 (October 9, 1915), reprinted in *Crystal Eastman on Women and Revolution*, pp 237–241.

15 Wilson was one of the founders of the Fellowship of Reconciliation, a Christian group committed to absolute pacifism, in Cambridge in late December 1914. For an appreciation of Wilson's blending of her literary talents and pacifism, see Angela Ingram, " 'In Christ's Name – Peace!': Theodora Wilson Wilson and Radical Pacifism," in *Rediscovering Forgotten Radicals: British Women Writers, 1889–1939* (Chapel Hill: University of North Carolina Press, 1993), pp 175–204. Rosa Manus,

"International Women's Congress, Holland, April, 1915," *Jus Suffragii*, 9 (March 1, 1915), pp 245–246. The preliminary program is also in International Congress of Women, *Report*, pp 281–283.

16 Ibid., p xl. Also, Anna Petterson, "Letter from a Swedish Member of The Hague Congress," *Jus Suffragii*, 9 (June 1, 1915), p 305.

17 Michael Jürgs, *Der Kleine Frieden im Grossen Krieg; Westfront 1914: Als Deutsche, Franzosen und Briten Gemeinsam Weihnachten Fierten* (Munich: C. Bertelsmann, 2003), is the most recent of at least four books on the Christmas truce of 1914. The *New York Times*, December 31, 1914, p 3, reprinted from the London *Daily News* two of several eyewitness accounts of the truce. K.D. Courtney, *Extracts from a Diary during the War* (privately printed, 1927), p 28. Hereafter *War Diary*.

18 Jacobs, Boissevain, and Manus to Addams (cablegram), February 22, 1915, Addams Papers, Box 5; WPP Assistant Secretary to Catt, March 2, 1915, WPP Correspondence; *Chicago Tribune*, March 6, 1915, p 1; *New York Times*, March 6, 1915, p 10.

19 Addams to Balch, March 13, 26, 1915, Balch Papers, Box 6.

20 Ibid.; Addams to Mrs J. Malcolm Forbes, March 25, 1915, JAMC.

21 Catt to Jacobs, November 13, 1914, *Politics and Friendship*, p 149; Catt to Addams, December 29, 1914, and January 4, 16, and 27, 1915, Addams Papers, Box 5.

22 Shaw to Jacobs, January 4, 1915, *Politics and Friendship*, p 150.

23 Doris Groshen Daniels, *Always a Sister: The Feminism of Lillian D. Wald* (New York: Feminist Press at the City University of New York, 1989), p 129; Siegel, *Lillian Wald of Henry Street*, p 122; Balch, *Women at The Hague*, pp 1–2; Addams to Balch, March 13 and 26, 1915, Balch to

Ellen F. Pendleton, March 30, 1915, and Pendleton to Balch, April 1, 1915, Balch Papers, Box 6.

24 Balch, Personal and Local, Neighbors & Memories Mr Dole [1947], ibid., Box 20; Balch to Addams, February 27, 1915, WPP Correspondence, Jane Addams File.

25 Balch, Diary Notes, September 27, 1896, January 1, April 9, 29, and July 15, 1899, January 8, 1901, and August 28, 1904, Balch Papers, Box 19. Also, Mercedes M. Randall, *Improper Bostonian: Emily Greene Balch* (New York: Twayne, 1964), chs 1, 2, 18, the last one providing an overview of Balch's "inner life."

26 Autobiographical fragment, undated, Balch Papers, Box 20. Among her prewar works, see especially *Our Slavic Fellow Citizens* (New York: N.Y. Charities Publication Committee, 1910); and, for a contemporary survey, her article, "Racial Contacts and Cohesions As Factors in the Unconstrained Fabric of a World at Peace," *The Survey*, 33 (March 6, 1915), pp 610–611. Background on her early professional career is in Randall, *Improper Bostonian*, chs 3–4.

27 Balch, Diary Notes, November 29, 1899, Balch Papers, Box 19. For Dole's involvement in peace and anti-imperialist movements, see *Biographical Dictionary of Modern Peace Leaders*, pp 219–220. For his long-term influence on Balch, see Randall, *Improper Bostonian*, pp 16, 24, 48, 119, *passim*. Balch (and 11 other women) to Members of Congress, February 27, 1914, Anna Garlin Spencer Papers (Swarthmore College Peace Collection), Box 4. In 1933, Balch wrote: "For some time [before the war] I had been interested in the peace movement, as expressed, for instance, in the Hague Congresses [of 1899 and 1907] and the growing provision for arbitration, and had taken these up with my students as practical social problems, but I had not come to

the conviction, which later I gradually but inevitably reached, that there is no half-way house and that resort to war can and must come to an end." Quoted in *Beyond Nationalism: The Social Thought of Emily Greene Balch*, ed. Mercedes M. Randall (New York: Twayne Publishers, Inc., 1972), p 77.

28 See Madeleine Z. Doty, *The Central Organisation for a Durable Peace (1915–1919): Its History, Work and Ideas* (Geneva: University of Geneva [1945]), pp 24–38, *passim*. Andrews later described her priorities, not always very precisely, in her *Memory Pages From My Life* (Boston: Talisman Press, 1948).

29 International Congress of Women, *Report*, pp 266–270, contains brief résumés of the 47 American delegates. Francis Balch to Balch, April 7, 1915, Balch Papers, Box 6; Journal of Miss Emily Greene Balch, 1915, ibid., Box 19; Sicherman, *Alice Hamilton*, pp 185, 188; and Doty, quoted in New York *Evening Post*, May 24, 1915, p 2.

30 Lochner to Lucia Ames Mead, October 9, 1914, Lucia Ames Mead Papers (Swarthmore College Peace Collection); Lochner, "Wanted: Aggressive Pacifism," *Advocate of Peace*, 77 (February 1915), pp 36–38; New York *Evening Post*, April 7, 1915, p 1; Minutes of the Executive Committee of the Chicago Peace Society, April 8, 1915, CPS Papers; Lochner, *Always the Unexpected*, p 52.

31 Quotations in Patterson, *Toward a Warless World*, p 182; and Davis, *American Heroine*, pp 222–223; and Roosevelt's "base and silly" comments are in his letter to Juliet Barrett Rublee, February 9, 1915, Lochner Papers. Also see "Is the Women's Peace Movement 'Silly and Base'," *Literary Digest*, 50 (May 1, 1915), pp 1022–1023, and Patricia O'Toole, *When Trumpets Call: Theodore Roosevelt After the White House* (New

York: Simon & Schuster, 2005), pp 283–289.

32 New York *Evening Post*, May 13, 1915, p 5; Journal of Miss Emily Greene Balch, Balch Papers, Box 19.

33 Hamilton to Mary Rozet Smith, April 22, 1915, Sicherman, *Alice Hamilton*, pp 185–186; Vorse to Joe O'Brien, [April 1915], Mary Heaton Vorse Papers (Archives of Labor and Urban Affairs, Wayne State University), Box 55; also see Dee Garrison, *Mary Heaton Vorse: The Life of an American Insurgent* (Philadelphia: Temple University Press, 1989), pp 88–89.

34 New York *Evening Post*, May 13, 1915, p 5; Garrison, *Mary Heaton Vorse*, pp 90–91; Balch, Minutes and Notes of American delegation to The Hague, 1915, and Journal of Miss Emily Greene Balch, Balch Papers, Box 19; several entries from the latter are reproduced in Randall, *Improper Bostonian*, pp 149–151. Mrs Pethick-Lawrence was only a little less controversial than Schwimmer. Vorse also labeled both Pethick-Lawrences "bores" (Vorse to Joe O'Brien, [April 1915], Vorse Papers, Box 55), but Emmeline also developed firm friendships with Madeleine Doty and other women.

35 Wales to Committee, April 15, 1915, Wales Papers, Box 1; Alice Thatcher Post, "A Pacifist Journey in War Time," *The Public*, 18 (May 21, 1915), p 494; Angela Morgan to her mother, April 28, 1915, Angela Morgan Papers (Bentley Historical Library, University of Michigan), Box 3; Addams to Jordan, April 9, 1915, Jordan Peace Correspondence, Box 3; Addams to Mary Rozet Smith, April 22, 1915, Addams Papers, Box 5.

36 Link, *Wilson*, 3, pp 356–359; New York *Evening Post*, May 13, 1915, p 5; Hamilton to Mary Rozet Smith, April 22, 1915, Sicherman, *Alice Hamilton*, pp 187–188.

37 Ibid.; Balch, *Women at The Hague*, pp 4–6.

38 International Congress of Women, *Report*, p 34; Steven C. Hause with Anne R. Kenney, *Women's Suffrage and Social Politics in the French Third Republic* (Princeton, N.J.: Princeton University Press, 1984), pp 192–193.

39 Richard J. Evans, *Comrades and Sisters: Feminism, Socialism and Pacifism in Europe, 1870–1945* (New York: St. Martin's Press, 1987), pp 122–128, 131, 135 (first quotation on p 131); Charles Sowerwine, *Sisters or Citizens? Women and Socialism in France since 1876* (Cambridge: Cambridge University Press, 1982), pp 143–149 (second quotation on p 148).

40 Charles Sowerwine, "Women Against War: A Feminine Basis for Internationalism and Pacifism?" *Proceedings of the Sixth Annual Meeting of the Western Society for French History*, 6 (1978–79), pp 361–370 (quotation on p 363). After the Hague congress, Jacobs wrote Saumoneau to suggest that they keep in touch on matters of common concern, but Saumoneau apparently did not respond. Ibid., p 363.

41 Ibid., *passim*; Hause, *Women's Suffrage and Social Politics in the French Third Republic*, pp 67–70, 164–166, 191–197; Jacobs, *Memories*, pp 84, and later historians' commentaries, ibid., pp 203, 220n23, 231n13. Examples of affinity between the peace-oriented socialist and bourgeois women included greetings sent by the Berne conference to the Hague meeting (International Congress of Women, *Report*, pp 118–119) and, later, a formal protest by French socialist women against the police search of the French section of the International Women's Committee for Permanent Peace, which the Hague congress had created (Sowerwine, *Sisters or Citizens?*, p 152; the quotation is on p 145). Another perspective on the absence of French women at the Hague assemblage is Cooper, *Patriotic Pacifism*, p 200.

42 International Congress of Women, *Report*, pp 238, 239, 241; Lida Gustava Heymann (with Anita Augspurg), *Erlebtes – Erschautes: Deutsche Frauen Kämpfen für Freiheit, Recht, und Frieden, 1850–1940* (Meisenheim am Glad: Anton Heim, 1972), pp 137–147. An English translation of much of this section of Heymann's memoir is in Kathryn Kish Sklar, Anja Schüler, and Susan Strasser, eds., *Social Justice Feminists in the United States and Germany: A Dialogue in Documents, 1885–1933* (Ithaca, N.Y.: Cornell University Press, 1998), pp 189–196. Zetkin was soon released from prison because of seriously failing health (which incapacitated her for the rest of the war), and Saumoneau was released because of the government's fears that her continued imprisonment was calling attention to the antiwar movement, which thus far had received little public support, and making her a martyr among left-wing socialists. Sowerwine, *Sisters or Citizens*, pp 149–152; Sowerwine, "Women Against War," pp 364–366; Evans, *Comrades and Sisters*, pp 125–127, 131–137.

43 International Congress of Women, *Report*, pp 190–199, 220–221, 306–315 (first quotation on p 314); Hause, *Women's Suffrage and Social Politics*, pp 192–193 (second quotation on p 193); Jacobs, Notes of Journey to Berlin, Vienna, Bern, Rome, Paris, London, May 19–June 18, 1915 (hereafter Jacobs, Notes), Aletta Jacobs Papers (International Archives of the Women's Movement, Amsterdam); Pichon Landry and de Witt Schlumberger (Union Française pour le Suffrage des Femmes), "French Women and The Hague Congress," *Jus Suffragii*, 9 (June 1, 1915), p 308; [fifty-seven French women], "Manifesto of French Women Addressed to The Hague Congress," ibid. (July 1, 1915), pp 324–325 (third quotation on p 324). In addition to Halbwachs, other prominent French suffragists who continued to remain pacifists after 1914—although not always unwaveringly—were Jeanne Mélin, Gabrielle Duchêne, Hélène Brion, and Madeleine Pelletier. Dr Jacobs unsuccessfully tried to recruit Mélin, then a refugee from German troops occupying her Ardennes homeland, to attend the Hague congress. Judith Wishnia, "Feminism and Pacifism: The French Connection," in *Women and Peace*, pp 103–113, traces the antiwar travails particularly of Brion and Saumoneau. Grayzel, *Women's Identities at War*, ch 5, is mainly a case study of Brion's pacifism and the French prosecution of her for treason in 1917–1918.

44 A spokeswomen for the League of German Women's Associations affirmed the international solidarity of women and hoped for renewed postwar feminist contacts, but called the purposes and proceedings of the Hague congress "superfluous, . . ., untimely, . . ., impossible, . . ., tactless." Gertrude Baümer, "Der Bund Deutscher Frauenvereine und der Haager Frauencongress," *Die Frauenfrage*, 17 (1915–1916), pp 82–85. An English translation of extracts from this article is in *Social Justice Feminists*, eds. Sklar, *et al.*, pp 197–202. Also see *Character Is Destiny: The Autobiography of Alice Salomon*, ed. Andrew Lees (Ann Arbor: University of Michigan Press, 2004), pp 110–111; and Evans, *Comrades and Sisters*, pp 127–129.

45 Sandra Stanley Holton, *Suffrage Days: Stories from the Women's Suffrage Movement* (London: Routledge, 1996), pp 210–221; and Wiltsher, *Most Dangerous Women*, pp 61–72; Fawcett, undated statement [December 1914], and George G. Armstrong to Fawcett, February 12, 1915, Millicent Garrett Fawcett Papers (The Women's Library), Box 89.

Fawcett's December 15 letter to Catt is quoted in full in Oldfield, *Spinsters of This Parish*, pp 190–191. Fawcett's strong views on the controversy are presented in "The National Union of Women's Suffrage Societies and the Hague Congress," *The Englishwoman*, no 78 (June 1915), pp 193–200.

46 Courtney to Fawcett, February 25, 1915, quoted in Fawcett to Miss Alnuson, February 19, 1916, Fawcett Papers, Box 89.

47 NUWSS Executive Committee to Fawcett, undated [April 1915], ibid., named 10 women resigning from the NUWSS executive committee. Accounts of Maude Royden's antiwar career are Sheila Fletcher, *Maude Royden: A Life* (Oxford: Basil Blackwell, 1989), ch 6, *passim*; and Oldfield, *Women Against the Iron Fist*, ch 3. In late 1916, Kathleen Courtney tried to reconcile with Fawcett, but the latter believed that Courtney was one of the few resigning members who had "intentionally" wounded her. When Courtney responded, "I never thought of wounding you," Fawcett accepted that Courtney's wounding was "not intentional" and was prepared to cooperate where possible and "remember to forget." Leaf to Fawcett, November 2, 1916, Fawcett to Leaf, November 3, 1916, Courtney to Fawcett, November 26, 1916, and Fawcett draft letter to Courtney, undated, Fawcett Papers, Box 89. Some—Swanwick, for instance—restored a semblance of cordial relations with Fawcett despite their basic disagreement in 1915. Swanwick to Fawcett, November 4, 1916, ibid.; and Swanwick, *I Have Been Young*, p 259. Wiltsher, *Most Dangerous Women*, pp 72–81 (Leaf's April 5 letter to Marshall is quoted on p 77). Not all progressive suffragists resigned from the NUWSS. After considerable soul-searching, some like Selina Cooper, a radical suffragist in northern England, nonetheless

stayed with the society. She valued her income as a half-time NUWSS organizer and hoped that its democratic procedures would allow for a more leftward direction in the future. Jill Liddington, *The Life and Times of a Respectable Rebel: Selina Cooper (1864–1946)* (London: Virago Press, 1984), pp 262–265.

48 According to Fawcett, the NUWSS was asked to send one or two delegates; but as she learned that anyone paying the registration fee would be a delegate, she also argued, correctly as it turned out, that the representation at the Hague meeting would inevitably be badly skewed in favor of the Dutch contingent. "Therefore, had we accepted the invitation, we should have incurred responsibility, without any practical opportunity of controlling the results." Fawcett, "National Union of Women's Suffrage Societies," pp 195–196. Regarding the backgrounds and views of British women who supported the international congress at The Hague, see the Appendix.

49 Quoted in Sybil Oldfield, "England's Cassandras in World War I," in *This Working-Day World: Women's Lives and Culture(s) in Britain, 1914–1945*, ed. Sybil Oldfield (London: Taylor & Francis, 1994), p 92. An overview of Lady Courtney's pacifist and humanitarian activities is Sybil Oldfield, *Women Against the Iron Fist: Alternatives to Militarism, 1900–1989* (Oxford: Basil Blackwell, 1989), ch 2. Lady Courtney was no relation to the much younger Kathleen Courtney.

50 Courtney, *War Diary*, pp 34–35. The travail of the British would-be travelers to the Hague congress is recounted in Helen Ward, *A Venture in Good Will: Being the Story of the Women's International League for Peace and Freedom, 1915–1929* (London: Women's International League, 1929), pp 1–13. Also see

International Congress of Women, *Report*, pp 239–241; and Swanwick, *I Have Been Young*, pp 258–259. The catalyst prompting the Admiralty's closing of the channel was almost certainly the imminent women's congress at The Hague, but the Asquith government never explained its decision.

51 Jacobs, *Memories*, p 83. Dr Jacobs thanked these foreign women more effusively in her remarks at the close of the Hague congress. International Congress of Women, *Report*, p 177.

52 Ibid., pp 33–34, 73, 126; Balch, *Women at The Hague*, p 9. Regarding the pacifist orientation of Stöcker (and Heymann and Augspurg), see Regina Braker's two articles, "Bertha von Suttner's Spiritual Daughters: the Feminist Pacifism of Anita Augspurg, Lida Gustava Heymann, and Helen Stöcker at the International Congress of Women at The Hague, 1915," *Women's Studies International Forum*, 18 (March/April 1995), pp 103–111; and "Helene Stöcker's Pacifism in the Weimar Republic: Between Ideal and Reality," *Journal of Women's History*, 13 (August 2001), pp 70–97.

53 The Dutch committee making the arrangements for the congress had already asked Addams to serve as presiding officer if Mrs Catt could not attend. Addams to Mrs J Malcolm Forbes, March 25, 1915, JAMC. One example of Addams' skillful leadership at the congress occurred during discussion over a resolution urging a state monopoly of the manufacture and control of arms and munitions. Elizabeth Glendower Evans proposed an amendment calling for an international agreement whereby all neutral nations immediately placed an embargo on munitions of war. Addams admitted that she personally supported an embargo, but she ruled that the amendment clearly involved a judgment on the nations' conduct

of the present war and therefore was out of order. Embarrassed at ruling against Mrs Evans' criticism of her own country, Addams tactfully suggested that the delegates could at least partially resolve the dilemma by adding "traffic" to the list of government control over armaments, and the congress accepted her suggestion. On another occasion, she ruled that a proposal for no transference of territory without a plebiscite of the inhabitants, which was enthusiastically backed by the Finns, Belgians, and Poles, was out of order, but she condoned the speeches in support, saying they expressed genuine national needs. Evans, "The International Congress of Women," p 6; International Congress of Women, *Report*, pp 70, 122–125; Quotation from American delegates praising Addams in her role as chair are Alice Thatcher Post, "A Chapter in the New Internationalism," *The Public*, 18 (May 28, 1915), p 519; New York *Evening Post*, May 21, 1915, p 4; Wales to Committee, May 11 and 13, 1915, Wales Papers, Box 1; Hamilton to Mary Rozet Smith, May 5, 1915, Addams Papers, Box 5; and Post, "Pacifist Journey in Wartime," p 495.

54 Quotations in Mary Heaton Vorse, *A Footnote to Folly: Reminiscences of Mary Heaton Vorse* (New York: Farrar & Rinehart, 1935), pp 79–81; her account and further details in the text here are derived directly from her contemporary typescript, 1915 Hague Congress of Women, Vorse Papers, Box 190. The following also commented on the caution and fears of the European neutrals: Balch, *Women at The Hague*, p 17; Hamilton to Mary Rozet Smith, May 5, 1915, Addams Papers, Box 5; Wales to Committee, May 11, 1915 and June 4–15, 1915, Wales Papers, Box 1; and Post, "Chapter in the New Internationalism," p 521.

55 For the resolutions (and all quota-

56 tions), see International Congress of Women, *Report*, pp 35–41; for the debate, see ibid., pp 78–161, 168. Also, *New York Times*, April 30, 1915, p 3.

56 International Congress of Women, *Report*, pp 2, 42, 161–163 (quotations on p 42). The International Committee initially consisted of Leopoldine Kulka and Olga Misar (Austria), Eugénie Hamer and Marguerite Sarten (Belgium), Thora Daugaard and Clara Tybjerg (Denmark), Anita Augspurg and Lida Gustava Heymann (Germany), Chrystal Macmillan and Kathleen Courtney (Great Britain), Vilma Glucklich and Rosika Schwimmer (Hungary), Rosa Genoni (Italy), Aletta Jacobs, Hanna van Biema-Hymans, and Mia Boissevain (Netherlands), Emily Arnesen and Louise Keilhau (Norway), Anna Klemen and Emma Hansson (Sweden), and Jane Addams and Fannie Fern Andrews (United States).

57 Post, "Chapter in the New Internationalism," p 518; New York *Evening Post*, May 22, 1915, p 4; quotations in International Congress of Women, *Report*, pp 281, 136, 36.

58 Ibid., pp 154–156; Wales to Committee, May 11, 1915, Wales Papers, Box 1.

59 International Congress of Women, *Report*, pp 169–171; Hamilton to Bowen, May 16, 1915, Addams Papers, Box 5.

60 Wales to Committee, May 14, 1915, Wales Papers, Box 1; International Congress of Women, *Report*, pp 169–176 (first two quotations, pp 172, 174); Lola Maverick Lloyd Diary, May 1, 1915, Schwimmer-Lloyd Papers, Box O112. The voting, by raising of hands, was undoubtedly close, as the counting had to be taken twice.

61 International Congress of Women, *Report*, pp 176, 316–317. This total of 25 includes only the interviews with monarchs, prime ministers, and foreign secretaries as well as with the Pope and his secretary of state, but does not include the envoys' many meetings with other cabinet officials, ministers, and ambassadors in each capital, and multiple interviews with the same person. Jacobs Notes, Jacobs Papers.

3 PRIVATE DIPLOMACY IN EUROPE

1 Addams to Smith, May 9, 1915, Addams Papers, Box 5. Jill Conway also quotes this letter in her article, "The Woman's Peace Party and the First World War," p 55. Given her generally harsh evaluation of Addams, Conway then comments, "Of course she had lost her head. There was not one chance in a million of a women's mission or any other making peace in May of 1915." Such criticism ignores the symbolic importance of the women activists' efforts in trying to keep alive the prospect of peace talks well beyond the spring of 1915 and the belief of others, including Woodrow Wilson, that neutral mediation might ultimately succeed. More recently, Conway calls Addams "my great heroine." If not a new view, it may suggest that Conway has admired Addams for her achievements outside the peace movement. Conway, "Points of Departure," in *Inventing the Truth: The Art and Craft of Memoir*, ed. William Zinsser (New York: Houghton Mifflin, 1998 edition), p 47.

2 Stevenson, *Cataclysm*, pp 78, 82, 124, 125, 128, 163–165, 373–374; Hew Strachan, *The First World War* (Oxford: Viking Penguin, 2004), pp 144–145, 163–168; Richard Bessel, "Mobilizing German Society for War," in *Great War, Total War: Combat and Mobilization on the Western Front, 1914–1918*, eds. Roger Chickering and Stig Förster (Cambridge:

Cambridge University Press, 2000), p 446.

3 Addams, *Women at The Hague*, p 82.

4 Vorse, 1915 Hague Congress of Women, typescript, Vorse Papers, Box 190. Balch's concern for "fresh" approaches is in Paul U. Kellogg to Addams, October 24, 1914, Wald Papers (NYPL); Balch to Lochner, June 1, 1915, Wilson Papers, Reel 320; and Balch to Oswald Garrison Villard, September 28, 1915, Oswald Garrison Villard Papers (Houghton Library, Harvard University). Wales and Macmillan are quoted in Wales' letter to Committee, May 13, 1915, and June 4–15, 1915, Wales Papers, Box 1 (emphasis Wales'). Dickinson explained the "governmental mind" (or "governmental theory") in his article, "The War and the Way Out," *Atlantic Monthly*, 114 (December 1914), pp 820–837. Also see text herein, p 183 (including note 4, p 382). The British minister in Copenhagen was Mansfeldt Findlay who pushed for rigorous restrictions on Danish commerce with neighboring Germany, even to the point of risking possible German military occupation of their country, and he criticized the British minister in Stockholm, Esme Howard, for not taking tougher positions against Swedish trade with the enemy. Senior diplomats at Whitehall understood, however, that Sweden was a much larger and strategically important trading link not only to Germany but to allied Russia as well, and they appreciated Howard's mostly successful efforts in balancing assertions of Britain's restrictions on neutral commerce with acquiescence in some Swedish trade with the enemy. His even-handed approach helped to keep Sweden neutral throughout the war. Unlike Howard and other experienced British diplomats who subsequently moved on to more important posts (Howard served as an adviser at the Paris Peace

Conference and as ambassador in Washington in the 1920s), Findlay was not rewarded, remaining at Copenhagen until his retirement in 1923. Some of Findlay's complaints are in his personal letters to Howard (Esme Howard Papers, Cumbria Record Office, Carlisle, DHW 4/1/18); also see B.J.C. McKercher, *Esme Howard: A Diplomatic Biography* (Cambridge: Cambridge University Press, 1989), pp 148, 153, 155, 159–160, 167–169, 200.

5 Balch to Lochner, June 1, 1915, Wilson Papers, Reel 320. Rumors of the Gerards' reactions may have been exaggerated, but were in keeping with the ambassador's undiplomatic diplomacy.

6 Jacobs Notes, Jacobs Papers; Jacobs, *Memories*, pp 166, 85; *New York Times*, May 8, 1915, p 1.

7 *New York Times*, May 11, 1915, p 3.

8 Page's aversion to peace proposals of any kind shows through in his personal correspondence. See, especially, Page to House, undated, *The Life and Letters of Walter H. Page* (3 vols, Garden City, N.Y.: Doubleday, Doran, 1924–1926), vol 2, pp 13–17.

9 Eric Drummond to Addams, May 12, 1915, Addams Papers, Box 5; Jacobs Notes, Jacobs Papers.

10 Hamilton, *Exploring the Dangerous Trades*, p 167. H.M. Swanwick, *I Have Been Young* (London: Victor Gollanz, 1935), p 241, attributes the "twittering" comment to Asquith. John Fisher, *That Miss Hobhouse* (London: Secker & Warburg, 1971), p 237, says Asquith compared the women with "the twittering of sparrows."

11 James W. Gerard, *My Four Years in Germany* (New York: George H. Doran, 1917), p 412; Gottlieb von Jagow, Memorandum on Jane Addams and Aletta Jacobs, May 22, 1915, German Foreign Office Papers (National Archives), Reel 2075/D

935536–39. Hereafter cited as GFO Papers.

12 Jacobs Notes, Jacobs Papers; Courtney, *War Diary*, pp 42–43, is a detailed summary of Addams' talk about her European pilgrimage to members of the British executive committee of the Women's International League on June 23, 1915. Also, Jane Addams' interview in *New York Times*, June 24, 1915, p 3.

13 Addams Notes [July 8, 1915], Addams Papers, Box 5.

14 *New York Times*, June 11, 1915, p 24; Courtney, *War Diary*, pp 46–47.

15 Addams Notes [July 8, 1915], Addams Papers, Box 5; Jacobs Notes, Jacobs Papers; *New York Times*, June 4, 1915, pp 5, 11; Courtney, *War Diary*, pp 43–44.

16 Ibid., p 44. Although not identifying Stürgkh by name, she also quoted him more fully: "That door opens from time to time, and people come in to say, 'Mr Minister, we must have more men, we must have more ammunition, we must have more money or we cannot go on with this war.' At last the door opens and two people walk in and say, 'Mr Minister, why not substitute negotiations for fighting?' They are the sensible ones." Addams, *Women at The Hague*, pp 96–97.

17 Jacobs Notes, Jacobs Papers; Courtney, *War Diary*, pp 44–45; Addams Notes [July 8, 1915], Addams Papers, Box 5.

18 Courtney, *War Diary*, p 44; Jacobs Notes, Jacobs Papers; *New York Times*, June 24, 1915, p 3; Hamilton, *Exploring the Dangerous Trades*, pp 174–175.

19 Balch and Macmillan to Addams, June 8, 1915, and Addams to Mary Rozet Smith, June 18, 1915, Addams Papers, Box 5; Henrietta Barnett to Balch, July 10, 1915, Balch Papers, Box 7.

20 Schwimmer to Addams, August 4, 1915, Addams Papers, Box 5; Davis, *American Heroine*, pp 219, 222.

21 Grey to Addams, June 20, 1915, Addams Papers, Box 5; Grey to Drummond, June 20, 1915, British Foreign Office Papers, 800/95 (British National Archives). Hereafter FO.

22 Crewe's memorandum of her conversation with Addams, June 22, 1915, ibid., was read by Asquith, Grey, and Lord Haldane; Courtney, *War Diary*, pp 46–47.

23 Balch to Lochner, June 1, 1915, Wilson Papers, Reel 320.

24 Balch to Addams [July 3, 1915], Addams Papers, Box 5. The statement by the Danish Prime Minister Zahle and Foreign Secretary Scavenius, May 28, 1915, is ibid. English translations appear ibid. and in the Jacobs Papers.

25 Balch to Addams [July 3, 1915], Addams Papers, Box 5.

26 Ibid.; unsigned memorandum of the interview in Swedish, June 2, 1915, Swedish Foreign Office Papers (Archives of the Ministry of Foreign Affairs, Stockholm), 21 U 50. Hereafter SFO Papers.

27 Balch to Addams [July 3, 1915], Addams Papers, Box 5. Balch's extended report of their interview with Sazonov, which she wrote on July 3, 1915, in Amsterdam, is reproduced in Randall, *Improper Bostonian*, pp 190–192; also handwritten copy of Sazonov's statement, SFO Papers, 21 U 50.

28 Balch to Addams [July 3, 1915], Addams Papers, Box 5.

29 Wales to Committee, May 13, 1915, Wales Papers, Box 1; Macmillan, memorandum to Jane Addams [May 1915], Addams Papers, Box 5; and Macmillan and Schwimmer, Report of the Delegates' Interviews with the Governments, August 2, 1915, ibid. The summary of this consensus is in Macmillan's handwritten report, Visit to London of E. Balch & C. Macmillan, undated, Jacobs Papers.

30 Ibid.; and Balch to Addams [July 3, 1915], Addams Papers, Box 5.

31 Schwimmer and Macmillan, Report of the Delegates' Interviews with the Governments, August 2, 1915, and Schwimmer to Addams, August 4, 1915, ibid.

32 Macmillan, Visit to London of E. Balch & C. Macmillan, Jacobs Papers (emphasis Macmillan's); Jacobs, *Memories*, p 91. The other quotations are in Drummond to Macmillan, July 22, 1915, reproduced in Report of the Delegates' Interviews with the Governments, August 2, 1915, Addams Papers, Box 5.

33 Aletta Jacobs mentioned only Chrystal Macmillan as seeing Grey, but she wrote her notes from Macmillan's account of the interview. Jacobs Notes, Jacobs Papers. Randall, *Improper Bostonian*, p 187, assumes, however, that Balch alone saw Grey at about this time, but does not cite evidence for such a meeting. Unfortunately, Macmillan's report, Visit to London to E. Balch & C. Macmillan, Jacobs Papers, ends abruptly after the heading, "In the private interview with Sir Edward Grey," which may suggest that Macmillan did not see Grey, but passed on Balch's account of the interview to Jacobs. Balch later remarked that "we" (unidentified but presumably referring to Macmillan and herself) saw Grey. Cited in *Beyond Nationalism*, ed. Randall, p 78.

34 The Jane Addams Papers (SCPC) contain several letters from IWSA members opposing the International Congress of Women and the envoys to the governments. For example, Mona Taylor to Addams, May 11, 1915, which lists leaders of several British women's organizations opposed to any peace talk, and Elizabeth Banks to Addams, May 12, 1915, Box 5.

35 Hobhouse to Addams, July 5, 1915, ibid.; *New York Times*, June 24, 1915, p 3. In England alone, Addams conferred with more than 40 British liberals, socialists, pacifists, and others, both in and out of government. In addition to those mentioned here in the text, she saw Lord Bryce, well-known intellectual and former diplomat; William L. Massingham, editor of *The Nation*; Francis W. Hirst, editor of *The Economist*; G. Lowes Dickinson; H.N. Brailsford, author of the best seller, *The War of Steel and Gold*, an incisive criticism of the economic motive behind imperialism; J. Allen Baker, M.P. and a founder of the World Alliance of Churches for Promoting International Friendship; the Fabians, Sydney and Beatrice Webb; pacifist philosopher Bertrand Russell; Noel Buxton, M.P.; Lord Courtney, pacifistic husband of Lady Courtney; the political theorist Graham Wallas; E.D. Morel, Arthur Ponsonby, M.P.; Helena Swanwick; Olive Schreiner; Mary Sheepshanks; and Catherine Marshall. Addams' speech in London is reproduced in "Women and Peace," *The Christian Commonwealth*, 35 (May 19, 1915), pp 418–419.

36 Balch to Marie Louise Degen, undated, quoted in Marie Louise Degen, *The History of the Woman's Peace Party*, in *The Johns Hopkins University Studies in Historical and Political Science* (Baltimore: The Johns Hopkins Press, 1939), p 93.

37 Balch, *Women at The Hague*, p 109; Addams, ibid., p 98.

38 Perhaps because Schwimmer and Macmillan wanted to justify their deepening commitment to the dream of an early peace, their summary of all the envoys' interviews, Report of the Delegates' Interviews with the Governments, August 2, 1915, Addams Papers, Box 5, while factually accurate, consistently interpreted the results of these interviews in the most favorable light. For this reason their interpretation is less reliable. The women circulated this document confidentially to several European governments.

39 Addams, *Women at The Hague*, p 97; Schwimmer to Knut Wallenberg, August 22, 1915, SFO Papers, 21 U 50. The women envoys did not press the belligerent authorities on their nations' war (or peace) aims. With a few exceptions, such as France's demand for Germany's return of Alsace-Lorraine, the warring powers had not publicly stated their territorial, colonial, financial, and other claims or guarantees. Their war aims were in fact continuously expanding as the compacts on each side increasingly made assurances and concessions to the other allies in these areas to sustain the war effort. The women knew nothing of course of the secret understandings, which would greatly complicate prospects for any successful mediation, remote though that prospect was in the spring and summer of 1915. Two of David Stevenson's books, *French War Aims Against Germany, 1914–1919* (Oxford: Clarendon Press, 1982) and *Cataclysm*, ch 5, provide informed discussions of the belligerents' evolving war aims. Also see the text below, including notes 41 and 42.

40 Of the many studies relating Tisza's powerful role in the last years of the Dual Monarchy, see, for example, Leo Valiani, *The End of Austria-Hungary* (New York: Alfred A. Knopf, 1973), pp 39–40, 42–44, 47–48, 332–3.

41 Fritz Fischer, *Germany's Aims in the First World War* (New York: W.W. Norton, 1967 edition), pp 103–106, 110–113 (quotation on p 106); Roger Chickering, *Imperial Germany and the Great War, 1914–1918* (Cambridge: Cambridge University Press, 2004 edition), pp 60–64; and Karl E. Birnbaum, *Peace Moves and U-Boat Warfare: A Study of Imperial Germany's Policy towards the United States, April 18, 1916–January 9, 1917* (Stockholm: Almqvist & Wiksell, 1958), pp 11–21, 28–29, and the German documents reproduced ibid., pp 340–344.

42 Ibid., pp. 340–342. Cornelis Victor Lafeber, *Vredes-en Bemiddelingspogingen uit het Eerste Jaar van Wereldoorlog I, Augustus 1914–December 1915* (Leiden: Universitaire Pers, 1961), pp 65–71, 189, 192, 197–198, 203, 214, provides an account of Andersen's wide-ranging peace efforts. Also see L.L. Farrar, Jr., *Divide and Conquer: German Efforts to Conclude a Separate Peace, 1914–1918* (Boulder, Col.: East European Quarterly, 1978), ch 2; and Wilhelm Ernst Winterhalter, *Mission für den Frieden: Europäische Mächtepolitik und Dänische Friedensvermittlung im Ersten Weltkrieg vom August 1914 bis zum Italienischen Kriegseintritt May 1915* (Stuttgart: Franz Steiner, 1994), *passim*.

43 In his memoirs Grey wrote: "the Allies soon became dependent for an adequate supply [of munitions] on the United States. If we quarreled with the United States we could not get that supply. Blockade of Germany was essential to the victory of the Allies, but the ill will of the United States meant their certain defeat. It was better, therefore, to carry on the war without blockade, if need be, than to incur a break with the United States about contraband and thereby deprive the Allies of the resources necessary to carry on the war at all or with any chance of success." Grey also recognized the influence of the United States on smaller neutrals: "The very fact that the United States was in a sense a trustee of the rights of the weaker neutrals made its government disposed to champion those rights." Viscount Grey of Falloudon, *Twenty-Five Years, 1892–1916* (2 vols, New York: Frederick A. Stokes Company, 1925), 2, pp 107, 110. Also, Link, *Wilson*, 3, pp 336, 599, 602–605, 615–616.

44 Grey to House, August 26, 1915, Edward M. House Papers (Yale University Library).

45 A.G. Schmedeman (US Minister to Norway) to Secretary of State, December 28, 1914, *Foreign Relations, 1914, Supplement*, pp 159–161; Maurice Francis Egan to Secretary of State, January 6, 1915, *Foreign Relations, 1915, Supplement*, pp 7–8; Schmedeman to Secretary of State, February 12, 1915, ibid., p 101; Ira N. Morris (US Minister to Sweden) to Secretary of State, February 16, 1915, ibid., p 109; Morris to Secretary of State, February 18, 1915, ibid., pp 139–140; Schmedeman to Secretary of State (telegram), March 20, 1915, ibid., p 146; Schmedeman to Secretary of State, March 23, 1915, ibid., p 158; C. Brun (US Minister to Denmark) to Secretary of State, December 28, 1914, ibid., pp 159–161.

46 "Taken separately the small neutrals obviously did not have a chance against the great belligerents. Even if several small nations combined, their strength would have proven inadequate. Of all the world's neutrals, just one had its neutrality balanced by a sufficient force to have the laws obeyed, the United States." Nils Orvik, *The Decline of Neutrality, 1914–1941: With Special Reference to the United States and the Northern Neutrals* (Oslo: Johan Grundt Tanum Forlag, 1953), p 89.

47 Loudon to Sir Edward Grey, May 18, 1915, and W.L.F. van Rappard to Loudon, October 26, 1915, *Bescheiden Betreffende de Buitenlandse Politiek van Nederland, 1848–1919*, ed. C. Smit ([third period, 1899–1919, 6 vols.] 's-Gravenhage: Verkrijgbaar bij Martinus Nijhoff, 1964), 4, pp 365–366, 460–463. Hereafter *Bescheiden*.

48 "Five Hundred Peace Meetings on One Day," *The Survey*, 34 (August 14, 1915), p 439; Wallenberg to Deputation of the Peace Meeting at Varberg, July 17, 1915, SFO Papers, 21 U 50. The German minister in Stockholm had earlier reported that Wallenberg had informed him that he

had told the women envoys of his complete disinterest in peace talks. Assuming the minister reported the Swedish leader correctly, then Wallenberg was playing a double game, privately encouraging the women's search for peace while officially denying any attempt to influence the belligerents' war plans. German Ministry in Stockholm to Bethmann-Hollweg, June 5, 1915, GFO Papers, D935575, Reel 2075. Also, Lafeber, *Vredes-en Bemiddelingspogingen*, pp 213–214.

49 Ibid.; Sketch of Note to Monseigneur Nolens, April 15, 17, 1915, J. Loudon to Nolens, April 18, 1915, Cardinal Gasparri to Loudon, May 3, 1915, Loudon to Queen Wilhelmina, May 9, 1915, Loudon to Gasparri, May 16, 1915, Loudon to L.W.H. Regout (with enclosure), August 6, 1915, and Regout to Loudon, September 13, 1915, all in *Bescheiden*, 4, pp 350–352, 354–355, 359–360, 363, 405–406, 435–439. Regout died in late October 1915, but the full exchange of information continued under the chargé d'affaires, Schuller tot Peursum, and the new minister, O.F.A.M. van Nispen tot Sevenaer, through the rest of 1915 and 1916. Ibid., pp 478, 517–519, 527–529, 553–555, 559–562.

50 Amry Vandenbosch, *Dutch Foreign Policy Since 1815: A Study in Small Power Politics* (The Hague: Martinus Nijhoff, 1959), pp 140–146.

51 *New York Times*, January 31, 1915, p SM1. Cort van der Linden is quoted in "The Dutch Government with Regard to Future Attempts towards the Reestablishment of Peace," *Holland News*, new series, no 8 (July 15, 1915), p 2. Loudon to Grey, May 18, 1915, *Bescheiden*, 4, pp 365–366; F. W. Fox to Loudon, July 22, 1915, ibid., pp 398–399.

52 Wales to Committee, May 13, 1915, Wales Papers, Box 1; B. de Jong van Beek en Donk's statement, August 3, 1915, Balch Papers, Box 1; *New York*

Times, August 15, 1915, p 2. Jacobs Notes, August 12, 1915 (Jacobs' emphasis), Jacobs Papers; Jacobs, *Memories*, p 91. Battin, who became a "traveling secretary" of the World Alliance, also tried to draw religious leaders' attention to the deplorable treatment of prisoners of war. His European activities can be followed in Henriette A. Neuhaus to William I. Hull, October 28, 1914, Hull Papers, Box 2; W.H. Dickinson to Frederick Lynch, January 29, 1915, ibid., Box 3; Addams to Wald, May 12, 1915, Wald Papers (NYPL); Elizabeth Balmer Baker and P.J. Noel Baker, *J. Allen*

Baker, Member of Parliament: A Memoir (London: The Swarthmore Press, 1927), pp 237–239; and Bengt Sundkler, *Nathan Söderblom: His Life and Work* (London: Lutterworth Press, 1968), pp 180–181.

53 Wales to Committee, June 4–15, 1915, Wales Papers, Box 1; C.F. de Klercker (Swedish Minister in The Hague) to Swedish Foreign Office (telegram), August 15, 1915, SFO Papers, 21 U 50; Wallenberg to Swedish Ministry in The Hague, August 16, 1915, ibid.; Esme Howard to Wallenberg (enclosing memorandum), August 25, 1915, ibid.

4 PEACE WORKERS AND THE WILSON ADMINISTRATION

1 Press Conference, April 13, 1915, *PWW*, 32, p 516. Memorandum authorized by President Wilson, November 14, 1914, in reply to unsigned, typewritten memorandum, undated, Department of State Papers, 763.72119/115; Joseph E. Willard to William Jennings Bryan (telegram), December 7, 1914, and Bryan to Willard (telegram), December 8, 1914, *F.R., 1914, Supplement*, pp 146–147.

2 A recent evaluation of Wilson's inexperience in foreign matters is H.W. Brands, "Woodrow Wilson and the Irony of Fate," *Diplomatic History*, 28 (September 2004), pp 503–512.

3 House Diary, September 28, 1914, *PWW*, 31, p 95; Link, *Wilson*, 3, pp 58–70, 167–170.

4 House Diary, November 6, 1914, and November 14, 1914, *PWW*, 31, pp 274–275, 320; Edwin A. Weinstein, *Woodrow Wilson: A Medical and Psychological Biography* (Princeton: Princeton University Press, 1981), pp 20, 23, 38–39, 63, 69, 73, 123, 254–260.

5 Link, *Wilson*, 3, pp 11–19.

6 Arthur S. Link, *Wilson: The Road to the White House* (Princeton, N.J.: Princeton University Press, 1947), pp 1–2. Wilson's recollections of his

Civil War experiences are summarized in Knock, *To End All Wars*, pp 3–4. A PBS television documentary in The American Experience series of Wilson's life, *Woodrow Wilson* (2002), stresses the impact of the Civil War on Wilson's intellectual development.

7 Diary of Nancy Saunders Toy, January 3, 1915, *PWW*, 32, pp 8–9; and especially Mulder, *Woodrow Wilson*, pp xiii–xiv, 269–271.

8 Ibid., pp 44–53, *passim*. Among many accounts of Burke's influence on Wilson, see John A. Thompson, *Woodrow Wilson* (London: Longman, 2002), pp 20, 33–34, 37, 50, 57.

9 Patterson, *Toward a Warless World*, pp 208ff.; Robert Erskine Ely to Wilson, March 25, 1907, *PWW*, 17 (1974), pp 92–93; and Benjamin F. Trueblood to Wilson, September 19, 1908, ibid., 18 (1974), pp 419–420; Wilson's addresses at a synagogue in Trenton [September 7, 1911], ibid., 23 (1977), pp 305–308, and to the Universal Peace Union in Philadelphia [February 19, 1912], ibid., 24 (1977), pp 181–183. Like many university presidents, Wilson was also aware of the Cosmopolitan Club movement, but apparently did not promote it at Princeton, perhaps because there were so

few foreign students enrolled there. Syngman Rhee to Wilson, July 7, 1910, ibid., 20 (1975), p 556.

10 Wilson to Ellen Axson, March 4, 1884, ibid., 3 (1967), pp 60–61, and February 24, 1885, ibid., 4 (1968), p 287.

11 Weinstein, *Woodrow Wilson*, p xiii, provides a convenient chronology of Wilson's major illnesses, including his strokes in 1896, 1904, 1906, 1907, 1908, 1910, and 1913, and the author's narrative treats the strokes, including their possible impact on Wilson's behavior, in careful detail. Of course, an emphasis on Wilson's physical and psychological problems is somewhat controversial because his illnesses were mostly not medically diagnosed or, if treated, physicians' records about them have not survived. Particularly in his pre-presidential years, Wilson often tried to avoid medical help for his physical problems, but Wilson's own letters and surviving comments by friends and family members provide considerable evidence of their relative severity. Often at the brink of completely debilitating mental or physical breakdown, Wilson managed to back away from his work. Trips to Great Britain (1896, 1899, 1906, 1908) and Bermuda (1907, 1908), for example, restored his faculties and re-energized him for his next challenges in public life. While mindful of Wilson's physical and psychological problems, this study says little about them because, once he overcame his depression in the months immediately after Ellen's death, they did not seem obvious in his behavior during the period of U.S. neutrality. Mulder, *Woodrow Wilson*, pp 53–54, 64–65, 68, 131–132, 139, 145–150, 155–156, 185–186, 189–190, 202–203, 241–244.

12 This dualism is a prominent theme in August Heckscher, *Woodrow Wilson* (New York: Random House, 1991), pp 28, 154–155, 187, *passim*; also,

Louis Auchicloss, *Woodrow Wilson* (New York: Viking, 2000), p 23, and, more nuanced, Thompson, *Woodrow Wilson*, pp. 17–18, 21, 37–38, 53–54, 76–77.

13 Quoted and analyzed in Daniel M. Smith, *Robert Lansing and American Neutrality, 1914–1917* (Berkeley: University of California Press, 1958), p 80. Even Professor Link, early in his researches on Wilson, seems to have agreed: "When reason clashed with his intuition, reason had to give way." Arthur S. Link, *Woodrow Wilson and the Progressive Era, 1910–1917* (New York: Harper & Row, 1954), p 32.

14 Wilson to Bryan, April 27, 1915, *PWW*, 33 (1980), pp 81–82.

15 Memorandum by Herbert Bruce Brougham (*New York Times*), December 14, 1914, ibid., 31, pp 458–460; Jackson Day Address, January 8, 1915, ibid., 32, pp 40–41; Wilson to Mott (with enclosure), September 17, 1914, ibid., 31, pp 40–41, and note 1. After his European trip, Mott reported to Wilson that the Europeans generally praised the president's neutrality policy and, while pessimistic about mediation for the foreseeable future, he counseled that the United States would have a "unique opportunity" at the end of the war because of the exhaustion of the warring nations. Charles R. Crane to Wilson, January 10, 1915, ibid., 32, pp 52–53, and note 1.

16 Bryan to Wilson, December 14, 1914, Department of State Papers, 763.72119/35–1/2e; House Diary, December 16, 1914, *PWW*, December 16, 1914, 31, pp 469–470, and A Draft Pan-American Treaty [December 16, 1914], ibid., pp 471–473. A fuller discussion of the origins of the Wilson administration's pan-Americanism is in *The Intimate Papers of Colonel House: Arranged as a Narrative*, ed. Charles Seymour (4 vols, Boston: Houghton Mifflin,

1926–1928), 1, pp 209–210, 233–234; Arthur S. Link, *Wilson: The New Freedom* (Princeton, N.J.: Princeton University Press, 1956), pp 324–327 (hereafter Link, *Wilson*, 2); and, particularly as it relates to Wilson's emerging "new diplomacy," Knock, *To End All Wars*, pp 39–45, 65–74, 81–84, *passim*. The four-part draft pan-American treaty was communicated to the governments of Argentina, Brazil, and Chile on February 1, 1915.

17 Arthur Link argues that it is "strongly possible" that Bernstorff telephoned Wilson on May 28, saying he had with him a secret emissary from the Imperial Chancellor and requested an interview. According to Link, Wilson cancelled his other appointments that day and had Bernstorff and Gildemeester quietly escorted into his office. The Dutchman then gave Wilson his impressions of German attitudes toward the war, as noted below in the text. *PWW*, 33, pp 280–282, including notes. In his book, *Imperial Challenge: Ambassador Count Bernstorff and German-American Relations, 1908–1917* (Chapel Hill: University of North Carolina Press, 1989), pp 104–107, 295–297 (notes 31–38), Reinhard R. Doerries acknowledges Link's sleuthing and ingenious conclusions but from his own additional research, especially the transcripts of secret telephone recordings of the German Embassy at the time, is clearly skeptical about the meeting. He shows that Gildemeester did not see Wilson before May 30 and probably not at all. Both accounts also cite other historians' references to the "mysterious" behavior of Gildemeester and Bernstorff in this episode. The propaganda purposes of Gildemeester's visit are further suggested in the correspondence cited in the following note.

18 Adolph Caspar Miller to Bryan, June

3, 1915, *PWW*, 33, pp 332–333; and Gildemeester to Wilson, June 7, 1915, ibid., pp 361–362.

19 Bernstorff to German Foreign Office, May 29, 1915, ibid., pp 283–284.

20 Bernstorff to German Foreign Office, June 2, 1915, ibid., pp 318–320.

21 Gildemeester remained in the United States and worked with a pro-German group, Friends of Peace, which excluded him, however, from its deliberations for fear he was a British spy! Later he returned to Holland only to be expelled by the Dutch government possibly for allegations of smuggling goods into Germany. *New York Times*, September 5, 1915, p 3, and December 12, 1915, p 1.

22 Jane Addams, "The Revolt Against War," *The Survey*, 34 (July 17, 1915), pp 355–359. A slightly revised text is Addams, *Women at The Hague*, ch 3. She also gave her impressions of her European experience in an interview with the *New York Times*, July 11, 1915, p SM1. Elshtain, *Jane Addams and the Dream of American Democracy*, p 314, note 43, quotes Addams on the downplaying of the maternal instinct.

23 Criticisms of Addams can be followed in *New York Times*, July 13, 1915, p 10; July 14, 1915, p 8; July 15, 1915, p 8; July 30, 1915, p 3; August 5, 1915, p 10; August 17, 1915, p 8 (editorial); August 23, 1915, p 8; August 27, 1915, p 8; October 17, 1915, p SM4; and October 23, 1915, p 10. Addams' attempted clarifications are ibid., August 15, 1915, 2, p 3; August 18, 1915, p 10; and October 23, 1915, p 10. Several biographies of Addams, especially Davis, *American Heroine*, pp 223, 226–231, and Elshtain, *Jane Addams and the Dream of American Democracy*, pp 226–235, detail the long-term fallout from her address. Davis also mentions those friends who stood by her. Muted explanations or strong defenses of her views are in *New York Times*, July 16, 1915,

p 8; July 22, 1915, p 5; and July 23, 1915, p 2; Wald to Addams, July 14, 1915, Coss, *Lillian D. Wald*, pp 50–51; Hamilton to Addams, July 20, 1915, *Alice Hamilton*, ed. Sicherman, p 195; and Elizabeth Glendower Evans to Addams, July 22, 1915, Addams Papers, Box 5. On the ready availability of alcohol and drunkenness among the troops, see Niall Ferguson, *The Pity of War* (New York: Basic Books, 1999), pp 351–352.

24 Montgelas to Lochner, May 17, 1915, Ford Peace Plan Papers (Manuscript Division, Library of Congress), Box 1. Hereafter, FPP Papers. Lochner to Wilson, June 25, 1915, enclosing Balch to Lochner, June 1, 1915, Wilson Papers, Reel 320. Lochner sent this letter special delivery to Wilson at his Cornish retreat just when Wilson was scheduled to go there. Lochner reasoned that official mail forwarded from Washington might not yet have caught up with him and that Wilson might personally open a special delivery letter. Lochner's ingenuity seems to have worked. He later recalled incorrectly that he sent the letter to Wilson at his summer home on the New Jersey shore, but he obviously meant Cornish because Wilson did not vacation in New Jersey until 1916. Lochner, *Always the Unexpected*, pp 52–53.

25 Crane to Wilson, July 2, 1915, Wilson to Crane, July 3, 1915, and Wilson to Wald, July 3, 1915, *PWW*, 33, pp 469, 471, 472.

26 Hapgood to House, July 16, 1915, House Papers; Diary, July 17, 1915, ibid.; House to Wilson, July 17, 1915, *PWW*, 33, p 516.

27 Godfrey Hodgson, *Woodrow Wilson's Right Hand: The Life of Colonel Edward M. House* (New Haven, Conn.: Yale University Press, 2006), pp 1–12, *passim* (quotations on pp 6 and 7).

28 For discussions of Colonel House's ideas and actions relating to *realpoli-*

tik, neutral rights, and mediation, see ibid., chs 8–10, *passim*, and Link, *Wilson*, 3, pp 47–48, 110–114, 172–173, 202–208, 218–231, 375, 392–395, 598–599. Some of House's letters best expressing these ideas are cited in the following three notes.

29 House to Wilson, May 25, 1915, *PWW*, 33, p 254.

30 Link, *Wilson*, 2, pp 314–318.

31 House to Wilson, May 9, 11, 14, 25, June 16, 1915, *PWW*, 33, pp 134, 158–159, 197–198, 253–254, and 405–407.

32 Link, *Wilson*, 3, *passim*.

33 For examples of House's flattery of his mentor, see House to Wilson, July 1, 1914, *PWW*, 30, p 242; House to Wilson, September 18, November 30, 1914, ibid., 31, pp 45, 370; House to Wilson, January 29, 1915, ibid., 32, p 162; and House to Wilson, November 10, 1915, ibid., 35 (1980), p 186. For House's promotion of Wilson's peacemaking skills, see House to Wilson, January 8, April 11, 14, 1915, ibid., 32, pp 42, 504, 522; and House to Wilson, April 20, May 7, 1915, ibid., 33, pp 47–48, 123.

34 House to Wilson, July 17, 1915, ibid., pp 516–517. Earlier, House had advised Wilson to keep Secretary Bryan out of any mediation diplomacy. Wilson entirely agreed, but House often reminded him of Bryan's unsuitability. For instance, after Wilson offered his good offices to the belligerents on August 4, 1914, House urged the president to "make it clear that what you have done was at your own instance. If the public either here or in Europe thought that Mr Bryan instigated it, they would conclude that it was done in an impractical way and was doomed to failure from the start." House to Wilson, August 5, 1914, ibid., 30, p 349. Also, House to Wilson, August 1, 1914, ibid., p 327; and House Diary, December 3, 1914, ibid., 31, p 385.

35 House Diary, July 17, 1915.

36 Hamilton to Addams, July 20, 1915, *Alice Hamilton*, ed. Sicherman, p 194.

37 Wilson's confidential journal, October 20, 1887, *PWW*, 5 (1968), p 619; Wilson to Charles W. Kent, May 29, 1894, ibid., 8 (1970), pp 583–584; Wilson to Witter Bynner, June 20, 1911, ibid., 23 (1977), p 160; Wilson to Edith M. Whitmore [February 8, 1912], ibid., 24 (1977), p 140; also Weinstein, *Woodrow Wilson*, ch 5.

38 Diary of Nancy Saunders Toy, January 6, 1915, *PWW*, 32, p 21. In 1912, Wilson framed the question of women's place in the (private) home versus her outside (public) role to Max Eastman: "In demanding their rights, aren't women proposing to neglect their duties?" Quoted in Max Eastman, *Love and Revolution: My Journey through an Epoch* (New York: Random House, 1964), p 32.

39 Remarks to a Woman Suffrage Delegation, June 30, 1914, *PWW*, 30, pp 226–228 and 228n1.

40 House Diary, July 19, 1915. House to Wilson, July 19, 1915, *PWW*, 33, pp 532–533, briefly summarized House's interviews with Villard and Addams.

41 Arthur S. Link, *Wilson: Confusions and Crises, 1915–1916* (Princeton, NJ: Princeton University Press, 1964), pp 101–113. Hereafter Link, *Wilson*, 4.

42 Wilson to Lansing, August 7, 1915, Wilson Papers, Reel 72.

43 House Diary, July 19, 1915.

44 Link, *Wilson*, 3, p 591.

45 For this theme, see John Morton Blum, *Woodrow Wilson and the Politics of Morality* (Boston: Little, Brown, 1956).

46 Kellogg to Lochner, July 21, 1915, Lochner Papers. Also, Minutes of Peace Meeting at Henry Street Settlement, July 20, 1915, Balch Papers, Box 6.

47 Link, *Wilson*, 3, pp 161–167.

48 "Civilization's Peril," *The Survey*, 33 (February 6, 1915), p 518; "America and Peace: 1915," ibid. (January 2,

1915), pp 387–388. The Reverends Walter Rauschenbusch, of German descent, and Charles F. Aked, of English background, issued a joint statement condemning the American trade in arms. New York *Evening Post*, July 13, 1915, p 9. Aked later became a member of the Ford peace expedition.

49 Jordan to A.G. Gardner, October 15, 1915, Jordan Peace Correspondence, Box 4. The World Peace Foundation and the New York Peace Society opposed any legislation on neutral rights. In the latter group this consensus ranged from the hawkish Anglophile Lyman Abbott at one extreme to pacific-minded individuals like Reverend Frederick Lynch and Rabbi Stephen S. Wise on the other. Other members opposing an embargo were John Bates Clark, Samuel Train Dutton, William H. Short, Hamilton Holt, and George W. Kirchwey. *New York Times*, February 20, 1915, p 2, June 14, 1915, p 9, and September 6, 1915, p 5; "What Ought We to Do?" *The Independent*, 82 (April 26, 1915), pp 131–132; and "Selling Death," ibid., 83 (September 6, 1915), pp 312–313.

50 *New York Times*, September 5, 1915, p 3.

51 Link, *Wilson*, 3, pp 62–64, 132–136, 169, 381, 389.

52 *New York Times*, July 22, 1915, p 2; *Washington Post*, July 22, 1915, p 4; Addams to Kellogg, July 27, 1915, Wald Papers (NYPL). Also, Addams to Marcet Haldeman, July 25, 1915, JAMC.

53 Addams' earlier consideration of variations of the proposal for an official neutral conference, is in Courtney, *War Diary*, p 43; and Memorandum for Executive Committee on American Action in Line with Miss Addams' Suggestions [late July or early August 1915], Wales Papers, Box 1. Kellogg to Lochner, July 21, 1915, and Kellogg to Addams, August

4, 1915, ibid., describe her alternative scheme in detail.

54 Formulation of August 4, 1915, Wilson Papers, Reel 72. This memorial contained the signatures of Jane Addams, Leo Arnstein, Emily Greene Balch, Edward T. Devine, John Palmer Gavit, John Haynes Holmes, Hamilton Holt, Frederic C. Howe, William I. Hull, Florence Kelley, Paul U. Kellogg, William Kent, George W. Kirchwey, Samuel McCune Lindsay, Owen R. Lovejoy, Julian W. Mack, George H. Mead, George W. Nasmyth, George Foster Peabody, Graham Taylor, Oswald Garrison Villard, Lillian D. Wald, Mornay Williams, and Stephen S. Wise.

55 Addams to Kellogg, July 27, 1915, Wald Papers (NYPL); Memorandum for Executive Committee on American Action in Line with Miss Addams' Suggestions, undated, Wales Papers, Box 1. In an apparent attempt to appease proponents of other approaches, this memorandum also subscribed to "concurrent action" on a conference of American nations to formulate sea law for the Western hemisphere, voluntary cooperation with like-minded groups and individuals in neutral and belligerent nations, exchange of ideas with other groups like the Dutch Anti-War Council "looking toward the substitution of law for war," and inquiries at the state department on the feasibility of two friendly neutrals serving as the diplomatic agents for exchanges on peace terms by each belligerent side. But the memorandum made them lesser priorities for the immediate future, and the written proposal to the Wilson administration did not mention any of them.

56 Lansing Desk Diary, August 6, 1915, Robert Lansing Papers (Manuscript Division, Library of Congress). Hereafter, Lansing Desk Diary.

Villard to Balch, August 10, 1915, Villard Papers, Folder 120.

57 Lansing to Wilson, August 6, 1915, *PWW*, 34 (1980), p 110; Wilson to Balch, August 2, 1915, ibid., p 58; Wilson to Lansing, August 7, 1915, Wilson Papers, Reel 72.

58 House Diary, August 16, 1915.

59 Lochner to Juliet Barrett Rublee, July 23, 1915, Lochner Papers.

60 Balch to Addams, August 17, 1915, Addams Papers, Box 5.

61 Martin, *Peace Without Victory*, p 95; also see House to Wilson, March 8, 1915, *PWW*, 32, pp 340–341.

62 All this memoranda, totaling 13 pages, is in the Wilson Papers, Reel 72.

63 Balch to Addams, August 19, 1915, Addams Papers, Box 5.

64 Wilson to Galt, August 18, 1915, *PWW*, 34, p 243. For the romance, see Phyllis Lee Levin, *Edith and Woodrow: The Wilson White House* (New York: Scribner, 2001).

65 Since Lansing's opinion was dated August 18, 1915, the same day as Emily Balch's interview with the President, it is possible that it reached Wilson who might have read it before seeing her at 2:00 p.m. (Appointment Books, Wilson Papers, Reel 3). If so, he did not use any of Lansing's arguments or objections to an international commission in the interview, although he wrote his secretary of state the next day that he liked his presentation. Nor did he mention Lansing's note in his letter to Galt the same evening as the interview (see p 129).

66 Lansing to Wilson, August 18, 1915, *PWW*, 34, pp 236–237.

67 Smith, *Robert Lansing and American Neutrality*, pp 6–9; Larry Zuckerman, *The Rape of Belgium: The Untold Story of World War I* (New York: New York University Press, 2004), p 130.

68 Wilson to Lansing, August 19, 1915, *PWW*, 34, pp 236–237.

69 See above pp 112–113; and Link, *Wilson*, 3, pp 554–587, 645–681.

70 Wilson to Galt, August 19, 1915, *PWW*, 34, pp 260–261 (emphasis Wilson's).

71 Jacobs, *Memories*, p 91; Jacobs to Addams, August 26, 1915, Addams Papers, Box 5.

72 Wilson to Balch, August 28, 1915, *PWW*, 34, p 350; Wilson to Lansing, August 31, 1915 [September 1, 1915], ibid., p 399.

73 Memorandum, Interview of Dr Jacobs and Miss Balch with Secretary Lansing, August 31, 1915, Villard Papers, Folder 120. Balch probably wrote the report that Dr Jacobs undoubtedly approved. Lansing to Wilson, September 1, 1915, Robert Lansing Papers (Princeton University Library), Box 2, confirms the accuracy of Balch's facts (if not always the tone) and adds a few details. Hereafter, Lansing Papers (PU).

74 Ibid. Lansing's firm opposition to collaboration with the European neutrals on mediation reflected his disdain for any kind of cooperative or parallel action with them in the defense of their common neutral rights under international law. A critical evaluation of Lansing's evasive and discouraging responses to the European neutrals' requests for U.S. cooperation on neutral rights is Orvik, *Decline of Neutrality*, pp 96–103.

75 Balch to Villard, September 28, 1915, Villard Papers, Folder 120. In later interviews with Lansing, other peace people confirmed Balch's judgment. After Chrystal Macmillan saw him (Lansing Desk Diary, November 2, 1915), she wrote: "Lansing I found, if possible, more of a formalist than he has been described. He seemed to consider nothing but the purely technical aspect of the situation." Macmillan to Jordan, November 3, 1915, Jordan Peace Correspondence, Box 5; also, Macmillan to Kellogg, November 3, 1915, FPP Papers, Box 1. And when Lochner saw public officials in Washington (Lansing Desk Diary, November 13, 1915) in an attempt to learn the attitude of the Wilson administration on mediation, he concluded of his efforts: "Lansing was the least satisfactory. He is just all the time thinking in ruts." Lochner to Wales, November 13, 1915, Wales Papers, Box 1. Needless to say, peace advocates thereafter refrained from further contact with the secretary of state.

76 House Diary, September 1, 1915.

77 Schwimmer to Addams, August 20, 1915, enclosing Minutes of ICWPP Board of Officers Meeting, August 18, 1915, Addams Papers, Box 5; Macmillan to Addams (cable), August 21, 1915, Addams Papers, Box 5; Jacobs to Addams, September 8, 1915, and Hobhouse to Jacobs, August 21, 1915, *Politics and Friendship*, pp 157–159.

78 Mary R. Smith to Balch (telegram), August 26, 1915, Balch Papers, Box 7; Mary R. Smith to Mabel L. Hyers, August 26, 1915, WPP Correspondence, Addams file; Addams to Jacobs (telegram), September 13, 1915, Jacobs Papers.

79 Jacobs to Schwimmer and Macmillan, September 13, 1915, *Politics and Friendship*, p 160; Jacobs to Addams, September 13, 1915, Addams Papers, Box 5.

80 Jacobs to Addams, September 15, 1915, Addams Papers, Box 5. (An extract is printed in *PWW*, 34, p 473.)

5 MORE MOMENTUM AND NEW DIRECTIONS

1 Appointment Books, September 20, 1915, Wilson Papers, Reel 3; Battin to Cort van der Linden and Loudon, October 4, 1915, J. Loudon Papers

(Netherlands Ministry of Foreign Affairs); an extract is printed in *PWW*, 35, pp 20–21.

2 Wilson to Addams, September 23, 1915, Jacobs Papers.

3 Addams to Kellogg, September 24, 1915, Wald Papers (NYPL); Memorandum on Henry Street Meeting, September 27, 1915, Schwimmer-Lloyd Papers, Box A62. Regarding the peace activism of Holmes and Peabody, see *Biographical Dictionary of Modern Peace Leaders*, pp 422–424 and 732–734.

4 Balch to Kellogg, September 25, 1915, Schwimmer-Lloyd Papers, Box A62.

5 Kellogg to Addams, September 29, 1915, Survey Associates Papers (Social Welfare History Archives, University of Minnesota), Reel 1; Memorandum on Henry Street Meeting, September 27, 1915, Schwimmer-Lloyd Papers, Box A62, and Kellogg to Schwimmer, October 11, 1915, ibid., Box A63.

6 Balch to Lochner, June 1, 1915, Wilson Papers, Reel 320. Balch noted the worsening prospects for future mediation moves when she said that the next month might be "a crucial time" for the mediation advocates. Balch to O.G. Villard, September 28, 1915, O.G. Villard Papers, Folder 120. Also, see her article, "The Time to Make Peace," *The Survey*, 35 (October 2, 1915), pp 24–25. Similarly, when Jane Addams recounted her travels through the belligerent nations, she stressed the suppression of liberal and peace sentiment and the growing number of extreme proposals for a purely military solution. See her articles, "The Revolt Against War," p 356; "Peace and the Press," *The Independent*, 84 (October 11, 1915), pp 55–56; and "The Food of War," ibid. (December 13, 1915), pp 430–431.

7 Jane Addams' interview, *New York Times*, July 11, 1915, p SM1; Balch,

"The Time to Make Peace," p 24. Also, see, Randall, *Improper Bostonian*, p 211n.

8 *New York Times*, January 24, 1915, p III3; *San Francisco Chronicle*, July 7, 1915, p 11; Sewall to Lochner, January 10, 1916, Lochner Papers; May Wright Sewall, *Women, World War and Permanent Peace* (San Francisco: John J. Newbegin, 1915), pp xi–xxx, 164–165, 178–191.

9 *Proceedings of the Fifth American Peace Congress, held in San Francisco, California, October 10–13, 1915*, eds. H.H. Bell and Robert C. Root (New York: Church Peace Union, 1915), *passim; San Francisco Chronicle*, October 14, 1915, p 3. These biennial conferences began in 1907; the 1915 meeting would be the last one.

10 The manifesto, signed by Addams, Balch, Jacobs, Macmillan, and Schwimmer, appeared in the *New York Times*, October 16, 1915, p 3, and most other metropolitan newspapers. Paul Kellogg apparently first suggested the joint manifesto. Kellogg to Addams, September 21, 1915, Wald Papers (NYPL).

11 New York *Evening Post*, October 5, 1915, p 1, October 9, 1915, p 9, and October 15, 1915, p 1.

12 *New York Times*, November 4, 1915, p 4; Sewall to Lochner, January 10, 1916, Lochner Papers.

13 Herbert Hoover, *The Ordeal of Woodrow Wilson* (New York: McGraw Hill, 1958), p 2. Hoover's date for his visit to the United States to see Wilson is off by several months, but other sources, including the President's Appointment Books (Wilson Papers, Reel 3), confirm their meeting on November 3, 1915. In a letter to his fiancé, November 3, Wilson noted that his "most interesting interview to-day" was with Hoover and went on to sing the praises of Hoover and his work, but did not directly mention their discussion of mediation prospects. *PWW*, 35, p 165.

14 Patterson, *Toward a Warless World*, pp 207, 209–210, 221, 233–234.

15 Lochner to Jordan, June 29, July 8, 1915, Jordan Peace Correspondence, Box 4; Lochner to Balch, August 16, 1915, Balch Papers, Box 1. Printed copies of this petition, which listed several reasons why "the civil authorities as well as the well-informed citizenship in each of the belligerent countries" would respond favorably to a mediation offer by the United States alone or in conjunction with other neutrals, are in the Balch Papers, Box 1, and the Addams Papers, Box 5. Petitions containing more than 200 signatures of college professors and a few administrators from more than 50 colleges and schools are in the Lochner Papers, and the FPP Papers, Box 1.

16 Jordan to Wilson, September 28, 1915, U.S. Department of State Files, 763.72119/85. Jordan advanced similar reservations concerning peace moves when he saw Jane Addams on his way to Washington for his interview with the President. Addams expressed "large hopes" for a conference of neutrals and hoped Jordan might become one of the delegates, but Jordan was more cautious: "Nous verrons bien," he wrote his wife, "but I am not over hopeful. Germany's peace suggestions seem pretty raw." Jordan to Jessie Jordan, October 22, 1915, Jordan Peace Correspondence, Box 4.

17 House Diary, October 25, 1915; Jordan to Addams, October 26, 1915, WPP Correspondence, Jordan File.

18 Lochner to Wales, October 28, November 2, 3, 1915, Wales Papers, Box 1; Lochner to Jordan, November 2, 1915, Jordan Peace Correspondence, Box 5; Lochner to Wales, November 4, 1915, Wales Papers, Box 1.

19 Lochner to Jordan, November 2, 1915, Jordan Peace Correspondence, Box 5, best describes Lochner's campaign. Copies of the circular letter, sample telegraph messages to newspapers and President Wilson, a statement of the case for continuous neutral mediation, background material on previous actions of the mediation movement, and other data, totaling 16 pages, are preserved in the University of Chicago Library and the Lochner Papers.

20 Macmillan to Schwimmer, November 3, 1915, FPP Papers, Box 1. There are several favorable replies to Lochner's circular letter in the Lochner Papers. A sampling of newspapers suggests that the resolution was widely endorsed but with little enthusiasm. *Dayton Daily News*, November 8, 1915; *Cincinnati Times-Star*, November 8, 1915; Cleveland *Plain Dealer*, November 9, 1915; and *Boston Herald*, November 9, 1915. Also, George W. Nasmyth to Wales, November 9, 1915, Wales Papers, Box 1. A six-page typewritten statement listing 202 telegrams for President Wilson asking for a conference of neutral nations, November 9, 10, 11, 1915, is in the FPP Papers, Box 1. Apparently this list was compiled from telegrams to Lochner by individuals and groups informing him of their action, although this fact is not noted on the list.

21 LaFontaine to Lochner, November 14, 1915, FPP Papers, Box 1; Theodore D.A. Cockerell to Lochner, November 2, 1915, ibid. (emphasis Cockerell's).

22 Wales to Lochner, November 1915, quoted in Walter I. Trattner, "Julia Grace Wales and the Wisconsin Plan for Peace," *Wisconsin Magazine of History*, 24 (Spring 1961), p 212.

23 L. Hollingsworth Wood (with 24 others) to Lochner, December 9, 1914, Lochner Papers; New York *Evening Post*, December 10, 1914, p 1, and December 19, 1914, p 3; "To Promote Preparedness for

Peace," *The Survey*, 33 (January 9, 1915), pp 394–395; and Wald, *Windows on Henry Street*, pp 288–290.

24 Jordan to Wilson, telegram, August 13, 1915, Wilson Papers, Reel 325; Peabody to Joseph P. Tumulty, October 16, 1915, and Jenkin Lloyd Jones to Wilson, November 10, 1915, ibid., Reel 326; and Stephen S. Wise to Wilson, November 12, 1915, *PWW*, 35, pp 194–195; *New York Times*, June 16, 1915, p 4, June 28, 1915 (letter), p 8, November 5, 1915, p 1, and November 8, 1915, p 8.

25 Villard to Wilson, September 7, 1915, Wilson Papers, Reel 326; Villard to Wilson, October 30, 1915, *PWW*, 35, pp 141–143; Villard to Tumulty, November 17, 1915, Wilson Papers, Reel 375; *New York Times*, November 9, 1915, p 4, November 11, 1915, p 5, November 13, 1915, p 6, and November 16, 1915, p 9; "Recommendations," *The Survey*, 35 (December 4, 1915), pp 232–233. Villard also wrote an eight-part series on the military preparedness question in New York, *Evening Post*, October 23, 1915, p 9, October 27, 1915, p 9, October 30, 1915, p 9, November 3, 1915, p 9, November 6, 1915, p 11, November 10, 1915, p 9, November 13, 1915, p 9, and November 17, 1915, p 11.

26 Lochner to Wales, November 3, 4, 1915, Wales Papers, Box 1.

27 Lochner, Memorandum of White House Interview, November 12, 1915, *PWW*, 35, pp 195–199.

28 Lochner, Additional Data Regarding Our Interview [November 13, 1915], extract in *PWW*, 35, pp 199–200. Jordan likewise told Colonel House that he had found the President "greatly interested and sympathetic, but without committing himself by word of mouth to anything." House Diary, November 18, 1915.

29 Ray Stannard Baker, who first gained access to Wilson's personal papers in the 1920s, wrote on the top of the packet, "Never opened or read by

W.W. RSB." Lochner to Wilson, November 13, 1915, Wilson Papers, Reel 74.

30 Link, *Wilson*, 4, pp 106–107.

31 Ibid., pp 101–113.

32 Additional Data Regarding Our Interview [November 13, 1915], Lochner Papers.

33 *New York Times*, April 11, 1915, p SM14, and August 23, 1915, p 3.

34 Ibid., September 9, 1915, p 1, September 18, 1915, p 5, and August 23, 1915, p 3.

35 Lochner, Additional Data Regarding Our Interview [November 13, 1915], Lochner Papers.

36 Lochner to Henry C. Morris, September 15, 1915, CPS Papers, vol 1; G. S. Anderson (secretary to Henry Ford) to Jordan, November 2, 1915, FPP Papers, Box 1; Henri LaFontaine to Ford (draft of letter), November 11, 1915, ibid.; Warren Worth Bailey to Ford, September 16, November 4, 1915, William Jennings Bryan to Ford, November 2, 1915, and G.S. Anderson to Bailey, November 12, 1915, Warren Worth Bailey Papers (Princeton University Library), Box 7. E.G. Liebold, another of Ford's aides, claimed that since Ford's announcement of his ten-million dollar endowment, he had received an average of 600 letters daily. *New York Times*, September 21, 1915, p 11. Holbrook to Schwimmer, September 17–18, 1915, Schwimmer-Lloyd Papers, Box A62.

37 Jane Campbell, The Making of a Radical Pacifist: Rebecca Shelley 1914–1920 (Senior honors thesis: University of Michigan, 1974), pp 9–16; Rebecca Shelley to her father, October 11, 1915, Rebecca Shelley Papers (Michigan Historical Collections), Box 1. Shelley added the second "e" to her surname sometime after the Great War. I have used her later spelling throughout this study.

38 Willmann's many letters (in German)

to Shelley between 1911 and 1915 are preserved ibid. (She unfortunately did not keep copies of her letters to him.) An engraved announcement of their engagement is ibid.; Franz Willmann to Parent-in-law, February 22, 1914, ibid.; and Shelley to Franciska Schwimmer, October 27, 1956, ibid., Box 10.

39 W.H. Worrell to Shelley, January 1, 1912, and Shelley to Florence Shelley, November 12, 1912, ibid., Box 1. Beginning in December 1912, Franz Willmann addressed her as "Liebe Rebecca" and "Mein Liebling" and used the more familiar "du" and "dein."

40 Emma Willmann to Shelley, April 28, 1913, and Lella Secor to Shelley, March 14, 1915, ibid. Franz Willmann escaped death on the battlefield, but died of encephalitis shortly after the war. Shelley later wrote Franz's mother: "The chasm between my radical pacifism (for want of a better term) and Franz'[s] support of the war seemed too wide to attempt to bridge. The passing years have only confirmed my conviction that war is a crime in which no one should participate, no matter what the provocation." Shelley to mother of Franz [probably 1922], ibid.

41 Shelley to Franciska Schwimmer, October 27, 1956, ibid., Box 10.

42 Ibid.

43 Shelley to her father, October 11, 1915, ibid., Box 1.

44 *Detroit News*, November 2, 1915, p 7, November 6, 1915, p 1, November 7, 1915, p 15, and November 13, 1915, p 1. A summary of Shelley's activities at this time appears in the New York *Evening Post*, November 23, 1915, p 3.

45 Shelley to Mercedes M. Randall, January 14, 1958, Balch Papers,

Folder 350. Edith Wynner, Schwimmer's private secretary in later years, has supported Schwimmer's assertion that it was she who first saw Ralph Yonker about obtaining an interview with Ford, but Shelley's version seems to make more sense because she was better acquainted with the names of the newsmen in the motor city and from her first-hand experiences already knew those tactics that were doomed to failure and those that might succeed. Shelley was also less inclined than Schwimmer to claim credit for the successes of the peace movement. Edith Wynner to Rebecca Shelley, May 31, 1965, Shelley Papers, Box 10; and Edith Wynner, "Out of the Trenches by Christmas," *The Progressive*, 29 (December 1965), pp 31–32.

46 The story of Ford's conversion to active support of the neutral conference is most fully told in Rosika Schwimmer, "The Humanitarianism of Henry Ford," *B'nai B'rith News*, XI (October–November 1922), pp 9–10, which incidentally gives her version of the origins of Ford's anti-Semitic pronouncements in the early 1920s. For corroborative evidence of Ford's conversion, see *Detroit News*, November 17, 1915, p 1, and November 19, 1915, p 1; Frederic C. Howe, *The Confessions of a Reformer* (New York: Charles Scribner's Sons, 1925), pp 247–248; Lochner to Wales, November 18, 21, Wales Papers, Box 1; and Lochner to Jordan, November 20, 1915, Jordan Peace Correspondence, Box 5. Also, see, Beth S. Wenger, "Radical Politics in a Reactionary Age: The Unmaking of Rosika Schwimmer, 1914–1930," *Journal of Women's History*, 2 (Fall 1990), pp 66–99.

6 CLIMAX AND ANTICLIMAX

1 Lochner, *America's Don Quixote*, pp 14–16.

2 House Diary, November 21, 1915.

3 Addams to House, November 23, 1915, House Papers. For similar arguments by mediation proponents, see the text pp 138–139.

4 Lochner, *America's Don Quixote*, pp 20–21.

5 House Diary, November 22, 1915.

6 John M. Blum, *Joe Tumulty and the Wilson Era* (Boston: Houghton Mifflin, 1951), pp 3, 11–12, 20–24, 37–67, *passim* (quotation on p 59).

7 Wilson's and Tumulty's notes, attached to Alfred Lucking to Tumulty, November 21, 1915, Wilson Papers, Reel 74.

8 Notes by Wilson and Charles L. Swem, November 23, 1915, ibid. Ford's latest joke was about the man who asked to be buried with his Model T because it had gotten him out of every hole he'd been in. Wilson may have recited his favorite limerick:

> "For beauty I am not a star,
> There are others more handsome by far,
>   But my face, I don't mind it
>   For I am behind it—
> It's the fellow in front that I jar."

Quoted in Barbara S. Kraft, *The Peace Ship: Henry Ford's Pacifist Adventure in the First World War* (New York: Macmillan, 1978), p 66.

9 The quoted passage in Lochner, *America's Don Quixote*, p 24, is taken verbatim from the author's undated typescript [November 23, 1915], Lochner Papers.

10 Quotations in Lochner, *America's Don Quixote*, pp 24–25, are taken verbatim from Lochner's undated typescript [November 23, 1915], Lochner Papers.

11 Kraft, *Peace Ship*, p 65.

12 Lochner, *America's Don Quixote*, pp 19–20; Kraft, *Peace Ship*, pp 63–65.

13 *New York Times*, November 25, 1915, p 1.

14 Less than a month earlier, Schwimmer had argued that an unofficial conference had not the "slightest hope" of success, as she believed belligerents would not listen to proposals made by unofficial people and the European neutrals also would not object, though she conceded an unofficial agency might be feasible sometime in the future. Schwimmer to Kellogg, October 27, 1915, Schwimmer-Lloyd Papers, Box A63; Schwimmer to Katherine Lecki, November 11, 1915, ibid., Box A64.

15 Schwimmer to Wilson, October 31, 1915 (marked "not sent"), and Macmillan to Schwimmer, November 3, 1915, ibid., Box A63.

16 Pipp to George E. Miller, November 11, 1915 (telegram), Miller to Pipp, November 12, 1915, and Pipp to Miller, undated [November 13, 1915], ibid.; Shelley to Schwimmer, November 12, 1915, ibid., Box A64; Wilson's note, attached to Alfred Lucking to Tumulty, November 21, 1915, Wilson Papers, Reel 74. To maintain studious neutrality, the President's "official" position was in fact not to see nationals from belligerent countries who were not accredited representatives of their governments nor even to acknowledge their correspondence, but his acquiescence in this upcoming interview was an exception. There were others too – see pp 38, 275–276, and 291–294.

17 Schwimmer to Snowden, November 15, 1915, Schwimmer-Lloyd Papers, Box A63; and Snowden to Schwimmer, November 16, 1915, ibid., Box A64; Detroit *News*, November 19, 1915, p 1; Schwimmer to Shelley (telegram), November 21, 1915, Shelley Papers, Box 1. Snowden is quoted in *New York Times*, July 6, 1915, p 2.

18 Several newspapers stated that Mrs Ford's gift amounted to ten thousand dollars, but Addams' figure of eight thousand dollars is probably more accurate. Jane Addams, *Peace and Bread in Time of War* (New York: Macmillan, 1922), p 27. The initial telegram read: "For the sake of all the anxious mothers dreading that their sons may be added to the ten millions already killed or crippled in this war, will you strengthen the appeal to be made next Friday by Ethel Snowden of England and Rosika Schwimmer of Hungary to President Wilson by telegraphing him immediately at Washington somewhat as follows: 'We urge a conference of neutral nations dedicated to find a just settlement of the war.' " Quoted in New York *World*, November 24, 1915, p 4.

19 Addams, *Peace and Bread*, pp 27–28; New York *World*, November 26, 1915, p 4.

20 Washington *Star*, November 26, 1915, pp 1, 2.

21 New York *World*, November 27, 1915, p 1; Mrs Snowden's typewritten statement of the interview, quoted in Detroit *News*, November 28, 1915, p 1.

22 Mrs Philip Snowden, *A Political Pilgrim in Europe* (New York: George H. Doran, 1921), pp 45–46. Snowden likely used her typewritten account of the interview cited in the previous note as the basis for her published account.

23 Schwimmer to Wales, November 26, 1915 (telegram), Wales Papers, Box 1; Washington *Star*, November 26, 1915, p 1; New York *World*, November 27, 1915, p 3.

24 *New York Times*, November 30, 1915, p 1.

25 Among the many studies of and reminiscences about Henry Ford, I have particularly relied on Allan Nevins and Frank Ernest Hill, *Ford: Expansion and Challenge, 1915–1933* (New York: Charles Scribner's, 1957), the second of a three-volume biography; Keith Sward, *The Legend of Henry Ford* (New York: Rinehart, 1948), a debunking but still perceptive biography; Anne Jardim, *The First Henry Ford: A Study in Personality and Business Leadership* (Cambridge, Mass.: The MIT Press, 1970), which takes a psycho-biographical approach; and Lochner, *America's Don Quixote*, for a close-up view of Ford during his peace ventures.

26 Lochner to Jordan, November 20, 1915, Jordan Peace Correspondence, Box 5.

27 Samuel S. Marquis, *Henry Ford: An Interpretation* (Boston: Little, Brown, 1923), p 50. Frederic Howe, who frequently attempted to win Ford's endorsement of liberal causes, concurred with that judgment: "His mind leaped from starting-point to conclusion. Intermediate factors were as though they did not exist." Howe, *Confessions of a Reformer*, p 247.

28 Kraft, *Peace Ship*, p 62. Nevins and Ernest Hill, *Ford: Expansion and Challenge*, pp 31–32, suggest that Ford may have derived his pacifist sympathies from his parents, who had little love for the military, and from his reading of antiwar selections from McGuffey readers in school, but these explanations are not convincing. Ford never acknowledged their influence and, as Nevins and Hill admit, other evidence is speculative.

29 Lochner, *America's Don Quixote*, pp 6–8; Kraft, *Peace Ship*, 85.

30 Ibid., pp 67–68.

31 Lochner, *America's Don Quixote*, pp 30–32, 36–37; The Reminiscences of Mr. E.G. Liebold (Ford Motor Company Archives, Oral History Section), January 1953, p 258.

32 Clara Ford, note attached to Ellen Starr Brinton to Clara Ford, April 28, 1948, Fair Lane Papers (Ford Motor Company Archives), Box 53. Edsel Ford was 22 years old at the time.

33 Lochner, *America's Don Quixote*, pp 6–7, 26.

34 In this view, according to Jardim, *First Henry Ford, passim*, the key element was Ford's childhood, which involved his unwarranted rejection of his father. Following his father's death in 1905, the son, suffering from a guilty conscience, sought to make amends for his faults by producing the Model T and the tractor, both of which were intended to alleviate the drudgery of farm work which his father had endured. The same sense of guilt led him to other good works, including a five dollar a day pay for his employees (a very progressive innovation in his time) and his peace ship. And when the latter effort failed, he came increasingly narcissistic in the late 1910s and projected his aggressive feelings against others, including his own company associates and the Jews, and even his own son. The result in Ford's later years was a serious decline in the fortunes of his car company.

35 See, for example, Kay R. Jamison, *Exuberance* (New York: Alfred A. Knopf, 2004) and John Gartner, *The Hypomanic Edge* (New York: Simon and Schuster, 2005). Gartner's book, a study of American historical personalities with hypomanic symptoms, includes a brief discussion of Henry Ford. A layman's summary of the emerging literature on hypomania is in the *New York Times*, March 22, 2005, p D1.

36 *New York Times*, November 13, 1915, p 6.

37 A biography touting his populism is Steven Watts, *The People's Tycoon: Henry Ford and the American Century* (New York: Alfred A. Knopf, 2005).

38 Ford's benevolence toward his workers ("people") was matched by his suspicions about them. Thus when he announced in January 1914 the five-dollar day for workers at his plants, thereby doubling their wages, he also introduced a "sociological department" to spy on workers' homes for evidence of drinking (Ford was a prohibitionist), marital problems, and other examples of "unwholesome living." Workmen who did not pass the "character" test, perhaps 5 to 10 percent, had their wages cut in half. Sward, *Legend of Henry Ford*, ch 4.

39 Two interpretations of the development of Ford's anti-Semitic views are Albert Lee, *Henry Ford and the Jews* (New York: Stein and Day, 1980), and Neil Baldwin, *Henry Ford and the Jews: The Mass Production of Hate* (New York: PublicAffairs, 2001).

40 Lochner to Jordan, November 27, 28, 1915, FPP Papers, Box 1; Jordan to Jessie Jordan, November 26, December 1, 2, 1915, Jordan Peace Correspondence, Box 5; Holt to Ford, November 26, 1915, FPP Papers, Box 1; Anna Garlin Spencer to Ford, December 1, 1915, and Lucia Ames Mead to Lochner, [*c.* late November 1915], ibid., Box 3.

41 Bryan to Ford, November 29, 30, 1915, Wald to Ford, November 30, 1915, and John Haynes Holmes to Ford, November 30, 1915, ibid.

42 Crystal Eastman Benedict to Jane Addams, November 27, December 3, 1915, WPP Correspondence, New York Branch File. In addition to Holt, Wald, and Eastman, other Henry Street conferees declining Ford's invitation included Villard, Peabody, Kirchwey, Balch, and Kellogg. Kraft, *Peace Ship*, pp 82, 83.

43 Detroit *News*, November 27, 1915, p 1; *New York Times*, December 1, 1915, p 3. Addams recounted her health problems in some detail in letters to her niece, Marcet Haldeman, September 11, 1915, October 3, 10, 1915, and January 26, 1915, JAMC. Harriet P. Thomas to Lucy Biddle Lewis, February 1, 1916, WPP Correspondence, Lucy Lewis File, gives the doctor's diagnosis of Addams'

illness. Her retrospective account is Addams, *Peace and Bread*, pp 33–41.

44 Besides Sewall, Wales, and Schwimmer's friends—Holbrook, Lloyd, and Shelley—the only other woman who was part of both the earlier Hague congress and the Ford peace ship was Wales' friend, Grace DeGraff. Kraft, *Peace Ship*, pp 81, 90, 107, 112–114.

45 Ibid., pp 68–71, 84–87, 115–117.

46 Secor to Loretta Secor, January 10, 1916, *Lella Secor: A Diary in Letters, 1915–1922*, ed. Barbara Moench Florence (New York: Burt Franklin, 1978), p 25. Two decades later, Secor continued to bewail her colleagues' shoddy reporting: "I don't suppose half a dozen ever tried to discover just what the promoters of the expedition had in their minds, or to examine dispassionately the merits or flaws of their proposals . . . I feel ashamed of the unscrupulous behaviour of my colleagues. We were treated with extraordinary kindness . . . This was repaid, on our part, by insolence and scandal-mongering . . . With the exception of a half dozen journalists, hardly a fair and decent story was sent out from the Ford Peace Ship." Lella Secor Florence, "The Ford Peace Ship and After," *We Did Not Fight: 1914–18 Experiences of War Resisters*, ed. Julian Bell (London: Cobden-Sanderson, 1935), pp 100–101, 106.

47 In addition to other sources cited in this chapter, complementary accounts documenting dissension in the Ford party are: Elmer Davis, The Ford Peace Ship (Columbia Oral History Research Project, 1959), *passim*; The Reminiscences of Ben W. Huebsch (Columbia Oral History Research Project, 1965), pp 130–166; Julia Grace Wales, A Condensed Statement of my Experience with the Ford Conference, undated Wales Papers, Box 1; Lewis A. Maverick Diary, Schwimmer-Lloyd Papers, Box E11; and Burnet Hershey, *The Odyssey of*

Henry Ford and the Great Peace Ship (New York: Taplinger, 1967), pp 99–189.

48 Lochner, *America's Don Quixote*, pp 60–64, 70–75; Secor to Lida Hamm, December 9, 1915, *Lella Secor*, pp 11–13; and Secor's press release to Washington state newspapers, December 13, 1915, ibid., pp 276–278. Synopses of personal and editorial reactions, mostly unfavorable, to the peace ship are "Henry Ford in Search of Peace," *Literary Digest*, 51 (December 11, 1915), pp 1333–1338, and "Rocking the Peace-Boat," ibid., 52 (February 5, 1916), pp 341–343.

49 Marquis, *Henry Ford*, p 19; Lochner, *America's Don Quixote*, pp 85–91.

50 *New York Times*, January 3, 1916, p 1.

51 Irving Caesar, Diary, March 5, 1916, Accession 167 (Ford Motor Company Archives), Box 1; Kraft, *Peace Ship*, pp 126, 132–133, 139–141, 180–181.

52 Quoted ibid., p 138. The *New York Times*, January 31, 1916, p 2, reproduced one of Bullitt's detailed dispatches. Lochner, *America's Don Quixote*, p 75.

53 Kraft, *Peace Ship*, pp 123–124.

54 Plantiff to Liebold, January 7, 1916, quoted in Kraft, *Peace Ship*, p 182.

55 Ibid., pp 168–169, 184–186, 190, 192–193.

56 Quoted ibid., p 124.

57 Caesar, Diary, March 5, 1916, Ford Archives, Box 1.

58 Quoted in Kraft, *Peace Ship*, p 138. The *New York Times*, January 31, 1916, p 2, reproduced one of Bullitt's detailed dispatches.

59 Quoted in Lochner, *America's Don Quixote*, p 66.

60 Caesar, Diary, December 13, 1915, Ford Archives, Box 1; Aked is quoted ibid., February 24, 1916.

61 Irving Caesar manuscript, How I Stopped World War I (1947) (Ford Motor Company Archives), pp 20–21.

62 Caesar, Diary, February 6, 29, March 5, 1916, *passim*, Ford Archives, Box 1.

63 Wales to Lochner, February 25, 1916,

Lochner Papers; Lochner to Ford, March 13, 1916, FPP Papers, Box 6; Lochner to Addams, March 14, 1916, Addams Papers, Box 6.

64 Kraft, *Peace Ship*, pp 175–179, 189; Lochner, *America's Don Quixote*, p 114; Bryan to Jordan, May 6, 1916, Jordan Peace Correspondence, Box 6.

65 Kraft, *Peace Ship*, pp 189–198, 201–206.

66 Ada Morse Clark to Addams, February 20, 1916, Lochner Papers.

67 Lochner, *America's Don Quixote*, p 115; Kraft, *Peace Ship*, pp 207–209. A list of the members is ibid., pp 306–309.

68 Ibid., pp 207, 217–227; quotation in Lochner, *America's Don Quixote*, pp 138–140.

69 *New York Times*, March 12, 1916, p 5, and March 17, 1916, p 20; Clark to Shelley, June 5, 1916, Shelley Papers, Box 1; quotation in Lochner, *America's Don Quixote*, pp 141–145.

70 Lochner to Ford, March 30, 1916, FPP Papers, Box 6 (emphasis in original); *New York Times*, April 20, 1916, p 7, and June 18, 1916, p 3; B. de Jong van Beek en Donk, "Reorganized Neutral Conference," typescript, May 25, 1916, Balch Papers, Box 22; Lochner, *America's Don Quixote*, pp 145–151; Kraft, *Peace Ship*, pp 209–210.

71 Clark to Jordan, July 6, 1916, Jordan Peace Correspondence, Box 6; Kraft, *Peace Ship*, pp 230–231; Balch to Jacobs, November 15, 1916, Jacobs Papers.

72 Liebold, Reminiscences, pp 265–266, Ford Archives; Lochner to Liebold, February 14, 28, and March 1, 1916 (telegrams), FPP Papers, Box 6; Lochner, *America's Don Quixote*, pp 120–122.

73 *New York Times*, May 18, 1916, p 4; Jordan to Jessie Jordan, April 3, 1916, Jordan Peace Correspondence, Box 6.

74 Lochner, *America's Don Quixote*, pp 168–171.

75 Lochner to Ford, August 10, 1916, FPP Papers, Box 6.

7 TWO DISCOMFITING EPISODES

1 *Year Book of the Woman's Peace Party, 1916*, pp 48, 54–57; Steinson, *American Women's Activism*, pp 130–148.

2 *Washington Star*, January 13, 1916, p 11.

3 Addams made this statement to a Senate committee on January 13, 1916, only a few hours after seeing Wilson. *Hearing Before the Committee on Military Affairs, United States Senate, Sixty-fourth Congress, First Session: Conference of Neutral Nations* (Washington: Government Printing Office, 1916), p 8. She quoted Wilson's remarks again, adding the "much handled and read" part, in *Report of the International Congress of Women, Zurich, May 12 to 17, 1919* (Geneva: Women's International League for Peace and Freedom [1920]), p 196. Still later, she wrote that Wilson told her at their meeting "in August [actually July], 1915, that they were the best formulation he had seen up to that time." *Peace and Bread*, p 59. Perhaps he told her that then (as well as in January 1916), but more likely she recalled the sequence of events incorrectly.

4 Regarding Dickinson, see note 4, p 362; Baker to Wilson, January 6, 1915, and Wilson to Baker, January 11, 1915, *PWW*, 32, pp 24, 53; Swartz, *Union of Democratic Control*, pp 30, 63, 96. It is also possible that Wilson read newspaper accounts of the planks of the newly founded Woman's Peace Party in Washington, DC, in January 1915, which formed the basis for the women's Hague resolutions a few months later. Knock, *To End All Wars*, pp 34–38, is more

persuasive on Wilson's conclusions, by the first months of 1915, on the need for new measures to reform the dysfunctional international system than on the crystallization of specific principles, which he would not forcefully expound upon until 1917–1919. Addams to Marcet Haldeman, April 11, 1916, JAMC. Two months later, Addams was still having occasional "hemorrhaging" attacks. Grace Abbott to Balch, June 12, 1916, Balch Papers, Box 7.

5 New York *Call*, March 4, 1915, p 4.

6 Morris Hillquit, *Loose Leaves from a Busy Life* (New York: Macmillan, 1934), pp 160–161. The manifesto differed from the women's Hague resolutions only in demanding no indemnities and "industrial democracy" and in omitting any reference to the national manufacture of munitions and freedom of the seas.

7 Harry Lane (D, Ore.) introduced the same resolution in the Senate. *Congressional Record*, 64th Congress, 1st session, 53 (December 6, 1915), p 32, and (December 13, 1915), p 328. The resolutions died in committee. Testimony supporting the resolutions is in *Hearings Before the Committee on Foreign Affairs, House of Representatives, Sixty-fourth Congress, First Session: Commission for Enduring Peace* (Washington: Government Printing Office, 1916), and Senate Committee on Military Affairs, *Conference of Neutral Nations*.

8 Walter Lanfersiek (executive secretary of the Socialist party) to Wilson, January 15, 1916, *PWW*, 35, p 487.

9 Hillquit, *Loose Leaves from a Busy Life*, p 161; New York *Call*, January 26, 1916, p 1.

10 Hillquit, *Loose Leaves from a Busy Life*, pp 161–162. A less detailed version of the same interview is James H. Maurer, *It Can Be Done: The Autobiography of James H. Maurer* (New York: Rand School Press,

1938), pp 215–216. Maurer also wrote that he met again with Wilson on mediation and preparedness [e]xactly a month later" (p 216), but his name does not appear on the President's schedule (Wilson Papers, Reel 3). Maurer had difficulty recalling events for his memoirs, which he began writing more than a decade later, and may have confused it with other meetings he had with the President. Hillquit to Maurer, May 13, 1927, Morris Hillquit Papers (Wisconsin Historical Society), Reel 3.

11 Link, *Wilson*, 4, pp 115–141, 164. A full discussion of this problem is also in *Intimate Papers of Colonel House*, 2, pp 271–292.

12 New York *Evening Post*, December 10, 1914, p 1, and December 19, 1914, p 3. Jane Addams, Lucia Mead, Anna Garlin Spencer, Alice Thacher Post, and Sophonisba P. Breckinridge to Wilson, October 29, 1915, *PWW*, 35, pp 134–135. For the extensive correspondence on military preparedness, some of it friendly, between Wilson and antipreparedness and peace advocates from late 1914 through 1915, see above pp 144–145.

13 For the preparedness movement, see John Patrick Finnegan, *Against the Specter of a Dragon: The Campaign for American Military Preparedness, 1914–1917* (Westport, Conn.: Greenwood Press, 1974), which includes a chapter on the antipreparedness opposition; and Marchand, *American Peace Movement and Social Reform*, pp 238–248.

14 Pinchot to Wilson, January 27, 1916, *PWW*, 36 (1981), pp 22–23, and Wise's statement in *Hearings Before the Committee on Military Affairs, House of Representatives, Sixty-fourth Congress, First Session: To Increase the Efficiency of the Military Establishment of the United States* (Washington: Government Printing Office, 1916), p 1332.

15 Specifically, the AUAM program

called for a congressional investigation of defense spending, nationalization of munitions-making, preparation for a "concert with South America" and a Pan American Union, and fellowship with Pacific and Asian peoples. (Also see note 20 below.) Crystal Eastman estimated that in the fall of 1916 (when the membership was likely at its peak) the AUAM had 1,000 contributing members and 5,000 noncontributing members. AUAM pamphlet, October 1916, reproduced in *Crystal Eastman on Women and Revolution*, pp 251–252.

16 High-minded, conservative college administrators Nicholas Murray Butler and Samuel Train Dutton were well-known spokesmen against increases in military preparedness, and they derided the military boosters, but they shied away from direct citizen protests. Moreover, Butler, a leader in the Republican party, backed away from antipreparedness when it became a political issue. More conservative "progressives" attacked preparedness in part because it conflicted with their opposition to big government. Thus Amos Pinchot expressed pronounced progressive views, but his radicalism (which included writing for the impertinent *Masses* magazine) was mostly cultural. Politically, he perceived the federal government's role as mainly negative in breaking up monopolies and special interests, and he rejected centralized authority, including socialism. Antipreparedness conformed to his notions of small government and equal opportunity.

17 Roy W. Howard to Pinchot, May 24, 1916, Amos Pinchot Papers (Manuscript Division, Library of Congress), Box 24; Finnegan, *Against the Specter of a Dragon*, pp 106–107.

18 Villard, "Preparedness Is Militarism," *Annals of the American Academy of Political and Social Science*, 66 (July 1916), pp 217–224. The latter slogan

was displayed at an antipreparedness rally on a banner stretching across Carnegie Hall. *New York Times*, April 7, 1916, p 3.

19 *New York Times*, February 14, 1916, p 2; John Spargo to Wilson, February 11, 1916, Wilson Papers, Reel 327; Crystal Eastman, in *Yearbook of the Woman's Peace Party, 1916*, p 17; Frederic Howe, "Democracy or Imperialism – the Alternative That Confronts Us," *Annals of the American Academy of Political and Social Science*, 66 (July 1916), pp 250–258. Howe, an AUAM stalwart, produced a full account of the role of economic interests in causing the World War. See his *Why War* (Seattle: University of Washington Press, 1916).

20 Liaison between the two groups also included the AUAM's renting of space in the WPP's New York office whenever it needed to hold meetings in New York instead of its Washington headquarters. Other parts of the AUAM program included creation of a joint commission to investigate increasing tensions between the United States and Asian nations, and the establishment of the principle that foreign investments should be made without any claim to military protection. Some AUAM flyers, broadsides, articles (mainly by Crystal Eastman), and correspondence are reproduced in Blanche Wiesen Cook, ed., *Toward the Great Change: Crystal and Max Eastman on Feminism, Antimilitarism, and Revolution* (New York: Garland, 1976), pp 213ff. Eastman is quoted in Cook's introduction, p 23. A WPP brochure featuring the dinosaur motif is in the Pinchot Papers, Box 26.

21 The testimony, respectively, of Addams, John A. McSparren, William I. Hull, Wald, Maurer, Wise, Howe, and Villard, among the more prominent pacifists and antimilitarists, is in *Hearings Before the Committee on Military Affairs, United States*

Senate, Sixty-fourth Congress, First Session: Preparedness for National Defense (Washington: Government Printing Office, 1916), pp 201–213, 1240–1246, 1265–1266, 1269–1273, 1323–1330, 1330–1337, 1357–1365, and 1367–1377, and of Villard, Wald, Maurer, and L. Hollingsworth Wood in *To Increase the Efficiency of the Military Establishment of the United States*. Moreover, in their testimony promoting the neutral conference proposal (see notes 3 and 7 above), pacifists often included antipreparedness arguments as part of their vision of international reform.

22 Link, *Wilson*, 4, pp 42–48. Wilson's speeches on the tour are in *PWW*, 36, pp 7–16, 26–48, 52–73, 75–85, 87–122. The quotations are from Wilson's speech in St Louis, p 120.

23 Wise, Pinchot, and Berle (except for one city) made the entire tour; the pacifist clergymen Charles E. Jefferson and John Haynes Holmes, Socialists Maurer and Allen L. Benson, Scott Nearing, professor of political economy at the University of Toledo, and the crusading reformer and Congregational minister Herbert Bigelow addressed one or more of the meetings. Antimilitarists' summaries of their tour include a long letter by Berle in the *Springfield Republican*, April 21, 1916, p 8; and "Swinging Around the Circle Against Militarism," *The Survey*, 36 (April 22, 1916), pp 95–96. A common complaint by the antimilitarist participants was that the local press in the cities deliberately ignored or downplayed the meetings.

24 Peabody to Tumulty, October 16, 1915, Wilson Papers, Reel 274; Jordan to Crystal Eastman, March 3, 1916, Jordan Peace Correspondence, Box 5.

25 Realizing he had exaggerated, Wilson substituted "most adequate" for "greatest" in the official published text. New York *Evening Post*, March 24, 1916, p 9; Link, *Wilson*, 4, pp 48n., 50. Concerning his statement, Wilson confessed to Walter Lippmann: "Oratorical afflatus, very endemic, ashamed." Diary of Walter Lippmann, March 22, 1916, *PWW*, 36, p 658.

26 *Washington Wife: Journal of Ellen Maury Slayden from 1897–1919* (New York: Harper & Row, 1962), p 280.

27 Link, *Wilson*, 4, pp 38–42; Wise to Wilson, November 12, 1915, and Wilson to Wise, November 18, 1915, *PWW*, 35, pp 194–195, 212.

28 On the tour Wise objected to the comments of Benson, who would soon become the Socialist party's nominee for president, for his criticism of Wilson, but other AUAM members came to Benson's defense. Cook, Woodrow Wilson and the Antimilitarists, p 60.

29 Hallinan to Wise, March 8, 1916, and Kellogg to Addams, March 9, 1916, Addams Papers, Box 6; Pinchot to Baker, March 10, 1916, Pinchot Papers, Box 26; Daniel R. Beaver, *Newton D. Baker and the American War Effort* (Lincoln: University of Nebraska Press, 1966), pp 1–3, *passim*. Baker was a student at Johns Hopkins University when Wilson was a visiting professor there. They apparently met then, but were not in regular contact until Baker's appointment as secretary of war.

30 *New York Times*, February 19, 1916, p 7.

31 Link, *Wilson*, 4, chs 5–6.

32 Wald to Wilson, April 21, 1916, *PWW*, 36, pp 524–525; Wilson's two notes to Tumulty, and Warren F. Johnson (Tumulty's secretary) to Wilson [all April 27, 1916], ibid., p 562; House Diary, April 2, 1916, ibid., p 402. Wilson had also refused antimilitarists' earlier requests for a hearing. L. Hollingsworth Wood (secretary of the American League to Limit Armaments) to Wilson, August 14, 1915, enclosing numerous citizens' petitions against preparedness,

and Jordan to Wilson (telegram), August 13, 1915, with undated notation on the latter by the President's stenographer that the President's "engagements prevent interviews of that sort." Wilson Papers, Reel 325.

33 Hallinan to AUAM members, May 2, 1916, Pinchot Papers, Box 24; New York *Evening Post*, February 15, 1916, p 1, and February 22, 1916, p 7; *New York Times*, February 23, 1916, p 7, and April 8, 1916, p 8; "Peace and Prohibition in Nebraska," *The Independent*, 86 (May 1, 1916), p 165; Ellis O. Jones, "Those Henry Ford Votes," ibid. (May 15, 1916), p 241.

34 Max Eastman substituted at the last minute for Maurer who fell sick and could not attend. Press reports named additional AUAM members at the interview; of those mentioned, Hallinan, Kellogg, Alice Lewisohn, and Crystal Eastman were in Washington the same day at AUAM meetings (AUAM minutes, May 8, 1916, Pinchot Papers, Box 24), but neither their actual presence at the interview nor that of others mentioned in newspaper accounts could be confirmed.

35 The AUAM memorial and interview is in *PWW*, 36, pp 632–648. The transcript incorrectly has Maurer in attendance (see previous note).

36 New York *Evening Post*, May 8, 1916, p 1; *New York Times*, May 11, 1916, p 2. Wald is quoted ibid., May 16, 1916, p 5. Max Eastman, "The Masses at the White House," *Masses*, 5 (July 1916), p 16.

37 *New York Times*, May 16, 1916, p 5; Cook, Woodrow Wilson and the Antimilitarists, p 66.

38 Slayden, *Washington Wife*, p 277.

39 Link, *Wilson*, 4, pp 327–338 (quotation on p 337).

40 Hallinan to Jordan, May 23, 1916, Jordan Peace Correspondence, Box 6; *New York Times*, May 19, 1916, p 1; *Chicago Tribune*, June 9, 1916, p 12; Hallinan and Eastman are quoted in AUAM minutes, August 7, 1916

and October 23, 1916, respectively, American Union Against Militarism Papers (Swarthmore College Peace Collection). In 1913, Hensley had persuaded the House to adopt a similar amendment (but not acted on in the Senate) endorsing a British proposal for a one-year "holiday" in battleship construction. Wilson had then liked Hensley's idea and also Secretary of the Navy Daniels' bolder proposal for hosting a disarmament conference in Washington, but nothing had come of these suggestions. Patterson, *Toward a Warless World*, pp 218–220; Charles H. Levermore to Wilson, March 24, 1916, and Wilson to Levermore, March 28, 1916, *PWW*, 36, pp 362–363, 374.

41 Arthur S. Link, *Wilson: Campaigns for Peace and Progressivism, 1916–1917* (Princeton, N.J.: Princeton University Press, 1965), pp 60–65. Hereafter Link, *Wilson*, 5.

42 Quoted in Tumulty, *Woodrow Wilson As I Know Him* (Garden City, N.Y.: Doubleday, Page, 1921), pp 157–160. Professor Link, who is skeptical about the authenticity of some of Tumulty's recollections of his meetings with Wilson, believes that Tumulty's account in this instance is genuine and questions the accuracy of only a few sentences on "valour" at the end, which are not quoted here. Link, *Wilson*, 4, pp 213–214.

43 Ibid., pp 206–218, 280–314. Besides Link, I have particularly benefited from Clarence C. Clendenen, *The United States and Pancho Villa: A Study in Unconventional Diplomacy* (Ithaca, N.Y.: Cornell University Press, 1961); Frank E. Vandiver, *Black Jack: The Life and Times of John J. Pershing* (2 vols, College Station: Texas A&M University Press, 1977), vol 2; and Friedrich Katz, *The Secret War in Mexico: Europe, the United States, and the Mexican Revolution* (Chicago: University of Chicago Press, 1981), pp 327–351.

44 On Peabody's business holdings in Mexico and his views on US–Mexican relations, see Louise Ware, *George Foster Peabody: Banker, Philanthropist, Publicist* (Athens: University of Georgia Press, 1951), pp 133, 141, 172–173, 192, *passim.*

45 Villard and 20 others (AUAM) to Wilson, June 21, 1916 (telegram), Religious Society of Friends to Wilson, June 21, 1916 (telegram), Seattle AUAM to Wilson, June 22, 1916 (telegram), WPP Massachusetts branch to Wilson, June 22, 1916 (telegram), and Frederick Lynch to Wilson, June 22, 1916 (telegram), Wilson Papers, Reel 214; quotation in *New York Times*, June 24, 1916, p 4. The Mexican representatives were Luis Manuel Rojas, director of the Biblico Nacional of Mexico, Modesto C. Rolland, a civil engineer from Yucatan who had a New York Office, and Dr Atl, editor of a labor journal.

46 *New York Times*, June 24, 1916, p 4, June 23, 1916, p 1, and June 26, 1916, pp 1, 3; Newton Baker to Wilson [June 24, 1916], *PWW*, 37 (1981), p 291; Lansing memorandum, June 26, 1916, ibid., pp 306–307; Link, *Wilson*, 4, pp 311–313.

47 *New York Times*, June 26, 1916, p 3, and June 28, 1916, p 3; David Starr Jordan, *The Days of a Man: Being Memories of a Naturalist, Teacher and Minor Prophet of Democracy* (2 vols, Yonkers-on-Hudson, New York: World Book Company, 1922), 2, pp 697–698, 812. In addition to Storey, Amos Pinchot was named as one of the replacement delegates. Because of demands on his legal services in New York, however, Pinchot soon resigned; Kellogg replaced him. Pinchot to Storey, July 6, 1916 (telegram), Pinchot Papers, Box 24.

48 *New York Times*, June 27, 1916, p 7; Pinchot to Wilson, June 28, 1916 (telegram), *PWW*, 37, pp 320–321.

49 A large sample is Leo S. Rowe to Wilson, June 23, 1916, Boston AUAM to Wilson, June 23, 1916 (telegram), New York AUAM to Wilson, June 23, 1916 (telegram), Chicago AUAM to Wilson, June 24, 1916 (telegram), Pennsylvania WPP to Wilson, June 26, 1916 (telegram), Religious Society of Friends to Wilson, June 26, 1916, George Burnham, *et al.*, to Wilson, June 26, 1916, Jordan to Wilson, June 26, 1916 (telegram), and Mrs J. Malcolm Forbes to Wilson, June 27, 1916 (telegram), Wilson Papers, Reel 80; *New York Times*, June 25, 1916, p 5. Also, WPP Executive Board to Wilson, June 27, 1916, Robert Underwood Johnson to Wilson, June 27, 1916, Arthur Hoag Howland to Wilson, June 27, 1916, John Palmer Gavit to Wilson, June 27, 1916, and Charles W. Eliot to Wilson, June 28, 1916, *PWW*, 37, pp 308, 309, 310–311, 313–314, 322.

50 Link, *Wilson*, 4, p 315.

51 For example, Resolutions of the New York AUAM, WPP, and other groups, June 28, 1916, Wilson Papers, Reel 214.

52 Overstreet, Fisher, and Gertrude Pinchot to Wilson, June 27, 1916, *PWW*, 37, pp 308–309, and pp 316–317n.; *New York Times*, June 30, 1916, p 3.

53 *PWW*, 37, p 316.

54 Frederic C. Howe to Wilson, June 28, 1916, Cleveland Hoadley Dodge to Wilson, June 29, 1916, John Temple Graves to Tumulty, June 29, 1916, and Warren Worth Bailey to Wilson, July 1, 1916, *PWW*, 37, pp 321, 330–331, 331–332, and 342–343. The journalist is quoted in Link, *Wilson*, 4, pp 315–316.

55 Link, *Wilson*, 5, p 51.

56 Wilson to Ralston, June 29, 1916, Wilson Papers, Reel 214; Wilson to Pinchot, June 30, 1916, Wilson to Eliot, June 30, 1916, and Wilson to Howe, June 30, 1916, *PWW*, 37, p 336.

57 Link, *Wilson*, 4, pp 314–318.

58 Jordan, *Days of a Man*, 2, pp 699–700; the quotation is on p 700. Leo S. Rowe to Storey, July 6, 1916, Moorfield Storey Papers (Manuscript Division, Library of Congress), Mexican Commission Correspondence, Box 4. Minutes of the unofficial commission's first two sessions, July 6 and 8, 1916, and Kellogg's letters to Storey, July 10, 25, and August 2, 1916, summarizing later sessions (which were sometimes held in New York and Boston), are ibid. Kellogg, "New Era of Friendship for North America," *The Survey*, 36 (July 15, 1916), pp 415–417.

59 *New York Times*, July 6, 1916, p 3; Clendenen, *United States and Pancho Villa*, p 201.

60 Steffens, "Into Mexico and – Out!" *Everybody's Magazine*, 34 (May 1916), pp 533–547; *The Letters of Lincoln Steffens*, eds. Ella Winter and Granville Hicks (2 vols, New York: Harcourt, Brace, 1938), 1, pp 361–376; *The Autobiography of Lincoln Steffens* (New York: Harcourt, Brace, 1931), pp 736–738.

61 Executive Office Diary, July 6, 1916, Wilson Papers, Reel 3; *Letters of Lincoln Steffens*, 1, pp 376–378; *Autobiography of Lincoln Steffens*, pp 738–740 (quotations on pp 738 and 739).

62 Link, *Wilson*, 5, pp 51–55, 120–123, 131–134, 328–338; Clendenen, *United States and Pancho Villa*, pp 286ff. Advocates of peace were still urging the withdrawal of all U.S. troops from Mexico into the new year. Gertrude M. Pinchot (for WPP, NY branch) to Wilson, January 5, 1917, *PWW*, 40 (1982), p 418.

8 REAPPRAISALS AND POLITICAL REALITIES

1 Casualty figure is from Keegan, *First World War*, pp 317–318. Quotations from House Diary, May 3, 1916, *PWW*, 36, p 600, and Baker memorandum [May 12, 1916], ibid., 37, pp 36–37.

2 Tumulty to Wilson, May 16, 1916, ibid., pp 58–60. Neither in his role in arranging Wilson's interviews with Schwimmer or Ford, nor in his argument for an early mediation initiative did Tumulty directly indicate any political motive for his chief's mediation move. Nevertheless, as an experienced tactician on domestic political matters, it is highly unlikely that he would have urged a Wilsonian mediation move if he did not believe it would redound in his mentor's favor during the coming re-election campaign. In early August 1916, Tumulty also had lunch at an inconspicuous hotel with Willem van Rappard, the Dutch minister in Washington, to discuss Wilson's possible peace initiatives. *PWW*, 38 (1982), p 53n2. Subsequently, even when not focused on mediation, he continued to stress the importance of foreign policy issues (or their relationship to domestic legislation) in the campaign. Tumulty to Wilson, October 23, 1916, ibid., pp 513–514. Tumulty's influence in the Wilson administration declined during the re-election campaign, however, as House lobbied successfully for his own choices for key campaign officials. After Wilson's re-election, he conspired with Mrs Wilson, who also disliked Tumulty, to oust him. Though Tumulty managed to survive as the President's secretary, his relationship with Wilson suffered thereafter. Blum, *Joe Tumulty and the Wilson Era*, pp 115–122.

3 Wilson to Tumulty, May 17, 1916, *PWW*, 37, p 62.

4 Florence, "The Ford Peace Ship and After," p 116. I am indebted here and below to Steinson, *American Women's Activism*, pp 95–105 (quotations of

p 99); and Steinson's article, " 'The Mother Half of Humanity'," pp 274–275.

5 Quotations in Steinson, *American Women's Activism*, pp 99, 100.

6 Ibid.; Addams to Wald, May 18, 1916, Wald Papers (NYPL).

7 Documentation on the organizing effort is in the WPP Correspondence, Neutral Conference 1916–1917 File; also, Kirchwey, Lynch, Holt, Walsh, and Shelley to Amos Pinchot, May 30, 1916, Pinchot Papers, Box 26; and *Lella Secor*, pp 75–105.

8 Shelley to Lloyd, April 24, 1916, Schwimmer-Lloyd Papers, Box O24; Shelley to Lloyd, June 17, 1916 (telegram), WPP Correspondence, Neutral Conference 1916–1917 File; Holt to Wilson, May 11, 1916, *PWW*, 37, p 75.

9 Steinson, *American Women's Activism*, pp 101–102.

10 The "Santa Claus" reference to Lynch may be Shelley's characterization some 60 years later. Ibid., p 97n. The Church Peace Union financial contribution to the ANCC was a loan. Holt to Schiff, August 2, 1916, WPP Correspondence, Neutral Conference 1916–1917 File; Minutes of the Fourth Meeting of the American Neutral Conference Committee, July 6, 1916, Hamilton Holt Papers (Mills Memorial Library, Rollins College), Box 66; Harriet P. Thomas to Addams, July 8, 1916, WPP Correspondence, Jane Addams File. The first quotation is in Florence, "The Ford Peace Ship and After," p 116; the second is from the letterhead of the committee's stationery.

11 Shelley to Wilson, June 13, 1916, Wilson Papers, Reel 338; Secor to Mother and All, June 18, 1916, *Lella Secor*, pp 77–79. The two women did no lobbying at the Republican convention, perhaps because of insufficient funds or their preoccupation with trying to influence Wilson and his party. Naomi W. Cohen, *Jacob H. Schiff: A Study in American Jewish Leadership* (Hanover, N.H.: Brandeis University Press, 1999), pp 91–95, 191–198. Schiff gave 500 dollars (and perhaps more) to the ANCC. Shelley to Schiff, September 11, 1916, WPP Correspondence, Neutral Conference 1916–1917 File; [Hamilton Holt] "For a Conference of Neutral Nations," *The Independent*, 87 (July 31, 1916), pp 143–144; and Irving Fisher, "Call a Neutral Conference Now," ibid., pp 153–154.

12 *Detroit News*, July 26, 1916, p 1; *Detroit Free Press*, July 27, 1916, p 1; Kraft, *Peace Ship*, pp 242–243. When Lochner read press clippings of Aked's remarks to the press, he commented to a friend: "Dr Aked certainly did everything possible to disrupt the work. He has issued a series of damnable lies that make my blood boil." Quoted in Carol W. Gelderman, *Henry Ford: The Wayward Capitalist* (New York: The Dial Press, 1981), p 128.

13 Quoted in Kraft, *Peace Ship*, pp 242–243; Lochner to Addams, July 2, 1916, Addams Papers, Box 6.

14 Addams to Wilson, August 2, 1916, and Wilson to Addams, August 5, 1916, *PWW*, 37, pp 515, 527–528; Executive Office Diary, Wilson Papers, Reel 3; Balch to Polk, August 22 [1916], and Polk to Balch, September 30, 1916, Frank L. Polk Papers (Yale University Library), Drawer 81, File 244.

15 Schwimmer to Ford, July 31, 1916, August 1, 2, 8, 1916, and Schwimmer to Addams, August 10, 19, 21 (telegram), 1916, Addams Papers, Box 6. Addams gave two rather weak excuses for not asking Ford to see Schwimmer: she was an outsider and thus "utterly unable to follow the developments of the expedition and really ought not to jump in now," and Ford, "firmly" believing she had exaggerated her illness when failing to sail with the *Oscar II*, would

"have very little respect for the opinion of such a quitter." Addams to Schwimmer, August 22, 23, 1916, Schwimmer-Lloyd Papers, Box A86.

16 Addams to Balch, August 23, 1916, Balch Papers, Box 7; Gelderman, *Henry Ford*, p 128; *New York Times*, July 8, 1916, p 3; Shelley to Balch, July 21, 1916 (telegram), July 24, 1916 (telegram), and Balch to Shelley, undated draft telegram, Balch Papers, Box 7; Holt to Jacob Schiff, August 2, 1916, WPP Correspondence, Neutral Conference 1916–1917 File; Randall, *Improper Bostonian*, p 218.

17 Secor's quotations from her letters to Loretta Secor [June 1916], and to Laura Kelley and Lida Hamm, September 4, 1916, *Lella Secor*, pp 75, 87, 86; also, Shelley to Lloyd, August 27, 1916, Schwimmer-Lloyd Papers, Box O26. Balch's long article, New York *Evening Post*, October 4, 1916, p 9; Balch quotations from her article, "The Stockholm Conference," *New Republic*, 8 (September 9, 1916), pp 141–142. Holt to Schiff, August 2, 1916, WPP Correspondence, Neutral Conference 1916–1917 File. Addams' comment is in her undated letter to Balch [September 5, 1916], Balch Papers, Box 7. Holt was then 44, or only 15 years older than Secor and Shelley, so their age difference was not significant; but the two women perceived him as "old" because of his involvement with the prewar peace movement and the League to Enforce Peace, each of which had been (or was) dominated by older males.

18 Holt, *et al.*, to Wilson, August 14, 1916, Wilson to Tumulty, August 17, 1916, Shelley to Wilson, August 28, 1916, and Wilson to Shelley, August 29, 1916, Wilson Papers, Reel 320. Of the 20 participants, the following have already been identified in this study: Balch, Dutton, Fisher, Huebsch, Holt, Jordan, Lynch, Secor, Shelley,

Fanny Villard, and Woolley. The others were Benjamin Brewster (Catholic Bishop, Maine), Desha Breckinridge (ed., Lexington, Ky. *Herald*), Philander C. Claxton (US Commissioner of Education), Herbert J. Friedman (attorney, Chicago), Sidney L. Gulick (secretary, American branch of the World Alliance for Promotion of Friendship through the Churches), John Harvey Kellogg (surgeon and author, Michigan), John Nolen (city planner, Massachusetts), Arthur W. Pope (assistant professor of philosophy, University of California, Berkeley), and Frederick Starr (associate professor of anthropology, University of Chicago). Seven others also planned to attend, but other commitments apparently prevented their participation. A list of the 27 is in the WPP Correspondence, Neutral Conference 1916–1917 File.

19 Actually, Jordan, the only presenter who mentioned Latin America, said representation from the region could be limited to the three largest ones— Argentina, Brazil, and Chile—but Wilson countered that the smaller Central and South American states were "very jealous of the ABC powers," and the United States would lose all influence with the smaller ones if they were excluded. "We have either got to invite all of them or none of them," and for Wilson the former was the less undesirable option.

20 In his last comment, Wilson may have picked up on a recent comment by the Dutch minister in Washington, as reported to him by House: "He contends, with truth, I think, that if you could get them to parley, it would be impossible for them to resume fighting no matter how impossible it was for them to arrive at terms." House to Wilson, August 19, 1916, *PWW*, 38, p 53. The White House stenographer's transcript on the entire interview is printed as A

Colloquy with Members of the American Neutral Conference Committee, August 30, 1916, ibid., pp 108–117. The stenographer's report has Holt making the first presentation when Holt only said a few words before introducing Professor Fisher as the initial speaker.

21 Wilson to Schiff, August 31, 1916, *PWW*, 38, p 123.

22 Battin to Wilson, August 29, 1916, ibid., p 104. In this letter, Battin said he would not confide the substance of his interviews with European leaders in July and August, which were only for the President if he wanted them. He was not part of the ANCC delegation to the White House.

23 Reminiscences of Ben W. Huebsch, p 170.

24 Secor to Laura Kelley and Lida Hamm, September 4, 1916, *Lella Secor*, p 94.

25 Reminiscences of Ben W. Huebsch, p 170–171.

26 Shelley to Hull, September 9, 1916, Hull Papers, Box 1, is one of several letters to supporters summarizing this consensus.

27 Jordan to Jessie Jordan, August 31, 1916, Jordan Peace Correspondence, Box 6.

28 Jordan to Tumulty, September 3, 1916, Wilson Papers, Reel 237.

29 Shelley to Hull, September 9, 1916, Hull Papers, Box 1.

30 Secor to Laura Kelly and Lida Hamm, September 4, 1916, *Lella Secor*, p 94; Schiff to Wilson, August 31, 1916, *PWW*, 38, p 123; Shelley to Schiff, September 11, 1916, WPP Correspondence, Neutral Conference 1916–1917 File; Cohen, *Jacob H. Schiff*, p 196.

31 Addams to Wald, May 12, 16, 1916, Wald Papers (NYPL).

32 Lochner to Ford, September 27, 1916, FPP Papers, Box 6.

33 Addams to Balch, August 26, 1916, and Wald to Balch, September 5, 1916, Balch Papers, Box 7; Lochner

to Ford, September 25, 1916, FPP Papers, Box 6.

34 *New York Times*, September 8, 1916, p 5; Wald to Balch, September 5, 1916, Balch Papers, Box 7; Shelley to Herbert J. Friedman, October 19, 1916, WPP Correspondence, Neutral Conference 1916–1917 File; and Jordan's letter cited in note 27 above.

35 *Crystal Eastman on Women and Revolution*, pp 6–7, 16; the quotations are in Cook, Woodrow Wilson and the Antimilitarists, pp 151–154.

36 Pinchot to Wilson, August 9, 1916, Wilson to Pinchot, August 11, 1916, Wilson to James Hay, August 11, 1916, Hay to Wilson, August 14, 1916, and Hallinan to Tumulty, August 18, 1916, Wilson Papers, Reel 343; Wilson to Pinchot, August 19, 1916, *PWW*, 38, p 52; Pinchot to Wilson, August 18, 1916 (telegram) and Hallinan to Tumulty, August 23, 1916, Wilson Papers, Reel 343.

37 The letters and telegrams, from August–December 1916, are ibid.

38 Wald raised the issue through their mutual friend, Henry Morgenthau, who served as intermediary in the correspondence. Wald to Morgenthau, September 18, 1916, Morgenthau to Wilson, September 20, 1916, and Wilson to Morgenthau, September 22, 1916, ibid.; and Wald to Morgenthau, September 25, 1916, Lillian D. Wald Papers (Columbia University Library).

39 Wise to Kellogg, August 4, 1916, Pinchot Papers, Box 24.

40 The Republican party platform had in fact been carefully crafted to repudiate Roosevelt's pro-war stance. Its call for "honest" neutrality and its condemnation of Wilson's interference with Mexico were deliberate appeals to antiwar and German-American voters, and its endorsement of "adequate" preparedness effectively conceded the issue to Wilson in return for trying to win the hyphenated voters. But party platforms were

not taken seriously in election campaigns, and in any case Hughes often departed from it by demanding a much larger army and criticizing hyphenated Americans. Cook, *Woodrow Wilson and the Antimilitarists*, pp 152, 155; Finnegan, *Against the Specter of a Dragon*, pp 159–160.

41 *New York Times*, September 18, 1916, p 5 October 15, 1916, p A12; Harriet P. Thomas to Addams, September 28, 1916, WPP Correspondence, Jane Addams File; Jordan to Jessie Jordan, November 13, 1916, Jordan Peace Correspondence, Box 7; Warren F. Kuehl, *Hamilton Holt: Journalist Internationalist, Educator* (Gainesville, Fla.: University of Florida Press, 1960), pp 61–62; Max Eastman, *Love and Revolution*, p 32. Villard privately condemned Wilson as a political opportunist, duplicitous on preparedness, and "shameful" in his treatment of African-Americans, but his newspaper endorsed Wilson in October. He never thereafter cast his vote for a victorious presidential nominee. Villard to Tumulty, February 19, 1916, and November 10, 1916, Wilson Papers, Reel 375; Cook, *Woodrow Wilson and the Antimilitarists*, pp 166–167; and Michael Wreszin, *Oswald Garrison Villard: Pacifist at War* (Bloomington: Indiana University Press, 1965), pp 61–63, *passim*. Also, *PWW*, 38, p 445n1. Allen F. Davis, "The Social Workers and the Progressive Party, 1912–1916," *American Historical Review*, 69 (April 1964), pp 671–688, describes the social workers' disillusionment with Roosevelt and his Progressive party. Of the prominent peace people in this study who voted for Wilson in 1916, only Lochner, Jordan, Peabody, and Rabbi Wise are known to have endorsed him in 1912.

42 AUAM minutes, September 7, 1916, AUAM Papers; Why Wilson? A Statement by Social Workers, manuscript in Survey Associates Papers,

Folder 329. The statement was published as an advertisement on the back page of *The Survey*, 37 (October 28, 1916).

43 Thompson, *Woodrow Wilson*, pp 128–130 (quotation on p 128).

44 *New York Times*, October 3, 1916, p 1, October 7, 1916, p 3, and October 25, 1916, p 1. Ford ran a half-page advertisement in several metropolitan newspapers (for example, ibid., November 5, 1916, p E6) entitled "Humanity – and Your Vote," explaining why he was going to vote for Wilson. For the likelihood of the two's discussions of mediation at these meetings, see ch 9.

45 New York *World*, October 7, 1916, p 2; *New York Times*, October 25, 1916, p 1.

46 Link, *Wilson*, V, pp 108–112, 160–164.

47 *New York Times*, October 20, 1915, p 1; Harriet P. Thomas to Addams, September 28, 1916, WPP Correspondence, Addams File; Hapgood to Wilson, September 16, 1916, *PWW*, 38, pp 178–179; *Crystal Eastman on Women and Revolution*, pp 16–18.

48 Wilson's speeches, ibid., pp 161–164, 481–489, and 526–533; *New York Times*, September 9, 1916, p 2. For the full limerick, see ch 6, note 8.

49 Meyer Jonah Nathan, The Presidential Election of 1916 in the Middle West (PhD dissertation, Princeton University, 1966), pp 15–26, 45–53, 122–140, 148–149, 215–252, and 270–274.

50 *New York Times*, November 10, 1916, pp 5, 12, and November 12, 1916, p 1. The only gender breakdown in the voting was in Illinois (women could vote only in presidential and local elections necessitating separate ballots), which showed that a slightly higher percentage of women than men voted for Hughes, but further west the newspaper found women much more supportive of Wilson. It also reported that the Woman's Party

(the national arm of the Washington-based Congressional Union), which had attacked the party in power for

failing to obtain women's suffrage, had failed miserably in trying to get women to desert Wilson for Hughes.

9 PEACE FEELERS IN EUROPE

1 Keegan, *First World War*, pp 306–308, 316–319, 321.

2 Roger Chickering, *Imperial Germany and the Great War, 1914–1918* (Cambridge: Cambridge University Press, 1998), pp 151–154; Stevenson, *Cataclysm*, pp 106–110, 219–230.

3 British Committee of the Women's International Congress, *Towards Permanent Peace: A Record of the Women's International Congress held at The Hague, April 28th–May 1st, 1915* (1915); Ward, *Venture in Goodwill*, pp. 14–15; the British WIL's mission statement is quoted in H.M. Swanwick, "The Women's International League," *The U.D.C.*, 1 (January 1916), p 26.

4 Ward, *Venture in Goodwill*, pp 19–20.

5 Ibid.; Wiltsher, *Most Dangerous Women*, pp 131–138; Fletcher, *Maude Royden*, pp 135–136; Barbara Winslow, *Sylvia Pankhurst: Sexual Politics and Political Activism* (New York: St Martin's Press, 1966), pp 84–88.

6 Courtney's correspondence and diaries for this period are in the Kathleen Courtney Papers (The Women's Library). Hereafter Courtney Papers, WL.

7 Swanwick, *Women and War, passim.* Examples of Royden's writings at the time include *The Women's Movement of the Future; The Making of Women: Oxford Essays in Feminism*, ed. Victor Gollancz (London: George Allen & Unwin, 1917), ch 5, and *Women and the Sovereign State* (New York: Frederick A. Stokes, 1917). British women over 30 were granted the suffrage in 1918.

8 Both quotations, in letters to Marshall, and analysis are in Fletcher, *Maude Royden*, p 137.

9 Ibid., pp 135–137; Thomas C. Kennedy, *The Hound of Conscience: A History of the No-Conscription Fellowship, 1914–1919* (Fayetteville: University of Arkansas Press, 1981), pp 146–152, 216–221, *passim* (quotation on p 147).

10 The following pages owe much to Swartz, *Union of Democratic Control*, pp 58–104, 235–237.

11 Morel to Trevelyan, June 9, 1915, quoted in Blanche Wiesen Cook, "Democracy in Wartime: Antimilitarism in England and the United States, 1914–1918," *American Studies*, 13 (Spring 1972), p 62.

12 Quotations in Swartz, *Union of Democratic Control*, p 69; and Russell to Ottoline Morrell, July 11, 1915, *The Autobiography of Bertrand Russell* (London: George Allen, 1968), vol 2, pp 52–53. Russell also found his nonresistant acquaintances too mild: "so Sunday-schooly – one feels they don't know the volcanic side of human nature, they have little humour, no intensity of will, nothing of what makes men effective." Ibid., p 53. Russell's emotional and intellectual turnings during the war years are treated in Jo Vellacott, *Bertrand Russell and the Pacifists in the First World War* (New York: St. Martin's Press, 1980), pp 12–14, 18–20, 23, *passim.*

13 Quotation in Swartz, *Union of Democratic Control*, p 71n.

14 Quotation ibid., pp 100–101.

15 Quoted ibid., p 81.

16 Liddington, *Road to Greenham Common*, pp 112–125. Quotations from the memorial are from "Peace by Negotiation," *The U.D.C.*, 1 (June 1916), p 82, and Ward, *Venture in Goodwill*, pp 14–15. Promoters of

the memorial for peace negotiations gave somewhat different numbers of signatories; another estimate for late 1916 claimed 150,000 (see below, p 278). By the fall of 1917, 221,617 individuals had signed the memorial, which also had received endorsements from labor groups totaling 900,000 members. Martin Ceadel, *Semi-Detached Idealists: The British Peace Movement and International Relations, 1854–1945* (Oxford: Oxford University Press, 2000) pp 223–224.

17 A full account of Hobhouse's background and wanderings in 1915–1916, summarized here and below, is in Fisher, *That Miss Hobhouse*, ch 13. Additional details are in A. Ruth Fry, *Emily Hobhouse: A Memoir* (London: Jonathan Cape, 1929), ch 16, *passim*; John V. Crangle and Joseph O. Baylen, "Emily Hobhouse's Peace Mission, 1916," *Journal of Contemporary History*, 14 (October 1979), pp 731–744; and Jennifer Hobhouse Balme, *To Love One's Enemies: The Work and Life of Emily Hobhouse Compiled from Letters and Writings, Newspaper Cuttings and Official Documents* (Cobble Hill, Canada: Hobhouse Trust, 1994), ch 31, *passim*.

18 Schwimmer to Hobhouse, August 18, 1914, Hobhouse to Schwimmer, August 19, 20, 21, 1914, and Schwimmer to Hobhouse, August 22, 1914, Schwimmer-Lloyd Papers, Box A41. Regarding the Christmas letters, p 52 above.

19 Quoted in Fry, *Emily Hobhouse*, p 267; for her religious outlook, also see ibid., pp 31–32, 299.

20 Quoted in Balme, *To Love One's Enemies*, p 546 (italics in text).

21 Quoted in Fisher, *That Miss Hobhouse*, p 237.

22 Henry Wickham Steed, *Through Thirty Years, 1892–1922: A Personal Narrative* (2 vols, Garden City, NY: Doubleday, Page, 1925), 2, pp 38–39, 72.

23 Macmillan to Addams, January 14,

1916, Addams Papers, Box 6. Quotations in Hobhouse to Jacobs, August 21, 1915, *Politics and Friendship*, p 159; Balme, *To Love One's Enemies*, p 548; and Courtney, *War Diary*, p 65.

24 Hobhouse to Addams, November 4, 1915 (emphasis Hobhouse's), Jacobs Papers.

25 Later, in early December 1916, Lady Courtney recorded that Simon "evades any real talk, but did come out strongly about the resentment expressed toward any offer of mediation . . . He will soon be talking of peace negotiations, and I shall not remind him of his solemn warning to us 'not to mention the word peace.' " *War Diary*, p 103.

26 Quoted in Fisher, *That Miss Hobhouse*, p 240.

27 Quoted in Fry, *Emily Hobhouse*, p 271.

28 Quoted phrases in Fisher, *That Miss Hobhouse*, p 248.

29 Quoted in Fry, *Emily Hobhouse*, p 274.

30 Quoted in Fisher, *That Miss Hobhouse*, p 242.

31 Quotations ibid., p 244.

32 Macmillan to Addams, January 14, 1916, Addams Papers, Box 6; Balch to Jacobs, November 15, 1916, Jacobs Papers. Also see Bosch, *Een Onwrikbaar Geloof in Rechtvaardigheid*, pp 575ff.

33 Quotations in Balme, *To Love One's Enemies*, pp 553, 554.

34 Quotations in Fisher, *That Miss Hobhouse*, pp 246, 247, 248; and Balme, *To Love One's Enemies*, p 557.

35 Quotation from Hobhouse's journal, ibid., p 556.

36 London *Times*, October 18, 1916, p 7, October 20, 1916, p 9 and October 31, 1916, p 7. Was Hobhouse's reporting on Louvain accurate? Building on earlier books on the Louvain events, especially the conclusions published in 1958 of an investigation by a Belgian–German committee of historians, two historians have since developed a compelling case that the Belgian citizenry

there offered no resistance to the German occupiers, who for various reasons—for example, stories of French *francs-tireurs* in the earlier Franco-Prussian war of 1870–1871 that had severely harassed occupying German troops and their easy assumption that the Belgians must have similar guerrilla units in place, panicky (and sometimes drunken) German soldiers retreating to Louvian from a counterattack by the Belgian army, the hostility of the German Protestant-dominated units to the university, a Catholic institution run by prominent Catholic clergy and professors, and friendly fire incidents—proceeded to go on a rampage, terrorizing, even summarily executing, innocent citizens. They also note that the German army deliberately set fire to parts of Louvain, including the university library, and that about one-sixth of the city was destroyed. (For her one-eighth estimates, Hobhouse had written, "I use of course approximate figures.") John Horne and Alan Kramer, *German Atrocities, 1914: A History of Denial* (New Haven, CT: Yale University Press, 2001), pp 38–42, 74–76, 105, 107, 120–122, 217–219, 412–417, *passim* (quotation in text on pp 218–219). This definitive account of German military behavior in the first stage of the war concludes that overall Entente propaganda greatly exaggerated the extent and brutality of civilian atrocities, but the German army did kill nearly 6,500 civilians, including priests, women, and children, in Belgium and France, mostly in a 10-day period in August 1914.

37 Quotation in Fisher, *That Miss Hobhouse*, p 243; also, London *Times*, November 3, 1916, p 5, November 14, 1916, p 7, November 15, 1916, p 11, and November 16, 1916, p 9.

38 Quotations in Fry, *Emily Hobhouse*, p 276; and Fisher, *That Miss Hobhouse*, p 257.

39 London *Times*, November 13, 1916, p 9 (and other London newspapers); and Hobhouse, "A German Official's View of Peace," *The Nation* (London), 20 (October 21, 1916), pp 113–114.

40 Quotation in London *Times*, November 3, 1916, p 5.

41 Ibid., November 8, 1916, p 5.

42 David Lloyd George, *War Memoirs, 1915–1916* (Boston: Little, Brown: 1933), pp 280–282 (quotation on p 281); Emmeline Pethick-Lawrence, "The Lloyd George Interview," *The Nation* (London), 20 (October 7, 1916), pp 19–20; Swartz, *Union of Democratic Control*, pp 80–81, 94, 135.

43 Lloyd George, *War Memoirs, 1915–1916*, pp 282–284 (quotation on p 283). Lloyd George also claimed in his memoirs that the course of events, which eventually resulted in a U.S. break of relations with Germany followed by its declaration of war, proved Grey's fears groundless, but he conveniently overlooked the December 1916–January 1917 period when Wilson actively solicited Germany's support for his peace initiative and the German Government sought to exploit the President's seemingly more agreeable stance on mediation. Ibid., pp 284–286.

44 Lansdowne's memorandum is reproduced, ibid., pp 288–296.

45 Ibid., pp 297–316.

46 Lochner, *America's Don Quixote*, pp 177–178; Howard to Grey, August 18, 1916, FO 115/2053. By contrast, Ambassador Spring-Rice in Washington commented that "Mr Lochner and Madame Schwimmer have acted throughout under direct German influence and their proceedings are no doubt being carefully watched and perhaps controlled in German quarters." Spring-Rice to Grey, June 23, 1916, ibid.

47 Esme Howard, *Theatre of Life: Life Seen from the Stalls* (2 vols, Boston: Little, Brown, 1936), 2, pp 159, 165–166; McKercher, *Esme Howard*,

pp 25–27, 113–118; Leipnik to Howard, March 27 [1911], Howard Papers, DHW 4/27; William Tyrrell, Minutes of the British Foreign Office, November 30, 1916, FO 371/2801 (file 240229). An example of Leipnik's reporting is his article, "The Future of the Ottoman Empire," *Contemporary Review*, 97 (March 1910), pp 291–301. Leipnik's interest in Catholicism resulted in his essay written sometime before the Great War, Die Katholische Kirche in Ungarn (The Catholic Church in Hungary), manuscript in Wickham Steed Papers (British Library). Howard converted to Catholicism when he married an Italian countess from a devout Catholic family in 1898.

48 Leipnik to Howard, November 18 [1912] and December 5 [1912], Howard Papers, DHW 4/27.

49 Leipnik to Howard, September 25 [1914], ibid.

50 Leipnik's main contact at the *Times* was Wickham Steed, the paper's foreign correspondent and a historian of the Hapsburg Empire. Steed to Leipnik, January 31, 1915, February 1, 1915, and March 30, 1915, Leipnik Correspondence (British Library). Examples of Leipnik's articles (his byline identified him as a "former correspondent for the *Times*" or a very experienced "Hungarian publicist") are London *Times*, January 20, 1915, p 9, February 2, 1915, p 7, and April 13, 1915, p 7.

51 Lochner believed that because of Leipnik's knowledge of the Central Powers, the British intelligence service had offered him a job, which Leipnik turned down. Lochner, *America's Don Quixote*, pp 194–195. Leipnik was well known in British governmental circles and corresponded with Tyrrell about possible job openings before the war. Tyrrell to Leipnik, July 1, 1912, Leipnik Correspondence, and Leipnik to Howard, July 1 [1912], Howard

Papers, DHW 4/27. It is doubtful, however, that a government position would be held for an enemy alien, even one with well-known British sympathies. Perhaps Lochner was thinking of Leipnik's reports to the foreign office (see below in text), which were a form of intelligence and may have been submitted informally and without remuneration. Tyrrell to Leipnik, October 23, 1914 (telegram), September 18, 1916, and October 23, 1916, Leipnik Correspondence (quotation in last letter).

52 Lochner to Courtney, June 27, 1916, Courtney to Cecil, July 17, 1916, and Cecil to Courtney, July 27, 1916, FO 371/2803/4177.

53 Leipnik to Howard, December 28 [1914], Howard Papers, DHW 4/27. Leipnik also knew Rosika Schwimmer, a fellow Hungarian, and was aware of her mediation campaign at the outbreak of the war. Leipnik to Schwimmer, August 12, 1914, Schwimmer-Lloyd Papers, Box A40. He likely understood that Lochner's involvement with the neutral conference was an outgrowth of her earlier activism.

54 Leipnik summarized his criticisms of Lochner's plans in a memorandum to the British Foreign Office, September 29, 1916, FO 115/2053, pp 202–206. Also, Leipnik to Howard, April 8 [1916], September 25 [1914], and April 10 [1915], Howard Papers, DHW 4/27.

55 Steed to Leipnik, March 28, 1915, Leipnik Correspondence; Lochner, *America's Don Quixote*, pp 195–196.

56 Ibid., pp 180–181.

57 *New York Times*, October 6, 1916, p 1; Lochner, *America's Don Quixote*, p 181; Lochner to Plantiff, October 21, 1916, and Lochner to Members of the Neutral Conference, October 25, 1915, FPP Papers, Box 6.

58 The letters are all quoted in full in Lochner, *America's Don Quixote*,

pp 182–183; a copy of the last-named is also in the FPP Papers, Box 6.

59 Lochner to Plantiff, December 6 and 8, 1916, ibid., Box 7. Leipnik's initial stipend was to be 1,000 dollars (20,000 dollars) per month for three months (his contract was not extended beyond that). In that era, 3,000 dollars was equivalent to an annual salary of a well-paid professional, and indeed Leipnik noted a year later that he was still living on the Ford dollars and did not yet need to find new remunerative work. Leipnik to Howard, December 17 [1917], Howard Papers, DHW 4/27.

60 Lochner, *America's Don Quixote*, p 181.

61 Press reports of Ford's meetings with Wilson never mentioned any discussions on mediation. That they were concerned with domestic politics and not with the peace question is confirmed by Mrs Wilson who later wrote of one (probably the second) meeting: "My recollection is that Vance McCormick [Democratic Party national chairman] suggested and insisted Mr Wilson see Henry Ford, while we were at Shadow Lawn, hoping by so doing he, Ford, would suggest he would finance a newspaper campaign McCormick thought would be most helpful and which he had already discussed with Ford. He invited Ford to lunch, and when he came he said something about it; but Mr Wilson told me afterwards he did not follow the matter up as Ford's ideas seemed as visionary as the Peace Ship." Barbara Francke, quoting Edith Bolling Wilson to Ray Stannard Baker, April 8, 1934, Ray Stannard Baker Collection of Wilsonia (Manuscript Division, Library of Congress), Series I, Box 69. Of course, Ford went ahead anyway with his newspaper advertisements endorsing Wilson. Also, Wilson to Ford, September 20, 1916, *PWW*, 38, p 187 and nn 1 and 2.

62 Ada Morse Clark later affirmed that Lansing had sent her boss a letter asking all U.S. diplomats to cooperate with Lochner's peace efforts in every possible way. Clark to Alfred Kliefoth, January 6, 1917, FPP Papers, Box 7; Lochner, *America's Don Quixote*, p 184.

63 *New York Times*, December 2, 1916, p 2.

64 Lochner to Balch, December 8, 1916, Balch Papers, Box 7.

65 Bethmann Hollweg to Hindenberg, January 4, 1917, Carnegie Endowment for International Peace, *Official German Documents Relating to the World War* (2 vols, New York: Oxford University Press, 1923), 2, pp 1095–1097. Bethmann was responding to a German press report about Lochner's discussion with Zimmermann indicating Germany's interest in mediation.

66 In late 1914, for example, Zimmermann co-authored a memorandum calling for military control and economic penetration of Belgium in the event of a German victory; thereafter he showed some willingness to support the war aims of the military party. Hans W. Gatzke, *Germany's Drive to the West (Drang Nach Osten): A Study of Germany's War Aims during the First World War* (Baltimore: Johns Hopkins Press, 1950), pp 13–14, 79–80, 136–137. For Zimmermann's scornful attitude toward President Wilson, see Heinrich Kanner (editor of the Vienna newspaper, *Die Zeit*), memorandum of conversation with Zimmermann, October 25, 1915, *Fall of the German Empire, 1914–1918*, ed. Ralph Haswell Lutz (2 vols, Stanford, CA: Stanford University Press, 1932), 1, p 393.

67 *New York Times*, November 26, 1916, p A2, and November 28, 1916, p 1; Bernstorff to Bethmann Hollweg, December 11, 1916, *Official German Documents*, 2, pp 1040–1041.

68 Karl E. Birnbaum, *Peace Moves and U-Boat Warfare: A Study of Imperial Germany's Policy Towards the United States* (Stockholm: Almquist & Wiksell, 1958), pp 170–173, 217–218; and Link, *Wilson*, 5, pp 184–186.

69 Birnbaum, *Peace Moves and U-Boat Warfare*, pp 225–246; Link, *Wilson*, 5, pp 210–214; Matthew Stibbe, *German Anglophobia and the Great War, 1914–1918* (Cambridge: Cambridge University Press, 2001), pp 157–164; Chickering, *Imperial Germany and the Great War*, pp 90–91 (quotation on p 91).

70 Leipnik to British Foreign Office (draft) [October 1916], FPP Papers, Box 6.

71 Lochner, *America's Don Quixote*, pp 183, 186–187; Leipnik to Tyrrell, November 28, 1916, FO 371/2801 (file 240229).

72 Minutes of the British Foreign Office, November 30, 1916, ibid.

73 For Page's frustrating trip to the United States in the late summer of 1916, see Ross Gregory, "The Superfluous Ambassador: Walter Hines Page's Return to Washington 1916," *The Historian*, 28 (May 1966), pp 389–404. British authorities were well aware of Page's isolation from the Wilson administration. The foreign secretary wrote his ambassador in Washington: "Mr Page himself, on his last visit to the United States, found how difficult it was to make the British point of view understood at Washington." Grey to Spring-Rice, November 15, 1916, FO 115/2057.

74 Minutes of British Foreign Office, November 30, 1916, FO 371/2801 (file 240229).

75 C.F. (DMI) to Campbell, December 7, 1916, Harris (Home Office) to Under Secretary of State for Foreign Affairs, December 18, 1916, Drummond to Harris, December 28, 1916, and British Foreign Office to Sir A. Johnstone (British minister at The Hague), December 9, 1916, ibid.

76 Friedrich Rosen, *Aus einem Diplomatischen Wanderleben* (4 vols in 3, Weisbaden: Limes Verlag, 1931–1959), 3–4, pp 191–192.

77 Lochner to Plantiff, December 6, 8, 13, 1916, FPP Papers, Box 7.

10 WOODROW WILSON'S INDEPENDENT MEDIATION

1 Bernstorff to Bethmann Hollweg, December 11, 1916 (received in Berlin on January 26, 1917), *Official German Documents*, 2, p 1029–1042 (quotations on p 1037).

2 Doerries, *Imperial Challenge*, pp 199–200.

3 *New York Times*, November 25, 1916, p 1, November 27, 1916, pp 1, 3, December 2, 1916, p 2, December 5, 1916, p 4, December 10, 1916, pp 4, 22, December 11, 1916, p 2. The 16 "Cosmos" articles, all entitled "All Want Peace: Why Not Have It Now?" appeared in the same newspaper between November 25 and December 18. Press renderings of ANCC activities appear in several of the following notes.

4 House Diary, November 2, 1916, *PWW*, 38, pp 607–608.

5 House Diary, November 15, 1916, ibid., p 658; Link, *Wilson*, 5, pp 188–189.

6 House Diary, November 14, 1916, *PWW*, 38, pp 646–647.

7 Wilson to House, June 22, 1916, ibid., 37, pp 280–281.

8 House Diary, November 14, 1916, ibid., 38, pp 645–647 (quotation on p 646).

9 The press incorrectly reported on November 15 that the state department had already formally protested to Germany on the issue. Wilson was furious, but Lansing told him that the American embassy had thus far made only "representations" to the

German Government. House Diary, November 15, 1916, ibid., pp 656–657 (quotation on p 657); Link, *Wilson*, 5, pp 195–196.

10 Documentation on the U.S. response to the deportations is in *FR, 1916, Supplement*, pp 858–870; for a concise summary of the issue, see Waldo H. Heinrichs, Jr., *American Ambassador: Joseph C. Grew and the Development of the United States Diplomatic Tradition* (Boston: Little, Brown, 1966), pp 27–30 (quotation on p 28).

11 Draft Prolegomenon to a Peace Note [November 25, 1916], *PWW*, 40, pp 67–70. Addams' speech is summarized above, pp 113–114.

12 See above, p 110.

13 Florence Jaffray Hurst Harriman to Wilson, August 8 1915, and Wilson to Harriman, August 16, 1915, *PWW*, 34, pp 135–136, 217, House to Wilson, May 19, 1916 and June 25, 1916, ibid., 37, pp 77, 294–295. Later in the year, Angell forwarded Wilson a long, complicated memorandum, analyzing the international situation and urging his assertive leadership in promoting certain international reform principles on the belligerents. Angell, Memorandum [c. November 20, 1916], ibid., 40, pp 10–19. When Norman Hapgood arranged to get the memorandum to Wilson, he wrote at the top that he would like it returned to him, but the President kept it in his personal files. Angell's retrospective account of his U.S. stay is in *After All: The Autobiography of Norman Angell* (London: Hamish Hamilton, 1951), ch 6.

14 House to Wilson, June 25 and 27, 1916, Wilson to House, July 2, 1916, House to Wilson, July 5, 1916, Lane to Wilson, enclosing a memorandum by Buxton, July 6, 1916, Wilson to Lane, July 7, 1916, House to Wilson, July 11, 1916, *PWW*, 37, pp 294–295, 311–312, 345, 364, 370–372, 375, 402 (quotation on p 345); Buxton to House, June 29, 1916, July 10, 1916,

August 19, 1916, and November 20, 1916, House Papers.

15 House Diary, November 18, 1916, ibid.; House to Wilson, November 20, 1916, and Wilson to House, November 21, 1916, *PWW*, 40, pp 4–6, 20–21. In his letter to the President of his meeting with Whitehouse, House added that he pressed his visitor for an analysis of reactions in the House of Commons to a Wilsonian peace move, and Whitehouse conceded that the discussion there would probably result in the peace faction losing in a close vote, with "advanced" Liberals then resigning and their places being taken by reactionaries, followed by a military dictatorship. Wilson ignored the pessimistic scenario. Indeed, House, who was rapidly getting cold feet on a presidential mediation initiative, may have concocted (or at least exaggerated) the account of Whitehouse's negative prediction to suggest the downside to Wilson's proposed mediation. At any rate, neither House in his diary nor the Briton in his description of the same meeting mentioned any discussion of the future consequences in Britain of such action, and a few weeks later Whitehouse provided Wilson with a distinctly upbeat appraisal of the likely results in Britain following a presidential mediation initiative (see text, pp 281–282).

16 Trevelyan's undated paper is in the Wilson Papers, Reel 85; it is summarized with extensive quotations in *PWW*, 40, pp 124n–125.

17 A.J.A. Morris, *C. P. Trevelyan, 1870–1958: Portrait of a Radical* (Belfast: Blackstaff Press, 1977), pp 2–3, 71–72, 116–117, 127–128, *passim*. A Morris essay focusing on Trevelyan's pre-World War foreign policy views is "C. P. Trevelyan's Road to Resignation 1906–1914: The Odyssey of an Antiwar Liberal," *Doves and Diplomats: Foreign Offices and Peace Movements*

in Europe and America in the Twentieth Century, ed. Solomon Wank (New York: Greenwood Press, 1978), ch 5. Morris offers a broader perspective of radical prewar views on foreign policy among British Liberals in *Radicalism Against War, 1906–1914: The Advocacy of Peace and Retrenchment* (London: Longman, 1972). Quotation in Swartz, *Union of Democratic Control*, p 67.

18 Gavit to Wilson, November 21, 1916, Wilson to Gavit, November 22, 1916, Gavit to Wilson, December 2, 1916, and Wilson to Gavit, December 5, 1916, *PWW*, 40, pp 29, 36, 124–127, 164. The journalist was Charles T. Thompson, whom Gavit met on the train back to New York from Washington. The clergyman was D. Anderson, who has not been further identified.

19 Wilson to House, November [December] 3, 1916, ibid., p 131; Link, *Wilson*, 5, pp 206–208.

20 Addams to Dear Madam, November 20, 1916, WPP Correspondence, Neutral Conference 1916–1917 File; Secor to Loretta Secor, December 1916, *Lella Secor*, p 117; *New York Times*, November 24, 1916, p 1, and November 26, 1916, p 1; and quotation, ibid., December 4, 1916, p 6.

21 Shelley to Schiff, September 9, 1916, WPP Correspondence, Neutral Conference 1916–1917 File.

22 Shelley and Secor, for example, had an hour-long conversation with Whitehouse who they found "simply charming." Secor to Loretta Secor [September 4, 1916], *Lella Secor*, p 98. Her letter was more likely written sometime in October.

23 Trevelyan to Wilson, November 23, 1916, *PWW*, 40, pp 178–180 (quotations on p 179).

24 *New York Times*, December 5, 1916, p 3, summarized the letter with brief quotations; the full text is in "Hands Across the Sea: An Open Letter to Americans," *The Survey*, 37 (Decem-

ber 9, 1916), pp 261–262. Gavit was mortified, as he told Wilson, that the public release of Trevelyan's earlier message included mention that it had also "been presented to the President for his consideration." According to Gavit, this was "in direct violation of the pledge which was given to me before I consented to have anything to do with the matter." Gavit to Wilson, December 2, 1916, *PWW*, 40, p 124.

25 Buckler to House, November 24, 1916, ibid., p 180.

26 House to Wilson, November 30, 1916, ibid., pp 110–111.

27 House to Wilson, December 5 and 6, 1916, ibid., pp 172, 178; *New York Times*, December 5, 1916, p 3.

28 House to Wilson, December 7 and 9, 1916, *PWW*, 40, pp 185–186, 201. During the British cabinet crisis, House had written that if Lloyd George and his allies assumed control, "England will then be under the military dictatorship that Whitehouse spoke about." House to Wilson, December 3, 1916, ibid., p 139.

29 Wilson to House, December 8, 1916, ibid., p 189 (emphasis Wilson's).

30 Wilson to Lansing, December 9, 1916, and Lansing to Wilson, December 10, 1916, ibid., pp 197–200, 209–211 (quotation on p 209).

31 House Diary, December 20, 1916, ibid., pp 304–305.

32 Ibid., pp 256–262, 273–276; and the analysis in Link, *Wilson*, 5, pp 197–199, 218–219.

33 House Diary, December 21, 1916, *PWW*, 40, pp 304–305.

34 Lansing Diary, December 3, 1916, quoted ibid., p 310n (emphasis Lansing's). Lansing had earlier written, "That German imperialistic ambitions threaten free institutions everywhere apparently has not sunk very deeply into his [Wilson's] mind. For six months I have talked about the struggle between Autocracy and Democracy, but do not see that I have

made any great impression. However I shall keep on talking." Lansing Diary, September 1916 (Manuscript Division, Library of Congress).

35 Wilson also ignored a second letter from Lansing again asking for guidance on German submarine sinkings of Allied ships. Lansing to Wilson, December 8 and 21, 1916, *PWW*, 40, pp 190–191, 313–314.

36 Lansing to Wilson, December 10, 1916, ibid., p 209.

37 Wilson to Lansing, December 21, 1916, ibid., p 307, and note 1, pp 307–311. Wilson told House some weeks later that "Lansing was not in sympathy with his [own] purpose to keep out of the war. . . . I came very near to asking for his [Lansing's] resignation when he gave out the statement regarding the last note." House Diary, January 11, 1917, ibid., p 445. Link, *Wilson*, 5, pp 221–225.

38 Zimmermann to Bernstorff, December 26, 1916, *Official German Documents*, 2, p 1005.

39 The annexationists' aims were in fact breathtaking in their broad sweep, involving major territorial sacrifices from Belgium and Russia, control over Baltic areas, and an African colonial empire. Had they been known, they would also have solidified Allied opinion even more firmly against peace negotiations until Germany was thoroughly beaten. Ibid., pp 233–237 (quotations on pp 234, 236).

40 Ibid., p 237.

41 House to Wilson, May 3, 1916, *PWW*, 36, p 600; Wilson to House, June 22, 1916, and House to Wilson, July 30, 1916, ibid., 37, pp 280–281, 502.

42 House to Wilson, December 27, 1916, ibid., 40, p 337.

43 House Diary, January 3, 1917, ibid., pp 403–405.

44 House Diary, January 11, 1917, ibid., p 445. Afterward Wilson confirmed his main purpose: "The real people I was speaking to was neither the Senate nor foreign governments, as you will realize, but the *people* of the countries now at war." Wilson to Gavit, January 29, 1917, ibid., 41 (1983), p 55 (emphasis Wilson's).

45 Link, *Wilson*, 5, pp 249–255 (quotation on p 254).

46 Still opposed to peace talks, Lansing objected in each case to the use of U.S. transmission facilities until House, with the President's backing, overruled him. A less secure and uncertain alternative for German diplomatic exchanges was to send them via the wireless (radiogram).

47 House to Wilson, January 18, 1917, *PWW*, 40, p 516.

48 Gertrude Pinchot (for WPP of New York) to Wilson (telegram), January 5, 1917, ibid., p 418; Swartz, *Union of Democratic Control*, pp 135–137; *New York Times*, December 30, 1916, p 2, and pamphlet extracts, ibid., January 6, 1917, p 2. Kirchwey, president of the American Peace Society, also quoted Trevelyan's first letter and mentioned other British broadsides advocating peace talks, including Ponsonby's, in his letter published in the *New York Times*, January 7, 1917, p G2. The title of Ponsonby's pamphlet was *Why Must the War Go On?*, and of Buxton's, *Peace This Winter: A Reply to Mr Lloyd George* (September 1916); the ANCC reprinted both.

49 A young American woman acquaintance had brought Russell's letter from England and given it to the ANCC, which then staged a press event to provide maximum public attention. It arranged for the woman to enter an ANCC luncheon meeting at the Waldorf-Astoria Hotel and dramatically present the letter to ANCC officers. Reporters were summoned and given already prepared copies. Lella Secor Florence, "Ford Peace Ship and After," p 117; and *Autobiography of Bertrand Russell*, vol 2, pp 27–32. More context is provided in *Bertrand Russell's*

America: His Transatlantic Travels and Writings: A Documented Account, eds. Barry Feinberg and Ronald Kasrils (London: George Allen, 1973), vol 1, ch 5. *New York Times*, December 23, 1916, p 1, and *Los Angeles Times*, December 23, 1916, p 12, quoted the letter in full; it was summarized, among other places, in the *Atlanta Constitution*, December 23, 1916, p 2, *Christian Science Monitor*, December 23, 1916, p 1, and *Washington Post*, December 23, 1916, p 3.

50 The *Chicago Tribune*, December 24, 1916, p 5, reported that the deputation was told the President was out, so the three gave the letter to Tumulty to deliver to the President. Nearly 20 years later, Secor recalled the deputation as if she had been one of them. Wilson, she wrote, "listened to us with polite aloofness. He assured us he would be delighted to oblige us, but there were reasons which we could not understand that prevented him from doing so." Lella Secor Florence, "Ford Peace Ship and After," pp 117–118. She probably confused in her mind the ANCC group's interview with Wilson on August 30, which she attended, with this late December encounter, which likely did not take place. Russell's letter was not found in the Wilson Papers.

51 *New York Times*, January 6, 1917, p 2 (emphasis Buxton's).

52 Peabody to Wilson, January 13, 1917, and Wilson to Peabody, January 16, 1917, Wilson Papers, Reel 321.

53 House to Wilson, December 29, 1916, House to Wilson, January 5, 1917, and House Diary, January 11, 1917, *PWW*, 40, pp 358–362, 413–416, 445–447 and notes. House either forwarded the British radicals' letters or speeches to his chief or read them to him at the White House.

54 First quotation in Charles Merz's report of a news conference, January

8, 1917, ibid., p 423 (Merz, a *New Republic* reporter, capitalized this sentence presumably to draw his editors' attention to it); Wilson to Herbert Croly, January 25, 1917, ibid., 41, p 13. In this letter, Wilson was referring to one of two editorials, "Peace without Victory," *New Republic*, 9 (December 23, 1916), pp 201–202, or an untitled editorial, ibid. (January 6, 1917), pp 252–253.

55 Lochner to Plantiff, December 14, 1916, FPP Papers, Box 6; Lochner, *America's Don Quixote*, pp 195–196.

56 Drummond to Spring Rice, January 4, 1917, FO 115/2220/260–261, and Drummond, Minutes of the British Foreign Office, January 20, 1917, ibid., 371/3072 (file 14642).

57 Leipnik to Ada Morse Clark, January 4, 1917, FPP Papers, Box 7; Lochner, *America's Don Quixote*, pp 199–200. Lochner mistakenly recalled the date of the interview as January 19. His account of the interview, however, is probably accurate, as he wrote it immediately after the interview and read it to Leipnik, "who agreed that it was substantially correct." Ibid., p 201.

58 Ibid., pp 201–205. In Wilson's reply to Leipnik's query, the latter soon recorded, "He answered literally, 'Of course I cannot give you any proofs but I am firmly convinced that I shall get the fullest support of the American people.'" Leipnik to Howard, February 10, 1917, Howard Papers, DHW 5/34.

59 House Diary, November 26, 1916, Wilson to House, November [December] 3, 1916, and House to Wilson, December 4, 1916, *PWW*, 40, pp 85–87 (quotation on p 87n1), 131–132, 137–138.

60 Telegram 4149 from Berlin, July 24, 1916, reproduced ibid., 37, p 480; quotation in Lochner to Plantiff, December 6, 1916, FPP Papers, Box 6.

61 Lochner, *America's Don Quixote*, pp

201–205. Lange was a noted Norwegian historian of internationalism and secretary of the Interparliamentary Union from 1909 to 1933. He was awarded the Nobel Peace Prize for 1921.

62 Zimmermann to Bernstorff, January 7, 1917, *Official German Documents*, 2, pp 1012–1013; House to Wilson, January 15 and 16, 1917, *PWW*, 40, pp 477–478 (first two quotations on p 476, with emphasis House's), and 493 (third quotation). The "independence" of Belgium was not really a German concession, because a nominally independent Belgium to the annexationists would be subservient to Germany's predominant economic and security interests.

63 Wilson to House, January 16, 1917, ibid., p 491. On House's January 15 letter (note 62 above), Wilson had underlined two words and put question marks next to two of House's sentences: "His [Bernstorff's] Government are willing to submit to *arbitration* as a means of peace;" and "They propose that you submit a *program* for a peace conference and they agree to give it their approval." Bernstorff provided some clarification on these matters in his letter to House, January 18, 1917, ibid., p 525; also, Wilson to House, January 19, 1917, ibid., p 524.

64 In his July message (note 60 above), Gerard warned of "possibility Germany signing treaty and then starting submarine war." Moreover, in the conversation between Gerard, Bryan, and House which House had recounted to his chief (note 59 above), the ambassador had asserted that the signing of conciliation treaties with Germany and Austria-Hungary would make Wilson the "laughing stock of the world," because, he believed, Germany would begin unrestricted submarine warfare during the cooling-off period.

65 Wilson to House, January 17, 1917, *PWW*, 40, pp 507–508. In this letter, Wilson misidentified Leipnik as an "English Jew." That characterization, if he had known it, would have horrified Leipnik, a devout Catholic from Hungary. Given the absence of any advance White House staff work, however, Wilson's error was understandable, as Leipnik had spoken about his British contacts as if he was one of them. His identification as a "Jew" is more problematical; but Wilson noted that Leipnik spoke "with a very decided foreign twist to his tongue," as if he were perhaps an assimilated Jew, and his somewhat swarthy complexion (see the photograph, p 269) just gave him a different look from (Christian) English people he knew.

66 In his account to Minister Howard, Leipnik wrote that he also had another, earlier interview with Wilson. At the first meeting, Leipnik reported that they discussed the prospects for Germany becoming a democracy after the war, and Leipnik denied any such possibility. According to Leipnik, Wilson then said, "What you say reveals quite an original point of view which I have never encountered yet[,] and though your opinion is strictly at variance with all I have heard so far expressed[,] I think there is much in it." At the second interview, Leipnik said that Wilson, presumably referring to their first conversation, remarked, "I think you are right [about Germany]. You have helped me perhaps more than you think." Leipnik to Howard, February 10, 1917, Howard Papers, DHW 5/34. The earlier interview may have occurred, but it seems doubtful. For one thing, no other reference to such a meeting has been found. An earlier interview would also have made it less likely that Wilson, better acquainted with Leipnik's background, would have misidentified him as an "English Jew"

after the second one. It is more probable that Leipnik, with Lochner, only saw Wilson once and, though seemingly an honorable person, concocted the earlier one perhaps to magnify his own importance to his diplomatic friend but, more importantly, to reemphasize his Anglophilic (or Germanophobic) views after Germany's submarine campaign made his peace mission a futile exercise compared with the reality of Germany's purposeful expansion of the war. Leipnik's last quotation from Wilson cited above, for example, is very close to Lochner's recollection of Wilson's parting words at the conclusion of their meeting. If Leipnik did have two interviews with Wilson, it is just as likely that he inadvertently mixed up their order. In this scenario, the first one was with Lochner, and the second one occurred sometime between January 20 and 27 (Leipnik embarked on his return voyage to England on the latter date), when Wilson, suddenly warned by House of Germany's seeming unreliability, might have been inclined to ask his visitor for his views on prospects for German democracy.

Upon his arrival in England, Leipnik met with Tyrrell on February 8, and perhaps also the following day, before returning to Holland. Tyrrell to Leipnik, February 8, 1917, Leipnik Correspondence. Additional documentation on Leipnik's time in the United States and his return to Britain is in FO 115/2220, 371/2801, and 371/3702.

67 Zimmermann to Bernstorff, January 7, 1917, *Official German Documents*, 2, pp 1012–1013; and Doerries, *Imperial Challenge*, pp 207–210.

68 Link, *Wilson*, 5, pp 238–248 (quotation on p 244); Matthew Stibbe, "Germany's 'Last Card': Wilhelm II and the Decision in Favour of Unrestricted Submarine Warfare in January 1917," *The Kaiser: New*

Research on Wilhelm II's Role in Imperial Germany, eds. Annika Mombauer and Wilhelm Deist (Cambridge: Cambridge University Press, 2006), ch 9 (especially pp 226–234).

69 Wilhelm II to Houston Stewart Chamberlain, January 15, 1917, quoted in Strachan, *First World War*, 1, p 1137.

70 House to Wilson, January 20, 1917, enclosing Bernstorff to House, January 20, 1917, *PWW*, 40, pp 527–529 (quotations on pp 528–529); and Doerries, *Imperial Challenge*, pp 210–214.

71 Address to the Senate, January 22, 1917, *PWW*, 410, pp 533–539.

72 Wilson to Cleveland H. Dodge, January 25, 1917, ibid., 41, (1983), p 11.

73 Balch to Lochner, January 22, 1917 (emphasis Balch's), and Addams to Lochner, January 23, 1917, Lochner Papers.

74 Lillian Wald, Oswald Garrison Villard, Owen R. Lovejoy, Paul Kellogg, and Amos Pinchot to Wilson, January 24, 1917, *PWW*, 41, pp 7–8. Other expressions included Bryan to Wilson, January 26, 1917, and Gavit to Wilson, January 26, 1917, ibid., pp 29, 32.

75 Carnegie to Wilson, January 23, 1917, ibid., 40, p 560; Wald to Wilson, February 8, 1917, ibid., 41, pp 168–169. The European war in fact profoundly depressed Carnegie who fell ill and remained an invalid most of the war; he died in 1919. Interestingly, Wilson asked Wald to go through Carnegie, who had effusively praised his speech, rather than through the Carnegie Endowment for International Peace's most prominent leaders, Elihu Root and Nicholas Murray Butler, both heavyweights in the Republican party. In the spring of 1914, the endowment at its benefactor's instigation had distributed throughout the country 741,000 copies of Senator Root's speeches supporting Wilson's decision to ask for

congressional repeal of the Panama Canal tolls. Patterson, *Toward a Warless World*, pp 212–213, 234–235.

76 Lochner to Ford, January 24, 1917 (not sent), Lochner Papers; first quoted phrase in Lochner to Leipnik, January 23, 1917, ibid.; second quotation in Lochner, *America's Don Quixote*, p 206. Again, Lochner's correspondence is more accurate on chronology than his retrospective account of the events, which is sometimes off by several days.

77 Lochner to Leipnik, January 23, 1917, Lochner Papers, and Leipnik to Howard, February 10, 1917, Howard Papers, DHW 5/34.

78 Lochner to Jordan, January 30, 1917, Jordan Peace Correspondence, Box 7; quotation in Lochner to Leipnik, January 23, 1917, Lochner Papers; Lochner, *America's Don Quixote*, pp 206–214.

79 A WPP committee was also scheduled to meet with Wilson before Lochner's interview to discuss problems in U.S.–Nicaragua relations, but the women cancelled the meeting because of the German crisis. Executive Office Diary, February 1, 1917, Wilson Papers, Reel 3; Legislative Committee Report of the Women's Peace Party for 1917 [June 1917], WPP Correspondence.

80 House Diary, February 1, 1917, *PWW*, 41, p 87.

81 House Diary, January 4, 1917, ibid., 40, p 409.

82 Wilson to House, January 24, 1917,

ibid., 41, p 3 (emphasis Wilson's). Also see Link, *Wilson*, 5, pp 272, 277–278.

83 House Diary, February 1, 1917, *PWW*, 41, p 87.

84 Lochner's account of the interview, February 1, 1917, ibid., pp 89–92. Lochner did not ask Wilson, confronted by a sudden, weighty crisis, for a specific endorsement of the neutral conference, but instead put the question negatively: whether there was anything he did not like about it. But Wilson had already said that he was interested in principles and could not endorse any specific peace program. When Balch had met with Wilson in early August 1916, she presumably had also summarized the activities of Ford's neutral conference. Of course, much had happened in the mediation arena since then, but Wilson's professed ignorance to Lochner of its various activities suggests his earlier disinterest in it.

85 Kraft, *Peace Ship*, pp 265–271 (quotation on p 271).

86 Strachan, *First World War*, 1, pp 975–976 (quotation on p 975).

87 Ibid., pp 955–957.

88 David Englander, "Mutinies and Military Morale," in *World War I: A History*, ed. Hew Strachan (Oxford: Oxford University Press, 1998), ch 14; Ferguson, *Pity of War*, pp 345–346.

89 *Autobiography of Lincoln Steffens*, p 739.

90 House Diary, March 18, 1917, quoted in Hodgson, *Woodrow Wilson's Right Hand*, p 139.

11 AFTERMATH

1 Quoted in Link, *Wilson*, 5, p 288.

2 Quotations ibid., pp 294, 291, 295.

3 See above, p 109.

4 Link, *Wilson*, 5, pp 298–301.

5 Kellogg to Addams, February 9, 1917, Addams Papers, Box 6; Jordan to Wilson, March 16, 1917, Wilson Papers, Reel 237.

6 *New York Times*, February 8, 1917, p

22; Van Voris, *Carrie Chapman Catt*, pp 138–139.

7 Ibid., p 138.

8 Quotations in *New York Times*, February 9, 1917, p 11, and New York *Evening Post*, February 15, 1917, p 9. The Spencer–Catt exchanges are summarized in Harriet Hyman Alonso, *Peace As a Women's Issue: A*

History of the US Movement for World Peace and Women's Rights (Syracuse, NY: Syracuse University Press, 1993), pp 74–76.

9 Quotations in *New York Times*, February 22, 1917, p 20.

10 Van Voris, *Carrie Chapman Catt*, pp 138–139. Quotation in memorandum from Addams, *et al.*, to Catt, February 22, 1917, Addams Papers, Box 6. Ellen Slayden, observing Catt close up in the House gallery as they watched the final vote on the war resolution, well summarized moderate pacifists' views of Catt. Compared with the American women pacifist leaders Slayden admired, she found "more calculation in her eyes, less sweetness. Many kinds of strong women are coming to the front these days, but the bravest are still the tenderest." Slayden, *Washington Wife*, p 298.

11 AUAM Minutes, February 1, 1917, Pinchot Papers, Box 30. The statement, signed by 26 people, who were clerics like Frederick Lynch or John Haynes Holmes or AUAM or WPP stalwarts, appeared among other places in the *New York Times*, February 2, 1917, p 7, and New York *World*, February 2, 1917, p 7.

12 *New York Times*, February 3, 1917, p 12.

13 Ibid., p 11.

14 Ibid., February 6, 1917, p 5, and February 7, 1917, p 8.

15 Ibid., February 11, 1917, p A2; Bryan to Addams, February 17, 1917, WPP Correspondence. The notion of a nationwide referendum would attract widespread popular support well into the 1930s. See Ernest C. Bolt, Jr., *Ballots before Bullets: The War Referendum Approach to Peace in America, 1914–1941* (Charlottesville: University Press of Virginia, 1977).

16 Cook, *Woodrow Wilson and the Antimilitarists*, pp 182–184.

17 *Washington Post*, February 13, 1917,

p 4, and New York *Evening Post*, February 13, 1917, p 4.

18 Ibid., February 14, 1917, p 6, and February 20, 1917, p 4.

19 Peabody explained his position in a long, handwritten letter to Tumulty, who forwarded it to the President with his own very brief summary of its contents. Peabody to Tumulty, February 9, 1917, Wilson Papers, Reel 254.

20 *New York Times*, February 23, 1917, p 2.

21 Chicago *Tribune*, February 6, 1917, p 5, and *New York Times*, February 5, 1917, p 4.

22 Wald to Wilson, February 8, 1917, *PWW*, 41, pp 168–169, which enclosed a memorandum summarizing Hayes' paper and the galley proofs of the entire article published as "Which? War without a Purpose? Or Armed Neutrality with a Purpose?" *The Survey*, 37 (February 10, 1917), pp 535–538. Wilson to Tumulty [c. February 9, 1917], *PWW*, 41, p 167n1, contains his instructions for a reply to Wald. Hayes was one of the 26 signatories of the AUAM-sponsored advertisement at the very outset of the crisis (see n 11 above) and may have been an AUAM member.

23 House to Wilson, February 8, 1917, ibid., pp 164–165, and Lansing to Wilson, February 10, 1917, ibid., p 185.

24 Wilson to Tumulty [c. February 20, 1917], Charles Sumner Hamlin to Wilson, February 14, 1917, and Wilson to Hamlin, February 15, 1917, ibid., pp 257–258, 231–233. Hamlin, a Bostonian who had recently resigned as chairman of the Federal Reserve Board, relayed Forbes' request for advice to Wilson. Also see p 3 above.

25 Cook, *Woodrow Wilson and the Antimilitarists*, pp 185–186.

26 Germany's announcement defined broad zones around Britain, France,

Italy, and in the eastern Mediterranean, and provided for grace periods of different lengths for each zone for ships already at sea (Leipnik who left New York for England on January 27 was a beneficiary), and allowed one American passenger liner a week to travel between New York and Falmouth, if it was clearly marked and the U.S. Government certified that no contraband was on board.

27 Link, *Wilson*, 5, pp 340–342, 346–349; Peabody to Wilson, February 26, 1917, Wilson Papers, Reel 254; Lynch quoted in *New York Times*, February 27, 1917, p 2; Jordan to Jessie Jordan, February 26, 1917, Jordan Peace Correspondence, Box 7.

28 See above, pp 130–131, and also pp 218–219.

29 *PWW*, 41, pp 46–48, 50–51n1, 80–81.

30 Hodgson, *Woodrow Wilson's Right Hand*, pp 136–139.

31 Max Eastman's paper is in *PWW*, 41, pp 305–308.

32 Of the delegates, all but Lynch apparently made presentations. They are summarized in an article in a Quaker journal, reproduced ibid., February 28, 1917, pp 302–304. Quotations from the much later accounts by Hull and Addams of Wilson's responses are also ibid., pp 304–305, and n 3.

33 Different interpretations of Addams' comment are Knock, *To End All Wars*, pp 120–121, for Wilson's ego, and Thompson, *Woodrow Wilson*, pp 147–148.

34 Diary of Thomas W. Brahany, *PWW*, 41, March 31, 1917, p 515.

35 John Milton Cooper, Jr., *The Warrior and the Priest: Woodrow Wilson and Theodore Roosevelt* (Cambridge, Mass.: Harvard University Press, 1983), pp 322–323. Wilson's war message only substituted "her" and "she" for Luther's "me" and "I."

36 David M. Kennedy, *Over Here: The First World War and American Society* (Oxford: Oxford University Press,

1980), pp 18–24 (quotation on p 23). Rankin served one term but, elected again to the House in 1940, cast the lone vote against war following the Japanese attack on Pearl Harbor.

37 Quoted in Thompson, *Woodrow Wilson*, p 158.

38 Arthur S. Link, *Wilson the Diplomatist: A Look at His Major Foreign Policies* (Baltimore: The Johns Hopkins Press, 1957), p 99, citing approvingly a quip by an unnamed Briton during the American military involvement.

39 Quotations in Flag Day address, June 14, 1917, *PWW*, 42 (1983), p 504, address to American Federation of Labor, ibid., 45 (1984), November 12, 1917, p 14, and annual State of the Union message, December 4, 1917, ibid., p 195.

40 Quoted in Wreszin, *Oswald Garrison Villard*, p 101.

41 Wilson to House, March 22, 1918, *PWW*, 47 (1984), p 105; quotations in House Diary, January 13, June 1, 1918, House Papers.

42 F.L. Leipnik, *A History of French Etching from the Sixteenth Century to the Present Day* (London: John Lane, 1924). Leipnik dedicated the book to Esme Howard.

43 Wald, *Windows on Henry Street*, pp 307ff.

44 Secor to Dr James Harvey Kellogg, April 13, 1917, EPF Papers. Philip Florence had been born in the United States to an American father and English mother. After his father died when he was two, his mother had returned to England and raised him there. After attending the University of Cambridge, he returned to the United States to attend graduate school at Columbia University. When delivering the pamphlets, he met Secor and was immediately attracted by her. He began calling on her and often brought dinner to her office as she worked well into the night. Secor at first seemed uninterested, believing

her feminism would preclude her ever getting married. But his persistence and devotion soon won her over. In the interwar years, she was active in the British section of the Women's International League for Peace and Freedom, the founding of which is described in the text below. During the Second World War, she and her husband wrote books promoting Anglo-American cultural ties and political friendship. Florence, *Lella Secor*, pp 124, 140, 143, 153–160, *passim*.

45 Ibid., pp 174 (n 16) and 200 (nn 31, 36, and 41). Shelley, *I Confess* (Colombes: A Cary, 1967), briefly recounts her peace interests after the First World War and, in greater detail, her political activity against the Vietnam War. A photograph of her as an antiwar activist dressed in mourning is in the Swarthmore College Peace Collection.

46 For two examples, see Johanna Alberti, *Beyond Suffrage: Feminists in War and Peace, 1914–28* (New York: St. Martin's Press, 1989), pp 267–271; and J. Stanley Lemons, *The Woman Citizen: Social Feminism in the 1920s* (Urbana: University of Illinois Press, 1973).

47 On Villard, see Harriet Hyman Alonso, *The Women's Peace Union and the Outlawry of War, 1921–1942* (Syracuse, NY: Syracuse University Press, 1997). Webb is quoted in Oldfield, *Women Against the Iron Fist*, p 45.

48 On Royden's postwar interests, see Fletcher, *Maude Royden*, chs 7–12 (quotations on pp 202 and 274, capitalization Royden's); on British pacifism, see Martin Ceadel, *Pacifism in Britain 1914–1945: The Defining of a Faith* (Oxford: Oxford University Press, 1980).

49 Concerning the suffragists' cleavage during the Great War, Courtney could remark more than a half century later: "We were all confused and emotionally upset by the war whose origins we so little understood. We were not quite responsible for our actions." Quoted in Francesca Wilson's draft biography of Courtney [c. early 1970s], Kathleen Courtney Papers (Lady Margaret Hall Library, University of Oxford). A similar comment by Courtney on her ninetieth birthday (1968) is quoted in Oldfield, *Spinsters of This Parish*, p 308.

50 Addams to Courtney, August 15, 1932, Courtney Papers, WL, Box 454.

51 Vera Brittain, a feminist and pacifist in the interwar period, wrote that Swanwick, finding the second war too much to bear, took her own life. Other historians (eg, Ceadel, *Pacifism in Britain*, p 240) have accepted her account, but Wiltsher (*Most Dangerous Women*, p 251, n 30), saying Brittain is the only source for this information, doubts her suicide. Wiltsher may be right, although Swanwick was clearly upset by the onset of the war and Brittain recorded her death as a "suicide" at the time in a matter-of-fact manner as if it was commonly accepted knowledge, and later unquestioningly repeated her account. Brittain, *Wartime Chronicle: Diary, 1939–1945*, eds. Alan Bishop and Aleksandra Bennett (London: Victor Gollancz, 1989), pp 36, 37; and Brittain, *Testament of Experience: An Autobiographical Story of the Years 1925–1950* (London: Victor Gollancz, 1957), p 266.

52 Swartz, *Union of Democratic Control*, ch 10 and conclusion.

53 For an American example, decades later, see Amy Swerdlow, *Women Strike for Peace: Traditional Motherhood and Radical Politics in the 1960s* (Chicago: University of Chicago Press, 1993). Also, see Naomi Black, "The Mothers' International: The Women's Co-operative Guild and Feminist Pacifism," *Women's Studies International Forum*, 7 (1984),

pp 467–476; and Liddington, *Road to Gresham Common*, pp 143–144, 153, *passim*.

54 Rupp, *Worlds of Women*, pp 131–134, 196–200 (quotation on p 133).

55 Catt to Courtney, September 12, 1940, Courtney Papers, WL, Box 456.

56 Van Voris, *Carrie Chapman Catt*, pp 174–177, 214, 218; Rupp, *Worlds of Women*, pp 196–200.

57 Ibid., p 29; Peter Pastor, "The Diplomatic Fiasco of the Modern World's First Woman Ambassador, Róza Bédy-Schwimmer," *East European Quarterly*, 8 (Fall 1974), pp 273–282; and Wenger, "Radical Politics in a Reactionary Age," pp 76–99.

58 Schwimmer, "The Cause and Cure of Peace," *World Tomorrow*, 16 (February 22, 1933), pp 181–183. Correspondence between Catt and Schwimmer in the interwar period is in the Catt Papers, Box 8.

59 Details on Balch's termination at Wellesley are in Patricia Ann Palmieri, *In Adamless Eden: The Community of Women Faculty at Wellesley* (New Haven, CT: Yale University Press, 1995), pp 238–244.

60 Quotations in Swanwick, *I Have Been Young*, p 318.

61 Quoted in Sklar, *et al.*, eds., *Social Justice Feminists in the United States and Germany*, p 67.

CONCLUSION

1 Slayden, *Washington Wife*, p 298; Patterson, *Toward a Warless World*, chs 3–4.

2 Jordan, *Days of a Man*, 2, pp 727–729.

3 On the movement during American belligerency, see, for instance, Frances Early, *A World Without War: How U.S. Feminists and Pacifists Resisted World War I* (Syracuse: Syracuse University Press, 1997); and Kathleen Kennedy, *Disloyal Mothers and Scurrilous Citizens: Women and Subversion during World War I* (Bloomington: Indiana University Press, 1999); of the many studies of the American peace movement in the interwar period, see Charles Chatfield, *For Peace and Justice: Pacifism in America, 1914–1941* (Knoxville: University of Tennessee Press, 1971); and Charles DeBenedetti, *Origins of the Modern American Peace Movement, 1915–1929* (Millwood, N.Y.: KTO Press, 1978).

4 Some examples are the comments above by Vorse on naïvité, and quotations by Addams and Balch respectively, pp 65, 66 and 64. Likewise, in confessing his "romanticism," Lochner feared he was "a bit off."

Lochner to Balch, March 1, 1917, Lochner Papers.

5 Quoted in Richard A. Rempel, "Bertrand Russell and Russia, 1914–1920," *The Pacifist Impulse in Historical Perspective*, ed. Harvey L. Dyck (Toronto: Toronto University Press, 1996), p 348.

6 Charles Chatfield has usefully distilled in various publications historians' insights on the ideas and goals of "community" and "polity" internationalists. See, for example, his *The American Peace Movement: Ideals and Action* (Boston: Twayne, 1991), pp 167ff.

7 A historian of the British peace movement writes: "At this juncture [1916–1917], the League of Nations tended to mean whatever anyone wanted it to mean. It was, therefore, a very useful idea; that is, until attempts were made to go beyond the stage of acclamation and discuss particulars." Robbins, *Abolition of War*, p 105.

8 See above, p 154.

9 Forcey, *Crossroads of Liberalism*, pp 263ff.

10 See above, p 108.

A NOTE ON THE SOURCES

In my research for this book, I have relied primarily on letters, telegrams, and other correspondence written by the principal actors. During the First World War era, letter writing was the main form of communication among literate people who were not regularly in face-to-face contact. There is very little evidence in the documents, for example, that the individuals relied on the telephone, especially for long-distance calls, as it was still a primitive communication tool and not widely used. Fortunately for the historian, the manuscript collections, often very extensive, of most of the central figures in my narrative have been preserved. Except for a few collections of selected letters of women participants and the *Papers of Woodrow Wilson* (which are available in 69 volumes), however, none of the personal papers consulted for this study have been edited and published; and even the published Wilson papers, as chief editor Arthur S. Link and his assistants have noted, are far from complete. Wherever possible, I have cited the printed volumes of the President's papers; I have used citations to his manuscript collection (on microfilm) for documents that are not included in the published volumes. Among government records relevant to this study, only some U.S. State Department and Dutch documents are available in published form. I conducted much of my research in private and government repositories. In the United States, the consulted collections stretched from New England to California. The Swarthmore College Peace Collection, which houses manuscript collections of many individual peace workers and peace organizations, was the richest resource; the Manuscript Division of the Library of Congress holds other important manuscript sources and also has microfilm copies of a few manuscript collections at Swarthmore and the Wisconsin Historical Society. The listing below identifies the entire range of repositories consulted for this study.

Internationally, my search for European source material took me to Amsterdam, The Hague, and Geneva, and, in the United Kingdom, repositories in London, Manchester, and Carlisle. I also collected government documents on microfilm from Stockholm and perused the microfilm copy of the German Foreign Office records for this period at the National Archives in Washington, DC. I also looked at the U.S. Department of State files, including those of several U.S. legations and embassies in Europe, at the National Archives.

A second important contemporary source was several daily newspapers and a few magazines, which I used to supplement information from other documents. Often the journalistic accounts provided fresh perspectives on individual actors and events. I have used them with some caution, however, because of possible errors from quick reporting or interpretive bias and have tried to corroborate the thrust of their stories, wherever possible, with other source material.

Also valuable for my purposes were autobiographies and reminiscences written by the participants. Composed after the events—sometimes long afterward—memoir accounts can be selective or distorted on specific episodes, even when they are not self-serving. I found them nonetheless helpful for background on the memoirists' careers, and their retrospective accounts, when used with discretion, are often quite reflective and serve as another frame of reference for evaluating their behavior and roles during the World War period.

In a study involving many individuals from several countries, this researcher soon realized that he could not look at every primary source. Some compromises, especially for secondary figures and themes, were required if I was ever to complete this study. I have thus consulted a wide range of excellent secondary works. If none centers directly on my subject, many were very helpful in providing well-documented background and detail on important parts of my story. Particularly useful were biographies of many participants—peace activists, suffragists, other reformers, diplomats, and political figures—as well as monographs on peace movements in specific countries, various governments' political and military policies, and diplomatic developments.

My research often led me to other sources from which I undoubtedly gained helpful insights, but I have cited in the endnotes only those most directly relevant or from which quotations have been taken. The following list includes all manuscript collections consulted, but from printed sources comprises only a selection of the most relevant ones used in this history. Additional printed citations appear in the endnotes.

BIBLIOGRAPHY

Note: For published materials, this listing does not include articles in contemporary magazines and newspapers.

MANUSCRIPT COLLECTIONS

Jane Addams Memorial Collection, Hull House Archives
Jane Addams Papers, Swarthmore College Peace Collection
American Union Against Militarism Papers, Swarthmore College Peace Collection
John A. Aylward Papers, Wisconsin Historical Society
Warren Worth Bailey Papers, Manuscript Division, Library of Congress
Ray Stannard Baker Papers, Manuscript Division, Library of Congress
Emily Greene Balch Papers, Swarthmore College Peace Collection
William Jennings Bryan Papers, Manuscript Division, Library of Congress
Irving Caesar Diary, Ford Motor Company Archives
Carrie Chapman Catt Papers, Manuscript Division, Library of Congress
Chicago Peace Society Papers, Chicago Historical Society
Kathleen Courtney Papers, Lady Margaret Hall Library, University of Oxford
Kathleen Courtney Papers, The Women's Library
Fair Lane Papers, Ford Motor Company Archives
Millicent Garrett Fawcett Papers, The Women's Library
Ford Peace Plan Papers, Manuscript Division, Library of Congress
Hamilton Holt Papers, Mills Memorial Library, Rollins College
Edward M. House Papers and Diary, Yale University Library
Esme Howard Papers, Cumbria County Record Office, Carlisle
William I. Hull Papers, Friends Historical Library, Swarthmore College
International Woman Suffrage Alliance Papers, The John Rylands University Library, University of Manchester
Aletta H. Jacobs Papers, International Archives of the Women's Movement
David Starr Jordan Peace Correspondence, Hoover Institution
La Follette Family Collection, Manuscript Division, Library of Congress
Robert Lansing Papers, Manuscript Division, Library of Congress
Robert Lansing Papers, Princeton University Library
Ferdinand L. Leipnik Correspondence, British Library
Louis P. Lochner Papers, Wisconsin Historical Society

J. Loudon Papers, Netherlands Ministry of Foreign Affairs
Lewis A. Maverick Diary, Ford Motor Company Archives
Edwin D. and Lucia Ames Mead Papers, Swarthmore College Peace Collection
Angela Morgan Papers, Bentley Historical Library, University of Michigan
Neutral Conference for Continuous Mediation Papers, Swarthmore College Peace
    Collection
Ralph W. Owen Papers, Wisconsin Historical Society
Amos Pinchot Papers, Manuscript Division, Library of Congress
Frank L. Polk Papers, Yale University Library
Rosika Schwimmer Papers, Hoover Institution
Schwimmer-Lloyd Papers, New York Public Library
May Wright Sewall Papers, Indianapolis Public Library
Rebecca Shelley Papers, Bentley Historical Library, University of Michigan
Anna Garlin Spencer Papers, Swarthmore College Peace Collection
Wickham Steed Papers, British Library
Moorfield Storey Papers, Manuscript Division, Library of Congress
Survey Associates Papers, Social Welfare History Archives, University of Minnesota
Oswald Garrison Villard Papers, Houghton Library, Harvard University
Mary Heaton Vorse Papers, Archives of Labor and Urban Affairs, Wayne State
    University
Lillian D. Wald Papers, Columbia University
Lillian D. Wald Papers, New York Public Library
Julia Grace Wales Papers, Wisconsin Historical Society
Woodrow Wilson Papers, Manuscript Division, Library of Congress
Woman's Peace Party Correspondence, Swarthmore College Peace Collection

ORAL REMINISCENCES

Irving Caesar, Reminiscences. Ford Motor Company Archives, December 1954
Elmer Davis, The Ford Peace Ship. Columbia Oral History Research Project, 1959
Ben W. Huebsch, Reminiscences. Columbia Oral History Research Project, 1965
Ernest G. Liebold, Reminiscences. Ford Motor Company Archives

GOVERNMENT DOCUMENTS AND PUBLICATIONS

Bescheiden Betreffende de Buitenlandse Politiek van Nederland, 1848–1919, ed. C. Smit. 6
    vols [third period, 1899–1919], s'-Gravenhage: Verkrijgbaar bij Martinus Nijhoff,
    1964.
Germany. Foreign Office Papers, Record Group 242, National Archives and Records
    Administration.
*Hearing Before the Committee on Military Affairs, United States Senate, Sixty-fourth
    Congress, First Session: Conference of Neutral Nations.* Washington, DC: Govern-
    ment Printing Office, 1916.
Hearings Before the Committee on Foreign Affairs, House of Representatives, Sixty-fourth

Congress, First Session: Commission for Enduring Peace. Washington, DC: Government Printing Office, 1916.

Hearings Before the Committee on Military Affairs, House of Representatives, Sixty-fourth Congress, First Session: To Increase the Efficiency of the Military Establishment of the United States. Washington: Government Printing Office, 1916.

Hearings Before the Committee on Military Affairs, United States Senate, Sixty-fourth Congress, First Session: Preparedness for National Defense. Washington: Government Printing Office, 1916.

Papers Relating to the Foreign Relations of the United States, 1914, 1915, 1916, and 1917, and *Supplements*. Washington, DC: Government Printing Office, 1922–1932.

Papers Relating to the Foreign Relations of the United States: The Lansing Papers, 1914–1920. 2 vols, Washington, DC: Government Printing Office, 1939–1940.

Sweden. Foreign Office Papers, Archives of the Swedish Ministry of Foreign Affairs.

United Kingdom. Foreign Office Records, National Archives.

United States. General Records of the Department of State, Record Group 59, National Archives and Records Administration.

AUTOBIOGRAPHIES, MEMOIRS, AND REMINISCENCES BY PARTICIPANTS

Jane Addams, *Peace and Bread in Time of War*. New York: Macmillan, 1922.

Jane Addams, Emily G. Balch, and Alice Hamilton, *Women at The Hague: The International Committee of Women and Its Results*. New York: Macmillan, 1915.

Fannie Fern Andrews, *Memory Pages of My Life*. Boston: The Talisman Press, 1948.

Norman Angell, *After All: The Autobiography of Norman Angell*. London: Hamish Hamilton, 1951.

Elizabeth Balmer Baker and P.J. Noel Baker, *J. Allen Baker, Member of Parliament: A Memoir*. London: Swarthmore Press, 1927.

Julian Bell, ed., *We Did Not Fight: 1914–18 Experiences of War Resisters*. London: Cobden-Sanderson, 1935.

Max Eastman, *Enjoyment of Living*. New York: Harper & Brothers, 1948.

Max Eastman, *Love and Revolution: My Journey Through an Epoch*. New York: Random House, 1956.

James W. Gerard, *My Four Years in Germany*. New York: George H. Doran, 1927.

Viscount Grey of Falloudon, *Twenty-five Years, 1892–1916*. 2 vols, New York: Frederick A. Stokes, 1925.

Alice Hamilton, *Exploring the Dangerous Trades: The Autobiography of Alice Hamilton, M.D.* Boston: Little, Brown, 1943.

Burnet Hershey, *The Odyssey of Henry Ford and the Great Peace Ship*. New York: Taplinger, 1967.

Lida Gustava Heymann (with Anita Augspurg), *Erlebtes – Erschautes: Deutsche Frauen Kämpfen für Freiheit, Recht, und Frieden, 1850–1940*. Meisenheim am Glad: Anton Heim, 1972.

Morris Hillquit, *Loose Leaves from a Busy Life*. New York: Macmillan, 1934.

Sir Esme Howard, *Theatre of Life: Life Seen from the Stalls, 1903–1936*. 2 vols, Boston: Little, Brown, 1936.

Frederic C. Howe, *The Confessions of a Reformer*. New York: Charles Scribner's Sons, 1925.

Aletta H. Jacobs, *Memories: My Life as an International Leader in Health, Suffrage, and Peace*, ed. Harriet Feinberg. New York: Feminist Press at the City University of New York, 1996.

David Starr Jordan, *The Days of a Man: Being Memoirs of a Naturalist, Teacher and Minor Prophet of Democracy*. 2 vols, Yonkers-on-Hudson, NY: World Book, 1922.

David Lloyd George, *War Memoirs*. 6 vols, Boston: Little, Brown, 1933–1937.

Louis P. Lochner, *Always the Unexpected: A Book of Reminiscences*. New York: Macmillan, 1956.

Louis P. Lochner, *America's Don Quixote: Henry Ford's Attempt to Save Europe*. London: Kegan Paul, Trench, Trubner, 1924.

Samuel S. Marquis, *Henry Ford: An Interpretation*. Boston: Little, Brown, 1923.

James Hudson Maurer, *It Can Be Done: The Autobiography of James Hudson Maurer*. New York: Rand School Press, 1938.

Emmeline Pethick-Lawrence, *My Part in a Changing World*. London: Victor Gollancz, 1938.

Friedrich Rosen, *Aus einem Diplomatischen Wanderleben*. 4 vols in 3, Wiesbaden: Limes Verlag, 1931–1959.

Alice Salomon, *Character Is Destiny: The Autobiography of Alice Salomon*, ed. Andrew Lees. Ann Arbor: University of Michigan Press, 2004.

Mrs Philip Snowden, *A Political Pilgrim in Europe*. New York: George H. Doran, 1921.

Lincoln Steffens, *The Autobiography of Lincoln Steffens*. New York: Harcourt, Brace & World, 1931.

H.M. Swanwick, *I Have Been Young*. London: Victor Gollancz, 1935.

Charles Trevelyan, *From Liberalism to Labour*. London: George Allen & Unwin, 1921.

Mary Heaton Vorse, *A Footnote to Folly: Reminiscences of Mary Heaton Vorse*. New York: Farrar & Rinehart, 1935.

Lillian D. Wald, *Windows on Henry Street*. Boston: Little, Brown, 1934.

COLLECTED LETTERS, DIARIES, AND PAPERS

Mineke Bosch, with Annemarie Kloosterman, eds, *Politics and Friendship: Letters from the International Woman Suffrage Alliance, 1902–1942*. Columbus: Ohio State University Press, 1990.

Blanche Wiesen Cook, ed., *Crystal Eastman on Women and Revolution*. New York: Oxford University Press, 1978.

Blanche Wiesen Cook, ed., *Toward the Great Change: Crystal and Max Eastman on Feminism, Antimilitarism, and Revolution*. New York: Garland, 1976.

K.D. Courtney, *Extracts from a Diary during the War*. Privately printed, 1927.

Barbara Moench Florence, ed., *Lella Secor: A Diary in Letters, 1915–1922*. New York: Burt Franklin, 1978.

Arthur S. Link, *et al.*, eds, *The Papers of Woodrow Wilson*. 69 vols, Princeton, NJ: Princeton University Press, 1966–1990.

Mercedes M. Randall, ed., *Beyond Nationalism: The Social Thought of Emily Greene Balch*. New York: Twayne, 1972.

Charles Seymour, *The Intimate Papers of Colonel House: Arranged as a Narrative*. 4 vols, Boston: Houghton Mifflin, 1926–1928.

Barbara Sicherman, ed., *Alice Hamilton: A Life in Letters*. Cambridge, MA: Harvard University Press, 1984.

Ellen Slayden, *Washington Wife: Journal of Ellen Maury Slayden from 1897–1919*, ed. Prescott Webb. New York: Harper & Row, 1962.

MISCELLANEOUS DOCUMENTARY COLLECTIONS, REPORTS, AND PAMPHLETS

British Committtee of the Women's International Congress, *Towards Permament Peace: A Record of the Women's International Congress held at The Hague, April 28th–May 1st, 1915* [1915].

Carnegie Endowment for International Peace, Division of International Law. *The Hague Conventions and Declarations of 1899 and 1907, Accompanied by Tables of Signatures, Ratifications, and Adhesions of the Various Powers, and Texts of Reservations*, ed. James Brown Scott. New York: Oxford University Press, 1915.

Carnegie Endowment for International Peace, *Official German Documents Relating to the World War*. 2 vols, New York: Oxford University Press, 1923.

International Congress of Women, The Hague—28th April–May 1st, 1915, *Bericht—Rapport—Report*. Amsterdam: Women's Committee for Permanent Peace [1915].

Ralph Haswell Lutz, ed., *Fall of the German Empire, 1914–1918*. 2 vols, Stanford, CA: Stanford University Press, 1932.

Nederlandsche Anti-Oorlog Raad, *Dutch Anti-War Council* [1915].

May Wright Sewall, ed., *Women, World War and Permanent Peace*. San Francisco: John J. Newbegin, 1915.

Women's International League for Peace and Freedom, *Report of the International Congress of Women, Zurich, May 12 to 17, 1919*. Geneva: Women's International League for Peace and Freedom [1920].

BIOGRAPHIES AND HISTORIES

Johanna Alberti, *Beyond Suffrage: Feminists in War and Peace, 1914–28*. New York: St Martin's Press, 1989.

Harriet Hyman Alonso, *Growing Up Abolitionist: The Story of the Garrison Children*. Amherst: University of Massachusetts Press, 2002.

Harriet Hyman Alonso, *Peace as a Women's Issue: A History of the US Movement for World Peace and Women's Rights*. Syracuse: Syracuse University Press, 1993.

Arina Angerman, Geerte Binnema, Annemieke Keunen, Vefie Poels, and Jacqueline

Zirkee, eds, *Current Issues in Women's History*. London: Routledge & Keegan Paul, 1989.

Katherine Arnup, Andrée Lévesque, and Ruth Roach Pierson, eds, *Delivering Motherhood: Maternal Ideologies and Practices in the 19th and 20th Centuries*. London: Routledge, 1990.

Ray Stannard Baker, *Woodrow Wilson, Life and Letters: Facing War, 1915–1917*. [Volume 5] Garden City, NY: Doubleday, Doran, 1937.

Ray Stannard Baker, *Woodrow Wilson, Life and Letters: Neutrality, 1914–1915*. [Volume 4] Garden City, NY: Doubleday, Doran, 1935.

Neil Baldwin, *Henry Ford and the Jews: The Mass Production of Hate*. New York: PublicAffairs, 2001.

Jennifer Hobhouse Balme, *To Love One's Enemies: The Work and Life of Emily Hobhouse Compiled from Letters and Writings, Newspaper Cuttings, and Official Documents*. Cobble Hill, Canada: Hobhouse Trust, 1994.

Olive Banks, ed., *Biographical Dictionary of British Feminists, 1800–1930*, Vol 1. New York: New York University Press, 1985.

Daniel R. Beaver, *Newton D. Baker and the American War Effort, 1917–1919*. Lincoln: University of Nebraska Press, 1966.

Carol R. Berkin and Clara M. Lovett, eds, *Women, War, and Revolution*. New York: Holmes & Meier, 1980.

Karl E. Birnbaum, *Peace Moves and U-Boat Warfare: A Study of Imperial Germany's Policy towards the United States, April 18, 1916–January 9, 1917*. Stockholm: Almqvist & Wiksell, 1958.

John M. Blum, *Joe Tumulty and the Wilson Era*. Boston: Houghton, Mifflin, 1951.

John M. Blum, *Woodrow Wilson and the Politics of Morality*. Boston: Little, Brown, 1956.

Ernest C. Bolt, Jr., *Ballots before Bullets: The War Referendum Approach to Peace in America, 1914–1941*. Charlottesville: University Press of Virginia, 1977.

Mineke Bosch, *Een Onwrikbaar Geloof in Rechtvaardigheid [An Unshakeable Belief in Justice]: Aletta Jacobs, 1854–1929*. Amsterdam: Balans, 2005.

Regina Braker, "Bertha von Suttner's Spiritual Daughters: the Feminist Pacifism of Anita Augspurg, Lida Gustava Heymann, and Helene Stöcker at the International Congress of Women at The Hague, 1915," *Women's Studies International Forum*, 18 (March/April 1995), pp 103–111.

Regina Braker, "Helene Stöcker's Pacifism in the Weimar Republic: Between Ideal and Reality," *Journal of Women's History*, 13 (Autumn 2001), pp 70–97.

H.W. Brands, "Woodrow Wilson and the Irony of Fate," *Diplomatic History*, 28 (September 2004), pp 503–512.

Renate Bridenthal and Claudia Koonz, eds, *Becoming Visible: Women in European History*. Boston: Houghton Mifflin, 1977.

Gisela Brinker-Gabler, *Frauen gegen den Krieg*. Frankfurt: Fischer Tauschenbuch, 1980.

Victoria Bissell Brown, *The Education of Jane Addams*. Philadelphia: University of Pennsylvania Press, 2003.

Gertrude Bussey and Margaret Tims, *Women's International League for Peace and Freedom, 1915–1965*. London: George Allen and Unwin, 1965.

F.L. Carsten, *War Against War: British and German Radical Movements in the First World War*. Berkeley: University of California Press, 1982.

Martin Ceadel, *Pacifism in Britain, 1914–1945: The Defining of a Faith*. Oxford: Oxford University Press, 1980.

Martin Ceadel, *Semi-Detached Idealists: The British Peace Movement and International Relations, 1854–1945*. Oxford: Oxford University Press, 2000.

Clarke A. Chambers, *Paul Kellogg and the Survey: Voices for Social Welfare and Social Justice*. Minneapolis: University of Minnesota Press, 1971.

Charles Chatfield, *For Peace and Justice: Pacifism in America, 1914–1941*. Knoxville: University of Tennessee Press, 1971.

Charles Chatfield and Peter van den Dungen, eds, *Peace Movements and Political Cultures*. Knoxville: University of Tennessee Press, 1989.

Roger Chickering, *Imperial Germany and a World Without War: The Peace Movement and Germany Society, 1892–1914*. Princeton, NJ: Princeton University Press, 1975.

Roger Chickering, *Imperial Germany and the Great War, 1914–1918*. Cambridge: Cambridge University Press, 1998.

Clarence C. Clendenen, *The United States and Pancho Villa: A Study in Unconventional Diplomacy*. Ithaca, NY: Cornell University Press, 1961.

Jill Conway, "Jane Addams: An American Heroine," *Daedalus*, 93 (Spring 1964), pp 761–780.

Jill Conway, *When Memory Speaks: Reflections on Autobiography*. New York: Alfred A. Knopf, 1998.

Blanche Wiesen Cook, "Democracy in Wartime: Antimilitarism in England and the United States, 1914–1918," *American Studies*, 13 (Spring 1972), pp 51–68.

Blanche Wiesen Cook, "The Woman's Peace Party: Collaboration and Non-Cooperation," *Peace and Change*, vol 1 (Fall 1972), pp 36–42.

John Milton Cooper, Jr., *The Warrior and the Priest: Woodrow Wilson and Theodore Roosevelt*. Cambridge, MA: Harvard University Press, 1983.

Sandi E. Cooper, "The Guns of August and the Doves of Italy: Intervention and Internationalism," *Peace and Change*, 7 (Winter 1981), pp 29–43.

Sandi E. Cooper, *Patriotic Pacifism: Waging War on War in Europe, 1815–1914*. New York: Oxford University Press, 1991.

Sandi E. Cooper, "Peace as a Human Right: The Invasion of Women into the World of High International Politics," *Journal of Women's History*, 14 (Fall 2002), pp 9–25.

Clare Coss, ed., *Lillian D. Wald: Progressive Activist*. New York: Feminist Press at The City University of New York, 1989.

Lela B. Costin, "Feminism, Pacifism, Internationalism and the 1915 International Congress of Women," *Women's Studies International Forum*, 5 (1982), pp 301–315.

John M. Craig, *Lucia Ames Mead (1856–1936) and the American Peace Movement*. Lewiston, NY: Edwin Mellen Press, 1990.

John V. Crangle and Joseph O. Baylen, "Emily Hobhouse's Peace Mission, 1916," *Journal of Contemporary History*, 14 (October 1979), pp 731–744.

Paul Crook, *Darwinism, War and History: The Debate over the Biology of War from the 'Origin of Species' to the First World War*. Cambridge: Cambridge University Press, 1994.

Doris Groshen Daniels, *Always a Sister: The Feminism of Lillian D. Wald*. New York: Feminist Press at the City University of New York, 1989.

Allen F. Davis, *American Heroine: The Life and Legend of Jane Addams*. New York: Oxford University Press, 1973.

Allen F. Davis, "The Social Workers and the Progressive Party, 1912–1916," *American Historical Review*, 69 (April 1964), pp 671–688.

Marie Louise Degen, *The History of the Woman's Peace Party*, in *The Johns Hopkins University Studies in Historical and Political Science*. Baltimore: Johns Hopkins Press, 1939.

Reinhard R. Doerries, *Imperial Challenge: Ambassador Count Bernstorff and German-American Relations, 1908–1917*. Chapel Hill: University of North Carolina Press, 1989.

Harvey L. Dyck, ed., *The Pacifist Impulse in Historical Perspective*. Toronto: University of Toronto Press, 1996.

Frances H. Early, *A World Without War: How U.S. Feminists and Pacifists Resisted World War I*. Syracuse: Syracuse University Press, 1997.

Wilfried Eisenbeiss, *Die Bürgerliche Friedensbewegung in Deutschland während des Ersten Weltkrieges: Organisation, Selbstverständnis und Politische Praxis, 1913/14–1919*. Frankfurt: Peter D. Lang, 1980.

Jean Bethke Elshtain, *Jane Addams and the Dream of Democracy: A Life*. New York: Basic Books, 2001.

Jean Bethke Elshtain, *Women and War*. New York: Basic Books, 1988.

Jean Bethke Elshtain and Sheila Tobias, eds, *Women, Militarism, and War: Essays in History, Politics, and Social Theory*. Savage, MD: Rowman & Littlefield, 1990.

Richard J. Evans, *Comrades and Sisters: Feminism, Socialism and Pacifism in Europe, 1870–1945*. New York: St Martin's Press, 1987.

L.L. Farrar, Jr., *Divide and Conquer: German Efforts to Conclude a Separate Peace, 1914–1918*. Boulder, CO: East European Quarterly, 1978.

John C. Farrell, *Beloved Lady: A History of Jane Addams' Ideas on Reform and Peace*. Baltimore: Johns Hopkins Press, 1967.

Barry Feinberg and Ronald Kasrils, eds, *Bertrand Russell's America: His Transatlantic Travels and Writings: A Documented Account*. London: George Allen, 1973.

Niall Ferguson, *The Pity of War*. New York: Basic Books, 1999.

John Patrick Finnegan, *Against the Specter of a Dragon: The Campaign for American Military Preparedness, 1914–1917*. Westport, CT: Greenwood Press, 1974.

Fritz Fischer, *Germany's Aims in the First World War*. New York: W.W. Norton, 1967 edition.

John Fisher, *That Miss Hobhouse*. London: Secker & Warburg, 1971.

Sheila Fletcher, *Maude Royden: A Life*. Oxford: Basil Blackwell, 1989.

Charles Forcey, *The Crossroads of Liberalism: Croly, Weyl, Lippmann and the Progressive Era, 1900–1925*. New York: Oxford University Press, 1961.

Robert Booth Fowler, *Carrie Catt: Feminist Politician.* Boston: Northeastern University Press, 1986.

A. Ruth Fry, *Emily Hobhouse: A Memoir.* London: Jonathan Cape, 1929.

Dee Garrison, *Mary Heaton Vorse: The Life of an American Insurgent.* Philadelphia: Temple University Press, 1989.

John Gartner, *The Hypomanic Edge.* New York: Simon and Schuster, 2005.

Hans W. Gatzke, *Germany's Drive to the West (Drang Nach Osten): A Study of Germany's Western War Aims during the First World War.* Baltimore: Johns Hopkins University Press, 1950.

Carol Gelderman, *Henry Ford: The Wayward Capitalist.* New York: Dial Press, 1981.

Joshua S. Goldstein, *War and Gender: How Gender Shapes the War System and Vice Versa.* Cambridge: Cambridge University Press, 2001.

J.L. Granatstein and R.D. Cuff, eds, *War and Society in North America: Papers Presented at the Canadian Association for American Studies Meeting, Montreal, Fall, 1970.* Toronto: Thomas Nelson, 1971.

Susan R. Grayzel, *Women's Identities at War: Gender, Motherhood, and Politics in Britain and France during the First World War.* Chapel Hill: University of North Carolina Press, 1999.

Ross Gregory, "The Superfluous Ambassador: Walter Hines Page's Return to Washington 1916," *The Historian,* 28 (May 1966), pp 389–404.

Verdiana Grossi, *Le Pacifisme Européen, 1889–1914.* Brussels: Bruylant, 1994.

Nicoletta F. Gullace, *"The Blood of Our Sons": Men, Women, and the Renegotiation of British Citizenship During the Great War.* New York: Palgrave Macmillan, 2002.

Francisca de Haan, Krassimira Daskalova, and Anna Loutfi, eds, *A Biographical Dictionary of Women's Movements and Feminisms: Central, Eastern, and South Eastern Europe, 19th and 20th Centuries.* Budapest: Central European University Press, 2006.

Harry Hanak, "The Union of Democratic Control during the First World War," *Bulletin of the Institute of Historical Research,* 36 (November 1963), pp 168–180.

Steven C. Hause with Anne R. Kenney, *Women's Suffrage and Social Politics in the French Third Republic.* Princeton, NJ: Princeton University Press, 1984.

August Heckscher, *Woodrow Wilson.* New York: Charles Scribner's Sons, 1991.

Sondra R. Herman, *Eleven Against War: Studies in American Internationalist Thought, 1898–1921.* Stanford, CA: Hoover Institution Press, 1969.

Margaret Randolph Higonnet, Jane Jenson, Sonya Michel, and Margaret Collins Weitz, eds, *Behind the Lines: Gender and the Two World Wars.* New Haven, CT: Yale University Press, 1987.

Margaret R. Higonnet, ed., *Lines of Fire: Women Writers of World War I.* New York: Penguin, 1999.

Godfrey Hodgson, *Woodrow Wilson's Right Hand: The Life of Colonel Edward M. House.* New Haven, CT: Yale University Press, 2006.

Deian Hopkin, "Domestic Censorship in the First World War," *Journal of Contemporary History,* 5 (January 1970), pp 151–169.

John Horne and Alan Kramer, *German Atrocities, 1914: A History of Denial.* New Haven, CT: Yale University Press, 2001.

Angela Ingram and Daphne Patai, eds, *Rediscovering Forgotten Radicals: British Women Writers, 1889–1939*. Chapel Hill: University of North Carolina Press, 1993.

Jerry Israel, ed., *Building the Organizational Society: Essays on Associational Activities in Modern America*. New York: Free Press, 1972.

Anne Jardim, *The First Henry Ford: A Study in Personality and Business Leadership*. Cambridge, MA: Massachusetts Institute of Technology Press, 1970.

B. de Jong van Beek en Donk, *History of the Peace Movement in the Netherlands* (1915), in *Peace Activities in Belgium and the Netherlands*, ed. Sandi E. Cooper. New York: Garland, 1972.

Harold Josephson, *et al.*, eds, *Biographical Dictionary of Modern Peace Leaders*. Westport, CT: Greenwood Press, 1985.

Katherine Joslin, *Jane Addams, A Writer's Life*. Urbana: University of Illinois Press, 2004.

Michael Jürgs, *Der Kleine Frieden im Grossen Krieg; Westfront 1914: Als Deutsche, Franzosen und Briten Gemeinsam Weihnachten Fierten*. Munich: C. Bertelsmann, 2003.

Margaret Kamester and Jo Vellicott, eds, *Militarism versus Feminism: Writings on Women and War*. London: Virago, 1987.

Friedrich Katz, *The Life and Times of Pancho Villa*. Stanford, CA: Stanford University Press, 1998.

David M. Kennedy, *Over Here: The First World War and American Society*. Oxford: Oxford University Press, 1980.

Thomas C. Kennedy, *The Hound of Conscience: A History of the No-Conscription Fellowship, 1914–1919*. Fayetteville: University of Arkansas Press, 1981.

Susan Kingsley Kent, *Making Peace: The Reconstruction of Gender in Interwar Britain*. Princeton, NJ: Princeton University Press, 1993.

Thomas J. Knock, *To End All Wars: Woodrow Wilson and the Quest for a New World Order*. New York: Oxford University Press, 1992.

Barbara S. Kraft, *The Peace Ship: Henry Ford's Pacifist Adventure in the First World War*. New York: Macmillan, 1978.

Warren F. Kuehl, *Hamilton Holt: Journalist, Internationalist, Educator*. Gainesville: University of Florida Press, 1960.

Cornelis Victor Lafeber, *Vredes-en Bemiddelingspogingen uit het Eerste Jaar van Wereldoorlog I, Augustus 1914-December 1915*. Leiden: Universitaire Pers, 1961.

Paul Laity, *The British Peace Movement, 1870–1914*. Oxford: Clarendon Press, 2001.

Albert Lee, *Henry Ford and the Jews*. New York: Stein and Day, 1980.

Vernon Lee, *Peace With Honour*. Union of Democratic Control, 1915.

Phyllis Lee Levin, *Edith and Woodrow: The Wilson White House*. New York: Scribner, 2001.

Jill Liddington, *The Life and Times of a Respectable Rebel: Selina Cooper (1864–1946)*. London: Virago Press, 1884.

Jill Liddington, *The Road to Greenham Common: Feminism and Anti-Militarism in Britain since 1820*. Syracuse: Syracuse University Press, 1991 edition.

Arthur S. Link, *Wilson: Campaigns for Progressivism and Peace, 1916–1917*. Princeton, NJ: Princeton University Press, 1965.

Arthur S. Link, *Wilson: Confusions and Crises, 1915–1916*. Princeton, NJ: Princeton University Press, 1964.

Arthur S. Link, *Wilson: The New Freedom*. Princeton, NJ: Princeton University Press, 1956.

Arthur S. Link, *Wilson: The Road to the White House*. Princeton, NJ: Princeton University Press, 1947.

Arthur S. Link, *Wilson: The Struggle for Neutrality, 1914–1915*. Princeton, NJ: Princeton University Press, 1960.

Michael A. Lutzker, "The Pacifist as Militarist: A Critique of the American Peace Movement, 1898–1914," *Societas*, 5 (Spring 1975), pp 87–104.

Michael A. Lutzker, "Present at the Outbreak: American Witnesses to World War One," *Peace and Change*, 7 (Winter 1981), pp 59–70.

C. Roland Marchand, *The American Peace Movement and Social Reform, 1898–1918*. Princeton, NJ: Princeton University Press, 1972.

Albert Marrin, *Sir Norman Angell*. Boston: Twayne, 1979.

Laurence W. Martin, *Peace without Victory: Woodrow Wilson and the British Liberals*. New Haven, CT: Yale University Press, 1958.

Arno J. Mayer, *Political Origins of the New Diplomacy, 1917–1918*. New Haven, CT: Yale University Press, 1959.

B.J.C. McKercher, *Esme Howard: A Diplomatic Biography*. Cambridge: Cambridge University Press, 1989.

Brock Millman, *Managing Domestic Dissent in First World War Britain, 1914–1918*. London: Frank Cass, 2001.

David J. Mitchell, *Women on the Warpath: The Story of the Women of the First World War*. London: Cape, 1966.

Annika Mombauer and Wilhelm Deist, eds., *The Kaiser: New Research on Wilhelm II's Role in Imperial Germany*. Cambridge: Cambridge University Press, 2006.

A.J.A. Morris, *C. P. Trevelyan, 1870–1958: Portrait of a Radical*. Belfast: Blackstaff Press, 1977.

A.J.A. Morris, *Radicalism Against War, 1906–1914: The Advocacy of Peace and Retrenchment*. London: Longman, 1972.

John M. Mulder, *Woodrow Wilson: The Years of Preparation*. Princeton, NJ: Princeton University Press, 1978.

Allan Nevins and Frank Ernest Hill, *Ford: Expansion and Challenge, 1915–1933*. New York: Charles Scribner's Sons, 1957.

David Paull Nickles, *Under the Wire: How the Telegraph Changed Diplomacy*. Cambridge, MA: Harvard University Press, 2003.

Sybil Oldfield, *Spinsters of This Parish: The Life and Times of F. M. Mayor and Mary Sheepshanks*. London: Virago Press, 1984.

Sybil Oldfield, *Women Against the Iron Fist: Alternatives to Militarism, 1900–1989*. Oxford: Basil Blackwell, 1989.

Sybil Oldfield, ed., *Women Humanitarians: A Biographical Dictionary of British Women Active between 1900 and 1950*. London: Continuum, 2001.

Sybil Oldfield, ed., *This Working-Day World: Women's Lives and Culture(s) in Britain, 1914–1945*. London: Taylor & Francis, 1994.

Nils Orvik, *The Decline of Neutrality, 1914–1941: With Special Reference to the United States and the Northern Neutrals*. Oslo: Johan Grundt Tanum Forlag, 1953.

Patricia O'Toole, *When Trumpets Call: Theodore Roosevelt After the White House*. New York: Simon & Schuster, 2005.

Sharon Ouditt, *Fighting Forces, Writing Women: Identity and Ideology in the First World War*. London: Routledge, 1994.

Patricia Ann Palmieri, *In Adamless Eden: The Community of Women Faculty at Wellesley*. New Haven, CT: Yale University Press, 1995.

Peter Pastor, "The Diplomatic Fiasco of the Modern World's First Woman Ambassador, Róza Bédy-Schwimmer," *East European Quarterly*, 8 (Fall 1974), pp 273–282.

David S. Patterson, *Toward a Warless World: The Travail of the American Peace Movement, 1887–1914*. Bloomington: Indiana University Press, 1976.

David S. Patterson, "Woodrow Wilson and the Mediation Movement, 1914–17," *The Historian*, 33 (August 1971), pp 535–556.

Anne Phillips, ed., *Feminism and Equality*. New York: New York University Press, 1987.

Ruth Roach Pierson, ed., *Women and Peace: Theoretical, Historical and Practical Perspectives*. London: Croom Helm, 1987.

Martin Pugh, *Electoral Reform in War and Peace, 1906–18*. London: Routledge & Kegan Paul, 1978.

Martin Pugh, *Women and the Women's Movement in Britain, 1914–1999*. New York: St Martin's Press, 2000.

Ludwig Quidde, *Der Deutsche Pazifismus Während des Weltkrieges, 1914–1918*, ed. Karl Holl. Boppard am Rhein: Boldt, 1979.

Mercedes M. Randall, *Improper Bostonian: Emily Greene Balch*. New York: Twayne, 1964.

Rose Rauther, "Rosika Schwimmer: Stationen auf dem Lebensweg einer Pazifistin," *Feministische Studien*, 3 (May 1984), pp 63–75.

Keith Robbins, *The Abolition of War: The "Peace Movement" in Britain, 1914–1919*. Cardiff: University of Wales Press, 1976.

Robert I. Rotberg, *A Leadership for Peace: How Edwin Ginn Tried to Change the World*. Stanford, CA: Stanford University Press, 2007.

Constance Rover, *Women's Suffrage and Party Politics in Britain, 1866–1914*. London: Routledge & Kegan Paul, 1967.

Leila Rupp, *Worlds of Women: The Making of an International Women's Movement*. Princeton, NJ: Princeton University Press, 1997.

Linda K. Schott, *Reconstructing Women's Thoughts: The Women's International League for Peace and Freedom before World War II*. Stanford, CA: Stanford University Press, 1997.

James D. Shand, "Doves Among the Eagles: German Pacifists and Their Government During World War I," *Journal of Contemporary History*, 10 (January 1975), pp 95–108.

Beatrice Siegel, *Lillian Wald of Henry Street*. New York: Macmillan, 1983.

Gerard E. Silberstein, *The Troubled Alliance: German-Austrian Relations, 1914–1917*. Lexington: University of Kentucky Press, 1970.

Kathryn Kish Sklar, "Jane Addams's Peace Activism, 1914–1922: A Model for Women Today?" *Women's Studies Quarterly*, 23 (Fall/Winter 1995), pp 32–47.

Kathryn Kish Sklar, " 'Some of Us Who Deal with the Social Fabric': Jane Addams Blends Peace and Social Justice, 1907–1919," *Journal of the Gilded Age and Progressive Era*, 2 (January 2003), pp 80–96.

Kathryn Kish Sklar, Anja Schüler, and Susan Strasser, eds, *Social Justice Feminists in the United States and Germany: A Dialogue in Documents, 1885–1933*. Ithaca, NY: Cornell University Press, 1998.

C. Smit, *Hoogtij der Neutraliteitspolitiek: Der Buitenlandse Politiek van Nederland, 1899–1919*. Leiden: A.W. Sijthoff, 1959.

Daniel M. Smith, *Robert Lansing and American Neutrality, 1914–1917*. Berkeley: University of California Press, 1958.

Charles Sowerwine, *Sisters or Citizens? Women and Socialism in France since 1876*. Cambridge: Cambridge University Press, 1982.

Barbara J. Steinson, *American Women's Activism in World War I*. New York: Garland, 1982.

David Stevenson, *Cataclysm: The First World War as Political Tragedy*. New York: Basic Books, 2004.

David Stevenson, *French War Aims Against Germany, 1914–1919*. Oxford: Clarendon Press, 1982.

Hew Strachan, *The First World War; Volume I: To Arms*. Oxford: Oxford University Press, 2001.

Hew Strachan, ed., *World War I: A History*. Oxford: Oxford University Press, 1998.

Marvin Swartz, *The Union of Democratic Control in British Politics during the First World War*. Oxford: Clarendon Press, 1971.

John A. Thompson, *Woodrow Wilson*. London: Longman, 2002.

Walter I. Trattner, "Julia Grace Wales and the Wisconsin Plan for Peace," *Wisconsin Magazine of History*, 24 (Spring 1961), pp 203–213.

Jacqueline Van Voris, *Carrie Chapman Catt: A Public Life*. New York: Feminist Press at the City University of New York, 1987.

Amry Vandenbosch, *Dutch Foreign Policy Since 1815: A Study in Small Power Politics*. The Hague: Martinus Nijhoff, 1959.

Jo Vellacott, *Bertrand Russell and the Pacifists in the First World War*. New York: St. Martin's Press, 1980.

Jo Vellacott, *From Liberal to Labour with Women's Suffrage: The Story of Catherine Marshall*. Montreal: McGill-Queen's University, 1993.

Solomon Wank, ed., *Doves and Diplomats: Foreign Offices and Peace Movements in Europe and America in the Twentieth Century*. New York: Greenwood Press, 1978.

Helen Ward, *A Venture in Goodwill: Being the Story of the Women's International League, 1915–1929*. London: Women's International League, 1929.

Louise Ware, *George Foster Peabody: Banker, Philanthropist, Publicist*. Athens: University of Georgia Press, 1951.

Steven Watts, *The People's Tycoon: Henry Ford and the American Century*. New York: Alfred A. Knopf, 2005.

Edwin A. Weinstein, *Woodrow Wilson: A Medical and Psychological Biography*. Princeton, NJ: Princeton University Press, 1981.

Stanley Weintraub, *Silent Night: The Story of the World War I Christmas Truce*. New York: Free Press, 2001.

David Welch, *Germany, Propaganda and Total War, 1914–1918: The Sins of Omission*, New Brunswick, NJ: Rutgers University Press, 2000.

Beth S. Wenger, "Radical Politics in a Reactionary Age: The Unmaking of Rosika Schwimmer, 1914–1930," *Journal of Women's History*, 2 (Fall 1990), pp 66–99.

Christl Wickert, *Helene Stöcker, 1969–1943, Frauenrechtlerin, Sexualreformerin, und Pazifistin: Eine Biographie*. Bonn: J.H.W. Dietz, 1991.

Anne Wiltsher, *Most Dangerous Women: Feminist Peace Campaigners of the Great War*. London: Pandora Press, 1985.

Barbara Winslow, *Sylvia Pankhurst: Sexual Politics and Political Activism*. New York: St Martin's Press, 1996.

Wilhelm Ernst Winterhalter, *Mission für den Frieden: Europäische Mächtepolitik und Dänische Friedensvermittlung im Ersten Weltkrieg vom August 1914 bis zum Italienischen Kriegseintritt May 1915*. Stuttgart: Franz Steiner, 1994.

Michael Wreszin, *Oswald Garrison Villard: Pacifist at War*. Bloomington: Indiana University Press, 1965.

William Zinsser, ed., *Inventing the Truth: The Art and Craft of Memoir*. New York: Houghton Mifflin, 1998 edition.

Dragan R. Zivojinovic, *The United States and the Vatican Policies, 1914–1918*. Boulder, CO: Colorado Associated University Press, 1978.

Larry Zuckerman, *The Rape of Belgium: The Untold Story of World War I*. New York: New York University Press, 2004.

UNPUBLISHED STUDIES

Jane Campbell, The Making of a Radical Pacifist: Rebecca Shelley 1914–1920. Senior honors thesis, University of Michigan, 1974.

Blanche Wiesen Cook, Woodrow Wilson and the Antimilitarists, 1914–1917. PhD dissertation, Johns Hopkins University, 1970.

Madeleine Z. Doty, The Central Organisation for a Durable Peace (1915–1919): Its History, Work and Ideas. PhD dissertation, University of Geneva [1945].

Jack Frooman, The Wisconsin Peace Movement, 1915–1919. MA thesis, University of Wisconsin, 1949.

Marvin Howard Kabakoff, The Composition of the Anti-War Movement in France in World War One. PhD dissertation, Washington University, 1975.

James Parker Martin, The American Peace Movement and the Progressive Era, 1910–1917. PhD dissertation, Rice University, 1975.

Meyer Jonah Nathan, The Presidential Election of 1916 in the Middle West. PhD dissertation, Princeton University, 1966.

Peter G. Tuttle, The Ford Peace Ship: Volunteer Diplomacy in the Twentieth Century. PhD dissertation, Yale University, 1958.

INDEX